GLOBAL FINANCE

GLOBAL FINANCE

Second Edition

Maximo V. Eng

Francis A. Lees

Laurence J. Mauer

St. John's University

ADDISON-WESLEY

An imprint of Addison Wesley Longman, Inc.

Reading, Massachusetts • Menlo Park, California • New York • Harlow, England
Don Mills, Ontario • Sydney • Mexico City • Madrid • Amsterdam

Senior Editor	Denise Clinton
Associate Editor	Julie Zasloff
Supplements Editor	Joan Twining
Senior Production Supervisor	Nancy H. Fenton
Marketing Manager	Jodi Fazio
Manufacturing Supervisor	Hugh Crawford
Cover Designer	Regina Hagen
Project Coordination	Interactive Composition Corporation

Cover Image © Lonny Kalfus, Tony Stone Images

Library of Congress Cataloging-in-Publication Data

Eng, Maximo.
    Global finance/Maximo V. Eng, Francis A. Lees, Laurence J.
Mauer. — 2nd ed.
      p. cm.
    Includes bibliographical references and index.
    ISBN 0-321-01377-8
    1. International finance.   I. Lees, Francis A.   II. Mauer,
Laurence J.   III. Title.
HG3881.E53   1998
332'.042—dc21   97-31208
                                     CIP

1 2 3 4 5 6 7 8 9 10—CRW—01 00 99 98 97

BRIEF CONTENTS

CONTENTS

5   CURRENCY FUTURES, OPTIONS, AND SWAPS

PART III   INTERNATIONAL BANKING

9   GLOBAL BANKING: OVERVIEW   246

PREFACE TO SECOND EDITION

Global finance is one of the new, dynamic areas of finance and international business curricula. Today, the financial marketplace is indeed global. It is impossible for a student of finance or international business to understand contemporary events and market trends without a background in global finance. After studying this text, the student reader should be able to understand and evaluate international financial information found in major financial publications.

PREMISES OF GLOBAL FINANCE

A book about global finance embodies several premises. First, finance is a "glue" that binds together many diverse domestic and international activities and processes. Therefore, the reader will "travel" to many countries to illustrate these activities and processes. Second, formerly distinct areas of finance (financial markets, banking, corporate financial management, and portfolio investment) are becoming more integrated due to the introduction of new financial instruments, innovative financial techniques, and the multinational and multidisciplinary approach of financial management decision making. Third, financial activities themselves are becoming more integrated. As a result, borrowers must consider the impact of system and industry debt patterns on financial statements, and pure lenders may take on managerial functions to strengthen the quality of credits. Bankers, cross-border investors, and portfolio managers must have an understanding of political, economic, and financial dimensions. Finally, the world financial environment is changing dramatically. For example, many developing nations are shedding their regulatory restrictions on finance and commerce, allowing new global financial institutions, markets, and instruments to influence their economies.

Global Finance seeks to integrate these financial activities, trends, and developments into a meaningful whole. To accomplish this task, it focuses on key concepts, analytical approaches, and practical applications.

Global Finance focuses on five closely interrelated areas of the international financial infrastructure. First, it includes the environment of international finance, particularly the international monetary system. Second, it examines international financial markets, including foreign exchange, derivatives, Eurocurrencies, and international bonds. The third, fourth, and fifth sections focus on international banking, international corporate finance, and international portfolio management, particularly portfolio investment in emerging markets. These latter areas incorporate the activities of important financial players. After reading this text, the student should understand the activities, operations, and decision-making processes of these three key players in the international financial arena.

INNOVATIVE FEATURES

This text contains many distinctive features. Within the framework of the five interrelated areas of study, *Global Finance* also:

1. Shows how evolution of the international monetary system provides challenges, and also opportunities, for the key players in the field.
2. Develops a clear distinction between performance and structure in balance of payments analysis.

3. Presents a comparative analysis of three major international financial centers: New York, London, and Tokyo.

4. Provides a comprehensive analysis of the Eurocurrency market and offshore banking.

5. Integrates analysis of Eurobonds, foreign bonds, and global bonds within the context of international bond markets.

6. Provides an analysis of bank profit sources in foreign exchange and Eurocurrency dealing.

7. Analyzes the effect of the Basle agreement for uniform bank capital standards on asset preference.

8. Includes international comparisons of bank cost of capital, and impact on their competitiveness.

9. Presents a risk-return analysis to understand the shift of direct investment to the United States during the 1980s and 1990s.

10. Shows how the US tax code impacts multinational corporations.

11. Through an integrated example, presents an international capital budgeting case under alternative foreign exchange rate and inflation scenarios.

12. Describes the market sectors and channels available for international portfolio diversification.

13. Integrates discussion of leading contributions concerning international portfolio diversification.

14. Presents analysis of performance evaluation of international investment managers.

15. Analyzes how the principal dealers in financial market sectors generate profits.

16. Provides an analysis of how exchange traded financial futures work, in the case of cross-border currency and interest rate arbitrage.

17. Focuses on the growing role and importance of emerging debt markets for a wide range of participants.

18. Analyzes the increasing role of emerging equity markets for global portfolio managers.

19. Establishes a framework for understanding the shift toward investment banking on the part of large commercial banks.

LEARNING AIDS AND PEDAGOGY

In an effort to produce a book that is useful to a wide range of students, we have broken down complicated financial concepts into a series of easy learning steps. Also, numerous examples and short illustrations explain the many principles and concepts covered in the text.

The following represent our efforts to enhance the usefulness and ease of reading and understanding the material in *Global Finance:*

1. generous use of illustrations and brief descriptions of real world situations;

2. timely introduction and analysis of financial concepts; frequent use of tables and figures that make these concepts clear to the reader;

3. generous use of questions and short problems;

4. frequent use of box illustrations that focus on managerial practices and real world issues and decision problems;

5. Instructor's Manual that contains solutions to end-of-chapter review questions, and tips for presenting materials found in each chapter; and,

6. Student Workbook that provides information on research, overview of each chapter, review questions, multiple choice questions, and homework problems. The New Student Workbook contains innovative features. These include:

   a.   Brief overview of global finance.

   b.   Section on how to pursue research projects in global finance.

   c.   How to use the Internet for research.

    d.   Key Internet websites in the field.

    e.   Tear-out homework and problem assignments.

TO THE INSTRUCTOR

We designed this text to accommodate a wide variety of classroom applications. Instructors, whose teaching experience may focus on two or three areas of the finance discipline such as banking, international corporate finance, or portfolio investment, will find *Global Finance* particularly useful. This text, through its survey approach to international finance, will enable them to augment their areas of expertise and guide their students through the instantaneous, intricate, and ever-expanding global financial network where today's successful multinational corporations and institutions thrive.

    The following suggestions represent the selectivity and flexibility of this textbook.

1. It can be used for a comprehensive international finance course on a selective basis.
2. It can be used for a course in international financial markets with Part II and other selected chapters.
3. It can be used for a course in international banking with Part III and other selected chapters.
4. It can be used for a course in international corporate finance with Part IV and other selected chapters.
5. It can be used for a course in international portfolio management with Part V and other selected chapters.

STRONGLY RECOMMEND USE OF *THE FINANCIAL TIMES* AND SIMILAR NEWS SOURCES

Global finance is an area with an unusually high level of financial innovation. One of the ways to capture this important dimension is to follow emerging issues and trends through the active use of the financial press. In this regard, we strongly recommend the use of *The Financial Times (FT)* newspaper as a daily source of information on global finance. The *FT* provides excellent coverage of daily news and also, several times a week, special industry and market studies. The *FT* can be used to supplement the instructor's classroom presentations and may be a basic research tool for student research reports. The *FT* may be obtained through subscription or may be accessed over the Internet at http://www.ft.com.

READERS FEEDBACK

We encourage our readers to write us concerning suggestions for improving this text or expanding its coverage. Also, we look forward to hearing from our readers concerning questions or problems they encountered while using this text. Through your advice and suggestions, we can make important improvements to *Global Finance* for our global readers.

ACKNOWLEDGMENTS

We wish to thank the many individuals who assisted us in the development of this manuscript and provided information and constructive suggestions. These include:

    Alan Alford, Northeastern University
    John Atkin, Schroder's, London
    John M. Atkin, Citibank, UK
    James C. Baker, Kent State University
    Stefano Balsamo, Morgan Guaranty Trust Company, Rome
    Dan Berg, Alternate Director (United States), EBRD
    Robert W. Boatler, Texas Christian University
    William Bokos, Citibank, USA

Paolo Bovone, Coopers & Lybrand, Italy

Simon Bradford, NatWest Securities, Edinburgh

Anne Brien, International Financial Review, UK

Todd Burgman, Union College

M. Martin Byrne, Loyola Marymount University

Thomas Chadwick, Merrill Lynch, London

George J. Clark, Citicorp, New York, USA

Bernadette Connolly, Deutsche Morgan Grenfell, London

Dorothy Conway, University of Central Florida

Jan Dauman, InterMatrix, Inc.

Matteo Del Fante, J.P. Morgan Securities, Ltd., London

Frank A. Elston, Eastern New Mexico University

Daniel Fan, North American Trade Finance, Citibank, N.A. Citicorp, USA

Charles Ford, US Embassy, London

Martin S. Fridson, Merrill Lynch, New York

Rick Haller, Deutsche Morgan Grenfell, UK

Robert Hartmann, Emerging Markets Group, Chase Manhattan Bank, London

Bart Hellendoorn, European Bank for Reconstruction & Development, London

Charles W. Hultman, University of Kentucky

Georg Inderst, Foreign & Colonial, UK

Lee Jackson, Alternate Director (United States), EBRD

Kurt Jesswein, Texas A&M International University

Lin Jiang, Center for Hong Kong-Macau Studies, Zhong Shan University, Guangzhou, China

Stephen A. Johnson, The University of Texas

James B. Kehr, Miami University

Joel Kibazo, *Financial Times,* UK

Yong H. Kim, University of Cincinnati

David N. Klaer, Revlon Corporation

Robert T. Kleinman, Oakland University

V. Sivarama Krishnan, Cameron University

David F. Lomax, National Westminster Bank, UK

David Lord, Standard-Chartered Capital Markets Ltd., UK

F. John Mathis, American Graduate School of International Management

Donna Mayatt, Bank of England

Daniel L. McConaughy, Rosary College

Sam O. McCord, Auburn University

Boris Milner, Russian Academy of Sciences, Institute of Economics, Moscow

Kerry Morris, Hongkong Shanghai Banking Corp., London

Paul S. Nadler, Rutgers University

John Nelson, Barclays Bank PLC, UK

Huub Nielssen, Borden, Inc.

John P. Olienyk, Colorado State University

Akira Onishi, Soka University, Tokyo, Japan

Debra Moore Patterson, Trinity University

Gerald Perrotta, Fuji Capital Markets, London

Devendra Prasad, University of Texas

Kumoli Ramakrishnan, University of South Dakota

Robert Ryan, Bank of New York
Anthony Scaperlanda, Northern Illinois University
Massimo Scialla, Banca di Roma
Robert Smolik, US Embassy, Italy
Martin Snow, Baring Securities Ltd., UK
Marjorie T. Stanley, Texas Christian University
Nicola Stoch, Banca di Roma
Jahangir Sultan, Bentley College
George W. Trivoli, Jacksonville State University
Howard E. Van Auken, Iowa State University
David Walker, Scottish Financial Enterprise, Edinburgh
Gordon Young, Smith New Court, UK

Also, we wish to express our gratitude to the many companies, financial institutions, government agencies, and organizations that provided information required for this volume. These include:

Bank for International Settlements
Bank of England
Bank of Japan
Chicago Mercantile Exchange
Citicorp
Deutsche Bundesbank
Economist Intelligence Unit, London
Emerging Markets Traders Association, New York
Federal Reserve Bank of Chicago
Federal Reserve Bank of New York
Federal Reserve Bank of San Francisco
ING Barings, London
International Finance Corporation
International Monetary Fund
London International Financial Futures Exchange, London
London Stock Exchange
J.P. Morgan
Morgan Stanley
National Westminster Banks
New York Stock Exchange
Salomon Brothers
Securities Exchange Commission
The Prudential Group, London
Tokyo Stock Exchange
United Nations Center for Transnational Corporations
United Nations
World Bank

Finally, we would like to express our special appreciation to the Addison Wesley Longman team that has given us so much support and assistance. Special thanks to Julie Zasloff, Joan Twining, and Nancy Fenton for their personal attention to *Global Finance*.

MAXIMO V. ENG, PH.D.

Maximo Eng is Distinguished Adjunct Professor of Economics and Finance at the Graduate School of Business and College of Business Administration, St. John's University, New York. A former Chairman of the Economics and Finance Department, his principal areas of teaching and research include domestic and international financial markets, international banking, international financial management, international trade and investment, and global capital movements. He has published a number of books, numerous articles, and chapters on US overseas banking, international lending, international financial markets, international capital flows, and economic developments. Dr. Eng was formerly an economic advisor for Citibank. He has served as consulting and contributing editor for International Publications, Inc. He has also served as a consultant to the United States and state government agencies. He is currently coeditor of *Journal of Emerging Markets*. Dr. Eng has frequently visited the Asia-Pacific area, Latin America, Europe, and Russia for research, academic seminars, and professional presentations. He holds his MBA and Ph.D. from the Stern School of Business, New York University.

FRANCIS A. LEES, PH.D.

Francis A. Lees is Professor of Economics and Finance at the Graduate School of Business, St. John's University. Dr. Lees formerly served as Chairman of the Economics and Finance Department, and Assistant Dean of the Graduate School of Business. His principal areas of research and teaching include global investment, country risk analysis, international banking, and development finance. He has published numerous books and articles including *Banking and Financial Deepening in Brazil* (1990), *Foreign Multinational Investment in the U.S.* (1986), and *International Lending, Risk, and the Euromarkets* (1979). Dr. Lees has served as a consultant for the Central Intelligence Agency of the US Government, The Conference Board, Royal Commission on Electric Power (Toronto), Central Bank for Cooperatives (Denver), and New York Clearing House Association. Currently, he is coeditor of *Journal of Emerging Markets*. Dr. Lees has traveled widely to Latin America, Asia, Europe, and Africa in research and consulting. He has been recognized for his professional accomplishments in *Who's Who in America*. Dr. Lees hold his Ph.D. from the School of Graduate Arts and Sciences, New York University.

LAURENCE J. MAUER, PH.D.

Laurence J. Mauer is Professor of Economics and Finance at the Graduate School of Business, St. John's University. Dr. Mauer formerly served as Associate Vice President and Dean, College of Business Administration, St. John's University. His teaching areas include international corporate finance and money and capital markets. He holds the Ph.D. degree from the College of Business Administration, University of Tennessee. He joined St. John's University in 1983. From 1979 to 1983, he worked with the GTE Corporation Corporate Planning Office, where he assisted in the preparation, coordination, and evaluation of strategic plans for GTE's international operations. From 1973 to 1979, he served as Vice President for the Northern Trust Company of Chicago. In that capacity, he was the international economist for this large financial services corporation, working closely with both the Foreign Exchange/Money Market Division and with the International Banking Department. Dr. Mauer was associated with the United Nations Industrial Development Organization in Vienna, Austria, as Industrial Development Officer and Research Consultant in 1969-1970.

From 1967 through 1973, Dr. Mauer held the position of Associate Professor and Chairman of the Department of Economics at Northern Illinois University in De Kalb, Illinois. He was awarded a National Science Foundation Grant to study "The External Effects of the European Economic Community," over the period 1969-1973. He has published extensively in professional journals and has also given numerous presentations before scholarly/professional groups, including testimony before the Committee on Finance, United States Senate, in Washington, DC, July 1985, on proposed legislation which subsequently was enacted as the "Tax Reform Act of 1986."

To Our Wives

Margot Eng, Kathryn Lees, and Karen Mauer,

with love

PART ONE

Environment
of Global Finance

*I*n this section we examine the environment that sets the conditions for global financial market growth and impacts decisions made by banks, corporate treasurers, and investors. Our study of the environment includes the evolving international monetary system, the international payments positions of individual nations, and economic growth patterns in the major regions and countries of the world. The following three chapters consider how the environment of global finance influences market conditions in the foreign exchange, Eurocurrency, and other financial markets. Furthermore, these chapters analyze the impact of environmental changes on three major participants or players in global finance: banks, multinational corporations, and portfolio investors plus international official borrowers.

ENVIRONMENT OF GLOBAL FINANCE

INTERNATIONAL FINANCIAL MARKETS	INTERNATIONAL BANKING
INTERNATIONAL CORPORATE FINANCE	INTERNATIONAL PORTFOLIO MANAGEMENT

CHAPTER 1

Global Finance and the World Economic Environment

INTRODUCTION

In the decades since World War II, the world economic environment has experienced tremendous change. In the 1950s business corporations were busy rebuilding their domestic markets. In the 1960s business firms expanded internationally, attracted by rapidly growing international trade and markets abroad. In the 1970s business organizations became multinational, investing abroad in manufacturing facilities and distribution centers.

Since 1980 rapid growth of both international trade and capital flows have compelled many large business and financial firms to go global in their outlook and organization. The typical slogan in this period has been to adopt "global strategies for profits." Underlying this globalization of business and finance have been the following: technological advances such as computers and telecommunications; deregulation of business and financial markets by industrialized countries such as the United States, the United Kingdom, and Japan; and an escalation of cross-border capital flows such as bank lending, international bond issues, and mutual fund portfolio investment.

These trends are integrating the world economy in the flows of goods, services, capital, and people. The globalization of business and the increasing need for global finance have become part of the typical landscape in the 1980s and 1990s and will continue to be important as we enter the twenty-first century.

What is global finance? We deal with four important aspects. First, global finance analyzes the domain of finance globally, embracing the environment, international financial markets, international banking, international corporate finance, international investment management, and their relations. This concept of global finance is represented in Exhibit 1.1 that depicts all four key aspects of this book.

Second, global finance explains the interactions of financial activities on a global basis, whether these occur in major industrialized nations, newly industrialized countries, developing nations, or newly converted free market economies in transition, such as Russia and the Eastern European countries or the People's Republic of China.

Third, global finance provides an integrated analysis of micro and macro financial activity. On the micro financial level, emphasis is given to detailed activities in

Economies in transition

Former communist countries in Eastern Europe and Russia which have gradually transformed their centrally-planned economies to free market economies in the 1990s.

EXHIBIT 1.1   **Five Major Components of Global Finance**

ENVIRONMENT OF GLOBAL FINANCE

| INTERNATIONAL FINANCIAL MARKETS | INTERNATIONAL BANKING |
| INTERNATIONAL CORPORATE FINANCE | INTERNATIONAL PORTFOLIO MANAGEMENT |

the realms of corporate finance, financial markets, banking, and portfolio invest-ment management. At the same time, careful attention is given to macro financial activity, since it is necessary to understand the larger picture in order to compre-hend the workings of global financial management and financial markets.

Fourth, global finance is a continuous process, creating further change as it takes place. In recent years, cross-border financial transactions have become one of the most dynamic forces, transforming domestic financial systems and the linkages that connect one country's financial system with that of another. Developments in global finance have become an important source of financial innovations. These, in turn, have impacted regional financial systems and contributed to a greater integra-tion of national financial markets. For example, the development of the Eurobond market has had a great impact not only on European securities markets, but also on domestic financial markets in the United States and Japan.

The following sections of this chapter provide an overview of the interrelations between the world economic environment and global finance. Changes in the world economic environment have posed significant challenges to governments, businesses, and world financial institutions.

LEARNING OBJECTIVES IN THIS CHAPTER

1. To explain the drastic changes in the world economic environment after World War II and to describe how the concept and practices of global finance have emerged in the integrated world economy.

2. To define four important aspects of global finance and to explain how they are interrelated with changes in the world's economic structure.

3. To describe the role of world capital flows in the growth of the world economy, the globalization of financial markets, and their new developments.

4. To explore serious challenges to governments, businesses, and financial institutions as the result of continuous technological advances, financial innovations, and integration on a global basis.

5. To select chapters in the book suitable for course purposes.

KEY TERMS AND CONCEPTS

- Marshall Plan in Europe
- Club of Rome
- Multinational corporations
- Oil shocks in 1974 and 1979
- "Twin deficits"
- Group of seven

- Globalization of financial markets
- Note issuance facilities
- Financial engineering
- Transitional economies
- Unified European market
- Emerging markets

ACRONYMS

OPEC	Organization of Petroleum Exporting Countries	**GDP**	Gross Domestic Product
EC	European Community	**SWIFT**	Society for Worldwide Interbank Financial Telecommunications
IMF	International Monetary Fund	**G-7**	The Group of Seven (comprising Canada, France, Germany, Italy, Japan, United Kingdom, and the United States)
IBRD	International Bank for Reconstruction and Development		
GATT	General Agreement on Tariffs and Trade	**NAFTA**	North American Free Trade Agreement
UN	United Nations		
MNC	Multinational Corporation	**APEC**	Asia-Pacific Economic Cooperation
LDCs	Less Developing Countries		
GNP	Gross National Product	**WTO**	World Trade Organization

Changes in World Environment and Economic Structure

After the painful lessons of the Great Depression of the 1930s and World War II, the United States undertook a leadership role to assist countries in Western Europe and Asia rebuild their war-torn economies. These efforts by the U.S. government took the form of the *Marshall Plan in Europe* and various relief programs in Asia, especially in Japan and China. Several important world organizations were established to further institutionalize international cooperation and assistance, including the International Monetary Fund (IMF) in 1944, the International Bank for Reconstruction and Development (World Bank) in 1945, the General Agreement on Tariffs and Trade (GATT) in 1948, the United Nations (UN) in 1949 and the World Trade Organization (WTO) in 1995.

In the postwar years between 1950–1990, the world has experienced tremendous changes in global environment and economic structure. The drastic growth of world trade, the rapid flow of international capital, the quickening pace of technology, and the shift of the Communist system to the market economy in Eastern Europe and Russia have accelerated regional cooperation and global integration. As a result of these developments, the world presents many challenges and opportunities to bankers, corporations, and investors.

CHANGES IN WORLD ECONOMIC ENVIRONMENT

These postwar developments set the stage for the world environment that we know today. We provide an overview of the evolution of the International Monetary System (IMS) in Chapter 2. Here, we offer a brief history so that we can appreciate the changes which have swept over the world economic environment in the past 35 years. This understanding is critical since, as we move through the 1990s, we may expect this rapid pace of change to continue and even to accelerate. Some of the developments that have signaled significant changes in the world economic and financial environment are:

1. The emergence of the Eurodollar market in 1957 in London, in response to British capital controls imposed on pound sterling (see Chapter 6);

2. The formation of the European Economic Community (EEC) in 1958 that has come to be known as the European Common Market and is now simply called the European Community (EC);

3. From the mid-1950s, the rush by U.S. corporations to establish operations overseas; Japanese and European corporations also shifting toward a multinational orientation, and foreign multinational corporations (MNCs), challenging U.S. companies in the United States as well as overseas;

4. The development of new business opportunities in the Far East stimulated by rapid economic progress in Japan since the 1960s;

5. The international financial crises in 1971 and 1973, leading to the collapse of the Bretton Woods System, and the formal shift from a fixed exchange rate system to floating exchange rates;

6. Substantial pressures on the world economic system from the first and second oil shocks in 1974 and 1979; the Organization of Petroleum Exporting Countries (OPEC) increased prices of oil substantially in these two years;

Debt service

Total debt at the year-end in percent of exports of goods and services in year indicated.

7. Onset of the world debt crisis in 1982, due to widespread debt service problems facing the developing nations;

8. Emergence of Japan as a leading international financial power and source of global capital in the 1980s;

9. In February 1987, seven countries (G-7) reached the "Louvre Accord" in Paris. They planned to support the falling U.S. dollar by pegging exchange rates within a narrow range. They also intended to bring their economic policies into line.

10. In 1987, the European Community's passage of the Single Europe Act, calling for the creation of a Unified European Market by 1992 that would fundamentally change the Western European economic and financial landscape;

11. In 1989–1992 East Europe's Communist countries' change of their political systems from Communist to multiparty governments, and conversion of centrally planned economies to free market economies; these changes have exerted profound influences on world politics, economy, and finance; and,

12. The unified European Market after 1992, the approval of the North American Free Trade Agreement (NAFTA) in November 1993, and the Conference of Asia-Pacific Economic Cooperation (APEC) in the United States in 1993 have intensified regional development in the 1990s.

13. Increasing importance of emerging capital markets as a part of global finance in the 1990s.

North American Free Trade Agreement (NAFTA)

The United States, Canada, and Mexico signed an agreement allowing free flows of trade and capital among these three countries in 1993.

Asia Pacific Economic Cooperation (APEC)

Countries around the Pacific Ocean in Asia, America, and Australia would meet from time to time for economic consultation and cooperation.

Emerging capital markets

Emergence of capital markets in developing countries resulting from their rapid economic growth have attracted international lenders and borrowers to these markets.

CHANGES IN WORLD ECONOMIC STRUCTURE

How products are produced and sold fundamentally influences the world economic structure. Generally, the pattern and trend of world production and trade does not change much from one year to the next. However, from a long-term perspective, changes in these trends have been demonstrated to have important effects on the magnitudes and pattern of global financial flows.

Over the past two decades, four major structural trends have been identified:

+ the changing relationship between the primary-product economy and the industrial economy;
+ a shift within the industrial economy toward greater knowledge requirements in production;
+ international capital movements becoming more important than international trade; and
+ development of more diversified activities by multinational corporations, including joint venture international investment and partnership agreements.[*]

Traditionally, there has been a strong relationship between the primary-product economy and the industrial economy. The pattern has been that the primary-product producing countries export their products to the industrial countries, and in turn use the proceeds to import manufactured goods. These trends have changed since the collapse of nonoil commodity prices. In the mid-1970s, a group of European intellectuals known as the Club of Rome predicted global shortages of most natural resources by 1987. Based on this view, many primary-product producing nations hoped to cartelize primary commodity supplies and to increase their foreign exchange earnings. This intent follows the example of OPEC. However, this hope has not been realized. In 1986, the United Nations's measure of primary-product prices was at an index of 50, compared with its 1971–1981 average value of 100.[†] The protracted decline in primary product prices can be related to changes in supply and demand. The expectation of higher prices in the 1970s led to increases in investment and overcapacity, especially in the world metals industries. Technological changes also affected demand. For example, telecom-

---

[*] Three of these four changes are identified in Peter F. Drucker, "The Changed World Economy." *Foreign Affairs.* (Spring 1986): 768–91.

[†] *World Economic Survey,* United Nations, New York, 1987.

munications companies are now using fiber optics to install cable where once they used only copper wire. Technology has also helped many countries to increase their domestic production of basic grains and foods, reducing international trade in foodstuffs.

A second change in world economic structure is the shift in employment patterns from labor-intensive to knowledge-intensive jobs. Increased automation, computerization, and robotization in industrialized countries have resulted in more white-collar but less blue-collar employment. Ease in communication stimulates entrepreneurship, small business, and individual creativity. To utilize these knowledge-intensive approaches requires workers with high skills and education. As a result, labor cost has become less important. Instead, capital investment and human capital have become more important for overall productivity and competitiveness.

The third major change is that the world has been experiencing a greater growth in international capital movements than in international trade. According to the IMF *International Financial Statistics,* world exports reached a level of about $2 trillion in 1981, declined a bit in 1982–1983, but climbed back to $3,568 billion in 1991 and $4,367 billion in 1994. There was not much change except in the shares or proportions of exports among countries. However, in the same period international capital flows increased dramatically. This increase is reflected in the Eurocurrency market, international bond markets, and the foreign exchange market. The net size of the Eurocurrency market expanded from $1,155 billion in 1981 to $3,660 billion in 1992 and to $5,830 billion in 1994. International bond issues surged from $23 billion to $427 billion in the same period. Moreover, daily turnover of foreign exchange in three leading international financial markets increased significantly. In the period 1986–1995, London's average daily foreign exchange turnover increased from $90 billion to $464 billion. In the same period, New York's daily turnover climbed from $50 billion to $244 billion. Tokyo's turnover increased from $48 billion to $161 billion in 1995 alone.*

The fourth major change in economic structure is the growing importance of MNCs and their joint ventures among nations. Essentially, MNCs extended their organization, production, and marketing in foreign countries, facilitating the flow of goods, services, capital, and technology among nations. In the 1960s, this aspect of international business was dominated by American-based MNCs. By the 1980s multinational companies based in other countries had taken on a more important role. Brazilian and Korean multinationals operating in the United States are cases in point. Joint ventures have become a popular means of entering global business. Since 1980 joint venture agreements between major multinational companies now number in the hundreds.

Examples of joint ventures include the GM-Toyota investment to produce automobiles in the United States. American manufacturers substantially increased market penetration in Western European countries with joint ventures to produce computers. America's Eli Lilly and the Hungarian government formed a joint venture in Budapest to produce pharmaceutical products. To the extent that joint ventures reduce the necessity of shipping products from one country to another, such agreements reduce the volume of international trade but increase international investment (e.g., the GM-Toyota joint venture in the United States).

---

* *Financial Times,* (March 13, 1996): 10.

Growth of the World Economy and Capital Flows

VARIATIONS IN GROWTH RATES AND IMPLICATIONS FOR CAPITAL FLOWS

During the 1970s and 1980s there were substantial changes in economic growth rates of nation-states and world regions. Economic growth rates play an important role in influencing the way that nation-states participate in world trade and investment. Generally, high domestic growth rates bring about an upward shift in a nation's imports of goods and services. This shift may be accompanied by an increased need to borrow from the rest of the world. The opposite takes place when lower growth rates reduce borrowing requirements. However, growth rates are only one influence on international capital flows. Other factors include trade policy, deregulation of financial markets and financial transactions, and changes in investment opportunities. Since 1978 all of these factors have tended to expand international capital flows.

Since the 1980s the developed market economies have experienced a greater variability in annual growth rates. Growth in gross domestic product for these economies slipped from 4.3% in 1988 to 3.3% in 1989 and 2.4% in 1990. The growth rate declined to 1.4% in 1991 but increased to 2.7% in 1994.

These forces have been even more marked in the case of the developing nations, where growth rates in the 1980s fell to about three-fourths of their levels in the 1970s. Growth rates were particularly low for LDCs in the Western Hemisphere. By contrast, the South and East Asian nations—including Singapore, Hong Kong, Taiwan, and South Korea—managed to maintain growth rates (1988–1994) in the range of 5.5% to 8.0% (Exhibit 1.2).

The former centrally planned economies of Eastern Europe have experienced lower growth rates in recent years. Besides their domestic economic difficulties, slower growth among the developed market economies has curtailed the growth of exports from the Eastern European nations to the West. These factors have reduced Eastern European growth from an average 3.7% in 1988 to negative rates in 1990–1994.

Developments in the People's Republic of China (PRC) stand in sharp contrast to the Eastern European experience. Through the global introduction of market economy and relaxation of central planning, the PRC has maintained a high rate of economic growth, from 11.3% in 1988 to 11.8% in 1994 (Exhibit 1.2).

Mirroring the reduction in the trend rate of GDP growth, world trade volume experienced slower growth in the early 1980s. According to IMF data, world trade growth rates declined from an average 5.0% in the 1970s to an average 2.7% per annum in the early 1980s, but expanded to an average 6.0% in 1984–1994. It is expected that world trade volume may increase in 1995–1996 period due to the new effort made by the World Trade Organization (WTO). The WTO is designed to facilitate trade negotiation and dispute settlement among its members. Its charter explicitly links it to the decisions and customary practice under the GATT, including the dependence on consensus in reaching decisions. As reported by IMF International Financial Statistics, total world exports of goods increased from $3,568 billion to $4,367 billion over the 1991–1994 period. During this time the share of industrial countries decreased from 70% to 66.6%, but the share of developing countries increased from 30% to 33.4%. In 1994 Asian developing economies such as China, Hong Kong, Korea, Singapore, and Taiwan accounted for 12.7% of

EXHIBIT 1.2   Growth of Population and Output by Region, 1987–1994

	Population 1990 (Millions)	Population growth rate (annual percentage)	Gross domestic product (Billions of 1980 dollars)	RATES OF CHANGE OF GROSS DOMESTIC PRODUCT (ANNUAL PERCENTAGE)						
				1987	1988	1989	1990	1991	1992	1994
World	5,292	1.8	—	2.6	4.3	3.0	1.0	0.0	2.1	3.1
Developed market economies	813	0.6	7,640	2.4	4.3	3.3	2.4	1.4	3.0	2.7
North America	276	0.8	2,866	2.8	4.4	2.5	1.0	1.0	3.1	3.5
Western Europe	358	0.2	3,467	1.8	3.8	3.4	2.7	1.2	2.3	2.1
Developed Asia	144	0.5	1,060	3.8	5.4	4.6	5.0	3.1	4.1	3.4
Eastern Europe and the Soviet Union	405	0.6	—	2.7	3.7	1.4	−6.3	−9.5	−4.5	−8.3
Developing countries	4,074	2.1	2,780	3.0	5.0	3.4	2.9	3.5	5.0	5.6
Western hemisphere	432	2.1	815	1.2	0.8	1.1	−0.7	1.5	3.0	2.8
Africa	606	3.1	336	1.2	2.1	3.3	3.4	3.0	3.0	3.3
West Asia	130	3.0	357	−1.6	1.1	2.4	0.0	−0.5	7.0	0.4
South and East Asia	1,686	2.2	662	5.3	8.7	6.0	6.1	5.5	6.0	8.0
China	1,139	1.5	470	10.0	11.3	3.3	4.8	5.5	6.0	11.8
Mediterranean	81	1.5	141	3.2	1.4	1.0	−0.7	2.0	4.0	−2.8
Memorandum items: Heavily indebted countries	612	2.3		1.0	1.2	1.5	−0.8	1.5	1.4	4.4
Sub-Saharan Africa	383	3.2		1.4	3.0	2.7	1.9	3.0	0.0	2.1

SOURCE: UN/DIESA. Data on population growth rates are those published by the Department in World Population Prospects, Estimates and Projections, as assessed in 1984 (United Nations publication sales No. E.86.XIII.3). As reported by the United Nations, World Economic Outlook, 1994, 1995.

9

the total world exports due to the growth of their economies and exports of manufacturing goods in recent years.

WORLD CAPITAL FLOWS

From a theoretical standpoint, we would expect international capital to flow to places where yields and productivities are relatively high. Moreover, we would expect the worldwide structure of yields on productive assets to be rather stable, since these are closely tied to underlying productivities. With this theoretical framework in mind, we would not expect massive changes in international capital flows. Yet several such changes have taken place over the past two decades. One of these changes involves the United States.

Since 1983 international credit flows to the United States have increased without interruption (Exhibit 1.3). In the period 1983–1990, world capital flows to the United States aggregated $879 billion; of this sum, Japan accounted for $327 billion or 37%, the EEC 16%, and offshore banking centers and developing countries 47%. Most foreign capital flows to the United States were invested in U.S. government bonds, corporate bonds, corporate stocks, and direct investment across several industries.* This sizeable inflow of foreign funds helped to finance the U.S. government budget deficit. The relationship between these "twin deficits" is complex and discussed in later chapters. At this juncture, it is sufficient to indicate that twin deficits can be expected to contribute to instability as well as downward pressure on the U.S. dollar in the foreign exchange market. This instability could be aggravated if foreign investors withdraw funds previously invested in the United States.

Since 1991 the direction of world capital flows has changed from the United States to the developing countries. As shown in Exhibit 1.4, capital flows to developing countries increased from $93 billion to $155 billion in the period 1991–1993 but receded to $125 billion in 1994. Of these flows direct investment accounted for 45%, and 49% was portfolio investment. The remaining 6% consisted of short-term credit flows. It is noted that capital flows to developing countries (emerging markets) increased more drastically for portfolio investment than for direct investment in this period due to the growth of securities markets in the developing countries.

There was a marked regional difference in the composition of capital flows to developing countries. In 1994 Asia took 58% of the total capital flows ($125 billion), the Western Hemisphere shared 31%, and others absorbed 11%. It is also noted that the Western Hemisphere relatively received more portfolio investment than direct investment in the 1991–1994 period while an opposite pattern prevailed in Asia.

There have been four basic reasons for the surge of capital flows to the emerging markets in the developing countries in the 1991–1994 period. First, many developing countries have initiated sound macroeconomic policies and structural reforms including financial sector reforms. These facilitated the reentry into international capital markets. Second, economic fluctuations in industrial countries encouraged the outflow of capital to emerging market countries for higher rates of returns. For example, the decline in interest rates in the industrial countries including the United States in the early 1990s contributed to the increases in portfolio investment in emerging market countries. Third, diversification of institutional portfolios (securities houses,

Twin deficits

The U.S. federal government deficits and the U.S. international balance of payments deficits.

---

* U.S. Department of Commerce, *Survey of Current Business* (various issues).

EXHIBIT 1.3 **Net Resource Transfers to the United States by Region, 1980–1990 (Billions of Dollars)**

	1980	1981	1982	1983	1984	1985	1986	1987	1988	1989	1990[1]
Canada	-0.5	0.3	7.1	9.0	12.3	13.1	10.2	8.0	7.1	5.1	4.0
Japan	9.5	14.5	15.5	24.6	42.1	51.3	52.1	53.4	47.3	41.5	32.6
Western Europe	-16.7	-9.0	-2.7	5.4	21.4	31.1	34.8	32.2	18.7	1.7	-1.8
of which:											
Germany	2.4	2.9	5.3	8.3	13.2	15.9	20.0	21.4	18.1	13.8	—
United Kingdom	-2.2	1.1	2.9	2.8	3.0	5.3	5.6	4.7	—	-4.1	-3.9
Latin American and the Caribbean	-2.2	-6.3	4.7	18.0	20.6	16.6	12.7	15.3	10.2	10.7	10.7
of which: Mexico	-2.7	-5.5	4.2	10.1	7.90	7.5	7.3	8.3	5.6	5.2	—
Major oil exporters of Africa and Asia[2]	36.7	24.9	5.8	0.8	5.2	3.1	2.3	7.2	5.7	11.2	14.8
Other developing countries	-4.7	-0.6	1.1	9.4	21.3	22.1	31.6	42.1	34.7	35.6	35.6
Eastern Europe and USSR	-2.7	-2.9	-2.8	-1.7	-2.1	-1.4	—	-0.2	-1.6	-3.5	-2.2
Other countries[3]	-0.1	-4.7	-4.4	-8.0	-11.0	-12.9	-3.4	-4.9	-6.6	-7.8	-8.0
Total[4]	19.4	16.1	24.3	57.6	109.8	123.0	140.4	153.1	115.5	94.4	85.8

[1] Preliminary estimate, full country breakdown unavailable at this time.

[2] Comprising OPEC member countries, excluding Ecuador and Venezuela.

[3] Including net transactions with international organizations and unallocated amounts.

[4] Differs slightly from total in Table A. 28 because certain private transfers are unavailable on a geographical basis.

SOURCE: UN/DIESA, based on data of United States Department of Commerce, Survey of Current Business. As reported by the United Nations, *World Economic Outlook*, 1992.

EXHIBIT 1.4	Capital Flows to Developing Countries (in billions of U.S. dollars)				
	1990	1991	1992	1993	1994
All developing countries	39.8	92.9	111.6	154.7	125.2
Net foreign direct investment	19.5	28.8	38.0	52.8	56.3
Net portfolio investment	6.2	22.5	39.1	88.3	61.7
Other	14.1	41.6	34.5	13.6	7.2
Asia	25.6	50.7	39.2	72.0	73.4
Western Hemisphere	17.9	28.6	52.6	62.3	38.6
Other	−3.7	13.6	19.8	20.4	13.2

SOURCE: International Monetary Fund.

pension funds, mutual funds, insurance companies, banks, etc.) has encouraged capital flows to emerging market countries. Fourth, impressive economic growth rates in many emerging market countries such as China, Malaysia, Thailand, and Singapore have attracted multinational corporations to invest funds in these countries for profitable endeavors in the local markets or regional markets.

GLOBALIZATION OF FINANCIAL MARKETS

Since the 1980s financial markets have operated on a global basis such as the Eurocurrency and the Eurobond markets. In the 1990s several other financial markets achieved "global status." The following are examples of these markets. In the period 1990–1994, the world derivative markets rose from $2,290 billion to $8,837 billion.[*] International repurchase agreements (Repos) surged from $1,208 billion to $7,300 billion.[†] Value traded on stock exchanges in all emerging market countries increased from $894 billion to $1,679 billion.[††] These phenomena can be achieved only under the following five conditions.

International repurchase agreements (Repos)
International repos are conducted by international financial institutions mostly with government securities similar to the domestic repos in the U.S. but sometimes involving central banks between nations.

First and foremost is deregulation among countries. Deregulation efforts by many nations have eliminated capital controls and allowed funds to flow freely among different national markets. Second, the global presence of international financial institutions such as commercial banks, investment banking houses, and mutual funds have provided global competition in financial services that tend to lower the costs of capital for borrowers and increase the rates of return for investors. Third, financial instrument innovations such as Euro-medium term notes, global bonds, interest rate futures and options, international repos, and stock index futures, provide a wide range of alternatives to international lenders and borrowers for their portfolio choices. Fourth, modern technology such as telecommunications and computerized information have quickened cross-border transactions and minimized transaction costs. For example, an investment banker can now settle international financial transactions in bonds and foreign exchange through the SWIFT (Society for Worldwide Interbank Financial Telecommunications) system (discussed in Chapters 6 and 8). Commercial banks can issue letters of credit electronically from their head offices to their overseas branches; these communications can in turn be transmitted through computers to local importers or exporters (discussed in

[*] Bank for International Settlements Annual Report.

[†] *Financial Times,* March 1, 1996.

[††] International Finance Corporation Factbook.

Chapter 10). Fifth, geographic linkages among major financial markets have helped international financial managers in banks, corporations, investment banking houses, and government agencies conduct their international financial operations more efficiently and effectively. Since capital flows, interest rates, and foreign exchange rates are volatile in the changing political, economic, and financial environment, it is not unusual that international financial managers maintain a 24-hour alert among the major financial markets such as New York, San Francisco, Tokyo, Hong Kong, Singapore, Frankfurt, Paris, and London. Geographic linkages are particularly important to financial strategists for global lending and funding activities, global arbitrage, speculation, and risk management.

Challenges to Governments, Business, and World Financial Institutions

The preceding discussion indicates that the world economic environment and structure have changed dramatically over the past 40 years. These changes have altered the direction and magnitude of world capital flows. The growth of world capital depends on savings out of current income. These savings can be channeled to ultimate investors through the international financial system. Governments encourage the saving-investment process and, in so doing, spur capital accumulation. To this end, governments must provide favorable legal, political, social, economic, and financial environments in which both domestic and international business can function and develop fully.

When changes take place in a nation's balance of payments, they are accompanied by large movements of capital from one country to another. One of the most significant shifts has been the rapid increase in the U.S. trade deficit following 1982. This caused the United States to absorb a large share of world capital. As a result, the United States quickly became a large international debtor nation (since 1986). The continued growth of U.S. external indebtedness in the 1990s poses a problem for policymakers around the world.

DEVELOPED MARKET ECONOMIES

The developed market economies account for about 65% of total world output (Exhibit 1.2). This group has a vital influence on the economic affairs of other nations through international linkages of trade, capital flows, and technology. At present, the developed market economies face many problems. The major challenges to specific developed economies are:

1. *The United States.* During the past decades, the United States has been running a large structural federal budget deficit of about $120 billion and a deficit in international payments on the current account also of $120 billion. In order to maintain economic growth without inflation, these "twin deficits" must be reduced in the 1990s.

2. *Japan.* This country is the second largest producer after the United States. The challenge facing the Japanese is to find ways to channel the current account surplus into productive loans and investments in other countries. Japanese capital must be channeled to nations facing a shortage of capital. Appreciation of the

Japanese yen and maintenance of noninflationary economic growth in Japan will be factors complicating fiscal and monetary policy. Economic decline in the Japanese economy in 1992–1994 revealed certain weaknesses of the Japanese financial system that must be addressed in the 1990s.

3. *The European Community.* The EC countries have enjoyed moderate economic growth with declining inflation. High unemployment rates have persisted. The German government has been conservative in using fiscal stimulation because of the traditional abhorrence of inflation. Coordination of economic and financial policies among EC economies under the Unified European Market in 1992 will play an important role in influencing trade and investment flows. However, the currency crisis in September 1992 signaled a warning that the road to European monetary union by 1999 will not be a smooth one.

DEVELOPING COUNTRIES (LDCs)

During the 1970s the LDCs borrowed large sums of money to develop their economies and to pay for oil imports. By 1982 LDC debt reached unmanageable proportions (Exhibit 1.5). LDCs saw their total external indebtedness surge from $130 billion in 1973 to $1,114 billion in 1986, to $1,336 billion in 1990 and to $1,623 billion in 1994. Since the LDC debt service burden increased, the terms of trade for these nations have been negative, that is, LDC export prices fell relative to import prices. Since the international credit worthiness of LDCs has come into question, the international financial community has become less willing to lend or invest in some LDCs. Consequently, investment spending has fallen and economic growth in these nations has slowed.

The challenge to the LDCs is to find ways to work out from under these international debt obligations, while at the same time maintaining social and political stability. The governments of these debtor nations have moved to improve economic efficiency by relying more on private sector initiatives. Privatization of government enterprises is one direction taken in this broad area of activity. Also, some LDCs have moved to improve the climate for foreign investment and trade through regional integration. The *North American Free Trade Agreement (NAFTA)* is a case in point. Under this agreement there will be a free flow of goods and services among the United States, Canada, and Mexico.

NEWLY INDUSTRIALIZED COUNTRIES (NICs)

In the 1980s the term "newly industrialized countries" was applied to countries in both East Asia and Latin America. Four economies were cited as representatives of this category due to their remarkable economic growth primarily by export-led growth strategies: Singapore, Hong Kong, Taiwan, and Korea.

In the 1990s several additional nations earned this distinction: China, Malaysia, Thailand, and Indonesia. According to IMF statistics, in the period 1992–1994, average annual economic growth rates were: 13% in China: 8.3% in Malaysia; 8.2% in Thailand; 6.5% in Indonesia; 6.5% in Korea; 8.0% in Singapore; 6.3% in Taiwan; and 5.0% in Hong Kong. The recent economic growth rates in these countries have been attributed to their high domestic saving and investment rates, imports of foreign capital and technology, and exports of more manufacturing goods. However, these countries are confronting many challenges in the late 1990s. China, Malaysia, and Thailand have to deal with domestic inflation resulting from economic prosperity. Hong Kong was returned to China by the British

EXHIBIT 1.5	**Indicators of LDC Debt and Debt Service, 1973–1994**				
	1973	**1980**	**1986**	**1990**	**1994**
LDC Debt (Billions)	$130	$634	$1114	$1336	$1623
Debt Service Ratio[1]	15.9	17.6	23.0	17.6	15.8
Terms of Trade	+13.3	−16.3	−18.1	−0.4	−0.3

[1] Debt service ratio is the required debt service as a percent of export revenues.

SOURCE: IMF, *World Economic Outlook* (1983, 1991, and 1995).

after July 1, 1997. Singapore, Korea, and Taiwan have encountered more trade competition within the region and from external trading blocs such as European Community (EC), North American Free Trade Agreement (NAFTA), and Japan.

Latin America, Mexico, Brazil, and Argentina are included in the NICs category. These countries have demonstrated relatively strong economic growth rates in the 1992–1994 period but were affected by the Mexican peso crisis in December 1994 to May 1995. High inflation and volatile capital inflows continue as major problems for these nations. Economic, financial, and social reforms remain as long-term challenges for these countries.

Mexican peso crisis

Drastic decline in value of the Mexican peso in December 1994–early 1995 affected many emerging capital markets in Latin America including Mexico, Brazil, and Argentina.

TRANSITIONAL ECONOMIES

In the 1990s Eastern European countries are in the process of transforming from centrally planned economies to free market economies. This change implies that these countries need more inflows of foreign capital to support their transition. As shown in Exhibit 1.1, Eastern European countries and Russia have had negative economic growth in the 1990–1993 period. These countries, except Russia, managed modest economic growth in 1994.

The basic economic problems of the former centrally planned economies are shortages of consumer goods, wasteful use of resources, inadequate or depleted infrastructure, and difficulty in generating and applying technological innovations. The lack of economic incentives and outdated technology are key factors contributing to these problems. Among this group, Poland, Hungary, China, and Russia have called for decentralization of domestic economic management, privatization of certain sectors of the economy such as agriculture and services, tax incentives to foreign investment, and the use of new technologies.

Unfortunately, reforms initiated in many ex-Communist countries have not been successful. Many Eastern European countries such as Poland and Hungary require further political and economic reforms, especially the privatization of their state-owned industries. In addition, these countries will require substantial investments in infrastructure, modern capital equipment, and advanced production techniques for many years to come.*

MULTINATIONAL CORPORATIONS

Since the early 1960s when American firms rushed to establish their operations overseas, multinational corporations have become an important international phenomenon. At that time U.S. firms provoked considerable controversy concerning

---

* *The Banker* "Journey into the Unknown," (October 1989): 42–56.

the impact of their operations on home and host country economies. The role and competitive status of U.S. multinational companies has changed. First, U.S. multinationals have encountered severe competition in many markets from companies based in Japan, Europe, and even some developing countries. Second, foreign multinationals have invested in the United States, attracted by favorable market opportunities. According to the U.S. Department of Commerce, foreign direct investment in the United States surged from $1,193 billion in 1986 to $2,613 billion in 1994. Third, U.S. multinationals have turned inward after 1980 because 1) tax reform adopted by the U.S. government favors domestic investment, 2) after 1985 a weak dollar made U.S. overseas investment more expensive, and 3) low petroleum prices cut oil company investment abroad. In the period 1986–1994 U.S. direct investment abroad has increased from $1,250 to $2,233 billion. This trend tends to increase international competition in the U.S. marketplace.

Structural changes have forced multinationals to reevaluate their competitive strategies. The challenging questions facing these companies include how to form joint undertakings with local or multinational companies to maximize resource allocation, for example, Japanese capital and technology and American management and marketing (described in Chapters 14 and 18). Other challenges are: how to produce new products to increase market share, such as joint ventures in West Europe; how to use the global capital market for low-cost financing (discussed in Chapter 15); and how to use modern technology to lower cost and avoid adverse foreign exchange and interest rate fluctuations (discussed in Chapters 16–17).

FINANCIAL INSTITUTIONS: INTERNATIONAL BANKS AND PORTFOLIO MANAGERS

Internationally oriented private financial institutions face tremendous challenges as a result of deregulation, technological change, rapid growth in capital flows, financial innovations, and the volatility of foreign exchange and interest rates. Commercial banks must deal with the restructuring of LDC debt, as well as increased competition with investment banks and foreign-based commercial banks. Japanese banks and securities firms have become strong competitors in global financial markets. The trend of securitization has imposed formidable pressures on both international commercial banks and investment banks to serve their customers in volatile markets.

With the globalization of financial markets and related financial innovations, international portfolio managers of insurance companies, pension funds, and mutual funds need high level financial skills to make timely decisions in rapidly changing financial markets. International portfolio investment is explored in detail in Chapters 18, 19, and 20.

INTERNATIONAL FINANCIAL INSTITUTIONS: THE IMF

As stated in the beginning of this chapter, the role of the International Monetary Fund is of critical importance in world finance. The challenges confronting the IMF for the present and near future are many. Three challenges are likely to remain as central issues. The first is to maintain stability and a viable international payments system in the foreign exchange market. Since the adoption of floating exchange rates after 1973, uncertainty in the foreign exchange market has persisted. A drastic change in the value of a key currency such as the U.S. dollar or German mark may cause a stormy reaction in world financial markets. To alleviate the foreign exchange risk, central banks have diversified their reserve holdings and business firms and banks have hedged their foreign currency operations. Under this system the worldwide supply and demand for specific currencies are critical to the efficient working of the international currency market. One source of IMF concern in this regard is its limited ability to influence national government intervention in the foreign exchange markets. For example, a central bank may manipulate a floating exchange rate favorable to its own currency. This practice is referred to as "dirty float" and not allowed by the IMF.

Dirty float

Central bank of a nation intervenes in the foreign exchange market under the floating exchange rate system without legitimate reason purely for the benefit of its own currency.

The second challenge to the IMF is the question of a member nation borrowing funds from the IMF. IMF conditionality involves the IMF establishing policy guidelines for members seeking to borrow reserve funds. Developments in Russia and the Eastern European countries since 1990 require special measures on the part of the IMF.

The third challenge to the IMF is how the IMF, and other international financial institutions (e.g. BIS) and major financial powers (e.g. U.S.), could prevent any major international financial crisis such as the Mexican peso crisis.

Global Finance: A Continuous Challenge

Looking ahead, the challenging areas in global finance may include the following:

1. The approval of NAFTA will stimulate flows of goods, services, and capital among the United States, Canada, and Mexico; what industries will be helped or hurt financially remains to be seen.
2. The strong growth of national economies and financial markets in Far Eastern countries has opened business and financial opportunities for foreign investors. However, problems persist in the form of high risk, internal competition, and diverse cultural patterns and business practices.
3. Newly converted market economies in Eastern European countries, Russia, and China are eager to welcome foreign investors, but the systemic gaps between these former Communist countries and western industrialized nations must be narrowed.
4. The recent global growth of derivative markets has accelerated cross-border capital flows and competition. Furthermore, the lack of regulation in the derivative markets raises questions of safety for international financial players.
5. Floating foreign exchange rates and volatile interest rates in the international financial markets have increased uncertainty and made planning more difficult for corporate and financial institutional investors.
6. Increasing importance of emerging capital markets and international repurchase agreements are new realities in global finance.

SUMMARY

The world financial environment has been changing rapidly over the past several decades. These changes include growth of the Eurocurrency market, development of the European Common Market, growth in importance of multinational corporations, international financial crises, a series of oil shocks, the international debt crisis, and the collapse of Communism in Russia and Eastern Europe and the orientations to market economy.

The world has been experiencing greater growth in international capital movements. In part, this shift has resulted from variations in economic growth rates of nation-states.

During the 1980s international capital flows to the United States increased without interruption. This increase has contributed to a globalization of financial markets in the leading international financial centers. Tighter connections between these international centers has produced a financial revolution, consisting of an increased global presence of financial institutions, financial integration, and the rapid pace of financial innovations.

These developments pose challenges in the 1990s to governments, businesses, financial institutions and world organizations. The United States has been running large budget and foreign trade deficits. Japanese payments surpluses must be channeled into productive investments in other countries. Developing countries must find ways to service an inflated external debt, as well as pay for the increasing costs of importing goods and capital. The transitional economies in Eastern Europe must reestablish themselves within the free market system.

The IMF plays a critical role in world finance. First, it must work to maintain a viable international payments system. Second, it must apply appropriate policy guidelines for member countries seeking to borrow hard currency funds and it must act as coordinator of global financial policies among member countries.

REVIEW QUESTIONS

1. In what ways has the world financial environment been changing in recent decades?
2. Why has the global economy been experiencing a greater growth in international capital movements?
3. What qualitative changes have been taking place in international capital flows?
4. What are the most serious challenges facing governments, businesses, financial institutions, and world organizations as a result of the changing global economy?
5. What role does the IMF play in the dynamic environment of global finance?

SELECTED BIBLIOGRAPHY

Angelini, Anthony, Maximo Eng, and Francis A. Lees. *International Lending, Risk and Euromarkets.* London: Macmillan, 1979.

Bank for International Settlements. *Annual Report,* Basle, various issues.

Bryant, Ralph C. *International Coordination of National Policies.* Washington, D.C.: Brookings Institution, 1995.

Eng, Maximo, and Vladimir Simunek. "Inflow of Capital and Financing Needs of the U.S. Economy." *Journal of North American Economics and Finance,* December 1988.

Eiteman, David K., Arthur I. Stonehill, and Michael H. Moffett. *Multinational Business Finance.* 7th ed. Reading, MA: Addison-Wesley, 1995.

Grabbe, Orlin J. *International Financial Markets*. New York: Elsevier, 1996.

International Finance Corporation, *Emerging Stock Markets Fact Books,* 1995.

International Monetary Fund. *World Economic Outlook,* Washington, D.C., various issues.

International Monetary Fund. *International Capital Markets.* Washington, D.C., various issues.

Hirtle, Beverly. "Factors Affecting the Competitiveness of Internationally Active Financial Institutions." *Quarterly Review,* Federal Reserve Bank of New York (Spring 1991).

Morgan, J. P. *World Financial Markets,* New York: various issues.

Levi, Maurice D. *International Finance*. 2d ed. New York: McGraw Hill, 1990.

Madura, Jeff. *International Financial Management*. 4th ed. St. Paul, Minn.: West Publishing Co., 1995.

Melvin, Michael. *International Money and Finance*. 2d ed. New York: Harper & Row, 1989.

Organization for Economic Cooperation and Development. *Financial Market Trends*. Paris: various issues.

Root, Franklin R. *International Trade and Investment*. 7th ed. Cincinnati: Southwestern, 1995.

Shapiro, Alan C. *Multinational Financial Management*. 2d ed. Boston: Allyn & Bacon, 1995.

Solnik, Bruno. *International Investment*. Reading, MA: Addison-Wesley, 1996.

CHAPTER 2

International Monetary System

INTRODUCTION

The international monetary system has undergone significant change, both in its structure and in the way in which it operates. The pace of change has accelerated during the past four decades. The dollar, which was the only strong currency at the end of World War II, now stands in the mid-range of currencies in terms of relative hardness. Similarly, American financial institutions have suffered relative decline with American banks, capital market sectors, and the U.S. money market all playing a somewhat less important role than 30–40 years ago. On the ascendancy are the European and Japanese capital market sectors, the Eurocurrency money market mechanism, stock markets in the developing nations, and international banks from almost all continents of the world.

In this chapter we provide an overall perspective on how the international monetary system has evolved. We then focus in greater detail on the interworking of the present system and its major components.

LEARNING OBJECTIVES IN THIS CHAPTER

1. To understand the role and importance of the international monetary system to the successful conduct of business and financial activities.
2. To appreciate the steadily evolving nature of the international monetary system and the changes that have taken place since the gold standard years, through World War II and the postwar era.
3. To analyze the current structure, operation, and major components of the international monetary system, including the International Monetary Fund, foreign exchange market, and other components.
4. To define the role played by the European Monetary System as a regional stable exchange rate mechanism and forum for monetary cooperation.

The Role of the International Monetary System

The international monetary system is analogous to the domestic monetary system. It carries out similar functions. In the domestic monetary system the functions that must be carried out include 1) providing for the transfer of purchasing power, that is, money payments to cover transactions, 2) providing a stable unit of value, and 3) providing a standard for deferred payments. For example, if a Philippine company borrows Peso 200 million, the domestic monetary system provides the money, checkbook money or currency, with which to make payments. If the Philippine company repays the loan over a five-year period, the bank lender will hold a claim of peso 200 million, which hopefully will be measured by a stable unit of value, the peso. Finally, the monetary system provides a standard—the dollar in the United States, the pound sterling in the United Kingdom, the peso in the Philippines—by which deferred payments can be measured.

The domestic monetary system generally works well in the absence of inflation. Inflation is a particularly serious problem with respect to the second and third functions of the domestic monetary system. Given a high rate of inflation in the United States, the dollar will not maintain a stable purchasing power and will not function as an adequate standard of deferred payments.

The international monetary system operates in a manner analogous to the domestic system. The same basic functions must be served by the international monetary system, namely, making payments to cover transactions, providing a stable unit of account, and providing a standard of deferred payments. The major difference in the international monetary system is that cross-border payments generally involve a foreign currency transaction for at least one of the parties involved in the transaction. Foreign currency transactions generally are channeled through the foreign exchange market. The foreign exchange market is one of the principal components of the IMS.

Let us again examine the case of a Philippine company borrowing funds, in this case the equivalent of Peso 200 million from a U.S. bank headquartered in Hong Kong. We assume the loan is denominated in U.S. dollars, and is for \$10 million (\$10 million $\times$ 20 Peso/\$ = Peso 200 million). The loan is to be repaid over a five-year period with the Philippine company bearing full foreign exchange risk. At the time of the loan, the U.S. dollar-Philippine peso rate of exchange is as follows:

$$\$U.S. \ 0.05 = Peso \ 1.00 \ or$$

$$Peso \ 20.00 = \$U.S. \ 1.00$$

Amortization of the loan principal is straight-line over the lifetime of the bank loan, with equal amounts of principal repaid year-end in each of the five years over the lifetime of the bank loan. Interest at 9% is also paid at year-end on the outstanding principal.

At the end of two years, the Philippine company has lost Peso 5,440,000 as a result of depreciation of the peso against the dollar in the foreign exchange market. Over the five-year period the accumulated loss is Peso 47,200,000, or 23.6% of the original amount borrowed. It can thus be observed that the IMS clearly poses serious problems for the conduct of international business. In this case, the Philippine company suffered serious financial loss as a result of peso depreciation. This loss will interfere with the ability of the Philippine company to remain competitive in domestic and export markets.

This example helps us identify some of the key performance characteristics required for an IMS to operate effectively. These include:

1. *Provision of adequate liquidity*. This provision takes the form of adequate units of official reserves held by governments of countries involved in foreign trade. It also

EXHIBIT 2.1	**Effect of Philippine Peso Depreciation on Local Currency Cost of Servicing a U.S. Dollar Debt**						
	Dollar Principal to be Repaid (Thous.)	Remaining Principal Amount (Thous.)	Yearly Interest	Total Debt Service (Thous.)	FX Rate Peso vs $	Peso Debt Service (Thous.)	Planned Debt Service (Thous.)	Increase in Debt Service (Thous.)
Year 0		$10,000						
Year 1	$2,000	8,000	$900,000	$2,900	20	P58,000	P58,000	0
Year 2	2,000	6,000	720,000	2,720	22	59,840	54,400	P 5,440
Year 3	2,000	4,000	540,000	2,540	24	60,960	50,800	10,160
Year 4	2,000	2,000	360,000	2,360	26	61,360	47,200	14,160
Year 5	2,000	0	180,000	2,180	28	61,040	43,600	17,440
							Total	P47,200

NOTE: Cumulative increase in cost of debt service in Philippine pesos: P47,200
Cumulative increase in cost of debt service as percent of original borrowing: 23.6%

requires incentives for commercial banks operating as foreign exchange dealers to hold sufficient foreign exchange reserves to satisfy the requirements of the private sector. In the period 1992–1996 U.S. current account deficits averaged over $120 billion per year. As a result of these deficits, nonresident holders, including foreign central banks and commercial banks, accumulated this amount of dollars, adding to the dollar holdings of these entities. Given the central role of the U.S. dollar in international finance and payments, the world experienced sizable increments to official reserves and liquidity as a by-product of U.S. payments deficits.

2. *Operation of a smooth adjustment mechanism.* This objective requires that individual nations carry out economic and financial policies conducive to maintaining reasonably well-balanced international payments systems, or that financial mechanisms operate to provide payments adjustment, or that governments act to preserve equilibrium in the foreign exchange markets. The adjustment mechanism has not worked well in the past decade. For example, a growing U.S. trade deficit—imports in excess of exports—has remained virtually unaffected by a substantial depreciation of the U.S. dollar. In the period 1985–1996, the dollar fell sharply in value against the yen (from 250 yen to 105 yen per dollar), the pound sterling, the German mark, the French franc, and other major currencies.

Adjustment Mechanisms

Processes in the economy that work to assure a nation's external economic equilibrium.

The persistent trade and current account deficits of the United States in the face of a depreciating dollar raise serious questions concerning the adjustment mechanism and the efficiency of the floating rate system. It was thought that a floating dollar would find its own level, that the exchange value would equilibrate the U.S. payments position. Several factors help to explain the "failure" of the floating rate adjustment mechanism. Among these are trade barriers and the practices followed by multinational corporations (MNCs).

Common external tariff

For each commodity class, the EC countries maintain the same tariff rate for imports from outside the EC. There are no tariffs on trade among EC countries.

Trade barriers include the Japanese resistance to allow increased imports, the common external tariff of the European Community, and the lack of purchasing power in debt-ridden developing countries of Latin America. Given these barriers, a significant depreciation of the U.S. dollar seems to have little effect on increasing U.S. exports or on curbing U.S. imports.

MNCs follow practices relating to their investment, production, and logistics. MNCs set up their production facilities in selected countries, and these investments involve long-term commitments of large amounts of funds. These "sunk investments" must be utilized, irrespective of temporary exchange rate shifts. For example, many U.S. exporters decided in 1983–1984 to shift some of their production facilities to Western Europe, locating them inside the Common Market. Beginning in 1985, the depreciation of the dollar could have no influence on these logistics. Production facilities in Western Europe had to be utilized, even though the condition of the "overvalued dollar" of 1983–1984 had been reversed. The shift of U.S. production bases to Western Europe meant that this component of the former U.S. export potential was lost, irrespective of the depreciating dollar after 1985.

3. *Confidence in the system.* If private sector business firms and investors believe that governments will follow policies conducive to a well-balanced international payments system, they will have confidence in the system. International organizations such as the International Monetary Fund seek to promote such policies on the part of governments. In addition, governments undertake cooperative arrangements with one another to build confidence in the existing system.

During the postwar period confidence in the IMS has been associated with the status of the U.S. dollar, which plays a central role in the system. High inflation in the United States tends to undermine confidence in the future value of the dollar. In 1971 this loss of confidence took the form of a speculative bearish attack against the dollar, at which time speculators sold dollars in exchange for other currencies. Holders of dollars sought to shift their assets to nondollar form. This compelled leading central banks to suspend convertibility of dollars into other currencies at fixed exchange rates.

Early History and Postwar Evolution

All international monetary systems must incorporate the basic functions and qualities previously described in order to be effective. Historically, several distinct sets of international monetary arrangements have fulfilled these functions. We will now examine the historical progression of the IMS from the late nineteenth century through the present era. This focus on IMS arrangements, institutional structures, and issues and events will increase appreciation of the dynamic IMS environment within which global finance occurs.

The international monetary system is an evolving mechanism. It is constantly changing due to the actions of governments which affect its operational performance, and the trends and events taking place in the world economy.

THE GOLD STANDARD AND THE SPECIAL ROLE OF BRITAIN

International Gold Standard

The golden years of the international monetary system.

Imperial preferences

Imports from British colonies favored; tariffs and quotas on noncolony imports.

In the 40 years prior to 1914, the IMS was largely a British sterling-influenced system. Called the international gold standard, this system included Great Britain and many leading industrial countries, all of which 1) defined their currency units by a fixed gold content, 2) permitted free coinage of gold at the mint, and 3) allowed unrestricted export and import of gold.

The dominant role of Great Britain in world finance was based on a global colonial system and the widespread use of sterling in international finance. As was noted at that time, "the sun never sets on the British Empire." The British colonial system provided a strong foreign trade position, protected behind a wall of imperial preferences. British investment in the colonial areas was an important aspect of the ascendancy of the pound sterling in international finance. Foreign investment provided a constant return flow of income. That provided the British with financial resources to pay for imports from the rest of the world and with funds for further investment. During this period, London served as banker for the world; sterling deposits in London were considered equivalent to monetary gold.

The basic rules of the game previously described fulfilled two requirements. First, each country chose gold as the ultimate standard of value by maintaining the unit of its currency equal to a defined weight of gold. Second, each country permitted the free export and import of gold. To keep all money including coins, currency, and bank deposits equal in value, a country may: Mint gold coins containing the amount of gold specified by law as the standard unit of value, Instruct the national treasury to buy or sell gold at a fixed price (bullion), or maintain the parity in value of its currency and gold by buying or selling, at a fixed price, the currency of a country on the gold standard. During the 1800s, the gold standard was in effect a sterling standard since many countries kept their currencies stable in value in terms of sterling.

In the period 1870–1914, Great Britain tied the pound sterling closely to gold. During this period Great Britain had the advantage of not being invaded in wars, which added to its image as the model of financial security and prudence. According to Kindleberger and Lindert, the success of the gold standard in this period is explained in part by the tranquility of the era.* The world economy was not exposed to excessive shocks as severe as World War I and the Great Depression.

At times Great Britain was called upon to curb outflows of gold reserves. The Bank of England displayed an impressive ability to halt gold outflows via monetary tightening. This tightening attracted large volumes of short-term capital from abroad, even when central banks in other countries raised their interest rates along with the Bank of England. The ability to attract short-term capital seems to have been linked with London's role as the reserve center for the world's money markets.† When this system broke down during and after World War I, the United States inherited the role of world banker.

After World War I a number of problems emerged that made it difficult for gold standard countries to return to this system. First, differential inflation experienced by countries formerly on the gold standard raised the question of the appropriate pattern of exchange rates. Second, the United States was not an experienced world banker. The country engaged in foreign lending during the 1920s, and many of those loans went into default. Third, the Great Depression of the 1930s led to a severe contraction of world trade and investment. Finally, several countries attempted to solve their international payments deficits by engaging in competitive currency devaluations and restrictive trade practices. These disruptions and instabilities eroded confidence and led to further cutbacks in international lending and investment. The IMS did not operate effectively in facilitating the growth of world trade and payments until the conclusion of World War II.

Toward the conclusion of World War II the international monetary conference at Bretton Woods, New Hampshire, led to the creation of two new institutions: the International Monetary Fund and the World Bank. The former of these has come to play a pivotal role in postwar international finance.

Devaluations and trade restrictions

Sometimes called "beggar thy neighbor" policies.

Bretton Woods, NH

Conference in 1944 establishing foundation for postwar international monetary system.

---

* Kindleberger, C.P., and P.H. Lindert. *International Economics,* Homewood, IL: Dow Jones-Irwin, 1978, 391.

† ————. p. 394.

POSTWAR EVOLUTION

The end of World War II in 1945 presented the world with an opportunity to restore a stable financial environment. During the war years strong inflationary pressures became established around the world. Inflation did and can still place severe pressure on foreign exchange relationships and tends to inject an element of riskiness into the conduct of foreign trade and overseas business dealings.

The IMS has evolved and changed since 1945, affected by the:

1. changing role of the United States and the U.S. dollar in world finance;
2. growth in importance of international financial markets;
3. opportunities for expansion of international banking operations;
4. new requirements and opportunities perceived by multinational corporations;
5. emergence of financial crises brought on by changes in the basic economic relationships between countries; and,
6. growing importance of foreign investment, particularly international portfolio investment.

In the following discussion we examine this postwar evolution of the IMS, in particular noting roles of the various forces described.

Dollar Shortage: 1946–1952   At the termination of World War II the two major poles of economic potential, the United States and Western Europe, were in opposite positions regarding their ability to function as foreign traders and investors. In 1946 the United States economy was producing at a high level. The postwar transition to a peacetime economy was being carried out smoothly, and the rest of the world needed American goods and services. For this reason the dollar demand exceeded supply to an extent that economists named this period the "dollar shortage" era.

In contrast, the Western European economy was in a state of turmoil. The ravages of war had destroyed numerous factories and productive infrastructure. There were shortages of many goods, requiring high levels of imports. Postwar Europe had an inflated demand for imports, but a depressed capacity to produce for export.

In addition, the Western European currencies were weak and unstable in value. At this point these currencies were inconvertible due to the unwillingness of foreign traders and financial institutions to accept them as payment for exports.

The dollar shortage provided American banks with the opportunity to monopolize the financing of foreign trade where U.S. exports and imports were concerned. American banks found themselves in a commanding position where foreign credits were involved. Their position was secure because dollar credits were heavily demanded and there were few if any competing lenders.

Stability: 1953–1957   By 1952 Western Europe had regained prewar levels of industrial production. This was facilitated largely by generous provision of dollar credits and aid under the European Recovery Program of 1947–1952, also referred to as the Marshall Plan. From 1948–1951, $14 billion of this aid was provided to Western European nations to finance exports of manufactures, coal, and food items from the United States.

With Europe regaining its productive capacity, intra-European trade flourished and industrial competition became a more important factor leading to a healthy and

Dollar Shortage
Protracted period after World War II when world demand for U.S. dollars exceeded supply.

stable economic environment. Gradually, European currencies became more stable, and the foreign exchange markets in Europe were liberalized so that nonresident and resident money transfers could be made more freely. By 1957 the European currencies were ready for full convertibility status. This meant that European currency holders faced no restrictions in how and where they used their currency. With this liberalization, international lending and foreign exchange trading expanded as underlying economic transaction volume grew.

Emerging Payments Problems: 1958–1963   The strengthening and stabilization of the foreign exchanges culminated in official convertibility status for the principal European currencies in 1958. This set the stage for the Common Market. Originally, the Common Market was a six-country grouping (West Germany, France, Italy, Belgium, Luxembourg, and Netherlands) in which all tariffs on industrial products within the group were gradually removed over a ten-year transition period. In addition, a common external tariff was set in place. Formation of the Common Market presented a problem for American corporations. Prior to 1958 American companies enjoyed a profitable export market in Europe. Now the Common Market established a regional trade integration scheme that would discriminate against U.S.-based manufacturers.

> **Common Market**
>
> In addition to economic benefits, CM brought countries of Europe closer politically.

American manufacturers had little choice but to consider investing in production facilities within the six-country group. This move would provide them with equal access to the prosperous Common Market. Between 1959 and 1964, U.S. manufacturers accelerated their direct business investment in the Common Market, giving American banks the opportunity to finance some of this investment. American banks also began to see the need to establish closer contacts in Western Europe in the form of representative offices and branches.

The sharp increase in capital outflows from the United States to Western Europe imposed pressures on the U.S. balance of payments. These conditions included not only the original financial outflows, but also a number of related trade flow effects. American manufacturers, setting up production facilities in Europe, ordered capital equipment from U.S. suppliers, thus increasing the exports of U.S. capital goods. Gradually these European production facilities displaced some exports from the United States resulting in an unsatisfactory balance of payments performance. In the early 1960s larger outflows of portfolio investment from New York investment firms, in the form of foreign bond flotations, placed additional pressure on the U.S. balance of payments position.

Capital Controls: 1964–1970   The balance of payments (BOP) deficit became an issue in the presidential election of 1960. Democratic candidate John F. Kennedy blamed the BOP deficit on faulty economic policies. However, the Democratic election victory did not reverse basic economic trends that included a rising volume of capital outflow from the United States in the form of foreign bond issues placed in New York.

> **Capital controls**
>
> Government regulations and legislation to influence FX market supply and demand.

In 1963 the Kennedy administration proposed an Interest Equalization Tax (IET) that Congress enacted in the subsequent year. The tax was an excise on American residents' purchases of bonds and stocks issued by foreign entities. The tax was aimed at equalizing the cost of funds in New York and in Europe where interest rate levels were higher. Initially foreign stock and bond purchases were taxed at a rate of 15%. On a 15- to 20-year bond issue, this tax raised the cost of funds to European borrowers by about 1% per year. While the American investor paid the tax, the ultimate burden of the tax was shifted to the foreign borrower. This effect is outlined in Exhibit 2.2.

EXHIBIT 2.2	Effect of Interest Equalization Tax on Cost and Yield of New York Funds	
	Before IET	**After IET**
Par value of bond	$1,000	$1,000
Annual coupon on bond	60	70
Cost to American investor	1,000	1,150
Effective annual cost to borrower	6.00%	7.00%
Yield to American investor	6.00%	6.08%

U.S. balance of payments problems continued as alternative forms of capital outflows increased. As a result, two additional forms of capital control were imposed early in 1965. These were a restraint on U.S. banks lending to offshore borrowers (among these, European affiliates of American corporations) and limits on direct U.S. business investment overseas.

The controls provided strong incentives for the development of offshore financial markets, including the Eurocurrency and Eurobond markets. Also, American banks began to establish offshore branches for use as lending platforms to avoid violating the capital controls program. Finally, American multinational corporations found it possible to use specialized financing affiliates to borrow in offshore markets in order to channel funds to operating affiliates.

International Financial Crises: 1971–1973   The Bretton Woods financial system was based on a structure requiring a stable and strong U.S. dollar. Confidence in the system depended on holders of dollar assets being able to rely on the unimpaired value of these assets in the future. During the 1960s rising inflation, the deterioration of the U.S. trade balance, and overall payments deficits led to a persistent accumulation of liquid dollar holdings by official and private holders outside the United States. In the late 1960s it was openly discussed that the dollar had become overvalued and might have to be devalued to restore equilibrium in the U.S. balance of payments. During the period 1968–1970 confidence in the existing exchange parity of the dollar in relation to other leading currencies had begun to ebb.

In 1971 there was a breakdown of confidence in the dollar. Many private holders of dollars sought to convert them to hard European currencies. The speculation against the dollar was so intense that the German central bank had to close down the foreign exchange market in Frankfurt for a brief period of time. In effect, the free convertibility of the dollar was interrupted. The role of the Group of Ten in the 1971 crisis is outlined in Exhibit 2.3.

As a result of this crisis a series of currency revaluations took place with the dollar devalued against the major European currencies by approximately 8%. In addition, gold convertibility of the dollar was suspended. By the end of 1971 leading industrial nations negotiated the Smithsonian Agreement, whereby the dollar was devalued and a wider band of currency rate fluctuation was permitted (2.25% instead of 1% in each direction).

The Smithsonian Agreement was important for several reasons. First, it represented the first multilateral action to cope with a loss of confidence in the Bretton Woods System and U.S. dollar weakness. Second, it recognized the need for an improved adjustment mechanism. The wider 2.25% band of fluctuation in either direction made it more costly for speculative action and also introduced more flexibility into exchange rate relationships. In 1973 a second currency crisis took place, and

Revaluation

Upward change in value of a currency. Opposite of devaluation.

Smithsonian Agreement, December 1971.

"Gold as a reserve asset has an uncertain value. Central banks do not wish to have gold back again center stage." (Japanese financial adviser)

EXHIBIT 2.3		**Chronology of Events in 1971 Leading to the Collapse of the Bretton Woods System**			
January–March	**April**	**May 3–5**	**May 10**	**June–July**	**August 15**
Large flows of interest-sensitive liquid funds from United States to Europe placed pressure on dollar in the fixed exchange rate system.	Large U.S. official reserve deficit occurred in first quarter; open speculation in foreign exchange market against U.S. dollar.	German Bundesbank was forced to purchase $1 billion of U.S. dollars. Bundesbank suspended dollar support operations in its exchange market. Other leading European central banks stopped support of dollar.	Foreign exchange markets reopened. European currencies were revalued or allowed to float against dollar.	Large increase occurred in U.S. official reserves deficit; large U.S. trade deficit in second quarter. U.S. gold stock fell as speculative flows continued.	In the United States, President Nixon announced major stabilization program. This program included 90-day freeze on wages and prices, 10% temporary surcharge on imports, tax measures, and temporary suspension of dollar convertibility into gold.
August 28	**September 15**	**October–November**	**December 1**	**December 17–18**	**April 1973**
Japan suspended official intervention in foreign exchange market, and yen increased in value.	At Group of Ten finance ministers meeting, no agreement was reached on policy. United States insisted on revaluation of major currencies vis-a-vis dollar.	Pressure was placed on United States to take measures to end the crisis. Currency speculation intensified as U.S. official reserves deficit rose in third quarter.	At Group of Ten finance ministers meeting in Rome, U.S. treasury secretary suggested a 10% devaluation (rise in dollar price of gold).	Last ditch effort by the G10 finance minister to save the Bretton Woods system by raising the price of gold to $38 an ounce from $35; by setting a multilateral realignment of exchange rates; and by ending the import surcharge.	Following the G10 meeting in Rambouillet (France), the exchange rates of all major industrial countries began to float against the dollar.

the United States was forced to devalue the dollar again. Shortly after, foreign currency markets moved toward a general floating of major currencies.

OPEC

Members are: Algeria, Iraq, Kuwait, Libya, Qatar, Saudi Arabia, United Arab Emirates, Gabon, Indonesia, Iran, Nigeria, Venezuela, and Ecuador.

Jamaica Agreement, 1976

Formal adoption of floating rates.

Petrodollar Recycling: 1974–1981   Early in 1974 the Organization of Petroleum Exporting Countries (OPEC) quadrupled the price of crude oil exports, creating the first international oil shock. The trade balances of many oil-consuming nations swung sharply to deficit. In response, the IMF set up its "oil facility" in mid-1974 to help "recycle" surplus funds from the OPEC countries to those needing to borrow. The oil crisis contributed to a number of changes in the IMS, including adoption of a formal system of floating exchange rates (the Jamaica Agreement of January 1976), a liberalized definition and use of the special drawing rights, and abolition of the official price of gold.

A second oil shock came in 1978–1979. The rise in oil prices placed many oil-importing nations under pressure to borrow funds to pay for oil imports. The onset of the oil crisis necessitated that the United States abandon its system of capital controls. Petroleum is a dollar-oriented commodity, and the dollar surpluses earned by the oil exporters had to be recycled, that is, loaned to oil-importing nations to help the adjustment process. These dollar surpluses are called petrodollars. The principal mechanisms for recycling the financial surplus were 1) the New York money market and banking sector, 2) the London money market, and 3) the Eurocurrency market. United States authorities moved quickly to suspend the capital controls, making it possible for American banks to increase their loans to all oil-importing countries, free of capital control limitations. As a result American banks were free to compete for petrodollar deposits and to lend these proceeds internationally without restriction. During the next several years there was a boom in international bank lending as the syndicated Euroloan market expanded to meet the needs of petrodollar recycling.

International Debt Crisis: 1982–1983   By 1981 it was becoming apparent that some developing country borrowers had gone beyond the practical limits of their debt-bearing capacity. In 1982 the international debt crisis became a reality when the government of Mexico announced it would be unable to make scheduled payments of interest and principal on external debt. Other debtor countries followed Mexico in announcing that their external debt service requirements had grown beyond their foreign exchange resources.

The 1982 shock had several causes. First, between 1978 and 1981 global inflation pushed interest rates on international loans and credits to record levels. Second, Euroloans were generally structured with floating interest rates based on fairly sensitive indicator rates such as LIBOR (London Inter Bank Offer Rate). Therefore, borrowing countries quickly felt the impact of higher interest rates in the form of rising debt service payments. Third, world commodity prices were declining, and debtor countries found export revenues shrinking due to weak prices of export commodities.

In the years following 1982, the international financial community witnessed frequent debt service problems and reschedulings. Debtor countries negotiated with creditors for longer periods in which to repay outstanding debts. Bank lenders earned front-end fees in return for providing rescheduling arrangements. In addition, many debtor nations agreed to IMF stabilization programs requiring financial austerity measures. These programs typically required debtor countries to reduce domestic monetary expansion and government budget deficits. In return, the Fund would provide medium-term credit facilities. These terms permitted debtors to continue purchasing necessary imports such as food, fuel, and industrial spare parts, thus keeping their economic systems moving forward.

FX Market Evolution   Over the period 1981–1984, the Reagan administration followed a "hands-off" approach toward intervening in the foreign exchange market. However, the appreciation of the U.S. dollar in 1982–1984 made imported goods cheaper and more attractive to American buyers. As a result, the trade deficit increased at an alarming rate. The automobile, textile, and agricultural sectors felt the strongest foreign competition and became more vocal in demanding protective legislation.

At the Group of Five (G-5) meeting held at New York's Plaza Hotel in 1985, the United States, the United Kingdom, France, Germany, and Japan announced there would be joint intervention in the foreign exchange market to bring about dollar depreciation, which marked a return to the earlier practice of attempting to influence exchange rate movements.

The dollar dropped steadily over the next eighteen-month period, causing a number of major industrial countries to feel the strong pressure of international competition. In response they followed moderately restrictive monetary policies. Meanwhile, the United States was pursuing a policy of lower interest rates accompanied by a

Stabilization program
IMF loan to member country based on it adopting austerity measures.

Intervention
Central bank buying or selling its currency in the foreign exchange markets.

Plaza Accord, 1985
Joint intervention and efforts to lower U.S. dollar value.

depreciating dollar. United States policy became a topic of criticism due to the apparent inconsistency of allowing the dollar to depreciate (expecting to improve the U.S. trade balance) while pushing down U.S. interest rates, which led to increased expenditure and U.S. imports.

The finance ministers of leading countries met in Paris in February 1987. They issued a statement entitled the "Louvre Accord" calling for stabilization of exchange rates around prevailing levels. The accord also called for target bands of +5% and −5% around current exchange rate levels. These goals were achieved for several months following the Paris meeting. However, in October 1987 exchange rate stability ended with the U.S. stock market's plunge.

Since 1987, a combination of "tools" has served as the basis for maintaining a degree of exchange rate stability among currencies of the major industrial nations. During this period the rules of coordination were not well defined. A sufficient degree of responsiveness is evidence that communication of national economic and social policy needs among nations has occurred. For example, in 1995 U.S. authorities actively participated in talking down the dollar's value against the yen as a way to pressure Japan into reducing its nontariff barriers to imports in several manufacturing and service product areas. A second purpose for this U.S. action was to encourage Japanese authorities to adopt a more aggressive stance toward spurring growth in the Japanese economy. The exchange rate slipped to a low of Y 85 per dollar in May and June 1995, from the Y 100–Y 110 range over the previous two years. Progress was made toward reducing nontariff barriers, and Japanese economic growth did increase. Subsequently, the dollar exchange rate returned to the Y 100–Y 110 range.

Securitization and Rescheduling   The international debt crisis of the early 1980s left a legacy of troubled loan situations in the developing nations. In reaction, international banks turned to securitization to convert financial claims into a form more easily traded as marketable securities. This trend was reinforced in several developed nations by severe balance sheet pressures on banks arising from the restructuring of national financial systems. In the U.S., for example, the collapse of the savings and loan industry and the depletion of the resources of the Federal Deposit Insurance Corporation (FDIC) led government banking regulators to place an emphasis on capital adequacy.

These pressures have led international banks to give direct lending a lower priority and to focus more attention on fee-earning services. Provision of these services permits the banks to avoid direct credit exposures, but earnings can simultaneously be generated from fees based on financial services provided. These services include: restructuring customer loan and asset portfolios (in part through interest rate swaps and currency swaps); providing financial backup for customers who are tapping the international capital markets; and assisting customers to reduce risks related to fluctuating exchange and interest rates.

Also, international banks have been busy in rescheduling outstanding loans to international borrowers. Generally these reschedulings involve three basic components: 1) revising or extending maturities so that borrowers have smaller units of debt principal to repay each year; 2) renegotiating interest spreads and fees; and 3) providing additional short-term credits to cover immediate and near-term trade financing and payment arrears.

In 1987 two events forced bank creditors and governments to rethink their policies about LDC debt: the large loan loss write-off of LDC debt paper by Citibank, and a debt-for-bonds exchange that Morgan Guaranty had structured for Mexico. By 1987, economic growth had fallen below population growth in a number of debtor countries, and it was feared that socio-political stability might be undermined. The Brady Plan was aimed at debt reduction. Key aspects of this plan included substantial credits by international organizations and commercial bank debt reduction or interest charge reduction.

A validation of these concerns emerged with the Mexican currency crisis in late 1994. Following a period of persistent capital flight, Mexican authorities devalued the peso by over 50% against the dollar. As a result, an acceleration of net capital outflows threatened to seriously undermine the Mexican economy. To stabilize this situation, American authorities worked together with the International Monetary Fund to establish a $20 billion safety-net plan. As recovery progresses, one outlet for Mexico will be exports to U.S. and Canadian markets within the framework of the North American Free Trade Association.

The EMS and Maastricht Treaty   During the 1980s the EMS countries experienced increasing convergence of their interest rates. By 1991 member countries were close to agreement on implementing a plan leading to monetary integration. The Maastricht Treaty was signed in February 1992. This introduced a program— the European Monetary Union (EMU)—that would advance economic and monetary union within the European Union (EU). Under Maastricht, candidate nations are required to meet the convergence criteria, including restriction on a prospective candidate country's monetary and fiscal policies. However, some nations are not prepared to relinquish this control. For this reason, Danish voters rejected the treaty in June 1992, and the U.K. and Italy withdrew in September 1992. Despite these significant setbacks, there is a general expectation that the EMU will be implemented in some form on January 1, 1999.

Maastricht Treaty, 1992
Agreement among European Union nations to work toward full economic and monetary union.

The EMU convergence criteria are: 1) Inflation should not exceed that of the three best-performing states by more than 1.5%; 2) The nominal long-term interest rate must not exceed that of the three best-performing states by more than 2%; 3) The fiscal deficit must not exceed 3% of GDP; 4) The gross government debt must not exceed 60% of GDP; and 5) The exchange rate must have respected the normal fluctuation margins in the ERM for at least two years.

Principal Components of the IMS

In the first section of this chapter, we describe the role of international monetary systems and identify several key performance characteristics. In this section we focus on our present IMS, which has been shaped by a rich course of events and forces as summarized in the preceeding brief historical review.

The present IMS possesses five important operational components:

1. International Monetary Fund (IMF)
2. Foreign exchange market
3. Official reserves
4. Private demand for foreign exchange
5. Intervention and swap network

These work together to provide liquidity, to facilitate adjustment of temporary imbalances, and to instill confidence in the system.

INTERNATIONAL MONETARY FUND

Bretton Woods System   In 1944 representatives of 44 nations met at Bretton Woods, New Hampshire, for the purpose of establishing a more orderly and better functioning world monetary system. They sought to create an institutional mechanism that would provide liquidity, payments adjustments, and increased confidence in the newly created payment mechanism. Considering the currency instability experienced in the interwar period, they hoped to design a monetary system that would foster financial stability, full employment, and external balance for all nations.

The system established at Bretton Woods called for fixed exchange rates of currencies for the U.S. dollar and a stable dollar price of gold. Countries were to hold their official reserves in gold or U.S. dollars and could exchange dollars for gold without limit at the U.S. Treasury.

The Bretton Woods conference led to the organization of the International Monetary Fund. The IMF structure focused on both providing better financial discipline among member countries and ensuring more stable exchange rates. Exchange rate discipline would be backed by countries following monetary policies conducive to price level stability and balance of payments equilibrium. If a country allowed inflation to reach an excessive level, it would experience a decline in exports and a surge in imports. As a result, it would lose international reserves and become unable to support the external value of its currency.

The fixed price of gold ($35 an ounce) would operate as a constraint on U.S. monetary policy. If the Federal Reserve created too many dollars, prices would rise and the U.S. payments position could deteriorate. Foreign central banks could accumulate dollars and convert them into gold. U.S. gold reserves would decline.

The IMF began operations at the end of World War II. Operating as an international financial institution, the Fund now has more than 160 member nations. The Fund was established to promote exchange rate and financial stability and to increase monetary cooperation among member nations. In a positive way, the IMF was established to overcome the problems of currency inconvertibility, trade and payments restrictions, and foreign exchange market instabilities that had prevailed in the 1930s and 1940s. The agency operates from its headquarters in Washington, D.C., where the largest part of its administrative and financial operations are planned and carried out.

Obligations of Member Countries   Member countries take on certain obligations when they join the IMF, including financial, behavioral, and economic responsibilities. Financial obligations include payment of cash to the Fund based on the size of the member's quota. The United States has the largest quota; and the 10 largest industrial countries have combined quotas equivalent to 55% of total quotas (Exhibit 2.4).

IMF quota

For each country, assigned under a complex formula based on national income, international monetary reserves, imports, and exports.

Members can draw on Fund resources based on the amounts in their quota subscriptions. On joining the IMF, the new member is required to pay 25% of its quota into the Fund in gold. Thus, a member with a $200 million quota will initially pay $50 million in gold and $150 million in its own currency in the form of non-interest bearing demand notes into the Fund. A quota is divided into four quarters known as tranches. The first tranche, referred to as the gold tranche, can be drawn on by a member automatically. All members can count on being able to

EXHIBIT 2.4	General Quotas of Selected IMF Members, February 1996
All Countries	**US$213.429 billions**
United States	38.958
Germany	12.104
Japan	12.104
France	10.889
United Kingdom	10.888
Saudi Arabia	7.536
Italy	6.742
Canada	6.345
Netherlands	5.058
China	4.972
Belgium	4.556
India	4.487
Australia	3.427
Brazil	3.189
Venezuela	2.865
Mexico	2.575
Argentina	2.257

SOURCE: International Monetary Fund, *International Financial Statistics,* April 1996.

draw this amount without question. As the amount of money a member desires to draw increases, the Fund's standards of financial conduct become more demanding. Conditionality standards also increase in the third and fourth tranche drawings.

In addition to extending financial assistance to its members through drawings, the Fund often enters into standby arrangements. In such cases members receive an assured line of credit rather than immediate cash. Under a standby arrangement the member is able to draw a specified sum with stated conditions. Standby credits can be renewed beyond the original period of time negotiated and may continue for several years.

Behavioral obligations include the responsibility of member nations to liberalize their current trade and payments relations with other countries. Also, members are expected to follow policies conducive to maintaining financial equilibrium. These actions might include fiscal policies leading to removal or reduction of deficits in the national budget and monetary policies that avoid inflation. At times when member nations wish to draw on the liquidity resources of the IMF, the Fund may set specific conditions for eligibility for such credits. This conditionality might include the country agreeing to specific economic policy targets such as reducing the national budget deficit to a specific percentage of GDP, improving the trade balance by a certain dollar amount, and curbing money wage increases to a certain percentage level. The IMF programs are generally labeled austerity programs due to the more constrained standard of living imposed on countries with payments deficits.

Economic obligations also apply to surplus countries that are to manage their national economic systems to facilitate the adjustment of deficit countries. For example, countries with a balance of payments surplus must keep their economies expanding so that their imports will expand, making it possible for deficit countries to expand exports and work themselves out of the deficit position.

The Bretton Woods system imposed dual stability conditions (Exhibit 2.5). This required that the United States pursue policies that maintained confidence in the fixed exchange rate and dollar price of gold. It also required that member countries

| EXHIBIT 2.5 | Dual Stability Conditions Under the Bretton Woods System |

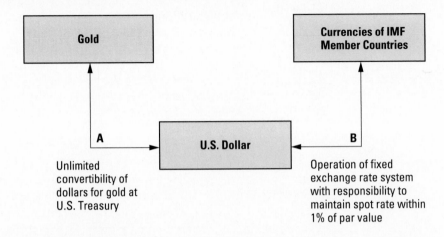

Dual stability conditions operate at points A and B. The first stability condition requires that the United States pursue financial policies that maintain confidence in the fixed dollar price of gold. The second stability condition requires that all member countries (including the United States) pursue financial policies that permit maintenance of their fixed exchange rate relationship in comparison with the U.S. dollar.

pursue policies permitting maintenance of their fixed exchange rate relationship with the U.S. dollar. However, the United States failed to maintain confidence in the fixed rate of the dollar against gold and other currencies, and the system disintegrated.

The U.S. currency played a central role and therefore the United States had unique obligations. These included the following:

- **U.S. Financial Obligation**—to convert dollars into gold for foreign governments and central banks.
- **U.S. Behavioral Obligation**—to manage the U.S. payments position so that the supply of dollars matches well with the needs of the rest of the world and to hold appropriate amounts of gold and other official reserve assets.
- **U.S. Economic Obligation**—to manage the U.S. economy in a manner facilitating easy adjustment of payments deficits and surpluses of countries that carry out substantial trade and investment with the United States.

We can summarize the functions of the IMF as follows:

International liquidity

Foreign exchange reserves and gold held by the national government.

1. provides liquid resources to member countries which are short in international liquidity or purchasing power;
2. monitors members' trade and payment systems to ensure they are maintained on a liberal and free transaction basis;
3. urges members to follow financial policies that will lead to stable economic relationships with the rest of the world, and thereby build confidence in the present system of currency and external payments arrangements; and
4. encourages members to adopt economic programs that will facilitate balance of payments adjustment.

FOREIGN EXCHANGE MARKET

The foreign exchange market is the framework for trading foreign currencies. In this market one currency is the commodity traded, while another currency is the active money ingredient. The foreign exchange market is the largest financial market in the world with daily trading in excess of $1 trillion.

The foreign exchange market is operated by large commercial banks that trade currencies in the form of sight deposits in other banks. Sight deposits are subject to immediate transfer or withdrawal, as contrasted with time deposits which cannot be withdrawn until maturity of the deposit. The market operates like an over-the-counter market with trading conducted over the telephone or telex, with no central or physical market location. The foreign exchange market:

1. transfers purchasing power from one country to another.
2. provides a means of hedging open currency positions. This function is carried out primarily through forward exchange transactions.
3. provides a clearing mechanism for international payments. Trading banks buy and sell each currency they trade with only a relatively small change in their net position by the end of the trading day.
4. provides a credit facility whereby banks can purchase time drafts drawn in foreign currency. A time draft is an order to pay a check, drawn on a bank, with a specified future maturity. This instrument is discussed in greater detail in Chapter 4.

The foreign exchange market is one important part of a complex financial process, and as such, the foreign exchange market reflects disequilibrium by the frequency and intensity of exchange rate movements. Changes in exchange rates in the market provide central banks, governments, and the IMF with a mechanism through which balance of payments problems can be partially corrected. Finally, the foreign exchange market is an important component of the private international financial markets, reinforcing close links between the various international money market sectors.

OFFICIAL RESERVES

Governments hold official reserves, international money, in various forms. Official reserves function like international money by their general acceptability. One central bank will readily accept reserves from another to complete international settlements. Exhibit 2.6 indicates that at April 1996 official reserves of all countries aggregated $1,420 billion, representing slightly over one-fifth of world exports. Official reserves consist of four separate and distinct components.

The first component is the reserve position in the Fund. This represents quotes of IMF member countries freely available to them to supplement their liquid resources. In 1995, this reserve amounted to $54.1 billion.

Special Drawing Rights (SDRs)

A form of international reserve asset. Its value is based on a portfolio composite of widely used currencies, created by the IMF in 1967.

The smallest component is special drawing rights, also referred to as paper gold. SDRs were created to supplement international liquidity at a time when it was thought official reserve growth would be inadequate to meet global needs. SDRs reflect bookkeeping entries within the IMF, which members in deficit can use to settle international payments at the official level (central bank of one country transferring SDRs to central bank of another country).

EXHIBIT 2.6	Official Reserves: Global Total, October 1995

Major Components:	
Reserve Position in Fund[1]	US$ 54.1 billion
Special Drawing Rights[2]	29.1
Foreign Exchange[3]	1297.1
Total Reserves Minus Gold	720.6
Gold[4]	48.4
Total Reserves	1402.4
Total Reserves as % World Exports	27.7%

[1] Reflects members' unused quotas subject to automatic access.

[2] Bookkeeping entries created in IMF system that countries can use to settle payments at official level.

[3] Approximately three-fourths of this amount is held in U.S. dollars.

[4] Valued at less than $40 per ounce.

The largest component consists of foreign exchange held by governments and their central banks. During the mid-1990s close to three-fourths of this amount had been denominated in U.S. dollars, although other currencies used included deutsche marks, pound sterling, yen, and French francs.

Finally, a part of official reserves is held in the form of monetary gold. Monetary gold reserves present a measurement problem due to the fluctuating value of gold in the world commodity markets. If these gold reserves were valued at current market prices, the dollar value of monetary gold reserves would represent over half of the total official reserves.

Official reserve holdings are fairly concentrated. In 1995 the ten countries for which data are provided in Exhibit 2.7 held $630 billion or 50% of the global total.

Governments hold official reserves for numerous reasons. Some governments are more concerned with the need to cover external debt payments, while others are more interested in being able to cover the cost of necessary imports such as food and fuel. Factors influencing governments to hold official reserves include:

1. to be able to carry out international transactions including imports without any delay in payments;
2. to improve the international credit standing of the nation;
3. to provide resources for foreign exchange market intervention, when needed; and,
4. to assure and facilitate external debt service payments.

PRIVATE DEMAND FOR FOREIGN EXCHANGE

The private demand for foreign exchange refers to the foreign currency balances held by foreign exchange banks. The term private demand is used in contrast with official demand, where official reserves are held by governments. Private demand results from the risk versus profit judgments of the private trading banks. When a large number of dealing banks become uncertain of the near future prospects for a currency in the market, they may shorten their deposit holdings of that currency. This move could place downward pressure on that currency in the exchange market.

More than 200 major international banks from only three dozen nations dominate this foreign exchange market. They represent the big players in the market, and include banks such as Sumitomo, a Japanese bank with approximately 20 money market and foreign exchange dealing rooms around the world where foreign

EXHIBIT 2.7	**Official Reserves of Selected Countries Year-End 1995**

United States	US$ 88.4 billion
Germany	90.0
France	31.1
Italy	38.4
Japan	184.5
Switzerland	40.8
United Kingdom	43.0
Singapore	68.7
Saudi Arabia	8.9
Spain	35.3

Other holders of large official reserves include

People's Republic of China,	US$76.0
Netherlands	35.7
Canada	15.2
Australia	12.3
South Korea	32.7

SOURCE: International Monetary Fund, *International Financial Statistics,* April 1996.

"FX market settlement risk is an emerging issue." (Member, F.R. Board of Governors)

exchange trading takes place. A bank like Sumitomo will, on a reciprocal basis, maintain foreign currency deposits in banks in all of the countries where foreign currency trading services must be operated (perhaps two dozen or more countries). Sumitomo's sterling balances may be held in National Westminster Bank, London, while reciprocally National Westminster will maintain yen deposits in Sumitomo's Tokyo office. The aggregate holdings of these 200 or more banks in yen, sterling, or deutsche marks represents the "private demand."

In effect, the foreign exchange market is an over-the-counter market (OTC) where market makers are the dealing banks. If the dealer organization becomes sour on a particular asset holding in the OTC market, they sell off. This action is quickly reflected in the valuation of that asset. In this regard the concept of private demand helps us to understand the high sensitivity of foreign exchange rates.

INTERVENTION AND SWAP NETWORK

A swap involves a standby credit agreement between two (or more) countries. The swap is used to borrow or lend foreign currency in exchange for domestic currency with a commitment to reverse the exchange in three months. A foreign exchange swap is a spot purchase of a currency coupled with a forward sale. The calculations involved in various types of swaps are discussed in a later chapter. Central banks use swaps to provide foreign currency resources to one another, which are used to intervene in the foreign exchange market.

To see how the swap network operates, suppose the United States wants to sell 200 million deutsche marks to support the U.S. dollar. What actually happens is the U.S. Federal Reserve sells the Bundesbank (German Central Bank) US $100 million (assume the rate is DM 2.00 = $1.00) in exchange for DM 200 million, with an agreed reversal in three months at a fixed rate. The Bundesbank's official reserves rise by US $100 million and those of the Federal Reserve rise by DM 200 million. The Federal Reserve can now sell the deutsche mark in the foreign exchange market, with the purpose of driving up the value of the U.S. dollar.

The technique of central bank swaps was first developed by the U.S. Federal Reserve in the early 1960s. The Federal Reserve has negotiated agreements with

15 central banks and the Bank for International Settlements (located in Basel, Switzerland). These banks provide more than $30 billion in foreign exchange resources for the defense of the dollar. Other countries also have put together swap arrangements to provide funds for currency market intervention.

FIVE COMPONENTS OF THE IMS AND THEIR INTERACTION

The interaction of the five components of the IMS is illustrated in Exhibit 2.8. Each year a large volume of international financial transactions takes place. These transactions may be 100–150 times as large as total official reserves held by all countries participating in these transactions. This exchange includes foreign trade and foreign investment transactions, payments for services (tourism, shipping, insurance), and remittances of income on foreign investments. These transactions are settled and cleared through the foreign exchange market. Private commercial banks that buy, sell, and hold foreign currency balances support the foreign exchange market in carrying out these financial operations (flow (1) in Exhibit 2.8).

Discrepancies in any particular country's demand and supply for foreign exchange can be balanced off by that country drawing on (activating) its stock of official reserves. In cases of excess demand, the central bank can sell foreign exchange

EXHIBIT 2.8	**Composition of International Monetary System**

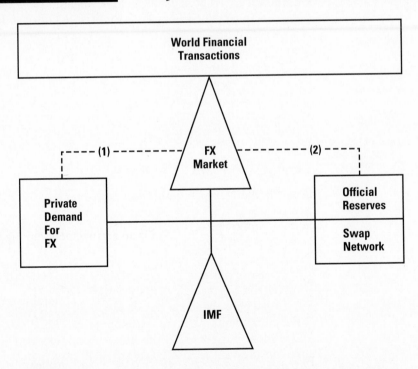

(1) Private commercial banks buy, sell, and hold foreign currency balances. The amounts of a particular currency they are willing to hold constitutes the private demand for that currency.
(2) The central bank can sell foreign exchange to the commercial banks from its official reserves. Official reserves are held in part in the form of foreign exchange balances, as deposits, or as liquid money market investments.

to its commercial banks from its official reserve holdings. This operation is shown in Exhibit 2.8, flow (2). Countries in the swap network can also draw on swap facilities with central banks in other countries. Finally, the IMF can provide short-term assistance (activate drawing facilities) for individual member countries in need of these financial resources.

An example will clarify this concept. Say that Denmark experiences a temporary shortfall in its foreign exchange earnings needed to pay for imports and debt service. Denmark's commercial banks are finding that they have to pay higher foreign exchange rates (in Danish krone) to purchase sufficient dollars to meet the needs of their commercial and investment customers. In effect, the Danish krone is depreciating in relation to the U.S. dollar. Over time this depreciation could correct the shortfall in foreign exchange earnings by discouraging imports of goods that cost more in Danish currency with the depreciation of the krone. The Danish central bank can release official reserves that it holds partly in the form of U.S. money market investments (U.S. Treasury bills). The Treasury bills can be cashed in for liquid bank deposits. In turn these can be sold as foreign exchange to Danish commercial banks. Finally, Denmark can make a drawing of dollars and other currencies from the IMF, based on its quota with that organization.

European Monetary System

European Monetary System

A monetary alliance among European Community members to maintain exchange rates within specified margins about fixed central rates.

Following the international financial crises of 1971 and 1973, the countries of the European Community (EC) agreed to cooperate among themselves in preserving monetary and foreign exchange rate stability. With the advent of floating rates in the mid-1970s, the EC operated as an exceptional grouping of countries whose exchange rate movements were limited within the framework of the European Monetary System (EMS) to small percentage changes around parity rates. In 1992 and 1993 the EMS experienced severe crises. In 1992 two members left the fixed rate mechanism, and in 1993 the members agreed to work under wider bands of currency rate fluctuation.

BASIC STRUCTURE OF EMS

In March 1979 nine members of the European Community launched the European Monetary System. The EMS is an arrangement among member nations to limit fluctuations in their currencies and achieve monetary stability. It was intended that foreign trade among the participating nations would be improved if exchange rates were stabilized. The EMS contains several important features, including a common currency unit, regulation of fluctuations of member currencies, mutual credit facilities, and the creation of a central reserve fund. Refer to selected key dates in the development of the EMS in Exhibit 2.9.

ECU

European Currency Unit.

Divergence indicator

The DI system is used to determine which nations are to alter economic policies to maintain the fixed parity values.

European Currency Unit (ECU)   The European Monetary System is based on a central reserve fund of gold, dollars, and member currencies. The common denominator of the system is the European Currency Unit (ECU). While the ECU is not money, it does serve important monetary functions:

1. a numeraire (yardstick of value) for the exchange rate mechanism;
2. the basis for a divergence indicator;

EXHIBIT 2.9	European Monetary System: Selected Key Dates				
March 1979	**February 1986**	**December 1991**	**June 1992**	**September 1992**	**January 1993**
European Monetary System comes into operation. Currencies originally in EMS include Belgium-Luxembourg franc, Danish krone, French franc, German mark, Irish punt, Italian lira, and Netherlands guilder.	Single European Act ratified following Delors Plan proposal which schedules liberalization of capital flows in 1990, and free movement of labor and capital in 1992.	Treaty on European Union ratified at Maastricht summit. Requires national referenda.	Danish voters reject Maastricht Treaty.	British pound and Italian lira temporarily withdrawn from European fixed exchange rate mechanism.	European Community officially becomes a single market.
August 1993	**October 1993**	**November 1993**	**January 1994**		**January 1, 1999**
Second ERM crisis within 12-month period. Currency bands widened to 15%, except for German mark and Netherlands guilder, which retain bilateral bands of 2.25%.	German Constitutional Court rejects claims that Maastricht Treaty involved a dissolution of German national sovereignty.	Maastricht Treaty enters into force.	Stage two of the EMU begins. European Monetary Institute organized (precursor to the European Central Bank). First steps to common monetary policy.		Start of third EMU stage. Countries lock exchange rates together. Binding rules in macroeconomic and budgetary areas. Common monetary policy under the European Central Bank. Exchange intervention in third currencies the responsibility of the ECB Council.

3. the denominator for operations in the intervention and credit mechanism; and,

4. a means of settlement among monetary authorities of the European Community.

The ECU is equivalent to a weighted average of a base of EMS currencies. Weights assigned to each currency are based upon the gross domestic product of each country and its share in European trade. The dollar value of the ECU can be calculated by multiplying the exchange rates of the EC currencies by their weighted value in the basket of ECU currencies. The dollar value of the ECU on April 19, 1996, was approximately $1.2410. The appendix illustrates value calculations.

The ECU Is a Monetary Asset The ECU functions as a monetary asset. The EMS nations hold ECU balances as part of their official reserves. The EMS central banks lend, borrow, and use ECU balances as a means of settling debts among themselves. It is possible in the future that nonmember central banks could use ECU as an international reserve asset, similar to their current use of the SDR issued by the International Monetary Fund.

EXHIBIT 2.10	**European Monetary System Central Rates, % Change from Central Rate, and Divergence Indicator, April 18, 1996**

	ECU Central Rates	Currency Amounts Against ECU 18 April 1996	% Change from Central Rate	% Spread Versus Weakest Currency	Divergence Indicator
Spain	162.493	158.532	−2.44	4.36	17
Netherlands	2.15214	2.12759	−1.14	3.00	8
Belgium	39.3960	39.0875	−0.78	2.62	6
Austria	13.4383	13.3827	−0.41	2.24	3
Germany	1.91007	1.90299	−0.37	2.20	4
Portugal	195.792	195.204	−0.30	2.13	2
France	6.40608	6.45552	0.77	1.04	−6
Denmark	7.28580	7.34522	0.82	1.00	−6
Ireland	0.792214	0.806634	1.82	0.00	−12
Non ERM Members					
Greece	292.867	305.386	4.27	−2.35	—
Italy	2106.15	1981.06	−5.94	8.25	—
UK	0.786652	0.835326	−6.19	−4.11	—

ECU central rates set by the European Commission. Currencies are in descending relative strength. Percentage changes are for ECU; a positive change denotes a weak currency. Divergence shows the ratio between two spreads: the percentage difference between the actual market and ECU central rates for a currency, and the maximum permitted percentage deviation of the currency's market rate from its ECU central rate.

(17/9/92) Sterling and Italian lira suspended from ERM. Adjustment calculated by the *Financial Times*.

SOURCE: *Financial Times,* 19 April 1996.

Central exchange rates

The fixed par values, with respect to ECU, among exchange rates of participating countries.

The ECU serves as an accounting unit for calculating the central exchange rates of the individual currencies of EMS members (see Exhibit 2.10 for ECU central rates as of April 1996). Each of the central banks of the EMS has formally defined the value of its currency in terms of the number of units of that currency which equals one ECU. The currency rates are reexamined every six months, taking into account the evolution of each member's balance of payments situation and economic conditions.

There are two reasons for converting EMS member currencies into their ECU equivalents. First, it permits establishing a central rate for each currency that is then used to calculate the system of ECU-based exchange rates linking member currencies (Exhibit 2.10). Second, it provides a benchmark in measuring fluctuations in exchange rates. In turn these fluctuations are used to determine when the "threshold of divergence" of the currency is reached. When the currency reaches the threshold of divergence (a deviation of 75% of the agreed maximum fluctuation—1.69% of the 2.25% for most currencies), the government of that country must take action within agreed limits to maintain the value of its currency.

European Monetary Cooperation Fund

Provides EMS settlement resources, based on specified revolving swap arrangements.

EMS Payment Procedures   Countries in the EMS are required to contribute 20% of their gold and U.S. dollar holdings to create a special reserve. This amount is held in the European Monetary Cooperation Fund (EMCF). In return members receive credit in ECUs. This exchange of reserve assets is updated quarterly as members' official reserves increase or decline.

Members are expected to extend short-term credits to other EMS countries when monetary conditions call for such support. When an EMS member must intervene in the foreign exchange market to stabilize its currency rate in relation to other members, the intervening country must advise the central banks of other EMS countries. When intervening and making funds available, the lending central banks consider this as short-term financing. Prevailing interest rates are charged against the borrowing country whose currency has been supported by intervention.

Should a member country borrow for intervention purposes, its debt is denominated in ECUs. The debtor country can repay the debt in ECUs or the borrowed currency. If the debtor country possesses no ECUs and wishes to acquire some, it may apply to the central banks of EMS countries or to the EMCF. In the case of acquiring ECU from the EMCF, the acquiring central bank pays for these ECUs by contributing gold and dollar reserves.

ECUs are used in settlement of intra-community debt, as agreed upon by the EMS countries. EMS central banks can transfer ECUs to one another against dollars, EMS currencies, SDRs, or gold.

OPERATION OF EMS

Until September 1992 the European Monetary System included all 12 EC member countries. However, Greece had not yet joined the exchange rate mechanism (ERM), preferring to allow its currency to float freely. The currencies of the most recent entrants (Spain 1989, United Kingdom 1990, and Portugal 1992) were temporarily permitted a wider band of fluctuation.

When the EMS was initiated, many observers doubted that this experiment in regional fixed exchange rates could be successful. In 1979 there were great pressures on exchange rates due to wide differences in inflation rates and interest rates among member countries. In the period prior to the crisis of September 1992, the EMS had made use of several defense mechanisms to keep it afloat:

1. wide bands of exchange rate flexibility for members (2.25% to 6%);
2. ability of France and Italy to utilize selected exchange controls during the initial years;
3. periodic exchange rate realignments; (for example, in 1987 there was a realignment of the French franc due to strikes and demonstrations in France. In 1990 there was a realignment of the Italian lira when the lira's band was reduced to 2.25%.)
4. closer monetary cooperation among member nations. (Some observers suggest this control means that the German central bank tends to dominate European monetary policy.)

To date, the EMS has been moderately successful. Members have aligned their monetary policies more closely. Inflation rates and interest rates have moved more closely over the years in a period characterized by many strains and pressures on exchange rates.

With the liberalization of capital movements and the reunification of Germany, both in 1990, extreme pressures were brought to bear on the fixed exchange rate mechanism. In addition, in 1992 the referendum on ratification of the Maastricht Treaty in member countries led to speculative pressures on individual currencies. In 1992 and 1993 several crises led to two members temporarily withdrawing from the fixed rate mechanism, and the widening of bands to 15%.

Since the crisis of September 1992, member countries have affirmed their intent to continue the process of economic and financial integration. In November 1993, the Maastricht Treaty entered into force, and in January 1994 stage two of the EMU began (Exhibit 2.9). January 1999 is the target date for the start of the third stage of EMU. The following countries are expected to participate at that time: Germany, France, Belgium, Netherlands, Luxembourg, Austria and Ireland. Four other countries for which EMU membership is a high priority are: Italy, Spain, Portugal, and Greece. Other countries expressing a commitment are: Sweden, Finland, Denmark, and the United Kingdom.

SUMMARY

The international monetary system is analogous to the domestic monetary system. The major difference is that in the IMS, cross-border payments involve a foreign currency transaction. Key performance characteristics of the IMS include provision of adequate liquidity, operation of a smooth adjustment mechanism, and confidence in the continued viability of the system.

The present IMS includes five operational components. These are the International Monetary Fund (IMF), the foreign exchange market, official reserves, private demand for foreign exchange, and the intervention-swap network. The Bretton Woods conference led to organization of the IMF that was established to overcome the problems of currency inconvertibility and foreign exchange market instabilities. Members can borrow liquid resources from the IMF to relieve payments difficulties. In return, the Fund expects members to pursue economic policies that will assist in eliminating payments deficits. Under the Bretton Woods fixed exchange rate system, dual stability conditions persisted, that is, the dollar had to be kept convertible into gold, and members had to maintain spot rates of their currencies within 1% of par value.

Postwar evolution of the IMS reflects the changing role of the United States and the dollar in world finance, the growth of international financial markets, the expansion of international banking, new needs of multinational corporations, and the growing importance of foreign investment. The international financial crises of 1972–1973 led to the replacement of the fixed exchange rate system with a floating exchange rate mechanism.

In 1979 nine European countries launched the European Monetary System to limit fluctuations of member currencies and to achieve a measure of monetary stability. The EMS is based on a central reserve, with a common denominator—the European Currency Unit (ECU). While the ECU is not money, it does serve important monetary functions, including as a numeraire or standard of value for the exchange mechanism, a basis for the divergence indicator, a denominator for intervention, and a means of settlement among monetary authorities of the European Community.

APPENDIX

RECOMPOSITION OF THE ECU

The European Currency Unit value is subject to recomposition at five-year intervals. The following describes the weighted basket and currency recomposition over the period since 1979 when this system was introduced.

EXHIBIT 2.11   **Appendix**

RECOMPOSITION OF ECU

The European Currency Unit (ECU) is a weighted basket containing fixed amount of each of the 12 EC countries. These fixed amounts are reviewed every five years and can be changed only by official action. The weights of the 12 currencies are calculated by converting their fixed amounts into common currency at current market exchange rates. This means that a currency's weight can move in response either to a change in its fixed amount, or to a change in its market exchange rate. Official recompositions are intended to correct changes in ECU weights caused by currency movements that can be justified by underlying economic criteria. The last recomposition took place on 21 September 1989, when the ECU basket was enlarged to include the Spanish peseta and the Portuguese escudo. In 1992 the 12 EC currencies were given the following fixed amounts and weights in the ECU.

	ECU PERCENTAGE WEIGHTINGS AT RECOMPOSITION			Fixed Currency Amount in ECU 21 Sep 1989	Actual FX Rate against DM 17 Dec 1992	Value of component in DM	Effective Weighting 17 Dec 1992
	13 Mar 1979	17 Sep 1984	21 Sep 1989				
German mark	33.0	32.0	30.1	0.6242	1.00	0.624200	31.9
French franc	19.8	19.0	19.0	1.332	3.419	0.389588	19.9
British pound	13.3	15.0	13.0	0.08784	0.407	0.215867	11.0
Italian lira	9.5	10.2	10.15	151.8	898.7	0.168911	8.6
Dutch guilder	10.5	10.1	9.4	0.2198	1.125	0.195378	10.0
Belgian/Lux franc	9.7	8.5	7.9	3.431	20.52	0.167203	8.5
Danish krone	3.1	2.7	2.45	0.1976	3.860	0.051197	2.6
Irish punt	1.1	1.2	1.1	0.008552	0.3776	0.022647	1.2
Greek drachma	—	1.3	0.8	1.440	132.5	0.010868	0.6
Spanish peseta	—	—	5.3	6.885	70.99	0.096985	4.9
Portuguese escudo	—	—	0.8	1.393	89.11	0.015631	0.8

17 Dec 1992 DM/ECU = 1.958474

In between these official recompositions, a currency's ECU value and thus its weight in the ECU will fluctuate in step with changes in market exchange rates. These market-induced changes in ECU weights will remain small in the absence of a realignment of ERM central rates. Since the recomposition on 21 September 1989, the effective weight of the mark in the ECU has increased from 30.1% to 31.9%.

REVIEW QUESTIONS

1. The following table indicates external debt outstanding and official reserves of selected countries. Discuss the significance of these amounts to a prospective bank lender and to a U.S. Treasury official proposing to increase American government loans to these countries.

Country	OFFICIAL RESERVES ($ billion)	EXTERNAL DEBT ($ billion)
Brazil	$7.7	$110.0
Chile	1.8	12.6
Costa Rica	0.7	3.4
Indonesia	2.6	28.4
Mexico	5.8	96.0
Philippines	0.4	25.0

2. How might each of the following organizations be affected by full implementation of monetary union in the year 1999?
   a. European-based commercial bank
   b. European-based investment bank
   c. European-based pension fund
   d. European-based manufacturing company

3. Explain how the transition toward the European Monetary Union might affect the practices of European companies seeking to borrow funds to finance their expanding operations.

4. What is the role of gold as a component of official reserves in our present international monetary system? Is it possible that forward foreign exchange contracts and options may provide an alternative approach to fulfill this role?

5. Critically evaluate the following statement: "In today's foreign exchange markets, central banks are important in influencing the course of foreign exchange rates. Thus, central banks are relegated to the status of FX rate followers, not leaders."

6. What are the forces that have driven many countries to participate in regional currency blocs?

7. The Bank of England wishes to prevent further strengthening of the pound against the dollar. To do this the BOE sells sterling for dollars in the spot market. Simultaneously, the BOE sells U.K. Treasury bills as a way to soak up excess liquidity in the British money market. What is the net effect of these actions on the dollar/pound exchange rate?

8. Under the Gold Standard international monetary system, what were the "rules of the game" that the central banks of participating countries were called upon to undertake?

9. What were the factors that led the U.K. and Italy to withdraw from the European Monetary Union in 1992? What were the implications of this action for the EMU evolution?

10. You are the CFO of a major U.S.-based multinational corporation. The company is considering investment in a new manufacturing facility to be located in Europe. How will the formation of the EMU and its movement to a single European currency influence your choice of country location?

11. What are the main components of official reserves? Explain why nations hold official reserves. What is meant by the private demand for foreign exchange?

12. In 1995, the IMF recommended that the government of Egypt devalue the pound in order to spur its economy. The Egyptian monetary authorities refused to heed this advice. Why? Do you think their reluctance to devalue the Egyptian pound was a wise decision? This question is a current problem faced by many emerging economies and relates to the Mexican peso situation in 1994–95.

SELECTED BIBLIOGRAPHY

Abuaf, Niso, and Philippe Jorion. "Purchasing Power Parity in the Long Run." *Journal of Finance,* 45 (March 1990): 157–74.

Arshanapalli, Bala and John Doukas. "Integration of Euro-Money Markets." *Journal of Multinational Financial Management,* (1993): 2:107–126.

Bertola, Giuseppe and Ricardo Caballero. "Target Zones and Realignments." *American Economic Review,* 82 (June 1992): 520–36.

Bloughton, James M. (ed). *Fifty Years After Bretton Woods: the Future of IMF and the World Bank.* Washington, D.C.: International Monetary Fund, 1995.

Claassen, Emil-Maria. *International and European Monetary Systems.* New York: Praeger, 1990.

Cooper, Richard N. *The International Monetary System: Essays in World Economics.* Cambridge, Mass.: MIT Press, 1987.

DeCecco, Marcello, and Alberto Giovanni (eds). *A European Central Bank? Perspectives on Monetary Union After Ten Years of the EMS.* Cambridge: Cambridge University Press, 1989.

DeGrauve, Paul. *The Economics of Monetary Integration.* Oxford: Oxford University Press, 1992.

Deutsche Bundesbank. "Freedom of Germany's Capital Transactions with Foreign Countries." *Monthly Report,* 37 (July 1985): 13–23.

Diebold, Francis X., Steven Hustel and Mark Rudon. "Real Exchange Rates under the Gold Standard," *Journal of Political Economy,* 99 (December 1991): 1252–71.

Engel, Charles M., and James D. Hamilton. "Long Swings in the Dollar: Are They in the Data and Do Markets Know It? *American Economic Review,* 80 (September 1990): 689–713.

Frankel, Jeffrey. "The Japanese Cost of Finance: A Survey." *Financial Management,* 20 (Spring 1991): 95–127.

Fratianni, Michele, and Jurgen von Hagen. "German Dominance in the EMS: The Empirical Evidence." *Open Economies Review,* 1 (1990): 67–87.

Grabbe, Orlin. *International Financial Markets.* New York: Elsevier, 1991.

Graboyes, Robert F. "The EMU Forerunners and Durability," Federal Reserve Bank of Richmond *Economic Review,* (July/August 1990).

Lewis, Karen K. "The Behavior of Eurocurrency Returns Across Different Holding Periods and Monetary Regimes." *Journal of Finance,* 45 (September 1990): 1211–36.

Marston, Richard C. *International Financial Integration,* Cambridge: Cambridge University Press, 1995.

Suzuki, Yoshio, Junichi Miyake and Mitsuaki Orabe. *The Evolution of the International Monetary System: How Can Efficiency and Stability Be Attained?* Tokyo: University of Tokyo Press, 1990.

Svensson, Lars E.O. "The Simplest Test of Target Zone Credibility." *IMF Staff Papers,* 38 (September 1991): 655–65.

Ungerer, Horst. "Europe: The Quest for Monetary Integration," *Finance and Development,* (December 1990).

Wolfson, Martin H., and Mary M. McLughlin. "Recent Developments in the Profitability and Lending Practices of Commercial Banks." *Federal Reserve Bulletin,* 75 (July 1989): 461–73.

CHAPTER 3

Balance of Payments Analysis

CONCEPTS AND ACCOUNTING RELATIONSHIPS

OVERVIEW

Balance of payments

Statistical estimate of the transactions between residents of one country and residents of the rest of the world.

A nation's balance of payments is an estimate of the transactions between residents of that country and residents of the rest of the world. We should note that all types of transactions are included in this definition: merchandise trade, shipping services, financial services, tourism, remittances, profits, and financial transactions.

We should also recognize the importance of residence status in defining balance of payments. In estimating the U.S. balance of payments, residents of the United States include individuals, corporations, government entities, and financial institutions. When a corporation or financial institution has an overseas branch or affiliate for balance of payments purposes, that overseas unit is a nonresident. For example, Dow Chemical U.S. is a resident, but Dow Chemical Europe is a nonresident. Chase Manhattan Bank NY is a resident, but Chase Manhattan London Branch is a nonresident.

We should note further that balance of payments numbers are estimated. A comprehensive reporting system is used by the government of a nation to estimate that nation's balance of payments. There can be and generally is a margin of error in these estimates. This margin is included in the balance of payments and labeled "errors and omissions" or "discrepancy". We return to this later when we discuss the double entry nature of balance of payments accounts.

LEARNING OBJECTIVES IN THIS CHAPTER

1. To comprehend the definition and conceptual basis of the balance of payments.
2. To appreciate the many uses and purposes of balance of payments analysis.
3. To develop an ability to work with the balance of payments accounts of a country and to be able to construct a balance of payments when given a series of transactions.
4. To understand the key economic forces that impact a nation's balance of payments.

5. To analyze a country's balance of payments accounts and to evaluate balance of payments performance from the perspective of economic policy, financial trends, and structural relationships.

KEY TERMS AND CONCEPTS

- ◆ balance of payments equilibrium
- ◆ basic balance
- ◆ capital account
- ◆ capital inflow
- ◆ capital outflow
- ◆ current account balance
- ◆ direct investment
- ◆ double entry

- ◆ errors and omissions
- ◆ immature debtor
- ◆ mature creditor
- ◆ official settlements balance
- ◆ payments
- ◆ receipts
- ◆ unilateral transfer

Sources and Uses of Funds

The term balance of payments refers to an accounting system that is analogous to the sources and uses of funds statement often used to depict the performance of a business entity. In the case of a nation's balance of payments, the performance is concerned with receipt and payment transactions. Although the typical analysis of a nation's balance of payments appears to be based on the supposition that cash is exchanged in all transactions, this exchange may not take place in every instance. For example, a company may make a direct business investment in the form of capital goods exports to the host country, with no cash transfers.

Receipt transaction

Transaction that results in receipt of funds by a resident.

Payments transaction

Transaction that results in payment of funds by a resident.

A receipt transaction is one that gives rise to the receipt of funds by a resident, and a payments transaction is one that results in payment of funds by a resident. In the United States balance of payments accounts in 1994, merchandise exports totaled $502 billion (Exhibit 3.1, line 3). American residents are presumed to have received that amount of cash as a result of their export activities. Similarly, in the same year American residents paid $668 billion for merchandise imports (line 4). American residents are presumed to have paid that amount of cash as a result of their import activities.

Receipt transactions include merchandise exports, exports of services (including shipping and tourism), receipt of income on foreign investments, and capital inflows (foreign purchase of domestic assets). Payments transactions include merchandise imports, imports of services, and capital outflows (resident purchases of foreign assets).

Double entry accounting

Every BOP transaction has two sides, a debit and a credit.

The balance of payments uses double entry accounting; therefore, every transaction has two sides, a debit and a credit. Under this accounting system total debits should always equal total credits. The equality of debits and credits has no special significance, but is based on the accounting logic that debits (payments) equal credits (receipts).

The balance of payments accounting system is used by economists as a measuring device and tool of analysis. Therefore we should understand the economists'

EXHIBIT 3.1   Summary of U.S. International Transactions

Millions of dollars

Item credits or debits	1992	1993	1994
1 Balance on current account	−61,348	−99,925	−151,245
2 Merchandise trade balance	−96,106	−132,618	−166,099
3 Merchandise exports	440,352	456,823	502,485
4 Merchandise imports	−536,458	−589,441	−668,584
5 Military transactions, net	−2,142	448	2,148
6 Other service transactions, net	58,767	57,328	57,739
7 Investment income, net	10,080	9,000	−9,272
8 U.S. government grants	−15,083	−16,311	−15,814
9 U.S. government pensions and other transfers	−3,735	−3,785	−4,247
10 Private remittances and other transfers	−13,330	−13,988	−15,700
11 Change in U.S. government assets other than official reserve assets, net (increase, −)	−1,661	−330	−322
12 Change in U.S. official reserve assets (increase, −)	3,901	−1,379	5,346
13 Gold	0	0	0
14 Special drawing rights (SDRs)	2,316	−537	−441
15 Reserve position in International Monetary Fund	−2,692	−44	494
16 Foreign currencies	4,277	−797	5,293
17 Change in U.S. private assets abroad (increase, −)	−68,115	−182,880	−130,875
18 Bank-reported claims[1]	20,895	29,947	915
19 Nonbank-reported claims	45	1,581	−32,621
20 U.S. purchases of foreign securities, net	−46,415	−141,807	−49,799
21 U.S. direct investments abroad, net	−42,640	−72,601	−49,370
22 Change in foreign official assets in United States (increase, +)	40,466	72,146	39,409
23 U.S. Treasury securities	18,454	48,952	30,723
24 Other U.S. government obligations	3,949	4,062	6,025
25 Other U.S. government liabilities[2]	2,180	1,706	2,211
26 Other U.S. liabilities reported by U.S. banks[1]	16,571	14,841	2,923
27 Other foreign official assets[3]	−688	2,585	−2,473
28 Change in foreign private assets in United States (increase, +)	113,357	176,382	251,956
29 U.S. bank-reported liabilities[1]	15,461	20,859	114,396
30 U.S. nonbank-reported liabilities	13,573	10,489	−4,324
31 Foreign private purchases of U.S. Treasury securities, net	36,857	24,063	33,811
32 Foreign purchases of other U.S. securities, net	29,867	79,864	58,625
33 Foreign direct investments in United States, net	17,599	41,107	49,448
34 Allocation of special drawing rights	0	0	0
35 Discrepancy	−26,399	35,985	−14,269
36 Due to seasonal adjustment	. . .	. . .	. . .
37 Before seasonal adjustment	−26,399	35,985	−14,269
MEMO *Changes in official assets*			
38 U.S. official reserve assets (increase, −)	3,901	−1,379	5,346
39 Foreign official assets in United States, excluding line 25 (increase, +)	38,286	70,440	37,198
40 Change in Organization of Petroleum Exporting Countries official assets in United States (part of line 22)	5,942	−3,717	−1,184

[1] Reporting banks include all types of depository institutions as well as some brokers and dealers.

[2] Associated primarily with military sales contracts and other transactions arranged with or through foreign official agencies.

[3] Consists of investments in U.S. corporate stocks and in debt securities of private corporations and state and local governments.

SOURCE: U.S. Department of Commerce. Bureau of Economic Analysis. *Survey of Current Business.*

terminology for the two sides of transactions in the balance of payments. These terms include:

Receipts	Payments
sources of funds	uses of funds
exports of goods and services	imports of goods and services
inflows of capital	outflows of capital
credit	debit

Receipt transactions include exports of goods and services and inflows of capital. Receipt transactions constitute a source of funds. Payment transactions include imports of goods and services, and outflows of capital. Payment transactions constitute a use of funds.

USES OF BALANCE OF PAYMENTS INFORMATION

Many banks, financial institutions, companies, portfolio managers, and government agencies work with balance of payments data for a wide range of applications. The balance of payments data is used to:

1. evaluate a country's credit worthiness;
2. serve as a business indicator in the analysis of national economic trends;
3. project pressures on foreign exchange rates;
4. anticipate government policy actions;
5. develop a better understanding in country risk analysis; and,
6. assist in evaluating the national economy's state of health.

Balance of Payments Accounting

CURRENT ACCOUNT AND CAPITAL ACCOUNT

The current account includes all transactions that influence the balance of payments in the year or time period in which they take place, but not in subsequent years or time periods. In contrast, capital account transactions typically require repayment at a future time period, which influences the balance of payments in subsequent years or time periods. The current account and capital account are defined further in Exhibit 3.2.

The current account includes merchandise exports and imports, exports and imports of services (including tourism, shipping, and insurance), and foreign investment income. The current account also includes unilateral transfers on private and official account—remittances, pensions, gifts, and government grants. Government grants and gifts are included in the current account, they require no repayment in a subsequent period.

Trade balance

Goods exports minus goods imports.

The trade balance, consisting of goods exports minus goods imports, dominates the current account of most nations. Exceptions include nations that export and import large amounts of services (financial, management, and marketing).

Capital outflows

Transfers of capital funds (asset holdings) to other (host) countries.

Capital inflows

Transfers of funds to the (home) country whose BOP is being estimated.

The capital account includes various types of loan and investment transactions. Capital outflows reflect transfers of capital funds (asset holdings) to host countries. Capital inflows reflect transfers of capital funds to the home country where balance of payments is being estimated. Capital transactions can be carried out by the

EXHIBIT 3.2	**Terminology Used in the Balance of Payments**
Current Account	Includes transactions that are completed within the time period. They are recorded in the balance of payments, with no effect on balance of payments in subsequent time periods.
Capital Account	Includes long-term and short-term investment transactions. These effect the international investment position of the country. Subsequent time period balance of payments effects will take place as a result of income flows or reversal of investments made in earlier years.
Direct Investment	Control investment in a foreign company or enterprise.
Portfolio Investment	Investment in securities (stocks and bonds) involving no control of a foreign enterprise
Unilateral Transfer	A transfer (gift or cash) for which no payment is made by the recipient. May include government aid to other countries or private transfers (contributions and donations).

private sector or by the government. Government loans via the Export-Import Bank or special lending agencies must be distinguished from official settlements that are discussed in the following section.

From the point of view of the U.S. balance of payments, capital outflows include the following types of transactions:

1. direct investment overseas by American firms;
2. acquisition of foreign stocks and bonds by American investors;
3. loans to foreign-based borrowers by American lenders; and,
4. acquisitions of bank deposits in offshore banks by American residents.

Capital inflows include the following types of transactions:

1. direct investment in the United States by foreign firms;
2. acquisition of U.S. stocks and bonds by foreign investors;
3. loans to U.S.-based borrowers by foreign lenders; and,
4. acquisition of bank deposits in U.S.-based banks by nonresidents.

The current account is the most widely publicized of the international payments balance concepts because of its focus on goods, services, and income—elements related to the international transfer of real consumer goods or productive resources. A second widely used concept is the basic balance, which is defined as the sum of the current account and long-term capital account balances. Here the focus is on the basic, long-term trends in international transactions. More volatile, short-term private capital movements and government official settlements transactions are excluded from the basic balance. The third payments concept is the official settlements balance that reflects the efforts of governments and central banks to provide foreign exchange resources in order to balance or "settle" residual needs not immediately financed by private sector capital flows.

Basic balance

Sum of the current account and long-term capital account balances.

OFFICIAL SETTLEMENTS

Official settlements balance

Net transactions by government of a monetary nature.

The official settlements balance is the net amount of transactions by governments. These represent the final settlement of transactions, and require that official reserves be used to effect payments. For example, the central bank may sell foreign exchange to its commercial banks when there is an expansion of imports or capital outflows. In this case the central bank holdings of official reserves provides a means for residual settlements of international payments.

Official settlements can involve the government spending reserves when there is an excess of private sector international expenditures over receipts. Official settlements can also involve the government accumulating reserves when there is an excess of private sector receipts over expenditures.

The point is that official settlements may only become necessary when a country experiences an imbalance in international transactions. In the case of a payments surplus, official reserves are accumulated. This situation is equivalent to a capital outflow—an accumulation of foreign exchange claims against nonresidents. In the case of a payments deficit, official reserves are utilized or drawn down. This circumstance is equivalent to a capital inflow or a reduction of foreign exchange claims against nonresidents.

CONSTRUCTING THE BALANCE OF PAYMENTS

We will now describe some sample transactions in a hypothetical country. We shall construct its balance of payments accounts.

There are two entries in each of the following transactions. The first represents the transaction taking place and the second represents the financing or financial side of the transaction. For example, when we indicate that a nonresident has purchased domestic government bonds (a portfolio investment inflow), we must also indicate that this purchase was financed by a reduction in foreign bank deposits held in the country receiving the portfolio investment.

The following transactions take place for Mightyland, a mythical country that uses the dollar as its local currency.

1. A European importer buys equipment from a Mightyland manufacturer worth $3 million. Payment is made by the European importer buying dollar deposits held by European banks in Mightyland banks, and then paying these dollars to the Mightyland manufacturer.

Credit: Merchandise exports	$3,000,000
Debit: Short-term liabilities to foreigners	$3,000,000

2. Mightyland importers purchase food from Latin American suppliers worth $1.2 million. Payment is made by transfer of dollar funds to Latin American exporters, who sell the dollar funds to Latin American banks who hold these short-term funds.

Credit: Short-term liabilities to foreigner	$1,200,000
Debit: Merchandise imports	$1,200,000

3. Mightyland tourists travel to Europe and spend $400,000 for travel expenses, hotels, and meals. They exchange dollar traveler's checks for European currency at various European banks. The European banks deposit the traveler's checks in other accounts in Mightyland banks.

Credit: Short-term liabilities to foreigners	$400,000
Debit: Tourist expenditures overseas	$400,000

4. Residents of Mightyland receive interest and dividends of $200,000 on their portfolio investments made in London, Paris, Zurich, and Frankfurt. The funds

are made available through clearing accounts held by European banks in local Mightyland banks. European banks experience reduced claims on Mightyland banks.

Credit: Investment income received	$200,000
Debit: Short-term liabilities to foreigners	$200,000

5. A Mightyland firm purchases 60% of the voting stock in a European manufacturer for $800,000. Payment is made by transfer of Mightyland dollars to the seller. The seller exchanges the dollars for local (European) currency, and the European banks accumulate the dollars purchased in deposits in Mightyland banks.

Credit: Short-term liabilities to foreigners	$800,000
Debit: Direct investment outflow	$800,000

6. The government of Mightyland provides foreign aid to the Philippines in the form of a unilateral transfer of agricultural products worth $300,000. No cash payment is received from the Philippines, but the unilateral transfer is recorded in the Mightyland balance of payments.

Credit: Merchandise exports	$300,000
Debit: Unilateral transfers	$300,000

7. The Bank of England (UK central bank) purchases 100,000 Mightyland dollars from British commercial banks, payment made in local (sterling) funds.

Credit: Short-term liabilities to official foreigners	$100,000
Debit: Short-term liabilities to private foreigners	$100,000

8. Mightyland banks loan $50,000 to Argentina. The Argentine borrower temporarily deposits the dollars in a Mightyland bank.

Credit: Short-term liabilities to foreigners	$50,000
Debit: Medium-term bank claims on foreigners	$50,000

9. European investors purchase $80,000 of common stocks listed and traded on the Mightyland stock exchange. European investors make payments purchasing dollars from European banks that draw down their dollar accounts held in Mightyland banks.

Credit: Portfolio investment inflow	$80,000
Debit: Short-term liabilities to foreigners	$80,000

We take these nine typical transactions and construct a balance of payments for Mightyland. The completed balance of payments is presented in Exhibit 3.3. Parts I, II, and III of the exhibit present current account transactions and the current account balance. Current transactions generate a surplus of $1,900,000 and unilateral transfers produce a deficit of $300,000, leaving the current account balance at $1,600,000. Note that credit and debit transactions and the net balance are all separately recorded.

Parts IV, V, and VI present capital account transactions. Long-term capital flows are presented in Part IV, lines 8, 9, and 10. These outflows provide a balance on long-term capital of $770,000 (net outflows). By combining the current and long-term capital account sectors that are defined in Exhibit 3.2, we have the basic balance. Mightyland's basic balance is positive $830,000. The basic balance is an indicator of how a country is performing in its international transactions, including current and

EXHIBIT 3.3	Balance of Payments of Mightyland, Constructed from Nine Typical Transactions		

Transaction	Credit	Debit	Net Balance
I. Current Transactions			
1. Merchandise exports	(1,6) $3,300,000	—	$3,300,000
2. Merchandise imports		(2) 1,200,000	−1,200,000
3. Tourism		(3) 400,000	−400,000
4. Investment Income	(4) 200,000		200,000
5. Subtotal	3,500,000	1,600,000	1,900,000
II. Unilateral Transfers			
6. Official		(6) 300,000	−300,000
III. Current Account			
7. Balance			1,600,000
IV. Long-Term Capital			
8. Direct Investment		(5) 800,000	−800,000
9. Portfolio Investment	(9) 80,000		80,000
10. Other (Bank Loans)		(8) 50,000	−50,000
11. Subtotal	80,000	850,000	−770,000
V. Basic Balance			
12. Current Account minus			
long-term Capital	830,000		830,000
VI. Private Short-Term Capital			
13. Net change in liabilities to foreigners		930,000	−100,000
VII. Official Reserve Assets & Liabilities			
14. Short-Term Liabilities to	(7) 100,000		
Foreign Officials			
VIII. Total			
15. Total Receipts & Payments	3,680,000	3,680,000	0

(1) This is a net figure, reflecting receipts of 2,450,000 and payments of 3,380,000.

EXHIBIT 3.4	Gross Credit and Debit Entries for line 13, Net Changes in Liabilities to Foreigners

Short-Term Inflows	Short-Term Outflows
1,200,000	3,000,000
400,000	200,000
800,000	100,000
50,000	80,000
2,450,000	3,380,000
	2,450,000
Net Debits (Short-Term Capital Outflows)	930,000

NOTE: Exhibit 3.4 provides a recapitulation of the clearing-settlement transactions, which are reflected in the balance of payments of Mightyland as a net change in liabilities to foreigners (line 13, Exhibit 3.3). The gross outflows (reduced liabilities to foreigners) exceed the gross inflows (increased liabilities to foreigners) by $930,000. This is included in Exhibit 3.3, line 13.

long-term capital transactions. The basic balance also shows balance of payments performance before considering both private short-term capital and the official settlements transactions. A recapitulation of these transactions is found in Exhibit 3.4.

Part VI indicates private short-term capital flows. Foreign banks maintain short-term claims on Mightyland in the form of deposits in banks or investments in the local money market. An increase in the short-term claims becomes a credit or receipt item in Mightyland's balance of payments. A decrease in these short-term claims becomes a debit or payment item in Mightyland's balance of payments. In the case of Mightyland banks maintaining short-term claims overseas, a credit reflects a reduction of assets held in foreign financial centers, and a debit shows an increase of assets held in foreign financial centers. Line 13 indicates a large volume of clearing and settlements transactions as foreign banks increase and reduce their short-term assets in Mightyland. For example, a nonresident sale of goods to a buyer in Mightyland is likely to increase foreign bank deposits maintained in Mightyland. A nonresident purchase of goods from a seller in Mightyland is likely to decrease foreign bank assets maintained in Mightyland.

Changes in official reserve assets and liabilities, also referred to as official settlements, are illustrated in line 14. In this case, the Bank of England purchased dollars from British banks. These additions to British government official reserves are equivalent to a short-term capital inflow to Mightyland. Alternatively, if Mightyland's central bank increases its official reserve assets in the form of deposits of foreign currency overseas, this would be entered as a debit on line 14.

The U.S. Balance of Payments

DETAILS OF U.S. PAYMENTS

We are now ready to examine the U.S. balance of payments accounts. The balance of payments of the United States is presented in Exhibit 3.1. We will now examine various sectors of these accounts.

In 1994 the balance on current account recorded a deficit of $151 billion (line 1). This deficit could be attributed in large part to the U.S. trade deficit ($166 billion) shown on line 2. Other components of the current account sector registered surpluses—military transactions and other service transactions. Investment income transactions recorded a net debit of $9 billion (line 7). United States government grants (line 8) and private transfers (line 10) registered deficits aggregating $20 billion. In 1992 the current account deficit was much smaller ($61 billion).

United States government capital transactions (line 11) recorded small deficits in the years 1992–1994. United States private capital transactions are reported on lines 17–21. Overall they reflect an outflow of U.S. investment capital of $182 billion in 1993 and $130 billion in 1994. The largest outflow in these years was U.S. purchases of foreign securities (line 20). Close behind was direct investment abroad (line 21). Foreign investment inflows in the United States were $176 billion in 1993 and $251 billion in 1994 (line 28). In 1993 the largest investment inflow was purchases of U.S. securities (line 32). In 1994 the largest inflow was increase in U.S. bank-reported liabilities (line 29).

Official reserve transactions include changes in U.S. government official reserve assets (lines 12–16), and changes in foreign government official assets held in the United States (lines 22–27). United States official reserve assets increased in 1993 by $1.3 billion and decreased in 1994 by $5.3 billion. (line 12). Declines reflect the overall payments position that required the U.S. government to draw on its foreign exchange reserves.

In 1993 foreign official reserve assets increased by $72 billion and in 1994 by $39.4 billion (line 22). In part these increases represent the foreign exchange intervention of foreign central banks in supporting the U.S. dollar in the foreign exchange markets.

SIMPLIFIED RESTATEMENT OF U.S. BALANCE OF PAYMENTS FOR 1994

A simplified restatement of the U.S. balance of payments is presented in Exhibit 3.5. Several important observations should be made. First, the current account deficit was quite substantial in 1994, approximately 30% of merchandise exports. This

EXHIBIT 3.5	**Simplified Restatement of U.S. Balance of Payments for 1994 (Billions of U.S. dollars)**		
	Credits	**Debits**	**Net**
Merchandise Trade	502.4	668.5	−166.1
Services Net			59.8
Investment Income Net			−9.2
Unilateral Transfers Net			−35.7
Current Account Balance			−151.2
U.S. Private Assets Abroad		130.8	
Foreign Private Assets in U.S.	251.9		
Change in U.S. Government Assets		0.3	
Capital Account Balance			120.8
Change in U.S. Official Reserve Assets	5.3		
Change in Foreign Official Assets in U.S.	39.4		
Official Balance			44.7
Statistical Discrepancy			−14.3

SOURCE: Table 3.1.

contrasts sharply with 1992 when the current account deficit was only 13% of exports, and in 1993 when it was 22% of exports. Second, in 1994 substantial private sector inward capital transfers ($251 billion) took place. These were considerably larger than U.S. private outflows of $130 billion. This left a surplus in the capital account of $120 billion. Third, the 1994 balance on current account plus capital account was in deficit by $30 billion. This deficit was financed by drawing on U.S. official reserve assets ($5.3 billion), and increases in foreign official assets in the United States ($39.4 billion). The statistical discrepancy (errors and omissions) was a relatively low $14 billion, representing 2.8% of merchandise exports.

EQUILIBRIUM/DISEQUILIBRIUM

The preceding analysis of the U.S. balance of payments position indicates an expanding current account deficit between 1992 and 1994. The U.S. current account deficit was only $61 billion in 1992 and deteriorated markedly to $151 billion in 1994. The balance on current plus capital account moved from a deficit of $16.3 billion in 1992 to a deficit of $30.1 billion in 1994.

Before commenting further on this deterioration in the U.S. payments position, we should note the general conditions that must exist for a nation's balance of payments to be considered in a state of equilibrium. Three conditions must prevail:

1. The appropriate balance concept is zero—basic balance or official settlements balance, depending on the economy's structure and the business or public policy perspective of the analysis;
2. full employment in the country; and,
3. absence of serious restrictions on international transactions.

If the first condition does not exist and there is a deficit, for example in the basic balance, transactions based on long-term conditions point to problems of a fundamental nature. In addition, the country may be using its official reserves to settle the claims of nonresidents who will be seeking to exchange holdings of that country's currency for their own or convertible currencies. If there is surplus, the country may be accumulating foreign exchange reserves, and pressures may develop in the foreign exchange market for its currency to appreciate in value.

Full employment is a prerequisite for balance of payments equilibrium. A country can achieve "balance" in its basic transactions by restricting economic expansion. This option may lead to unemployment, a high price to pay for balancing the international accounts.

Another means that countries can use to balance international accounts is to restrict international transactions. Such controls can take the form of tariffs, quotas on imports, various nontariff barriers, or restrictions on capital transactions. These controls prevent buyers and sellers from trading goods, services, and capital to their best advantage. This option also suggests that a high price will be paid to achieve balance in the international accounts.

Evaluating the Balance of Payments Position

The evaluation of a country's balance of payments position must include consideration of the structure, performance, and economic forces that control international transactions flows. In this section we consider the structure and performance dimensions from the standpoint of the four phases of evolution in the balance of payments. Also, we make several country comparisons and consider how economic forces affect the balance of payments.

STRUCTURE VERSUS PERFORMANCE

The analysis of the U.S. balance of payments accounts must focus on 1) consideration of the relation between economic structure and balance of payments structure, and 2) how the U.S. balance of payments reflects operational performance. It is important to untangle two complex, interrelated elements in balance of payments analysis. These are the operational performance and the structure of the economy.

The operational performance of the economy can be viewed in a static way by examining the balance of payments flows in a given time period. Alternatively, the operational performance can be viewed in a dynamic way by examining the changes in balance of payments flows over a sequence of time periods. In the previous discussion we followed the static approach concerning the U.S. balance of payments. In a later section we will shift to the dynamic approach where we consider comparisons over time, specifically by examining the balance of payments in Brazil. Key components in analysis of the operational performance of a nation's balance of payments are outlined in Exhibit 3.6.

The structural approach involves making comparisons of different countries while noting how the structure of each country's balance of payments represents that nation's stage of economic development. We will examine the structural approach in a following section when we focus on four phases of balance of payments development.

FOUR PHASES IN THE BALANCE OF PAYMENTS

It is important to distinguish between economic structure and operational performance when carrying out balance of payments analysis. Economic structure can influence whether a country will have a trade surplus or deficit, whether it will

EXHIBIT 3.6	Performance and Structural Analysis of the Balance of Payments	
Evaluation Approach	**Method of Analysis**	**Approach Used by Analyst**
I. Operational (Performance)		
A. Static	Relationships between account categories	1. Judge effectiveness in financing current account deficit
		2. Analyze extent to which balance of payments position departs from equilibrium (basic balance)
B. Dynamic	Time series available	1. Evaluate whether balance on current transactions is improving or deteriorating
		2. Judge effectiveness of economic policies of government (reversing deterioration in trade balance)
		3. Analyze possible changes in international credit worthiness of nation
		4. Anticipate future strength or weakness of currency of nation
II. Structural	Four phases of development. Key variables include trade balance, balance on long-term capital, and balance on foreign investment income	1. In what phase of balance of payments evolution is this country at present?
		2. Given the balance of payments phase, are the interrelationships among the key variables satisfactory?

enjoy capital inflows or outflows, and whether the net balance on foreign investment income will be positive or negative. By contrast, operational performance focuses on whether poor economic management has inflated the economy and reduced the trade surplus, or if temporary tight monetary policy has induced larger than ordinary capital inflows. Structural analysis focuses on balance of payments flows influenced by long-term economic forces, while performance analysis concentrates more on balance of payments relationships subject to shorter term economic pressures.

The key structural relationships in the balance of payments are outlined in Exhibit 3.7. These include 1) trade balance, 2) long-term capital flows, and 3) foreign investment income. These three relationships evolve over time as a national economy develops. Over the past 200 years the U.S. balance of payments has moved through all four stages identified in Exhibit 3.7. As the U.S. balance of payments has evolved through the four phases characterized in Exhibit 3.7, the shifts in U.S. payments reflect changes in industrial development, technology status, resource endowments, and other fundamental shifts in the U.S. economy.

In the late eighteenth century the United States was a new nation, lacking adequate capital for investment, and having limited capacity to produce manufactured goods. Principal exports were limited to agricultural products. The trade balance was negative, and large amounts of imports of manufactured goods were needed. Foreign investment flowed into the United States at this time, providing an overall balance between the deficit on current account and surplus on capital account. The United States remained in the immature debtor phase with a trade

Immature debtor
BOP phase with trade deficit and surplus on capital account.

EXHIBIT 3.7	Comparison of Balance of Payments Structure of Countries in Four Stages of Development			
	Immature debtor (1)	Mature debtor (2)	Immature creditor (3)	Mature creditor (4)
Trade balance	−	+	+	−
Foreign investment income		−		+
Long-term capital	+	−	−	+

deficit and surplus on capital account until the 1870s. This status is outlined in Exhibit 3.7.

By the 1870s the U.S. economy was industrializing rapidly. The transcontinental railroad system was nearly complete, enabling continued growth of agricultural exports from interior regions. Rapid development of the iron, steel, textile, and other manufacturing sectors provided import substitution and export opportunities. The trade balance shifted into surplus during the 1870s, making the United States a mature debtor nation. With this shift emerged a negative balance on foreign investment income. (Exhibit 3.7, Column 2). This negative balance reflected interest and dividends paid to foreign investors.

United States residents continued borrowing from overseas while continued inflows of foreign investment resulted in a growing negative balance of net foreign investment income. The interest and dividends paid by the United States to foreign investors and lenders was substantial by the 1870s, representing an offset to the surplus on trade that emerged at that time.

The United States continued as a mature debtor for several decades, but American investors were going overseas. By the eve of World War I the United States had become a substantial foreign investor. Nevertheless, foreign investments in the United States still exceeded U.S. foreign investments by a wide margin. The United States was slowly reducing its net debtor position, however, by increasing its foreign investment.

Events during World War I accelerated the gradual shift of the United States to net creditor status. United States exports to France and Great Britain increased during the war due to their expanded need for supplies and a partial cutoff of international shipping. Also, Great Britain and France liquidated some of their investment assets in the United States because they needed money to pay for American supplies. By the conclusion of the war in 1918, the United States had become an immature creditor nation (Exhibit 3.7, Column 3).

As an immature creditor nation, the United States enjoyed a trade surplus and was a net investor and lender to the rest of the world. During the 1920s, foreign loans distributed in the United States increased. However, by the end of the decade there was growing evidence of weak credits, and many American investors found that borrowers were unable to keep up with scheduled interest and principal repayments. During the Great Depression of the 1930s international capital flows came to a halt. American investors curtailed their activities, and capital tended to return to the United States. This change was related to the devaluation of the dollar (1934), the currency uncertainties in other countries, and the political turmoil (dictatorships) in Europe.

Mature debtor
BOP phase with trade surplus and deficit on foreign investment income account.

Immature creditor
BOP phase with trade surplus and deficit on capital account.

In the decades after World War II, the U.S. balance of payments position continued to reflect that of an immature creditor. There was a large trade surplus and substantial transfers of capital to the rest of the world. After several decades of postwar experience the trade position of the United States displayed a tendency to change. During the 1960s the trade surplus narrowed, and in 1970–1971 shifted into deficit.

The negative trade deficit persisted in the two decades following 1970. Nevertheless, the United States had a large accumulation of foreign investments that generated substantial investment income. The balance on foreign investment income in this period was positive, offsetting much of the trade deficit. At this time, the U.S. balance of payments conforms to the model of a mature creditor—trade deficit and surplus on foreign investment income. This position is shown in Exhibit 3.7, Column 4.

Mature creditor
BOP phase with trade deficit and surplus on foreign investment income account.

In the late 1980s the U.S. trade deficits widened considerably. At the same time there were large capital inflows to the United States, and the United States again became a net debtor nation.

COMPARATIVE ANALYSIS OF A COUNTRY'S BALANCE OF PAYMENTS

In this section we compare the balance of payments of several countries. We will show that the operation of the world payments system involves a meshing together of the different positions of countries, all at different phases of their balance of payments evolution.

Exhibit 3.8 presents the balance of payments of eight countries, all displaying different structural positions and different phases of balance of payments evolution. In addition, Venezuela, an oil exporter, and Switzerland, a financial entrepôt (or intermediary center of trade), are represented. The financial entrepôt conforms to the mature creditor (stage 4) model, and displays a balance of payments structure with large two-directional capital flows. In Switzerland this consists of net outflows of direct investment and portfolio investment, and net inflows of other long-term capital (mostly bank loans). The balance of payments data in Exhibit 3.8 provide gross flows inward and outward (liabilities and assets), and in Switzerland the gross flows in each direction are much larger than the net flows. The net flows are the difference between inflows and outflows. Switzerland's net errors and omissions represent 1.1% of exports, indicating moderate underreporting of some transactions, considered to consist primarily of short-term capital transactions.

As an oil exporter Venezuela enjoys a substantial trade surplus ($7.6 billion). However, the current account shows a smaller surplus ($2.4 billion). Venezuelan residents make large service payments for shipping, business services, and tourism.

The balance of payments of Uruguay reflects the position of an immature debtor. Uruguay has a large trade deficit, financed in part by external borrowing. A larger part of Uruguay's current deficit was financed by foreign grants (unilateral) or transfers (line 8). Errors and omissions (line 17) were 4.9% of exports, representing substantial unrecorded capital transactions.

Chile's balance of payments reflects the position of a mature debtor. Chile had a moderate-sized trade surplus. The current account deficit was financed by private capital inflows (lines 12, 14, and 16). Chile enjoys a fairly stable financial and political environment, and as a result capital inflows play an important role in the overall balance of payments structure.

Japan is an immature creditor. A large trade surplus is balanced with substantial capital outflows.

EXHIBIT 3.8   Comparative Analysis of Balance of Payments of Eight Countries

	Uruguay 1	Chile 2	China 2	Japan 3	Germany 3	United Kingdom 4	Venezuela PETRO	Switzerland FINL ENTR
1. Goods exports	1913	11,538	102,561	384.2	430.3	206.1	15,890	82,625
2. Goods imports	−2585	−10,879	−95,271	−238.3	−379.8	−222.2	−8,199	−79,294
3. Trade balance	−672	659	7,290	145.9	50.5	−16.1	7,691	3,330
4. Services credit	1246	2,846	16,503	60.5	61.0	60.5	1,307	22,785
5. Services debit	−818	−2,827	−16,201	−110.1	−100.1	−54.7	−4,389	−12,691
6. Income credit	283	498	5,854	155.4	75.4	119.8	1,627	26,980
7. Income debit	−488	−2,271	−6,873	−115.1	−70.6	−103.7	−3,570	−18,434
8. Current transfers credit	67	358	874	1.5	19.4	8.2	444	2,571
9. Current transfers debit	−8	−20	−915	−9.0	−57.3	−16.4	−660	−6,046
10. Current account	−389	−757	6,532	129.2	−21.7	−2.4	2,450	18,495
11. Direct invest abroad	—	−925	−2,000	−17.9	−14.6	−25.3	−525	−10,549
12. Direct invest inward	170	1,795	33,787	0.9	−3.0	10.1	764	3,684
13. Portfolio invest assets	—	−351	−380	−83.2	−53.1	26.6	7	−16,818
14. Portfolio invest liabilities	158	1,373	3,923	34.4	27.2	45.2	246	912
15. Other invest assets	80	−141	−1,189	−46.4	−0.0	−62.5	−3,685	−22,441
16. Other invest liabilities	−23	−2,690	−1,496	26.1	67.9	−18.6	−433	28,743
17. Errors-omissions	94	−471	−9,100	−17.8	−5.5	7.9	−298	−876
18. Overall balance	90	3,213	30,453	25.3	−2.1	−18.9	−1,484	1,105
19. Line 17 as % Line 1	4.9%	4.1%	8.9%	4.6%	1.3%	3.8%	1.9%	1.1%
20. Lines 12 & 14 as % Line 10	84%	419%	Surplus	Surplus	114%	2290%	Surplus	Surplus

NOTE: All data apply to 1994. Data for Uruguay, Chile, China, Venezuela, and Switzerland in millions of U.S. dollars. All others in billions of U.S. dollars.

LEGEND: 1 Denotes immature debtor, 2 denotes mature debtor, 3 denotes immature creditor, 4 denotes mature creditor, PETRO denotes petroleum exporter, FINL ENTR denotes financial entrepôt country.

SOURCE: International Monetary Fund, *International Financial Statistics*.

61

Germany is an immature creditor. As such, its balance of payments position consists of a trade surplus ($50 billion), and direct investment capital outflows. For several decades Germany has enjoyed large balance of payments surpluses. This has permitted Germany to make large investments overseas, and provides substantial official gifts or transfers (line 9) of $57 billion. Since 1990, and following the unification of East and West Germany, the German balance of payments position has been modified so a current account deficit is likely to show up in the payments position.

The United Kingdom's balance of payments structure conforms to the mature creditor model. This includes a trade deficit and a surplus on foreign investment income. In 1994 this surplus on foreign investment income was $16 billion. Errors and omissions were 3.8% percent of exports, suggesting moderate unrecorded short-term capital flows. Given the importance of London in Eurodollar, foreign exchange, and Eurobond trading, the United Kingdom plays an important role as financial entrepôt.

Economic Forces and the Balance of Payments

The previous discussion illustrates that balance of payments accounts must reflect an equality between receipt and payment transactions. This accounting equality is distinguished from the concept of economic equilibrium. In the sections that follow, we will review our definition of economic equilibrium in the balance of payments, describe the main types of economic forces that impact balance of payments transactions, and consider how these forces can bring about an adjustment in the overall balance of payments position of a country.

CONDITIONS FOR EQUILIBRIUM

In economics the essential meaning of equilibrium is balancing opposite forces. In the context of balance of payments, there is equilibrium when the nation's economy is in basic adjustment to the rest of the world. Using balance of payments terminology, this state means that the aggregate of receipts transactions equals the aggregate of payments transactions.

The concept of balance of payments equilibrium is closely tied to how free markets interact. Departures from the operation of free and competitive market systems raise a question of whether an equilibrium condition exists. When balance of payments receipts and payments are equal, but under conditions where markets are not free and competitive, we cannot conclude there is equilibrium in the balance of payments. From a balance of payments perspective, governments tend to interfere with markets in at least two fundamental ways:

1. Governments may restrict domestic economic activity to achieve a better overall balance on external accounts. We refer to this restriction as the unemployment effect.
2. Governments may place quotas or tariffs on merchandise imports to improve the overall balance of payments performance. We refer to this action as the controls effect.

We have seen that at least three requirements must be met before a country's balance of payments is in equilibrium. First, the total of basic or official settlements receipts and payments transactions must be in balance. This function could be interpreted to mean that there is a zero or close to zero balance in basic or official settlements transactions. Second, the domestic economy must be at full employment. It should be clear that a nation can "force" its balance of payments into what appears to be equilibrium. This circumstance could be accomplished through policies aimed at compressing domestic demand leading to high and unacceptable levels of unemployment of domestic resources (labor and capital). Third, the country should allow all sectors to operate on the basis of free and competitive markets. Any serious interference with the free operation of markets can be interpreted as a departure from balance of payments equilibrium. This interference can take the form of controls on payments, imports, or foreign investment flows, or restrictions on any type of international transaction.

ECONOMIC FORCES

Four key economic forces influence a country's balance of payments flows. These are the inflation rate, real GNP growth rate, interest rates, and the spot rate of exchange (Exhibit 3.9).

The inflation rate should be considered in a relative sense. For example, if France has an annual inflation rate of 3%, and the United Kingdom has an annual inflation rate of 10%, the excessive level of price increases in the United Kingdom will have an effect on the competitiveness of United Kingdom versus French goods and services. Eventually, a number of United Kingdom goods and services will lose their competitive position to similar French goods and services. United Kingdom imports

---

EXHIBIT 3.9   **Balance of Payments Adjustment to Economic Forces**

ECONOMIC FORCES

Relative Inflation Rate	Real GNP Growth Rate	Relative Interest Rate	Spot Exchange Rate
Differences between countries' inflation rates affect competitiveness of exports/ imports	Differences in countries' income growth exert greater or lesser pull on imports	Differences and expectations in countries' interest rates lead to capital flows	Actual and expected changes in exchange rates affect trade flows and capital flows
Price Level Mechanism	Economic Activity Mechanism	Capital Flow Mechanism	Exchange Rate Mechanism

Balance of Payments Position
Receipts — Payments

from France will rise. The balance of payments of the United Kingdom will reflect this increase in imports. Similarly, the balance of payments of France will experience an increase in exports. At the same time U.K. exports to France may level off and decline. While French imports from the U.K. will decline.

Real GNP growth affects the level of goods and services imports. A country experiencing high and rising real GNP growth tends to have a higher volume of imports. A country with a lower real GNP growth tends to import fewer goods and services.

Differences in interest rate levels can exert a powerful effect on international capital flows. Countries experiencing a high or rising level of interest rates usually experience capital inflows, based on the desire of nonresidents to benefit from the higher interest rates available. These transaction flows are represented in the capital account of the balance of payments. Countries with relatively low interest rates can expect to experience capital outflows based on the actions of investors seeking to maximize income.

In a world of floating exchange rates, upward or downward changes in the spot rate can affect export and import transactions. The current level of spot exchange rates affects the relative cost of imports versus domestic goods. A high current level of the spot rate for a foreign currency discourages imports and encourages exports. A low exchange rate for a foreign currency encourages imports and discourages exports.

The future expected level of the spot rate may result in more complex balance of payments effects. Here expectations play an important role in affecting capital account as well as current transactions. For example, Mr. Jones is a resident of the United States. He is considering investing in the bond market. When he is researching bond investments he finds that good quality bonds in the United States offer a yield of 10.0%, and that similar quality bonds in the United Kingdom offer a yield of 12.0%. Mr. Jones is uncertain about the foreign exchange risk, which he has not researched, and tentatively decides to invest in the United States where the yield is 10.0%. However, prior to the investment he calls his investment broker. The broker has just learned that the British government has imposed a series of policy measures aimed at strengthening and stabilizing the pound. According to the information the investment advisor provides, Mr. Jones modifies his expectations about the future level of the spot pound. He now expects the pound to remain stable or even rise in value in relation to the U.S. dollar. Mr. Jones decides to invest in the U.K. bonds yielding 12.0%. This example depicts a balance of payments transaction, that is, a portfolio capital outflow in the U.S. balance of payments and a portfolio capital inflow in the U.K. balance of payments.

PROCESS OF ADJUSTMENT

The balance of payments of a country is undergoing continuous adjustment. This adjustment is in response to the various economic forces that impact a country's balance of payments (Exhibit 3.9).

Inflation and changes in relative prices bring about changes in balance of payments transactions. Differences in inflation from country to country affect the competitive position of goods and services that are traded. With excessive inflation countries tend to experience an increase in imports and a decline in exports. We can refer to changes in balance of payments due to differences in inflation as part of a price level mechanism.

Differences in real economic growth between countries also impact their respective balance of payments. Countries with slow growth in real income generally experience similar slow growth in imports. Conversely, countries with high income growth tend to experience more rapid growth in imports. Finally, countries with high growth rates may exhibit high real interest rates in their respective capital markets. High real interest rates attract capital inflows. We refer to these balance of payments influences based on differences in economic growth rate as an economic activity mechanism.

Countries with high or rising interest rate levels tend to experience capital inflows. By contrast, countries with low or declining interest rate levels tend to experience capital outflows. In recent years, the volume of cross-border capital flows based on interest rate differences appears to have been increasing. These capital flows operate as a balancing or financing component in a nation's balance of payments. In effect, a capital flow mechanism influences the balance of payments position and that works through changing levels of investment inflows and outflows.

Changes in foreign exchange rates also influence balance of payments transactions. A rise in the value of a nation's currency reduces the competitiveness of that nation's exports and also makes imports more attractively priced to residents. In contrast, a fall in the value of a nation's currency enhances the competitiveness of that nation's exports and makes imports less attractive to residents. This exchange rate mechanism plays an important role in adjusting a country's balance of payments position.

Comparisons and Government Policies

Balance of payments data is used to make comparisons of a nation's performance over time. Another important use is to analyze the effect of government policy on the balance of payments and to plan government policy to impact the BOP.

Brazil's balance of payments is presented in Exhibit 3.10, covering the period 1988–1994. Brazil is the largest debtor among the developing nations of the world and also one of the highest ranking developing nations in terms of GDP. Brazil's balance of payments structure conforms to that of a mature debtor, with a trade surplus and a deficit on foreign investment income.

Brazil was one of the largest international borrowers until 1982, the first year of the debt crisis. With the debt crisis there followed a period of economic stagnation and subsequently high inflation. The government froze prices, squeezed credit, and exchanged new currency units for old currency due to the inflation.

Brazil has a strong capacity to manage its trade balance, in part due to a diversified and productive economic base. As we can observe in Exhibit 3.10 lines 2 and 4, goods exports can grow impressively on a year-to-year basis. The trade balance was in surplus every year over the period 1988–1994.

Brazil suffers from a large deficit on foreign investment income averaging $9–12 billion a year. Over the period 1988–1994 Brazil displayed a capacity to attract increasing amounts of foreign investment, especially portfolio investment. By 1994 Brazil was receiving gross capital inflows of $50 billion, most in the form of portfolio investment. With the ability to generate a current account surplus, as in 1992–1993, Brazil may be able to experience a favorable balance of payments performance throughout the 1990s.

EXHIBIT 3.10	**Brazil's Balance of Payments, 1988–1994**						
	1988	**1989**	**1990**	**1991**	**1992**	**1993**	**1994**
1. Current account	4,156	1,002	−3,823	−1,450	6,089	19	−1,153
2. Goods exports	33,773	34,375	31,408	31,619	35,793	39,630	44,102
3. Goods imports	−14,605	−18,263	−20,661	−21,041	−20,554	−25,301	−33,241
4. Trade balance	19,168	16,112	10,747	10,578	15,239	14,329	10,861
5. Services credit	2,279	3,132	3,762	3,319	4,088	3,965	4,908
6. Services debit	−5,302	−5,917	−7,523	−7,210	−7,430	−9,555	−10,254
7. Income credit	771	1,310	1,157	904	1,118	1,307	2,202
8. Income debit	−12,851	−13,856	−12,765	−10,555	−9,115	−11,630	−11,293
9. Current transfers credit	127	238	840	1,556	2,260	1,704	2,577
10. Current transfers debit	−36	−17	−41	−42	−71	−101	−154
11. Direct invest abroad	−175	−523	−665	−1,014	−137	−491	−1,037
12. Direct invest inward	2,804	1,131	989	1,103	2,061	1,292	3,072
13. Portfol invest assets	—	−30	−67	—	—	−606	−3,052
14. Portfol invest liabilities	−498	−391	579	3,808	7,366	12,928	47,784
15. Other invest assets	−1,994	−894	−2,864	−3,140	−99	−2,696	−4,368
16. Other invest liabilities	−9,347	−11,818	−3,539	−4,886	−2,675	−2,823	−34,434
17. Errors-omissions	−827	−819	−296	852	−1,393	−814	−442
18. Overall balance	−5,878	−12,319	−9,651	−4,685	11,266	6,890	6,543
19. Line 17 as % Line 2	2.4%	2.4%	0.9%	2.7%	3.9%	2.1%	1.0%
20. Line 12 and 14 as % Line 1	Surplus	Surplus	41%	295%	Surplus	Surplus	4410%

NOTE: Amounts are in millions of U.S. dollars.

SOURCE: International Monetary Fund, *International Financial Statistics.*

SUMMARY

The balance of payments is a statistical estimate of the transactions between residents of one country and the rest of the world during a specific time period. Generally we look at balance of payments data covering a full year period.

Residence is an important aspect of balance of payments definitions. A corporate entity can have several centers of residence. For example, a bank like the Chase Manhattan head office has residence in the United States, but foreign branches have residence in the country of location.

The balance of payments is divided into three major sectors: the current account, the capital account, and the official reserves account.

Since the balance of payments is a double entry bookkeeping system, debits always equal credits. The accounting equality should not be confused with the economic concept of equilibrium. From an economic point of view, a condition of balance of payments equilibrium holds when three conditions are met: a basic or official settlements balance of zero, full employment, and an absence of restrictions on international transactions.

In evaluating balance of payments performance, we must distinguish between structure and performance. Operational performance can be determined by analyzing comparisons over time or relationships between specific balance of payments accounts. The structural approach involves making comparisons of different countries or noting how the structure reflects the nation's stage of economic development.

The balance of payments of a nation may be expected to evolve through four phases. These include immature debtor, mature debtor, immature creditor, and mature creditor.

A number of economic forces influence a country's balance of payments flows: the relative inflation rate, real GNP growth, interest rates, and the spot rate of exchange. The balance of payments is continuously adjusting to these economic forces.

REVIEW QUESTIONS

1. What is the balance of payments?

2. What is the current status of the U.S. balance of payments?

3. What do we mean when we say the balance of payments accounts are based on a double entry accounting system?

4. Must all countries evolve through the four stages of balance of payments? Explain.

5. Distinguish between balance of payments structure and performance.

6. How would you define balance of payments equilibrium?

7. If a country has a surplus on current account, what is likely to be the status of its capital account?

8. How might the international debt crisis affect a debtor country's balance of payments?

9. If a country has a current account surplus, is it likely to be a lender to or borrower from the rest of the world?

10. What are some uses of balance of payments analysis?

11. What key economic forces impact the balance of payments? Explain briefly how the balance of payments adjusts to changes in these economic forces.

12. A country has the following entries in its balance of payments: current account balance: −$1200; gross capital inflows: $1400; gross capital outflows −$500. Comment on the state (equilibrium) of this country's balance of payments position.

13. A country has the following entries in its balance of payments: trade balance: $750; balance on other current transactions: −$320; capital inflows: $1240; capital outflows: −$680. Comment on the state (equilibrium) of this country's balance of payments position.

14. A country has the following entries in its balance of payments: trade balance: −$550; capital inflows: $840; capital outflows: −$110. In what phase of the balance of payments evolution is this country? Explain.

15. You are given the balance of payments statistics for Amazonia and Belgoland. Answer the following.
    a. Does Amazonia have a surplus or deficit in
       1. current account,
       2. basic balance?
    b. In what stage is Belgoland's balance of payments?

    c. Is Amazonia's balance of payments in the same stage of evolution?

    d. Compare and contrast the ability of each country to finance its current deficit.

    e. Using the BOP as a general indicator of country risk, compare and contrast these two countries.

Type Transaction	Amazonia	Belgoland
Merchandise: Exports	23	64
Merchandise: Imports	−38	−91
Service: Exports	6	3
Service: Imports	−5	−7
Unilateral Transfers	2	6
Private Capital		
Direct Investment, Residents	−1	0
Direct Investment, Nonresidents	9	4
Portfolio		
Residents	0	0
Nonresidents	5	2
Other capital	−1	3
Official Settlements	0	16

Note: Amounts in millions of local currency units.

16. Between 1990 and 1994 the components of Mexico's gross domestic product moved as indicated in the table. This is stated as a percent of GDP.

    a. What implications are there for changes in Mexico's trade balance? BOP equilibrium?

    b. Mexico's financial crisis of Dec. 1994–May 1995 was viewed as a panic by foreign investors. Some economists interpreted the crisis as mainly a condition of excess domestic absorption. Which view is more correct?

	1990	1994
Private consumption	70.9%	71.0%
Government consumption	8.4	11.3
Total investment	21.9	23.6
Aggregate	101.2	105.9

SELECTED BIBLIOGRAPHY

Bank for International Settlements. *Annual Report,* Basle, various issues.

Bergsten, C.F. and S. Islam. *The U.S. As a Debtor Nation.* Washington, D.C.: Institute for International Economics, 1989.

Carvounis, Chris. *The United States Trade Deficit of the 1980s.* Westport, Conn.: Quorum Books, 1987.

Chrystal, K. Alec and Geoffrey E. Wood. "Are Trade Deficits a Problem?" In R. Kolb, *The International Finance Reader.* Atlanta: Kolb Publishing, 1991.

International Monetary Fund. *Balance of Payments Yearbook, 1994–1996* Washington, D.C., annual.

International Monetary Fund. *International Financial Statistics,* Washington, D.C., monthly, various issues.

Khan, M. "The Macroeconomic Effects of Fund Supported Adjustment Programs." *IMF Staff Papers,* September 1990.

Kindleberger, Charles P. "Balance of Payments Deficits, and the International Market for Liquidity." *Essays in International Finance.* Princeton: Princeton University, May 1965.

Koray, Fail. "The Trade Balance and the Exchange Rate." *Journal of Microeconomics,* Spring 1990.

Kubarych, Roger M. "Financing the U.S. Current Account Deficit." *Federal Reserve Bank of New York Quarterly Review,* Summer 1984.

Meade, J. *The Balance of Payments.* London: Oxford University Press, 1951.

Meyer, Stephen A. "The U.S. As a Debtor Country: Causes, Prospects, and Policy Implications." In R. Kolb, *The International Finance Reader.* Atlanta: Kolb Publishing, 1991.

Nawaz, S. "Why the World Current Account Does Not Balance," *Finance and Development,* September 1987.

Rosenberg, Michael R. "The Balance of Payments Flow Approach to Exchange Rate Determination." In *Currency Forecasting.* Homewood, ILL.: Irwin Professional Publishing, 1996.

Stern, R.M. "The Presentation of the U.S. Balance of Payments." *Essays in International Finance.* Princeton: Princeton University Press, 1977.

U.S. Department of Commerce, Office of Business Economics. *Survey of Current Business,* monthly, various issues.

U.S. Department of Commerce, *The Balance of Payments of the United States: Concepts, Data, Sources, and Estimating Procedures.* Washington, D.C., May 1990.

PART TWO

International Financial Markets

*I*n this section we analyze the major components of the international financial markets. *These markets play a key role in the following ways: They mobilize and allocate funds globally; they provide a valuation or pricing function that reflects a balancing of return required relative to the riskiness of the asset; they represent perceptions of market participants regarding future changes in interest rates and foreign exchange rates; and they finance balance of payments deficits of individual nations. These five chapters explore the foreign exchange market, Eurocurrency market, and international bond market, hedging markets for futures and options, and the three major global financial centers, namely, New York, London, and Tokyo.*

ENVIRONMENT OF GLOBAL FINANCE

INTERNATIONAL FINANCIAL MARKETS

INTERNATIONAL BANKING

INTERNATIONAL CORPORATE FINANCE

INTERNATIONAL PORTFOLIO MANAGEMENT

CHAPTER 4

Foreign Exchange Market

INTRODUCTION

The foreign exchange market is the largest single financial market in the world. This market plays an important role in linking together the many varied parts of the world's financial markets. In this chapter we focus on the basic functions of the market as well as its links with other markets. A detailed presentation shows the mechanics of the market as well as the types of transactions that take place. The chapter also provides an analytical view of how spot rates are determined under alternative exchange rate systems, and how parity relations explain exchange rate behavior.

LEARNING OBJECTIVES IN THIS CHAPTER

1. To understand the basic nature of the foreign exchange market, its role and importance, and principal market participants.
2. To appreciate the complex nature of this market, the three levels of trading, and the growth and size of the market on a global basis.
3. To examine the distinction between spot and forward exchange, why there may be differences in rates of exchange spot and forward, and the matrix of spot rates.
4. To discern the different types of transactions that take place in the market and how trading banks generate profits.
5. To identify the factors that determine exchange rate changes.
6. To comprehend the parity relationships that can be used to explain the interrelations between the spot rate and forward rate.
7. To value the importance of and techniques used to forecast foreign exchange rates.

Nature of Foreign Exchange Market

The basic commodity of foreign exchange is any financial claim that is denominated in a foreign currency. Technically, in the United States the following vehicles qualify under this definition: securities issued by non-U.S. borrowers denominated

Foreign exchange

A financial claim denominated in a foreign currency.

in foreign currencies (e.g., German government bonds denominated in deutsche mark), bills of exchange calling for payment in pound sterling, currency issued by the government of France, and shares of stock issued by Unilever N.V., a Dutch corporation valued in Netherlands guilders. While it is important to understand the many forms foreign exchange may take, we focus on the form that tends to dominate market transactions—sight deposit claims denominated in foreign currency.

Although this summary describes foreign exchange from the perspective of the United States, in Great Britain foreign exchange includes U.S. government securities denominated in dollars, currency issued by non-British governments such as those of France or Italy, and bills of exchange calling for payment in Dutch guilders or Japanese yen.

From a market mechanism point of view, the definition of foreign exchange might be the exchange of the currency of one country for the currency of another.

Sight deposits

The "commodity" traded in the foreign exchange market.

Dealer bank

Foreign exchange market maker, buys and sells currency balances.

Sight deposits are the stock in trade of banks that deal in the foreign exchange market. Bank dealers maintain these foreign currency deposits with correspondent banks located in other financial centers where that particular currency is the domestic currency. For example, a large U.S.-based dealer bank might have foreign currency deposits in several dozen non-dollar currencies in banks located in financial centers where these currencies are the domestic currency. Other U.S.-based banks also maintain such deposits in banks in foreign financial centers. In this way the U.S. banks would be in a position to sell foreign exchange by instructing their foreign correspondents to deliver the sight deposit funds to the purchaser or a designated third party. Similarly, U.S. banks could purchase foreign exchange, whereby the seller would deliver the foreign exchange to a bank in a foreign financial center for the account of the U.S. bank.

Bank dealers, nondealer banks, exporters, importers, multinational companies, financial institutions, investors, and government agencies all participate in the foreign exchange market. These participants often have diversified needs in the market including the need to hedge open or exposed foreign currency positions, to invest funds in other parts of the world, and to shift purchasing power from one country to another.

The largest foreign exchange banks operate trading sections in several of the leading financial centers (London, New York, Tokyo, Frankfurt, Singapore, Hong Kong). In major centers, particularly London and New York, these banks have 30–40 traders operating in their dealing rooms, covering different currency sectors of the foreign exchange market. The largest banks may make markets in 50 or more separate currencies.

Early in the working day before the local financial market has opened for business, these traders are on the telephone talking to their counterparts in other parts of the world. They share information and written reports regarding the developments, trends, and happenings in centers where trading has commenced. They combine this information with technical analysis, data on economic fundamentals, and changing political conditions to develop a better understanding of market conditions. On the basis of this analysis, traders are better informed and prepared for subsequent market trading activity.

The foreign exchange market operates without the benefit of a centralized trading facility like the New York Stock Exchange, where buyers and sellers congregate and deal in full view of one another. For this reason it resembles an over-the-counter market rather than an organized securities exchange. Electronic communications and computer support facilities provide a necessary backup to foreign exchange traders, who are on the telephone or utilize similar telecommunications equipment much of the day. High-speed information systems are vitally important to traders working in the dealing rooms of market-making banks. Prices in the market are sensitive and can change quickly. Therefore banks must be able to contact counterparties in the market without delay and then complete the trade as quickly as possible. This need is prompted in part by the risk exposure that market-making banks face when they hold foreign currency positions. These are risky assets, and value can change abruptly. Hence, dealer banks must be in a position to adjust their positions quickly, before the market moves to a price level that leaves the dealer bank with a loss.

GLOBAL SYSTEM

The foreign exchange market consists of many national foreign exchange markets, all of which are more or less integrated into a global system. The global system permits a bank in a given national foreign exchange center to carry on transactions that take place on the following basis:

Level 1: *Retail level*. Transactions are in one national market where a dealer bank buys or sells in relation to a customer.

Level 2: *Wholesale interbank*. Transactions are in one national market where two dealer banks deal in relation to one another with the assistance of a foreign exchange broker. Essentially, this is an interbank market.

Interbank market

Interbank market refers to the over-the-counter foreign exchange market, where dealer banks play a major role.

Level 3: *International level*. Transactions between two or more national markets where dealer banks in different centers trade with one another. This transaction could involve two-market arbitrage, or three-market arbitrage.

Arbitrage

Purchase of securities, including foreign exchange, on one market for immediate resale on another at a more advantageous price.

In this global system there is a tendency for the "law of one price" to prevail. Therefore the exchange rate relation in New York between U.S. dollars and pound sterling, and between U.S. dollars and deutsche mark will prevail in London and Frankfurt as well. This takes place through a process of arbitrage. If any discrepancy develops in the price relationship between these currencies, bank dealers or other market participants will buy and sell currencies in an effort to generate profits from such discrepancies.

MARKET SIZE AND GROWTH

The foreign exchange market is the largest financial market in the world. London is the largest foreign exchange and trading center in the world. Its leading status is supported by the historic international role of the London money market, the concentration of wholesale Eurodollar trading in London, and the exchange market's role as a trading center and as an issuer of international securities (Eurobonds). The large number of foreign banks with offices in the city further supports London's central status in world foreign exchange. These banks use their London offices to clear and settle foreign exchange transactions.

In 1996 the Bank for International Settlements reported that daily turnover in global foreign exchange markets reached $1,200 billion in 1995. In its report the BIS noted that foreign exchange market growth is beginning to slow, but dealers and investors are becoming more sophisticated in their use of related (derivatives and swap) instruments. The BIS foreign exchange survey indicated that in constant

| EXHIBIT 4.1 | **Volume of Foreign Exchange Transactions, by Financial Center and by Category of Transaction** |

A. Daily Trading Volume in Selected Financial Centers (Billion US Dollars)

	1969	1977	1979	1980	1983	1984	1986	1989	1992	1995
New York	0.8	5.0	17	18	26	35	50	130	192	244
London			25		50	49	90	187	303	464
Tokyo			2	6.7		8	48	115	128	161
Subtotal			44			92	188	432	623	869
Frankfurt			11			17				60
Zurich			10			20				66
Paris			4			5				58
Singapore			3			8				105
Hong Kong			3			8				72
Total			75			150				1230

Estimated annual trading: $640 × 250 days = $160,000 billion.

The data in this table comes from Federal Reserve and central bank surveys conducted at different times, covering different periods of years. In some cases the data includes only Federal Reserve estimates of trading in New York. In other cases several central banks cooperated to provide estimates of trading volume in a number of important financial centers.

1995 figures are from *Financial Times* and Bank for International Settlements.

B. Annual Trading Volume by Category of Transaction, 1995

	TYPE OF FOREIGN EXCHANGE TRANSACTION	
	US $ (billion)	% of Total
1. Merchandise trade	4,300	1.4
2. Service[1]	900	0.3
3. Income from foreign investment	900	0.3
4. Long-term capital flows	900	0.3
5. Financial transactions[2]	293,000	97.7
Total	300,000	100.00

[1] Shipping, tourism, financial services

[2] Eurocurrency dealing, portfolio investment, and financial settlements and clearings

SOURCE: New York Federal Reserve Bank, Group of Thirty, *Financial Times,* and Bank for International Settlements.

dollar terms the foreign exchange market grew between 1992 and 1995 by 30%, about the same rate as in 1989–1992 (Exhibit 4.1).

The BIS survey showed that the dollar, involved on one side of 83% of all transactions worldwide, is by far the most important currency in the market. The study shows London the leading forex center, accounting for 30% of global turnover (more than New York and Tokyo, the next biggest markets, combined).

London, Singapore, and Hong Kong are the most global of the leading centers, with the domestic currency involved in less than 20% of deals. By contrast in New York and Tokyo the domestic currency is involved in more than 80% of deals.

The forward market is larger than the spot market, accounting for 56% of turnover. Eighty-five percent of the forward market consists of swaps, involving exchange of two currency amounts on a specific date and a reverse exchange for the same amount at a later date. Automated or electronic trading now accounts for 4–6 percent of total turnover in London, New York, and Tokyo.

Foreign exchange market trading volume includes a wide range of activities. Financial transactions (Exhibit 4.1) account for more than 90% of the market's volume. World export volume in 1995 was approximately $4,300 billion, representing about 1.4% of the base of estimated foreign exchange market trading. Service transactions such as foreign investment income flows, shipping services, and tourism together account for approximately one percent of market volume.

Daily trading volume has grown rapidly. Subtotals for the three largest markets indicate that trading volume more than doubled between 1979 and 1984, and again between 1984 and 1986 (Exhibit 4.1). Similarly, data for trading in the eight largest centers in the period 1979–1984 indicate equally high growth rates of trading volume.

EXOTIC CURRENCIES

"Without doubt, Eastern Europe is becoming the more prominent region for exotic currency trades." Economist at London office of largest American forex trader.

Exotic currencies of the developing (emerging) and transitional economies are fast becoming an essential part of full service foreign exchange business. While Asia and Latin America have enjoyed active currency trading, the *big growth in the 1990s has come in Polish zlotys, the Czech koruna, and the South African rand*. Trading volume has risen by 440% a year for many of the so-called exotics.

Daily foreign exchange turnover exceeds $1 billion for the currencies of South Africa, Malaysia, Thailand, Indonesia, Turkey, India, and South Korea. Increasing numbers of foreign exchange dealing room personnel are now committed to exotic currencies.

"Trading these currencies is a never-ending system of opportunities, but also a never-ending stream of risk." Head of Emerging Markets Currency Group, leading Hong Kong Bank.

Market estimates indicate that total daily turnover in the leading 20 exotic currencies is about $40 billion. This is approximately 3% of the daily turnover of $1,200 billion in *the 26 leading markets surveyed by the BIS*. In many cases these currency trades take on the character of structured trades, with traders taking several days to a week to come up with a price.

MONEY TRANSFERS

Participants in the foreign exchange market carry out a number of basic functions. These functions include money transfer, hedging, clearing, and credit. The transaction most easily understood is that of money transfer. If a British business firm must make payment to a French firm in French currency, it becomes necessary to transfer money (funds) from Britain to France. This international shift of purchasing power is accomplished through the foreign exchange market.

The British firm buys spot French francs in the London foreign exchange market. A spot transaction is for delivery now. A forward transaction is for delivery in the future. The London bank (Barclays) maintains franc deposits in a Paris correspondent (Banque National de Paris—BNP). These sight deposits are released to the British firm when Barclays instructs BNP to make the franc transfer. The British firm can transfer the francs to the French firm by simply advising the French bank to carry out the transfer of deposit funds.

Tourists also require transfer of purchasing power services. Generally, tourists purchase foreign currency banknotes rather than deposits denominated in foreign currency. American tourists traveling to the United Kingdom require pound sterling to pay for accommodations, meals, local travel, and entertainment. A purchase of sterling in the form of banknotes or deposits permits them to transfer purchasing power to the United Kingdom.

In hedging, participants in the foreign exchange market protect against an open currency position, called a currency exposure. An American importer purchasing merchandise from a Japanese supplier, with the sale invoiced in yen, has an open position in that currency. The American importer knows that in two months he will have to make payment in yen and for that period faces a currency exposure position.

The risk is that the yen could appreciate against the dollar, raising the dollar cost of the imported merchandise. In this case, the American importer can hedge by buying yen for future delivery. This purchase of forward yen locks in the dollar cost of the merchandise and protects against the currency rate risk.

The foreign exchange market provides a clearing mechanism for international payments. This mechanism operates through the turnover of foreign currency deposits that banks maintain with their correspondent banks in other international finance centers. For example, a German bank dealing in dollars in the Frankfurt market will be buying and selling dollars in relation to counterparties. These transactions will be cleared by debits and credits to that German bank's sight deposits (U.S. dollars) maintained in New York banks.

Clearing mechanisms permit a large volume of transactions with only small amounts of net settlements or fund transfers. For example, two Frankfurt banks may carry out the following transactions on a given morning of trading dollars against deutsche mark:

	Buy Dollars	Sell Dollars	Net Buy
Bank A	$120 million	$100 million	+ $20 million
Bank B	$ 90 million	$ 95 million	− $ 5 million

A total of $405 million has been traded through the dealings of the two banks, but the change in ownership has been very small. Bank A increases its dollar position by $20 million and Bank B reduces its dollar position by $5 million. Now let us consider afternoon trading of dollars by the same banks:

	Buy Dollars	Sell Dollars	Net Buy
Bank A	$110 million	$135 million	− $25 million
Bank B	$105 million	$ 90 million	+ $15 million

A total of $440 million has been traded, and again the change in ownership is very small. In afternoon trading, Bank A reduced its dollar position by $25 million, while Bank B increased its dollar position by $15 million. Even more interesting is that through trading Bank A reversed its dealing position. In the afternoon it was a net seller of dollars when in the morning it had been a net buyer. Through the day Bank A was a net seller of $5 million. Similarly, Bank B was a net seller of dollars in the morning, but a net buyer of dollars in the afternoon. Therefore both banks traded $845 million of dollars, but over the whole trading day one bank proved to be a net seller of dollars (Bank A) of $5 million, and one bank proved to be a net buyer (Bank B) of $10 million. A smaller net change in position could be accomplished if these banks traded dollars directly with one another, Bank B selling $5 million to Bank A. In that case the only change in position after the entire trading day would be Bank B accumulating $5 million.

Finally, the foreign exchange market provides credit. Credit is provided when an exporter draws a foreign currency time draft on the buyer or the buyer's bank. A sight draft is payable today, whereas a time draft is payable at a specified or predetermined future date. If the exporter draws a time draft (as opposed to a sight draft), it is discounted, sold in the bill market, and the exporter is paid the discounted value. Since it is denominated in foreign currency, the bank negotiates the draft for the exporter. By negotiating the foreign exchange instrument for the exporter, the bank facilitates the export transaction financing. The time draft becomes an acceptance, purchased in the money market by an investor, thereby financing the transaction. We describe this type of operation in detail in Chapter 10 that addresses foreign trade finance.

Time draft

Order to pay, drawn on a party, bank or nonbank, with a stated future maturing date.

Sight draft

Order to pay, drawn on a party, bank or nonbank, payable at sight.

FOREIGN EXCHANGE MARKET LINK WITH THE EUROCURRENCY MARKET

The foreign exchange market's closest links are with the local money market and the Eurocurrency market. The incentives that can exist for interest arbitrage are one basic reason for the strong link with local money markets. We referred to foreign exchange arbitrage earlier in this chapter. Whereas in foreign exchange arbitrage we seek profits from discrepancies in currency rates, in interest arbitage we seek profits from discrepancies in interest rates—usually between domestic and foreign money markets.

When interest rates are higher in one money market (London) than another (New York), investors seek to benefit from this discrepancy. They will shift funds from the low interest rate market to the high interest rate market. If investors are risk averse, they will avoid an exposed position in the high interest rate currency by selling it forward. The simultaneous spot purchase and forward sale of the foreign currency by the party seeking higher interest income is called a swap. A swap can have a cost attached to it when the foreign currency buyer pays a spot purchase price that exceeds the lower forward selling price. Given higher interest rates in London than New York, investors will arbitrage funds from New York to London. This move will usually push down interest rates in London and push up interest rates in New York. In effect arbitrage movements of funds through the foreign exchange market tend to realign interest rates in the two money markets.

Similarly, interest rate differentials in the Eurocurrency market provide incentives for interest arbitrage flows. In this case investors can arbitrage funds between various Eurocurrency sectors. In a later section we note that swap costs function as a stabilizing effect on those interest arbitrage flows.

Eurocurrency and foreign exchange trading have certain similarities in that dealer banks make up both types of markets, and the same major currencies play a key role. However, Eurocurrency and foreign exchange trading do differ. In the Eurocurrency market the basic commodity is time deposits that earn interest. In the foreign exchange market the basic commodity is sight deposits that do not earn interest.

Swap
Simultaneous spot purchase and forward sale of foreign currency.

Mechanics of the Market

INSTRUMENTS OF FOREIGN EXCHANGE

Foreign exchange is defined as any asset or financial claim denominated in a foreign currency. These vehicles include foreign currency deposit balances, foreign government bonds, or shares (German bearer shares denominated in deutsche marks). In examining the specific workings of the market, banks employ the most important instruments:

- cable or electronic transfers of sight deposit funds
- banker's sight drafts
- commercial drafts.

A cable transfer or electronic transfer is a method of payment whereby the buyer pays the selling bank for the needed foreign currency, and the bank telexes or electronically communicates payment instructions to its correspondent bank where the foreign currency deposit is held. This method is commonly used to transfer large amounts of funds.

| EXHIBIT 4.2 | **Society for Worldwide Interbank Financial Telecommunications (SWIFT)** |

SWIFT is the most important communications network for international transactions. SWIFT is a private nonprofit corporation headquartered near Brussels, Belgium. It is owned by more than 2,000 members, most of which are banking institutions. It operates message switching centers in the Netherlands and in Culpepper, Virginia. Operating centers are connected by international transmission lines to regional processors in most member countries. The SWIFT system has operated for more than 15 years.

Modernization of SWIFT provides almost unlimited capacity to transmit information relative to foreign exchange transactions, payments confirmations, securities confirmations, international trade documentation, and other financial information. SWIFT is the most widely used international message transfer system. However, there are several alternative systems, including a service developed by Reuters, a British company. The Reuters service provides current financial market information and allows traders to interact with one another.

The SWIFT network interacts closely with daily currency settlement and clearing systems. For example, in New York 140 banks that are serviced by SWIFT settle foreign exchange and Eurodollar transactions through the Clearing House Interbank Payments System (CHIPS). Foreign exchange transactions account for over half of CHIPS messages by number and dollar values. The New York Clearing House Association operates CHIPS in cooperation with the Federal Reserve Bank of New York.

Specialized computer-operated telecommunications facilities have been developed to speed the flow and improve the accuracy of messages from one bank to another. For example, the Society for Worldwide Interbank Financial Telecommunications (SWIFT) operates an international message transfer system that reduces errors and delays in foreign exchange trading (see Exhibit 4.2).

An alternative to electronic transfer would be mail transfer. In this case the instructions are mailed, or a bankers' sight draft is issued to the buyer who then sends the draft via airmail to the party to whom payment must be made. For example, a U.S. importer may have arranged to mail a bankers' sight draft to a foreign supplier for pound Sterling 138,000. The U.S. importer first purchases this sight draft from Chase Manhattan Bank in New York. Chase issues the sight draft drawn on its account at National Westminster Bank, London. The draft is then mailed to the foreign seller, who can negotiate the draft in London and be paid sterling funds.

Commercial drafts are drawn by exporters on the buyer or buyer's bank. If these drafts are drawn in foreign currency, they are foreign exchange. The exporter can request one of the banks servicing the transaction to negotiate the draft, that is, to purchase or discount the draft. We discuss this procedure in Chapter 10, chapter on foreign trade finance.

SPOT EXCHANGE

There are three forms of foreign exchange trading: outright spot (delivery now), outright forward (delivery in the future), and swaps. A swap is a simultaneous buy and sell at different maturities. In this section we consider trading in outright spot. Trading in the other forms is considered in other sections of this chapter.

Actual foreign exchange market quotations are presented in Exhibit 4.3, as printed in the *New York Times*. The left side of the exhibit presents dollar prices of foreign currencies (the direct method of quoting), while the right side displays foreign

SWIFT

Society for Worldwide Interbank Financial Telecommunications. Computerized message and payments instruction system operated by and for foreign exchange banks.

Bankers sight draft

Means by which foreign exchange bank issues draft drawn against its foreign currency balances on deposit in a foreign financial center.

EXHIBIT 4.3	Foreign Exchange Rates in New York Market			
	FGN. CURRENCY IN DOLLARS		DOLLAR IN FGN. CURRENCY	
	Fri.	Thu.	Fri.	Thu.
f-Argent (Peso)	1.0100	1.0100	.9901	.9901
Australia (Dollar)	.6785	.6782	1.4738	1.4745
Austria (Schilling)	.0839	.0839	11.918	11.918
c-Belgium (Franc)	.0283	.0283	35.30	35.28
Brazil (CruzeiroR)	.0036	.0036	280.99	280.99
Britain (Pound)	1.5020	1.5040	.6658	.6649
30-day fwd	1.4993	1.5010	.6670	.6662
60-day fwd	1.4969	1.4987	.6680	.6672
90-day fwd	1.4946	1.4964	.6691	.6683
Canada (Dollar)	.7506	.7544	1.3323	1.3255
30-day fwd	.7502	.7540	1.3330	1.3262
60-day fwd	.7498	.7536	1.3337	1.3269
90-day fwd	.7496	.7534	1.3341	1.3273
y-Chile (Peso)	.002420	.002420	413.14	413.14
China (Yuan)	.1725	.1725	5.7955	5.7955
Colombia (Peso)	.001464	.001464	683.24	683.24
c-CzechRep (Koruna)	.0343	.0343	29.17	29.17
Denmark (Krone)	.1509	.1508	6.6275	6.6330
ECU	1.13630	1.13630	.8800	.8800
z-Edudr (Sucre)	.000508	.000508	1967.03	1967.03
d-Egypt (Pound)	.2994	.2994	3.3405	3.3405
Finland (Mark)	.1770	.1768	5.6485	5.6570
France (Franc)	.1734	.1734	5.7680	5.7680
Germany (Mark)	.5898	.5900	1.6955	1.6950
30-day fwd	.5881	.5883	1.7005	1.6999
60-day fwd	.5867	.5869	1.7044	1.7038
90-day fwd	.5857	.5859	1.7075	1.7069
Greece (Drachma)	.004112	.004105	243.20	243.60
Hong Kong (Dollar)	.1295	.1295	7.7215	7.7225
Hungary (Forint)	.0102	.0102	98.28	98.28
y-India (Rupee)	.0322	.0322	31.034	31.034
Indnsia (rupjah)	.000476	.000476	2102.78	2102.78
Ireland (Punt)	1.4322	1.4350	.6982	.6969
Israel (Sherkel)	.3441	.3441	2.9059	2.9059
Italy (Lira)	.000602	.000602	1660.00	1660.00
Japan (Yen)	.009019	.009042	110.88	110.60
30-day fwd	.009002	.009034	111.09	110.69
60-day fwd	.008990	.009024	111.23	110.81
90-day fwd	.008977	.009013	111.39	110.95
Jordan (Dinar)	1.4535	1.4535	.68799	.68799
Lebanon (Pound)	.000584	.000584	1712.00	1712.00
Malaysia (Ringgit)	.3899	.3899	2.5645	2.5645
z-Mexico (Peso)	.321234	.321234	3.1130	3.1130
N. Zealand (Dollar)	.5588	.5588	1.7895	1.7895
NethrInds (Guilder)	.5263	.5260	1.9000	1.9010
Norway (Krone)	.1359	.1358	7.3600	7.3640
Pakistan (Rupee)	.0334	.0334	29.96	29.96
y-Peru (New Sol)	.4785	.4785	2.090	2.090
z-Philpins (Peso)	.0363	.0363	27.56	27.56
Poland (Zlofy)	.000050	.000050	20180	20180
Portugal (Escudo)	.005774	.005774	173.19	173.19
a-Russia (Ruble)	.000800	.000800	1250.00	1250.00
Saudi Arab (Rival)	.2666	.2666	3.7515	3.7515
Singapore (Dollar)	.6285	.6285	1.5910	1.5910
SlovakRep (Koruna)	.0303	.0303	32.98	32.98
So. Africa (Rand)	.2965	.2965	3.3730	3.3730
f-So. Africa (Rand)	.2273	.2255	4.4000	4.4350
So. Korea (Won)	.001238	.001238	808.00	808.00
Spain (Peseta)	.007161	.007161	139.65	139.65

(Continued)

EXHIBIT 4.3	**(Continued)**			
	FGN. CURRENCY IN DOLLARS		**DOLLAR IN FGN. CURRENCY**	
	Fri.	Thu.	Fri.	Thu.
Sweden (Krona)	.1217	.1220	8.2174	8.1955
Switzerland (Franc)	.6954	.6976	1.4380	1.4335
30-day fwd	.6946	.6968	1.4397	1.4352
60-day fwd	.6941	.6963	1.4407	1.4361
90-day fwd	.6938	.6959	1.4413	1.4369
Taiwan (NT $)	.0375	.0375	26.69	26.69
Thailand (Baht)	.03929	.03929	25.45	25.45
Turkey (Lira)	.000070	.000070	14198.00	14198.00
U.A.E. (Dirham)	.2723	.2723	3.6720	3.6720
f-Uruguay (Peso)	.229885	.229885	4.35	4.35
z-Venzuel (Bolivar)	.0095	.0095	105.3500	105.3500

ECU: European Currency Unit, a basket of European currencies. The Federal Reserve Board's index of the value of the dollar against 10 other currencies weighted on the basis of trade was 94.86 Thursday, off 0.50 points or 0.52 percent from Wednesday 95.36. A year ago the index was 91.15

a-fixing, Moscow Interbank Currency Exchange

c-commercial rate, d-free market rate, f-financial rate, y-official rate, z-floating rate.

Prices as of 10:00 a.m. Eastern Time from Telerate Systems and other sources.

SOURCE: *New York Times.*

currency prices of the dollar (the indirect method). We can explain how these two prices or exchange rates are related, if we understand that these rates are reciprocals of one another. For example, the spot rate on German deutsche marks was $0.5898, that is, the fraction $/DM. The reciprocal is obtained by dividing this rate into 1.000. This yields DM 1.6955 per U.S. dollar or the fraction DM/$.

Similarly, we can verify that the dollar price of French franc of $0.1734 has a reciprocal rate of FF 5.7670 by dividing the first rate (0.1734) into 1.000. Essentially the foreign exchange market works on the basis of this system of reciprocal rates. Arbitrage between various foreign exchange market centers maintains the fine equilibrium in the market so that there are no discrepancies in these reciprocal rates.

Complicated arbitrage involving three or more currencies can take place thus keeping the rates in equilibrium across all market centers. For example, if the rates in Exhibit 4.3 are operating, and a trader in Frankfurt purchases Dutch florin (guilders) at a rate of Fl 1.20 per deutsche mark, profit can be made by arbitrage. The Frankfurt trader can purchase florin at Fl 1.20 per deutsche mark and can sell them in New York against dollars at $0.5263. At the same time the dollars can be converted into deutsche mark at $0.5898. Now let us calculate the amount of profit that can be generated if the original transaction involves a purchase of Fl 1.2 million.

The profit calculation is summarized in Exhibit 4.4. In Frankfurt, DM 1 million is used to acquire Fl 1.2 million. At this point the Fl 1.2 million is sold in New York for $631,560. The dollar proceeds are then used to purchase deutsche mark. A profit of DM 70,804 is generated.

An alternate calculation is to obtain the cross rate on deutsche mark and Dutch florins in New York. The cross rate is obtained by multiplying two rates to obtain a third rate. In this case, we obtain the cross rate of florin/DM by multiplying the florin/$ rate by the $/DM rate, as follows:

$$\text{Cross rate of florin/DM} = \text{florin/\$} \times \text{\$/DM}$$

Reciprocal rates

A pair of currencies exhibit two rates of exchange in comparison with one another, which are reciprocals of one another.

Cross rate

Rate obtained by multiplying two foreign exchange rates.

EXHIBIT 4.4	**Calculation of Arbitrage Profit: Purchase of Florin and Arbitrage through Dollars into DMarks**		
DMark cost of florin		DM	1,000,000
Amount of florin purchased		Fl	1,200,000
Dollars received on sale of florin			631,560[1]
DMarks received by purchase in New York		DM	1,070,804[2]

[1] $0.5263 × 1.2 million
[2] $631,560 divided by 0.5898

To calculate florin/$ rate obtain reciprocal of $/florin rate. This is given as Fl 1.9000. Therefore

$$1.9000 \times 0.5898 = 1.12062$$

Since we can purchase florin in Frankfurt at Fl 1.2 per deutsche mark, the advantage is as follows:

$$\frac{1.2 - 1.12062}{1.12062} \quad \text{or} \quad 7.08\%$$

Therefore a DM 1,000,000 investment should generate a profit of DM 70,800 (the difference is due to rounding in calculations).

Note that these calculations ignore transactions costs that can reduce the profitability of the arbitrage. Transaction costs exist because bank dealers buy and sell foreign exchange at slightly different prices to provide a spread or profit margin. Dealers buy at a bid price and sell at an ask price. Taking the quoted bid-ask rates between the dollar and pound sterling of $1.5020–$1.5030, we have a spread of $0.0010, or 0.066%. This is approximately 1/15th of 1%. While this amount appears as a trading cost in the market, it represents a profit margin to dealing banks. Banks generate substantial foreign exchange trading profits from the large transactions volume in the market (Exhibit 4.1).

Spread

Dealer banks quote bid and ask prices for a currency, the difference or spread providing a trading profit.

Matrix of Spot Rates

The market system of exchange rates can be visualized better if we examine a matrix of spot rates (Exhibit 4.5). If we are given the top row (row A) of rates, we can calculate the column 1 rates by obtaining reciprocals of the rates in row A. For example, the rate $/DM is $0.590 in row A. The reciprocal rate DM/$ in column 1 is obtained by:

$$1/0.590 = 1.695 = DM/\$$$

and the $/FF rate of $0.1733 in row A can be converted into the FF/$ rate by:

$$1/0.1733 = 5.770 = FF/\$$$

Exchange rates in column 2 (Swiss Franc/£) are cross rates from row A ($/£) and column 1 (Swiss Franc/$).

$$SwFr/£ = SwFr/\$ \times \$/£ = 1.435 \times 1.504 = 2.158$$

EXHIBIT 4.5	Matrix of Spot Rates					
	U.S. Dollar (1)	Pound Sterling (2)	Deutsche Mark (3)	Swiss Franc (4)	Canadian Dollar (5)	French Franc (6)
A. U.S. Dollar	—	1.504	0.590	0.697	0.754	0.1733
B. Pound Sterling	0.665	—	0.392	0.463	0.502	0.1152
C. Deutsche Mark	1.695	2.548	—	1.181	1.278	0.2936
D. Swiss Franc	1.435	2.158	0.847	—	1.082	0.2487
E. Canadian Dollar	1.326	1.994	0.783	0.924	—	0.2298
F. French Franc	5.770	8.678	3.406	4.021	4.352	—

SOURCE: *Financial Times.*

Proceeding further, all remaining rates (not found in row A or in column 1) can be obtained by using this method of calculating cross rates. For example, the cross rate FF/Cdn$ can be obtained by:

$$FF/Cdn\$ = FF/\$ \times \$/Cdn\$ = 5.770 \times 0.754 = 4.352$$

This is the rate found in Exhibit 4.5, at row F, column 5.

FORWARD EXCHANGE

Foreign exchange market participants trade currency in spot and at the forward. Spot exchange is traded for delivery on a value date, usually two working days after the date the transaction is concluded.

Forward exchange

Contract to buy or sell a currency for future delivery.

Forward exchange is traded for delivery at some time in the future. An American importer may have to pay French francs to a French supplier and therefore will purchase spot French francs. The New York bank may issue the buyer a sight draft drawn on its French correspondent bank. The importer can mail sight draft to the supplier. Alternately, the New York bank may provide a cable transfer by advising the French bank via telex to transfer the designated amount of French francs to a specific party.

However, the American importer may be required to pay the French supplier in one, two, or possibly three months time. If the importer fears a rise in the price of the French franc and wants to lock in the currency cost now, he has two alternatives. In this example the buyer has the choice of buying the French francs spot and investing them in Paris until payment is to be made, or of buying the francs forward. In buying the francs forward, the importer obtains a contract from the New York bank that locks in the dollar price of the francs and calls for delivery to the importer at a stipulated date in the future.

The importer will be inclined toward the forward purchase of francs if the spot rate on francs is expected to be higher in the near future than it is at present. If many American importers believe that spot francs will rise in value and accordingly purchase francs forward, this practice will tend to drive up the price of forward francs. In this way a wedge is driven between the spot and forward rates based on price expectations. Conversely, if American importers believe that spot francs will fall in value, they will not purchase forward francs, and there will be no reason for the forward franc to rise in value.

Relative cost factors may be the determinant of which alternative the importer chooses. This question can be examined in relation to the opportunity cost relationships. For example, let us assume that the importer is faced with the interest rates

EXHIBIT 4.6	**Opportunity Costs Determining Choice of Spot or Forward Purchase of French Francs (3-Month Maturities)**

Interest rate in New York	8.5%
Interest rate in Paris	9.2%
Spot rate, $/FF	$0.200
3-Month forward rate, $/FF	$0.199
Annualized discount on forward franc	2.0%

Spot cover: Borrow dollars at 8.5%; convert into French francs; invest at 9.2%; gain of 0.7%

Forward cover: Buy French franc forward at annualized discount of 2.0%

EXHIBIT 4.7	**Basic Formula Used to Calculate Annualized Premium or Discount on Forward Exchange Rate**

$$\text{Annualized premium} = \frac{F - S}{S} \quad \times \quad \frac{12}{n} \quad \times \quad 100$$
$$\text{or discount}$$

Calculate decimal value	Annualize based on number of months to maturity	Convert decimal to %

and foreign exchange rates in Exhibit 4.6. A spot purchase of French franc and investment in Paris offers an annualized net gain of 0.7% (9.2% − 8.5%) for the American importer. A forward purchase of French franc offers the American importer a net gain of 2.0%. Therefore the alternative of purchasing French franc forward is preferable to purchasing francs spot.

The calculation of the 2.0% net gain is based on the following formula that converts the discount on forward francs to a number that is comparable with interest rates. Interest rates are always expressed as annualized percentages. In the equation, S represents the spot rate for the French franc stated in terms of U.S. dollars, F the forward rate, and n the number of months maturity of the forward contract. (Exhibit 4.7).

$$\frac{F - S}{S} \times \frac{12}{n} \times 100 = \text{annualized discount (or premium) on forward exchange.}$$

$$\frac{0.001}{0.200} \times \frac{12}{3} \times 100 = 2.0\%$$

Forward exchange rates can be at a discount or premium relative to the spot rate. For currencies that are widely traded, including sterling, dollar, deutsche mark, yen, French franc, and Swiss franc, forward rates tend to respond quickly to changes in interest rates. Simply stated, interest rate differentials between money centers tend to drive forward rates to premiums or discounts. The mechanism that brings about this adjustment is interest arbitrage.

SWAPS

Interest arbitrage

Moving short-term investment funds to obtain higher net return.

Interest arbitrage involves investors shifting liquid funds to the highest net advantage. As shown in Exhibit 4.8, interest rates that can be earned on short-term sterling assets are at 5.32%, and on short-term dollar assets, 3.19%. Investors are inclined to swap dollars into sterling for short-term investment.

There are two parts to the swap. First, investors purchase pound sterling spot for investment in London. Second, they simultaneously sell sterling for future delivery (forward). The swap is used to avoid exposure to the risk of currency rate changes. In carrying out the swap, the investor buys sterling spot, uses the funds to purchase short-term sterling assets, and sells sterling forward. The sale of sterling forward protects the investor against a decline of the dollar price of sterling should that decline take place while invested in sterling assets.

Analysis of the swap activity is the key to understanding how the discount develops in forward sterling. Continuous swap activity places upward (buying) pressure on spot sterling, and downward (selling) pressure on forward sterling. This opens a discount on forward sterling that increases until it is no longer profitable for investors to arbitrage dollars into sterling investments.

Returning to our illustration of swapping dollars into sterling, we can calculate the net advantage for the dollar-based investor. The net advantage will be:

Net advantage

Difference between interest rate differential and cost of swap, resulting from interest arbitrage.

Net advantage = Interest differential in favor of London minus cost of the swap

Net advantage = (5.32% − 3.19%) − 2.00% = 2.13% − 2.00% = 0.13%

The net advantage is not large at 0.13%. In general we find this situation in most sectors of the foreign exchange market. That is, arbitrage activity by banks and other participants in the market drives the forward rate to a discount on the high interest rate currency. When a large discount develops on the high interest rate currency, this "cost of the swap" tends to offset the advantage of earning a high interest rate on that currency.

In Exhibit 4.8 we see the cost of the swap on high interest rate currencies and the profit on swaps into low interest rate currencies (column 3). This is a comparison

EXHIBIT 4.8	**Relationship between Interest Rates and Forward Rates**			
Currency	Interest Rate (Eurocurrency) (1)	Interest Differential vis-a-vis Dollar (2)	Forward Rate Expressed as Discount or Premium Relative to Spot Rate (3)	Forward Discount or Premium as % of Interest Differential vis-a-vis Dollar (4)
Spanish peseta	8.56%	5.37	5.7% discount	106%
Italian lira	8.00%	4.81	5.1% discount	106%
Deutsche mark	6.08%	2.81	2.8% discount	100%
Pound sterling	5.32%	2.13	2.0% discount	94%
Swiss franc	4.13%	0.94	0.9% discount	96%
U.S. dollar	3.19%	0	0	0
Japanese yen	1.06%	−2.13	2.2% premium	106%

SOURCE: *Financial Times.*

to interest rates on U.S. dollar denominated short-term assets. The exhibit also shows that the forward discounts and premiums represent between 94% and 106% of the respective currencies' interest differential against U.S. dollar assets. In short, there is a high correlation between interest rate differentials and the forward premiums and discounts on these currencies.

We conclude by noting that several factors influence spot-forward rate relationships. These include interest rate differentials, expectations concerning changes in the spot rate, and changes in interest rates. Nevertheless, as observed in Exhibit 4.8, when we take pairs of currencies and examine the basic relationships there is a high conformity between costs and profits on swaps and the respective interest differentials.

Foreign Currency Futures and Options

We have already considered use of the forward (interbank) market in hedging foreign currency positions. An alternative is futures trading in foreign currencies on the Chicago Mercantile Exchange (CME) or futures exchanges in other countries. In 1972 the CME initiated trading in foreign currency futures contracts on the International Monetary Market (IMM).

Trading on the IMM has grown rapidly, especially since the adoption of floating exchange rates in 1973. More than 700 IMM members act as floor brokers in the execution of trades. Members must carry accounts with clearing members to conduct personal transactions. Clearing members represent major securities firms, subsidiaries of bank holding companies, and commercial trading firms.

FX Futures

Contract trading foreign currency on an organized exchange where a standardized contract is utilized.

The currency futures contract provides for the future delivery of a specified amount of a foreign currency at a specific date, time, and place. The contract is fulfilled by accepting or making delivery of the currency on the value date of the contract. A buy or sell position can be closed out by making an offsetting purchase or sale of an equivalent contract prior to expiration of trading for the contract. Futures contracts must be backed by margin deposits, the amounts set by the exchange. In Chapter 5, we discuss the mechanics and use of currency futures and options in detail.

Transactions in the Market

The foreign exchange market permits participants to transfer purchasing power, to hedge, to speculate on currency rate changes, to engage in covered interest arbitrage, and to speculate on interest rate changes. The following discussion elaborates on the nature of these transactions.

Transfer of Purchasing Power

In the internationally integrated world we live in, it is often necessary to shift purchasing power from one country to another. Importers must shift their purchasing power to the country of the exporter. Tourists must shift purchasing power to countries they visit. A simple spot purchase of foreign currency will accomplish this shift, whereas a purchase of forward exchange will transfer purchasing power at a future date.

HEDGING AND SPECULATION

Hedging

Covering an open or uncovered currency position.

Hedging is the art of covering an open or uncovered position. Importers paying foreign currencies may wish to hedge against an increase in value of the currency in which the sale is denominated. In this case they may buy the foreign currency forward. Exporters receiving foreign currencies may wish to hedge against a decrease in value of the foreign currency they will receive from their export activities. In this case they may sell the currency forward.

For example, a French importer who needs to pay deutsche mark 200,000 in three months time has three alternatives. First, the importer can borrow French francs, convert into deutsche marks, and invest in the Frankfurt money market. Second, the importer can purchase deutsche mark forward, and take delivery at maturity of the contract. Finally, the importer can do nothing, that is, make a decision to not hedge the open position.

The cost/return from each of the three alternatives can be calculated when we make certain assumptions concerning interest rate levels and exchange rates (Exhibit 4.9). If the spot deutsche mark rises from French franc 3.00 to FF 3.06, the cost of purchasing deutsche mark spot rises at a rate of 2%, or 8% annualized. By comparison the cost of the hedge (purchase of deutsche mark forward) is 1%, or 4% annualized. The cost of borrowing French franc and purchasing deutsche mark spot, and then investing the deutsche mark is 3.5% (9.0 − 5.5). Under these conditions the best course of action would be to hedge via borrowing in the money market at a cost of 3.5%. The cost of doing nothing would have been 8% annualized.

Speculation

Taking an uncovered currency position for profit.

Speculation is based on the expectation of a currency rate change, and positioning oneself to benefit from the expected change. For example, we may expect that the spot sterling will fall from $1.7500 now to $1.6000 in three months. An appropriate action would be to sell sterling forward. Let us assume the forward sterling is sold for $1.735. Not considering transaction costs and the possible requirement of margin deposits by trading banks, if the spot rate declines to $1.6000 as projected, the profit on this speculation can be calculated as follows:

Rate at which sterling sold forward	$1.7350
Rate at which forward sterling contract is covered by spot purchase	$1.6000
Profit per pound	$0.1350

COVERED INTEREST ARBITRAGE

As might be expected, money flows to where it can obtain the highest return. In the global context money can flow to any of a number of local financial markets, and the range of interest rates (returns) available in the world's various money markets is quite large.

EXHIBIT 4.9	Hedging Alternatives	
	Now	**3 Months Later**
Foreign exchange rates		
Spot Deutsche Mark	FF 3.00	FF 3.06
3-month Deutsche Mark	FF 3.03	
Interest rates		
Paris	9.0%	
Frankfurt	5.5%	

| EXHIBIT 4.10 | Interest Arbitrage Incentives (3-Month Maturities) | | | | |

Money Market	Annualized Discount or Premium on Forward (swap cost or profit)	Currency	Interest Rate in Local Money Market	Interest Differential vis-a-vis New York	Net Advantage of Arbitrage[1]
Milan	5.1	Lira	8.32	5.07	−0.03
Paris	3.3	French franc	6.50	3.25	−0.05
Frankfurt	2.8	DMark	6.08	2.83	0.03
Amsterdam	2.4	Guilder	5.62	2.37	−0.03
London	2.0	Sterling	5.25	2.00	0.00
Zurich	0.9	Swiss franc	4.25	1.00	0.10
New York	0	U.S. dollar	3.25	0	—
Tokyo	1.2[2]	Yen	2.06	−1.19	0.01

[1] Minus sign indicates advantages to New York.

[2] There is a profit swapping dollars into yen.

SOURCE: *Financial Times.*

In Exhibit 4.10 we present data reflecting local money market returns, swap profit and cost factors, and net advantage derived from interest arbitrage. As shown, in 1993 interest rates on the New York money market were lower than rates in most of the other money markets. In six cases—Milan, Paris, Frankfurt, Amsterdam, London, and Zurich—money market rates were higher than New York. In one case, Tokyo, money market rates were lower than New York. This occurrence might suggest that in the case of New York investors, money arbitrage would flow to the high interest rate centers (Milan, Paris, Frankfurt), but not to the low interest rate center (Tokyo). On an uncovered (unhedged) basis this outcome might be true. But investors seeking to preserve capital and earn higher returns will engage in covered interest arbitrage.

Covered interest arbitrage

Swapping one currency into another on a hedged basis to benefit from interest differential.

Covered interest arbitrage involves swapping one currency into another. This arbitrage involves two steps: 1) Buying foreign currency spot (transfer purchasing power), and 2) selling foreign currency forward (hedge position). By these two steps the investor is swapped, and has no currency rate exposure. Without hedging the position, the investor could take a substantial loss if the foreign currency depreciates in value against the investor's home currency.

The swap activity tends to have the following effect. Purchase of a high interest rate currency spot tends to push the spot rate higher. Sale of a high interest rate currency forward pushes the forward rate lower. This move drives the forward rate to a discount relative to the spot rate. This discount is the "cost of the swap." This cost factor must be subtracted from the "favorable interest spread" obtained by interest arbitrage to arrive at the "net advantage." The following illustration makes this clear.

In Exhibit 4.10 we find that interest rates in the Zurich money market are 4.25% compared with 3.25% in New York, providing a 1.00% interest spread in favor of Zurich. On that basis we might expect that money will flow from New York to Zurich. The annualized cost of a three-month swap of U.S. dollars to Swiss francs is 0.9%. The net advantage of arbitrage from New York to Zurich is:

Net advantage (New York to Zurich) = Interest spread − Cost of swap

$$= 1.00\% - 0.90\% = 0.10\%$$

By contrast arbitrage from New York to Paris provides a negative net advantage as follows:

$$\text{Net advantage (New York to Paris)} = (6.50\% - 3.25\%) - 3.30\%$$

$$3.25\% - 3.30\% = -0.05\%$$

In short, there is no golden rule that guarantees a profit on swaps from low interest to high interest rate currencies. Interestingly, in the case of three currencies, there is a net advantage of arbitrage from New York to the other centers (Frankfurt, Zurich, Tokyo). In all three cases, the net advantage is very narrow.

SPECULATION ON CHANGE IN INTEREST RATES

The close ties between the international money markets and foreign exchange trading come into view when we consider the possibilities for speculation on a change in interest rates. In our illustration of this transaction, we assume perfect equilibrium exists between the money markets (interest rate spreads) and the forward exchange market (spot-forward rate relationship). In perfect equilibrium there is no advantage from covered interest arbitrage. Interest spreads between two financial centers are exactly offset by the discount (or premium) on the forward rate of exchange. This we identify as interest rate parity.

The equilibrium is reflected in Exhibit 4.11, where the cost of a swap of dollars to sterling is 4% annualized at all maturities. This relationship is charted in Exhibit 4.12. A forward transaction curve is plotted based upon information in Exhibit 4.11. The curve has a constant slope, $0.0060 for each monthly extension of the forward maturity. Six-month sterling priced at $1.7640 represents a 4% discount. Similarly, 12 month sterling at $1.7280 also represents a 4% discount. Forward transaction curve I is based on a uniform discount at all maturities, 4% per annum. The discount of 4% represents the interest differential between London and New York.

Our forecast is that *the interest rate spread will change*. We expect the interest rate spread to decline from 4% to 2%. If it does, the discount on forward sterling will also decline to 2% as indicated in Exhibit 4.11. Similarly, the forward transaction curve II will become the relevant curve, since the forward discounts will have become smaller and the forward transaction curve will have shifted upward.

Interest rate parity equilibrium

Where there is no advantage to engage in interest arbitrage on covered basis.

EXHIBIT 4.11	Basic Data for Speculation on Interest Rate Change	
	Now (I)	**Projected (II)**
Interest Rates		
London	13.0%	12.0%
New York	9.0%	10.0%
Interest spread	4.0%	2.0%
FX Rates		
Spot pound	$1.8000	$1.8000
1 month forward	1.7940	1.7970
6 month forward	1.7640	1.7820
12 month forward	1.7280	1.7640
Monthly charge	0.0060	0.0030

| EXHIBIT 4.12 | Forward Transaction Curves |

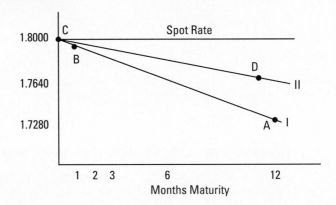

| EXHIBIT 4.13 | Swap Positions Taken in Interest Rate Speculation |

Day 0:	Sell 1-month sterling at $1.7940	Buy 12-month sterling at $1.7280
Day 30:	Buy spot sterling at $1.8000	Sell 11-month sterling at $1.7670
Loss	$0.0060	Gain $0.0390

Overall profit = $0.0390 − $0.0060 = $0.0330 per pound

Speculation on an interest rate change will be done in the absence of currency rate risk; therefore a swap must be used (Exhibit 4.13). On Day 0, our speculator initiates swap number one (points A and B on Exhibit 4.12). Here we are buying sterling at the lowest rate possible within a 12-month time frame, and selling sterling at the highest rate possible while leaving one month for the forecasted interest rate change to take place. Assuming that interest rates change as expected and that the New York-London interest spread narrows to 2%, we enter into swap number two on day 30 (points C and D in Exhibit 4.12).

Swap number two is necessary to cover the sale of one-month sterling that comes due for settlement on Day 30. Therefore a spot purchase of sterling is necessary on Day 30 to deliver against the sale of one-month sterling made on Day 0.

Second, a sale of 11-month sterling is necessary to maintain the swapped (hedged) position. The maturity of the 11-month sale coincides with the maturity remaining on the original 12-month buy (point A).

According to the information in Exhibit 4.13, the overall profit on this speculation is $0.0330 per pound sterling positioned. However, if the interest rate spread had increased rather than declined, the speculator would have experienced an overall loss.

CENTRAL BANK FOREIGN EXCHANGE OPERATIONS

Central banks are active participants in the foreign exchange market. Their activities include market intervention aimed at preventing wide and abrupt swings in currency values, and interbank swaps to augment the foreign exchange resources of other central banks. A reciprocal currency arrangement between the 14 largest central banks and the Bank for International Settlements provides for drawings between central banks of more than $30 billion. The reciprocal arrangements involve central banks swapping their respective currencies with one another, with a reversal of the swap at a later date.

Governments and central banks intervene under floating currency systems and fixed exchange rate systems. When governments and central banks intervene in a floating rate system, we refer to this as a "managed float." This denotes the fact that the currency is floating freely, but the float is being managed or guided by central bank intervention. The Group of Seven nations have been intervening actively in the foreign exchange market since the Louvre Accord. Intervention is necessary to operate a fixed exchange rate system. As noted in Chapter 2, central banks in EMS countries must carry out a large amount of this activity.

Managed float

Governments and central banks intervene in the foreign exchange market to influence exchange rate value.

Central banks can intervene quite actively in periods when large pressures build up against a particular currency. For example, market weakness developed in relation with the U.S. dollar in October-November 1988 due to a slowing U.S. economy, less favorable international interest rate differentials, renewed strength in German and Japanese trade surpluses, and a widening of the U.S. trade deficit. The dollar decline gained momentum through October 1988. United States monetary authorities intervened in the foreign exchange market to counter downward pressure on the dollar by purchasing $350 million against yen during the first two days of November. The dollar continued to come under selling pressure, and from November 9–16, U.S. authorities purchased another $625 million against yen in coordination with the Bank of Japan. Near mid-November selling pressure on the dollar intensified, and U.S. authorities broadened their intervention operations to include the mark. Between November 17 and December 2 they purchased $630 million against marks and $795 million against yen, all in coordination with other foreign central banks.

Monetary authorities generally include the central bank, and an exchange stabilization fund in cases where the national government has established one. The British Exchange Equalization Account (EEA) was established early in the 1930s, as was the U.S. Exchange Stabilization Fund (ESF).

Monetary authorities are responsible for the investment of foreign currency resources. For example, the Federal Reserve and ESF regularly invest their foreign currency balances in a variety of instruments that yield market-related rates of return and possess a high degree of quality and liquidity. These investments include securities issued by foreign governments. At the end of January 1989, holdings of such securities by the Federal Reserve amounted to $1.4 billion (equivalent), and holdings by the ESF to $1.8 billion.

Policy coordination is important to reinforce exchange intervention carried on by central banks. Policy coordination by the G-7 countries includes efforts to maintain interest rate relationships between their currencies to limit sharp shifts in foreign exchange rate relationships. G-7 country representatives meet several times each year to promote this policy coordination.

Determination of the Spot Rate of Exchange

Here we consider exchange rate behavior under three different kinds of exchange systems: floating, fixed, and controlled. Foreign exchange is traded (bought and sold) in the market at a price called the rate of exchange. The exchange rate is the price of foreign currency measured in domestic money. When currencies are traded in free market systems, daily quotations of foreign exchange are based on the price of bank transfers, whereby the selling bank sends a payment instruction to a depository institution. Bank dealers quote only a spot rate of exchange for most currencies traded in the foreign exchange market. Forward rates are quoted for a limited number of currencies. The analysis that follows refers to the spot rate only.

Floating rates

Exchange rate is free to find its level based on demand and supply forces.

In this discussion we consider three models of exchange rate determination: 1) freely floating rates, 2) fixed exchange rates, and 3) controlled rates. In a system of freely floating rates individuals can carry out foreign exchange transactions, and there is an absence of government activity in the market (except in the case of a managed float). In a fixed exchange rate system individuals can carry out foreign exchange transactions, and the government is active in stabilizing rate movements within agreed upon rate limits. In a controlled rate system individuals are restricted in exchange dealing, and the government holds a virtual monopoly over the allocation of foreign exchange.

FREELY FLOATING RATES

In a free market, in the absence of government stabilization, the exchange rate is determined by the supply and demand for foreign exchange. The amount of foreign exchange demanded at any time will depend on the volume of international transfers requiring payments to nonresidents. These transactions may include purchases (imports) of goods and services, and purchases (capital outflows) of financial assets. The quantity of foreign exchange demanded will vary inversely with its price. A high exchange rate makes foreign goods and services and financial assets more expensive, and the quantity demanded of these items will be lower. By contrast a low exchange rate tends to increase the amount of foreign exchange demanded.

The demand relationships described in the preceding paragraph are indicated in Exhibit 4.14. Two changes in demand are possible, as shown in Exhibit 4.14. These include a change in quantity demanded as a result of a change in price (exchange rate). In this case if the dollar price of deutsche mark rises from OS to OT, a smaller quantity of deutsche mark will be demanded (ON rather than OM).

A second change in demand occurs when the entire demand curve shifts. This demand shift can be caused by changes in income, price levels, interest rates, or consumer tastes. For example, in Exhibit 4.14 the shift to a higher demand for deutsche mark (dd to d'd') could be brought about by an increase in U.S. income levels, a higher price level in the United States relative to the price level in Germany, lower interest rates in the United States (making deutsche mark interest-earning assets relatively more attractive), or a change in consumer tastes favoring German-made goods.

The supply of foreign exchange comes from international transactions calling for money receipts from nonresidents. The amounts of foreign exchange supplied varies directly with the rate of exchange.

The quantity of foreign exchange supplied at any time will depend on the volume of international transfers generating receipts of funds from nonresidents. These transactions may include sales (exports) of goods and services, and sales (capital inflows) of financial assets to nonresidents. We must remember that supply of foreign exchange is initiated by nonresidents who want domestic goods and services. When the rate of exchange is high, domestic prices appear low to nonresidents, since they can purchase a unit of domestic money with a relatively small amount of their money. This trend stimulates domestic exports of goods and services and sales of financial assets to nonresidents, leading to a larger supply of foreign exchange coming into the market. By contrast a low exchange rate will dampen exports and lower the amount of foreign exchange offered in the market.

| EXHIBIT 4.14 | **Demand for Deutsche Mark Exchange in United States** |

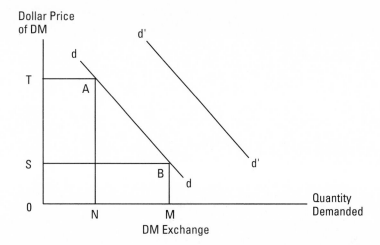

The demand schedule for deutsche mark exchange slopes downward from left to right. The amount demanded at a higher rate (point A) is less than the amount demanded at a lower rate (point B). An increase in the demand for deutsche mark is depicted by a shift in the curve from dd to d'd'. A decrease in demand for deutsche mark is depicted by a shift in the curve from d'd' to dd.

This supply relationship is indicated in Exhibit 4.15. At a high exchange rate (point A) there is a larger supply of foreign exchange available in the market (larger amount of exports of goods and services to Germany) than at a lower exchange rate (point B). This relationship occurs because at a higher exchange rate German buyers of dollars obtain a greater quantity of dollars in exchanging deutsche mark for dollars. Thus they are more willing to make the exchange.

A downward shift in the supply of deutsche mark (from ss to s's') takes place when income levels in Germany fall, reducing U.S. exports to that country. Other causes of downward shift in the supply of deutsche mark include a change in relative prices favoring German purchase of German goods and services over U.S. goods and services, or a change in German tastes shifting away from U.S. goods.

The rate of exchange is determined by the interaction of demand and supply. In Exhibit 4.16 the initial rate of exchange is set at point T, where quantity of deutsche marks demanded and supplied are equal. The exchange rate OS "clears the market" with OM quantity of deutsche marks traded. Suppose that demand for deutsche marks in the United States shifts up to d'd. This shift could follow from 1) a burst of inflation in the U.S. that makes German goods relatively more attractive, or 2) an upward shift in interest rates in Germany that makes German interest-bearing securities relatively more attractive.

Since foreign exchange fulfills the role of standard of deferred payments and store of value, demand and supply can shift easily. These shifts are in response to changed expectations concerning future inflation rates and interest rates. For example, if Germans are persuaded that inflation will become more subdued in the United States than in Germany, they will regard the dollar as a better store of value

EXHIBIT 4.15	Supply of Deutsche Mark Exchange in United States

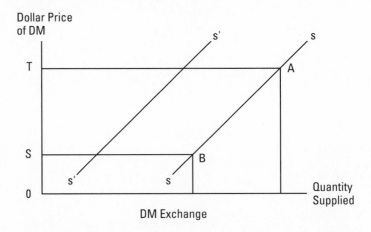

The supply schedule for deutsche mark exchange slopes upward from left to right. At a high exchange rate domestic prices of goods, services, and financial assets appear lower to nonresidents. This stimulates exports and brings a larger quantity of foreign exchange into the market (point A). By contrast lower rates reduce exports and bring in a smaller quantity of foreign exchange (point B). A decrease in supply is indicated by a shift of the curve from ss to s's'. An increase in supply is indicated by a shift of the curve from s's' to ss.

EXHIBIT 4.16	Determination of Equilibrium Exchange Rate for Deutsche Mark in New York Foreign Exchange Market

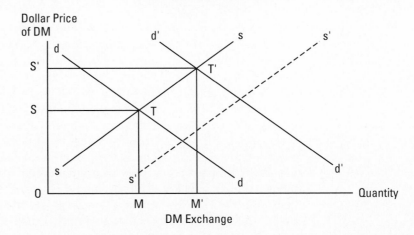

than the deutsche mark. This trend will result in a shift of the supply of deutsche mark outward to the right (s's' in Exhibit 4.16) and will tend to lower the dollar price of deutsche marks.

In Exhibit 4.17 we present a summary of the most important factors that affect exchange rate relationships. In Exhibit 4.17a, rising U.K. inflation brings about a decline in the pound sterling exchange rate. In Exhibit 4.17b, falling U.S. interest rates

EXHIBIT 4.17	**Factors Influencing Spot Exchange Rates**

A Inflation Rates:

U.K. inflation rises relative to U.S. inflation. U.S. demand for pounds shifts to d'd', while U.K. supply of pounds shifts to s's'. Exchange rate falls to E'.

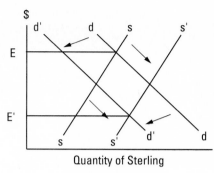

B Interest Rates:

U.S. interest rates fall relative to U.K. interest rates. U.S. demand for pounds shifts to d'd', while U.K. supply of pounds shifts to s's'. Exchange rate rises to E'.

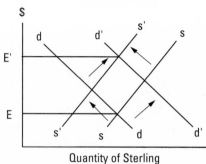

C Macroeconomic Activity:

U.S. income level rises relative to U.K. income level which remains unchanged. U.S. demand for pounds shifts to d'd', while U.K. supply of pounds is unaffected. Exchange rate rises to E'.

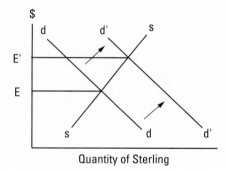

lead to a rise in the pound sterling exchange rate. In Exhibit 4.17c, rising U.S. income levels lead to a rise in the value of the pound relative to the dollar.

FIXED EXCHANGE RATES

Fixed rates

Government establishes par value for currency, and actively intervenes in market to maintain this valuation.

A review of the history of international financial arrangements over the past 180 years quickly tells us that a system of fixed exchange rates has been the operating mechanism for all but a few years. In the hundred years prior to World War I fixed exchange rates operated under the international gold standard. Governments of leading trading nations fixed their currency values in terms of gold. In turn, their fixed value in gold gave these currencies a common denominator of value and yielded a system of fixed exchange rates. The gold standard was restored after World War I and endured until the early 1930s. Since that time exchange rates have been stabilized by government intervention.

At the end of World War II the Bretton Woods system was created. This system was designed to promote fixed exchange rates between the leading currencies.

Countries established par values for their currencies and were required to pursue financial policies that were conducive to exchange rate stability. The IMF monitored exchange practices of member countries and provided liquid resources to countries experiencing difficulties in their current payments. Countries were required to maintain their currency values within a range of ±1% of par values. In this Bretton woods system, governments were expected to actively intervene in the exchange market to maintain spot currency rates within a narrow range of values.

The Bretton Woods system met its demise in the 1970s and was largely replaced by a floating rate system. However, in 1979 a number of European countries adopted an exchange rate mechanism, the European Monetary System (described in detail in Chapter 2). The EMS has operated much like the Bretton Woods system, with the exception that the permitted fluctuation in currency values has been larger (2.25% rather than 1%). The general operation of the EMS until August 1993, when very wide fluctuations in rates became accepted, is depicted in Exhibit 4.18.

In Exhibit 4.18, the FF/DM exchange rate moves within a relatively narrow range. Whenever it reaches or comes close to the upper or lower limits of permitted fluctuation, central bank stabilization comes into play. For example, in year 1 when the deutsche mark is at its upper limit against the French franc, the French central bank is selling deutsche mark in the Paris foreign exchange market, preventing the deutsche mark from moving through the ceiling of permitted rate movements.

For a fixed exchange rate system to work well, it is necessary for governments to maintain financial policies that promote stable exchange rates. Monetary expansion rates and macroeconomic growth rates cannot be too far out of line between the European Community countries in the EMS. Extreme differences in monetary and fiscal policies will result in greater discrepancies between inflation rates and interest rates, and place heavy pressure on exchange rates. Also, these differences in policies will lead to shifts in the demand and supply schedules of the respective currencies. We can observe this in Exhibit 4.18. Between year 1 and year 3 the FF/DM rate of exchange moved from the upper limit to the lower limit of the permitted range of values. Underlying this is the downward shift of French demand for deutsche mark (d_1 to d_3), and the outward shift of German supply of deutsche mark

---

EXHIBIT 4.18   **(a) EMS Fixed Exchange Rate System**
(b) Interaction of Demand and Supply under a Fixed Rate System

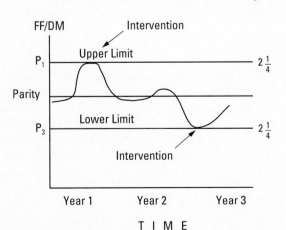
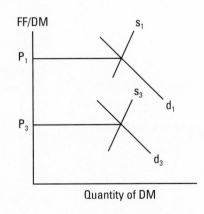

(s_1 to s_3). Both the floating and fixed exchange rate systems operate as free exchange markets. The major difference is the active intervention (stabilization) of governments in the market where there are fixed rates.

CONTROLLED EXCHANGE RATES

A third type of exchange rate system operates on the basis of government control and inconvertibility. Under an exchange control system the government authority enjoys exclusive power to determine the allocation and use of available foreign exchange. Residents of exchange control countries are not free to engage in foreign exchange transactions. Capital inflows and exports of merchandise generate available foreign exchange. The control authority must allocate foreign exchange due to the imbalance between available foreign exchange and the quantity demanded. Exchange control systems are designed to restrict private sector transactions. Demand and supply are not free to determine exchange rates and do not play a dominant role in allocating the uses of foreign exchange.

Exchange control

Government has exclusive power to determine the allocation and use of foreign exchange.

Exchange control systems must deal with disequilibrium conditions or imbalances of demand and supply of foreign exchange. In the case of a peso currency country, this imbalance is measured by the length MN in Exhibit 4.19. An excess of demand over supply generally applies due to the overvalued local currency (in this case the peso). The equilibrium exchange rate is OE, but the peso price of dollars is set at an artificially low level of OS. The government is unwilling to depreciate the peso for several reasons. First, the depreciation is likely to fuel inflationary pressures, as imported necessities such as fuel and food will increase in peso price. Second, increases in prices of necessities will lead to workers demanding higher wages, further aggravating inflation.

In Exhibit 4.19, given the exchange rate OS, the supply of foreign exchange will be OM, but the quantity of foreign exchange demanded will be ON. The exchange control authority must ration dollar exchange (in the amount of OM) based on government-established priorities.

EXHIBIT 4.19   **Demand and Supply of Dollars under a System of Exchange Controls—Overvalued Peso**

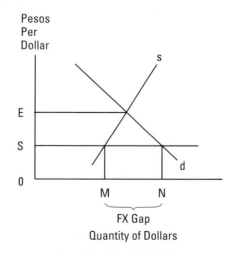

A controlled rate of exchange usually produces the following conditions: a) local currency tends to remain overvalued, b) the generation of foreign exchange is limited due to the low peso price of dollars and the lack of incentive to export, and c) international transactions usually remain at a lower level due to the resulting scarcity of dollars and need to ration foreign exchange for import and other payments transactions.

Parity Relationships and the Forward Market

In the previous section we considered the determination of the spot exchange rate under three types of exchange systems. Here we consider the interrelations between the spot rate and the forward rate and two other variables, namely, the interest rate and the inflation rate. We label these relationships "parity relationships."

Four types of parity relationships are described and analyzed in this section (Exhibit 4.20). Purchasing power parity (PPP) considers the relation between inflation and the spot rates of exchange. The International Fisher Effect considers the relationship between changes in the spot rate and interest rates. Interest rate parity considers the relation between the interest rate and forward rate premiums and discounts. Finally, the Fisher Effect considers the relation between inflation and interest rates.

These four parity relationships form the basis of a simple model of the international monetary environment. It is useful to understand these relationships, since they can play an important role in influencing asset prices and returns on assets.

Four variables interact according to these parity relationships. The spot exchange rate tells us the amount of foreign currency one unit of domestic currency can buy

---

EXHIBIT 4.20   Parity Relationships

Country and Currency	Nominal Interest Rate	Inflation Rate	Inflation Differential With United States	Current Spot Rate	Expected Spot Rate	Current Forward Rate	Real Return Required Investor
Germany Dmark	4.0%	1.0%	−5.0%	$0.60	$0.630	$0.630	3.0%
France Franc	7.0	4.0	−2.0	$0.20	$0.204	0.204	3.0
U.S. Dollar	9.0	6.0	0	1.0	1.0	1.0	3.0
Canada Cdn. Dollar	9.5	6.5	0.5	$0.80	$0.796	$0.796	3.0
U.K. Pound	11.0	8.0	2.0	$1.80	$1.764	$1.764	3.0

Fisher Effect

Purchasing Power Parity

Interest Rate Parity

International Fisher Effect

NOTES:

1. All foreign exchange rates are U.S. dollars per currency unit.

2. Expected spot rate is calculated according to International Fisher Effect. This reflects differences in nominal interest rate with the United States.

3. Real return is calculated by substracting inflation rate from nominal interest rate.

EXHIBIT 4.21	**Possible Effect of Differential Inflation on Spot Exchange Rates**					
	PRICE INDEX		**OLD RATE**		**NEW RATE**	
	France	Germany	FF/DM	DM/FF	FF/DM	DM/FF
Before Inflation	100	100	5.000	0.200		
After Inflation	135	110			6.136	0.163

for immediate delivery. The spot rate of exchange for the deutsche mark might be $0.60, indicating that one deutsche mark is worth $0.60 in U.S. currency. The forward exchange rate tells us the amount of foreign currency one unit of domestic currency can buy for delivery at a future date. The forward rate for the deutsche mark for delivery in one year might be $0.63 in U.S. currency. The differential between the spot and forward rates of exchange can be explained according to parity conditions. The interest rate is usually quoted as an annualized rate. The one-year rate on German money market paper may be 4.0%, whereas the one-year rate on U.S. money market paper may be 9.0%. In this case the interest differential is 5.0%. The inflation rate may be expressed as the rate of increase in consumer prices over a defined period (let us say one year). The inflation differential is equal to the difference in inflation rates between two countries. For example, the inflation rate might be 6.0% in the United States, and 1.0% in Germany, yielding a differential of 5.0%.

PURCHASING POWER PARITY

Purchasing power parity

Model that explains how exchange rate adjusts to differences in inflation, keeping prices of traded goods equal in all countries.

Purchasing power parity is a model that explains how spot exchange rates adjust to differences in inflation, keeping the prices of internationally traded goods equal in all countries. The PPP model explains how in the case of two countries their respective currencies will display exchange rate relationships that in the long run equalize the purchasing power of their respective currencies. The following formula represents the PPP relationship:

$$S = S_{t-1} \times \frac{P_d}{P_j}$$

where S is the new or current exchange rate, S_{t-1} is the old exchange rate, P_d is the price index at home, and P_j is the price index in the second country.

An example can illustrate how purchasing power parity works. Suppose the price of a basket of goods in France is 100 francs, and the price of a similar basket of goods in Germany is 20 deutsche marks. Further, the exchange rate is FF5.0/DM (Exhibit 4.21).

What might happen with differential inflation in the two countries? Suppose in Germany inflation is 10% and in France is 35%. The adjustment of exchange rates needed to restore purchasing power parity between the two currencies would be:

$$\frac{Price\ Index\ France}{Price\ Index\ Germany} \times Old\ Rate = New\ Rate$$

The deutsche mark appreciates against the franc by 22.7% (Exhibit 4.22).

The logic of PPP lies in the competitive effects differential inflation can have on trade flows and trade balances. While it can be difficult to find empirical tests that validate PPP, it is widely utilized as an indicator of future currency strength and weakness.

EXHIBIT 4.22   **Purchasing Power Parity after Inflation**

Before Inflation

Exchange rate: FF5.0/DM or Dm0.20/FF

Cost of French goods = FF100 (index value 100)
Cost of German goods = DM20 (index value 100)

Cost of French goods for Germans = FF100÷FF/DM (5.0) = DM20
Cost of German goods for French = DM20÷DM/FF (0.20) = FF100

PPP exists where DM20 and FF100 have equivalent purchasing.
power in both countries at prevailing exchange rates.

After Inflation

Exchange rate: FF6.136/DM or DM0.1629/FF

Cost of German goods = DM22 (index value 110)
Cost of French goods = FF135 (index value 135)

Cost of French goods for Germans = FF135÷FF/DM (6.136) = DM22
Cost of German goods for French = DM22÷DM/FF (0.1629) = FF135

PPP exists where DM22 and FF135 have equivalent purchasing
power in both countries at prevailing exchange rates:
$135/110 \times 5.0 = 6.136$

The rate FF/DM of 6.136 represents an appreciation of 22.7
Percent calculated as follows:
percent appreciation of Dmark = New rate/Old rate − 1
$= 6.136/5.0 - 1.0 = 1.227 - 1.0$
$= 22.7\%$

FISHER EFFECT

Fisher Effect

Nominal interest rate equals the investors required return plus the expected rate of inflation.

Named after economist Irving Fisher, the Fisher Effect holds that nominal interest rates (i) in a given country are equal to the investors required real rate of return (R) plus the expected rate of inflation (f).

$$i = R + f$$

Investors acquiring financial assets expect to be rewarded with a positive real return on their investment. Inflation often brings the real return on a financial asset (bond or bank deposit) below the nominal interest rate earned on that asset. Nominal interest rates are generally affected by inflation, rising above inflation to leave the investor with a positive real return. In countries with high inflation rates, investors respond quickly to changes in perceived inflation rates, bidding prices of financial assets to levels providing the necessary or desired real return.

If investors in the United States perceive a 5% inflation rate and desire at least a 4% real return, they will bid financial asset prices to a level where nominal interest rates approximate 9%. In Germany if investors perceive a 2% inflation rate and desire at least a 4% real return, they will bid financial asset prices to a level where nominal interest rates approximate 6%. Interest rate differences reflect inflation differentials. In each country nominal interest rates and inflation rates operate to provide some balance or equilibrium between countries. This balance can operate through the perceptions investors have regarding possible real versus nominal returns on financial assets denominated in different currencies. Differences in interest rate levels between countries indicate changes in inflation rate levels between the same countries.

INTERNATIONAL FISHER EFFECT

International Fisher Effect

Equilibrium between present and future spot exchange rates based on interest rate difference between two countries.

The *International Fisher Effect* defines an equilibrium between present and future spot rates and differences in interest rates in two countries. The exchange rate adjustment will be equal and opposite to the interest rate differential. Investors holding foreign securities must be rewarded with higher interest rates to be willing to hold financial assets denominated in currencies expected to depreciate against the investor's home currency. For example, if we expect the dollar to depreciate against the deutsche mark by 6% over the next year, we should expect that German investors will have to earn at least 6% higher interest rates on dollar denominated assets to be willing to hold these securities.

The parity relationship is based on investor needs and the competitive pricing of investment assets between countries. If, for example, the Swiss franc is expected to appreciate against the pound sterling by 5% over the next year, we can understand that international investors will price sterling financial assets to provide a nominal return 5% higher than Swiss franc financial assets.

INTEREST RATE PARITY

The *interest parity* condition holds that in free and competitive financial markets the interest rate differential will equal the forward exchange rate premium or discount. Interest rate differentials on different currency of denomination assets will bring about interest arbitrage flows of capital. As previously discussed, interest arbitrage is likely to be carried out on a covered (hedged) basis.

Covered interest arbitrage often results in premiums and discounts in the forward exchange market more or less equal to the interest differential. Interest rate parity relationships are closely related to the freedom of investors to make cross-border investments.

SYSTEM OF PARITY CONDITIONS

The system of parity conditions can be illustrated using the information provided on page 98 (Exhibit 4.20) concerning monetary conditions in Germany and the United States. These are the conditions in that illustration:

	Nominal Interest Rate	Inflation Rate	Inflation Differential	Current Spot Rate	Expected Spot Rate	Present Forward Rate	Real Return Required by Investor
Germany	4.0%	1.0%	5.0%	$0.60	$0.63	$0.63	3.0%
United States	9.0%	6.0%					3.0%

The Fisher Effect tells us that nominal interest rates equal the investor's required real return plus the expected rate of inflation. In Germany with nominal interest rates at 4.0% and the inflation rate at 1.0%, we can infer that investors require a real return of 3.0%. German investors can swap funds to the United States based on a higher nominal rate of interest. However, this swap will lead to a forward rate of $0.63 for one-year forward contracts. This interest parity condition applies equally to U.S. investors seeking to arbitrage money to Germany. The International Fisher condition states that the higher interest rate in the United States, as compared with Germany, represents expected depreciation of the spot dollar, in direct comparison with the deutsche mark. The expected future spot rate is $0.63. This rate coincides with the current forward rate. Finally, the purchasing power parity tells us that differential inflation between Germany and the United States should result in an appreciation of the deutsche mark. The appreciation should be equal to the inflation differential (5%).

Alternative Exchange Rate Forecasts

Forecasting the spot rate of exchange is a hazardous undertaking. Exchange rates are volatile, tend to overshoot projections, and are influenced by a mixture of fundamental, expectational, and technical factors. Many companies, banks, financial institutions, and economic research groups engage in currency forecasting.

BUSINESS FORECASTING APPROACHES

Currency forecasters employ several different approaches in developing exchange rate projections. We focus first on approaches based on balance of payments. This approach uses balance of payments statements of the sources and uses of foreign exchange reserves. Two techniques are commonly used. In the first, each of the components of the BOP is estimated, the total BOP is assembled, and a balance of payments "gap" is identified. The gap is the difference between forecasted receipts and payments. It indicates whether the currency in question is expected to appreciate or depreciate. A second balance of payments approach involves construction of a comprehensive econometric model. Numerous behavioral relationships are built into the equations of the model, including how trade flows respond to price and income changes. Simultaneous changes in transaction flows and an adjustment in the rate of exchange bring current and capital account components in the BOP into equilibrium.

Balance of payments forecasts have the advantage of providing a comprehensive approach. Unfortunately, they are very detailed and costly.

The forward rate approach uses actual market data without entering into complicated estimates. When using this approach a forecaster asks the question, "What exchange rate forecast is built into today's market quotation?"(assuming risk neutrality). The forward rate can be regarded as the expected value of the future spot rate. In the case of currencies with well-developed forward markets, we may utilize the given forward rate. With currencies lacking well-developed forward markets, we may use the interest parity calculation. For example, assuming the dollar and peso one-year interest rates are 8.0% and 14.0%, respectively, and the spot rate is peso 20/$, the implied market prediction for the peso/$ rate one year later is:

$$S_{t+1} = S_t \times \frac{1 + ip}{1 + i\$}$$

Inserting values into the equation we have:

$$20 \times \frac{1.14}{1.08} = 21.11$$

Studies have shown that forward exchange rates are poor indicators of future spot rates. This tendency may be due to the occurrence of unexpected news (central bank policy initiatives or slower economic growth) and its influence on spot rates.

Another approach can be based on several different parity models. One model—purchasing power parity (PPP)—is based on the relation between relative inflation in two countries and the associated change in spot rates of their currencies. Relative purchasing power parity can be expressed by:

$$\hat{S} = \hat{P}_\$ - \hat{P}_\text{p}$$

where $\hat{S}$ denotes percent change in dollar price of peso, $\hat{P}_\$$ denotes percent change in price level in the United States, and $\hat{P}_\text{p}$ denotes percent change in price level in Pesoland. Given an initial exchange rate of \$0.20/peso, and expected annual inflation rates in the U.S. of 7% and in Pesoland of 48%, the estimated one-year percent change in exchange rate is:

$$7\% - 48\% = -41\%$$

The exchange rate is expected to fall by 41%, from \$0.20 to (\$0.20-0.082), or \$0.118/peso. Economic research suggests that PPP works better for high inflation cases than for low inflation cases. That is, the estimated or forecasted exchange rate is closer to the actual rate. Also PPP seems to provide better, long-term estimates than short-term estimates. PPP has not been supported by empirical tests. One reason for this may be the presence of lags in the effects of prices on trade flows, and in turn on exchange rates.

A third approach—lead indicators—has its parallel in many other aspects of forecasting and shares similar advantages and disadvantages. Data is easy to collect but may not provide sufficient early warning. A final business forecasting approach—technical analysis—bases predictions on data found within the market that it is forecasting. Technical analysis has been widely applied in the stock market and in commodities forecasting. One technique used is plotting short-run and long-run moving averages. Crossovers of these moving averages are interpreted to indicate an approaching turning point in price. Technical analysis is widely used because of its simple approach.

ECONOMIC MODELS FOR FORECASTING

Economists have developed a number of theoretical models of exchange rate determination (Exhibit 4.23). These can be applied to forecast future spot rates. Previously we examined the PPP model and BOP model. The Mundell-Fleming model has gained wide acceptance because of its ability to incorporate the impact of monetary and fiscal policy and to allow for differences in degree of capital mobility. A depiction of how the exchange rate may be influenced by an expansionary fiscal policy is provided in Exhibit 4.24. The Mundell-Fleming model explains the breakdown in 1992–1993 of the European Exchange Rate Mechanism due to the inability of European monetary policies to continue to move accordingly with Germany's tight monetary policy. Following German unification, Bundesbank monetary policy progressively tightened to counter excess demand resulting from Germany's expansionary fiscal policy.

The monetary approach (Exhibit 4.23) gained a wide following from the 1960s onward. Unfortunately, this approach only offers a partial picture of exchange rate determination. In the flexible price monetary model, rising interest rate differentials cause a decline in the domestic currency value. This reflects differences in expected inflation rates, which in turn reflect differentials in expected future monetary growth rates. A rise in domestic inflation expectations will lead to a depreciation of

Mundell-Fleming Model

A model of exchange rate determination with floating rates and capital mobility.

Monetary approach

A model of exchange rate determination focusing on the impact of money creation and money demand.

EXHIBIT 4.23   Six Models of Spot Rate Determination

Model	Key Variables	Explanation	Problems and Shortcomings
I. Purchasing Power Parity	Price index in home country. Price index overseas.	Law of one price prevails in all countries. Exchange rate of home currency varies directly with the ratio of price level overseas relative to the price level at home.	1. Price indexes in countries have different compositon. 2. Nontradable goods. 3. Tends to ignore role of capital flows.
II. Balance of Payments Flow Model	Level—Aggregate demand and supply for home currency in forex markets. Volatility—The elasticity of demand and supply.	Trade and capital flows make up the demand and supply for a given currency.	1. Tends to ignore distinction between stocks and flows (of financial assets).
III. Mundell-Fleming Model	Monetary Policy-a. interest rate b. economic activity Fiscal Policy-a. output level b. interest rate. Impact of monetary and fiscal policy changes on exchange rates.	One of first models to give capital account a major role. Monetary expansion leads to a depreciation of the domestic currency, the magnitude of change dictated largely by degree of capital mobility. More mobile capital, the greater the exchange rate response. Exchange rate response to expansionary or contractionary fiscal policy is ambiguous. Fiscal stimulus will appreciate the domestic currency if capital mobility is high. Otherwise, currency will depreciate.	1. Comprehensiveness impairs use for forecasting purposes. 2. Limited capacity to explain role of changing risk premiums on exchange rate shifts.
IV. Monetary Approach	Money demand a function of income and interest rate.	Relative demand and supply for money in two countries determines exchange rate. Rise in domestic money supply leads to a depreciation of the exchange rate. Secondary effects on exchange rate work through liquidity and interest rate changes, and resulting capital flows. When these influences reinforce inflation, can lead to currency overshoot.	1. Offers partial view of what essentially must be a general equilibrium proceed. Supply and demand for goods and services are as important as supply and demand for money. 2. With floating, the monetary approach fails to provide an adequate explanation of exchange rate movements. 3. Monetary model omits number of key factors that are important to determination of exchange rates.
V. Currency Substitution	Demand for domestic and foreign money. Expected rate of change in relative currency values.	With an expected depreciation of the domestic currency, residents will switch from domestic to foreign currency balances as a hedge. Currency substitution can play a role in exchange rate determination in both developed and less developed countries.	1. Evidence supporting currency substitution in developed nations is not as clear cut as in less developed nations. For example, the elasticity of substitution between the U.S. dollar and Canadian dollar has not been found to be very high.
VI. Portfolio Balance Approach	Relative to supplies of financial assets denominated in domestic and foreign currencies.	The exchange rate is the relative price of bonds denominated in different currencies. Interaction of demand and supply of financial assets that are denominated in different currencies determines the exchange rate. Financial assets denominated in different currencies are imperfect substitutes. The relative risks and rewards are viewed differently from one currency group of bounds to another. Changes in wealth level bring shifts in relative asset demand.	Econometric tests of the Portfolio Balance model generally show poor results.

EXHIBIT 4.24 | Expansionary Fiscal Policy Impact on Exchange Rate According to the Mundell-Fleming Model

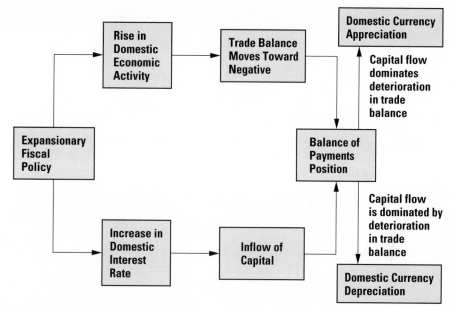

SOURCE: Adapted by authors from various sources.

the domestic currency. In the monetary model a relative rise in economic activity results in a rise in the domestic currency value, while a relative rise in domestic interest rates results in a depreciation of the domestic currency value. This contrasts directly with the BOP model, where a relative rise in domestic activity results in a depreciation of the domestic currency, and a relative rise in domestic interest rates results in an appreciation of the domestic currency.

Currency substitution

A model that deals with the substitutability of currencies on the demand side.

The currency substitution approach is partly an extension of the monetary model. Increasing inflation in developing countries and related *dollarization* of their economic systems has given this approach greater credibility. Unfortunately, this approach is more appropriate for explaining currency rate changes for developing countries than currencies of industrial nations.

According to some analysts, there are basically three view-points in explaining the determination of exchange rates. The first takes the exchange rate as the relative price of money (monetary approach). The second takes the exchange rate as the relative price of goods (PPP). The third takes the exchange rate as the relative price of

Portfolio balance model

A model of exchange rate determination that treats bonds denominated in different currencies as imperfect substitutes.

bonds (portfolio balance approach). The portfolio approach explains exchange rate determination by the interaction of the supply and demand for financial assets. It treats domestic and foreign currency bonds as imperfect substitutes. Investors view relative risks and rewards on domestic and foreign bonds differently. Risk averse investors will diversify bond portfolios and reweigh these portfolios as relative currency risks shift. Also, in the portfolio approach wealth can be shifted from country to country based on current account balance surpluses and deficits. Therefore the wealth transfer mechanism will play a part in exchange rate determination.

SUMMARY

The foreign exchange market operates on a global basis. Dealer banks link together foreign exchange market centers and financial markets. The market carries out several functions including transfer of purchasing power, hedging, clearing, and credit.

The law of one price prevails in the market. This law applies to arbitrage between exchange market centers and currency sectors. The many channels through which this arbitrage operates can be visualized by constructing a matrix of spot rates. Reciprocal and cross-rate relationships become evident within this matrix.

Foreign exchange transactions include outright spot, outright forward, and swaps. Transactions are undertaken in the market for many reasons including transfer of purchasing power, hedging, speculation, and interest arbitrage.

Interest arbitrage can yield a net advantage based upon the difference between two spreads, namely, the spread on interest rates between two currency centers and the spread between spot and forward rates of exchange.

It is possible to use the foreign exchange market to speculate on interest rate changes. This instrument requires that the speculator position himself initially in a foreign exchange swap based upon opportunities that can be visualized on a series of forward trading curves.

The spot rate of exchange is determined under three different systems—floating, fixed, and controlled rate systems. Demand and supply ultimately shape possible exchange rates and are more or less free to operate under these alternate systems. Demand and supply have the greatest possibility of determining rates under the floating rate system. Under a fixed exchange rate system countries must carefully follow financial policies to facilitate stable exchange rates.

Analysis of parity conditions provides a systematic model of international monetary relations. In this model four key variables interact—spot rate, forward rate, interest rates, and inflation rates.

Exchange rate forecasting utilizes simple as well as complex approaches. One of the simplest is to employ the forward rate as the expected value of the future spot rate. Six economic models provide a wide range of approaches to understanding how exchange rates are determined. These include the purchasing power parity model, balance of payments model, the Mundell-Fleming model, monetary approach, currency substitution, and portfolio balance approach.

APPENDIX

FORWARD RATE AS AN UNBIASED PREDICTOR OF FUTURE SPOT RATES

Close examination of interest rate parity and the International Fisher Effect conditions suggest a close relationship between interest rate differentials and exchange rates. Equation 1 states the interest rate parity condition. Interest rate parity tells us there should be an equilibrium where the difference between dollar and sterling interest rates is equivalent to the spread between the forward and spot exchange rate (dollars per pound). Therefore with dollar and sterling interest rates at 6% and 10% and the spot pound at $1.800, the equilibrium forward rate would be $1.728.

$$i_\$ - i_f = \frac{F - S_o}{S_o} \qquad (1)$$

The International Fisher Effect describes an equilibrium between national interest rate differentials and the spread between present and future spot rates. Equation 2 illustrates the International Fisher Effect. Using the previous example, with dollar and sterling interest rates at 6% and 10%, and with the spot pound at $1.800, the expected future spot rate would be $1.728.

$$i_\$ - i_f = \frac{S_1 - S_o}{S_o} \tag{2}$$

If we compare Equations 1 and 2, we note that only one term is different in the equations. Equation 1 uses the forward rate (F), whereas Equation 2 uses the expected future spot rate (S_1). In effect, we can set the right side of Equation 1 equal to the right side of Equation 2. This analysis indicates that the forward rate may serve usefully as a predictor of the future spot rate.

REVIEW QUESTIONS

1. Why is the foreign exchange market the largest financial market in the world?

2. What are the most important functions of the foreign exchange market?

3. Why is the foreign exchange market referred to as an interbank market? Why are correspondent bank relationships important in this market?

4. If the U.S. dollar price of the deutsche mark is $0.5892, what is the deutsche mark price of the U.S. dollar?

5. If the deutsche mark price of pound sterling is DM3.240, what is the sterling price of the deutsche mark?

6. If the U.S. dollar price of pound sterling is $1.8500 and the U.S. dollar price of the French franc is $0.111624, what is the French franc price of sterling?

7. In the preceding question assume that the Paris market quotes sterling at 11.3800. Explain what arbitrage opportunity exists, and the profit from taking $10 million and trading through the markets.

8. A company must pay 30 million German marks to a supplier in 90 days. The company wishes to lock in the dollar price of this payment using existing exchange rates. The spot rate is $0.6140, the forward rate of 90 days maturity is $0.6210, and interest rate in New York and Frankfurt is 10.0% and 7.0%, respectively. What is the lowest dollar cost of covering the payment in 90 days? What steps will the company take to lock in this cost?

9. You can borrow/invest in New York at 7% and in Paris at 13%. The spot French franc is valued at $0.1600 and the three-month franc at $0.1570. Will interest arbitrage flows take place? In which direction?

10. The $/f rate is $0.1680 the FF/f rate is FF 9.250, and $/f rate is $1.5240. Is profitable arbirtage possible? Starting with $1 million, calculate the profit from a round of three-corner arbitrage.

11. Interest rates are 13.8% in London and 7.5% in New York. The spot pound is $1.9540 and the six-month forward pound is $1.9268. Mr. Jones has $5 million, and can invest in New York or swap funds for investment in London. What is the gain from investment in New York? What is the gain from investment in London?

12. What are the reasons for differences between spot and forward rates of exchange? Explain.

13. A U.S. bank expects the interest rate in London to decline from 14% to 12%. The interest rate in New York is 10.0% and not expected to change. The spot pound is $2.00 and interest rate parity operates perfectly. Explain how the bank would position itself to take advantage of the expected change in interest rates.

14. The spot rate of the French franc is $0.1598. This equilibrium rate of exchange is the result of demand and supply interacting under a freely floating rate system. How might each of the following affect the demand for French francs, the supply of French francs, and the rate of exchange?
    a. a decline in interest rates in France
    b. an increase in consumer spending in the United States
    c. a sudden upward spurt in inflation in the United States
    d. an income tax reduction in France
    e. an increase in the French GNP real growth rate
    f. a shift in consumer tastes away from French wine and toward California wine

15. The expected annual inflation rate is 5% in the U.S. and 2% in Germany. The current exchange rate is DM1.65/$. Assume that purchasing power parity is applicable. What is the expected exchange rate in one year?

16. The spot rate is $0.6500/DM. Interest rates in New York are 9.0% and are 6.5% in Frankfurt. Assume that the International Fisher Effect is operative. What might we expect the DM rate of exchange to be in one year? Does International Fisher indicate that investor behavior is rational? Explain.

17. Distinguish between forward exchange, currency futures, and currency options.

CASE 1

Countryside Foreign Exchange Advisory Service

Michael Pearce, a lifelong money broker, has achieved the dream of many London professionals. Instead of enduring the discomfort of central London congestion, he is now able to work in his comfortable farmhouse in the delightful village of Aldbury, Hertfordshire. At his elbow are the tools of his trade—a telephone, a fax machine, a desktop computer, and a Reuters financial information screen.

From Aldbury, Pearce has been using his modern communications tools to keep a watchful eye on foreign exchange and interest rate movements. He advises his growing list of industrial and commercial clients who find themselves exposed to the williwaws that blow through foreign currency markets. One is a cheesemaker who exports one-third of his production primarily to Europe. After setting his price list twice a year he is now following Pearce's advice and trading in the European Currency Unit (ECU).

The cheesemaker borrows ECUs against anticipated income in European currency over the coming half-year. The incoming currencies are sold spot and the proceeds are used to repay the ECU loan.

The main point according to Pearce is that this approach allows the cheesemaker continue with making and selling cheese rather than spending time and energy worrying about foreign exchange problems.

Pearce's ideas for running an independent foreign exchange and interest rate advisory service from a location removed from the hurly-burly of central London were crystallized during a one-year Master of Business Administration course at Cranfield School of Management in 1987–1988. When he started his new advisory service he had no idea that it would catch on as well as it has. At Cranfield, Pearce concluded there were many companies too small to employ corporate treasurers or financial officers with expertise in the

(Continued)

CASE 1 (Continued)

money markets but that could benefit from regular consulting and advice. He targeted companies with sales turnover of less than £25 million a year, and wrote to more than 40 of these, offering his professional services. Seven companies took up his services in the beginning. Since then he has added many new clients.

Pearce emphasizes that he is neither a soothsayer nor an economist. What he offers is his extensive knowledge of currency instruments, close day-to-day monitoring of trends, and an understanding of how to minimize risks. Pearce's foreign exchange and currency advice is not expensive compared with many professional fee scales. He charges companies £1,000 initially to make a study of their business. He then takes a retainer of £550 a month for a trial period of six months. He expects his fee income to rise to £100,000 in the third year.

SOURCE: Adapted from *Financial Times,* 25, March 1989.

CASE 2

Escargot Finance Menu

Caspar Truffault was running out of time. Tomorrow morning he would have to make recommendations concerning the financing of Escargot, a French publishing subsidiary of Snail Communications, a U.K. publishing/media corporation. Escargot sold books principally to consumers through retail distributors.

Truffault was administrative assistant to the treasurer of Escargot. The treasurer indicated that the firm required FF 10 million to bridge working capital requirements over the next six months. Truffault was leaning toward recommending a FF 10 million six-month loan from Credit Commercial in Paris, the key banking contact of the company. This loan would cost 9.75%. Since tomorrow's meeting would be attended by financial officers from the London headquarters of Snail Communications, Truffault was concerned about questions concerning alternative financing possibilities. First, should Escargot borrow in France in local currency? Should it borrow in the Euromarket, and what risks could be incurred from a Euromarket borrowing?

Caspar Truffault had obtained the following data on six-month interest rates:

Bank Deposit Rates:	(Annual Rate)
Domestic franc deposits	8.23
EuroFrench franc deposits	8.50
Bank Loan Rates:	
Domestic franc loan	9.75
EuroFrench franc loan	8.88

The key question was, which currency should Escargot borrow? Truffault understood that the Eurosterling market might be an alternative. However, he remembered learning in a finance course at the university that the existence of efficient markets should preclude the possibility of borrowing in alternative currency sectors on a covered basis at different cost levels. Borrowing on an uncovered basis presented an exchange risk, which might be challenged by the parent company finance section. Truffault was worried about the exchange risk associated with borrowing sterling on an uncovered basis.

According to the forecasts, the pound was expected to fall against the French franc. One possibility to consider would be to borrow Eurosterling on a covered basis. An alternative would be to borrow Eurosterling uncovered on the expectation that the forecasted decline in sterling would prove correct.

How can we help Caspar Truffault formulate recommendations for the meeting tomorrow?

Euromarket Rates (six-month maturity, annual rate):	
Eurosterling loan rate	10.25
EuroFrench franc loan rate	8.88
Cost of forward cover	2.00
(Premium on forward French franc)	

Foreign Exchange Rates:	Sterling per FF	FF per Pound Sterling
Spot rate	.833	12.00
Six-month forward rate	.840	11.88
Forecast of spot rate in six months	.859	11.64

(The exchange rates shown are reciprocal rates).

18. Compare and contrast the monetary and portfolio balance approaches to determination of the spot rate. What happens to the dollar/sterling exchange rate under the following changed conditions according to each approach.
    a. the Fed engages in an open market purchase
    b. the British government expands rate of spending
    c. interest rates on U.K. bonds shift up

19. Compare and contrast the Mundell-Fleming and monetary approaches to determination of the spot rate. If the British government expands expenditures, trace the impact on exchange rates according to each of these approaches.

SELECTED BIBLIOGRAPHY

Bank for International Settlements. *Annual Reports,* various issues.

Broaddus, J. Alfred, and M. Goodfriend. "Foreign Exchange Operations and the Federal Reserve." *Federal Reserve Bank of Richmond Economic Quarterly,* Winter 1996.

Crystal, K.A. "A Guide to Foreign Exchange Markets." *Federal Reserve Bank of St. Louis Review,* March 1986.

Coninx, R. *Foreign Exchange Dealer's Handbook.* Homewood, ILL: Dow-Jones-Irwin, 1986.

Coughlin, C.C., and K. Koidyk. "What Do We Know About the Long Run Real Exchange Rate?" *Federal Reserve Bank of St. Louis Review,* January-February 1990.

Dooley, M. P., and P. Isard. "Capital Controls, Political Risk, and Deviations from Interest Rate Parity." *Journal of Political Economy,* April 1980.

Edwards, Sebastian. *Exchange Rate Misalignment in Developing Countries.* World Bank Paper No. 2. Baltimore, Johns Hopkins, 1988.

Froot, Kenneth, and Kenneth Rogoff. "Perspectives on PPP and Long Run Real Exchange Rates." NBER Working Paper 4592, 1994.

Gawith, Philip. "Exotic but Not for Faint Hearts." *Financial Times,* London, May 15, 1996.

Glassman, Debra. "Exchange Rate Risk and Transactions Costs: Evidence from Bid-Ask Spreads." *Journal of International Money and Finance,* December 1977.

Humpage, Owen F. "Exchange Market Intervention: The Channels of Influence." *Federal Reserve Bank of Cleveland Economic Review,* 1986.

Humpage, Owen F. "Intervention and the Dollar." In R. Kolb, *The International Finance Reader.* Atlanta: Kolb Publishing, 1991.

Krugman, Paul. *Exchange Rate Instability.* Cambridge: MIT Press, 1989.

Kubarych, Roger M. *Foreign Exchange Markets in the United States.* Revised edition, Federal Reserve Bank of New York, 1983.

Lapper, Richard, and Philip Gawith. "Forex Market Growth Slowing, Says BIS." *Financial Times,* London, May 31, 1996, p. 4.

MacDonald, Ronald, and Mark Taylor. "The Monetary Approach to the Exchange Rate: Rational Expectations, Long Run Equilibrium, and Forecasting." IMF *Staff Papers,* March 1993.

Rogalski, R. J., and J. D. Vinso. "Price Level Variations as Predictors of Flexible Exchange Rates." *Journal of International Business Studies,* Summer 1977.

Rosenberg, Michael R. *Currency Forecasting.* Chicago: Irwin Professional Publishing, 1996.

Shapiro, Alan C. "What Does Purchasing Power Parity Mean?" *Journal of International Money and Finance,* December 1983.

Sweeney, Richard J. "Reading the Foreign Exchange Market." *Journal of Finance,* March 1986.

Walmsley, Julian. *The Foreign Exchange and Money Market Guide.* New York: Wiley, 1992.

CHAPTER 5

Currency Futures, Options, and Swaps

INTRODUCTION

Derivatives markets have grown rapidly, providing greater flexibility for those seeking to hedge risk or take speculative positions for gain. This growth has been impressive both for exchange traded and over-the-counter traded instruments. We begin this chapter with an overview of derivatives markets and a discussion of market structure. We also consider regulatory issues. Derivative instruments are available to hedge interest rate, currency, and stock market positions. In this chapter we focus on currency-related derivatives and we will discuss other types of derivatives in later chapters.

With the advent of floating currency relationships in the 1970s, increased attention has been given to finding methods to hedge foreign currency risk. In addition, internationally-oriented risk takers have taken positions in foreign currencies for speculative gain. Two general approaches have been used. The first involves customized deals either through forward exchange contracts negotiated with large foreign exchange banks in the interbank market, or through currency swaps arranged between two counterparties willing to exchange debt service obligations in two different currencies. These methods are outlined in Exhibit 5.1.

A second approach involves trading standardized currency contracts on markets organized for that purpose. Here competitive markets exist for currency futures contracts, options, and options on futures. The various contracts are standardized in this second approach so that a high degree of liquidity and market efficiency exists.

In Exhibit 5.1 we describe five alternative methods to hedge foreign currency risk. Forward contracts and currency swaps are customized deals arranged with bank intermediaries. Forward contracts are described in the previous chapter. They are created in the interbank foreign exchange market with amounts and maturity dates established according to the needs of the market participant. Currency swaps are also customized to the needs of the counterparty. We discuss currency swaps in detail later in this chapter. Futures contracts, option contracts, and options on futures are described in the following sections of this chapter.

EXHIBIT 5.1	Methods Available to Hedge Foreign Currency Risk

Method	Description
1. Forward contract	Customized contract that facilitates buying or selling foreign currency delivery set on given forward date.
2. Futures Contract	Standardized contract for foreign currency futures that can be purchased or sold. Purchase of futures contract gives buyer a long position in that currency; sale gives seller a short position.
3. Option Contract	Standardized contract that gives holder right to buy (call option) or sell (put option) foreign currency at fixed price.
4. Option on Futures	Standardized contract that gives holder right to buy or sell futures contract on foreign currency.
5. Currency Swap	Customized contract to exchange debt service payments on specific debt, where debt of each party is denominated in different currency.

LEARNING OBJECTIVES IN THIS CHAPTER

1. To consider the growing role of derivative instruments.
2. To understand the various methods available to hedge foreign currency risk.
3. To appreciate the mechanics of using exchange-traded, foreign currency futures, the various protections afforded participants in this market, and the importance of contract specifications in trading standardized hedging instruments.
4. To detect the important elements in the purchase of an option contract and the factors that influence the pricing of an option.
5. To comprehend the similarities and differences in using futures and options as hedging or speculative instruments.
6. To realize the special role of currency futures as a means of modifying currency exposure.

KEY TERMS AND CONCEPTS

- at the money
- Black-Scholes
- call
- Commodity Exchange Act
- currency swap
- derivative instrument
- exercise
- forward
- future
- in the money
- initial margin
- intrinsic value
- maintenance margin
- option

- option on future
- out of the money
- premium
- put
- speculator

- strike price
- time value
- volatility
- writer

ACRONYMS

IMM   International Monetary Market

CME   Chicago Mercantile Exchange

LIFFE   London International Financial Futures and Options Exchange

Derivatives Markets

OVERVIEW

Derivative instrument

Financial claims with value based on that of the underlying securities.

The decades of the 1980s and 1990s have witnessed rapid growth in the volume and variety of use of derivative instruments. This is related to the increased importance of financial markets around the world, securitization of previously nontradable financial instruments and obligations, and the need for borrowers and investors to hedge against volatility in the securities markets.

Derivative instruments are financial claims with value based on that of the underlying securities. Therefore a change in the value of an underlying security (T-Bond) is expected to be accompanied by a similar change in the value of the related derivative instrument (T-Bond future). Derivatives are originated and traded both on organized exchanges and over the-counter. Exchange traded instruments have an aggregate value that is somewhat less than over-the-counter traded instruments (Exhibit 5.2).

Interest rate futures account for more than 65% of the value of exchange traded derivatives. These include short-term interest rate instruments and longterm (bond futures). Short-term instruments account for 94% of all interest rate futures, and Eurodollar futures represent nearly half of short-term futures. Euroyen futures are half as large as Eurodollar futures, and Euro DM futures are approximately one-third as large as Euroyen futures.

"It is certainly true that real exchange rates have been more volatile under floating rates than they were in the Bretton Woods period." Andrew Crickett, Executive Director, Bank of England.

In addition to these two interest rate futures, two other financial futures occupy this field. These include currency futures and stock market index futures (Exhibit 5.2). We discuss these in subsequent chapters.

Exchange-traded instruments also include interest rate options, currency options, and stock market index options. The largest of these in value are the interest rate options.

Over-the-counter instruments include interest rate swaps, currency swaps, and other swap-related derivatives (caps, collars, floors, and swaptions).

As shown in the exhibit, the value of exchange-traded instruments has been growing explosively, almost doubling every two years. Similarly, over-the-counter traded instruments have been growing rapidly, but at a lesser rate than instruments traded on organized exchanges.

EXHIBIT 5.2	**Markets for Selected Financial Derivative Instruments**

	NOTIONAL PRINCIPAL OUTSTANDING IN BILLIONS OF US DOLLARS					
Instruments	**1989**	**1990**	**1991**	**1992**	**1993**	**1994**
Exchange-traded instruments	1,766.6	2,290.2	3,518.8	4,632.5	7,760.8	8,837.8
Interest rate futures	1,200.8	1,454.5	2,156.7	2,913.0	4,942.6	5,757.4
Interest rate options[1]	387.9	599.5	1,072.6	1,385.4	2,362.4	2,622.8
Currency futures	15.9	16.9	17.9	24.9	32.2	33.0
Currency options[1]	50.2	56.5	62.8	70.9	75.4	54.5
Stock market index futures	41.3	69.1	76.0	79.7	109.9	127.7
Stock market index options[1]	70.6	93.7	132.8	158.6	238.3	242.4
Over-the-counter instruments[2]	—	3,450.3	4,449.4	5,345.7	8,474.6	—
Interest rate swaps	1,502.6	2,311.5	3,065.1	3,850.8	6,177.3	—
Currency swaps[3]	449.1	577.5	807.2	860.4	899.6	—
Other swap-related derivatives[4]	—	561.3	577.2	634.5	1,397.6	—

[1] Calls and puts.

[2] Data collected by the International Swaps and Derivatives Association (ISDA) only; the two sides of contracts between ISDA members are reported once only.

[3] Adjusted for reporting of both currencies; including cross-currency interest rate swaps.

[4] Caps, collars, floors and swaptions.

SOURCE: Futures Industry Association, various futures and options exchanges, ISDA and BIS calculations. BIS, *annual Report 1995*: 184.

MARKET STRUCTURE

A basic function of exchange-traded derivatives markets is to provide liquidity through large volume, standardized contracts, price transparency, and the interposition of the clearing house as a central counterparty. By contrast, over-the-counter markets provide users with contracts that can be tailored to individual requirements. These services tend to be complementary, so that growth on one side of the market usually supports expansion in other sectors.

In exchange traded markets the exchanges have formed trading alliances and links that facilitate 24-hour trading. Agreements between European and Asian exchanges capitalize on the growth of cash and forward European currency trading in Asia, and on the development of markets in yen products in Europe. Bilateral trading links have become a widespread means of facilitating round-the-clock trading and wider access. Leading exchanges include the Chicago Mercantile Exchange (CME), Chicago Board of Trade (CBOT), and the London International Financial Futures and Option Exchange (LIFFE).

REGULATORY DEBATE

Events in 1994–1995 constitute a watershed for the derivatives markets. The 1994 reversal in interest rates caught many market participants by surprise, resulting in sizeable losses among end-users and market intermediaries. Adverse publicity and earnings volatility caused several major intermediaries to reduce the resources committed to derivatives-related activities. Losses on derivatives were attributed to inadequate internal controls, inappropriate use, and excessive risk positioning. This gave emphasis to central bank and regulatory criticism of risk exposure. Despite the several incidents where large losses took place, the financial markets worked through these events quite well.

"Long before 2020, credit risks will be disaggregated into discrete attributes that will be readily traded, unbundled, and rebundled." Charles S. Sanford, Jr., Chairman, Bankers Trust, New York.

Surveys of risk management practices were undertaken. The 1993 Group of Thirty report on derivatives focused on practical problems faced by users and market participants. The report recommended that dealers and market participants formulate policy on derivatives trading and risk-taking at the highest corporate level of responsibility, that companies implement quantitative measures of risk, estimate potential losses using mark-to-market accounting, and that specific counterparty risks should be evaluated. The report further suggested that regulators permit netting arrangements, remove legal uncertainties in use of derivatives, and avoid tax regulation that would increase the cost of using derivatives.

Banks and market participants can more easily ride through turbulent episodes in these markets if they have sufficient capital to absorb losses. Since 1988 banks have been subject to capital requirements under the Basle Capital Accord relative to exposures on derivatives (Chapter 9). In 1994 the Basle Committee on Banking Supervision recognized bilateral netting of credit exposures for capital adequacy purposes. In 1995 the same committee refined its methodology for assessing potential credit exposures in derivatives. The Basle Committee has been working to extend the Capital Accord to market risks (this is also discussed in Chapter 9). In this case banks will be able to use internal risk management systems as a basis for calculating market risk capital charges.

Capital Accord

International agreement that introduced minimum capital for banks relative to the riskiness of their assets.

International securities regulators also have been working to develop and refine capital adequacy criteria for derivatives and other trading activities. Also, official policy has been leaning toward imposing market discipline through improved transparency. This is based on the view that markets function best when participants are able to make well-informed investment and trading decisions.

FURTHER DISCUSSION

Further consideration of derivatives is organized as follows. The remainder of this chapter focuses on currency-related derivatives. In Chapter 7 we consider use of bond futures and swaps. In Chapter 9 we take up the matter of derivatives risk as it relates to international bank supervision and capital adequacy. In Chapter 11 we examine short term interest rate futures. In Chapter 20 we consider stock index futures and options to achieve portfolio insurance.

Currency Futures

FUTURES MARKETS—ROLE OF THE EXCHANGE

In the United States currency futures contracts are traded on the International Monetary Market (IMM), a division of the Chicago Mercantile Exchange (CME). Eight foreign currency futures contracts are traded including the Australian dollar, British pound, Canadian dollar, Deutsche mark, French franc, Japanese yen, Swiss franc, and European Currency Unit (ECU). Currency futures are similar to *forward contracts*. They make it possible to lock in the price of a given currency where delivery takes place at a future point in time. Unlike a forward, *futures contracts* are standardized and are traded on an organized exchange. The ability to buy and sell futures contracts in an exchange market gives futures an advantage over forward contracts, namely, market liquidity. The holder of a futures contract can sell the contract in a liquid market, providing an additional advantage in the form of flexibility to alter the hedging or speculative position as conditions or needs change.

Corporate or institutional investor participants can benefit significantly by hedging in financial futures. Trading currency futures can help a multinational company offset exchange risk related to an investment position. Portfolio managers can offset currency exposure positions or take on currency investment positions by buying and selling currency futures.

Futures contracts provide important services to those who make use of the exchange market. These include: 1) price discovery, that is, hedgers and speculators come together to discover the future price of a currency; 2) liquidity, the ability of market participants to buy and sell at any time when the market is open for trading; and 3) customer protection. Customer protection is provided by the enforcement of exchange rules. The CME makes use of the following to assure a high level of customer protection:

1. Margin requirements
2. Protection against insolvency
3. Protection against default
4. Clearing system

Initial margin

Cash payment required when futures position is taken, imposed by exchange on which such contracts are traded.

Maintenance margin

Cash payment required when price of futures contract moves up or down. Needed to maintain "equity" position of trader.

Commodity Exchange Act

U.S. federal law that regulates commodities trading.

Margin Requirements   The first level of protection in trading currency futures is the initial margin. The exchange enforces margin requirements relative to each clearing member firm. In turn that member firm enforces margin requirements on the customer (buyer or seller of the futures contract). These requirements minimize potential injury to customers in the event of any member firm's financial reversal or insolvency. In addition to initial margin, there are maintenance margin requirements. These are based on day-to-day gains or losses in value of the futures contract. The exchange imposes these requirements on member firms, and the member firms enforce maintenance of margin requirements on customers by means of a daily settlement.

Protection Against Insolvency   The Commodity Exchange Act is the federal law that regulates commodities trading. This law requires that member firms of futures exchanges maintain capital at prescribed levels, and that customers' funds be segregated from a member firm's funds. This measure is intended to ensure that customers will not be adversely affected in the event of insolvency of an individual clearing member firm.

Protection Against Default   The CME Clearing House deals directly with its own member firms and not individual market participants. The exchange secures payment directly from clearing members (Exhibit 5.3). In this way the exchange does not rely on the trading public to make good on funds due to its member firms. This "independence" permits the CME to substitute itself in every transaction and make good payment to the member firm, regardless of any possible default by the party with the opposite position.

Clearing System   The clearing house functions as guarantor of performance for each futures and options contract. As delivery agent for contracts that entail physical delivery, the clearing house ensures timely delivery by the seller and full and timely payment by the buyer. Most futures contracts are liquidated before expiration.

EXHIBIT 5.3	**The Order Process in Trading Foreign Currency Futures**

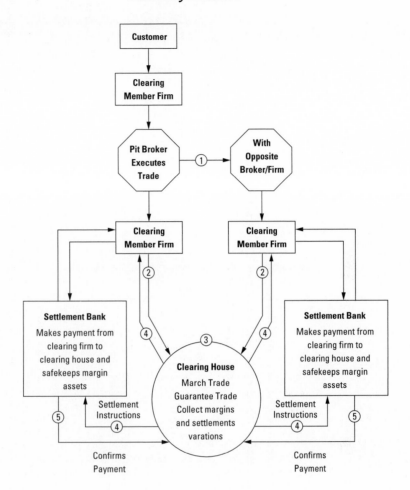

CONTRACT SPECIFICATIONS

Standardized futures contracts contain numerous features that are defined by the exchange. The standardized features of foreign currency futures cover 1) trading unit or size of contract, 2) method of price quotation, 3) minimum price change, 4) price limits, 5) maturities, 6) specified final trading date, 7) settlement date, and 8) collateral or margin requirements. Treatment of the preceding items on the CME is summarized in Exhibit 5.4.

The following summary defines several aspects of futures contract specifications on the CME.

Trading Unit On the IMM, Swiss franc and German mark contracts are for 125,000 units. French franc contracts are larger (250,000 units), while British pound contracts are smaller (62,500 units).

Method of Quotation All currency contracts traded on the IMM are quoted in U.S. dollars.

EXHIBIT 5.4 Foreign Currency Futures—Contract Specifications

Chicago Mercantile Exchange Currency Futures and Options Contract Highlights

CME CURRENCY FUTURES

	Ausralian Dollar (AD)	British Pound (BP)	Canadian Dollar (CD)	Deutsche Mark (DM)	French Franc (FF)	Japanese Yen (JY)	Swiss Franc (SF)	DM/JY (DJ)
Trading Unit	AD 100,000	BP 62,500	CD 100,000	DM 125,000	FF 500,000	JY 12,500,000	SF 125,000	DJ 125,000
Quotations	US$ per AD	US$ per BP	US$ per CD	US$ per DM	US$ per FF	US$ per JY	US$ per SF	US$ per DM
Minimum Price Change	.0001=$10.00	.0002=$12.50	.0001=$10.00	.0001=$12.50	.00002=$10.00	.000001=$12.50	.0001=$12.50	.01=JY1.250
Months Traded				March, June, September, December[1]				
Trading Hours[3] (Chicago Time)	7:20am-2:00pm[3]	7:20am-2:00pm[3]	7:20am-2:00pm[3]	7:20am-2:00pm[3]	7:20am-2:00pm	7:20am-2:00pm[3]	7:20am-2:00pm[3]	7:20am-2:00pm[3]
Last Day of Trading				The second business day immediately preceding the third Wednesday of the contract month[4]				

[1] Additional valid contract months (not actively traded): Jan, Apr, Jul, Oct and Spot Month.

[2] Trading will end at 12:00 noon on the business day before a CME holiday and on any U.S. bank holiday that the CME is open.

[3] This contract also is traded on the GLOBEX[7] system. Contact your broker or the CME for specific GLOBEX trading hours.

Canadian dollars *only*—Futures trading shall terminate on the business day preceding the third Wednesday of the contract month for contracts expiring in or after December '94.

This information has been compiled by the Chicago Mercantile Exchange for general information purposes only. Although every attempt has been made to ensure the accuracy of the information, the CME assumes no responsibility for any errors or omissions. All matters pertaining to rules and specifications herein are made subject to and are superceded by official CME rules. Current CME rules should be consulted in all cases concerning contract specifications (12/93).

Source: Chicago Mercantile Exchange

Maturities IMM contracts have a standard maturity date. Currency futures contracts mature on the third Wednesday of the month in which the contract expires.

Specified Final Trading Date IMM contracts may be traded until two business days before the Wednesday on which they mature. Generally these contracts trade until the Monday preceding the Wednesday maturity date.

Settlement Date This date is the third Wednesday of the delivery month. We emphasize that only a small proportion of futures contracts are settled by physical delivery of currency between buyer and seller. Most often buyers and sellers offset their original position prior to the delivery date by taking an opposite position.

UNDERSTANDING MARKET QUOTATIONS

Market quotations for currency contracts traded on the IMM are published in the financial section of daily newspapers. In Exhibit 5.5 we have IMM currency futures prices as of 15 November 1990 for the deutsche mark.

As we note in Exhibit 5.5 deutsche marks are traded in contracts of DM 125,000. The dollar prices are also indicated in Exhibit 5.6. Information refers to contracts expiring in December, March, and June. December 1990 contracts opened

EXHIBIT 5.5	IMM Currency Futures Prices—15 November 1990 Deutsche Mark (DM 125,000), Price in $ per Mark

| | | | | | | LIFETIME | | OPEN |
	Open	High	Low	Settle	Change	High	Low	Interest
Dec 1990	.6769	.6799	.6769	.6795	+.0036	.6799	.5764	78,170
Mar 1991	.6750	.6799	.6750	.6774	+.0034	.6779	.5820	2,884
June 1991	.6738	.6756	.6738	.6750	+.0032	.6756	.6163	139

Estimate Volume 28,030; Volume Tues 27,025; Open interest 81,203 + 4,218.

SOURCE: *Wall Street Journal*

EXHIBIT 5.6	Premiums on Deutsche Mark Currency Options, 15 November 1990 U.S. Cents per Unit

| | | CALLS | | | PUTS | | |
Underlying Price	Strike Price	Nov	Dec	March	Nov	Dec	March
67.96	66	2.01	2.12	2.71	r	0.26	1.82
67.96	66.5	1.52	1.81	s	0.04	0.40	s
67.96	67	0.96	1.44	r	0.07	0.54	r
67.96	67.5	0.50	0.96	s	0.11	0.73	s
67.96	68	0.24	0.81	1.70	0.33	0.92	2.00
67.96	68.5	0.07	0.54	s	r	r	s
67.96	69	r	0.46	1.26	r	r	r

r = not traded.
s = no option offered.

SOURCE: *Wall Street Journal.*

trading at $0.6769/DM. The highest trading price during the day was $0.6799/DM, and the lowest trading price was $0.6769/DM. Settle refers to the settlement price or daily closing price used by the clearing house. This price is used for determining margin calls and invoice prices for deliveries. The trading price used for December contracts at the conclusion of trading was $0.6795/DM. The change is the difference between the previous day and current day settle.

Lifetime high and low refers to the highest and lowest prices at which a contract traded since it was introduced. The December contract has traded as high as $0.6799 and as low as $0.5764. Open interest refers to the sum of long (buying futures) and short (selling futures) contracts outstanding. The last line reports trading volume for the day to which the table refers and for the preceding date.

Buying, Selling, and Closing Out a Futures Position

Investors, companies with overseas operations, exporters and importers, and speculators use foreign currency futures. Currency futures can be purchased or sold. A purchase gives the buyer a long position in the foreign currency and may be used to hedge against a future payment obligation in that same currency. For example, a U.S. importer may have contracted to purchase merchandise from a German supplier invoicing in deutsche mark. To hedge against a rise in the value of the deutsche mark, the U.S. importer can purchase a deutsche mark currency future contract or several contracts depending on the amount of deutsche marks to be settled in future. If the spot deutsche mark rises in value, the futures contract will also rise in value parallel to the spot rate. At the time when the importer must pay deutsche mark, a spot purchase of deutsche mark can be carried out for this purpose. The spot deutsche mark will be more costly, given the rise in the spot rate of exchange. But this price will be offset by an increase in the value of the futures contract purchased and held by the importer. The futures contract can be reversed, that is, sold in the market. The profit on the futures contract should approximately equal the additional cost incurred by purchasing spot deutsche mark.

A sale of a foreign currency future gives the seller a short position in the currency. For example, a U.S. exporter may have contracted to sell merchandise to a German buyer, invoicing in deutsche mark. To hedge against a fall in the value of the deutsche mark, the U.S. exporter can sell a deutsche mark currency future contract or several contracts, depending on the amount of deutsche mark position to be hedged. At a later time the exporter can buy a deutsche mark futures contract with a similar settlement date. In effect, this closes out the currency position.

Currency Options

Option Gives holder right to buy or sell the asset traded at a fixed or strike price.

Call option Gives holder right to buy underlying asset at strike price.

Writer Party that writes or issues the option to another party.

Currency options give the holder the right to exercise the option until its expiration. Call options give the holder the right, but not the obligation, to purchase the currency at a price set in the contract called the strike price. Put options give the holder the right, but not the obligation, to sell the currency at a price set in the contract. American style options can be exercised at any time until expiration of the option. By contrast European style options can be exercised only at the maturity date.

There are two parties to an option contract: the option seller or writer and the option buyer who can be a hedger or speculator. The buyer essentially purchases a commitment that the option writer will stand ready to sell or purchase a specified amount of the underlying currency on demand. The option buyer's cost for this right, the premium, is paid to the option writer. Currency options are purchased and traded either on an organized exchange, such as the Philadelphia Exchange, or in the over-the-counter market. Exchange-traded options are standardized contracts, in multiples of standard amounts, with predetermined exercise (strike) prices and standard maturities.

An important factor limiting the use of options as compared with futures is that they can be expensive to use. In other words, a substantial premium can be paid, and then the option may not be exercised. For this reason it is necessary to compare the option solution with alternative type hedges.

OPTION MARKET QUOTATIONS

Three elements are important in the purchase of an option contract, namely, the strike price, maturity date of the option contract, and premium paid for the option. The strike price is fixed in the option contract. As displayed in Exhibit 5.6, seven different strike prices are represented in the deutsche mark currency options, ranging from US$0.66/DM to US$0.69/DM. At mid-November 1990 the actual spot price of the deutsche mark was US$0.6796. Four of the strike prices were below the spot price and three were above it. The ability of the holder of the call or put option to buy or sell at the fixed strike price provides a hedge, or speculative position. In the case of a call option, if the actual price rises substantially above the strike price, the holder can sell the currency spot at a profit. Alternatively, the holder can observe a rising premium on the call option, and sell the contract, thereby receiving a profit. The profit should be approximately the same as if the holder had exercised the option and then sold the currency in the spot market.

Based on the relationship between the strike price and spot price of the underlying currency, an option can be in the money, at the money, or out of the money. An option where strike price is the same as the spot price of the currency is said to be at the money. An option that generates profit for the holder when exercised is said to be in the money. For call options this means that the strike price is below the spot price of the currency. In the case of put options, this means that the strike price is above the spot price. An option that yields a loss if exercised is said to be out of the money. In other words, the strike price is above the spot price for call options, and the strike price is below the spot price of the currency for put options.

Exhibit 5.6 depicts the premiums for deutsche mark options as of 15 November 1990. Note there are seven different strike prices ranging from US$0.66 to US$0.69 per deutsche mark. Anyone seeking to hedge an open or exposed position could purchase call or put options on the deutsche mark at any of the seven different strike prices.

If we consider the columns labeled November, December, March, we have call and put options with different maturities (November 1990, December 1990, and March 1991). A company or investor that wants to cover a short position in deutsche mark that matures in December could purchase a call option with a strike price of $0.67/DM for a premium of $0.0144. Since the deutsche mark option is traded in standard amounts of 62,500 DM per contract, purchase of a single call option contract will cost $900.00 ($0.0144 × 62,500).

The three columns at the right side of Exhibit 5.6 represent premiums on put options that have similar maturities and strike prices as the call options. For example, a December 1990 put option with a $0.67 strike price is priced at $0.0054 per

Premium
Price paid to writer of option contract.

Strike price
Price fixed in the option contract, at which holder can buy or sell asset.

In the money
An option that generates profit for the holder when exercised.

At the money
An option where strike price is the same as spot price.

Out of the money
An option that generates loss for the holder when exercised.

Put option
Gives holder right to sell underlying asset at strike price.

deutsche mark. A single put contract for DM 62,500 maturing December 1990 will cost $337.50 ($0.0054 × 62,500).

No margin is required to buy an option. The buyer pays a premium for the call or the put and if the holder sells the option back, there should be a receipt of funds based upon the premium on that particular option at that point in time.

FACTORS CONTROLLING OPTION PREMIUMS

Intrinsic value

Financial benefit to be derived if an option is exercised immediately. Generally the difference between spot price and exercise price.

Time value

Related to the possibility that the price of the underlying asset will change over remaining lifetime of the option contract.

According to the Bank for International Settlements publication *Recent Innovations in International Banking* (April 1986), the value of an option consists of two components: intrinsic value and time value. Intrinsic value can be defined as the financial benefit to be derived if an option is exercised immediately. Basically, intrinsic value reflects the difference between the exercise price and the market (spot) price of the underlying currency. For example, the intrinsic value of a call option on deutsche mark with an exercise price of $0.66 and a market price of $0.6796 would be $0.0196 (1.96 cents) per deutsche mark (Exhibit 5.7). The intrinsic value falls to zero when the market price equals the exercise price (Exhibit 5.6, all three call options with strike price of $0.68). Generally an option will sell for at least its intrinsic value.

The time value of an option is related to the possibility that the price of the underlying currency will change over the remaining lifetime of the option contract so as to give the option greater value. For example, an option that is out of the money can move into the money, or one already in the money can become more so. The time value of an option is always greater than zero. Therefore the selling price of an option generally exceeds its intrinsic value.

The time value and intrinsic value of an option can always be calculated separately. The following steps are involved in this calculation:

1. calculate the intrinsic value (spot price minus strike price);
2. take the difference between intrinsic value and total value; and,
3. the remainder in step 2 constitutes time value.

For example, in the three deutsche mark call options with strike price of $0.66 (Exhibit 5.7), the total value (premium) is given in column 1. The November 1990 call option has a total value of US 2.01 cents. The intrinsic value is calculated by taking the difference between the spot price of the underlying currency and the exercise price (67.96 − 66.00 = 1.96 cents). The time value is the difference between the total value, or premium, and intrinsic value (2.01 − 1.96 = 0.05), or US cents 0.05 per deutsche mark.

EXHIBIT 5.7	Calculation of Intrinsic Value and Time Value of Deutsche Mark Call Options—Cents per DM (Strike Price of $0.66)

Option Maturity Date	Total Value	Intrinsic Value	Time Value
	(1)	(2)	(1)−(2)=(3)
November 1990	2.01	67.96 − 66.00 = 1.96	0.05
December 1990	2.12	67.96 − 66.00 = 1.96	0.16
March 1991	2.71	67.96 − 66.00 = 1.96	0.75

Traders have used the Black-Scholes option pricing model to calculate the value of an option. Option pricing models try to explain the intrinsic value and time value of an option. Generally, these models must incorporate the following variables in explaining premiums on foreign currency options:

1. Spot price of underlying currency minus exercise price—the larger this differential, the larger the intrinsic value.

2. Time to maturity—all other things being equal, longer maturity option contracts contain greater value than shorter maturity options.

3. Relative interest rates on the two currencies included in the option contract—in the case of deutsche mark option contracts valued in U.S. dollars, call values rise and put values fall when the interest differential between the two currencies increase. This function is because a foreign currency normally is at a forward premium or discount in comparison with the domestic currency; the forward premium or discount is determined by relative interest rates.*

4. Price volatility (exchange rate) of the underlying asset—most of the time value of a currency option is related to changes in the price of the underlying asset. Option pricing takes into account the manner in which the price of the underlying asset may move. We refer to the variability of price movements of the underlying currency as volatility. Volatility can be measured or calculated by use of the standard deviation of price.

5. The balance between demand and supply for specific option contracts can vary due to a number of factors. These factors include seasonal, cyclical, or episodic events.

Volatility

Variability in price of the underlying asset. One factor that affects time value of option.

SPECULATING WITH CALL OPTIONS

Foreign currency options can be used to take a speculative position. A speculative buyer may exercise the option or allow it to expire. The speculator will exercise the option when it is profitable to do so, that is, when the option is in the money. As the spot price of the underlying currency moves up, the speculative holder of a call option will obtain greater and greater profit. Potential profit is unlimited. However, if the spot price of the currency moves down, the holder of the option can allow it to expire. In this case, the holder's loss is limited to the amount of the premium paid. Exhibit 5.8 illustrates this relationship.

Assume that a speculator has purchased a call option for £31,250, with a strike price of $1.90 and a maturity of three months. The cost of the option is $937.50 (3.0 cents per pound × £31,250). In Exhibit 5.8 we measure the profit or loss on the vertical axis, and illustrate spot prices on the horizontal axis. In this example the speculator would not exercise the option if the spot price was $1.84 at the time of expiration, since it would be possible to purchase pounds in the spot market at a lower price. The speculator's loss would be limited to the premium paid for the option. At the spot price of $1.90 or lower, the speculator's loss would be limited to the premium paid.

If at expiration of the option the spot price was $1.96, the speculator would exercise the option. The speculator would pay $59,375.00 to purchase £31,250 at the strike price of $1.90. The £31,250 could be sold in the spot market for $61,250.00 (1.96 × £31,250). This would yield a gross profit of $1,875.00, and a net profit of $937.50 after deducting the premium cost of $937.50.

---

* Bank for International Settlements. *Recent Innovations in International Banking.* (April 1986): 70–71.

EXHIBIT 5.8	**Call Option, Profit and Loss Generated at Selected Spot Prices of British Pound**

Currency: British Pound Sterling
Contract Size: £31,250 (Philadelphia Exchange)
Exercise (Strike) Price: $1.90
Premium (Price): 3.0 cents per pound ($937.50 per contract)

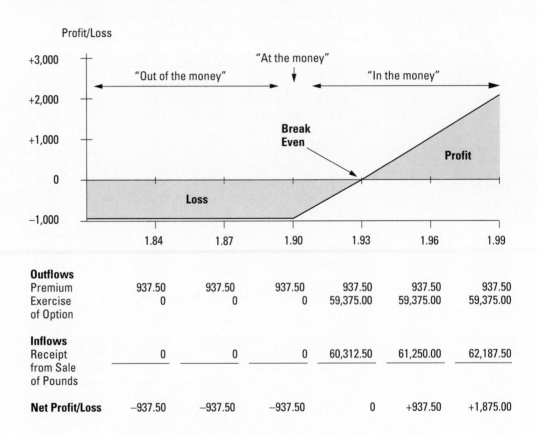

	1.84	1.87	1.90	1.93	1.96	1.99
Outflows						
Premium	937.50	937.50	937.50	937.50	937.50	937.50
Exercise of Option	0	0	0	59,375.00	59,375.00	59,375.00
Inflows						
Receipt from Sale of Pounds	0	0	0	60,312.50	61,250.00	62,187.50
Net Profit/Loss	−937.50	−937.50	−937.50	0	+937.50	+1,875.00

SPECULATING WITH PUT OPTIONS

Foreign currency *put options* can also be used for speculation. The possible outcome from taking a position as the buyer of a put is shown in Exhibit 5.9. The speculator holding the put option hopes to sell the underlying currency at the strike price when the market price falls below the strike price.

In Exhibit 5.9, the speculator has purchased a put option for £31,250, with an exercise price of $1.90. If the spot pound falls to $1.84, the holder of the put option can purchase £31,250 spot for $57,500 ($1.84 × £31,250), deliver the pounds to the writer of the put option and receive $59,375. This transaction will yield a net profit of $937.50.

There will be no incentive to exercise the put option at spot prices of $1.90 or higher. In that case the speculator loses the premium paid for the option. At spot prices between $1.87 and $1.90 the speculator will exercise the put option, recovering part of the premium originally paid for the option.

EXHIBIT 5.9	Put Option, Profit and Loss Generated at Selected Prices of British Pound

Currency: British Pound Sterling
Contract Size: £31,250 (Philadelphia Exchange)
Exercise (Strike) Price: $1.90
Premium (Price):   3.0 cents per pound ($937.50 per contract)

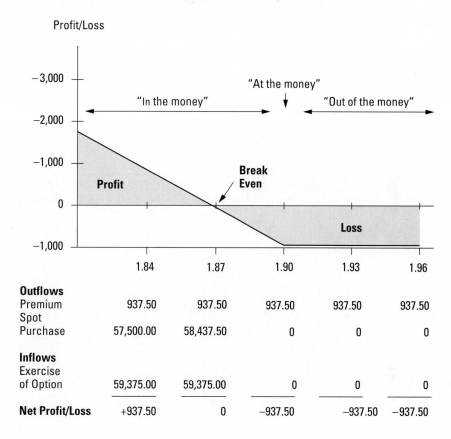

	1.84	1.87	1.90	1.93	1.96
Outflows					
Premium	937.50	937.50	937.50	937.50	937.50
Spot Purchase	57,500.00	58,437.50	0	0	0
Inflows					
Exercise of Option	59,375.00	59,375.00	0	0	0
Net Profit/Loss	+937.50	0	−937.50	−937.50	−937.50

COMPARISON OF OPTIONS AND FUTURES CONTRACTS

At this point we will compare currency futures and currency options. A company interested in hedging or speculating on an increase in the value of the pound sterling can purchase a pound sterling currency future, or purchase a pound sterling call option. The comparative position and cost facing this company is summarized in Exhibit 5.10. The call option carries a premium cost of $937.50, as compared with the interest cost implicit in the margin required for the future contract of $74.22. Further, if the acquisition of the currency future or call option is purely speculative, with no offsetting short position in that currency, the potential gain and loss is quite different for the future as compared with the call option. The currency future can increase or fall in value. Therefore both potential gains and losses are very large. By contrast the call option contains a limited loss (premium cost) but unlimited potential gain.

Finally, we can obtain an overview of the position of a buyer or writer of call and put options (Exhibit 5.11). Reviewing the pound sterling options cases in

EXHIBIT 5.10   Comparison of Cost in Currency Futures and Call Option Contracts

Cost of Futures Contract:	
Number of pound sterling units	£31,250
Dollar value per pound	$1.90
Value of contract in dollars	$59,375.00
5% margin	$2,968.75
10% interest on margin	$296.87
10% interest (three months)	$74.22
Cost of Call Option contract:	
Number of pound sterling units	£31,250
Premium paid (per currency unit)	3.0 cents
Basic cost of 3-month call option	$937.50
Multiple of Call Option Cost compared with	
Futures Contract Cost	
(937.50/74.22 = 12.6)	12.6

EXHIBIT 5.11   Overview of Possible Outcomes: Buyer and Writer of Call and Put Options

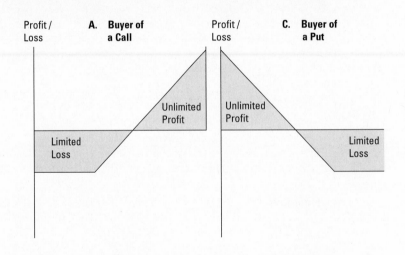

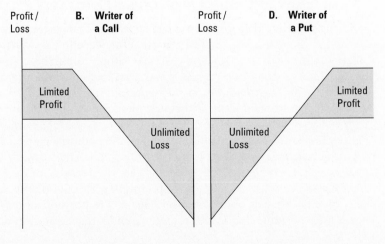

Exhibits 5.8 and 5.9, we see that the buyer of the call option faces a limited loss (based on the premium paid for the option), but an unlimited profit (Exhibit 5.11a). The writer of the call option faces a limited profit (premium) but potential unlimited loss (Exhibit 5.11b).

The buyer of the put option faces a limited loss (premium paid), but unlimited profit (Exhibit 5.11c). The writer of the put option faces a limited profit but unlimited potential loss (Exhibit 5.11d).

Options on Futures

We have noted that it is possible to use currency futures or currency options to hedge open currency positions or to speculate on price movements in particular currencies. A currency futures contract has a relatively modest transaction cost in the form of brokerage commissions paid to specialist firms that operate on the futures exchange (Exhibit 5.12). In addition there are initial margin and maintenance margin costs. If an offsetting transaction is not made prior to expiration of the futures contract, the contract holder will have to make settlement.

In the case of a currency option, an initial premium is paid to the writer of the option contract, and commissions are paid in the trading of currency options on the exchange (Exhibit 5.12). However, there is no margin. Furthermore, the holder of the option may abandon it and use the spot market if that alternative is advantageous.

Futures options

Option contracts where the underlying asset is a financial futures contract.

Options on futures contracts provide a third alternative for the hedger or speculator. If the hedger is short the currency amount and desires protection against an upward movement in price of that currency, the hedger can purchase a call option on a given futures contract in that currency. To illustrate, a U.S. multinational must pay DM 125,000 in January 1991, three months into the future. The spot mark is $0.6700, and the treasurer of the corporation is concerned that the deutsche mark will rise in value. The firm can purchase any of several call options (with January 1991 expiration), with strike prices ranging between $0.6600 and $0.6800.

Prices for call and put options on futures for deutsche mark are presented in Exhibit 5.13.

The strike price of 6600 in Exhibit 5.13 means that contracts have an exercise price of $0.6600/DM. Calls maturing in December were settled at 2.11 cents per mark on that day. December calls with strike prices ranging from 6600 to 6800 were

EXHIBIT 5.12	**Comparison of Exchange Traded Futures, Options, and Options on Futures**		
	Currency Futures	Currency Options	Option on Futures
Transaction Cost	Brokerage Commissions	Brokerage Commissions	Brokerage Commissions
Margin Required	Initial Margin and Maintenance of Margin	None	None
Premium Paid	None	Premium	Premium
Settlement at Maturity	Required if Offsetting Transaction Not Made	Not Required	Not Required

EXHIBIT 5.13	**Futures Options Prices Deutsche Mark (IMM)** **125,000 Marks, Cents per Mark**					
	CALLS-SETTLE			**PUTS-SETTLE**		
Strike Price	**December**	**January**	**March**	**December**	**January**	**March**
6600	2.11	2.23	2.72	0.16	0.50	1.02
6650	1.70	1.89	—	0.25	—	—
6700	1.34	1.57	2.13	0.39	0.84	1.41
6750	1.01	1.29	—	0.56	1.05	—
6800	0.74	1.04	1.63	0.79	1.30	1.89

Estimated volume 11,155; Tuesday volume 2,645 calls, 3,161 puts.
Open interest Tues 54,962 calls, 78,813 puts.

SOURCE: *Wall Street Journal.*

settled on that particular day at prices ranging from 2.11 cents down to 0.74 cents per mark.

The maturity of options on futures affects their value. This instrument works in a manner similar to the case of straight options (Exhibits 5.6 and 5.7). As the maturity lengthens the price of call and put options increases.

Let us assume a multinational corporation purchased a January call option on deutsche mark futures with a strike price of 6700 (for DM 125,000). It would pay DM 125,000 × $0.0157 = $1,962.50. If at maturity (January 1991) the deutsche mark was worth $0.71 the firm could exercise the option to acquire the future. It could then use the futures contract to acquire deutsche mark. Its profit would be the difference between the spot price and exercise price, less the castoff (a premium paid for option plus exchange commissions), all multiplied by the number of deutsche mark in the option and futures contracts. The calculations would be as follows:

$$\text{Profit} = [(\text{Spot Price} - \text{Strike Price}) - \text{Premium on Option}] \times 125,000$$

$$\text{Profit} = [(0.71 - 0.67) - 0.0157] \times 125,000$$

$$\text{Profit} = 0.0243 \times 125,000 = \$3,037.50 - \$50.00 \text{ (commission)}$$

$$\text{Profit} = \$2,987.50$$

Currency Swaps

Currency swap

Agreement between two counterparties to swap or exchange future cash flows denominated in two different currencies.

Since 1981 a substantial currency swap market has developed. We consider currency swaps at this point since they offer a means for modifying currency exposure, generally over a medium term or longer period. We consider interest rate swaps in Chapter 7 in connection with borrowing via the international bond market.

Currency swaps were first developed by the World Bank, one of the largest single borrowers in the global financial markets. The World Bank enjoys two basic advantages from currency swaps: 1) they improve the liquidity of the longterm market in major foreign currencies, and 2) they reduce the risk of foreign currency exposure more effectively than traditional alternatives.[*]

---

[*] Bock, D., and C. Wallich, *Currency Swaps.* World Bank, Staff Working Papers No. 640, 1984.

EXHIBIT 5.14	**Swaps: A Schematic Representation[1]**

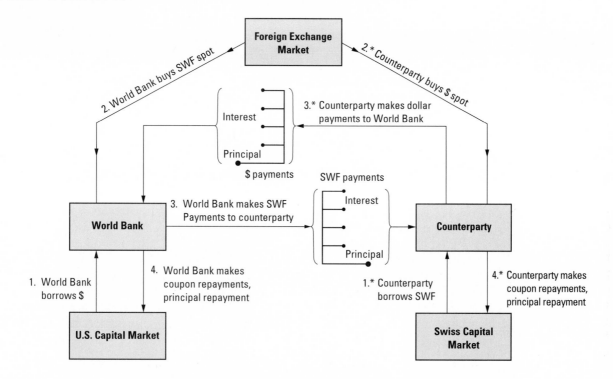

[1] This illustrates a typical swap of a new liability, involving fixed interest rate dollars and fixed interest rate Swiss francs.

* Refer to transactions of counterparty.

A market participant enters into a swap transaction to exchange one pattern of future cash flows denominated in one currency for another that is denominated in a preferred second currency. The World Bank has followed a common pattern in developing its swap transactions. The bank generally borrows a high nominal interest rate currency (U.S. dollars or sterling) in the Euromarkets or in a domestic capital market. It wants to convert the proceeds (U.S. dollars) into a preferred currency by selling the dollars in the spot foreign exchange market for that currency (Swiss franc).

During the 1980s the main objective of the World Bank was to operate as a lender in low coupon interest currencies such as deutsche marks or Swiss francs. As a result the borrowing country was less encumbered with debt service and in the long run can service a larger total amount of external debt.

To keep its own currency exposure position under control, the World Bank has made use of various hedging mechanisms including the currency swap. Currency swaps have enabled the World Bank to borrow high coupon dollar and sterling funds, enter into currency swaps with suitable counterparties (usually high credit quality borrowers with direct access to Swiss franc and deutsche mark capital markets), and lend the preferred currency to developing nation borrowers.

The following outlines a typical currency swap transaction (Exhibit 5.14). Assume the World Bank has borrowed U.S. dollars at a rate of 10.0%. A Swiss company has borrowed SF 100 million at a rate of 6.0% and wishes to swap the proceeds into dollars for use by its North American affiliate. Both parties agree to participate in a currency swap for SF 100 million as follows:

	Year	Amount Sold by World Bank to Counterparty	Amount Received by World Bank from Swiss Counterparty
Spot Exchange	0	$50.0 million[1]	SF100.0 million[1]
Forward	1	SF6.0 million	$5.0 million
Contract	2	SF6.0 million	$5.0 million
	3	SF6.0 million	$5.0 million
	4	SF6.0 million	$5.0 million
	5	SF106.0 million	$55.0 million

[1]Exchange rate at time of swap agreement is $1 = SF 2.0.

In this case each counterparty, the World Bank and the Swiss company, has borrowed funds from which they wish to swap. The proceeds from World Bank borrowing are used to purchase Swiss franc. Remember that in the typical currency swap there is no exchange of initial principal, only of debt service funds.

The typical transaction is depicted in Exhibit 5.14. Each counterparty has borrowed funds that it will swap away from (1 and 1*). Each counterparty uses borrowed funds to purchase the desired currency (2 and 2*). Forward contracts are concluded (3 and 3*) that call for payment of interest only in the first four years and repayment of principal and interest in the fifth year. The World Bank Swiss franc payments to the counterparty are used to repay the counterparty's Swiss franc obligation, and similarly, the World Bank's forward purchases of dollars from the counterparty are used to meet the Bank's dollar liabilities (4 and 4*).

SUMMARY

Since 1980 derivatives markets have grown at an explosive rate. With the introduction of floating exchange rates in the 1970s, increased attention has been given to finding methods to hedge foreign currency risk. Two approaches can be taken in hedging currency positions. One involves customized deals through forward exchange contracts. A second involves trading standardized currency contracts on markets organized for this purpose.

Currency futures contracts make it possible to lock in the price of a given currency where delivery is at a future point in time. Futures contracts are standardized and traded on an organized exchange. The holder of a futures contract can sell the contract in a liquid market, providing the ability to alter the hedge or speculative position as needed.

Futures contracts provide services to those who make use of the exchange market. These services include price discovery, liquidity, and customer protection. Margin requirements are one element of customer protection. The exchange on which futures contracts are traded establishes contract specifications.

Currency options give the holder the right to exercise the option until its expiration. Call options give the holder the right to purchase the currency at the strike price. Put options give the holder the right to sell the currency at the strike price. There are two parties to an option contract, the option seller (writer), and the option purchaser (hedger or speculator). Option premiums have two components—intrinsic value and time value.

Option on futures provide another alternative for the hedger. The purchase of an option on futures gives the holder the right to exercise the option, in which case

Option on futures

Right to buy or sell futures contract.

there will be the right to buy or sell a futures contract. Since 1981 a large market has developed in currency swaps. In a currency swap a counterparty uses borrowed funds to purchase the desired currency.

REVIEW QUESTIONS

1. Explain why derivative market activities have grown so rapidly in recent years. Distinguish between the role played by exchange traded as compared with over-the-counter instruments.

2. What types of hedging and speculative instruments have been developed with respect to foreign currency risk? Why have so many different types of instruments been developed?

3. What are the advantages of using foreign currency futures? How do they differ with foreign currency forwards?

4. How do futures exchanges provide customer protection? What types of risks are protected against?

5. Why are the contract specifications for currency futures so important?

6. A U.S. investor has purchased DMark denominated securities in the German capital market worth DM 10 million. The investor fears the deutsche mark may decline in value and can sell futures for six-month delivery at $0.6763. The current spot price is $0.6785. What is the annualized percentage cost of this hedge? Assume brokerage costs are $150.

7. A British company plans to import electronic components from a U.S. supplier worth $4,500,000. Payment will be due in approximately 75 days. The company decides to hedge its position with IMM futures. The spot rate at this time is $1.50 and the price on the futures contract suitable for hedging is $1.49. The company purchases the number of contracts that match the exposure as closely as possible to its $4.5 million exposure. Seventy days later the spot rate is $1.4620 while the futures price is $1.4540. Calculate the net gain or loss in terms of pound sterling of the hedged position at this time. Disregard any possible interest on margin funds used for the hedge.

8. What is the difference between purchasing a currency futures and a currency option? Which is better for speculation?

9. Distinguish between the position of a writer and purchaser of a currency option.

10. In purchasing a currency option, describe the three elements that govern the success of the purchaser's hedging or speculative activity.

11. What do we mean when we say an option is in the money, at the money, or out of the money?

12. A speculator purchases a call option on deutsche mark for $.03 per unit. The strike price is $.66, and the spot rate at the time of exercise is $.72. Assume there are 62,500 units in a deutsche mark option. What was the net profit of the speculator?

13. A speculator sold a call option on Swiss franc of $.01 per unit. The strike price was $.77 and the spot rate at the time of exercise was $.80. Assume the speculator purchased marks at the spot price of $.80 to make delivery under the exercised option. There are 62,500 marks in a deutsche mark option. What was the net profit to the seller of the call option?

14. A speculator purchases a put option on deutsche mark for $.02 per unit. The strike price was $.48, and the spot rate at the time of exercise was $.44. There

are 62,500 marks in a deutsche mark option. What was the net profit on the put option?

15. A speculator sold a put option on Swiss franc for $.04 per unit. The strike price was $.75, and the spot rate at the time of exercise was $.70. Assume the speculator sells the Swiss franc as it is received. There are 62,500 units in a Swiss franc option. What was the net profit to the seller of the put option?

16. Distinguish between intrinsic value and time value as determinants in pricing options. In the case of a pound sterling call option priced at 3.86 cents, with strike price of $1.80 and spot price of $1.83, calculate the intrinsic value and time value of the option.

17. Describe the various factors in the Black-Scholes option pricing model that can be used to explain the value of an option.

18. Explain how options on futures provide an opportunity for hedging a currency position. How do options on futures compare with straight options?

19. What is a currency swap? Why must two counterparties be matched with complementary needs to affect a currency swap?

20. Are currency swaps perfect substitutes for currency futures? Explain.

SELECTED BIBLIOGRAPHY

Bank for International Settlements. *Recent Innovations in International Banking*. Basle, April 1986.

Black, F., and M. Scholes. "The Pricing of Options and Corporate Liabilities." *Journal of Political Economy,* May-June 1973.

Bock, D., and C. Wallich. *Currency Swaps*. World Bank, Staff Working Papers No. 640, 1984.

Chicago Mercantile Exchange. *Spreads on Currency Futures*. Chicago: 1988.

Chicago Mercantile Exchange. *A World Marketplace*. Chicago: 1990.

Cornell, Bradford, and Marc Reinganum. "Forward and Future Prices." *Journal of Finance,* December 1981.

Garman, Mark, and Steven Kohlhagen. "Foreign Currency Option Values." *Journal of International Money and Finance,* December 1983.

Group of Thirty. *Derivatives Practices and Principles,* Washington, D.C.: 1993.

Hill, John. *Options, Futures and Other Derivatives*. England Cliffs: Prentice Hall, 1993.

Kuprianov, Anatoli. "Derivatives Debates Case Studies of Large Losses." *Federal Reserve Banks of Richmond Economic Quarterly,* Fall 1995.

LIFFE. *Investing With Confidence,* London: Cannon Bridge, 1995.

LIFFE. *Summary of Futures and Options Contracts*. London: Cannon Bridge, April 1996.

Loosigian, Allen M. *Foreign Exchange Futures*. Homewood, IL: Dow-Jones Irwin, 1981.

Schwartz, Robert, and Clifford Smith. *The Handbook of Currency and Interest Rate Risk Management*. New York Institute of Finance, 1990.

Smith, Clifford, Charles Smithson, and Sykes Walford. *Managing Financial Risk*. New York: Harper & Row, 1990.

Solnik, Bruno. *International Investments*. Reading, Mass.: Addison-Wesley, 1991.

Stoll, Hans R., and Robert R. Whaley. *Futures and Options*. Cincinnati: Southwestern, 1991.

CHAPTER 6

Eurocurrency Market and Offshore Banking

INTRODUCTION

This chapter has several objectives including: 1) to review the special characteristics of the Eurocurrency market and offshore banking within the context of global financial markets; 2) to examine the size, growth and development, and significance of the Eurocurrency market and offshore banking; 3) to analyze the structure and operations of the Eurocurrency market in relation to deposit instruments, interbank trading, and international lending; 4) to explain the specific banking and financial activities of major Eurocurrency and offshore banking markets; and 5) to briefly discuss international collaboration on financial market policies in the 1990s.

LEARNING OBJECTIVES IN THIS CHAPTER

1. To obtain an overview of the global financial markets and the interrelationships of the components.
2. To explain the special characteristics of the Eurocurrency market and offshore banking.
3. To understand the significance of the Eurocurrency market in connection with worldwide participants, international flows of funds, global economic developments, and national economic policies.
4. To examine different aspects of the Eurocurrency market: structures, functions, deposit instruments, lending instruments, sizes, operations, and risks.
5. To trace the process of syndicated loans in the multinational, multicurrency markets.
6. To study general characteristics, geographic locations, and continuous growth of the Eurocurrency and offshore banking markets that necessitate collaboration in financial market policies by governments, especially in times of international monetary crisis.

KEY TERMS AND CONCEPTS

- Eurocurrency
- Eurobanks
- Euro-CDs
- Euro-Commercial Paper (ECP)
- Eurocurrency Interbank Market
- Eurodollar Arbitrage
- Note Issuance Facilities (NIFs)
- Offshore Banking Market

- Petrodollar Recycling
- Primary Market Rate
- Regulation Q
- Revolving Underwriting Facilities (RUFs)
- Secondary Market Rate
- Syndicated Bank Loans

ACRONYMS

BIS	Bank for International Settlements	**LIBOR**	London Interbank Offered Rate
CD	Certificate of Deposit	**LIFFE**	London International Financial Futures and options Exchange
CHIPs	Clearing House Interbank Payments		
ECP	Euro-Commercial Paper	**LLR**	Lender of Last Report
ECUs	European Currency Units	**MTN**	Medium Term Note
GMAC	General Motors Acceptance Corporation	**RUFs**	Revolving Underwriting Facilities
IBFs	International Banking Facilities	**SHIFT**	System for Handling Interbank Transfer
IMM	International Monetary Market, a division of the Chicago Mercantile Exchange (CME)	**SIBOR**	Singapore Interbank Offered Rate
		SIMEX	Singapore International Monetary Exchange
JOM	Japan Offshore Market		

Global Financial Markets: An Overview

COMPONENTS OF GLOBAL FINANCIAL MARKETS

There are five major components of the global financial markets: the national financial markets, the traditional international financial markets, the international currency exchange markets, Euromarkets and offshore banking markets (Exhibit 6.1).

National financial markets include the short-term money market, the longterm capital market, the national foreign exchange market, and several derivative markets (including financial options and futures). These markets function within a national regulatory and economic framework subject to government policy.

The traditional international financial markets facilitate borrowing and investment transactions between residents of two countries denominated in a single currency. These transactions may be subject to regulations imposed by the two nations. For example, the Industrial Development Bank of Japan borrowed pound

EXHIBIT 6.1	**Global Financial Markets: An Overview**

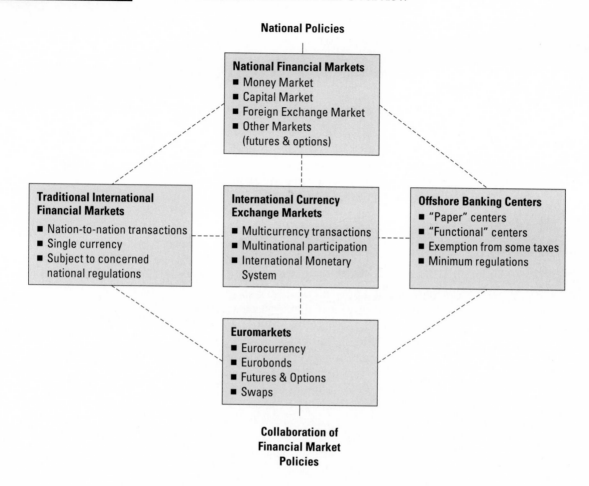

sterling from the London market in the nineteenth century to finance domestic economic development; the National Financial (development) Bank of Mexico obtained U.S. dollar loans in the 1960s to finance its imports; the Bank of China borrowed Japanese yen in Tokyo to purchase machinery for industrial development in the 1980s. The international currency exchange markets facilitate trading many currencies simultaneously in leading financial centers such as New York, London, Tokyo, and others where currency dealing takes place. Under the present international monetary system, international currency exchange is subject to the rules set forth by the International Monetary Fund, as discussed in Chapters 2 and 4.

The Euromarkets include the Eurocurrency market, Eurobond market, Eurodollar futures and options, and currency and interest rate swaps. Eurocurrency is a time deposit housed in a bank outside the currency-issuing country. We refer to U.S. dollars deposited in London banks, whether they are U.S. branch banks or other banks in London, as Eurodollars. Similarly, we refer to German deutsche marks deposited in Swiss banks as Euro-deutsche marks and Japanese yen deposited in Paris banks as Euroyen.

We may classify offshore banking centers as either "paper" or "functional." A paper center acts as a location of record, with little or no actual banking operations carried out. By contrast deposit and lending operations are carried out in a functional center. Both types of centers help channel funds from major international financial centers such as London and New York to final borrowers. Banks use paper centers such as the Bahamas and Cayman Islands to minimize taxes and escape regulation.

INTERRELATIONSHIPS BETWEEN EUROMARKETS AND OTHER MARKETS

The five major, interrelated components of global financial markets carry out different types of financial functions. The Euromarkets are generally free from national or domestic regulations such as reserve requirements and deposit insurance fees. For this reason Eurobanks can operate more efficiently and with lower costs than domestic banks. Eurobanks and domestic banks compete against one another. This competition ties Euromarket interest rates together with interest rates in related domestic money markets. For example, if the U.S. domestic CD rate is higher than the Euro-CD rate, U.S. domestic banks will borrow funds from the Euromarkets through their overseas branches. At the same time, Eurodollar arbitrage in the Euromarkets will keep lending and deposit rates within limits determined by effective domestic lending and deposit rates.

In addition, there is a close relationship between traditional international financial markets and Euromarkets. When an international borrower wants to raise a large amount of funds not easily provided by a single lender, syndicated loans from the Euromarkets may provide a solution. The Euromarkets and offshore markets share close ties. The same group of banks serves both markets. Both mobilize and mediate internationally liquid funds, and both are less subject to domestic regulation. International currency exchange markets play a unique role in the global financial markets. These markets are positioned at the center of all markets. While the Eurocurrency market is a market for loans and deposits, the international exchange markets provide the basic means of payment.

In recent years, the fabulous derivative markets for currency futures, options, and swaps have been growing fast and closely related to the Eurocurrency market. For example, Eurocurrency futures and options have been actively traded on exchanges in New York, Chicago, London, Paris, Singapore, and Hong Kong. These subjects are discussed in detail in Chapters 5, 9, and 16.

SPECIAL CHARACTERISTICS OF THE EUROCURRENCY MARKET AND OFFSHORE BANKING

The Eurocurrency market and offshore banking centers possess distinct characteristics including:

1. minimum government regulation and incentives for nonresidents to participate in the markets;
2. facilities to attract large international commercial banks, financial institutions, and multinational firms to utilize these markets on the spot;
3. a functional banking system conducive to international (cross-border) transactions;
4. provision of a variety of financial instruments by which both lenders and borrowers have freedom of choice, e.g., instruments, maturities, interest rates, and currencies are suitable for their "Eurograms";

Eurobank
Banks engaging in Eurocurrency, Eurobonds, and other Euro-transactions.

Eurodollar Arbitrage
Buying and selling Eurodollars in different Euromarkets for profit based on price differentials of the dollars.

Eurograms
A variety of financial instruments by which both lenders and borrowers have freedom of choice in the Euromarket.

5. domestic political stability to insure uninterrupted operations;

6. efficient and skilled work force and communication skills to work efficiently with the international banking community;

7. a code of conduct must be observed that permits minimum national, domestic regulation along with an absence of abuses in the markets; and,

8. absence of international regulation of the markets.

Eurocurrency Market: Origin, Size, and Significance

Eurocurrency

A collective term applicable to any major currency deposited outside the currency issuing countries.

Over the past four decades the Eurocurrency market has developed into a major channel for international financial intermediation. This development has been one of the most important events in the financial world. The following sections examine the origin, size, and underlying reasons for the rapid growth of the Eurocurrency market.

ORIGIN OF THE EUROCURRENCY MARKET

In the early 1950s Soviet banks in Western Europe preferred to place their holdings of U.S. dollars with British and French banks, protecting against the risk of possible seizure by U.S. authorities in case of crisis. Soviet banks avoided U.S. banks, since the United States and the Soviet Union were political adversaries. These early Eurobanks applied simple banking principles by charging small spreads between creditor and debtor rates of interest.

Three events provided the impetus for development of the Eurodollar market. First, the U.K. government announced in 1957 that British banks were not permitted to finance trade for nonresidents because of capital and foreign exchange controls. However, the U.K. banks were able to take advantage of the availability of U.S. dollar funds to finance their international customers. British authorities could have prevented development of dollar financing through U.K. banks, but realized the advantages of developing London into a leading Eurodollar market. Second, in 1958, during the formation of the Common Market, Germany, France, and Italy returned to currency convertibility. This change meant that their residents could place dollar holdings with commercial banks based on competitive interest rates instead of surrendering them to their central banks. Third, the Federal Reserve imposed interest rate ceilings for interest paid on time deposits in domestic banks. These ceilings encouraged the outflow of dollars to Europe for higher yields. London continued to enjoy its long-standing position in the international money market as international lenders and borrowers flocked to the city during the 1960s and 1970s. As the Eurodollar market continued to expand, other major currencies such as the German deutsche mark, Swiss franc, French franc, British pound sterling, and later the Japanese yen became widely used in the Euromarket and the broader term *"Eurocurrency"* came into use.

Size and Development   The Eurocurrency market has grown spectacularly from $12 billion in 1964 to $3.660 billion in 1995. The development of the Eurocurrency market reflects changes and trends in world events. Except for a temporary setback in 1990 due to worldwide economic recession, there have been four big "waves" influencing the ups and downs in the development of the Eurocurrency market: 1964–1973, 1974–1981, 1982–1984, 1985–1995.

EXHIBIT 6.2	Eurocurrency Market Size (in U.S.$ Billion)																
	1964	1973	1974	1981	1982	1983	1984	1985	1986	1988	1989	1990	1991	1992	1993	1994	1995
Net Market size	12	160	221	1,155	1,285	1,382	1,430	1,678	2,076	3,200	3,530	3,350	3,610	3,660	3,780	4,240	4,645
Eurodollar as % of all currencies	83%	73%	77%	79%	80%	81%	82%	75%	68%	63%	75%	59%	85%	85%	53%	52%	50%

SOURCES: 1964–1995 are from *BIS Annual Report*, various issues except 1981–1986 are from Morgan Guaranty Trust Company, *World Financial Markets*, various issues.

A deteriorating U.S. balance of payments position led to the imposition of various capital controls: the Interest Equalization Tax (IET) in 1963, the Voluntary Credit Control in 1965, and the mandatory credit control in 1968. These measures discouraged borrowers from using U.S. financial markets and stimulated the growth of the Eurocurrency market. Nonresident borrowers searched for alternative sources of funds, and the Eurocurrency market served as a flexible alternative. Under the mandatory controls in 1968, the U.S. government restricted U.S. capital investment overseas and forced many U.S. multinational corporations to borrow abroad. As a result, Eurodollar interest rates rose and more funds flowed into the market.

Due to a credit crunch in the United States in 1969, U.S. commercial banks borrowed a large amount ($16.5 billion) of funds from their foreign branches in Europe in order to ease their liquidity pressures at home. As a consequence, for the first time the U.S. Federal Reserve imposed reserve requirements on domestic banks borrowing funds from their foreign branches. From 1964 to 1973, the Eurocurrency market surged from $12 billion to $160 billion, a 13-fold growth due to an increase in lending and deposits. (Exhibit 6.2)

Perhaps the most spectacular growth in the Eurocurrency market was from 1974–1981, when the size of the market increased from $221 billion to $1155 billion, a five-fold growth caused primarily by petrodollar recycling and inflation. Following the oil crisis in 1974, the Organization of Petroleum Exporting Countries (OPEC) enjoyed a cumulative $320 billion surplus by 1981. These countries made substantial deposits in large international commercial banks that in turn made loans primarily to the developing countries needing to finance payment deficits. This large volume of world deposit and lending of Eurocurrencies stimulated rapid expansion in the Euromarkets.

Petrodollar Recycling

U.S. dollars received by Organization of Petroleum Exporting Countries (OPEC) and deposited in international banks which, in turn, lend to oil importing countries for payments of their oil.

A more moderate growth in the Eurocurrency market took place in the 1982–1984 period. This period also brought a fundamental change in the equation of supply and demand in the Eurocurrency market. First, the collapse of the OPEC cartel brought oil prices down from $33 per barrel to $12 per barrel. The disappearance of the OPEC surplus and the heavy debt service burden of the debtor countries like Mexico, Brazil, and Poland was accompanied by slower growth in the Eurocurrency market. The slower growth, from $1,285 billion in 1982 to $1,430 billion in 1984, was due to the fact that banks were reluctant to lend to developing countries. After 1981 Japan began to supply funds to the world financial markets due to the growing surplus in its balance of payments. U.S. corporations also became net suppliers of funds in the Eurocurrency market because of high interest rates in Europe and the appreciation of the U.S. dollar during the 1981–1984 period.

On the demand side, the role of Latin American countries diminished. The ongoing economic revitalization of the Eastern European countries led to increased borrowing in the market, while continued economic prosperity in the U.S. and the opening of the International Banking Facilities (IBFs) in New York attracted considerable funds to the U.S. markets.

The Eurocurrency market advanced rapidly in the period 1985–1989, from $1,678 billion to $3,530 billion. Primarily due to increases in interbank trading and syndicated loans to finance mergers and acquisitions. The supply of funds to the market in this period was mainly from developed countries such as the United States, Luxembourg, and the Netherlands. Taiwan was a new net supplier of funds because of its continued trade surplus. In 1990, the sluggish worldwide economy reduced the size of the Eurocurrency market to $3,350 billion. Gradual economic recovery in the 1992–1995 period helped improve the Eurocurrency market to a level of $4,645 billion. However, the shares of the U.S. dollar fell from 85% to 50% due to the increasing strength of German mark and Japanese yen.

Participants in the Market

One of the unique features of the Eurocurrency market is the diversity of participants. A wide range of borrowers and lenders use Eurobank services. Participants can operate on both sides of the supply-and-demand equation. They include international financial institutions such as the World Bank, central banks, and commercial banks. Nonbank financial institutions such as brokerage firms, insurance companies, business corporations, governments and government agencies, and wealthy individuals also participate in the Eurocurrency market. Borrowers, lenders, and financial intermediaries come from all over the world, making the Eurocurrency market truly a global financial market.

There are several reasons for the global spread of the market. First, borrowers and lenders seek business environments that have minimal regulation such as offshore banking centers. Also, Eurobanks have little or no pressure to favor one borrower over the other, operating under the concept of profit maximization and perceived risks. Fierce competition among financial intermediaries precludes the possibility of any one bank or institution dominating the market.

Against this backdrop, participants in the Eurocurrency market have included not only the developed countries but also the developing countries in Asia, Latin America, Eastern Europe and Russia. This will be elaborated in the section on syndicated loans.

Offshore Banking Centers

Special centers for international banking transactions with minimal government regulations.

Significance to the World Economy

Generally the Eurocurrency market is free from regulation and is exempt from national taxes and reserve requirements. These favorable conditions permit international banks to take advantage of the lower cost of funds. They can then lend to international borrowers at lower rates than those found in domestic money and capital markets. The cost effectiveness of this international financial intermediation has led to an increase of global depositors and lenders in the market. Eurobanks efficiently mobilize and channel world capital from areas of surplus to areas of deficit under extremely competitive conditions.

Eurobanks face difficulties that arise from the challenge of managing funding and lending efficiently and effectively on a global basis. These banks also accept calculated risks: country risk, legal risk, foreign exchange risk, sovereign risk, credit risk, and market risk.

The efficient allocation of funds by Eurobanks benefits both lenders and borrowers. Lenders obtain higher yields than those available in their domestic markets, while borrowers benefit from access to low cost funds. For example, many developing countries borrowed Eurodollars in the 1960s to promote domestic economic development. In the 1970s they borrowed Eurocurrency for trade financing. A capital-importing country may find that external credit boosts domestic production, employment, and the GNP; this credit may also help its income distribution should the economic pie grow larger.

Many industrialized countries have benefited from the Eurocurrency market. For instance, the United Kingdom has benefited financially because London has been the hub of the Eurocurrency market. Italian and French public utilities have frequently been borrowers in the market. Even U.S.-based multinational corporations use the Eurocurrency market as an important channel for storing surplus cash and financing worldwide operations. These corporate projects stimulate the worldwide economy.

Many developing countries have also benefited from the Eurocurrency market. As the B15 1995 annual report indicated, Thailand, Brazil, and Chile borrowed substantial amounts from the Eurocurrency market in 1995 for improving their national economies.

EFFECTS ON NATIONAL MONETARY POLICIES

According to a survey by the Federal Reserve Bank of St. Louis,* inflation results when spending grows faster than real output. If excess spending occurs because the quantity of money grows faster than the desire to hold money, Eurodollar transactions can increase inflation only if they reduce either the growth of output or people's desire to hold money, or increase the amount of money in existence. The extent to which the Eurodollar market has reduced the demand for domestic currencies remains uncertain. Consequently, if the Eurodollar market contributes to inflation, it must do so either by increasing the amount of money in existence or impeding control of the domestic money stock.

This study further argues that the Eurodollar system can expand credit by a multiple of its reserves but that it cannot create money since its liabilities, unlike those of domestic banks, are not generally acceptable as a means of payment. The multiplier framework presented in the study is used to examine Eurodollar-induced effects on the money stock. Based on estimates over the period 1973–1979—a period of rapid growth in the Eurodollar market—Eurodollar flows were shown to have only minor effects on the U.S. money stock. This evidence warrants the conclusion that the Eurodollar market does not pose a serious threat to the Federal Reserve's ability to control the money supply.

In regard to the interest rate effect on national monetary policy, a study appearing in the *Journal of Banking and Finance*† provided an interesting analysis. It was based on daily observations for three-month maturity yields on Eurodollar deposits and negotiable CDs during the period 2 July 1973 through 30 April 1984. The study

---

* Balbach, Anatoal B., and David H. Resler. "Eurodollars and the U.S. Money Supply." *Federal Reserve Bank of St. Louis Review.* June/July 1980.

† Swanson, Peggy E. "The International Transmission of Interest Rates." *Journal of Banking and Finance,* 12 (1988) 563–573.

found that the effectiveness of government policies was not heavily dependent upon the level of rates in existence or the degree of volatility exhibited by yields. In addition, domestic CD yields responded more slowly to changes in Eurodollar yields than Eurodollar yields responded to changes in domestic CD yields. No evidence is found to support the opposing conclusions. In other words the Eurodollar market adjusts more rapidly and more completely to changes in the domestic market than the domestic market adjusts to changes in the Eurodollar market. From the national policy standpoint the U.S. domestic market is not independent of external market disturbances, but the response to changes appears to be slower and of lesser magnitude than the response of external markets to domestic market changes.

The Eurocurrency and foreign exchange markets are interrelated. A loss of confidence in one of those markets can exert destabilizing pressures on the other. It is generally agreed that the Eurocurrency market can exert strong effects on the foreign exchange market, especially in times of financial crisis. For example, after the collapse of Bank Herstatt and Franklin National Bank in 1974–1975, investors borrowed funds from the Eurocurrency market and carried out speculation and arbitrage among major currencies such as the U.S. dollar and deutsche mark. United States monetary authorities had to mobilize $30 billion to defend the U.S. dollar in the international exchange markets in 1978.

Eurocurrency Deposit Instruments

The primary purpose of Eurobanks operating in the Eurocurrency market is to accept deposits, to adjust their liquidity positions in the interbank market, and to lend to ultimate borrowers for profit. Volatile interest rates and foreign exchange rates make operations in the market more precarious. The risk of overlending, overborrowing, or suffering a loss from maturity mismatches is always present. To balance their worldwide liability and asset management in this arena, banks must devote substantial resources to forecast market changes and environmental factors such as changes in government regulations and policies.

In terms of Eurocurrency deposit instruments, there are two types: time deposits and Euro-CDs.

TIME DEPOSITS

The principal instrument of the Eurocurrency market is the nonnegotiable time deposit. When investing in a Eurocurrency time deposit, the depositor commits funds for a certain period of time at a specified interest rate. The depositor cannot withdraw these funds before the maturity date. At maturity the depositor receives the principal plus the interest. Other instruments include negotiable certificates of deposit (NCDs or simply called CDs). The Eurocurrency market is a wholesale market, and demand deposits are not used. Based on Bank of England statistics, unsecured "clean" time deposits accounted for about 90% and CDs for about 10% of the total.

Most Eurocurrency time deposits mature in less than one year. As Exhibit 6.3 indicates, Eurocurrency time deposits have various maturities: call, overnight, one month, three months, six months, and 12 months. Time deposits with maturities over one year account for a very small percentage of the market. Exhibit 6.3 also shows that Eurocurrency deposit rates vary among currencies and maturities. Deposits are loosely related to the interest rates prevailing in the domestic market of the same currency denomination. The great bulk of Eurocurrency deposits carry

EXHIBIT 6.3   **Euro-Currency Interest Rates**

AUG 7	Short Term	7 DAYS Notice	One Months	Three Months	Six Months	One Year
Belgian Franc	3 11/32 - 3 5/32	3 9/32 - 3 3/16	3 11/32 - 3 7/32	3 3/8 - 3 1/4	3 13/32 - 3 3/8	3 5/8 - 3 19/32
Danish Krone	3 13/32 - 3 5/32	3 29/32 - 3 11/16	3 7/8 - 3 3/4	3 15/16 - 3 13/16	4 1/16 - 3 29/32	4 5/16 - 4 5/32
D-Mark	3 5/16 - 3 9/32	3 3/8 - 3 1/4	3 7/16 - 3 3/8	3 11/32 - 3 7/32	3 5/16 - 3 1/16	3 15/32 - 3 11/32
Dutch Guilder	2 7/8 - 2 1/4	2 15/16 - 2 13/16	2 31/32 - 2 29/32	3 1/32 - 2 31/32	3 3/16 - 3 3/32	3 7/16 - 3 11/32
French Franc	3 5/8 - 3 1/2	3 23/32 - 3 19/32	3 11/16 - 3 3/16	3 25/32 - 3 21/32	3 29/32 - 3 25/32	4 3/32 - 3 15/16
Portuguese Esc.	7 9/16 - 7 7/16	7 1/2 - 7 7/16	7 15/32 - 7 3/8	7 11/32 - 7 9/32	7 5/16 - 7 1/4	7 1/4 - 7 1/8
Spanish Peseta	7 17/32 - 7 7/16	7 1/2 - 7 11/32	7 7/16 - 7 5/16	7 5/16 - 7 3/16	7 1/4 - 7 1/8	6 1/16 - 6
Sterling	5 3/4 - 5 1/2	5 3/4 - 5 11/16	5 13/16 - 5 3/4	5 25/32 - 5 23/32	5 13/16 - 5 3/4	5 15/16 - 5 7/8
Swiss Franc	2 3/8 - 2 1/4	2 5/8 - 2 3/16	2 1/4 - 2 1/8	2 3/8 - 2 1/4	2 1/2 - 2 3/8	2 5/8 - 2 1/2
Can. Dollar	4 5/8 - 4 7/16	4 7/16 - 4 1/4	4 3/8 - 4 1/4	4 7/16 - 4 5/16	4 1/2 - 4 3/8	4 7/8 - 4 3/4
US Dollar	5 5/16 - 5 5/16	5 5/16 - 5 5/16	5 3/8 - 5 5/16	5 3/8 - 5 5/16	5 5/8 - 5 7/16	5 7/8 - 5 11/16
Italian Lira	8 7/8 - 8 3/4	9 1/4 - 8 15/16	8 29/32 - 8 3/4	8 17/32 - 8 13/32	8 7/16 - 8 11/32	8 9/32 - 8 5/32
Yen	15/32 - 11/32	17/32 - 13/32	17/32 - 13/32	3/4 - 1/4	25/32 - 5/8	1 1/8 - 1
Asian $Sing	3 1/4 - 3 1/8	3 3/8 - 3 1/4	3 1/2 - 3 3/8	3 1/2 - 3 3/8	3 1/2 - 3 3/8	3 5/8 - 3 1/2

Short term rates are call for the US Dollar and Yen, others: two days' notice.

SOURCE: *Financial Times,* 8 August 1996: p. 19.

a fixed maturity. Deposits are effective immediately or overnight. Normally the deposit will be effective two business days after the contract is in effect, and mature, for example, 90 days later. On maturity, payment is normally made by means of transfer in the currency's home country (e.g., United States for Eurodollars). The minimum practical period for delivery of funds is usually two days, similar to payments in the foreign exchange market where two working days are required for delivery.

CERTIFICATES OF DEPOSIT

Although the majority of Eurodeposits are in the form of time deposits, CDs play an important role in the market because of their liquidity in the secondary market. Banks often buy and sell their own CDs in a secondary market to assure the investor liquidity, making their CDs more attractive to short-term investors. When a Eurobank issues a new CD, it specifies the amount of the deposit, the maturity date, the rate of interest, and the term under which the interest is calculated. For example, if IBM places $5 million in a three-month CD with the Citibank branch in London at an interest rate of 10%, the interest due is simply calculated as follows:

$$\% \text{ interest} \times \frac{\text{days to maturity}}{1 \text{ year}} \times \text{deposit amount} = \text{earned interest}$$

$$\frac{10}{100} \times \frac{91}{360} \times \$5,000,000 = \$126,388.80$$

We refer to the interest rate on negotiable CDs as the primary market rate. This rate is determined by market forces and directly negotiated between the issuer and depositor. The CD rates shown in newspapers are usually the secondary market rates. Most CDs issued in London are denominated in U.S. dollars, but some are also denominated in British pound sterling, Japanese yen, Hong Kong dollar and

European Currency Units (ECUs). The West German and Swiss central banks have resisted the introduction of CDs denominated in deutsche mark and Swiss franc, since such a flexible and negotiable instrument could become a vehicle of currency speculation. Also, their existence might undermine efforts of monetary authorities to influence the foreign exchange and money markets. However, CDs have been popular in Singapore, Nassau, and Tokyo.

There are normally three types of CDs: "tap" CDs, "tranche" CDs, and "rollover" CDs. Tap CDs are fixed-time deposits. The conventional tap CDs are denominated in large amounts of $1 million or more. Tap CDs appeal to large international depositors.

The term "tranche" means that the CDs are divided into several portions, and appeal to investors who prefer an instrument with smaller denominations. Investors buy tranche CDs through brokers or investment bankers.

Rollover CDs are contractual deposits agreed to by issuer and investor. The investor will buy a CD from the issuer on a continuous basis with floating interest rates adjusted by market conditions when the CD matures, and rollovers (renewals) occur.

Many CDs, such as dollar CDs and yen CDs, are issued in London. According to the *Bank of England Quarterly Bulletin,* nonsterling CDs and other short-term paper (not Euro-commercial paper) issued in London increased from $114 billion in 1986 to $155 billion in 1988. The U.K. banks accounted for 50% of this total, with Japanese banks accounting for 24%, American banks 8%, and the remaining foreign banks 18%.* Eurobanks in London that issue Eurodollar CDs to raise funds for international lending enjoy many advantages. No interest is withheld on London CDs meeting the normal standards and with maturities over seven days, and there is no stamp tax levied on London CDs.

Settlement for dollar CDs is made by payment of funds in New York, usually through CHIPs (Clearing House Interbank Payments System), although some payments are made on Fedwire. The actual payment is made for value the same day the CD is presented in London for payment. First Chicago Clearing Center is currently the major clearing and settling organization. Only a small share of London CDs, perhaps 5–10%, is held in Euro-clear or Cedel.

Eurocurrency Interbank Market

Eurocurrency Interbank Market

Eurobanks trade Eurocurrency from each other for profit.

The Eurocurrency Interbank Market plays a dominant role in channeling funds from lenders in one country to borrowers in another country. More than 1000 banks from more than 50 different countries participate in this market. The major currencies used for interbank trading are U.S. dollars, Japanese yen, German marks, British sterling, Swiss francs, French francs, and Dutch guilders.

Eurodollar futures and options play an important role in the interbank market. These were initiated by the International Monetary Market (IMM) Division of the Chicago Mercantile Exchange (CME) in 1972. The Singapore International Monetary Exchange (SIMEX), in cooperation with the IMM, established its own financial futures and options market in 1984. The London International Financial Futures and options Exchange (LIFFE) opened in September 1982 and quickly became the largest futures exchange outside the United States. The U.S., U.K., and

---

* Bank of England, *Quarterly Bulletin,* (August, 1989): Table 3.1–3.6.

EXHIBIT 6.4	Interbank Lending between Banks in the BIS Reporting Area (in $ Billion)			
	FLOWS		TOTAL STOCK OUTSTANDING	
	1986	1990	1995	1995
Gross international lending	654	714	651	9,224
International interbank lending	520	396	337	4,579
Interbank lending as % of gross international lending	79%	55%	52%	50%

SOURCE: BIS *Annual Report,* various issues.

Singapore exchanges are in different time zones, facilitating interbank trading on a global basis.

The Clearing House for Interbank Payments (CHIPS) settles all Eurodollar market transactions for accounts in the United States. The Society for Worldwide Interbank Financial Transactions (SWIFT) provides important support for interbank payments and money transfers through its high-speed computerized message routing system (see description in Chapter 4). The SWIFT system connects several thousand banks located around the globe, providing rapid message delivery. These messages include payments instructions, acknowledgements of received funds, and clarification on how to make international payments.

IMPORTANCE OF THE MARKET

Exhibit 6.4 presents data on international interbank lending by amount and as percentage of gross international lending. In 1986 interbank lending represented 79% of total flows. In 1990 interbank lending represented 55% of total flows. In 1995 it represented 52%. The total market size of international interbank lending in 1995 was nearly $4.6 trillion, or 50% of the outstanding stock.

The *BIS Annual Report* points out that the rapid expansion of the interbank market in 1986 was largely the result of a surge in interbank business within the reporting area. This unusual buoyancy of the interbank market can be ascribed to several factors; the increased role of banks in the securities markets, interest rate expectations and arbitrage, the growing role of Japanese banks with a traditionally high share of interbank claims, and the opening of the Japan Offshore market (discussed later).

In 1990–1991, international bank lending declined due to economic slowdowns in the United States, Japan, and Europe. In 1995, reduction in international bank lending by Japanese banks was noticeable, but other banking groups such as German banks gained more market shares. (See Exhibit 6.5). This was known as "Japan Premium".

"Japan Premium"

The retrenchment in Japanese banks' foreign lending due to their domestic financial problems led to strong expansion in international lending of other banking groups, notably German banks.

DEFINITIONS OF INTERBANK MARKET

Interbank Eurocurrency trading is conducted both within a Eurocurrency center and between Eurocurrency centers. This trading includes placements with head offices and foreign branches of banks chartered in other countries as these banks finance

EXHIBIT 6.5	**Total International Bank Lending by Nationality of Reporting Banks***

Percentage shares; end of period

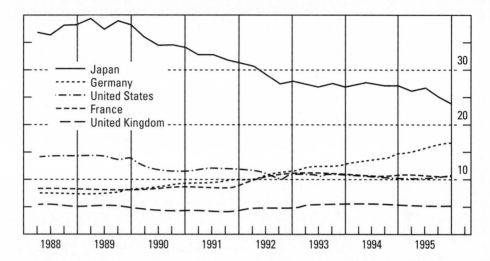

* Amounts outstanding at end of period of banks' cross-border claims and local claims in foreign currency.

SOURCE: BIS *International Banking and Financial Market Development*. Basle, May 1996: 7.

loans to nonbanks. Interbank trading tends to be concentrated in banks of industrial countries, particularly in the G-10 countries and Switzerland. As reported by the BIS, more than 50% of interbank claims of American banks were against banks in the big five: Canada, France, Germany, Japan, and the United Kingdom.

STRUCTURE AND FUNCTIONS OF THE MARKET

The players in the market include banks, money brokers, central banks or monetary authorities, and major corporations. In periods of high oil prices the monetary authorities of OPEC countries became important suppliers of funds to banks. At times some of these monetary authorities became borrowers. Multinational corporations have been major suppliers as well as borrowers of short-term funds to banks. Often banks use the services of international money brokers who have worldwide connections and can provide speedy execution in the volatile financial world. These transactions occur when banks find it important to handle interbank deals directly, especially when changing market conditions put a premium on speed of execution.

The Eurocurrency interbank market provides at least four interrelated functions.* The first is a distribution function. Banks in one country receiving funds from depositors may shift their liquidity to other banks for ultimate loan and investment. Second, the market performs a hedging function through which banks can buy and sell foreign currency assets and liabilities of different maturities. This function permits them to hedge their exposure to interest rate and foreign exchange risk. Third,

---

* For detail, see Anthony Saunders, "The Eurocurrency Interbank Market: Potential for International Crisis?" Federal Reserve Bank of Philadelphia, *Business Review* January/February 1988.

this market provides a convenient mechanism in which to borrow funds to adjust balance sheet positions. Fourth, channeling funds through the interbank market makes it possible to avoid regulations such as reserve requirements and deposit insurance fees, minimizing the cost of funds. International banks depend heavily on the international interbank market when funding loans to nonbanks abroad. For example, a bank will minimize taxes on profit. When it funds a loan in a high-tax country such as the United Kingdom, it books the loan in a center such as the Cayman Islands where taxes are low. This function permits the banks to widen the spread between borrowing and lending rates for higher profits.

How the Market Works

The Eurocurrency market works through a network of telecommunication lines. Banks in Eurocurrency centers throughout the world—especially in London, Tokyo, Hong Kong, Singapore, New York, Paris, and Zurich—bid for funds and offer funds to other banks.

Interbank deposits are normally limited to short-term placements at fixed rates. A bank's money traders, or money brokers, usually arrange these deposits in amounts of $5–10 million and sometimes up to $50 million. Trading is normally limited to institutions of good credit standing. Transactions are conducted on an informal basis, and no prior contract is required. Deals can be arranged in a matter of minutes or within an hour and are simply confirmed by telex between the parties involved. The bulk of the deposit placements are short-term, three months or less. Deposits of six months or a year are more rare. The bank's treasury department normally conducts the deals.

Interest rates in the Eurocurrency interbank market are very competitive. Differences among centers and between domestic and offshore markets tend to be arbitraged away in a short period of time, since the traders can obtain information about the ebb and flow of market demand and supply rather quickly from each other. For this reason, interbank margins are low or nonexistent.

Under normal circumstances the market not only keeps funds fully employed but also provides liquidity. To meet such requirements, banks ordinarily maintain only enough short-term deposits to provide loans and a comfortable cushion of liquid assets (including other banks' CDs and interbank placements of various maturities).

However, difficulties may occur in times of financial crisis. During the worldwide financial crisis in 1974–1975, there was a large amount of call deposits that could be withdrawn on only one day's notice by the depositor. When Bank Herstatt collapsed in 1974, the Eurocurrency interbank market adopted a practice of "tiering" deposit rates. That is, different tiers or levels of interest rates were applied to different Eurobanks depending on how other market participants evaluated each Eurobank's credit worthiness. At that time interbank deposit rates reflected the existence of six or more tiers of Eurobanks, depending on credit ranking.

International banks that need foreign currency normally find a swap transaction in the exchange market the most convenient method to obtain the required funds. Banks obtain funds but, lacking available nonbank borrowers, may use them in other markets such as the swap market. Arbitrage between deposits in two currencies in the swap market is illustrated in the following example.

A London bank is offered a three-month pound sterling deposit at the interest rate of 10%, but the bank has no lending opportunity for the funds at the present time. However, the London bank can accept the sterling deposit, sell the sterling for dollars, invest the dollars for three months in the U.S. money market, and cover with a forward contract. The bank checks the information in the foreign exchange market and money market. It can buy spot sterling at $1.5675 and sell it 90 days forward $1.5760. The bank would receive a premium of .0085 ($1.5760 − $1.5675) per pound for selling sterling forward. At the same time, the bank can lend three-month dollars in the United States at the interest rate of 12.5%.

The following calculation shows that to sell sterling spot and to buy it back forward will cost:

$$\frac{\text{forward rate} - \text{spot rate}}{\text{spot rate}} \times \frac{365}{90} \times 100 = \frac{.0085}{1.5675} \times \frac{365}{90} \times 100$$

$$= 2.199\%$$

The bank must pay 10% for the deposit plus 2.199% for the cost of the swap, making a total cost of $12.199%. Since the bank can lend at 12.5%, it will make profit of approximately 0.30% (12.5 − 212.199%) in this deal. If the sterling deposit is £1,000.000, the bank can make a total profit of £3,000 in this transaction.

In the international interbank market, Eurodollar arbitrage activities can be classified as "outward" or "inward" arbitrage, depending on the direction funds flow in response to interest rate incentives. A U.S. bank typically purchasing domestic funds by issuing large CDs and redepositing those funds with its offshore branches would be an example of outward arbitrage. If the branches then redeposit the funds in the interbank Euromarket or make new loans to nonbank borrowers, outward arbitrage will increase the size of the bank's worldwide consolidated balance sheet. While outward arbitrage is usually related to costs in the domestic CD market, the U.S. bank can utilize other domestic sources, e.g., bank holding company commercial paper.

Inward arbitrage primarily occurs when U.S. banks shift their funding from domestic to external sources. When domestic demands are strong and CD rates are high, active international banks in the United States are quick to tap the Eurodollar interbank market for cheaper funds. This technique of liability management represents the typical version of inward arbitrage and promotes a close relationship between the external and domestic costs of funds to U.S. banks.

RISKS IN THE MARKET AND LENDER OF LAST RESORT

Bank participants in the interbank market are confronted with several risks. These include credit (default) risk, market risk, country risk, foreign exchange risk, crisis-effort risk, liquidity risk, and political risk. These risks are described and illustrated in Exhibit 6.7.

To cope with these risks, banks in the interbank market often establish an "Asset-Liability" Committee composed of a bank's senior officers. The committee is assisted by a host of experts in different fields, e.g., economists, accountants, and lawyers. It is particularly important for the bank to collect information on any changes on a worldwide basis to carry out risk management policy and its implementation. The capability of a bank to handle crisis situations is enhanced by coordination with other affected banks and the central bank.

Since an interbank crisis can affect a nation's banking system and the international banking system, the central banks' role as lender of last resort becomes vitally

EXHIBIT 6.6 **Outward and Inward Arbitrage**

Incentives for outward and inward bank arbitrage can best be illustrated by using some numerical examples.

OUTWARD ARBITRAGE

Given the following information:

Three-month secondary certificate of deposit (CD) rate = 10.00%, (CD_{US})
Three-month Eurodollar bid rate = 12.00% (ED_{BID})
Federal Deposit Insurance Corporation (FDIC) Insurance premium = 0.037% (P_{FDIC})
CD reserve requirement = 8% = 0.08 (R_{CD})

To determine whether an outward arbitrage incentive exists, calculate the effective cost of domestic funds.

$$\text{Effective cost of domestic funds} = \frac{CD_{US} + P_{FDIC}}{1 - R_{CD}}$$

$$\frac{10.00\% + 0.037\%}{(1 - 0.08)} = 10.91\%$$

This calculation indicates that a bank could make a profit of 109 basis points

Profit on outward arbitrage = Eurodollar Bid Rate − Effective cost

= 12.00% − 10.91% on an outward arbitrage transaction. As banks begin to act on this opportunity, they will bid up CD rates and push down Eurodollar rates until the incentive is eliminated. For example:

Three-month secondary CD rate = 10.50%
Three-month Eurodollar bid rate = 11.45%

Now the effective cost of domestic funds is

$$\text{Effective Cost} = \frac{CD_{US} + P_{FDIC}}{1 - R_{CD}}$$

(10.50% + 0.037%)/(1 − 0.08) = 11.45%. The effective cost of domestic funds equals the external value of those funds to the U.S. bank; no incentive for outward arbitrage is present. Note that the Eurodollar-domestic rate differential has been narrowed from 200 to 95 basis points by bank arbitrage. Other things equal, this could imply reduced incentives for U.S. depositors to place funds offshore and increased incentives for U.S. borrowers to acquire funds offshore.

INWARD ARBITRAGE

Suppose the following information is known:

Three-month secondary CD rate = 10.00%
Three-month Eurodollar offer rate = 10.30%
FDIC insurance premium = 0.037%
CD reserve requirement = 12% = 0.12
Eurodollar reserve requirement = 6% = 0.06, (ED_{RR})

To determine whether an inward arbitrage incentive exists, the effective costs of both domestic and external funds must be calculated:

$$\text{Effective cost of domestic funds} = 10.00\% + \frac{0.037\%}{(1 - 0.12)} = 11.40\%$$

$$\text{Effective cost of external funds} = \frac{10.30\%}{(1 - 0.06)} = 10.96\%$$

Even though the nominal cost of Eurodollar funds in 30 basis points higher than the nominal cost of domestic funds, the **effective** cost of Eurodollar funds is actually 44 basis point **lower** than the effective cost of domestic funds. U.S. banks will have an incentive to obtain Eurodollars from their offshore branches in lieu of issuing new CDs. This activity will put upward pressure on the Eurodollar rate and downward pressure on the CD rate until effective costs are equalized. For example:

Three-month secondary CD rate = 9.90%
Three-month Eurodollar offer rate = 10.61%

$$\text{Effective Cost Domestic Funds} = \frac{CD_{US} + P_{FDIC}}{1 - R_{CD}}$$

$$\text{Effective Eurodollar Funds} = \frac{ED_{bid}}{1 - ED_{RR}}$$

The effective cost of domestic funds now equals (9.90% + 0.037%)/(1 − 0.12) = 11.29%, while the effective cost of Eurodollar funding has risen to (10.61%)/(1 − 0.06) = 11.29%. Since the effective costs have been equalized, no incentive for inward arbitrage remains. Note that the Eurodollar-domestic rate differential has been widened from 30 to 71 basis points by bank arbitrage. Other things equal, this could imply increased incentives for U.S. depositors to place funds offshore and reduced incentives for U.S. borrowers to acquire funds offshore.

SOURCE: Federal Reserve Bank of New York, *Quarterly Review* (Summer 1982): 12.

| **EXHIBIT 6.7** | **Risks Faced by Bank Participants in the Interbank Market** |

Bank participants in the interbank market are confronted with the following risks:

1. *Credit (default) Risk.* The borrowing bank or corporation may not be able to service or repay the loan. Loans and deposits in this market are uncollateralized.

2. *Market Risk.* Unexpected fluctuations in interest rates may cause problems in a bank's funding sources. Borrowers also may have difficulty in repaying, since the interbank market is based on floating interest rates (LIBOR or prime that are unstable, especially under inflationary conditions).

3. *Country Risk.* A country may prevent its banks from repaying loans or deposits received from banks in other countries (e.g., Russian revolution in 1919 and Cuba in 1961). A nation's worsening balance of payments position and drastic decrease in international reserves can also prevent the debtor (including government borrower) from servicing or repaying syndicated loans.

4. *Foreign Exchange Risk.* Drastic change in foreign exchange rates may make it difficult for a bank to manage interbank assets and liabilities. For example, the down valuation of the U.S. dollar and the up valuation of the Japanese yen in the period 1985–1987 adversely impacted the balance sheet structures of many international commercial banks and negatively affected their profits.

5. *Liquidity Risk.* A sudden withdrawal of interbank deposits by other banks may force a bank to sell other assets to meet its obligations at a loss.

6. *Crisis-effect Risk.* Whenever a worldwide financial crisis occurs—as in 1974 (Herstatt and Franklin National), or the LDC debt crisis in 1982 (Mexico and Brazil), or domestic bank failure in 1984 (Continental Illinois)—fear of the domino effect exists.

7. *Political Risk.* The U.S. authorities imposed freezes on Iranian (1979) and Libyan (1985) dollar assets.

---

important. As a lender of last resort, central banks assist banks that are illiquid by providing short-term credits. In this way, central banks help troubled banks and provide confidence to the banking community. For example, after the collapse of the Herstatt Bank in 1974, the Basle Committee, composed of central banks of the Group of 10 major industrial countries (under the auspices of the Bank for International Settlements) established principles for the supervision of banks by their respective central banks and supervision of liquidity by their respective monetary authorities.

Eurocurrency Lending

Lending in the Eurocurrency market has changed fundamentally over the past two decades. In the 1960s the major suppliers of funds in the market were central banks and financial institutions in Europe, while the major borrowers were U.S. commercial banks and multinational corporations involved in financing overseas direct investments. Other countries, such as Japan, also borrowed from the Eurocurrency market for purposes of trade financing. From 1970–1981 the main suppliers of funds were the OPEC countries and nonbanks, while the main borrowers of funds were oil importers from developing and developed countries. Canada and Japan also were net borrowers during this period. Eurocurrency lending fell into a state of recession from 1982 to 1983 due to the LDC debt crisis. In 1984–1985 major suppliers and borrowers in the market were the creditworthy developed countries such as

EXHIBIT 6.8	Borrowing on the Eurocurrency Market (in $ Billion)							
Instruments	**1986**	**1987**	**1988**	**1990**	**1991**	**1992**	**1994**	**1995**
Syndicated Loans	52.4	91.7	127.1	124.5	116.0	117.9	236.2	370.2
Note Issuance Facilities (NIFs)	24.8	29.0	13.2	4.3	1.9	1.7	—	—
Other Committed Facilities	4.5	2.2	2.3	2.7	5.8	5.0	4.9	3.8
Commercial Paper Programs	59.0	55.8	57.3	48.3	35.9	28.9	30.8	55.9
MTN programs	8.6	15.2	19.5	17.9	44.3	99.0	222.1	346.1
Total	149.3	193.9	219.4	197.7	203.9	252.5	494.0	776.0

NOTE: MTN = Medium-term note. In the 1990–1995 period, international bonds have also grown rapidly from $229.9 billion to $467.3 billion.

SOURCE: OECD *Financial Market Trends.* (February 1991, February 1993, and June 1996).

Sweden and the U.S. In 1986–1987 there was a shift in the composition of international credit flows away from long-term securities markets toward commercial bank mediation and short-term securities financing. In this period the major sources of funds were U.K. and U.S. nonbank entities while the largest borrowers were Japanese corporations and banks in the United States. As indicated in Exhibit 6.8, total borrowing in the Eurocurrency market increased, particularly in syndicated loans, commercial paper programs, and medium-term note programs. These instruments are analyzed in the following sections.

SYNDICATED BANK LOANS

Origin and Nature   In the late 1960s, Bankers Trust organized the first *syndicated bank loan* in an effort to arrange a large credit for Austria. Before this innovation borrowers could only obtain large amounts of funds by issuing Eurobonds. From the lender's viewpoint, banks use the syndication procedure to diversify the unique risk inherent in public-sector borrowers. This sector has accounted for more than 70% of syndicated lending. Syndication allows different sized banks, large or small, to participate in the loans and share the risk and profits in a single transaction. From the borrower's viewpoint, syndication allows for arrangement of a larger amount of funds than any single lender can possibly supply. This arrangement was an important consideration in the 1970s when the needs for financing balance of payments deficits by country borrowers were increasing. In the 1990s syndicated loans are important for financing mergers and acquisitions and national projects.

The life of a syndicated loan usually ranges from three to eight years. Syndicated loans comprise approximately 40–58% of Eurocurrency loans, as Exhibit 6.8 indicates. Borrowers located in the OECD area (see Exhibit 6.9) constitute the majority of the syndicated loans in the period 1987–1995. The second largest borrower group was the LDCs with acceptable credit standing. Loans not made in the form of syndicated credits bear shorter maturity. In such cases, borrowers are usually from the private sector, with loan funds used for trade financing or internationally related business transactions.

Growth and Development   According to BIS Annual Reports, the syndicated loan market grew rapidly from $4.7 billion in 1970 to $76 billion in 1980, due to

EXHIBIT 6.9	**Types of Borrowers in Syndicated Bank Loans**							
Borrowers	**1986**	**1987**	**1988**	**1990**	**1991**	**1992**	**1994**	**1995**
OECD area	36.3	66.8	105.5	101.0	87.8	99.1	211.5	328.2
Eastern Europe	2.7	2.9	2.7	3.0	0.1	0.2	0.8	0.5
OPEC	3.5	2.2	1.3	6.9	15.6	5.0	—	—
Other LDCs	8.4	17.9	14.0	12.9	11.1	11.5	23.6	41.5
International Development Institutions	—	1.6	2.5	0.4	0.6	1.0	0.3	—
Other	1.5	0.3	1.1	0.3	0.8	1.1	—	—
Total	**52.4**	**91.7**	**127.1**	**124.5**	**116.0**	**117.9**	**236.2**	**370.2**

SOURCE: OECD *Financial Market Trends* (February 1991, February 1993, and June 1996): 133.

Syndicated Bank Loans

A group of international banks join together and provide large amounts to international borrowers in the Eurocurrency market.

heavy borrowing from the nonoil developing countries. After the debt crisis of 1982 the volume of syndicated bank loans dropped to low levels from 1983–1985. They increased again after 1986, especially in 1988 when the volume reached $127 billion. In 1995 the volume was $370 billion. This was the highest level since the market's inception and was due to the extraordinary demand from nonbanks to finance mergers and acquisitions in Europe and in the United States, and to project financing in both developed and developing countries.

The Syndication Procedure   Although the syndicated Euroloan market is complex, its operation can be presented in a fairly simple fashion. An overview of the syndication procedure is presented in Exhibit 6.10.

1. The borrower must find a lead bank and discuss loan amount, currencies, and length of maturity of the desired credit.
2. The lead manager organizes the syndicate, consisting of lead manager (bank), comanagers (managing banks), and participating banks. Once the lead manager receives a mandate from the borrower, it issues a placement memorandum that invites other banks to participate in the loan. Participants in the loan are allocated to other banks who may be interested in taking up shares (the participating banks). It can take from 15 days to three months to arrange a syndication.
3. After arranging the loan the lead bank usually serves as agent to compute the appropriate interest rate charges. This term loan is usually repaid according to an amortization schedule that varies from loan to loan. Although the vast majority of syndicated loans are denominated in U.S. dollars, some are denominated in other acceptable currencies such as deutsche mark, Japanese yen, or Swiss franc. Sometimes multicurrency options are included in the legal agreements.
4. Payments schedule or loan rescheduling.

LIBOR

Short-term interest rates charged to banks in London when they borrow funds from each other.

The Pricing of Syndicated Loans   Interest on syndicated loans is usually computed by adding a spread to the London interbank offered rate (LIBOR), or by adding a spread to some other mutually agreed upon reference rate (United States prime rate, Singapore interbank offered rate (SIBOR), or U.K. base rate). Lenders usually offer many options to the borrower in relation to the cost structure of the loans and the location of the loans. Several factors determine the spread: 1) Is it the borrower's or the lender's market? 2) How strong is the borrower's credit standing? 3) What are the relationships between interest, maturity, and fee charges? For example, the longer the maturity, the higher the spread due to future uncertainty.

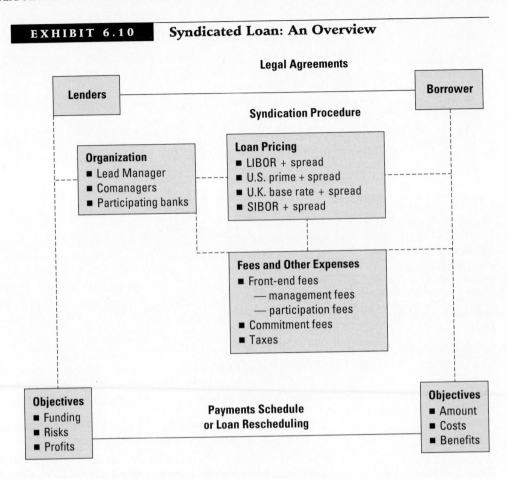

EXHIBIT 6.10 **Syndicated Loan: An Overview**

Some borrowers prefer higher fees but lower spreads in order to publicize lower spreads and the apparent better credit standing. The borrower is usually given a choice between a three-month or a six-month interest readjustment period under this pricing method. In general, the spreads range from 0.50% to 2.50% depending on the complexity of factors mentioned above.

In addition to the interest on a syndicated loan, the borrower can expect to pay management fees, participation fees, commitment fees, and taxes. Managing banks charge management fees for their services. These are one-time charges levied when the loan agreement is signed. Participation fees are divided among all banks in relation to their share of the loan. Commitment fees are charged to the borrower as a percentage of the undrawn portion of the credit and typically range from .25% to .50% annually. Other expenses include taxes which are a part of the overall cost of borrowing.

Loan Objectives Banks that participate in the Eurocurrency lending market must balance their liquidity positions and control their funding costs. Bank participation is based on the need to control revenues from the spread and fees. These revenues must be sufficient to overcome the risks confronting lenders in the market (Exhibit 6.11). Borrowers seek syndicated Eurocurrency loans based on loan costs versus the productivity of capital. Loan rescheduling is a last resort of the borrower if the borrower cannot meet scheduled payments set up in the loan agreement. The borrower seeks the lowest possible interest rate and loan costs over the life of the loan.

EXHIBIT 6.11	**Risk Protection Features of Syndicated Eurocredits**

Financial institutions participating in the Eurocurrency market normally face many risks. Compared with fixed rate credit arranged by an individual bank, the rollover syndicated Eurocredit reduces risk in several notable ways:

	LENDING RISKS	
Risk	**Source of risk**	**Risk reduction strategy**
Country risk	The ability and willingness of borrowers within a country to meet their obligations	Syndication of the credit and diversification of bank's loan portfolio
Credit Risk	The ability of an entity to repay its debts	Syndication of the credit and diversification of bank's loan portfolio
Interest risk	Mismatched maturities coupled with unpredictable movements in interest rates	Matching assets to liabilities by pricing credits on a rollover basis
Regulatory risk	Imposition of reserve requirements or taxes on the banks	A clause in the contract which forces the borrowers to bear this risk

SOURCE: Federal Reserve Bank of New York, *Quarterly Review* (Summer 1980):47.

NOTE ISSUANCE FACILITIES (NIFS) AND REVOLVING UNDERWRITING FACILITIES (RUFS)

NIFs are short-term notes underwritten by banks or guaranteed by bank standby credit arrangements. In 1985 many corporate borrowers found that it was difficult to borrow funds in the syndicated market that had suffered from the LDC debt crisis. NIFs were attractive to investors because they offered better liquidity through an active secondary market, better credits backed by banks, standby credits, and even higher yields. Principal arrangers of these transactions have been U.S. banks and investment banking houses that lost income as the syndicated market retrenched in the debt crisis. Another short-term innovation similar to NIFs is RUFs. Under the RUFs (Revolving Underwriting Loan Facility) arrangement, the lead manager is the sole placing agent. In this case a borrower uses a single bank to place its paper at a set price. All these Euronotes involve a variety of fees for underwriting commitments, management, and other services. Since 1994 the volumes of NIFs and RUFs have been categorically included into other committed facilities as shown in Exhibit 6.8.

EURO-COMMERCIAL PAPER

Commercial paper has been an important part of the U.S. money market for more than a century and was introduced to the Euromarket in the early 1980s. As Exhibit 6.8 shows, international borrowings through the issuance of Euro-commercial paper (ECP) have been sizable but fluctuating in the 1986–1995 period due to the competing popularity of Euro medium-term notes (MTN). This is discussed in the next section. This growth of ECP before 1988 was at the expense of the NIFs and RUFs (other commitment facilities). There have been several reasons for the growth of the ECP. First of all, there are many advantages to borrowers, corporations, and governments that can raise large amounts of funds with maturities suitable to their cash flows. The cost of funds is usually lower than bank loans and much less than syndicated loans. This arrangement does not require underwriting services such as NIFs. ECPs are mostly issued in U.S. dollars, and some of them are intended for swaps into other currencies. Another reason is that a commercial paper program can be set up in a few days, as opposed to more complex Euromarket instruments (syndicated loans). Also benefiting the ECP market is the publication of ECP rates by the Bank of England since 1987. The quality of the market has improved because all ECPs are rated by Moody's and Standard & Poor's. Although there are no publicly available statistics on the composition of the ECP investor base, it is internationally diversified with the largest pools of investors in Japan, Europe, and North America.

Special characteristics of the ECP differentiate it from domestic CP. Domestic CP is issued by large corporations, whereas ECP is issued by corporations and governments. ECP minimum denominations are $500,000, much larger than the $50,000 minimum for domestic CP. Domestic CP interest rates track close to CD rates, while ECP interest rates are closer to interbank rates. ECP may be issued in any currency, however, domestic CP is issued only in the national domestic currency.

According to the *BIS Annual Report* for 1992, both domestic CP and ECP have grown tremendously from 1986 to 1991. For example, in the United States, commercial paper increased from $325 billion to $528 billion. In the same period in Japan, the CP growth was from $0 to $99 billion, and ECP surged from $13 billion to $79 billion.

EURO MEDIUM-TERM NOTES (MTN)

MTN was pioneered by General Motors Acceptance Corporation (GMAC) in the United States domestic market (1978). MTNs were launched in Europe in 1986, but increased rapidly from $8.6 billion in 1986 to $346 billion in 1995 (see Exhibt 6.8).

From an issuer standpoint there are many advantages to MTNs. MTNs are flexible, liquid, and easy to issue. The maturities of MTNs range from nine months to 30 years, but two- to three-year maturity MTNs are most common. They can be issued in the form of zero-coupon bonds, or with floating or fixed rate and a tailored maturity. They can be issued with a range of currencies convenient for swaps. They are liquid because MTNs are listed on the Luxembourg exchange and to a lesser extent in London. MTNs are easy to issue because they can be placed through international bank dealers. Issuers include corporations and utilities from the United States, United Kingdom, France, Sweden, Japan, Australia, and Canada. The amounts range from $100 million to $1 billion.

Most investors (fund managers and trust companies) prefer two- to three-year alternative investments and anonymous "bearer" instruments. Financial institutions and central banks (including Japanese institutions) are also on the investment side for the flexibility and liquidity of MTN instruments.

Eurocurrency and Offshore Banking Centers

The Eurocurrency market is a part of the global financial market. Offshore banking centers are closely related to the Eurocurrency market. However, offshore banking centers can be regarded as a special category of international financial centers that serve as financial intermediaries primarily for nonresident borrowers and depositors. The primary attraction of an offshore banking center is the minimum amount of official regulation, including taxation and controls over portfolio decisions of banking units.

GENERAL CHARACTERISTICS

The emergence of offshore banking centers has been a special financial phenomenon since 1960 when the volume of Eurocurrency expanded rapidly. Many countries, especially small ones, discovered that by establishing offshore banking centers with operating advantages that attracted foreign banks, local employment could be increased. Also, through bank expenditures, licensing and other fees, these countries could improve their standard of living.

There are a number of characteristics that have contributed to the increase in offshore banking centers for Eurocurrency transactions. First, there is little or no regulation on the inflow and outflow of funds. Second, transactions must be purely international in nature without interfering with domestic economic and financial policies. Third, these centers offer efficient local and international communication and transportation facilities. Fourth, the offshore centers usually have good relations with key financial powers in industrial nations. Fifth, offshore centers enjoy domestic political stability and maintain financial transaction secrecy. Sixth, they maintain financial stability with a well-functioning central bank. Seventh, English is the major (or alternative) language. Eighth, offshore centers are easily accessible and are strategically located in time zones that often fall between major market time zones. Finally, these centers maintain a highly skilled work force.

THREE TYPICAL TYPES OF OFFSHORE MARKETS

There are three typical types of offshore markets. One approach involves special institutional arrangements within established financial centers such as Tokyo, New York, and Singapore. These markets all make provision for international banking facilities that have characteristics of offshore markets, as summarized in Exhibit 6.12. Under their rules special accounts are established separately from domestic ones, and these accounts can be exempt from restrictions that apply in the domestic financial market (for example, reserve requirements).

The second type is the London model. In London, Hong Kong, and other places, financial transactions are liberalized for both residents and nonresidents. In these locations, the "offshore" market is simply the onshore transactions between nonresidents since domestic and foreign transactions are integrated.

EXHIBIT 6.12	**Comparison of Types of Offshore Markets**					
	NEW YORK IBF TYPE (DOMESTIC & FOREIGN TRANSACTIONS SEPARATED)			**LONDON TYPE (DOMESTIC & FOREIGN TRANSACTIONS INTEGRATED)**		**TAX HAVEN TYPE**
Established Taxation:	**Tokyo Dec 1986**	**New York Dec 1981**	**Singapore Nov 1968**	**London End 1950s**	**Hong Kong 1957–1958**	**Bahamas and Caymans Late 1960s**
Corporate	yes	yes	yes	yes	yes	none
Other	local and stamp duty					Registration and licensing fees
Securities business allowed	none	none	yes	yes	yes	none

SOURCE: derived from *the Economist* (February 21, 1987):83.

The third type of offshore market is the tax haven. Offshore markets in the Bahamas and the Cayman Islands belong to this category. No tax is levied on transactions between nonresidents.

MAJOR OFFSHORE BANKING CENTERS

Offshore banking centers have grown considerably from the late 1960s to 1980s due to the growing Eurocurrency market, the advantages of establishing offshore banking units in some countries, and the efforts of some countries to attract offshore banking business to develop their own economic bases. Following Singapore and Bahamas in the late 1960s, Manila, Bahrain, and the Channel Islands established offshore banking markets in the 1970s. Latecomers were New York, Tokyo and Taipei (Taiwan) in the 1980s. Offshore financial centers continued to grow during the 1990s. For example, U.K. established three offshore financial centers: the Isle of Man, Jersey, and Guerney outside London; Malta and Cyprus are havens for Middle East and Russian Money; Bangkok International Banking facilities attract Asian and other foreign capital. Exhibit 6.13 indicates the selected Eurocurrency and offshore banking centers located in Europe, North and South America, and Asia. These centers play an important role in facilitating the flow of capital around the world for productive purposes.

Exhibit 6.14 shows the volume and shares of each of the Eurocurrency and offshore banking centers. The market share of the United Kingdom declined from 21.8% in 1986 to 16.3% in 1991 but regained its predominance in 1995. Japan increased its share from 10.5% to 15.1% but slid back to 10% in the same period. Simultaneously, the United States, ranking third, also experienced decreased shares from 14.4% to 9.4% but increased its share to 11.5% during the same period. Other offshore banking centers gained from 21.7% to 23%. These centers include Singapore, Hong Kong, and Taiwan, which are considered newly industrialized economies and active in offshore banking business.

EXHIBIT 6.13	**Location of Offshore Banking Centers**

As of the end of 1989, the noted Eurocurrency and offshore banking centers are as follows:

EUROPE

- London
- Paris
- Switzerland
- Luxembourg
- Frankfurt
- Brussels
- Amsterdam
- Channel Islands

WESTERN HEMISPHERE

- New York, Miami, Los Angeles, San Francisco
- Toronto
- Nassau
- Panama
- Cayman
- Bermuda
- Barbados
- Antigua
- Netherlands Antilles

ASIA

- Tokyo
- Singapore
- Hong Kong
- Taipei
- Manila
- Vanuatu
- Bahrain
- Bangkok

Due to limited space in this chapter, the following sections analyze a select few of the major offshore banking centers.

London   London is a major international financial center with well-developed capital, money, and foreign exchange markets. Here the Eurocurrency and offshore banking market is the largest in the world. London exhibits all the characteristics of an offshore banking center. These functions include providing a foreign currency market, serving as a net supplier of funds to world financial markets, and acting as an intermediary for international loan funds. London's prominent status as an off-shore market is attributable to the policy of the Bank of England in promoting the international role of London. Its liberal international banking policy has attracted a large number of foreign banks and international lenders as evidenced by the large foreign currency assets in the U.K. banking sector.

In the 1990s London still retained its predominance in the Eurocurrency and offshore markets owing primarily to the increased syndicated loans and derivative transactions plus speculative demand in currency and securities markets, as reflected in Exhibits 6.8 and 6.14.

Luxembourg   Luxembourg lacks the size and population of many of its European neighbors. Nevertheless, the nation has become a key player in the financial arena.

EXHIBIT 6.14	**External Lending**							

$ billions; *percentages in italics*

	STOCK	EXCHANGE RATE ADJUSTED FLOWS					STOCK	
	1986	1987	1989	1990	1991	1994	1991	1994
By center								
United Kingdom	*21.8*	90	55	86	−52	97	*16.3*	*17.9*
Japan	*10.5*	167	153	73	−36	22	*15.1*	*10.0*
United States	*14.4*	32	47	−28	7	−17	*9.4*	*11.5*
France	*6.2*	38	55	65	−15	−24	*6.6*	*7.7*
Switzerland	*3.3*	17	−6	46	−7	22	*6.3*	*4.7*
Germany	*4.4*	17	54	73	10	−13	*6.1*	*6.2*
Luxembourg	*4.3*	19	37	42	18	—	*5.0*	—
Belgium	*3.6*	17	20	23	2	—	*3.2*	—
Netherlands	*2.7*	9	22	22	7	−8	*2.9*	*2.3*
Italy	*1.8*	−2	19	2	5	−21	*1.5*	*3.2*
Offshore	*21.7*	182	211	183	−1	160	*23.3*	*23.0*
Other	*5.4*	11	19	23	6	49	*4.2*	*13.5*
Total	3,278	597	685	608	−56	267	6,240	7,135
Of which:								
Offshore	710	182	211	183	−1	160	1,456	1,636
Industrial area	2,568	415	474	425	−55	107	4,784	5,499
By currency								
US dollar	*58.3*	198	181	140	−78	127	*45.2*	*51.9*
Deutsche mark	*12.8*	35	64	67	−17	−15	*14.2*	*16.0*
Yen	*8.7*	128	113	43	−23	49	*13.7*	*5.1*
Swiss franc	*6.6*	2	−4	19	−7	−1	*5.1*	*3.3*
Sterling	*3.2*	14	24	34	−29	11	*4.2*	*3.1*
Ecu	*2.1*	8	21	21	16	−20	*3.6*	*4.2*
French franc	*2.1*	9	16	38	20	−40	*3.6*	*2.9*
Other	*6.2*	24	60	64	63	−4	*10.4*	*13.5*

NOTE: The first and last two columns indicate stock of outstanding lending. The middle five columns indicate annual flows of lending.

SOURCE: Bank of England, *Quarterly Bulletin* (May 1992):193. 1994 figures are calculated by the authors based on the BIS *Annual Report* 1995: 169–170.

In addition to being a major offshore banking center, Luxembourg is one of the founding members of the European Community (EC) and the headquarters of CEDEL (Eurobond Clearing) and the EIB (European Investment Bank).

Luxembourg, which has traditionally relied on the manufacturing industry as an important part of its economic base, has shifted its emphasis to developing financial service activities. Strategically located between France, Germany, and Belgium, its well-developed communications, multilingual residents, and relatively low cost of living have attracted many foreign banks, mutual funds, and investment companies. The strict practice of financial secrecy and low tax environment are keys to Luxembourg's success as an offshore banking center. For nonresident investors there is no withholding tax on investment income and bond coupons, no value added tax on physical gold transactions, no stamp duty, no capital gains tax, no dividend tax, no wealth tax, no exchange controls, or other restrictions on movement of funds. No other EC country except Holland offers these advantages. Many holding companies and foreign fund managers, particularly from the United States and the United Kingdom, have established tax-efficient bases in Luxembourg. As of 1995 there were more than 200 banks operating in Luxembourg.

Exhibit 6.14 shows that net lending to nonresidents from Luxembourg in the period 1987–1990 increased from $19 billion to $42 billion. It also shows that of the total international foreign currency lending, Luxembourg accounted for 5% of the total $6240 billion in 1991, ranking only behind the United Kingdom, Japan, United States, France, Switzerland, and Germany. The principal activities of banks in Luxembourg are in the Eurocurrency market, with the bulk of assets and liabilities denominated in deutsche mark. Of more than 200 banks, domestic and foreign, the largest local bank is the Caisse d'Eparque de L'Etat that conducts a large part of its activities with the nonbank resident sector. It also acts to help the quasi-central bank, the Institut Monetaire, to implement the government's interest rate policy.

According to the *Financial Times,* Luxembourg continues to enjoy its preeminence at the center of European investment funds, controlling 90% ($24 billion) of continental Europe's offshore fund assets. However, Luxembourg's greatest challenge is the arrival of the Euro in 1999 that may hit the banking sector, reducing foreign exchange dealing and Euromarket activities.*

Other European Offshore Banking Markets   France, Germany, and Switzerland are among other important international banking centers in Europe. According to Exhibit 6.14, France accounted for 7.7% and Germany for 6.2% of the total international lending market in 1994 while Switzerland shared 4.7%. There are many large French banks and foreign banks in Paris that have substantial foreign currency assets and lend actively to nonresidents. France does not offer a liberal banking regulatory environment to foreign banks, and the French franc is heavily protected and controlled.

Switzerland is a leading international banking center with liberal foreign exchange and tax regulation. Its foreign bond market is the largest followed by the United States and Japan. The Swiss stock market and gold market are also very active. The Swiss capital market provides an important alternative to Eurocurrency borrowers. Switzerland's most important international banking operations are its

---

* *Financial Times.* "Luxembourg" May 1996: II–III.

trustee accounts that are protected under the secrecy law via numbered bank accounts. Switzerland's international banking status owes much to the worldwide network of its "Big 3" commercial banks (Swiss Bank Corporation, Swiss Credit Bank, and Union Bank of Switzerland) that play a key role in managing the balance between inflows and outflows of international funds. In this environment international portfolio managers can flexibly invest funds in the capital market or deposit their liquid funds into the Eurocurrency market. The Appendix to Chapter 7, Switzerland—Financial Entrepôt, provides additional information concerning the international financial role of Switzerland.

Tokyo   Japan has played an increasingly important role in international finance since 1970, due to the strength of the yen, the rapid growth of exports and foreign exchange earnings, the aggressive competition among Japanese banks for global financial position, and the expansion of Japanese financial markets. Japan continued to play a leading role in international banking in the 1980s in view of its strong economic performance, huge current account surplus, enormous international banking assets, and the worldwide presence of its banks.

Japan has participated in the Eurocurrency market since the 1960s when it borrowed Eurocurrency to finance its domestic economy and overseas activities. The internationalization of the Japanese yen in the 1980s accelerated Japan's role in global finance. Exhibit 6.14 indicates the share of Japanese yen in international lending was 13.7%, second only to the U.S. dollar (45.2%) and deutsche mark (14.2%) in 1991, but declined to 5.1% in 1994.

The Japanese Offshore Market (JOM) was established on 1 December 1986 to promote the internationalization of the yen as well as to liberalize and internationalize Japan's financial markets, based on the model of New York's International Banking Facilities. The rapid growth of JOM is illustrated in Exhibit 6.15. In the period 1986–1988, Japan's international lending increased from $434 billion to $1155 billion, of which JOM's share increased from 26% to 48.0%. Since 1991 Japan's international lending declined but the JOM's share increased to over 60%.

As of June 1989, total assets of JOM were $461.8 billion (Exhibit 6.16), of which interoffice lending accounted for 53.1%, interbank deposits and call loans for 44.3%, and loans for 2.7%. In the borrower's category, the share of assets against nonresidents accounted for 77.8% of the total assets while residents accounted for 22.2%. In terms of currency, the yen shared 45.7% (and other currencies, 54.4%) of the total JOM assets in June 1989. Since 1990 no breakdowns of assets have been available in prevailing major publications.

EXHIBIT 6.15	**Japan's International Lending**					
	1986–1995 (in U.S.$ billion)					
	1986	**1987**	**1988**	**1991**	**1994**	**1995**
Total International						
Lending	434.0	768.8	1,155.0	942.4	1,007.6	1,099.3
Offshore Market	88.7	191.9	372.0	493.0	573.7	667.7
(as % of total)	(26.0)	(33.0)	(48.0)	(52.3)	(65.9)	(60.8)
Other	345.3	576.9	783.0	449.4	433.9	431.6
(as % of total)	(74.0)	(67.0)	(52.0)	(47.7)	(34.1)	(39.2)

SOURCES: Bank of England, *Quarterly Bulletin; Bank for International Settlements,* International Banking and Financial Market Development, various issues.

EXHIBIT 6.16   **Japan Offshore Banking Assets, June 1989 (in U.S.$ Billion)**

1) Type of Asset:

Interoffice Accounts	Total Assets	INTERBANK	
		Call Loans	Loans
245.1	461.8	204.4	12.3
(53.1%	100%)	(44.3%)	(2.7%)

2) Type of Asset: compared with opposite partner

Residents	Nonresidents
102.4	359.4
(22.2%)	(77.8%)

Yen	Others
211.2	250.6
(45.7%)	(54.3%)

NOTE: Nonresidents include foreign governments, foreign companies, international institutions, foreign banks, and overseas branches of Japan's foreign exchange banks.

In brief, JOM possesses many special characteristics.
* Like New York IBFs, JOM allows offshore banks to establish special accounts separately from domestic ones.
* Most (97.3%) of the transactions in JOM are, at present, interbank dealings rather than transactions with nonbank customers. Share of loans is very small possibly due to international debt problems.
* JOM has functioned as a subsidiary of domestic interbank market, particularly benefiting Japanese regional banks that do not have foreign branches but can take advantage of lower cost of funds than the domestic interbank market due to banking regulation.
* Share of yen-denominated assets has gradually been rising, especially in deposits and call loans. This means that more transactions with Japanese residents appear on the JOM horizon (e.g., borrow from Euroyens and transfer them to domestic market).
* Since April 1988, net transfer of funds between JOM and domestic markets was allowed to increase from maximum 5% to 10% of the average of assets against nonresidents during the preceding month. The relaxation of limits on net transfer of funds has enabled small and medium-sized foreign exchange banks to participate in JOM transactions. This has had a stimulative effect on the growth of JOM.

SOURCE: Bank of Tokyo, *Tokyo Financial Review* (October 1989):7–8.

Singapore   Singapore is a small island nation with a population of 2.7 million. Lacking natural resources, its economy relies on financial and business services along with manufacturing and construction. Singapore exports (including re-exports) approximately equal its gross domestic product (GDP) making this country one of the most open in the world. Singapore continues to benefit from its crossroad location in southeast Asia.

Singapore's government has played a key role in its economic expansion into the 1990s. There was an economic slowdown in 1985 and 1986, due primarily to the sluggishness of shipbuilding, oil refining, and construction. However, Singapore's economy rebounded in 1987–1995 with an average real GDP growth rate of 8%. Its per capita income was about $27,000 in 1995, giving Singapore the status of a newly industrialized country.

The government of Singapore has taken major steps to improve its status as an international financial center. These include:

Asian Dollar Market

A market for buying and selling U.S. dollars among banks in Singapore (and sometimes in Hong Kong) for profit.

* Singapore, aided by the Bank of America, established the Asian dollar market in 1968. Licenses have been issued to more than 170 domestic and foreign banking institutions to establish and operate offshore banks as Asian Currency Units (ACUs).

EXHIBIT 6.17	**Growth of Singapore's Asian Dollar Market Assets in Asian Currency Units, (U.S.$ Million)**
1968	30
1973	6,277
1981	85,775
1985	135,696
1986	177,979
1987	225,410
1988	263,529
1989	336,581
1990	390,395
1991	357,725
1993	306,703
1995	373,774

SOURCE: Monetary Authority of Singapore.

- The Monetary Authority of Singapore (MAS), established in 1971, is entrusted with promoting the financial markets and strengthening financial infrastructure.
- Tax structure is favorable to lower banking cost in Singapore.
- Exchange controls have been liberalized, permitting banks and others to engage in a wider range of activities including loans, Asian bond issues, and arbitrage.
- Financial futures, currency options, and swaps were traded on the Singapore International Monetary Exchange (SIMEX) in the 1990s.

As a result of the supportive government financial policy, there are more than 120 foreign banks in Singapore, of which about 80 are offshore banks. The strong presence of foreign banks and their participation in the interbank payment system called SHIFT (System for Handling Interbank Transfer) have facilitated Singapore's offshore banking activities. Exhibit 6.17 shows that the growth of the Asian dollar market has been most impressive. In 1968 Singapore's Asian dollar market was only $30 million. In 1995 the market size was $373 billion.

According to the Monetary Authority of Singapore, there is a high percentage of interbank activity, with interbank deposits and lending constituting about 75% of total assets/liabilities. Inflows of funds are mainly from London, the Middle East, New York, and Japan. These funds are directed to the Asian region for investment. In fact, Japanese firms such as Sony and U.S. electonics firms poured considerable amounts of funds into Singapore for manufacturing investment in the late 1980s and 1990s due to the appreciation of yen, higher labor costs in Japan, and worldwide demand for electronic products.

Singapore emphasizes wholesale offshore banking while Hong Kong stresses retail lending (e.g., trade financing). Singapore benefits from outside capital that has made its lending affordable at lower rates. In the 1990s Singapore must compete with other Asian offshore markets such as Hong Kong, Tokyo, Bangkok, and Malaysia.

The Singapore offshore banking market has been doing well, and the prosperity at home and in neighboring countries are favorable factors for its offshore banking activities. When the Baring Crisis occurred in early 1995 (failure of future contracts between Singapore and Tokyo by the British Baring Securities), the SIMEX handled the situation smoothly. This enhanced the reputation of Singapore as an orderly offshore market. SIMEX also quickly introduced several broad measures to strengthen its rules, reporting system and clearing system linking with the Chicago Mercantile Exchange, which provide mutual offset on the Eurodollar contract.

Hong Kong   From 1840 to June 1997, Hong Kong was a British colony that adjoins the Chinese province of Quangdong on the southeastern coast of the China mainland. After July 1, 1997, the British returned Hong Kong to China. It now holds the status of a Special Administrative Region.

Hong Kong has a population of 6 million with 98% Chinese residents. It traditionally adhered to a free enterprise system with no tariffs on imports, no exchange or capital controls, and no withholding tax on deposit interest. In the past 40 years, Hong Kong's economy has been transformed from entrepôt (reexport) trade in 1950–1960, to manufacturing in 1960–1970, and to financial services in the 1980s–1990s. The real average annual economic growth rate in the 1980s was about 8% while in 1990–1996 it was about 5%. Per capita income in 1996 was U.S. $26,000.

Hong Kong's economic prosperity is primarily based on real estate, manufacturing, foreign trade activities, and the diversity of its banking and financial institutions. As of 1996 under the supervision of Hong Kong Financial Secretary, there were 248 local banks and foreign banks, and 132 deposit-taking companies (DTCs). Hong Kong and Shanghsi Banking Corporation (HKSBC), with its head office in London, acted as an unofficial central bank for Hong Kong before July 1, 1997.

Liberal banking regulation and the presence of foreign banks from the United States, United Kingdom, Japan, Canada, France, and Singapore enable Hong Kong to provide a variety of banking services and activities. Since the Hong Kong stock market has been one of the most active in the Far East, it has attracted substantial numbers of international investment banking houses and portfolio managers. Its foreign exchange market and bond market have also been active. Since the 1970s Hong Kong dollar has linked closely in value to the U.S. dollar at the rate of H.K. $7.8 to U.S. $1. Hong Kong's offshore banking market is highly active in international syndicated loans, commercial paper, and certificates of deposit.

As Exhibit 6.18 indicates, the loan market in Hong Kong has grown rapidly from HK $500 billion in 1986 to HK $3,736 billion in 1995. However, the share of loans for use in Hong Kong in this period declined from 54% to 40.6% while the share of loans for use outside Hong Kong increased from 46% to 59.4% in the same period. This reflected the highly active offshore banking activities in Hong Kong as an international financial center. In fact, the share of loans for use in Hong Kong increased from 26.7% to 40.6% from 1992 to 1995 primarily due to increased borrowing from companies in mainland China. These companies have been financing alliances with Hong Kong companies ahead of the 1997 handover.

In 1995 offshore loans in foreign currency increased from 70% in 1991 to 99% (see Exhibit 6.19). This shows that offshore loans were borrowed by outsiders.

Based on the China-Britain Agreement of 1984, Hong Kong was transferred to the mainland Chinese government in 1997. There is concern whether the People's Republic of China will allow Hong Kong to keep its present capitalistic system for another 50 years (1997–2047) as a Special Administrative Region. Most financial market participants believe that the Chinese government will keep its commitment to the 1984 agreement since Hong Kong continues to be important to China's trade, finance, and especially to its foreign exchange earnings. It would even become a financial center of China.

EXHIBIT 6.18	Loan Market in Hong Kong (in HK$ Million)			
Year	Total Loans and Advances	Loans for Use in Hong Kong	Share of Hong Kong Loans	Share of Loans outside Hong Kong
1986	500,596	270,729	54.0	46.0
1987	778,782	352,685	45.2	54.8
1988	962,177	456,487	47.4	52.6
1991	2,243,773	816,767	26.7	73.3
1992	3,369,466	899,908	26.7	73.3
1995	3,735,859	1,517,497	40.6	59.4

SOURCE: *Asian Finance* (August 1989):58 and *Hong Kong Monthly Digest of Statistics* (March 1993 and March 1996).

EXHIBIT 6.19	Hong Kong Banking Sector's Total Offshore Loans (in HK$ Million)				
	In HK$	% of Total	In Foreign Currency	% of Total	Total Offshore Loans
1991	719.571	30%	1,524.12	70%	2,243.695
1992	812.088	33%	1,657.470	67%	2,469.558
1995	23.309	1%	2,143.053	99%	2,166.362

SOURCE: *Hong Kong Monthly Digest of Stastistics* (March 1993 and March 1996).

New York International Banking Facilities (IBFs)   In the late 1960s IBFs were proposed in response to the foreign lending restraints imposed on American banks as a consequence of the capital control program. Essentially, an IBF is a set of asset and liability accounts of an offshore banking unit. However, the Federal Reserve maintained its opposition on the basis that IBFs would interfere with the implementation of domestic monetary policy (leakage of funds between domestic and offshore markets).

The United States lifted the capital controls in 1974 and foreign capital (petrodollars) continued to be booked in Caribbean offshore banking centers. Under these circumstances the New York Clearing House Association strongly supported the IBF concept. Furthermore, the New York state legislature enacted a state/local tax exemption for the proposed IBFs. This exemption was in consideration of the beneficial employment and income effects expected from IBFs.

Finally, the Federal Reserve amended Regulations D and Q to permit establishment of international banking facilities in the United States as of 3 December 1981. The first IBFs were established in New York in December 1981 at a time of worldwide recession and inflation. Once IBFs were started in the United States, their assets/liabilities grew rapidly. As of 1994 the U.S. share in offshore lending accounted for 11.5% of total international lending, behind only the United Kingdom (see Exhibit 6.14). Deposits from and credit extended to foreign residents or other IBFs can generally be booked at these facilities free from domestic reserve requirements and interest rate limitations. Subject to conditions specified by the Federal Reserve, IBFs may be established by U.S. depository institutions, by Edge Act corporations, and by U.S. branches and agencies of foreign banks. Under the Edge Act (discussed in Chapter 9), federally chartered investment banking corporations can be organized.

The corporations carry on general investment banking activities and hold stocks of foreign banks and financial companies. Even though earnings from IBFs are exempt from state and local income taxes, they are subject to federal income tax.

Like Eurobanks, IBFs only offer time deposits. Time deposits offered to nonbanks are subject to a minimum maturity of two business days and require minimum deposit and withdrawal amounts of $100,000. In cases of time deposits offered to foreign banks, foreign central banks, official institutions, other IBFs, and U.S. parent banks, deposit maturities can be one day or longer. IBFs deal in U.S. dollars and foreign currencies. IBFs are permitted to accept only deposits related to operations outside the United States and extend credit only to finance operations outside the United States (that is, no conduit operations permitted). Funds shifted back to domestic banking channels are subject to normal Federal Reserve regulations. The FDIC does not insure IBF deposits.

Since the establishment of IBFs in the United States, their assets have increased from $55 billion in 1981 to $182 billion in 1985. As of 1995 total assets of IBFs in the United States was $301 billion, of which 82% was held in New York, 9% in California, 5% in Illinois, and 4–5% in other cities such as Miami, Houston, Atlanta, Boston, and Philadelphia.

At present, New York, London, and Tokyo are three pillars of global offshore banking. The strengths and limitations of U.S. IBFs are as follows.

Strengths:

• Sharing the same location with a U.S.-based parent bank can facilitate better management control.
• Political stability and a sound U.S. dollar provide confidence to foreign depositors putting funds in the U.S. offshore market.

Limitations:

• Unlike London IBFs, New York and other U.S. IBFs are not permitted to accept deposits from or extend credits to U.S. residents.
• U.S. IBFs offer no demand deposits and cannot issue CDs.
• U.S. IBFs are subject to federal income tax while the Bahamas and Caymans waive this type of tax.
• IBFs do not offer secret trust accounts such as those available in Switzerland.

Caribbean Offshore Markets   Caribbean offshore banking centers have played an important role in international lending, especially to Latin American countries during the petrodollar recycling of the 1970s. The Caribbean markets basically include the Bahamas, the Cayman Islands, the Netherland's Antilles, and Panama. The Netherlands Antilles concentrates on handling Eurobonds. During the 1980s many Caribbean offshore banking activities were affected by the changing economic and political climate in this area. The debt crisis and slow economic growth have definitely slowed market growth. There are also political problems resulting from alleged involvement of some government officials in narcotics trafficking.

The Cayman Islands are presently still attractive for bankers worldwide. The Caymans, like Bermuda, are ruled under the British Crown and are responsible for enacting their own laws. The Caymans are attractive to outside banks for many

| EXHIBIT 6.20 | **Assets/Liabilities of U.S. Branches and Agencies of Foreign Banks** |

1985–1995 (in $billion)

| Year | Number of reports filed | ALL STATES | | NEW YORK | | CALIFORNIA | | ILLINOIS | |
		Total including IBFs	IBFs only	Total including IBFs	IBFs only	Total including IBFs	IBFs only	Total including IBFs	IBFs only
1985	466	$311	$182	$231	$119	$40	$21	$16	$6
1986	487	396	198	293	154	55	25	21	9
1987	502	460	233	339	185	69	30	29	10
1988	517	513	247	376	194	74	33	36	12
1991	581	704	307	523	237	88	41	54	20
1995	526	761	301	590	248	70	28	59	16
As % of IBF Assets (1955)			100%		82%		9%		5%
Number of Reports (1955)				251		119		47	
As % of all reports	100%			48%		23%		9%	

SOURCE: *Federal Reserve Bulletin,* various issues

NOTE: Details may not add to totals because of rounding.

reasons including political stability, absence of taxation, banking confidentiality, and good transportation between the Islands and the United States. International telecommunications are also an important advantage vital to offshore markets. American banks are dominant forces in the Caribbean offshore markets.

According to BIS statistics, as of 1995 total international lending from the Bahamas was $185 billion, from the Cayman Islands was $411 billion, ranking only second to Hong Kong but ahead of Singapore.*

COLLABORATION ON FINANCIAL MARKET POLICIES

The rapid growth of the Eurocurrency market and offshore banking in the past 30 years can be attributed to differences in national regulation and the innovativeness of international financial institutions. The Eurocurrency market has contributed to growth of the world economy and international financial market integration. On the other hand there have been some negative aspects in the market. First, no reserve requirements exist on the Eurocurrency market. Each Eurobank has the potential to create large amounts of credit. This "pyramiding" of deposits is dangerous if bankruptcies occur among the Eurobanks. Another possible problem is that there is no direct regulatory oversight on the market's maturity structure; therefore, excessive maturity mismatches in the lending and funding process could easily cause liquidity problems. The lack of central bank control and regulations may allow banks in the Euromarket to overexpose themselves to such risks.

Monetary authorities in some major countries such as the United States and the United Kingdom have been aware of the benefits and possible problems created by the growing Eurocurrency market. Not until the banking crisis in 1974 was any

---

* BIS *International Banking and Financial Market Development.* Basle, May 1996, Table 2A.

collective action introduced. These crises included the collapse of the Herstatt Bank in West Germany and Franklin National in the United States. As a result, in 1975 common interest led 10 leading industrial countries to establish the Committee on Banking Regulation and Supervisory Practices, commonly known as the Cooke Committee, after its former chairman. Under the auspices of the Bank for International Settlements (BIS), the first step of the committee was a general statement on the joint responsibilities of host and parent authorities for supervision of foreign banking establishments, their liquidity, and their solvency. This international understanding was known as the "Basle Concordat".

During the LDC debt crisis in 1982, considerable debate took place on what could be done to protect the Eurodollar market.* No actions were taken in that period because of the complex or potentially explosive situation, since Poland, Mexico, Brazil, and Argentina had difficulties in meeting payments on their debt obligations to official and private international lenders. The widespread nature of these difficulties diminished the liquidity and profits of many large international commercial banks.

In the wake of the continued LDC debt problems and difficulties faced by creditor banks that encountered high loan-capital ratios, in 1986 the Basle Committee proposed a plan to harmonize capital adequacy standards for major banks in the G-10 countries. In March 1987 the United States and the United Kingdom reached agreement on common capital requirements for their own banks. By July 1988 all the countries represented in the Basle Committee reached a consensus on a similar basis and began to apply new capital adequacy standards to all internationally active commercial banks under their jurisdictions. The common requirement was that by 1992 banks must maintain minimum capital bases equivalent to 8% of their risk-adjusted assets.

At the end of 1995, the Basle Committee announced a major amendment to the Basle Capital Accord with the objective of setting capital charges for the market risks from bank trading activities and from their open position in foreign exchange and commodities markets. The Eurocurrency standing committee continued to monitor developments in international financial markets in light of the Mexican crisis, the collapse of Barings, and the tension in the foreign exchange markets in the spring of 1995.

SUMMARY

Global financial markets are composed of five distinct financial market sectors because of which the Euromarkets and offshore banking centers are truly global. Their widespread geographic location, worldwide participants, large-scale operations, sophisticated financial instruments, innovative capacity, and impacts on the world economy and finance have been unprecedented in financial market history.

The Eurocurrency market emerged on the international financial scene only after World War II, but its rapid growth and sheer size reflect intensive and extensive market activities around the globe. Eurocurrency market activities focus on: long-term and short-term international currency deposits; large-scale, cross-border

---

* Frydl, Edward J. "The Eurodollar Conundrum." Federal Reserve Bank of New York *Quarterly Review* (Spring 1982).

lending such as syndicated loans; and interbank market operations. These activities are dominated by international financial institutions that channel worldwide capital in an efficient and effective manner. However, banks must exercise prudence in this unregulated and precarious market as demonstrated by the LDC debt problems in the 1980s.

Offshore banking centers are by-products of the Eurocurrency market. They operate parallel to the national financial market but with limited national regulation in order to attract international lenders and borrowers. Exemption from local taxes is the common feature of almost all offshore banking centers. That feature is why even major financial markets like London, New York, and Tokyo find offshore banking a positive factor in strengthening their international competitive positions. Smaller countries such as Singapore, Luxembourg, and the Bahamas have also found beneficial effects from operation of offshore banking in their territories.

As a result of the enormous growth of the Eurocurrency and offshore banking markets, some problems have been inevitable. For smoother global capital flows and less negative impact on the world economy and finance, collaboration on financial market policies among industrial nations has been implemented by the Basle Committee at the Bank for International Settlements, Switzerland.

REVIEW QUESTIONS

1. What are the components of the global financial markets? Explain their respective characteristics.

2. What is the linkage between national financial markets and the Euromarkets? How do they influence each other?

3. What are the major differences between the paper center and the functional center in offshore banking? Give an example of each.

4. Explain:
    a. the origin of the Eurocurrency market;
    b. the major reasons for the growth of the Eurocurrency market in the 1960s and 1970s; and
    c. the major reasons for the slow growth of the Eurocurrency market in the first half of the 1980s.

5. Why is the Eurocurrency market so important to both developed and developing countries? Explain.

6. Is there any effect of the Eurocurrency market on national monetary policy? Give the rationale for your argument.

7. Explain the differences between domestic commercial paper and Euro-commercial paper.

8. What are the basic reasons for the expansion of the Eurocurrency interbank markets in the second half of the 1980s? Briefly explain.

9. Explain the major steps in the syndicated loan market. What are the crucial factors determining the pricing of syndicated loans?

10. What are the leading risks in the syndicated Eurocredits? How could financial institutions minimize the risks in a syndicated Eurocurrency loan?

11. Explain the three typical types of offshore markets. Give an example of each.

12. Explain the special characteristics of:
    a. The London Offshore Banking Market
    b. The Japan Offshore Market (JOM)
    c. The New York International Banking Facilities (IBFs)

13. A London Bank is offered a three-month pound sterling deposit at an interest rate of 8%, but the bank has no lending opportunity for the funds. It can swap the sterling into dollars. Spot sterling trades at $1.5075 and 90-day sterling trades at $1.5160. The bank can lend three-month dollars at the interest rate of 10.5%. Calculate the percentage profit and amount of profit when transacting 10 million pounds sterling.

14. A London bank is offered a six-month pound sterling deposit at an interest rate of 9%, but the bank has no lending opportunity for the funds. It can swap the sterling into dollars. Spot sterling trades at $1.5250 and 90-day sterling trades at $1.5460. The bank can lend three-month dollars at the interest rate of 12%. Calculate the percentage profit and amount of profit when transacting 20 million pounds sterling.

15. A U.S. bank faces the following market conditions: three-month CD rate is 9.0%, three-month Eurodollar bid rate is 11.0%, the FDIC insurance premium is 0.037%, CD reserve requirements are 6%.
    a. Determine whether an outward or inward arbitrage incentive exists.
    b. How much profit can the bank make from arbitrage?

SELECTED BIBLIOGRAPHY

Angelini, Anthony, Maximo Eng, and Francis A. Lees. *International Lending, Risk and Euromarkets.* London: MacMillan, 1979.

Bank of England. "The Market in Currency Options." *Quarterly Bulletin.* May 1989.

Bank for International Settlements. *Banking Innovations.* Basle, 1985.

Bryant, Ralph C. *International Coordination of National Stabilization Policies.* Washington, D.C.: Brookings Institution, 1995.

Clarke, Stephen V.O. *American Banks in the International Interbank Market.* A monograph published by the Graduate School of Business. New York: New York University, 1984.

Cole, David C., et al. (ed) *Asian Money Markets.* New York: Oxford University Press, 1995.

Dufey, Gunter, and Ian H. Giddy. *The International Money Market.* Englewood Cliffs, NJ: Prentice Hall, 1994.

Einzig, Paul. *The Eurodollar System.* London: MacMillan, 1970.

Eng, Maximo, and Francis A. Lees. "Eurocurrency Centers" *International Financial Handbook* (ed. by Abraham George and Ian Giddy). New York: John Wiley & Sons, 1983.

Federal Reserve Bank of New York. Research Paper. *The International Money Markets in London and First Chicago's Role in Clearing & Settling for Dollar Instrument.* May 1989.

Federal Reserve Bank of New York. Research Paper. *Clearing and Settling Euro-Securities Market: Euro-Clear and Cedel.* March 1989.

Federal Reserve Bank of New York. Staff Study. *International Competitiveness of U.S. Financial Firms.* May 1991.

Grabbe, J. Orlin. *International Financial Markets.* New York: Elserier, 1996.

International Monetary Fund. *International Capital Markets.* September 1995.

Organization for Economic Cooperation and Development. *Financial Market Trends*. February 1991, 1993, and 1996.

Ross, Stephen A. "Institutional Markets, Financial Marketing and Financial Innovations." *The Journal of Finance*. July 1989.

Rowley, Anthony. "Offshore Market: Convenience Store for Banks." *Far Eastern Economic Review*. 18 February 1993.

Saunders, Anthony. "The Eurocurrency Interbank Market: Potential for International Crisis?" Federal Reserve Bank of Philadelphia, *Business Review*. January–February 1988.

Sarver, Eugene. *The Eurocurrency Handbook*. New York: New York Institute of Finance. 1988.

Swanson, P. "Interrelationships Among Domestic and Eurocurrency Deposit Yields: A Focus on the U.S. Dollar." *Financial Review*. February 1988.

Terrell, Henry S., Robert S. Dohner, and Barbara R. Lowrey. "The Activities of Japanese Banks in the United Kingdom and in the United States, 1980–1988." *Federal Reserve Bulletin*. February 1990.

Walmsley, Julian. *The Foreign Exchange and Money Markets Guide*. New York: John Wiley, 1992.

CHAPTER 7

International Bond Market

INTRODUCTION

Until the early 1960s international bond issues were restricted to the foreign bond market centers of leading capital markets. These centers included the United States, Switzerland, West Germany, and the United Kingdom. Beginning in the 1960s a new component of the international bond market surfaced. Because its principal location of operations was Europe, this new market was given the name Eurobond market. Since 1960 the international bond market has demonstrated dynamic growth and change including the emergence of Eurobonds in 1963, foreign bond issues in Japan since the 1970s, and the introduction of Brady bonds and global bonds in the early 1990s. In this chapter we examine the structure and composition of the international bond markets, consider their role and importance, and analyze their operational aspects.

Close attention is given to the new issue or underwriting process, underwriting spreads, and the currency factor. Major instruments used in international bond issuance are analyzed and compared. Secondary trading of Eurobonds is analyzed, especially with reference to pricing of bond with accrued interest and to facilities for the clearing and settlements of bond transactions. Interest rate and currency swaps are analyzed as driving forces in new Eurobond issues. Global bond issues and emerging debt are also briefly examined.

LEARNING OBJECTIVES IN THIS CHAPTER

1. To differentiate and compare similarities between international bonds, domestic bonds, Eurobonds, foreign bonds, and global bonds.
2. To appreciate the role and importance of the international bond markets as a source of funds for borrowers, as an investment channel for lenders, and as a source of profit for banking institutions that service these markets.
3. To develop an awareness of the special role played by foreign bond markets, the type of borrowers that use these markets, and the mechanics of bond issuance.
4. To understand the basic nature of the Eurobond market, the reasons for its dynamic growth, and the special features of this market.
5. To sense the importance of the currency of denomination of international bond issues.

6. To examine the role played by interest rate and currency swaps, their relation to the international bond markets, and the characteristics of major types of swaps.

7. To consider the growing role and importance of global bonds and emerging debt markets.

KEY TERMS AND CONCEPTS

- Brady bond
- call premium
- Cedel
- convertible bond
- credit rating
- currency swap
- Emerging market debt
- Eurobond
- Euroclear
- floating rate note (FRN)

- foreign bond
- global bond
- interest rate swap
- international bond
- over-the-counter
- placement power
- plain vanilla
- syndicate
- underwriting spread

ACRONYMS

AIBD	Association of International Bond Dealers	**ISDA**	International Swap Dealers Association
ISMA	International Securities Market Association	**JGB**	Japanese Government Bond

Definition and Importance

FOUR DEFINITIONS

Foreign Bonds

Issued in a domestic bond market by a nonresident borrower and are denominated in the local currency of that bond market.

In this brief section we develop useful definitions of the foreign, Eurobond, and international bond markets. Foreign bonds are issued in a domestic bond market by a nonresident borrower and are denominated in the local currency of that bond market. Generally an underwriting syndicate (investment bank) of the domestic bond market is used, although its composition may be augmented by investment banking firms from the borrower's country. Local investors interested in bonds denominated in local currency are likely to purchase most of the foreign bond issue. For example, an American corporation may sell a Swiss franc denominated issue in the Swiss foreign bond market. These bonds will be underwritten by a primarily Swiss syndicate, and financial institutions located in Switzerland will purchase the bonds. In this bond issue example, the major distinguishing characteristics are 1) a nonresident borrower issues the bonds, 2) they are denominated in Swiss francs, and 3) a primarily Swiss banking syndicate underwrites the bonds.

Eurobonds

Issued in one or more foreign countries but currency denominations are other than that of the country or countries where the bonds are issued.

Unlike foreign bonds, Eurobonds are not issued on a single national bond market. Eurobonds are unique for two reasons. First, a multinational syndicate must be used to distribute the bonds in a number of national market sectors. Second, the currency of denomination, selected by the borrower and the managing bank, will not be a domestic currency for the majority of investors that purchase the bond.

The Eurobond market derived its early growth stimulus when the U.S. government proposed the Interest Equalization Tax (IET) on American resident purchases of foreign securities in 1963. This tax shifted foreign borrowing to the European markets and provided a steady demand for Eurobond financing. By the time the IET was removed in 1974, the Eurobond market had reached a level of $2 billion a year in new issues.

A borrower that is fairly well known to potential bond investors in a number of countries issues Eurobonds. Because a Eurobond issue will be distributed simultaneously in a number of countries, borrowers normally work through a large banking syndicate with multinational selling capacity. Generally Eurobonds are exempt from withholding taxes. Later in this chapter we will return to the taxation status of Eurobonds, the strategies of issuers and investors in the Eurobond market, and how the foreign currency nature of the bond fits into these strategies.

International Bonds

Include both foreign bonds and Eurobonds.

International bonds include both categories of bonds—foreign bonds and Eurobonds. In the early 1960s the volume of foreign bonds issued dwarfed Eurobonds. This trend has been reversed since 1982, and the annual amount of Eurobond issues is now several times as large as all other foreign bonds issued.

The first global bonds were introduced by the World Bank in September 1989. Global bonds are defined as very large issues sold simultaneously in the world's major capital markets in Europe, Asia, and the United States, with trading taking place both within and between these regions. The bonds are held and cleared through Cedel and Euroclear in Europe and through Fedwire or Depository Trust Company (DTC) in the United States. These bonds are listed on one or more of the major exchanges because liquidity is the crucial feature of global bonds. Global bonds have the combined, not separate, characteristics of Eurobonds and foreign bonds. They accounted for 11% of all international bonds in 1995.*

MARKET SIZE AND IMPORTANCE

Over the past several decades the international bond market has enjoyed dynamic growth, both in new issues and secondary trading. Growth in new issues broadly represents increasing needs for funds to finance higher levels of investment and international transactions. These needs come from governments, corporations, international financial organizations such as the World Bank, and other borrowers. However, to fully understand the growth of the market, the sides of both supply and demand must not be overlooked.

As indicated in Exhibits 7.1 and 7.2, during the 31-year period 1964–1995 international bond issues grew rapidly from $2.3 billion to $467 billion (200 times). It is noted that the growth rates between Eurobonds and foreign bonds were different, and that the major suppliers and borrowers in the international bond market have also changed from time to time.

In the period 1964–1974 total international bond issues increased from $2.3 billion to $6.8 billion (three times) but Eurobond issues increased faster (four times). Major borrowers were multinational corporations that shifted from the United States to the European capital market due to the U.S. capital controls. The formation

---

*OECD "The Rise of Global Bonds," *Financial Market Trends,* (June 1994): 55 and OECD *Financial Market Trends,* (June 1996): 68.

EXHIBIT 7.1	**Issues of International Bonds**

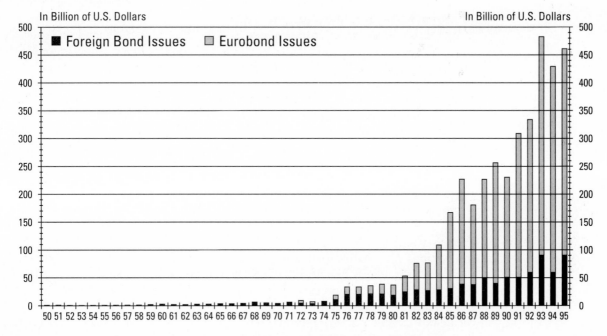

In Billion of U.S. Dollars

■ Foreign Bond Issues   □ Eurobond Issues

SOURCES: OECD, *International Capital Markets Statistics, 1950–1995.*

EXHIBIT 7.2	**International Bond Issues, 1964–1995 (in billions of U.S. dollars)**

	1964	1974	1975	1980	1982	1984	1986	1989	1991	1992	1993	1994	1995
Eurobonds	0.5	2.1	8.5	13.9	52	79	188	212	258	276	395	368	371
Foreign Bonds	1.8	4.7	21.4	17.9	26	28	38	42	51	58	86	60	96
International Bonds	2.3	6.8	29.9	41.8	78	107	226	254	309	334	481	428	467

SOURCE: OECD, *Financial Statistics,* OECD, *Financial Market Trends,* various issues.

of the European Community (EC) since 1958 attracted world capital suppliers with comparatively higher interest rates.

The increases in oil prices during the 1975–1982 period created a big pool of liquidity for international borrowers, especially the oil-importing countries. Eurobond issues in this period rose from $8.5 billion to $52 billion (six times) while foreign bond issues showed slower and uneven growth rates. Since 1982 the Eurobond issues have superseded the foreign bonds due to the flexibility of Eurobonds in terms of currency, location, and maturity plus other advantages that will be discussed in more detail later.

The collapse of some developing country borrowers (for example, Poland, Brazil, and Mexico) in 1982 ended the monopolistic petrodollars as the principal source of funds for international lenders. Instead, Japan became the largest international credit supplier due to its high domestic saving rates and continued trade surpluses in the 1982–1989 period. The LDC debt problem resulted in more cautious selection of international borrowers. Only high credit standing borrowers such as the Kingdom of Sweden, the World Bank, and IBM were welcomed in the global financial markets, including syndicated loan markets. Low credit rating borrowers had to pay higher spreads. Regardless of the LDC debt problems, the international bond issues continued to grow for different reasons. First, economic prosperity in industrial countries, such as the United States, Japan, Germany, and United Kingdom, encouraged international trade and investment, especially in view of the "single European market" by 1992. As a result, international bond issues surged from $78 billion in 1982 to $254 billion in 1989. The Eurobond issues were particularly strong owing to declining long-term interest rates and growing international business.

In the latest period of our analysis, 1990–1995, there have been many fundamental changes in the international bond market. First, the international political, economic, and financial environments have changed. Former communist countries in Russia and Eastern Europe have adopted more market oriented economies since 1991. The People's Republic of China also tended to pursue a more free market system. Gradually these countries have increased their borrowings in the international bond market. Second, many emerging market countries in Asia and Latin America increased their participation in the international bond market in order to obtain external funds for economic growth and developments. Some developing countries such as Singapore, Hong Kong, and Taiwan play the role of fund suppliers. Third, innovations such as global bonds and derivative financial instruments stimulated demand for funds by financial institutions. On the supply side, savings institutions such as pension funds, mutual funds, and life insurance companies have played an important role in the international bond market in the first half of the 1990s. As indicated in Exhibit 7.2, international bond issues grew in the period 1991–1995 but at a slower rate reflecting mild economic recessions in some countries including the United States in 1991 and high long-term interest rates in 1994.

The international bond markets play an important role in world finance as sources of medium and long-term capital. However, the Eurobond and foreign bond markets play somewhat different roles. Borrowers' access to foreign bond markets is somewhat more difficult than access to the Eurobond market. In part this difficulty is due to the institutional nature of the foreign bond market. Life insurance companies, savings banks, and pension funds are some of the more important buyers of bonds in the foreign bond markets; whereas individual investors and institutions better able to take on some degree of credit and currency risk form a large part of the investor base in the Eurobond market. As a result many non-U.S. corporations borrow in the Eurobond market, but might find a New York or Swiss bond market issue impossible or impractical due to difficulties in gaining access to these markets and to high cost factors.

Special Characteristics

The Eurobond market is less attractive to tax free institutional investors such as life insurance companies and pension funds, but it does attract investors that are subject to relatively high tax rates on reported income.

The Eurobond market is an extension of the offshore financial markets in which borrowing and lending take place at longer terms than in the Eurocurrency market. In this sense the Eurobond market is a special form of international financial intermediation. Operating as such, it has recycled petrodollars and intermediated other funds placed in the international bond markets. By contrast, the foreign bond market permits countries with current account payments surpluses or efficient capital markets to export capital to other parts of the world.

Eurobonds possess special characteristics that must be considered if we are to understand the role of this market in global finance. First, Eurobonds permit a choice of issuing currency and country. Moreover, the underwriting syndicate must be comprised of banks that ultimately will issue Eurobonds in the several national markets identified as good prospects for a particular issue.

Second, there is a high degree of currency flexibility. For example, a borrower can issue Eurobonds in London with currency denomination in U.S. dollar, German mark, or Japanese yen.

Third, the Eurobond market adds to the international mobility of capital by attracting a wider range of borrowers and investors than other internationally oriented financial markets. Fourth, Eurobonds can offer investors better portfolio diversification and higher yields after taxes (Chapter 20) than they can earn on domestic bonds. Fifth, there are strong links between the Eurobond and Eurocurrency market sectors. For example, Eurobond underwriters and dealers can borrow Eurocurrencies to finance their syndication and dealing operations. Finally, there is no withholding tax on Eurobond interest. This incentive, coupled with investor anonymity, provides important driving forces on the investor side of the market.

There are some disadvantages of Eurobond issues: shorter maturities (5–15 years) than domestic bonds (10–30 years); higher spreads charged by multinational underwriting syndicates for Eurobonds than domestic bonds due to higher risk; and currency risk if major currencies are used for the issues.

Mechanics of Foreign Bonds

MATURITY AND INTEREST COUPON

Foreign bond issues in New York, Frankfurt, Zurich, London, and Tokyo are generally offered through an underwriting mechanism. A lead or managing bank works closely with the borrower, planning sale of the issue in a manner that maximizes the likelihood of successful marketing of the bonds. At this point many details of the bond issue are considered including maturity, coupon interest, call protection and premium, and provisions for retirement.

Foreign bonds are usually issued with relatively long maturities, normally 20–30 years, due in part to the importance of institutional investors in the bond markets of New York, Frankfurt, and other foreign bond centers. These long maturity issues will carry interest coupons in line with the level of interest rates prevailing in these markets and with the credit standing of the borrower. Most central government borrowers and multilateral lending institutions (MLIs) issuing bonds in New York carry the highest "AAA" rating. The interest coupon will be marginally above what the U.S. Treasury must pay in the same market to borrow funds. By contrast, Canadian provinces and hydro-authorities will have bond credit ratings a notch below this level and will have to pay correspondingly more for funds borrowed in New York. Corporate borrowers are spread across a broad range of credit ratings, depending on their financial status as well as on the perceived country risk that affects their international credit worthiness.

Long-dated bonds usually offer the investor a certain amount of call protection. That is, borrowers often have the right to call bonds for early redemption and will do so when it is to their advantage. Borrowers will call bonds for early retirement when interest rates have fallen, and new borrowings can be carried out at lower cost than is being paid on outstanding debt. To protect as well as compensate the investor for having high coupon bonds called away, the bond issue may offer a five year (or longer) call protection, meaning the borrower cannot call the bonds during the first five years after issue. Further, early call (in the sixth year) must be at a premium over par. The call premium will likely be set at a level that considers the interest rate on the issue and possible loss from early call. In addition, the premium may decline over the lifetime of the bond issue.

UNDERWRITING

Once the managing bank has worked out the details of the issue with the borrower, an underwriting group can be assembled. The underwriting group will include investment banking houses that provide one or more of the following strengths:

1. underwriting power, namely, size (including capital base) and experience in underwriting similar bond issues
2. placement power with local institutional investors
3. placement power with home country (of borrower) investors

Placement Power

This refers to the strength and capacity of an underwriting group to place the bond issues with individual and institutional investors.

The underwriting group will consist of a number of domestic banks plus a generous mix of banks from the borrower's country and other countries where potential investors may be located.

The managing bank and underwriting group will enjoy compensation in the form of an underwriting spread. This means that if the bond issue is sold to investors at par ($1,000 per bond), the underwriting group pays the borrower an offer price minus the spread. A spread of 3/4 is $7.50 per bond, while a spread of 7/8 is $8.75 per bond. The way in which the spread is distributed is interesting. The managing bank receives approximately one-fourth of the total spread. This amount compensates the manager for negotiating and arranging the issue.

The underwriting fee is paid to participants in the underwriting group and may approximate one-fourth of the spread. This fee rewards the underwriting banks for taking risk by buying and holding bonds for resale. While the bonds are held for resale, interest rates could move up, and bond prices would decline leaving the underwriting banks with a loss on the bonds they hold. Finally, the selling commission and allowances absorb the remainder of the spread (more than one-half). This amount compensates bond sales associates who are paid commissions for bonds sold. Eurobond spreads are distributed somewhat differently than in the foreign bond market.

INTEREST RATES ON FOREIGN BONDS

Foreign bonds are issued in separate national capital markets. Therefore the interest rates on foreign bond issues are basically determined by the level of rates prevailing in each respective market. The general rule applies that stronger currencies carry lower interest rates, and softer currencies carry higher interest rates. Another way to look at it is to ask the question, "Is the local currency interest rate on government bonds (riskless securities for the domestic investor) likely to be enough to satisfy the global investor?" Comparative coupon interest rates and yields on benchmark government bonds are indicated in Exhibit 7.3 for 17 leading bond markets. These reflect local currency interest rates.

EXHIBIT 7.3		**Benchmark Government Bonds**					
	Coupon	Red Date	Price	Day's Change	Yield	Week Ago	Month Ago
Australia	6.750	11/06	90.5830	−0.060	8.12	8.07	8.79
Austria	6.250	05/06	98.8400	−0.140	6.31	6.28	6.56
Belgium	7.000	05/06	102.6000	−0.110	6.62	6.63	6.78
Canada*	7.000	12/06	97.9300	+0.080	7.29	7.30	7.72
Denmark	8.000	03/06	104.9600	−0.140	7.25	7.23	7.40
France BTAN	5.750	03/01	101.2500	+0.120	5.44	5.44	5.65
OAT	7.250	04/06	106.3000	+0.050	6.35	6.32	6.51
Germany Bund	6.250	04/06	99.6400	−0.130	6.29	6.27	6.55
Ireland	8.000	08/06	103.0500	+0.050	7.55	7.55	7.63
Italy	9.500	02/06	0.0000	—	0.00†	9.23	9.20
Japan No 140	6.600	06/01	119.4197	+0.020	2.16	2.22	2.29
No 182	3.000	09/05	98.7664	+0.070	3.18	3.22	3.24
Netherlands	8.500	06/06	115.7500	−0.070	6.29	6.25	6.48
Portugal	11.875	02/05	118.5600	—	8.68	8.70	8.71
Spain	8.800	04/06	99.1900	+0.250	8.90	8.90	8.86
Sweden	6.000	02/05	86.9868	+0.270	8.18	8.23	8.24
UK Gilts	8.000	12/00	103–11	−6/32	7.08	7.02	7.19
	7.500	12/06	97–22	−12/32	7.83	7.75	7.93
	9.000	10/08	108–02	−15/32	7.95	7.86	8.04
US Treasury*	7.000	07/06	103–04	+8/32	6.57	6.54	6.85
	6.750	08/26	99–21	+9/32	6.78	6.76	7.03
ECU (French Govt)	7.500	04/05	104.5200	+0.150	6.79	6.78	6.95

London closing, * New York closing   Yields: Local market standard.

† Gross (including withholding tax at 12.5 percent payable by nonresidents)
  Prices: US, UK in 32nds, others in decimal

SOURCE: *Financial Times*, (August 15, 1996): 16.

In the 1970s it was possible to say that the interest rate levels in the New York, Frankfurt, and Paris bond markets were set by domestic demand and supply. Foreign borrowers were price takers in these markets. However, in the 1980s foreign investor fund flows became a more important factor in shaping the interest rate levels in these markets. For example, in the first half of 1987 American authorities became concerned that a falling dollar would discourage foreign investor inflows to purchase U.S. Treasury securities. In turn, this decline would lead to a higher interest rate level in the U.S. bond market, with the spillover effects being greater difficulties for debtor countries trying to maintain interest payments on external debt.

ACCESS TO FOREIGN BOND MARKETS

Not all borrowers have ready access to the foreign bond markets in New York, Frankfurt, Zurich, and Tokyo. Many would like to borrow on such favored terms, but few are able to qualify. Borrowers have difficulty gaining access to the foreign bond markets. The Eurobond market is close behind the foreign bond markets in terms of international borrowers gaining access (Exhibit 7.4). The syndicated Euroloan market is more accessible to international borrowers (discussed in Chapter 12).

International borrowers have easiest access to short-term bank loans. In New York, Canadian entities such as provinces and hydro-authorities are important borrowers, along with central governments like France, Australia, and Sweden. In Zurich a somewhat more diversified mix of borrowers is willing to queue up and

EXHIBIT 7.4	**International Credit Market Sectors, in Descending Order of Accessability**

Top Tier	Foreign Bond Markets (New York, Switzerland, Frankfurt, London, Tokyo)	Very Difficult Access
Second Tier[2]	Eurobond Market	Somewhat Difficult Access
Third Tier[3]	Syndicated Euroloan Market	Moderately Easy Access
Fourth Tier[4]	Short-Term Bank Loans	Easiest Access

[1]Only top credits have access, in part due to restrictions operating on institutional investors in this market sector.
[2]Some corporate borrowers and most developing countries face difficulty accessing this market.
[3]Many developing countries encounter difficulty accessing this market.
[4]Most borrowers have some access to this source of funds.

EXHIBIT 7.5	**Foreign Bond Issues by Market (Billions in U.S. Dollars)**

	1991	1992	1993	1994	1995
United States	14.4	23.2	35.4	15.0	32.4
Switzerland	20.2	18.1	27.0	20.0	27.1
Japan	5.2	7.4	15.2	11.2	18.0
Luxembourg	5.5	5.5	3.5	11.0	13.8
Spain	2.7	1.6	3.0	1.6	2.3
Portugal	0.7	0.3	0.6	0.3	1.0
Austria	0.4	0.6	0.4	0.4	0.3
Netherlands	0.1	0.2	0.9	—	0.3
France	—	0.4	—	0.3	—
Other	1.4	0.3	0.4	0.4	0.8
Total	50.6	57.6	86.4	60.2	96.0

SOURCE: OECD, *Financial Market Trends,* (February and June 1996).

wait their turn. These borrowers include European regional institutions (European Economic Community, European Investment Bank), high credit-rated corporations, and governments. Tokyo has favored international organizations and regional development banks, but other borrowers attracted by the low rates are tapping the Tokyo market.

Access to the foreign bond markets is for the most part limited to the higher rated international credits. Developing country borrowers have only limited access to these markets. Only in rare cases do developing country borrowers obtain any access to these capital market sectors. A subtle screening process keeps lower rated credits away from the New York, Frankfurt, and Zurich markets. Interestingly enough, some of the borrowers who find themselves unable to tap the foreign bond markets are able to borrow in the Eurobond market.

Because only high credit-rated borrowers have access to foreign bond issues, borrowers usually enter any national financial markets with careful and comparative analyses. As indicated in Exhibit 7.5, the United States, Switzerland, and Japan accounted for about 80% of the total foreign bond issues in 1995 largely because of stable currency rates *for favorable variable* long-term interest rates, availability of funds, and good underwriting facilities in these countries.

Dynamics of Eurobonds

The Eurobond market originated in the early 1960s when a high level of investment spending in Western Europe could not be financed in local capital markets due to inadequate capital market capacity. In 1964, the capital controls imposed by the U.S. government, including the Interest Equalization Tax, accentuated the need for new sources of international capital at that time.

The Eurobond market characteristically lacks a physical location, although new bond issues primarily are organized in London and Luxembourg. Marketing of Eurobonds is a multicountry project. Given locational flexibility, this market remains largely unregulated, although following the Big Bang in London in October 1986 (reorganization of London stock exchange and securities industry) the British authorities have been seeking to tighten up on the procedures and practices in secondary trading of Eurobonds. The Eurobond market is multicurrency, with borrowers being able to designate any one of several currencies (or currency basket) to denominate the issue. The market offers the investor a high degree of anonymity.

Anonymity arises because Eurobonds are issued in bearer form. Ownership is evidenced by the fact that one has the bond in one's possession. Bearer bonds contrast with registered bonds; registered bonds have an ownership name assigned to the bond serial number, and the bond can be transferred only through formal procedure. Because bearer bonds are not registered, they are attractive investment assets for investors who wish to remain anonymous.

INTEREST RATES AND MATURITIES

Interest rates on Eurobonds tend to follow rates in the domestic capital market of the same currency. That is, yields on dollar Eurobonds follow yields in the New York bond market, whereas yields on deutsche mark Eurobonds follow yields in the German bond market. While Eurobond yields follow or parallel those in the respective domestic capital market, they are not rigidly locked together with these interest rates. Eurobond yields often can be lower than in the respective domestic capital market due to greater efficiency in the market. Also, the spreads between Eurobond interest rates and those prevailing in the respective domestic bond market can vary over time.

Eurobond issues generally have somewhat shorter maturities than foreign bond issues. Eurobond maturities can range from five years to ten or even 15 years final maturity. In some cases three-year notes are issued. This compares with 20–30 year maturities for most foreign bond issues.

The shorter maturities common for Eurobonds reflect the special role of the market, the interests of investors, and the need to keep risks under control. Individual investors may purchase a large percentage of Eurobonds. These investors seek the following benefits from their Eurobond investments:

1. tax anonymity, meaning that the coupon interest received represents a full measure of the current income
2. ability to cash in on speculative profit upon appreciation in value of the bond

The second benefit derives from the fact that most Eurobonds are denominated in foreign currency. A Belgian investor holding a dollar denominated Eurobond hopes that the dollar will appreciate against the Belgian franc, so that the Eurobond can be sold for speculative profit. One factor can interfere with this profit—an upward movement of dollar interest rates that cause the Eurobond to fall in value (interest rate risk). One way to minimize this "loss of liquidity" of the Eurobond is to issue it for a relatively short maturity so that interest rate swings are less likely to bring about sharp bond price fluctuations. In this way Belgian investors previously described can follow the strategy of seeking currency-related capital gains.

REASONS FOR MARKET GROWTH

Data provided in this chapter demonstrate the rapid growth of the Eurobond market. In the four-year period 1982–1986 the volume of new offerings increased from $52 billion to $188 billion. The sharp fall in long-term interest rates and the steep rise in bond prices since 1982 was important in underpinning bond market growth. Eurobonds exhibited strong growth in 1989–1995. This growth also was characteristic of earlier periods. A number of factors help explain this strong growth:

1. steadily growing demand for funds by multinational corporations, governments, and international organizations;
2. development of new sources of funds seeking investment outlets, including the oil surpluses of OPEC countries, new wealth accumulated in the emerging developing nations, and episodic flight capital;
3. ability of the market to operate more efficiently than foreign bond markets. This ability is attributed to the anonymity of investors and the absence of any direct application of income taxes on investment income, permitting investor and borrower both to obtain a better outcome than in domestic capital markets;
4. high degree of flexibility afforded by the market, whereby borrowers and investors can select from several possible currencies of denomination. In addition, the market affords the possibility of issuing new types of securities, including straight debentures, convertibles, bonds with warrants, and floating rate notes;
5. worldwide distribution of Eurobonds by multinational underwriting syndicate facilitates international capital flows;
6. efficient secondary markets in London, Luxembourg, and Belgium help liquidity settlements between buyers and sellers of Eurobonds.

UNDERWRITING PROCESS AND SPREADS

Eurobond underwriting is carried out in a process where the lead manager negotiates with the issuer and then organizes a syndication (underwriting) group. In addition, a selling group that may be quite large is organized to accomplish multinational distribution (Exhibit 7.6).

During the 1980s, discounting of bonds by Eurobond selling groups led to a sharp decline in the profitability of the new issue market. This decline led to the introduction of the fixed price reoffer syndication method in the 1990s. This method, imported from the United States, now dominates the market. In return for a lower issuing fee, lead managers are contractually obliged not to discount prices to final

| **EXHIBIT 7.6** | **Participants in a Eurobond Underwriting** |

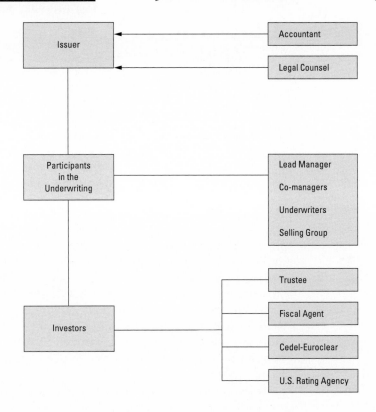

investors. This method is used in the majority of Eurobond issues and ensures banks a positive return on each transaction.

Eurobond underwritings are an international affair with banking houses from many countries included in the underwriting and selling groups. Rarely does the banking sector of any one country dominate in a particular Eurobond issue. A large underwriting group spreads the risks taken by underwriters. Also, successful marketing of Eurobonds requires that a number of national markets be covered. This arrangement is possible when there are several banks from each of a number of countries participating in the underwriting.

Underwriting Spread

The profit resulting from buying and selling Eurobonds by the underwriting group of the Eurobond issues.

Underwriting spreads in the Eurobond market are considerably larger than in the foreign bond markets. A basic reason for this difference is the greater risk involved in Eurobond underwritings as compared with foreign bond issues. In a domestic or foreign bond underwriting the basic risk is that interest rate levels in the local capital market will begin to rise at the time the underwriting group purchases the bond issue from the borrower. If this rise occurs, bond prices will fall and the underwriters may have to sell the bonds at a loss. The risk is one dimensional in this case, namely, a possible rise in local capital market interest rates.

Often underwriting spreads for Eurobonds are two times higher than foreign bond markets. These higher spreads compensate for the greater risks involved and for selling activities that must be organized on a multinational basis. In the case of a 1.75% to 2.0% underwriting spread in the Eurobond market, the management and

EXHIBIT 7.7	Yields on Eurobonds Before and After Rise in Level of Interest Rates on DMark Sector		
	Before	**Change**	**After**
Yield on:			
Dollar Issue	9.00%	9.00%	9.30%
DMark Issue	7.00%	7.30%	7.30%
Sterling Issue	10.00%	10.00%	10.30%

underwriting fee might each be 15–20% of the total spread, the remainder representing the selling commission (60–70% of the total). We should note that while the selling commission seems to be quite large, its share may be exaggerated due to the frequent practice of differential pricing by members of the selling group in a Eurobond underwriting.

The Eurobond market is organized somewhat differently than the foreign bond market. New bond issues can be denominated in any of several currencies. The price of a dollar denominated bond can be influenced by the change in price of a sterling or deutsche mark denominated bond. Investors in the Eurobond market are looking to buy bonds in whatever sector (or currency denomination) that offers prospects for best overall performance. In this case, if a borrower is planning to sell a sterling Eurobond, investors may require a yield of 10.0% but also will accept yields of 9.0% on dollar issues and 7.0% on deutsche mark issues. (Exhibit 7.7). In short this set of yields on the respective currency of denomination Eurobonds provides an equilibrium system in which investors are satisfied with their new portfolio holdings.

If the borrower proceeds with the sterling Eurobond issue, the underwriters will purchase the 10.0% sterling Eurobonds at let us say 98.5 (£985), for resale to investors at 100 (£1,000). The underwriting group can earn a spread of £15 per bond. But there are several risks. Interest rates in any of the three currency sectors may begin to rise, due perhaps to an increase in rates in the domestic capital market of the same currency of denomination. A rise in interest rates in New York would cause rates on dollar Eurobonds to rise also, and a rise in interest rates in the German capital market would cause rates on deutsche mark Eurobonds to rise, changing the relative attractiveness of Eurobonds denominated in these three currencies. Therefore in the case of the sterling Eurobond underwriting, a rise in interest rates in London, New York, or Frankfurt constitutes a serious risk factor—interest rate risk.

A weakening or strengthening of currency also poses a risk for Eurobond underwriting. If at the time of the sterling Eurobond underwriting, sterling exhibits signs of weakness, or alternatively the deutsche mark or dollar strengthens, investors will switch their purchases and holdings accordingly. This change will affect the relative success or failure of the new issue from the point of view of the bond underwriters. As this illustration indicates, there are several sources of risk related to interest rate changes and to relative strengthening and weakening of currency.

THE CURRENCY FACTOR

On a year-to-year basis, the relative role or importance of the leading currencies of denomination of Eurobonds changes. This year-to-year change in currency share is evident in Exhibit 7.8. Generally the U.S. dollar has accounted for the largest share of Eurobond issues while the deutsche mark has ranked second with approximately

EXHIBIT 7.8	**Type and Currency Structure of International Bond Issues**				
	1991	**1992**	**1993**	**1994**	**1995**
International Bonds (in $billion)	309	334	481	427	467
By Major Instruments (in percent)					
Straights	78.6	79.5	76.7	67.8	75.6
Floating rate	5.9	13.1	14.5	22.5	16.9
Convertibles	3.3	1.6	3.8	5.1	2.6
Equity Warrants	10.2	4.7	4.3	2.3	1.2
Zero Coupons	1.2	1.0	0.4	1.3	1.8
Other	0.7	0.2	0.3	1.0	1.8
Total	100.0	100.0	100.0	100.0	100.0
By Major Currencies (in percent)					
U.S. Dollar	29.7	36.9	35.9	37.5	39.5
Deutsche Mark	7.1	10.4	11.8	7.8	15.5
Yen	12.6	11.2	9.6	13.3	12.6
Sterling	8.8	7.6	10.8	8.8	5.9
Swiss Franc	7.1	5.8	6.1	4.8	5.6
Italian Lira	3.2	2.5	3.1	5.5	3.8
Dutch Guilder	1.1	2.0	2.6	3.0	3.2
Canadian Dollar	7.2	4.7	6.4	3.6	0.7
French Franc	6.1	7.5	8.7	7.0	2.8
Other	17.1	11.4	5.0	8.7	10.7
Total	100.0	100.0	100.0	100.0	100.0

SOURCE: OECD, *Financial Market Trends,* (February and June 1996).

9–15% of total issues. In the same period the yen took second place after the deutsche mark. The British pound followed closely behind. The following appear to be the major considerations influencing the share of any particular currency of denomination in Eurobond issues:

1. To be eligible as a currency of denomination there must be a fairly wide acceptance of the currency as a standard of value and a unit of account in which deferred payments can safely be denominated.

2. Very strong currencies are undesirable from the borrower's viewpoint, whereas very weak currencies are undesirable from the lender's viewpoint.

3. Comparing the relative merits of any two possible currencies of denomination, there is a coupon/currency strength tradeoff.

With respect to the first point, only currencies that have a broad acceptance in international transactions or in international investment are likely to be considered for use in denominating Eurobonds. All four of the leading Eurobond currencies listed (dollar, deutsche mark, sterling, yen) meet this requirement. The Swiss franc also meets this requirement, but the Swiss authorities have limited use of the Swiss franc since they do not wish to have their currency exposed to the pressures that accrue from serving as a currency of denomination for Eurobonds. This relationship is explained in closer detail in the appendix to this chapter titled "Switzerland—Financial Entrepôt."

The preferred currency of denomination of international bonds (and especially Eurobonds) varies considerably based on the country of residence of the bond issuer. This variation can be seen in the data summarized in Exhibit 7.9, covering the period 1994–1996. The four most preferred currencies of denomination are indicated for

EXHIBIT 7.9	**Rank Importance of Currencies of Denomination of International Bonds, By Country Borrower (1994–1996)**

Country Borrower	US$	SF	Yen	DM	Sterling	Other[1]			
Australia	2		3		4	1(1)			
Canada	1		3	4		2(2)			
France	2	4	4	3		1(3)			
Germany	2	3		1		4(1)			
Italy	2		1	4		3(4)			
Japan	1	3	2	4					
Sweden	1	3	2	4					
United Kingdom	2	4	3		1				
United States	1	4	3			2(4)			
Summary						EAu	ECU	FF	Cdn
Rank 1	4	—	1	1	1	1	—	1	—
Rank 2	5		2	—	—	—	1	—	1
Rank 3	—	3	4	1		—	1	—	—
Rank 4	—	3	1	4	1	1	1	—	—

SF denotes Swiss franc.
EAu denotes Euro-Australian dollar.
ECU denotes European Currency Unit.
FF denotes French franc.
Cdn denotes Euro-Canadian dollar.

[1] First number refers to rank importance. Second number (in parentheses) refers to the following: 1) = Euro Australian dollar, 2) = Euro Canadian dollar, 3) = French franc, and 4) = European Currency Unit.

SOURCE: OECD, *Financial Market Trends.* (June 1996): 92.

each of the nine countries that are important borrowers in the international bond markets. A "1" indicates borrowers in that country rank this currency of denomination as most preferred.

The results are not surprising. The dollar stands out as the first ranked in four cases, and second ranked in five cases. The Swiss franc and yen run close as second and third ranked currencies in overall preference, but German mark was increasingly important in 1995–1996.

Exhibit 7.9 reveals interesting information relative to the preferences of borrowers in using the deutsche mark and pound sterling as currencies of denomination. Only two countries rank the deutsche mark among the top four currencies of denomination, and only four countries rank the pound sterling. German borrowers rank the deutsche mark first in preference, and British borrowers rank the pound first in preference. This preference can be explained in part by the desire to avoid currency risk. Further, we might note that the perceived strength of the deutsche mark and potential weakness of the pound may place these currencies beyond the limits of acceptability for borrowers (in the case of the deutsche mark) or investors (in the case of the pound), thereby limiting their use as currencies of denomination.

Between 1981–1991 the European Currency Unit (ECU) was a more important currency of denomination for Eurobond issues. The first ECU denominated bonds were issued in 1981. The importance of ECU denominated bonds has declined since the European monetary crisis in October 1991 (Exhibit 7.10). As reported by the OECD Financial Market Trends, ECU denominated bonds only accounted for 1.7% of all international bonds in 1995. Another problem of the ECU denominated bonds in recent years is the uncertainty of the European Monetary union (EMU) in 1999. However, some international borrowers still issue ECU bonds because these bonds provide relatively high yields, coupled with low currency risk.

EXHIBIT 7.10   **The ECU Bond Bubble Bursts**

Over the 10 year period 1981–1991 the ECU component of the Eurobond market expanded dramatically. Early in 1981 it was stated "the ECU can be regarded as a sort of free lunch before European economic and monetary union." With ECU bond yields higher than those on German bonds, for example, yields were expected to drop as the European economies converged. This expectation was broken in October 1991.

In October conflicting and contradictory reports for plans to prepare the ECU for its pan-European role led to panic selling of ECU bonds. Sell-offs of ECU bonds occurred after several European government treasury and central bank officials gave speeches indicating support for a "freezing" of the ECU. A freezing of the ECU means that its currency basket will no longer be adjusted every five years. In fact, the ECU might be allowed to "depreciate" against individual component currencies of the ECU basket.

Bond dealers had been touting ECU bonds on the assumption that hardening the currency would be the policy followed. This view asserted that if the ECU were in fact hardened, European countries would have to align their economies with the strongest, whereas if the ECU were simply frozen,

they could converge at the median. A hard ECU would mean rapidly falling ECU interest rates, earning substantial profit for holders of existing bonds.

A flood of ECU and other international bond issues brought a rush of bankers into the market. At October 1991 there were some 40 licensed ECU market makers, double the number ten months earlier. Some banks that formerly dominated the market (for example, Paribas) were battling to maintain market position. With profits set to tumble as new Eurobond market makers entered the scene, a shakeout was expected for 1992. In late 1991 and 1992, ECU dealing houses were waiting patiently for signals from EC officials to calm the markets.

The referendum on the Maastricht Treaty further destabilized the ECU bond market in 1992. The big collapse occurred after June 1992, when Denmark voted against the treaty. A reversal of this decision in a second referendum in May 1993, along with rising hopes of the treaty being ratified, led to a modest recovery in the ECU market in 1993. Later that year, the German Constitutional Court removed the final barrier to the treaty, and thereby further stabilizied the ECU bond market.

SOURCE: *The Economist,* (October 19, 1991), p. 95.

Sovereign governments and supranational organizations have been quick to take advantage of ECU borrowing facilities given the built-in hedge against currency risk. For private sector corporations, the benefits of using ECU bonds depend on the ability to swap the proceeds of the issue into a useful operating currency. When currency and interest rate swaps (discussed in detail later in this chapter) are available, UK companies (British Telecom, Maxwell Communications) have been able to obtain floating rate sterling funding well below the London interbank offered rate. The opportunity to swap out of ECU depends on finding a counterparty willing to swap into ECU. Unfortunately, swap opportunities open up and also close down. As a result, the number of ECU bond issues by companies fluctuates on the basis of available offsetting swap opportunities.

For the borrower, the choice of currency of denomination is likely to be based on the following considerations. First, what is the expected cost of the bond issue? The cost is a combination of coupon interest plus the effects from currency rate change during the period the bond issue is outstanding. A French corporation borrowing in the Eurobond market might have the following choices:

U.S. dollar Eurobond issue—coupon	8.50%
Deutsche mark Eurobond issue—coupon	6.75%
French franc Eurobond issue—coupon	9.50%

Assuming that all three issues will be ten years to maturity, the basic question is: What currency rate changes are likely on average in the next ten years? This is a difficult question, but one that must be addressed. Let us assume the chief financial officer of the French corporation has the following projections of currency movements on which to base the decision.

1. Dollar will depreciate in relation to French franc 2.0% per year.
2. French franc will depreciate in relation to deutsche mark 2.8% per year.

The approximate currency adjusted cost of borrowing will be

1. U.S. dollar issue—6.50%
2. Dmark issue—9.55%
3. French franc issue—9.50%

Clearly, the dollar issue will be the most attractive from the point of view of overall cost considerations. But another set of considerations may be important, namely, the way that the selection of currency of denomination influences the overall currency exposure of the French corporation. Currency exposure management is explored in close detail in a later chapter. But let us look at the question of controlling currency exposure in an uncomplicated way.

The chief financial officer of the French corporation would have to ask two basic questions: 1) On a global basis, does the currency mix of our cash flows suggest anything in the way of preferred currency of denomination in borrowing? 2) On a global basis, does the currency mix of our assets and liabilities suggest anything in the way of a preferred currency of denomination in borrowing?

By way of example, let us assume that the French corporation has a large positive deutsche mark cash flow via a sales affiliate in West Germany, and a large U.S. dollar liability position due to extensive dollar denominated borrowing. These currency exposure positions call for more borrowing in deutsche marks, given the large deutsche mark cash flow generation. Also, they call for limiting future U.S. dollar borrowings due to the large existing dollar indebtedness.

If we put together the information concerning relative costs and currency exposure, we obtain a fairly mixed answer. Based on cost, dollar borrowings would be preferable. Based on the currency exposure situation, deutsche mark borrowings would be preferable. However, on an overall basis—combining expected currency rate movements and coupon interest—a French franc borrowing (9.50%) is no more expensive than deutsche mark issue (9.55%). Therefore a possible solution for the French corporation is to issue a French franc denominated Eurobond.

MAJOR INSTRUMENTS OF THE EUROBOND MARKET

The introduction of several new types of bond instruments has accompanied the growth and evolution of the Eurobond market. These different instruments satisfy the special needs of borrowers and lenders and inject an added dimension of flexibility to the market.

Exhibit 7.8 depicts the dollar amounts and percentage composition of international bond issues over the period 1991–1995. Straight fixed rate bond issues consistently represent more than 60% of new offerings. Bonds with equity warrants increased in importance over the short period 1987–1989 when the Tokyo stock exchange showed rising stock prices, but these issues declined in the period 1991–1995 due to excess value of Japanese stocks.

Floating rate notes (FRNs) occupy an important niche in the Eurobond market. These issues represent between 6% and 22% of total international issues. The FRN is a relatively short-term note that is automatically rolled over twice a year. The rollover rate is usually based on LIBOR plus a premium. The size of the premium depends on the quality of the bond or note issue. FRNs generally have a minimum rate. As a rule, the coupon interest does not fall below this minimum.

Convertible bonds have been a less important component of the Eurobond market. As Exhibit 7.8 indicates, these issues accounted for 2–5% of issues. The convertible Eurobond can be viewed as a straight bond with an option. In this case the option to convert the bond into stock of the same company has a potential value that results in a lower coupon on the convertible. In the early years of the Eurobond market American companies led in the use of convertible Eurobonds, followed by European and later Japanese companies.

Finally, zero coupon bonds make up a small (less than 2%) share of international bond issues.

Convertible Eurobonds offer an unusual currency play. A dollar denominated Eurobond will be convertible into the equity shares of the parent company. Convertibles issued by European or Japanese companies denominated in dollars offer a dual currency feature. Take the simple illustration in Exhibit 7.11. A French company can issue a dollar denominated Eurobond with a 4.5% coupon. Alternatively a straight Eurobond might call for a 9.0% coupon. The conversion rate is ten shares per bond. Note that the conversion premium is $200. Investors are paying $200 over current share value for the option to convert the bonds into shares. The shares will have to rise in value by $200 (FF1,000) for market share value to equal the bond issue price.

This illustration suggests a situation that occurs two years later where the shares appreciate in value in local currency by a wide margin of 65%. However, the French franc falls in value against the dollar to $0.167. As a result the Eurobond value (driven by underlying share values at this point) is $1100. Dollar-oriented investors have gained 10% through appreciation in bond value. But French franc-oriented investors have gained a full 32% appreciation.

Convertible Eurobonds present corporations with several benefits including the opportunity to sell shares indirectly at a double premium. The double premium arises due to 1) the conversion premium built into the pricing of the bond at issue, and 2) the prospects of currency gain that investors perceive due to the strength of the currency in which the underlying shares are valued at the time of issue.

EXHIBIT 7.11	**Convertible Eurobond Issued by French Corporation, Effect From Changes in Share Price and Foreign Exchange Rate**			
	WHEN BOND IS ISSUED		**TWO YEARS LATER**	
	$	FF	$	FF
Value of Bond ($)	1,000	5,000	1,100	6,600
Value of ten Shares of Stock	800	4,000	1,100	6,600
Conversion Premium	200	1,000		
Coupon on Bond	45	—	45	—
Yield on Bond	4.50	—	4.09	—
Foreign Exchange Rate ($/FF)	$0.20	FF5.00	$0.167	FF6.00
Price of Share (FF)		400		660

NOTE: Bond issued with conversion rate of ten shares of stock per bond.

EXHIBIT 7.12	**International Bond Offerings by Category of Issuer**				

	$ BILLION				
	1991	**1992**	**1993**	**1994**	**1995**
Governments[1]	44.4	64.0	106.3	90.5	75.9
Public Enterprises	48.3	51.2	64.9	52.1	56.7
Banks	55.9	67.6	110.2	133.5	154.0
Private Corporations	123.7	109.6	151.7	123.7	145.0
International Organizations	36.4	41.3	47.9	28.8	35.7
Total	**308.7**	**333.7**	**481.0**	**428.6**	**467.3**
Memorandum Item: Issues by Governments as a Percentage of Total	14.4	19.2	22.1	21.1	16.2

[1] Including central banks and state and local governments.

SOURCE: OECD *Financial Market Trends,* (February and June 1996).

CATEGORIES OF BORROWERS

Government share of all international bond offerings continued to decline in 1994–1995 (see Exhibit 7.12) while borrowings from public enterprises were relatively stable. Banks, especially German banks, needed funds to finance international credit expansion, particularly to finance the global wave of mergers and acquisitions. Banks borrowed $112 billion in 1993, $134 billion in 1994, and $154 billion in 1995. Private corporations stepped up borrowings in the international bond market to finance their worldwide investments, especially in the prosperous Asian countries. International organizations such as the World Bank and other regional development banks issued international bonds year by year—the amounts varying depending on their needs for project financing in the LDCs and on the cost of capital.

On an overall basis, the OECD area accounted for about 87% of total international bond offerings; non-OECD countries shared about 9%; and international organizations took 4% in the period 1991–1995.

TAXATION

Eurobonds are usually free of most taxes. From a legal standpoint syndicate managers take great care in preparing the issue to assure nonapplicability of withholding taxes. Because a substantial part of the investors are individuals, applicability of estate and gift taxes is minimized.

Many corporate borrowers issue Eurobonds through a finance subsidiary incorporated in a tax haven (for example, Netherlands Antilles). In this way the issue is not subject to income taxes or capital gains taxation. This procedure is an important requirement if the issuer (finance subsidiary) reloans the borrowed funds. All or some part of the interest spread charged could become subject to any income taxes applicable, reducing the benefits derived from this method of financing. In the case of a U.S. parent corporation using a foreign-based finance subsidiary to issue Eurobonds, there may be excess foreign tax credits in the U.S. tax reporting system. In order for the U.S. parent to utilize its excess foreign tax credits, the interest income of the finance subsidiary should be a foreign source.

International tax treaties can play a role in broadening the potential market for Eurobond issues. Such tax treaties reciprocally lower or remove the tax burden imposed on foreign source interest income of international investors.

Secondary Trading

The Eurobond secondary market operates like an over-the-counter market. There is no organized exchange or trading floor, and all trading is conducted by electronic communications and telephones. London has been the center for Eurobond trading due to the financial infrastructure, hands-off regulatory approach, and the availability of personnel to carry out dealing and related functions. A number of secondary market makers have closely related Eurocurrency and international banking operations in London as well.

The secondary market in Eurobonds provides an important liquidity service, enabling investors to buy and sell through the market maker. Market makers take on a number of costs in providing this liquidity service. These costs include 1) acquiring a nonoptimal portfolio from a liquidity point of view, 2) being forced to trade with some investors who may have superior information (insider trading is quite possible in the Eurobond market that enjoys no direct protection from the U.S. Securities Exchange Commission), and 3) the cost of running the dealing room and settlements system. Given these costs, if investors are not willing to pay them in the form of dealer spreads, market makers face the prospect of earning a subnormal return on their invested capital. Many Eurobond market makers have suffered losses on their secondary market operations in the past.

In 1968 the Association of International Bond Dealers (AIBD) was formed for the purpose of increasing the professional status of the market and to set rules for market makers. The market is spread out geographically. Therefore it might be difficult for investors located in countries more removed from the trading center, London, to stay in close contact with changing market conditions.

In 1991 the AIBD was reorganized into the International Securities Market Association (ISMA). ISMA has more than 500 members, but barely a dozen are market makers that provide continuous two-way price quotations. There are numerous reasons for the small number of market makers. Lack of profitability has been an important consideration. Eurobond dealing profits come from:

1. dealing spreads (bid/ask);
2. profit from changes in the value of inventory held, calling for holding a net short book when prices are falling, and a net long book when prices are rising; and
3. difference between the financing costs of bond holding, and the yield on these holdings. A major part of any dealer's inventory is financed by loans provided by the clearing system (Euroclear or Cedel). In turn profit is a function of the shape of the yield curve. An upward sloping yield curve permits profits from the balance between bond yield and financing cost.

Eurobond prices are quoted as a percent of face value. A bid/ask quote of 92-92.5 indicates a bid price of $920 and an asked price of $925 for a bond with face value of $1000. The spread on Eurobonds is .50%, but a range of spreads can exist depending on conditions in the market.

When a trade is made, settlement by exchange of bonds and cash takes place on the value date, approximately a week later. The standard-size Eurobond transaction is 100 bonds (with $100,000 of face value). Quoted prices apply to standard-size transactions. In other cases where smaller amounts of bonds are traded, prices must be negotiated and investors will experience a somewhat higher spread cost.

Secondary market purchase and sale is "with coupon." The buyer pays the seller the agreed price, plus interest that has accumulated since the last coupon interest payment. Several alternative methods can be used to calculate the accrued interest. For example, in the Eurobond market the conventional method applied to most Eurobonds and U.S. corporate bonds is the 30/360 method. This method considers each month to have 30 days. While there are 31 days (actual number) between 15 May 1996 and 15 June 1996, interest is allocated as if there were 30 days. Interest accrual for this period on an 8% coupon bond would be calculated as follows:

$$.08 \times 30/360 = .00667$$

Calculation of accrued interest and total purchase price of a Eurobond in the secondary market can best be described by an illustration.

On 15 October 1996 a bond trader buys 200 Eurobonds with a face value of $1000 each. The bonds have a 9% coupon, and the bond trader pays a price of 96. The bonds pay annual coupons on March 15. What is the bond trader's total cost?

The bond transaction is settled on October 22. There are 217 days (15 March 1996 to 22 October 1996), calculated on a 30/360 basis. The accrued interest is:

$$200 \times \$1,000 \times .09 \times 217/360 = \$10,850$$

The payment for the bond net of accrued interest is:

$$200 \times \$1,000 \times .96 = \$192,000$$

Total payment is $192,000 + $10,850 = $202,850

Euroclear

An international clearing system located in Brussels created by Morgan Guaranty Trust Company in 1968.

Cedel

An international clearing system located in Luxembourg created by a group of European banks in 1970.

Two international securities clearing systems were developed in 1968 and 1970, respectively. Euroclear was the first, set up in Brussels by Morgan Guaranty Trust Company. Two years later Cedel was established in Luxembourg. These clearing systems facilitate transfers of securities between buyer and seller in the form of book entries. Whereas the securities (Eurobonds) may be held in depositories in various countries, accounting for them is carried out in Brussels or Luxembourg. Cedel and Euroclear provide financing as well as settlement functions. The financing is based on the bond positions of market makers. The financing can be up to 90% of the collateral value at interest rates based on short-term interbank rates prevailing in the currency of denomination of the bonds.

Secondary market turnover as reported by the international clearing houses (Euroclear and Cedel) was $24.4 trillion in 1994 and $32.4 trillion in 1995.* The Eurobond turnover is the source of profit for Eurobond dealers in the secondary market. Secondary market data on International bonds is supplied by the ISMA and published in the Financial Times (see Exhibit 7.13).

From 1 June 1995 the ISMA shortened the settlement period for Euro securities to three business days, which paralleled similar moves by a number of national authorities such as the SEC in the United States.

---

*BIS Annual Report 1994 p. 177 and 1995, p. 46.

EXHIBIT 7.13   **Secondary Market Prices: International Bond**

FT/ISMA International Bond Service

Listed are the latest International Bonds for which there is an Adequate Secondary Market. Closing prices on August 21

	Issued	Bid	Offer	Chg	Yield
U.S. DOLLAR STRAIGHTS					
Abbey Natl Treasury $6\frac{1}{2}$ 03	1000	$98\frac{1}{8}$	$98\frac{3}{8}$	$-\frac{1}{4}$	6.85
ABN Amro Bank $7\frac{1}{4}$ 05	1000	$100\frac{5}{8}$	$100\frac{7}{8}$	$-\frac{1}{8}$	7.28
African Dev Bk $7\frac{3}{8}$ 23	500	$97\frac{1}{2}$	$97\frac{7}{8}$	$-\frac{1}{4}$	7.59
Alberta Province $7\frac{5}{8}$ 98	1000	$102\frac{3}{4}$	$102\frac{7}{8}$		6.23
Asian Dev Bank $6\frac{1}{4}$ 05	750	$96\frac{1}{8}$	$96\frac{1}{4}$	$-\frac{1}{8}$	6.94
Austria $8\frac{1}{2}$ 00	400	106	$106\frac{1}{4}$		6.47
Baden-Wuertt L-Fin $8\frac{1}{8}$ 00	1000	$104\frac{3}{4}$	$104\frac{7}{8}$		6.52
Bancomext $7\frac{1}{4}$ 04	1000	84	$84\frac{3}{8}$	$-\frac{1}{4}$	10.66
Bank Ned Gemeenten 7 99	1000	102	$102\frac{1}{4}$		6.25
Bayer Vereinsbk $8\frac{1}{8}$ 00	500	$104\frac{5}{8}$	$104\frac{3}{4}$		6.56
Belgium $5\frac{1}{2}$ 03	1000	$92\frac{1}{2}$	$92\frac{3}{4}$	$-\frac{1}{8}$	6.85
British Columbia $7\frac{3}{4}$ 02	500	$104\frac{3}{4}$	105	$-\frac{1}{8}$	6.73
British Gas 0 21	1500	$14\frac{3}{8}$	$14\frac{3}{4}$		8.00
Canada $6\frac{3}{8}$ 05	1500	$96\frac{5}{8}$	$96\frac{3}{4}$	$-\frac{1}{8}$	7.01
Cheung Kong Fin $5\frac{1}{2}$ 98	500	$96\frac{3}{4}$	$97\frac{1}{4}$		7.21
China $6\frac{1}{2}$ 04	1000	$94\frac{3}{4}$	$95\frac{1}{4}$		7.56
Credit Foncier $9\frac{1}{2}$ 99	300	$106\frac{3}{4}$	$107\frac{1}{8}$		6.46
Denmark $5\frac{3}{4}$ 98	1000	$99\frac{1}{2}$	$99\frac{3}{4}$		6.08
East Japan Railway $6\frac{5}{8}$ 04	600	$97\frac{3}{4}$	98	$-\frac{1}{8}$	7.01
EIB 6 04	500	$96\frac{1}{4}$	$96\frac{5}{8}$	$-\frac{1}{8}$	6.64
EIB $9\frac{1}{4}$ 97	1000	$103\frac{7}{8}$	$104\frac{1}{8}$	$-\frac{1}{8}$	5.86
Elec de France 9 98	200	104	$104\frac{1}{4}$		6.19
Ex-Im Bank Japan 8 02	500	$105\frac{7}{8}$	$106\frac{1}{4}$	$-\frac{1}{8}$	6.72
Export Dev Corp $9\frac{1}{2}$ 98	150	$105\frac{5}{8}$	$105\frac{7}{8}$		6.24
Exxon Capital 0 04	1800	$58\frac{1}{8}$	$58\frac{1}{2}$	$-\frac{1}{8}$	6.81
Fed Home Loan $7\frac{1}{8}$ 99	1500	$102\frac{1}{4}$	$102\frac{3}{8}$		6.36
Federal Natl Mort 7.40 04	1500	$103\frac{3}{4}$	$103\frac{7}{8}$		6.89
Finland $6\frac{3}{4}$ 97	3000	$100\frac{7}{8}$	101	$-\frac{1}{8}$	6.10
Ford Motor Credit $6\frac{1}{4}$ 98	1500	$100\frac{1}{8}$	$100\frac{1}{4}$		6.26
General Mills 0 13	1000	$24\frac{5}{8}$	$25\frac{3}{8}$		8.60
INI Finance $5\frac{1}{4}$ 98	650	$97\frac{3}{4}$	98		6.32
Inter-Amer Dev $6\frac{1}{8}$ 06	1000	95	$95\frac{1}{4}$	$-\frac{1}{8}$	6.96
Inter-Amer Dev $7\frac{1}{2}$ 05	500	$103\frac{1}{4}$	$103\frac{1}{2}$	$-\frac{1}{4}$	6.98
Intl Finance $5\frac{1}{4}$ 99	500	$98\frac{1}{8}$	$98\frac{3}{8}$		6.11
Italy 6 03	2000	$95\frac{1}{2}$	$95\frac{5}{8}$		6.92
Italy $6\frac{7}{8}$ 23	3500	$91\frac{1}{2}$	$91\frac{7}{8}$	$-\frac{1}{4}$	7.77
Japan Dev Bk $8\frac{3}{8}$ 01	500	$106\frac{1}{2}$	$106\frac{3}{4}$		6.63
Korea Elec Power $6\frac{3}{8}$ 03	1350	$95\frac{3}{8}$	$95\frac{3}{4}$		7.33
Matsushita Elec $7\frac{1}{4}$ 02	1000	$102\frac{1}{2}$	$102\frac{3}{4}$	$-\frac{1}{4}$	6.84
Ontario $7\frac{3}{8}$ 03	3000	$102\frac{7}{8}$	$103\frac{1}{8}$		6.93
Oster Kontroll bank $8\frac{1}{2}$ 01	200	$107\frac{1}{8}$	$107\frac{3}{8}$		6.62
Portugal $5\frac{3}{4}$ 03	1000	94	$94\frac{1}{4}$	$-\frac{1}{8}$	6.94
Quebec Hydro $9\frac{3}{4}$ 98	150	$106\frac{1}{8}$	$106\frac{3}{8}$		6.53
Quebec Prov 9 98	200	$103\frac{7}{8}$	$104\frac{1}{8}$		6.38
SAS 10 99	200	$107\frac{3}{8}$	$107\frac{3}{4}$		6.68
SNCF $9\frac{1}{2}$ 98	150	$105\frac{5}{8}$	106	$-\frac{1}{8}$	6.28
Spain $6\frac{1}{2}$ 99	1500	$100\frac{1}{2}$	$100\frac{5}{8}$		6.31
Sweden $6\frac{1}{2}$ 03	2000	$99\frac{1}{8}$	$99\frac{3}{8}$	$-\frac{1}{8}$	6.78
Tennessee Valley 6 00	1000	$98\frac{3}{8}$	$98\frac{1}{2}$		6.55
Tennessee Valley $6\frac{3}{8}$ 05	2000	$97\frac{1}{8}$	$97\frac{3}{8}$	$-\frac{1}{8}$	6.93
Tokyo Elec Power $6\frac{1}{8}$ 03	1000	$96\frac{3}{4}$	$97\frac{7}{8}$		6.72
Toyota Motor $5\frac{5}{8}$ 98	1500	$99\frac{3}{8}$	$99\frac{5}{8}$	$+\frac{1}{8}$	6.03
United Kingdom $7\frac{1}{4}$ 02	3000	$103\frac{5}{8}$	$103\frac{3}{4}$	$-\frac{1}{8}$	6.52
Walt Disney $6\frac{3}{8}$ 01	1300	$98\frac{5}{8}$	$98\frac{3}{4}$	$-\frac{1}{8}$	6.84
World Bank $6\frac{3}{8}$ 05	1500	$97\frac{3}{8}$	$97\frac{1}{2}$	$-\frac{1}{4}$	6.89
World Bank $8\frac{3}{8}$ 99	1500	$106\frac{1}{8}$	$106\frac{1}{4}$		6.27

(Continued)

EXHIBIT 7.13   **(Continued)**

	Issued	Bid	Offer	Chg	Yield
DEUTSCHE MARK STRAIGHTS					
Austria $6\frac{1}{2}$ 24	2000	$92\frac{3}{8}$	$92\frac{5}{8}$	$-\frac{5}{8}$	7.14
Baden-Wuertt L-Finance 6 99	2000	$103\frac{5}{8}$	104	$-\frac{1}{4}$	4.54
Credit Foncier $7\frac{1}{4}$ 03	2000	$104\frac{3}{4}$	$105\frac{1}{8}$	$-\frac{1}{2}$	6.33
Denmark $6\frac{1}{8}$ 98	2000	$103\frac{3}{8}$	$103\frac{1}{2}$	$-\frac{1}{8}$	3.95
Depfa Finance $6\frac{3}{8}$ 03	1500	$100\frac{3}{4}$	$100\frac{7}{8}$	$-\frac{3}{8}$	6.24
Deutche Bk Fin $7\frac{1}{2}$ 03	2000	$105\frac{7}{8}$	$106\frac{3}{8}$	$-\frac{1}{2}$	6.35
EEC $6\frac{1}{2}$ 00	2900	$104\frac{5}{8}$	$104\frac{7}{8}$	$-\frac{3}{8}$	5.03
EIB $6\frac{1}{4}$ 00	1500	$103\frac{7}{8}$	$104\frac{1}{8}$	$-\frac{1}{4}$	5.04
Finland $7\frac{1}{2}$ 00	3000	$107\frac{5}{8}$	$107\frac{7}{8}$	$-\frac{3}{8}$	5.01
Italy $7\frac{1}{4}$ 98	5000	$104\frac{3}{4}$	$104\frac{7}{8}$		3.84
LKB Baden-Wuertt $6\frac{1}{2}$ 08	2250	$98\frac{1}{4}$	$98\frac{3}{8}$	$-\frac{1}{2}$	6.71
Norway $6\frac{1}{8}$ 98	1500	$103\frac{3}{8}$	$103\frac{5}{8}$	$-\frac{1}{4}$	4.02
Ontario $6\frac{1}{4}$ 04	1500	$99\frac{3}{8}$	$99\frac{5}{8}$	$-\frac{1}{2}$	6.35
Spain $7\frac{1}{4}$ 03	4000	106	$106\frac{1}{8}$	$-\frac{1}{2}$	6.10
Sweden 8 97	2500	105	105		3.66
United Kingdom $7\frac{1}{8}$ 97	5500	104	$104\frac{1}{8}$		3.60
Volkswagen Intl Fin 7 03	1000	$103\frac{7}{8}$	$104\frac{1}{4}$	$-\frac{1}{2}$	6.27
World Bank 0 15	2000	31	$31\frac{3}{8}$	$-\frac{1}{8}$	6.25
World Bank $5\frac{7}{8}$ 03	3000	$99\frac{1}{2}$	$99\frac{3}{4}$	$-\frac{1}{2}$	5.96
SWISS FRANC STRAIGHTS					
Asian Dev Bank 0 16	500	36	$36\frac{3}{4}$	$-\frac{1}{2}$	5.39
Austria $4\frac{1}{2}$ 00	1000	$104\frac{1}{2}$	$104\frac{3}{4}$		3.11
Council Europe $4\frac{3}{4}$ 98	250	$102\frac{5}{8}$	103		2.91
Denmark $4\frac{1}{4}$ 99	1000	$103\frac{5}{8}$	$103\frac{3}{4}$	$-\frac{1}{8}$	3.01
EIB $3\frac{3}{4}$ 99	1000	$102\frac{1}{2}$	$102\frac{5}{8}$		2.67
EIB $6\frac{3}{4}$ 04	300	$112\frac{1}{2}$	$112\frac{3}{4}$		4.85
Finland $7\frac{1}{4}$ 99	300	$110\frac{1}{4}$	$110\frac{3}{4}$	$-\frac{1}{2}$	3.72
Iceland $7\frac{5}{8}$ 00	100	113			3.99
Inter Amer Dev $4\frac{3}{4}$ 03	600	104	$104\frac{1}{4}$		4.08
Ontario $6\frac{1}{4}$ 03	400	$110\frac{1}{2}$	$111\frac{1}{4}$	$-\frac{1}{8}$	4.34
Quebec Hydro 5 08	100	$100\frac{3}{4}$			4.91
SNCF 7 04	450	117	118		4.46
Sweden $4\frac{3}{4}$ 03	500	104	$104\frac{1}{4}$		4.08
World Bank 0 21	700	$26\frac{3}{4}$	$27\frac{1}{4}$	$-\frac{1}{4}$	5.36
World Bank 7 01	600	$113\frac{1}{4}$	$113\frac{1}{2}$	$-\frac{1}{8}$	3.76
YEN STRAIGHTS					
Belgium 5 99	75000	$110\frac{1}{4}$	$110\frac{1}{2}$		1.79
Credit Foncier $4\frac{3}{4}$ 02	75000	$109\frac{5}{8}$	110	$+\frac{1}{8}$	2.97
EIB $6\frac{5}{8}$ 00	100000	$116\frac{1}{4}$	$116\frac{1}{2}$	$+\frac{1}{8}$	1.87
Ex-Im Bank Japan $4\frac{3}{8}$ 03	105000	$109\frac{5}{8}$	$109\frac{7}{8}$	$+\frac{1}{8}$	2.86
Inter Amer Dev $7\frac{1}{4}$ 00	30000	$118\frac{3}{4}$	119		1.99
Italy $3\frac{1}{2}$ 01	300000	$104\frac{7}{8}$	$105\frac{1}{8}$		2.44
Italy 5 04	200000	$113\frac{1}{2}$	$113\frac{3}{4}$	$+\frac{1}{8}$	3.13
Japan Dev Bk 5 99	100000	$110\frac{1}{8}$	$110\frac{1}{4}$	$+\frac{1}{8}$	1.63
Japan Dev Bk $6\frac{1}{2}$ 01	120000	120	$120\frac{1}{8}$	$+\frac{1}{8}$	2.28
SNCF $6\frac{3}{4}$ 00	30000	$116\frac{3}{8}$	$116\frac{5}{8}$	$+\frac{1}{8}$	1.90
Spain $5\frac{3}{4}$ 02	125000	$116\frac{1}{4}$	$116\frac{1}{2}$	$+\frac{1}{8}$	2.59
Sweden $4\frac{5}{8}$ 98	150000	$105\frac{1}{4}$	$105\frac{1}{2}$		0.96
World Bank $5\frac{1}{4}$ 02	250000	$114\frac{3}{4}$	$114\frac{7}{8}$		2.41
OTHER STRAIGHTS					
Credit Foncier 7.60 02 LFr	2000	$102\frac{5}{8}$	$103\frac{1}{4}$		7.06
EIB $7\frac{1}{8}$ 05 LFr	3000	$104\frac{1}{2}$	105		6.45
World Bank $8\frac{1}{8}$ 04 LFr	2000	$110\frac{1}{8}$	$111\frac{1}{8}$		6.50
ABN Amro $6\frac{5}{8}$ 00 Fl	1000	$105\frac{1}{8}$	$105\frac{3}{8}$	$-\frac{1}{8}$	5.03
Austria $6\frac{1}{2}$ 99 Fl	1000	$104\frac{3}{4}$	105	$+\frac{1}{8}$	4.59
Bell Canada $10\frac{5}{8}$ 99 C\$	150	$111\frac{3}{8}$	$117\frac{7}{8}$	$-\frac{1}{8}$	6.21
British Columbia $7\frac{3}{4}$ 03 C\$	1250	$104\frac{1}{8}$	$104\frac{3}{8}$		7.10
Canada Mfg & Hsg $8\frac{1}{4}$ 99 C\$	1000	$106\frac{1}{8}$	$106\frac{3}{8}$	$-\frac{1}{8}$	6.03
EIB $10\frac{1}{8}$ 98 C\$	130	$107\frac{1}{4}$	$107\frac{5}{8}$		5.11
Elec de France $9\frac{3}{4}$ 99 C\$	275	$109\frac{7}{8}$	$110\frac{1}{3}$		6.10
KfW Int Fin 10 01 C\$	400	$112\frac{5}{8}$	113		6.66
Nippon Tel Tel $10\frac{1}{4}$ 99 C\$	200	$111\frac{1}{4}$	$111\frac{1}{2}$		6.21

(Continued)

EXHIBIT 7.13   (Continued)

	Issued	Bid	Offer	Chg	Yield
Ontario 8 03 C$	1500	$105\frac{3}{8}$	$105\frac{5}{8}$		7.08
Ontario Hydro $10\frac{7}{8}$ 99 C$	500	$111\frac{5}{8}$	$117\frac{7}{8}$	$-\frac{1}{8}$	5.90
Oster Kontrollbank $10\frac{1}{4}$ 99 C$	150	$110\frac{7}{8}$	$111\frac{1}{4}$		6.08
Quebec Hydro 7 04 CS	1000	98	$98\frac{1}{8}$	$+\frac{1}{8}$	7.47
Quebec Prov $10\frac{1}{2}$ 98 C$	200	$109\frac{5}{8}$	110		5.83
Council Europe 9 01 Ecu	1100	$111\frac{5}{8}$	112	$-\frac{1}{4}$	6.31
Credit Forcier $8\frac{3}{8}$ 04 Ecu	1000	$107\frac{1}{4}$	$107\frac{5}{8}$	$-\frac{3}{8}$	7.09
Denmark $8\frac{1}{2}$ 02 Ecu	1000	$110\frac{1}{8}$	$110\frac{1}{2}$	$-\frac{3}{8}$	6.31
EC 6 00 Ecu	1100	$101\frac{1}{2}$	$101\frac{3}{4}$		5.58
EIB 10 01 Ecu	1150	115	$115\frac{1}{4}$	$-\frac{1}{4}$	6.02
Ferro del Stat $10\frac{1}{8}$ 98 Ecu	500	$106\frac{3}{4}$	$107\frac{1}{4}$		4.91
Italy $10\frac{3}{4}$ 00 Ecu	1000	$115\frac{3}{8}$	$115\frac{5}{8}$	$-\frac{1}{8}$	5.93
United Kingdom $9\frac{1}{3}$ 01 Ecu	2750	$111\frac{3}{4}$	$117\frac{7}{8}$	$-\frac{3}{8}$	6.05
AIDC 10 99 A$	100	$106\frac{3}{8}$	$106\frac{3}{4}$	$+\frac{1}{8}$	7.41
Comm Bk Australia $13\frac{3}{4}$ 99 A$	100	$116\frac{5}{8}$	117	$+\frac{1}{8}$	7.50
EIB $7\frac{3}{4}$ 99 A$	350	$102\frac{1}{2}$	$103\frac{3}{8}$	$+\frac{1}{8}$	6.91
NSW Treasury Zero 0 20 A$	1000	$14\frac{5}{8}$	15	$+\frac{3}{8}$	8.25
R & I Bank $7\frac{3}{4}$ 03 A$	125	$98\frac{3}{4}$	$99\frac{1}{8}$	$+\frac{3}{8}$	7.99
State Bk NSW 9 02 A$	300	$105\frac{1}{2}$	$105\frac{7}{8}$	$+\frac{1}{4}$	7.82
Sth Aust Govt Fin 9 02 A$	150	$105\frac{3}{8}$	$105\frac{3}{4}$	$+\frac{3}{8}$	7.85
Unilever Australia 12 96 A$	150	$106\frac{7}{8}$	$107\frac{1}{4}$		7.31
Western Aust Trees $7\frac{5}{8}$ 98 A$	100	$100\frac{3}{4}$	$101\frac{1}{4}$	$+\frac{1}{8}$	7.12
Abbey Natl Treasury 8 03 £	1000	101	$101\frac{1}{8}$	$-\frac{1}{8}$	7.79
British Land $8\frac{7}{8}$ 23 £	150	$91\frac{1}{8}$	$91\frac{1}{2}$	$-\frac{3}{8}$	10.06
Denmark $6\frac{3}{4}$ 98 £	800	$100\frac{3}{8}$	$100\frac{1}{2}$		6.54
Depfa Finance $7\frac{1}{8}$ 03 £	500	$95\frac{7}{8}$	$96\frac{1}{8}$	$-\frac{1}{8}$	7.89
EIB 8 03 £	1000	$101\frac{7}{8}$	102	$-\frac{1}{8}$	7.63
Glaxo Wellcome $8\frac{3}{4}$ 05 £	500	$102\frac{1}{2}$	$102\frac{5}{8}$	$-\frac{1}{4}$	8.34
Hanson $10\frac{3}{8}$ 97 £	500	$104\frac{1}{8}$	$104\frac{3}{8}$		6.54
HBSC Holdings 11.69 02 £	153	$116\frac{1}{4}$	$116\frac{1}{2}$	$-\frac{1}{8}$	8.13
Italy $10\frac{1}{2}$ 14 £	400	$114\frac{1}{4}$	$114\frac{3}{8}$	$-\frac{1}{2}$	8.86
Japan Dev Bk 7 00 £	200	$99\frac{7}{8}$	$100\frac{1}{8}$	$-\frac{1}{8}$	7.03
Land Secs $9\frac{1}{2}$ 07 £	200	105	$105\frac{3}{8}$	$-\frac{1}{2}$	8.75
Ontario $11\frac{1}{8}$ 01 £	100	$113\frac{1}{8}$	$113\frac{3}{8}$		7.54
Powergen $8\frac{7}{8}$ 03 £	250	$104\frac{1}{8}$	$104\frac{3}{8}$	$-\frac{1}{4}$	8.03
Sevem Trent $11\frac{1}{2}$ 99 £	150	$110\frac{7}{8}$	$111\frac{1}{8}$		7.19
Tokyo Elec Power 11 01 £	150	$113\frac{1}{4}$	$113\frac{1}{2}$	$-\frac{1}{8}$	7.58
TCNZ Fin $9\frac{1}{4}$ 02 NZ$	75	$103\frac{1}{2}$	$104\frac{1}{2}$	$+\frac{1}{8}$	8.46
World Bank 9 99 NZ$	250	$102\frac{5}{8}$	103	$+\frac{1}{8}$	7.93
Credit Local 6 01 FFr	8000	$100\frac{7}{8}$	$101\frac{1}{8}$	$-\frac{1}{4}$	5.79
Denmark $5\frac{1}{2}$ 99 FFr	7000	$101\frac{1}{4}$	$101\frac{3}{8}$		5.06
Elec de France $8\frac{3}{4}$ 22 FFr	3000	117	$117\frac{3}{8}$	$-\frac{5}{8}$	7.27

FLOATING RATE NOTES

	Issued	Bid	Offer	C.cpn	
Abbey Natl Treasury $-\frac{1}{16}$ 99	1000	99.92	100.00	5.4766	
Bankamerica $\frac{1}{8}$ 99	750	99.95	100.05	5.7383	
Canada $-\frac{1}{4}$ 99	2000	99.67	99.74	5.2852	
CCCE 0 06 Ecu	200	99.58	99.76	4.2575	
Commerzbk O/S Fin $-\frac{1}{8}$ 98	750	99.83	99.90	5.3555	
Credit Lyonnais $\frac{1}{16}$ 00	300	98.14	98.57	5.9375	
Credit Lyonnais 0.30 98	1250	100.00	100.09	5.9406	
Denmark $-\frac{1}{8}$ 97	1000	99.97	100.03	5.4141	
Dresdner Finance $\frac{1}{32}$ 98 DM	1000	100.00	100.10	3.3750	
Fed Net Mort $-\frac{3}{16}$ 00	1000	99.71	99.81	5.0977	
Finland $-\frac{1}{8}$ 99	1500	99.94	100.00	5.4609	
Halifax BS 0 99	500	100.11	100.19	5.5391	
IMI Bank Intl $\frac{1}{4}$ 99	500	100.45	100.55	5.7305	
Italy $\frac{1}{16}$ 99	1500	100.29	100.35	5.6875	
LKB Baden–Wuert Fin $-\frac{1}{8}$ 98	1000	99.93	100.00	5.4766	
Lloyds Bank Perp 0.10	600	85.23	86.48	5.3500	
Malaysia $\frac{1}{16}$ 05	650	99.83	99.95	5.5625	
New Zealand $-\frac{1}{8}$ 99	1000	99.93	100.01	5.4453	
Nova Scotia $\frac{3}{16}$ 99	500	99.99	100.07	5.7266	

(Continued)

EXHIBIT 7.13	(Continued)			
	Issued	Bid	Offer	C. cpn
Ontario 0 99	2000	100.03	100.09	5.5000
Portugal 1_{16} 99 DM	2500	100.23	100.32	3.4492
Quebec Hydro 0 99	500	99.61	99.73	5.6875
Renfe 0 98	500	99.77	99.91	5.4375
Spain -1_{16} 02 DM	2000	100.07	100.13	3.3477
State Bk Victoria 0.05 99	125	100.01	100.11	5.8469
Sweden -1_8 01	2000	99.93	100.01	5.4141

CONVERTIBLE BONDS

	Issued	Conv. Price	Bid	Offer	Prem.
Allied–Lyons 6^3_4 08 £	200	6.04	94^1_4	95^1_4	+26.50
Gold Kalgoorlie 7^1_2 00	65	1.37	120^1_2	121^1_2	+9.30
Grand Metropolitan 6^1_2 00	710	4.37	115	116	+6.91
Hanson America 2.39 01	420	29.6375	85^7_8	86^3_8	
Honk Kong Land 4.01	410	31.05	85^3_4	86^1_2	−14.00
Land Secs 6^3_4 02 £	84	6.72	100^5_8	103^1_8	−0.70
Lasmo 7^3_4 05 £	90	5.64	92^7_8	94	
MBL Intl Fin 3 02	2000	22	110^1_4	110^3_4	+3.76
Mitsui Bank 2^5_8 03	200	2332.6	78^3_4	80^3_4	+40.22
Odgen 6 02	85	39.077	92^1_2	94	+85.37
Pennzoil 4^3_4 03	500	58.8097	107^1_2	108^1_2	+6.70
Sandoz Capital 2 02	750	1302.26	111^3_8	112^1_8	+4.08
Sappi BVI Finance 7^1_2 02	250	76	91^3_8	92^3_8	
Sapporo 1^3_8 00	40000	1059.4	104	105	+6.97
Sumitomo Bank 3^1_8 04	300	3606.9	82^5_8	83^5_8	+27.63
Sun Alliance 7^1_4 08 £	155	3.9	107^5_8	108^5_8	+14.37
Transatlantic Hldgs 5^1_2 09 £	250	5.05	82^7_8	84	+11.31

* No information available - previous day's price
‡ Only one market maker supplied a price

STRAIGHT BONDS: The yield is the yield to redemption of the bid-price; the amount issued is in millions of currency units. Chg. day=Change on day.

FLOATING RATE NOTES: Denominated in dollars unless otherwise indicated. Coupon shown is minimum. Spread=Margin above six-month offered rate (three-month §above mean rate) for US dollars. C.cpn=The current coupon.

Interest Rate and Currency Swaps

NATURE OF THE MARKET

Since 1981 the market for interest rate and currency swaps has grown at an exceptionally high rate. Starting at a zero base in that year, the global market was estimated by the Bank for International Settlements at $3 billion in 1982. In 1989 the International Swap Dealers Association's (ISDA) estimate of the market size was $1.5 trillion for interest rate swaps and $430 billion for currency swaps.

Interest rate and currency swaps are quite different from the foreign exchange swaps described in Chapter 4. Interest rate and currency swaps are related to existing and newly created debt, where the counterparties wish to change the nature of the debt service payments. The change can be related to the form of interest payment made (fixed versus floating interest), or to the currency of denomination of debt service.

In the past a large number of swaps have been related to new international bond issues. In such cases the borrower issued bonds with the intent of swapping the debt service into another interest form, currency, or both. In this connection it is

| **EXHIBIT 7.14** | **Three Types of Interest Rate Swaps** |

Example of Coupon Swap

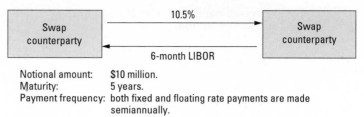

Notional amount: $10 million.
Maturity: 5 years.
Payment frequency: both fixed and floating rate payments are made
                              semiannually.

Example of Basis Swap

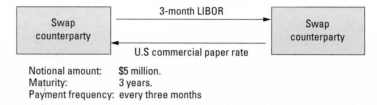

Notional amount: $5 million.
Maturity: 3 years.
Payment frequency: every three months

Example of Cross-Currency Interest Rate Swap

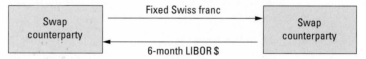

SOURCE: Bank for International Settlements.

necessary to consider the swap market as closely related to both the international bond market and the syndicated Euroloan market.

INSTRUMENTS AND MARKETS

A swap is a financial transaction in which two counterparties exchange payment streams over time. There are two major types of swaps: interest rate swaps and currency swaps.

An interest rate swap involves the exchange of interest payment streams of differing composition based on an underlying notional principal. No actual principal is exchanged in an interest rate swap. Interest rate swaps are of three main types: coupon swaps (fixed to floating rate); basis swaps (floating rate with one reference rate to floating rate with a different reference rate); and cross-currency swaps (fixed rate in one currency to floating rate in another currency). These three types of swaps are illustrated in Exhibit 7.14.

Currency swaps are transactions where two counterparties exchange specific amounts of two different currencies at the outset and repay over time following a predetermined pattern of interest and amortization. Generally fixed interest rates are used in each currency. In some currency swaps there may be no exchange of principal amount. Currency swaps have been discussed in detail in Chapter 5, and a typical World Bank swap transaction is described in that discussion.

CLASSIC OR PLAIN VANILLA SWAP

Plain Vanilla Swap

A five- to seven-year swap of floating rate funds against fixed rate funds to avoid interest rate risk.

The most common interest rate swap used in the early and mid-1980s has been referred to as the classic, or "plain vanilla" swap. It is a five- to seven-year swap of six-month LIBOR-based floating rate funds against fixed rate funds. These swaps were tied to Eurobond issues of the end users that provided fixed rate funds, but who wished floating rate funding at reduced costs. In such cases fixed rate borrowers, who had comparatively better access to floating rate funds, entered into swaps to obtain a lower cost substitute for bond finance, or to obtain fixed rate funding that was otherwise unavailable. Many Eurobonds are issued purely for the purpose of being swapped.

In Exhibit 7.15 we have an illustration of how the classic swap might work. The AAA borrower, possibly a large European bank, can borrow dollar funds in the Eurobond market at the fixed rate of 9.5% or floating LIBOR flat. The corporate borrower (lower quality credit) can borrow dollar funds in the Eurobond market at the fixed rate of 11.7% or floating at LIBOR + 1%. The corporation ultimately prefers to service fixed rate debt. The European bank is willing to service floating rate debt, since it can use a floating rate dollar loan as a hedge against interest rate risk. The differential in spread is 1.2%.

The swap transaction involves the AAA borrower taking on debt (fixed rate) at 9.5% and swapping against a counterparty for floating rate at LIBOR minus 0.5%. Also, the lower credit borrower takes on debt at floating rate (LIBOR + 1%); and swaps against a counterparty for fixed rate at 11.0%. The two parties (AAA borrower and lower credit) function as counterparties vis-a-vis one another. Alternately, a bank intermediary can serve as a counterparty for both borrowers. Both parties share in the reduced borrowing costs.

Since the beginning of the interest rate swap market in 1981, the variety of end users has increased, and counterparties have become reluctant to accept the credit risk in a purely brokered swap. This reluctance provided opportunities for large commercial and investment banks to take on an intermediary role by entering into

---

EXHIBIT 7.15	**Illustration of Plain Vanilla Swap, All Transactions in U.S. Dollars**	
	COST OF NEW BORROWING	
	Fixed Rate	**Floating Rate**
AAA Borrower (Bank)	9.5%	LIBOR
Lower Credit Borrower	11.7%	LIBOR+1%
Spread	2.2%	1%
Differential in Spread		1.2%
Swap Transaction:		
AAA Borrows Fixed at 9.5%	—Swaps for floating at LIBOR—0.5%	
Lower Credit Borrows Floating at LIBOR+1%	—Swaps for Fixed at 11.0%	
Cost Saving:		
AAA Pays under Swap LIBOR—0.5%, Saving 0.5%		
Lower Credit Pays under Swap Fixed 11.0%, Saving 0.7%		

two offsetting swaps. Intermediaries now act almost exclusively as counterparties. Frequently the bank intermediary is a high quality credit risk, and therefore a more acceptable counterparty.

Swaps are an attractive source of off balance sheet earnings. In addition, swaps facilitate other types of business for banks (Eurobond underwriting and trading derivative instruments such as futures and options). Commercial banks tend to use swaps as an extension of conventional banking activities. Banks can price the parts of a fixed rate loan (the floating rate loan and the swap) more efficiently by unbundling these components. Investment and merchant banks view swaps more as tradable securities. By standardizing swap contracts they improve the liquidity of the swap market.

Competition in International Bond Markets

The international bond markets exhibit and promote a high degree of competition in the global mobilization of capital. In the nineteenth century London was the unchallenged center for foreign bond issues. London's position was based on the pound sterling being the dominant currency in international finance and the willingness of British investors to acquire large portfolios of bonds issued by nonresident borrowers. By contrast in the twentieth century other foreign bond centers such as New York and Zurich emerged to challenge London's premier role. The first Eurobond issue appeared in 1963, denominated in U.S. dollars. This bond issue was at the same time the U.S. government proposed the Interest Equalization Tax (IET). Other currencies of denomination (deutsche mark, French franc, and Dutch guilder) also became popular in the Eurobond market in the 1960s. The first Japanese yen Eurobond appeared in the late 1970s. At present several foreign bond market sectors are competing with one another, namely, the Swiss franc market, the U.S. (Yankee) bond market, the deutsche mark market, and the yen (Samurai) market. After the financial market deregulation in the United Kingdom in 1979, London has regained some competitive edge in the Eurobond and foreign bond markets, as discussed in Chapter 8.

COMPETITION BETWEEN MARKET SECTORS AND FINANCIAL INSTITUTIONS

Selected international bond markets can be competitive for several reasons. To be successful as an international bond financing center, a nation must have a sound economic base and stable currency. Furthermore, international lenders and borrowers must have confidence in the issuing country's financial system and institutions through which the funds will be channeled. For these reasons many countries such as Britain, Japan, and Switzerland have liberalized their financial markets in order to attract more international financial business to their markets.

A favorable political, economic, and legal environment will have a positive effect on the ability of bond markets to compete for international financing. Part of this environment includes institutions, such as commercial and investment banks, that facilitate new bond issues and secondary trading.

International commercial and investment banks are major channels in facilitating the international flow of capital. These financial institutions compete and cooperate with each other for market share on a global basis. These institutions have

EXHIBIT 7.16	Top 20 Lead Managers in Eurobond Market		

Rank 1988	Rank 1992	Rank 1995
1 Nomura Securities	1 Deutsche Bank	1 Merrill Lynch
2 CSFB/Credit Suisse	2 Nomura	2 SBC Warburg
3 Deutsche Bank	3 Union Bank of Switzerland	3 CS First Boston
4 Daiwa Securities	4 Credit Suisse First Boston	4 JP Morgan
5 Yamaichi Securities	5 Banque Paribas	5 Morgan Stanley
6 Nikko Securities	6 Nikko Securities	6 HSBC Group
7 Merrill Lynch Capital Markets	7 Yamaichi Securities	7 Deutsche MG
8 Bankers Trust International	8 Daiwa Securities	8 Union Bank of Switzerland
9 Banque Paribas	9 Merrill Lynch	9 Nomura Securities
10 JP Morgan Securities	10 Goldman Sachs Intl	10 Banque Paribas
11 Industrial Bank of Japan	11 CCF	11 Daiwa Securities
12 Union Bank of Switzerland	12 Industrial Bank of Japan	12 Lehman Brothers
13 Salomon Brothers	13 JP Morgan	13 Barclays DZW
14 GS Warburg	14 SG Warburg	14 Goldman Sachs
15 Goldman Sachs International	15 Swiss Bank Corp	15 Dresdner KB
16 Dresdner Bank	16 Commerzbank	16 ABN Amro
17 Morgan Stanley International	17 Banque Nationale de Paris	17 CIBC Wood Gundy
18 Commerzbank	18 Credit Lyonnais	18 Industrial Bank of Japan
19 Swiss Bank Corp Investment Banking	19 Morgan Stanley	19 Saloman Brothers
20 Hambros Bank	20 Bankers Trust	20 Citibank

SOURCES: *The Economist, Institutional Investor, Financial Times.*

employed various strategies as competition has intensified between financial centers. A joint effort approach by financial institutions of two different nationalities, such as Credit Suisse/First Boston, Deutsche/Morgan Grenfell are not uncommon.

Banks participating in international bond financing may also provide advice to international corporations concerning mergers and acquisitions, financing strategies, issuance of securities in terms of volume, maturity, yield, currency of denomination, and marketplace. In order to compete successfully, these banks must give careful consideration to their capital resources, the quality of financial information and expertise, the adequacy of staff members, modern communication links, and good customer relations. The changing ranks of the top 20 lead managers in the Eurobond market between 1988–1995 reflect the keen competition among these banks (Exhibit 7.16).

Borrowers in the international bond markets include governments and their agencies, multinational firms, international organizations, and public utility companies. These borrowers are keenly aware of financing costs, sources of funds, and trends in financial structure and profits. Should a bond issue take place in London, Tokyo, New York, or Switzerland? Should the issue be placed by public underwriting or private placement? Should the bonds be at a fixed or floating rate? Should the bonds be convertible or attached with warrants or other features? Japanese firms employing warrants have increased the use of Euroyen bonds in recent years, indicating the importance of the borrowers' competitive strategies. The competitive market for international borrowers and investors is discussed further in Chapters 12 and 18.

Global Bonds

Large issues with one or more currency denominations sold simultaneously in the world's major capital markets. They combine the characteristics of Eurobonds and foreign bonds.

GLOBAL BOND ISSUES

Competition in international bond markets can stimulate innovative financing arrangements. One such innovation is the global bond issue. In brief, a global bond is a debt issue offered simultaneously in all major markets of the world. Global bond issues need many months of preparation before underwriting takes place. This time is required to negotiate the structure of primary distribution in some of the less open national markets. Also, local problems such as satisfying regulatory requirements must be solved.

International bonds have gained acceptance among investors located in many countries. These investors have indicated a willingness to acquire bonds denominated in leading currencies. Given the widespread acceptance of international bonds among investors around the globe, it should be expected that borrowers would attempt to tap the international capital market with a bond issue sold simultaneously around the world. Such a global bond issue could provide several advantages:

1. World wide distribution and high liquidity, (clearing through cedel and Euroclear).
2. Broader future market for borrower, based on publicity and enhanced credit standing. Borrower can select markets and investors to secure long-term bond programs.
3. Creation of a global benchmark issue.

Several key international benchmark government bond issues are identified (Exhibit 7.13). These bond issues play an important role in providing a reference point for pricing issues subsequently sold into the market sector occupied by the benchmark issue. To qualify as a benchmark the bond issue must be large so that a liquid market may develop. The issue must also be of high quality so that it can command one of the lowest interest rates accorded an issue in that market sector. In the absence of a government benchmark bond, a high quality nongovernment issue (for example, one World Bank bond) can be used.

The World Bank has taken a leading role as an issuer of global bonds. Reasons for this role include the following:

1. The World Bank has a large appetite for international capital, with an annual lending program of $10–12 billion.
2. The function of the World Bank is to obtain the lowest cost financing possible, so that these economies can be passed on to developing country borrowers who have limited debt service capacity.
3. The World Bank enjoys the AAA international credit rating.
4. This institution has been an innovator in international finance, developing the use of currency swaps in its borrowing program as early as 1981. In 1989 the World Bank introduced the practice of issuing global bonds.

Exhibit 7.17 outlines the terms and conditions of the World Bank's first global yen bond launched in 1992.

From the investor's point of view there are a number of advantages. First, 24 hours secondary market trading at uniform world prices provides supervisor liquidity, which is the most attractive feature in comparison to most other international bonds. Second, because global bonds are distributed in the world's major capital markets, the bonds trade as if they were "home market" instruments, allowing investors to deal with local market makers. Third, liquidity is important to institutional investors' active portfolio management approach. Fourth, global bonds provide a wider range of credit risk and yields offering investors more choice.

As Exhibit 7.18 indicates, global bonds have demonstrated tremendous growth from 1% of the total international bonds in 1989 to 11% in 1995.

EXHIBIT 7.17	World Bank's First Global Yen Bond—1992

Issuer:	International Bank for Reconstruction and Development
Amount:	Y250 billion
Spread at reoffer:	19 basis points through JGB 129
Coupon:	5.25%
Maturity:	Ten years
Joint lead-manager:	IBJI, JP Morgan, Nomura
Bond Placement:	20% in Japan
	17% in U.S.
	10% in Far East (excluding Japan)
	53% in Europe & Middle East

JGB=Japanese Government Bond

EXHIBIT 7.18	Offerings of Global Bonds by Category of Issuer

$ BILLION

	1989	1990	1991	1992	1993	1994	1995
Central Government	—	—	—	2.0	12.0	13.4	4.2
State and Local Government	—	—	—	3.0	10.7	5.5	1.7
Public Financial Enterprises	—	—	—	0.4	0.7	5.6	1.0
Public Enterprises	—	1.1	7.5	4.0	1.2	1.5	3.6
Banks	—	—	—	0.2	—	4.1	1.8
Private Financial Institutions	—	4.9	4.6	7.3	0.8	9.6	30.4
Private Corporations	—	—	—	1.0	1.0	2.9	1.0
International Organizations	1.5	3.6	3.3	7.2	8.0	6.4	7.3
Total	**1.5**	**9.6**	**15.4**	**25.1**	**34.4**	**49.0**	**51.0**
Global Bonds as Percentage of All International Bonds	1.0	4.0	5.0	7.5	7.2	11.4	11.1

SOURCE: OECD, *Financial Market Trends,* (February 1995): 68 and (June 1994): 57.

Since the first global bond was introduced by the World Bank in September 1989, public enterprises, private financial institutions, and international organizations were major issuers of global bonds in 1990–1991. The year 1992 witnessed more participants in the global bond market as reflected in the growing volume of the issues (7.5% of total international bonds). In 1993–1994 central governments were the largest borrowers in the global bond market, primarily for the purposes of replenishing their foreign exchange reserves and for financing government deficits. Issuance in 1995 became dominated by private financial institutions from the United States. These borrowers included U.S. government sponsored credit agencies which were innovative, creating a wide range of maturities, issuing callable bonds, and denominating in U.S. dollar and nondollar currencies. Several private financial institutions in the United States issued large-scale asset-backed global bonds. In the 1992–1995 period, many sovereign governments such as Canada, Finland, Italy, China, Sweden, Argentina, and Mexico also issued global bonds.

In terms of currency, the U.S. dollar accounted for more than 60% of issues, followed by the Canadian dollar, Japanese yen, and German mark. The majority of global bonds have been straight issues but there have been some floating rate and zero coupon offerings.

EMERGING MARKET DEBT

Beginning in 1989 the market for debt obligations of borrowers in emerging market countries took on new life. In that year Treasury Secretary Brady proposed a new approach to resolve the developing country debt problem and to restore the credit worthiness of restructuring countries. Under the Brady Plan, countries were encouraged to embark on reform efforts that would achieve domestic stabilization and external equilibrium. Several countries that mounted sustained reform efforts now benefit from growing market access on improving terms of borrowing. Brady emerging market debt operations catalyzed and accelerated this process.

Emerging Market Debt

It refers to debt issued by all developing countries in Asia, Latin America, and Europe in 1980s and 1990s being traded in international financial markets.

The Brady Plan introduced important innovations. Countries and bank creditor committees negotiated comprehensive packages that offered menus of debt and debt service reduction options. Those menus differed from case to case and gave banks a range of choices in exchanging debt for bonds. The restructurings usually securitized the claims, that is, converted the form of the claims from loans to bonds, lengthened the repayment periods, and converted much of the remaining exposure from floating to fixed-rate obligations.

Discount and par exchanges proved the most popular options. Creditors swapped existing loans for new bonds with lower principal amount (discount exchange) or with the same principal but fixed submarket interest rates (par exchange). Most commonly the principal would be fully backed by zero coupon U.S. Treasury bonds; the next 12 months of interest payments would be backed by high grade short-term securities. For the debtor the collateral effectively reduced the burden of the debt, as rebates of interest from the collateral accounts would cover the cost of funding these accounts.

The Brady Plan encouraged market reentry and debt conversion schemes, and improved debt servicing capacity. Brady restructuring countries now participate in diversified capital market financing. This financing includes international bond issues, international equity issues, and other capital market issues, as indicated in previous sections.

While investment in the emerging market securities will be analyzed in more detail in Chapter 20, the following section is intended to provide some highlights to the Brady bonds—the most liquid emerging markets' issues.

Brady Bonds

Bonds issued by developing countries and backed by U.S. Treasury bonds to replace commercial bank debt.

Because the Brady bonds are backed by U.S. Treasury bonds—limiting investors' exposures to the risk of default—the prices and rates of return on Brady bonds are affected by U.S. Treasury bond performance, as well as the financial conditions of the countries that issue the Bradys.

As Exhibit 7.19 indicates, Brady Bond Index rose rapidly in 1992–1993 mainly as the result of the declining long-term rates in the United States in this period. The

---

EXHIBIT 7.19	**Recent Brady Bond Performance**

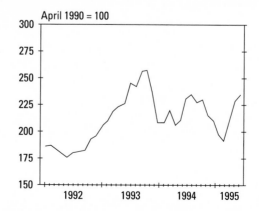

SOURCE: Salomon Brothers Brady Bond index.

BBI dropped in 1994, reflecting the high U.S. Treasury bond rate. The Mexican financial crisis from December 1994 to February 1995 aggravated the downturn in the Brady bond market. However, from March 1995 through July 1996 the BBI rose rapidly again primarily due to the low long-term Treasury bond rates. Also brightening the Brady bond market was the better economic conditions in Latin American countries including Mexico.

In the period 31 July 1995–31 July 1996, both the Brady Bond Index and the Emerging Money Market Fund (EMMF) Index showed continuous upward movement at higher levels than other bond indexes such as the High Yield Index and the World Government Bond Index. These reflected the optimistic and heavy trading in the emerging markets (Exhibit 7.20).

In the BBI family different issuing countries show different rate of return in different time periods. Argentina, Brazil, and Mexico are good examples, most notable is Mexico's lower rate of return after its financial crisis. These reflected credit spreads for these emerging markets (Exhibit 7.21).

EXHIBIT 7.20	**Salomon Brothers Total Rate-of-Return Indexes, 31 July 95–31 July 96**

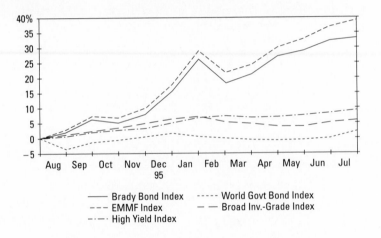

SOURCE: Salomon Brothers Inc.

EXHIBIT 7.21	**The Salomon Brothers Total Rate-of-Return Indexes, 31 July 96**

	July	3 Month	6 Month	Year-to-Date	12 Month
SB Brady Bond Index	0.55	4.69	5.38	14.67	33.07
SB Emerging Markets Mutual Fund Index	1.72	6.89	7.89	18.08	39.23
• BBI-Argentina	−2.96	−0.22	−2.26	4.51	29.02
• BBI-Brazil	1.07	7.09	7.54	17.81	38.04
• BBI-Mexico	0.27	−0.11	1.62	7.19	18.71
• BBI-Venezuela	2.92	11.40	18.32	27.92	51.14
• BBI-Latin	0.43	4.65	5.56	14.21	33.51
• BBI-Non-Latin	1.30	4.93	4.22	17.75	30.32
• BBI-Fixed-Rate	0.10	3.49	−0.64	8.16	29.00
• BBI-Floating-Rate	0.88	5.58	10.34	20.03	36.28
SB Broad Investment-Grade Bond Index	0.27	1.51	−1.67	−1.00	5.46
SB High-Yield Market Index	0.65	1.99	2.08	3.58	8.99
SB World Govt. Bond Index	1.92	2.74	1.67	0.41	2.05
S&P 500 Index	−4.42	−1.58	1.77	5.23	16.57

SOURCE: Salomon Brothers Inc. *Emerging Market,* (August 6, 1996).

Because Brady bonds have helped many emerging market countries to reenter the international bond markets, in 1996 Mexico and the Philippines have issued billions of dollars of Eurobonds in exchange for Brady bonds originally issued to replace commercial bank debt. As the emerging markets improve their credit standing, it is expected that Brady bonds will be replaced gradually by Eurobonds.

SUMMARY

The international bond markets include two key components: foreign bond markets and the Eurobond market. These components differ in a number of respects including currency of denomination, type of investors, average maturity of bonds, and taxation. The foreign bond markets (New York, London, Zurich) are much older, but the Eurobond market is now much larger.

The foreign bond markets tend to rely heavily on institutional investors and focus on longer maturity bond issues. Access to these markets is relatively easy for highly rated credits and quite difficult for lesser credits. Underwriting margins generally are below 1% in the foreign bond market but higher in the Eurobond market.

The Eurobond market has its origins in the early 1960s, partly associated with high levels of investment in Europe. The United States enacted capital controls in 1964 that gave the Eurobond market a strong boost. The leading currency of denomination in the market has been the U.S. dollar. Other important currencies include the deutsche mark, yen, and French franc. Issuance has been in shorter maturities. Interest rates on Eurobonds follow the rates in the home country of the currency of denomination.

Strong Eurobond growth reflects several trends, including a steady expansion in demand for funds by corporations, governments, and international organizations. In addition, the market has been fed by new sources of funds. The market offers a high degree of flexibility for borrowers and investors with respect to currency choice and types of securities (straight debentures, convertibles, warrants, and floating rate notes). The secondary market for Eurobonds has expanded rapidly, providing liquidity and greater market efficiency.

Since 1981 the market for interest rate swaps has grown rapidly. Interest rate swaps have been closely associated with new international bond issues. In such cases the borrower issues bonds with the intent of swapping the debt service into another interest form. End users utilize the swap market to obtain low cost financing, to obtain high yield assets, to hedge exposures, to implement short run asset/liability management, or to speculate.

In September 1989, global bonds were first introduced by the World Bank. The special characteristics of global bonds have encouraged many high credit standing borrowers to increase their issues in the 1990s.

Also in 1989 the Brady Plan introduced important initiatives toward debt reduction and resolving the debt crisis. Brady countries now participate in diverse capital market financings.

APPENDIX

SWITZERLAND—FINANCIAL ENTREPÔT

Switzerland plays a strategic role in the world of global finance. The large Swiss banks are part of a complex and comprehensive international financial mechanism.

There are four components of this mechanism, namely, the Swiss banks, the Swiss currency, the Swiss National Bank's (central bank) monetary guidance, and the political stability and conservatism of the Swiss government.

The Swiss currency is regarded to be one of the strongest and most stable currencies. A number of factors support this view including 1) the near absence of inflation in Switzerland and therefore the favorable international purchasing power of the Swiss franc, 2) the careful monetary management exercised by Swiss authorities, and 3) the insistence of the Swiss in insulating the currency from international pressures. At times substantial international pressures will be directed at the Swiss franc related to the large and often unpredictable flows of funds into the country. Swiss official reserves are quite substantial. In 1993 these were reported at $25 billion, equivalent to 34% of imports, and 10% of GDP.

By international comparisons Switzerland is a politically conservative and stable nation. The federal system does not allow rapid political change, and the nation has carefully preserved its neutrality and independence from entangling alliances with other nations.

Monetary guidance is carried out by the Swiss National Bank that regulates domestic credit expansion and informally consults with the banks to prevent disruption of domestic liquidity from international flows of investment and flight capital. This informal collaboration is one of the basic strengths of the Swiss financial system. This guidance requires close cooperation of the large banks that play a pivotal role in facilitating inflows and outflows of funds.

Fund inflows to Switzerland are persistent and large. These inflows tend to destabilize internal liquidity, the Swiss exchange rate, and interest rates in Switzerland. Often Swiss interest rates are among the lowest in the world. In part these low rates are due to the persistent fund inflows and resulting downward pressure on rates. To stabilize the Swiss financial system, the banks arrange fund outflows that are coordinated from the point of view of balancing total inflows with total outflows.

Inflows are related to the following:

1. Desire of investors to invest in Swiss franc denominated assets
2. Desire of investors to have funds managed by banks with expertise in global investment management
3. Flight capital
4. Funds seeking anonymity afforded by the Swiss banking system
5. Multinational corporations using the Swiss financial system to shield part of their corporate income from high taxation (See Exhibit 7A.1 with data on foreign direct investment.)
6. Swiss financial holding companies that maintain liquid investments in expectation of future needs
7. The Swiss franc is a small component of official reserves of governments and central banks
8. Investors seeking currency play with Swiss franc.

Clearly, fund inflows are based on widely varying motives.

Swiss banks channel funds from Switzerland in amounts required to keep the financial system balanced. The most important channels employed by the Swiss banks are:

1. Foreign bond issues denominated in Swiss franc, averaging more than $20 billion per year during the mid-1990s; borrowers are required to convert proceeds into other currencies without delay.

EXHIBIT 7A.1	**Switzerland—Selected Investment Flows**		
	1993	**1994**	**1995**
Swiss Franc Foreign Bonds[1] Valuation in Swiss Franc	SF39.9	SF27.0	SF31.7
Swiss Franc Foreign Bonds Valuation in U.S. Dollars	$27.0	$20.0	$27.1
Swiss Franc Foreign Bonds as a Percent of All Foreign Bonds Issued	31%	33%	28%
Foreign Direct Investment[2] Inflows	($83)	$2947	—
Foreign Direct Investment Outflows	$8765	$10554	—

[1] Bonds issued in Swiss Capital market by nonresident borrowers. Amounts are in billions of SF or U.S. dollars.

[2] Control business investment. Outflows represent Swiss-based corporate investment overseas. Inflows represent non-Swiss corporate investment in Switzerland. Amounts are in millions of U.S. dollars.

SOURCE: OECD, *Financial Market Trends* (June 1996): 38, 127.

2. Participation by Swiss banks in foreign loans.

3. Investment of funds in specialized international investment funds; these funds acquire securities traded in non-Swiss capital markets.

4. Management of personal investment funds for individuals; large amounts of these funds are invested in New York, London, Tokyo, and other stock and bond markets by offshore branches and securities affiliates of Swiss banks.

5. Placements of Euro-Swiss franc deposits offshore by banks; lacking an effective domestic money market, the Swiss banks accomplish international liquidity adjustment by this practice.

REVIEW QUESTIONS

1. What are the special characteristics of Eurobonds?

2. What are the special features of foreign bonds?

3. Explain the reasons for the growth of the Eurobond market in the 1980s.

4. Outline how the underwriting process takes place for a typical Eurobond issue. Why is the underwriting spread in the Eurobond market larger than in the foreign bond market?

5. Explain the different types of Eurobonds and the motivation of investors to buy these bonds.

6. Explain the marketing functions of the lead managers, syndicated group, and the selling group in the Eurobond market.

7. What are the major factors that international borrowers must consider when they borrow in the foreign bond market instead of the domestic market?

8. The Eurobond market is a competitive market. Identify three important lead managers in the Eurobond market from the following countries: the United States, West Germany, Switzerland, and Japan.

9. Why do U.S. corporations issue dollar denominated Eurobonds?

10. Why do Canadian provinces issue U.S. dollar bonds in the New York bond market?

11. What factors account for the growing popularity of ECU bonds in the period 1981–1991?

12. Explain the advantages of issuing global bonds by international borrowers and the motivation of investors to buy these bonds.

13. A U.S. corporation is considering financing with a mark denominated Eurobond. It would have to pay an 8% coupon. An equivalent U.S. dollar bond would cost 12%. In each case a five-year maturity would be used. A total financing of $25 million is required (DMark 50 million for the DM bond, with DM2.0 = $US1.0). The U.S. corporation has forecast the following exchange rates over the bond's lifetime.

Year	Exchange Rate
1	DM2.00
2	DM1.80
3	DM1.60
4	DM1.30
5	DM1.20

   a. Calculate the dollar cash flows required to service interest and principal repayment on each bond issue (Interest is paid once per year).
   b. Using a discount rate of 12%, calculate the present value of payment for each bond issue.

14. What is the difference between an interest rate swap and a currency swap?

15. What uses do bank intermediaries make of the swap market? Why is it desirable for a bank to have a high credit rating when dealing in the swap market?

16. What reasons are given for end users participating in the swap market?

17. Explain how a plain vanilla interest rate swap is used.

18. Atlas Company needs $50 million to finance expansion. Eurco requires a similar amount of funds. Atlas can issue dollar Eurobonds with fixed interest of 10.0%, or floating LIBOR + 1/2%. Eurco can issue dollar Eurobonds with fixed interest of 13%, or floating at LIBOR + 2%.
   a. Can these companies use interest rate swaps to mutual advantage?
   b. Indicate a possible set of interest rate swaps, where the interest savings are shared equally by both counterparties.

19. An investment banking syndicate in London launches a $100 million ten-year Eurobond issue. The syndicate consists of a lead manager, who receives half of the management fee, and three comanagers who split the remaining half of the management fee. The issue is underwritten by the four managing banks (who underwrite 45% of the issue), 40 major underwriters (who underwrite 40% of the issue), and 30 minor underwriters (who underwrite the remainder).

   The issue is sold as follows: the four managers sell $30 million, 40 major underwriters sell $35 million, 30 minor underwriters sell $20 million, and an additional 60 selling banks sell $15 million. Selling concession is divided among banks according to the amount sold. Assuming each bank in each group shares equally (except for the management fee), calculate the dollar amount of fees going to:
   a. the lead manager
   b. each of the comanagers
   c. each of the major underwriters
   d. each of the minor underwriters

e. each of the selling banks

Fee arrangements are as follows:

Management fee	3/8%
Underwriting allowance	1/4%
Selling concession	1 1/2%
Total	2 1/8%

20. A Eurobond with a face value of $1000 and an annual coupon of $120 is purchased when the current yield is 9%. Later the bond is sold for $975. What is the capital gain or loss?

21. A bond trader buys 300 Eurobonds in the secondary market at a price of 92, each bond has a face value of $1000, and a coupon of 11%. At the value date for the trade there will be 244 days elapsed since the last coupon. What must the trader pay for the bonds?

SELECTED BIBLIOGRAPHY

Bank for International Settlements, *66th Annual Report,* Basle, June 1996.

Boris, Antl, (ed.) *Swap Finance.* London: Euromoney Publications, 1986.

Bank for International Settlements. *Recent Innovations in International Banking,* Basle, April 1986.

Beidleman, Carl R. *Interest Rate Swaps.* Homewood, IL: Business One Irwin, 1991.

Bicksler, J., and A.H. Chen. "An Economic Analysis of Interest Rate Swaps," *Journal of Finance,* (July 1986).

Chase Manhattan Bank. *The Chase Handbook of Emerging Markets Debt. Risk* Magazine, London: (March 1993).

Clark, John. "Debt Reduction and Market Reentry under the Brady Plan," Federal Reserve Bank of New York *Quarterly Review,* (Winter 1993–1994): 38–62.

Eng, M., and F. Lees. *International Financial Markets.* New York: Praeger, 1975.

Fabozzi, Frank J. *Bond Markets Analysis and Strategies.* Englewood Cliffs, N.J.: Prentice Hall, 1996.

Fisher, F. *International Bonds.* London: Euromoney Publications, 1981.

Fridson, Martin S. "International Emerging Markets Debt in the Asset Allocation Process," *Journal of Emerging Markets,* (Spring 1996).

Grabbe, J.O. *International Financial Markets.* New York: Elsevier, 1996.

"Interest Rate Swap Volume Continues to Grow Rapidly," *The Journal of Commerce,* (November 5, 1987): 7a.

International Monetary Fund, *International Capital Markets: Developments and Prospects.* Washington, D.C., 1995.

Johnson, R; and R. Zuber. "Model for Constructing Currency Cocktails," *Business Economics,* (May 1979).

Lee, A.S. "International Asset and Currency Allocation," *Journal of Portfolio Management,* (Fall 1987).

Marr, M.W., R.W. Rogowski, and J.L. Trimble. "Competitive Effects of U.S. and Japanese Commercial Bank Participation in Eurobond Underwriting," *Financial Management,* (Winter 1989).

Quinn, Brian Scott. "The International Bond Market for the U.S. Investor," *Columbia Journal of World Business,* (Fall 1979).

Quinn, Brian Scott. *The New Euromarkets*. London: Macmillan, 1975.

Rogers, Jr., William P. "Regulation of Swaps in the United States," in Schwartz and Smith, *The Handbook of Currency and Interest Rate Risk Management*. New York: New York Institute of Finance, 1990.

Schwartz, R.J., and C.W. Smith, Jr. *The Handbook of Currency and Interest Rate Risk Management*. New York: New York Institute of Finance, 1990.

Solnik, Bruno. *International Investments*. Reading, MA: Addison-Wesley, 1996.

Temperton, Paul. "Structuring a Portfolio with Emerging European Bonds," in *Emerging European Bond Markets*. London: IFR Publishing, 1991.

Walmsley, Julian. *The New Financial Instruments*. New York: Wiley, 1988.

World Bank, *Annual Report 1995,* Washington, D.C.

CHAPTER 8

Major Financial Centers: New York, London, and Tokyo

INTRODUCTION

As indicated in Chapter 1, the most important changes in global finance in the past three decades have included the upsurge of international capital movements, the globalization of financial markets, and the changes in financial technology and government regulations. This chapter analyzes the process and prerequisite conditions to become a major international financial center. It provides the highlights of leading international equities markets, then examines three major financial centers—New York, London, and Tokyo—as representatives of the globalization of financial markets. Finally, this chapter compares these three major international financial centers in terms of their contributions to the evolution of the world economy. To increase understanding of the functions of these three financial centers and of other international financial centers, readers may consult articles and publications referenced in this chapter's bibliography.

LEARNING OBJECTIVES IN THIS CHAPTER

1. To show why New York, London, and Tokyo are leading international equities markets.
2. To explain the process of internationalization of financial markets and the important necessary conditions for a center to become an international financial center.
3. To gain a perspective on recent trends in the U.S. economy, financial system, and financial markets, and to understand how New York has been an international financial center, vigorously and efficiently serving the domestic and international financial communities since World War I.
4. To gain a perspective on recent trends in the U.K. economy, financial system, and financial markets, and to understand how London has maintained a sophisticated international financial marketplace within the new "European Single Market" in the 1990s.
5. To gain a perspective on recent trends in the Japanese economy, financial system, and financial markets, and to understand how Tokyo has been an international financial center since the 1970s, primarily supported by its strong economic

growth, high national savings, and huge trade surpluses. The strength and weaknesses of the Japanese economy and finance in the 1980s and 1990s are also examined.

6. To compare the three major financial centers' economic backgrounds, financial systems, and financial market sizes, and to see how these major financial centers have contributed in various ways to world finance and economies.

KEY TERMS AND CONCEPTS

- American Depository Receipts
- Building Societies
- Complementary (or Parallel) Money Market
- Financial Service Act of 1986
- Gensaki Market

- Gilt-edged Securities
- Meiji Restoration
- Samurai Bonds
- Shogun Bonds
- The "Big Bang"
- Yankee Bonds
- Zaibatsu

ACRONYMS

ADRs	American Depository Receipts	**NASDAQ**	National Association of Security Dealers Automated Quotations
AIM	Alternative Investment Market	**NSCC**	National Securities Clearing Corporation
CDs	Certificates of Deposit	**OECD**	Organization for Economic Cooperation and Development
DTI	Department of Trade and Industry		
FECDBA	Foreign Exchange and Currency Deposit Brokers Association	**PSBR**	Public Sector Borrowing Requirement
IBFs	International Banking Facilities	**SEAQ**	Stock Exchange Automated Quotations
ISE	International Stock Exchange	**SIB**	Securities and Investment Board
ISRO	International Securities Regulatory Commission	**SRO**	Self-Regulating Organization
LIFFE	London International Financial Futures Exchange	**TSA**	The Securities Association
		USM	Unlisted Securities Market

International Comparisons of Equities Markets

International equities markets have undergone some structural changes in the 1990s. First, the major industrial countries such as the United States, the United Kingdom, and Japan suffered short-term economic recessions in the early 1990s that hurt their equities markets, though recoveries occurred in the 1995–1996 period. Second, equities markets in the Western European countries such as Germany, France, and Switzerland have become more competitive in light of the European Monetary

EXHIBIT 8.1	International Comparisons of Equities Markets 1995 (£ Millions)					
	Domestic Equity Market Value of Listed Companies	TURNOVER VALUE			TOTAL NO. OF LISTED COMPANIES	
		Domestic	Foreign	Total	Domestic	Foreign
New York	3,714,090	1,820,232	168,747	1,988,979	2,428	247
NASDAQ	747,143	1,480,054	64,689	1,544,743	4,760	362
London	906,774	323,166	395,392	718,558	2,303	536
Tokyo	2,283,542	521,775	610	522,385	1,714	77
Germany	373,337	382,120	9,387	391,507	437	220
Switzerland	256,397	192,291	10,332	202,623	216	233
Paris	321,246	132,563	2,294	134,857	710	194

SOURCE: London Stock Exchange, *Fact Book* (1996): 49.

Union scheduled for 1999. Third, emerging equities markets in Asia, Latin America, and Eastern Europe, as explained in Chapters 1 and 18, have demonstrated significant growth due to their strong economic performance in the 1990s. In short, international equities markets have been growing in a global and competitive way.

Exhibit 8.1 shows the highlights of the world's major equities markets in 1995. In terms of domestic equity market value of listed companies, New York Stock Exchange (NYSE) ranked number one followed by Tokyo Stock Exchange (TSE), London Stock Exchange (LSE), and others. With regard to turnover value, NYSE was the leader followed by NASDAQ (National Association of Security Dealers Automated Quotations) in New York, London, and Tokyo. However, London has still retained its leading position over all other exchanges in the number of listed foreign companies and foreign equities transactions. In the category of total numbers of listed companies, domestic and foreign, NASDAQ had the largest number. However, the NASDAQ listings were relatively small in size while the NYSE, LSE, and TSE have been mostly dominated by large corporations, as reflected in their respective market values.

While equities markets in Germany, Switzerland, France, and many other countries have shown tremendous growth in recent years, New York, London, and Tokyo still enjoy their leading positions in the global marketplace.

To attain international status, a financial center must follow an appropriate evolutionary process and possess certain basic qualifications.

NASDAQ

National Association of Security Dealers Automated Quotations is a nationwide electronic quotation system that displays dealer quotations on terminals to securities firms across the United States for most actively traded OTC stocks.

Internationalization of Financial Markets

THE PROCESS OF INTERNATIONALIZATION

As a financial center becomes more international in status, normally the following route is taken: 1) develop a local financial market, 2) become a regional financial center, and 3) finally attain the mature level of international financial market.

The development of local financial markets takes place parallel to broad economic development. An efficient financial market mechanism is required to channel domestic savings or external capital for productive investment. Example of this process are the Japanese and American financial markets in the late nineteenth century, the Mexican and Brazilian capital markets in the 1960s, and the Chinese and Polish financial markets in the 1990s. Increased demand to service international capital transactions will result from increased international trade and cross-border flows of funds. This growth requires many nations to expand their financial market activities to include their regional neighbors. The United States stepped up its trade with Latin American countries and opened up the New York capital market to Latin American borrowers after World War I. Singapore expanded its markets in the 1960s for neighboring countries in Southeast Asia.

Inevitably many local and regional financial markets are involved in some global financial activities. For example, Philippine company stocks are listed on the U.S. stock exchanges and South African stocks are listed on London's International Stock Exchange. At present, many national financial markets such as Frankfurt, Paris, and Zurich are heavily involved in international transactions. However, very few countries have 1) a broad spectrum of financial market instruments, 2) worldwide participation in their domestic as well as foreign sectors, and 3) efficient international telecommunications systems. By all measurements and standards, only the United States, the United Kingdom, Japan, and some Western European countries at the present time meet the requirements to be considered major international financial centers.

Basic Conditions for an International Financial Center

It took several centuries for London to develop its international financial market. New York and Tokyo required approximately 100 years for this process. Berlin was a major European financial market, but declined in importance after World War II. Many offshore banking centers that function as international entrepôt centers (Hong Kong, Singapore, Bahamas) deal primarily with Eurocurrency banking. These centers are discussed in Chapter 6. Developing the financial institutions, instruments, and expertise needed for international status requires considerable time and effort. To be a major international financial center, several conditions are required.*

1. Economic freedom—no financial market can function without the freedom to work, to consume, to save, and to invest.
2. A sound legal system including settlement mechanisms to protect both lenders and borrowers.
3. A supportive domestic economy with a stable currency—a sound financial system and currency provides confidence for international investors.
4. Efficient and effective financial institutions and instruments channel savings into productive investment.
5. Broad, in-depth, and resilient markets—comprehensive markets such as long and short–term markets, options and futures markets, and commodity markets provide more opportunities for borrowers and investors. After the October 1987 stock market crash in New York, many investors shifted funds to the U.S. Treasury bond market and money market funds.
6. Technology and communications allow effective and efficient clearing operations and money payments.
7. Financial expertise and human capital result from training and education.

---

* These conditions are close to the ideas expressed in "Financial Centers Around the World," *The Banker* (August 1977): 75–77.

8. An environment conducive to international capital flow must evolve, and be supported by an appropriate legal, social, and political climate.

New York as a Financial Center

Throughout this chapter we refer to New York, London, and Tokyo financial markets. To some extent there are other financial centers of activity in the United States, United Kingdom, and Japan. For example, Chicago, San Francisco, and Miami are of growing importance as regional financial centers. Japan has the Osaka stock market, and the United Kingdom has the Scottish investment advisory services.

The discussions of each major financial center—New York, London, Tokyo—includes the analysis of the national economy that functions as the base of each center's financial markets, the financial system's framework for their respective financial activities, and the analysis of their different market sectors that have significant effects on the flow of funds in their economies.

U.S. ECONOMY, 1980–1995

After a decade of oil price shocks, worldwide inflation, financial crisis, and the petrodollar recycling of the 1970s, the world faced a recession and inflation in the early 1980s. As Exhibit 8.2 indicates, the U.S. economy was in recession in 1980. Consumer prices increased by 13.5%. The value of the U.S. dollar compared to ten major currencies was 87.3% of its 1973 value. The unemployment rate was relatively high by national standards (7%). Under these extraordinary circumstances, the U.S. government adopted a relatively drastic economic policy, the so-called "Reaganomics" at the beginning of the Reagan administration. Theoretically, Reaganomics consisted of: a tight monetary policy to check inflation, tax cuts to stimulate saving and investment, federal spending cuts to shift resources to the private sector, and deregulation to encourage market competition.

In general the results of these policies were satisfactory, considering the declining inflation level and falling short–term interest rates from 1980–1987. However, this economic improvement was not won without a price. In the same period, government deficit spending increased from $73 billion to $149 billion and the current account of the U.S. balance of payments registered deficits increasing from $8 billion in 1982 to $120 billion in 1988.

In the period 1983–1989 the U.S. economy continued to prosper without interruption. The GDP showed healthy growth. The stock and bond markets surged after a decade of sluggishness. The value of the U.S. dollar climbed from 1983 to 1985 due to inflows of foreign capital that financed federal budget deficits and trade deficits. A decrease in domestic saving rates (from 7.7% to 3.9% in 1980–1987) set the stage for large capital inflows. The New York financial markets shared in the economic prosperity in the period 1983–1989, and in the economic downturn in 1990–1991. The New York financial markets were bullish when the U.S. economy began to rebound from 1992 through 1996. It is expected that the U.S. economy will continue to enjoy moderate growth, about 2.3% in 1997 and 2.1% in 1998.

U.S. FINANCIAL SYSTEM

The United States financial system has three basic components: financial institutions, financial markets, and financial instruments. As Exhibit 8.3 indicates, financial

EXHIBIT 8.2 Selected United States Economic and Financial Indicators 1980–1995

Domestic	1980	1981	1982	1983	1984	1985	1986	1987	1988	1989	1990	1991	1992	1994	1995
Gross Domestic Product	−0.2	1.9	−2.5	3.6	6.8	3.5	2.7	3.7	4.4	2.5	1.0	−1.2	2.1	3.5	1.2
Consumer Price Index	13.5	10.3	6.1	3.2	4.3	3.6	1.9	3.7	4.2	4.8	4.3	3.1	2.9	2.7	2.5
Unemployment Rate (%)	7.0	7.5	9.5	9.5	7.4	7.1	6.9	6.2	5.3	5.3	5.7	6.7	7.4	6.1	5.6
U.S. Dollar Value (1973=100)	87.3	102.9	116.5	115.3	138.1	143.1	112.2	96.9	92.7	98.6	85.5	89.8	86.6	91.3	84.2
Government Surplus or Deficit (−)(in Bil. Dollars)	$ −73.8	−78.9	−127.9	−207.8	−185.3	−212.3	−220.7	−149.7	−155.1	−152.2	−123.8	−271.5	−290.1	−203.1	−163.8
Current Account (in Bil. Dollars) Surplus or Deficit (−) (in Bil. Dollars)	$ 1.9	6.9	−8.7	−46.2	−107.0	−116.4	−133.3	−143.7	−120.0	−106.0	−100.0	−3.7	−60.0	−153.2	−153.0
Flow of Capital (in Bil. Dollars)	$ −12.9	−10.6	−1.9	33.4	90.9	115.9	143.9	164.0	147.9	88.1	22.0	22.8	3.3	121.0	45.8
3-Month Treasury Bill Rate (%)	11.4	14.0	10.6	8.6	9.5	7.5	6.0	5.8	6.6	8.1	7.8	5.3	3.4	4.3	5.5
AAA Bond Rate (%)	11.9	14.2	13.8	12.0	12.7	11.4	9.0	9.4	9.8	9.3	9.3	8.7	8.1	8.0	7.6
30-Year Treasury Bond Rate (%)	11.5	13.9	13.0	11.0	12.4	10.6	7.7	8.4	8.8	8.5	8.7	7.8	7.0	7.1	6.6
Money Supply M1	7.5	5.2	8.7	10.2	5.3	12.0	15.6	6.2	4.1	0.6	4.8	8.6	14.0	1.8	2.1
Saving Ratio	7.3	7.7	7.0	5.5	6.3	4.6	4.5	3.9	4.9	5.4	5.5	4.7	4.9	3.8	4.5

$$\text{Saving Ratio} = \frac{\text{Savings}}{\text{Disposable income}}.$$

NOTE: All figures are in percent changes over the previous year except where indicated. Dollars ($) are in billions.

SOURCES: 1) *Survey of Current Business*, U.S. Department of Commerce, various issues.
2) *Federal Reserve Bulletin*, Board of Governors of the Federal Reserve System, various issues.

EXHIBIT 8.3   **U.S. Financial Institutions, Lenders and Borrowers, and Government Supervisory Agencies**

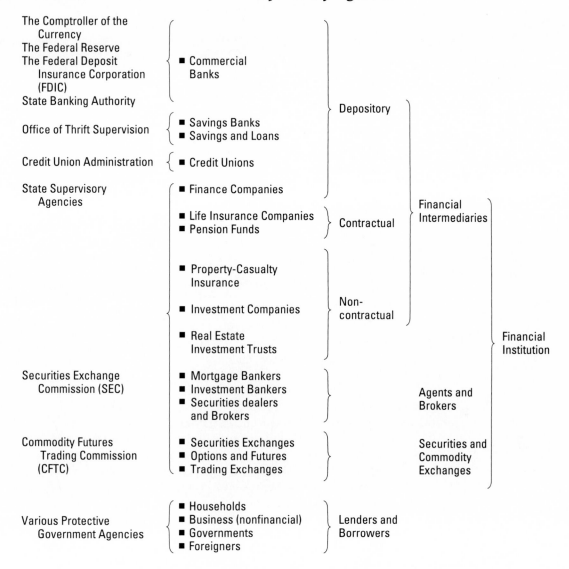

institutions include three broad categories: financial intermediaries, agents and brokers, and securities and commodity exchanges. The first category is consistent with depository institutions such as commercial banks and savings banks, contractual institutions such as life insurance companies and pension funds, and noncontractual institutions such as property casualty insurance and investment companies. The second category includes mortgage bankers, investment bankers, and securities dealers and brokers. The last category embraces securities exchanges and commodity exchanges including options, futures, swaps, and foreign currency trading.

The major function of these financial institutions is to channel savers' funds to borrowers for productive purposes. The size of their assets and liabilities reflects their relative importance in the free market economy. Exhibit 8.4 indicates that as of 1991, depository institutions accounted for 41% of the total financial assets, while

EXHIBIT 8.4	U.S. Financial Institutions: Financial Assets and Market Shares

31 December 1991–1995 (Billions of Dollars)

Depository Institutions	1991	1995	Growth Rate(%)
Commercial Banks	$3,458	$4,497	30%
Savings Institutions	1,172	1,030	−12
Credit Unions	237	311	3
	4,868	5,838	20
Insurance Companies			
Life Insurance Companies	1,518	2,085	37
Property-Casualty Insurance	563	743	32
	2,081	2,828	36
Pension Funds			
Private Pension Funds	1,427	2,625	84
State and Local Governments	877	1,388	58
	2,304	4,013	74
Other Financial Institutions			
Finance Companies	801	824	3
Mutual Funds	852	1,865	119
Money Market Funds	540	745	38
Securities Brokers and Dealers	315	561	78
	2,508	3,995	59
Total	$11,761	$16,674	42

SOURCE: *Federal Reserve Flow of Funds Accounts*

life insurance accounted for 13%. In 1995, assets of pension funds and mutual funds experienced higher growth rates than the depository institutions and insurance companies. As financial intermediaries, commercial banks play a key role in the short-term money market, while savings banks, pension funds, mutual funds, and life insurance companies mostly invest in long-term securities such as mortgages, corporate and government bonds, and corporate equities.

Various government supervisory agencies oversee and assure the proper functioning of financial institutions and markets. These agencies are outlined in Exhibit 8.3. Among the government supervisory agencies, the Federal Reserve System is the most influential because it is the central bank of the United States and also acts as the government fiscal agent. Its monetary policy is carried out through open market operations, changes in discount rates, and reserve requirements. The Federal Reserve influences the money supply and level of interest rates. In turn, these variables impact GDP, the price level, employment, and the value of the U.S. dollar.

The financial markets represent another important part of the U.S. financial system. In the United States we distinguish between long-term and short-term markets. The capital market, a long-term market, includes the equity (stock) market; the government, corporate, and foreign bond market sectors; the mortgage market; and consumer credit. The short-term market includes the money market, the foreign exchange market, and the financial options, futures, and swaps market.

Finally, the U.S. financial system employs various financial instruments. Short-term money market instruments include Treasury bills, certificates of deposit, bankers acceptances, commercial paper, federal funds, repurchase agreements, and loans to brokers and dealers.

Financial instruments are legal claims protected by law. Nevertheless, holders (investors) may be subject to a certain amount of credit risk. Investors obtain liquidity by selling credit instruments in the secondary market prior to maturity. Inflation,

EXHIBIT 8.5	Market Value of Stocks Traded on New York and Other Stock Exchanges in the United States 1995 (in Billions)			
	Market Value		Number of Shares	
New York Stock Exchange	$3,078	(84%)	90	(85%)
Other Stock Exchanges	610	(16%)	16	(15%)
Total	$3,688	(100%)	106	(100%)

NOTE: There were ten stock exchangers registered with the SEC in 1996.

SOURCE: United States Securities Exchange Commission. (SEC) Statistical Department, 1996.

changing levels of interest rates, and shifts in foreign exchange rates affect the effective yields on these financial instruments. Participants in the financial markets must be aware of the numerous risks present, including default or credit risk, reinvestment risk, inflation risk, political risk, and currency risk.

CAPITAL MARKET

The United States has an enormous capital market, the largest in the world. Exhibit 8.7 shows that in 1991 the total outstanding amount of securities including equity and debt was more than 15 trillion U.S. dollars. The capital market mechanism requires efficient financial institutions, a large amount of savings, and a strong demand for capital investment in land, plants, or equipment in order to maintain and increase long-term capital formation and economic productivity. New York is the center of the U.S. capital market. At present all large investment banking houses such as Salomon Brothers, Merrill Lynch, Goldman Sachs, Shearson Lehman, First Boston, and Morgan Stanley operate in New York to underwrite securities in the primary market and to act as brokers for customers in the secondary market. As dealers they trade securities for their own accounts. The growth of international capital flows has encouraged many foreign banks and investment banking houses to establish branches and affiliates in New York. They come from the United Kingdom, Western Europe, Japan, and countries all over the world.

The U.S. capital market is efficient due to the fact that domestic financial institutions channel new issues of bonds at low cost compared with other foreign markets.* In fact, in the primary market bond issues are more important than equity issues due to the huge volume of bond. However, in the secondary market the equity market is more significant due to the large volume of stock turnover in 1995 (Exhibit 8.5). As of 1995 the New York Stock Exchange accounted for 85% of share-trading and 84% of total volume in all securities exchanges in the United States. According to the New York Stock Exchange, the total market value of all stock listed on the New York Stock Exchange in 1995 was $6,279 billion with 2,922 companies (Exhibit 8.6).

The second largest capital market sector is the mortgage market that represented 56% of GDP in 1995 (Exhibit 8.7). Residential mortgages represent the largest part of the outstanding debt while government agencies such as Government National

* According to OECD Survey, *United States, 1987–1988,* p. 97, the cost of large bond issue was 0.98% of the total issue in the United States; 1.08% in the United Kingdom; 3.5+% in Japan. The cost of small and medium issue sizes also shows lower cost in the U.S. market than the other two financial centers.

EXHIBIT 8.6	**Stocks Listed on New York Stock Exchange 1995 (in Billions)**	
	Market Value	**Number of Companies**
U.S. Companies	$6,013	2675
Non-U.S. Companies	262	247
Total	$6,275	2922

SOURCE: New York Stock Exchange, *Fact Book* (1995): 42, 62.

EXHIBIT 8.7	**U.S. Capital Market Size, 1991–1995 (in Billions of Dollars)**		
Financial Instruments	**1991**	**1995**	**Growth Rate**
Common Stock	5,200	8,014	54%
Bonds			
U.S. Treasury Debt	2,759	3,609	31
State and Local Government Debt	902	1,063	18
Corporate Bonds	1,051	1,328	26
Foreign Bonds	124	282	127
Mortgages	4,037	4,700	16
Business Loans	724	848	17
Consumer Credits (installments and noninstallments)	796	1,116	40
Total Debt Outstanding Except Stock and Foreign Bonds	10,269	12,664	23
Total Outstanding as % of GDP	179%	175%	

NOTE: GDP, 1991 was $5,736 billion; 1995 was $7,248 billion.

SOURCES: *Federal Reserve Bulletin*, various issues; New York Stock Exchange *Fact Book*, various issues.

Mortgage Association (Ginnie Mae) and others have issued a tremendous amount of mortgage-backed securities.

The third largest borrower is the U.S. Treasury. Since 1983 the Treasury has stepped up its borrowings, a source of concern for many economists due to the "crowding out" of private sector borrowers and possible inflation effects. Foreign holders of Treasury securities are the second largest after the U.S. government agencies. The huge amount of government debt has impacted the value of the U.S. dollar in general and stock and bond markets in particular. The volatility of the U.S. bond market in recent years reflects foreign investors' sensitivity to the U.S. Treasury bond yields vis-a-vis yields in international financial markets, particularly in Tokyo and London.

The fourth largest amount is the corporate bond market. Increased bond issues in 1985 and 1987 included many "junk" bonds, with lower rating to finance corporate mergers and acquisitions. U.S. tax laws favor bond financing, since interest payments on bonds are tax deductible from corporate income tax and tend to lower the average cost of capital.

The volume of business loans and consumer credits usually reflects conditions in the national economy. In general, prosperity has encouraged individuals and businesses to borrow. Similarly, the declining interest rates since 1983 have also encouraged increased borrowing, in part to refinance debt at a lower cost.

Foreign bonds, the so called "Yankee Bonds"—U.S. dollar denominated bonds issued by foreigners in New York—are issued by Canadian provincial governments

EXHIBIT 8.8	U.S. Money Market 1991–1995 (in Billions Except Indicated in %)		
	1991	**1995**	**Growth Rate(%)**
Treasury Bills	590	760	29%
Federal Agency Securities	628	885	41
Negotiable Certificates of Deposit	356	421	18
Federal Funds and Repurchase Agreements	149	197	32
Bankers Acceptances	43	30	−30
Commercial Paper	530	675	27
Loans to Dealers and Brokers	106	84	−21
Total Size	2402	3,052	27
GDP	5736	7,246	26
Total Money Market 1995 Growth rate GDP	41.9	42.1	

NOTE: GDP 1991 was $5,736 billion; 1995 was $7,248 billion.

SOURCES: *Federal Reserve Bulletin,* various issues. *Economic Report of the President* (1993 and 1996).

and the European Investment Bank. Developing countries have limited access to the New York capital market because of strict SEC disclosure requirements and credit agencies' ratings (Moody's and Standard and Poor's).

MONEY MARKET

The United States domestic money market is the largest in the world by virtue of the sheer size of the U.S. economy. As shown in Exhibit 8.8, the total size of the U.S. money market at year end 1995 was 42.1% of the GDP. Economic prosperity usually needs liquidity to support its activities in the short-term market, for example, more CDs to finance business loans. Growing trends in the Treasury bill and government agency issues reflect increased government deficit financing. The federal funds market is a unique short-term money market in the United States. Basically it is a market where commercial banks lend and borrow excess reserve funds held as sight deposits in Federal Reserve banks. Federal funds and repurchase agreements increased substantially in 1995, primarily due to increase in demand for business loans.

The New York money market is vitally important in the United States. It is used by prime (top-rated) banks, corporations, and other participants to adjust short-term liquidity. The Federal Reserve Bank of New York is in the strategic position of conducting open market operations that are the mainstay of U.S. monetary policy and that directly impact money market liquidity. Open market operations are managed through the monthly meetings of the Open Market Committee of the Board of Governors of the Federal Reserve System in Washington.

Because the money market in the United States is a free market, it represents real market forces of supply and demand for funds. It also provides many alternatives to long-term lenders and borrowers. For example, when interest rates were high under inflationary conditions in the 1970s, funds shifted from the long-term to the short-term market. Many financial innovations such as money market mutual funds and options and futures trading are the result of the changing financial circumstances. In the supply and demand process, the Federal Reserve plays a key role

EXHIBIT 8.9	Value of the U.S. Dollar Against Major Currencies

1980–1995

	Value of U.S. dollar[1] 1973 = 100	$1 = Yen	$1 = DM	Value in £1 = U.S. $
1980	87.39	225	1.81	2.32
1985	143.01	238.47	2.9419	1.29
1991	89.84	134.59	1.5630	1.76
1995	84.25	93.96	1.4321	1.57

[1] Value of U.S. dollar against the average of ten currencies of leading industrial countries.

SOURCES: *Federal Reserve Bulletin,* various issues.

in controlling the flows of funds and the magnitude of money supply to influence short-term interest rates. For instance, in 1981, the Federal Reserve raised the discount rate to 14% and sold government securities to tighten the money supply in order to check inflation.

FOREIGN EXCHANGE MARKET

According to *The Financial Times* (London) 20 September 1995, foreign exchange turnover in New York on a daily average basis in April 1995 was $244 billion, second only to London (daily turnover $464 billion) but superseding Tokyo (daily turnover $161 billion). The most active currency in these three financial centers has been the U.S. dollar. Accounting for more than 60% of all international transactions, it is still the most popular currency in the world's financial markets. Chapter 4 explores these issues in detail.

Exhibit 8.9 shows the value of the U.S. dollar against the currencies of ten leading industrial countries. From 1980 to 1985 the dollar rose in value. From 1985 to 1995, the dollar declined against other currencies. In this 15-year period, the pound sterling depreciated against the U.S. dollar, while the yen appreciated against the U.S. dollar.

The foreign exchange markets in the United States are integrated with the foreign exchange markets in other countries and in the global market.* The national foreign exchange market includes bank-to-customer dealing (the retail sector), bank-to-bank dealing (the wholesale interbank sector), either direct or through brokers, and the central bank foreign exchange operations. These operations include intervention in the national exchange market, currency swaps with other central banks, and transactions with world financial organizations such as the World Bank and IMF. This global market covers worldwide transactions 24 hours a day. The foreign exchange market includes different time zones around the globe from New York to San Francisco, Tokyo, Hong Kong, Singapore, and London.

INTERNATIONAL LINKAGE

Three major "bridges" link the U.S. financial markets and international financial markets: financial institutions, business corporations, and securities markets.

---

* Kubarych, Roger M. *Foreign Exchange Markets in the United States.* Federal Reserve Bank of New York, 1978.

According to the *Annual Report* of the Board of Governors of the Federal Reserve System, 1995, there were 137 U.S. commercial banks with 802 branches in foreign countries; also, there were 76 Edge Act corporations doing banking business overseas. In the same year there were 761 foreign banking offices including International Banking Facilities (IBFs) in the United States, of which 590 offices were in New York. Both U.S. and foreign financial institutions are powerful vehicles for channeling funds between the United States and the rest of the world.

In the past three decades multinational corporations have built their global networks for production, marketing, trade, finance, and services. They have the flexibility of raising as well as investing funds in any national or international financial market sector. New York has provided an important operating base for U.S. and foreign multinationals in global finance.

The U.S. securities markets such as the equity and bond markets are another bridge linking U.S. financial markets and international financial markets. According to the *Fact Book 1995,* published by the New York Stock Exchange, in 1966 247 foreign companies from 39 countries had their stocks listed on the New York Stock Exchange in 1995. Their stocks had a total market value of $262 billion. Foreign companies can list their securities in the United States in the form of American Depository Receipts (ADRs). For example, in September 1988 the French government issued its treasury bonds on the New York Stock Exchange in the form of ADRs.*

The U.S. bond market also has strong international connections. Foreign investors hold substantial amounts of U.S. Treasury securities and U.S. corporate bonds. Foreign borrowers also issue foreign bonds (Yankee bonds) in the United States.

Modern technology such as telecommunications has contributed to these international linkages. Globalization of financial markets is impossible without rapid transfer of information and an efficient payments system among major international financial centers. At present the SWIFT network links all major international commercial banks, providing message switching that facilitates settlement of payments quickly. Several European and U.S. clearing organizations, including Euroclear in Brussels, Cedel in Luxembourg, the International Stock Exchange in London, and the international arm of National Securities Clearing Corporation (NSCC) of the United States handle Eurobond, foreign bond, and equity transactions across national boundaries every business day.

The New York financial markets are successful, in part due to a strong U.S. economic base and a comprehensive financial system. New York has fulfilled the role of a major financial center, servicing the net outflow of capital between 1950 and 1982, and the net inflow of capital between 1983 and 1995 as indicated in Exhibit 8.2.

American Depository Receipts

These represent shares of foreign stocks or bonds taken care of by American banks for U.S. residents who buy foreign securities without possession of the foreign securities.

"Yankee" bonds

U.S. dollar-denominated bonds issued by foreigners in New York.

London as a Financial Center

One of the amazing attributes of London as a world financial center is its capacity for "challenge and response" to any new situation or financial innovation.

During the Middle Ages when innovation was a forgotten word, the Magna Carta (Great Charter) was proclaimed by the English government (1215). This

---

* *The Economist* (September 24, 1988): 105. American Depository Receipts represent shares of foreign stock or bond custodied by American banks for U.S. residents who want to buy foreign securities without actual possession of the foreign securities. Interest is paid by foreign companies to U.S. investors through American banks.

charter guaranteed individual rights in England and that London would be a safe place for both domestic and foreign free traders.

Since then many major events have enabled London to continue unchallenged as an international financial center. The establishment of the Bank of England and the Royal Exchange in the 1690s laid the institutional foundations of the London financial markets. The mercantilist policies and the Industrial Revolution in Britain in the eighteenth century provided a strong commercial, financial, and economic base. London served as *the* world financial center for about 200 years—since the British gold standard was the cornerstone of international monetary systems, and sterling investment overseas dominated international trade, investment, and finance until World War I.

Between the First and the Second World Wars (1914–1945), New York emerged as an international financial center and challenged London's supremacy, especially its capital market. However, London managed its money market to service international trade financing, and its secondary trading market in international securities remained dominant because London was the focal point of Commonwealth and world banking.

After World War II the United Kingdom faced serious balance of payments deficits. To alleviate the problem of capital outflows, the British government imposed capital control on foreign exchange in 1957. The countries that had relied on the pound sterling to finance international trade were forced to use other currencies to meet their needs. The U.S. dollar was appropriate for this function. The increased demand for U.S. dollars in London increased the value of U.S. dollars. Since the 1960s London has become the hub of the Eurocurrency market of which about 75–80% is denominated in U.S. dollars.

The predominant position of London as leading the Eurocurrency market and its ability to serve a wide range of international needs were not sufficient to enable London to maintain its dominance as a capital market center. London's domestic capital market was losing ground to New York and Tokyo because of restrictive rules, including fixed commissions and the monopoly of stock transactions by jobbers (dealers) and brokers. In response to this challenge, the British government initiated the "Big Bang" in 1986. This action completely changed the structure of London's securities markets and created the new International Stock Exchange with completely computerized automatic quotations. London now competes with other markets for international securities trading activities.

"Big Bang"

Revolutionary structural changes in the U.K. securities markets under the Financial Services Act of 1986.

After the October 1987 stock market crash, securities trading volume in London declined. In 1988, the European Community (EC), including the United Kingdom, initiated plans for a unified market in Europe after 1992. Some question remains whether London will be able to maintain its edge over other continental financial centers such as Paris, Frankfurt, and Zurich in a unified European market.

To meet the new challenges for the European monetary union in 1999, the Bank of England and London Stock Exchange have initiated a number of innovations in the U.K. Securities markets. For example, the Bank of England has reformed the government securities (Gilts) such as the issuance of EMU Treasurer bills, increase in open market operations and repurchases agreements since 1995. The London Stock Exchange, supported by the Bank of England, introduced the new settlement system, CREST, in July 1996. This system provides electronic book entry transfer of registered stock, thereby reducing the movement of paper while still allowing shareholders the option of keeping share certificates. Participation in the system will be voluntary.

A three year independent study led by the London Business School concluded that most of London's international activities have been growing strongly over the past ten years. The commercial and technological forces supporting the concentration of financial business remain as strong as ever. The greater integration of the European economies is likely to create pressures for financial services to become more concentrated in London. However, the report also warned that shortcomings in transport, property, and promotion are the "key competitive threat" to London as a major international financial center. A special levy on business to help pay for improved public transport is a possibility.*

U.K. Economy

Until World War I, Britain played a major role in international economy and finance. Its economy began to experience problems after World War II: slow productivity growth in the 1960s, recurring inflation and government deficit spending in the 1970s, and relatively high unemployment in the 1980s. Several economists argue that the British economy has been revitalized since 1979 after Prime Minister Margaret Thatcher's economic reforms.†

In 1979 controls on foreign investment in the foreign exchange market were removed. Exhibit 8.10 shows that the British economy was in recession in 1980 and 1981. However, from 1982 to 1988, the economy expanded at a steady pace as inflation subsided, interest rates declined, and government deficits narrowed. Because of strong domestic demand, the British balance of payments on current account turned toward deficit since 1986. British privatization of government enterprises not only has stimulated economic competition, but has also reduced the public sector borrowing requirement (PSBR). In fact, money supply (M2) has grown steadily since 1981 in order to support the continued growing economy at lower interest rates. The strong demand for credit in the consumer, mortgage and business sectors has attracted many foreign financial institutions to London.

The financial sector has been the most dynamic in the British economy. It has maintained an importance in world financial markets while Britain's industrial base has lost its international competitive position. For example, in 1985 the U.K. financial sector share was 7.4% of GDP, while the financial sector in the United States and Switzerland only accounted for 4.7% and 6.9%, respectively.‡

From 1983 to 1988, the booming domestic economy in the United Kingdom and an aggressive privatization program reduced government deficits. However, the same economic boom has led to an increase in imports. The U.K. economy declined from 1990 to 1992 but rebounded from 1993 to 1996. Increased government spending played a key role in the economic upturn and decreased unemployment. This reflects the importance of the gilts market in recent years.§

U.K. Financial System

London's major role as an international financial center focuses world attention on U.K. monetary policy. In the past several decades several detailed analyses have been made of the financial system. For example, there was the MacMillan Report in

---

* *Finanical Times,* (March 13, 1995): 25.

† The problems are mentioned in Dornbusch, Rudiger, and Richard Layard (ed.) The Performance of the British Economy. Oxford: Clarendon Press, 1987. The revival of the British economy was described in Walters, Alan. Britian's Economic Renaissance. New York: Oxford University Press, 1986.

‡ OECD Economic Survey, *United Kingdom* (July 1987): 29.

§ OECD Economic Survey, *United Kingdom* (1996): 25.

EXHIBIT 8.10 Selected United Kingdom Economic and Financial Indicators

1980–1995

Domestic	1980	1981	1982	1983	1984	1985	1986	1987	1988	1989	1990	1991	1992	1994	1995
Gross Domestic Product	−2.5	−1.2	1.6	3.3	2.6	3.6	3.2	4.5	4.3	2.4	1.0	−2.1	−0.8	3.8	2.4
Consumer Price Index	18.0	11.9	8.6	4.6	4.9	6.1	3.4	4.1	4.9	7.9	8.2	6.9	4.4	2.4	2.8
Unemployment Rate	5.3	8.5	9.8	10.8	11.1	11.3	11.4	10.4	9.1	6.5	6.1	8.1	9.7	9.3	8.2
U.K. Sterling Exchange Rate (1975=100 for 1980–1987) (1985=100 for 1988–1992)(1990=100 for 1991–1995)	101.4	93.3	88.6	82.9	73.0	77.9	72.8	75.8	95.5	92.6	91.2	91.7	88.5	88.3	85.4
Government Surplus or Deficit (−)	L−2.5	−2.8	−2.7	−3.3	−3.1	−2.4	−2.2	−1.5	0.8	−0.1	−0.6	−2.0	−5.5	−4.7	−4.3
Current Account surplus or deficit (−)	L6.8	12.8	7.1	5.1	2.0	3.7	−1.4	−2.8	−26.3	−34.2	−25.7	−1.1	−2.1	−2.8	−8.7
3-Month Interbank Loan Rate	16.6	13.8	12.3	10.1	9.9	12.2	10.9	9.6	10.3	13.9	15.3	11.5	10.4	5.5	6.7
20-Year Government Bond Rate	13.8	14.7	12.9	10.8	10.7	10.6	9.9	9.5	9.4	9.8	10.6	10.1	9.3	8.0	8.2
Money Supply M2	4.4	10.7	8.6	10.3	12.7	9.3	14.4	10.5	16.9	9.9	11.0	5.8	3.2	7.0	6.3
Saving Ratio	14.2	13.0	12.2	10.5	10.5	9.2	7.5	5.9	5.4	6.7	8.4	10.7	12.3	9.5	10.1

NOTE: 1. All figures are in percent. Pound sterlings (L) are in billions.

2. For the U.S., M1 is currency in circulation plus domestic deposits; for the United Kingdom, M2 means M1 plus private sterling time deposits.

SOURCES: *IMF World Economic Outlook*, (1996) and OECD Financial Statistics; Central Statistical Office, Financial Statistics.

1931, the Radcliffe Report in 1959, and the Wilson Report in 1980, all of which suggested improvements for the British financial system and the financial market mechanisms.

Nevertheless, the complex financial mechanisms and institutions in London were outmoded by the late 1970s due to the rapidly changing international environment. In an effort to regain its role as an international financial center, the British government adopted a series of measures to revamp its financial system including: deregulation, securitization, and globalization of financial markets.

The removal of exchange controls in 1979 had positive as well as negative effects on the British financial system. On the one hand, restrictions on overseas investment were relaxed and more foreign bonds were issued in London. On the other hand, the erosion of exchange controls worldwide had encouraged the development of global trading in other international equity markets.

The Financial Services Act of 1986 represents the most comprehensive overhaul in regulating investment activities in the United Kingdom since the Second World War. Most of the powers to authorize and regulate investment business are given to the Securities and Investment Board (SIB),* while the Bank of England continues to carry on its responsibility for supervising the lending and deposit-taking activities of banks, the wholesale money markets, the foreign exchange markets, and the gilt-edged market.

The Building Societies Act of 1987 allows building societies to engage in some new financial activities including unsecured loans, insurance brokering, current account facilities and other financial services. Supervision of building societies has been vested in a new Building Societies Commission.

Under the Banking Act of 1987, the Bank of England is given power to obtain information regarding changes in stockholder control of U.K. banks. Bank shareholdings in investment firms are placed under the jurisdiction of the SIB.

The main purposes of these financial reforms are to strengthen and support the competitive capacity of U.K. financial institutions in increasingly globalized financial markets. As Exhibit 8.11 indicates, the Bank of England supervises and influences the banking sector through its monetary measures, and the SIB authorizes and regulates the nonbank long-term securities markets through many Self-Regulating Organizations (SROs) such as The Securities Association (TSA), International Securities Regulatory Organization (ISRO), and others.

In the banking sector, commercial banks are conglomerates acting in investment and merchant banking. Overseas banks compete in providing corporate financial services and in servicing the securities markets. United Kingdom building societies are becoming more like banks, while investment banks are becoming more like building societies. Furthermore, to support the securitization process in light of third world debt exposures, U.K. banks have become more active in placing paper, notes, and bonds issued by companies to generate fee income.

Exhibit 8.12 illustrates the relative importance of the U.K. financial institutions in terms of assets. For example, the monetary sector controls about 85% of domestic banking deposits while insurance companies and pension funds accounted for

* For a detailed explanation of the Financial Services Act 1986, see Lomex, David F. *London Markets after the Financial Services Act.* London: Butterworths, 1987. SIB reports to the Parliament via the chancellor of the exchequer. The governor of the Bank of England and the Secretary of State for Trade and Industry jointly approve the 18 members of the SIB Board. The SIB is the designated agency of the Secretary of State for Trade and Industry.

EXHIBIT 8.11	U. K. Financial Institutions and Government Supervisory Agencies

```
                    Chancellor                        Department of Trade
                     of the                            and Industry(DTI)
                    Exchequer


                  Bank of England            Securities and Investment
                                             Board (SI and B)


  Domestic Depository       International      • International Stock
  Institutions              Banks                Exchange (ISE)
                                               • London International
  • Clearing Banks          • Accepting Houses    Financial Futures
  • Building Societies        (Merchant Banks)    Exchange (LIFFE)
  • Discount Houses         • Overseas Banks    • Over-the-Counter (OTC)
  • Finance Houses          • Foreign Banks     • Commodity Exchange
  • Trustee Savings                             • Association of
    Banks                                         International
  • National Savings                             Bond Dealers
    and Girobanks                               • Investment and
    (They are Post                               Pension Fund
    Office Run                                   Managers
    Organizations)                             • Life Companies and
                                                 Unit Trust Managers
```

88% of the total assets of investing institutions in 1995. Among the investing institutions, pension funds, investment trusts, and unit trusts enjoyed the highest growth rates in the period 1991–1995.

Undoubtedly, the U.K. financial system has been revolutionalized beginning in the 1980s, especially after the Big Bang in October 1986. The first test of the new financial system was the October 1987 stock market crash.

Since 1995 many securities firms in London and other European financial centers (such as Amsterdam) use electronic connections to trade securities listed on London Stock Exchange but the transactions take place outside the LSE. This is known in Europe as "distant controlled membership."

Distant Control Membership

Securities firms in London and other European financial centers use electronic connections to trade securities listed on London Stock Exchange but outside the Exchange.

LONDON CAPITAL MARKET

Within the changing national economy and financial system, the London capital market changed drastically in the 1980s and 1990s. The highlights of the changes are:

• The Unlisted Securities Market (USM) was established in November 1980 and has successfully fulfilled the role of an organized equity market for small- and medium-sized companies. It is an over-the-counter market without the costly listing requirements of a regular stock exchange.

EXHIBIT 8.12	**U.K. Financial Institutions and Their Assets (in £ Billion)**

1991–1995

DEPOSIT-TAKING INSTITUTIONS				INVESTING INSTITUTIONS			
	ASSETS				ASSETS		
	1991	1995	Growth Rate		1991	1995	Growth Rate
Monetary Sector[1]	1,233.8	1,779.6	44%	Insurance Companies[3]	442.1	5,02.0	14%
				Pension Funds	302.7	447.9	48
Building Societies	248.4	297.3	20	Investment Trusts	22.5	40.0	78
Finance Houses[2]	9.5	15.3	61	Unit Trusts	55.1	88.4	60
Total	1,491.7	2,092.2	40	Total	822.4	1,078.3	31

[1] Monetary sector includes clearing banks, Trustee Savings Banks and discount houses.

[2] Finance houses are institutions which take deposits to provide industrial and consumer credit.

[3] Insurance companies include UK subsidiaries and branches of foreign companies.

SOURCES: Bank of England, *Quarterly Bulletin;* Central Statistical Office, Financial Statistics.

- In 1983, negotiated commissions replaced fixed commissions traditionally set by stock exchange brokers. Lower transaction costs have encouraged institutional investors and others to engage in securities trading.

- The inception of the London International Financial Futures Exchange (LIFFE) in 1981 has stimulated the London securities market in futures and options trading, parallel to developments in the United States.

- Since the Big Bang 27 October 1986, the name "London Stock Exchange" was changed to the "International Stock Exchange," that developed and introduced a terminal-based quotation system, Stock Exchange Automated Quotations (SEAQ). Under the new system, minimum commissions and the separation of member firms into brokers and jobbers were abolished. After the Big Bang, the market players on the ISE increased from seven to 35 including 21 from the United Kingdom, seven from the United States, and seven from Switzerland, Australia, and Hong Kong (*Financial Times,* October 27, 1986).

- In January 1987 the Third Market began trading. Small venture capital, speculative companies now have a forum for trading their shares.

- After the "Big Crash" on 19 October 1987, the volume of stock turnover was reduced in the first few months but gradually increased in 1988. However, investment houses suffered from loss of income.

- In 1990 merger of the USM and Third Market took place as a result of European Community regulatory directives on listing.

- In 1992 the LIFFE and London Traded Options Market merged.

AIM

The Alternative Investment Market is a new market established by the London Stock Exchange in June 1995 for smaller, young, and fast-growing companies, domestic and foreign.

- In June 1995 the alternative investment market (AIM) was established by the London Stock Exchange for smaller, young, and fast-growing companies. The USM set up in 1980 and closed at the end of 1996.

The following is a brief review of the London capital markets: the primary market, the secondary market, and other markets.

The Primary Market   This market includes new securities issued by the government, U.K. companies, and Eurobonds issued by foreign borrowers. According to Exhibits 8.10 and 8.13, government deficits gradually declined from 1985 through

EXHIBIT 8.13	**Funds Raised in the Primary Market (£ Million)**		
	1989–1995		
	1989	**1992**	**1995**
Public Sector (UK Gilts)	−10,219	27,043	29,720
UK Company Sector	17,135	10,871	12,807
Eurobonds	9,445	13,356	24,766
Total	16,361	51,271	67,293

SOURCE: The International Stock Exchange, (London) *Fact Book* (1996):57–58.

1990, and the money raised by the government in the primary market also decreased. However, government borrowings resumed in 1991 through 1995 for two reasons: 1) to revive the declining national economy and 2) to defend against the falling value of the British pound during the currency crisis in September 1992 and after.

In the United Kingdom company sector enterprises still rely on internal sources of funds. Nevertheless, external funding of companies continued to grow moderately in the capital market but more substantially through the commercial paper market since 1992.

Foreign borrowing in London through the issuance of Eurobonds demonstrated spectacular growth since the elimination of capital control in 1979. Exhibit 8.13 indicates the continuous growth in the period 1989–1995, second only to the funds raised by the public sector.

The Secondary Market   This market includes the trading of all outstanding securities on the London International Stock Exchange. After the Big Bang, securities trading volume increased significantly. Investment bankers now flock to London because it bridges the time period between the closing of Tokyo markets and the opening of New York markets. Furthermore, privatization in Europe necessitates that new private firms issue equities and find a liquid trading market for these securities outside their home countries. London is an attractive place for borrowers, investors, and financial intermediaries with its liberal regulatory framework, participation by well-known international investment bankers, and strong communications network.

The focal point of the London secondary securities market is the London Stock Exchange (LSE). The LSE covers four markets: domestic equities, gilt-edged and company fixed-interest securities, options, and foreign equities. The domestic equity market includes the listed market for well-established companies. The gilt market represents government bonds issued by the Bank of England. Gilts are bought and sold in huge quantities primarily by institutional investors. The options market was created in 1978. It provides investors with the means to hedge or protect their positions in underlying securities by buying or selling an option contract. As part of the London International Stock Exchange, foreign equities are traded on SEAQ International.

In Exhibit 8.14, we see there were 2600 companies listing their stocks and bonds on the International Stock Exchange as of 1995, with a total market value of over 1 trillion pounds.

Gilts

Gilt-edged stocks are bonds issued and guaranteed by the British government.

EXHIBIT 8.14	**Numbers of Listed Securities and Their Market Value**		

1995

	Number of Companies	Number of Securities	Market Value (£ Million)
Eurobonds	525	3,044	231,186
Equities	2,078	2,563	900,329
Fixed Interest	2,078	1,163	35,834
Total Listed Securities		6,770	1,167,349

SOURCE: The International Stock Exchange (London), *Fact Book* (1996):59.

LONDON MONEY MARKET

Among the three major international financial centers, the London money market is the oldest and most sophisticated. Its longevity can be attributed to the evolution of the market itself, the structure of the traditional money market and the complementary (or parallel) money market, and how the Bank of England exercises its supervisory role.

The Traditional Money Market   The Bank of England sits at the center of the British monetary system and exercises a number of important functions, including two major responsibilities: market operations and supervision. With respect to market operations, the Bank is responsible for financing the government deficit by borrowing in the gilt-edged market and smoothing the effects of daily flows between the government and banking system in the money markets. Market operators' responsibilities also encompass dealing in foreign exchange and gold markets for the government and other customers, and managing U.K. gold and foreign currency reserves. With regard to supervision, the Bank is responsible for protecting depositors and the health of the U.K. banking system under the 1887 Banking Act, supervising the wholesale markets in sterling, foreign exchange, and bullion (areas exempted under the Financial Act of 1986), and supervising the market makers including ISE money brokers and brokers operating in the gilt-edged market.

The Bank of England uses several credit control tools to influence the traditional money market: sales of Treasury bills to discount houses, buying and selling government securities through its open market operations, discounting eligible bills through the discount window for discount houses, and imposing reserve requirements for net sterling deposit liabilities in banks and licensed deposit-taking institutions. Since 1995 it has conducted more repurchase agreements.

Traditionally, the discount houses stand between the Bank of England and commercial banks and other banks in the system. As Exhibit 8.15 indicates, when the Bank of England sells Treasury bills, the discount houses borrow call money from banks. The profits of the discount houses in this case depend on the cost of money and the margin on the sales of the Treasury bills to investors including banks. Surplus funds at banks can be used efficiently on a day-to-day basis, but banks reserve the right to call back these funds if they are short of liquidity. In case of need for liquidity, only the discount houses—not the banks as in other countries—have the right of access to the Bank of England for last resort finance against the presentation of eligible securities at the Minimum Lending Rate.

EXHIBIT 8.15   **The Traditional London Money Market**

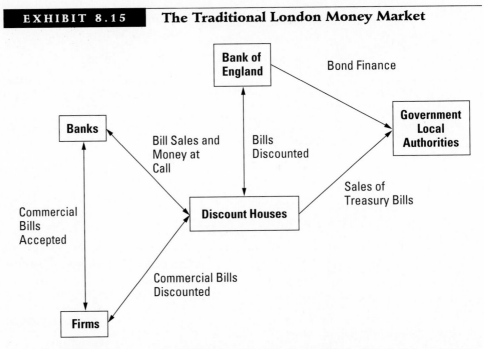

The Complementary or Parallel Money Market   While the traditional money market is a secured market, the complementary market is unsecured. It includes the interbank market, sterling certificates of deposit, dollar certificates of deposit, local authority funds, finance house funds, and intercompany funds. Euro-commercial paper was introduced to the London parallel market, and sterling commercial paper was also allowed by the Bank of England in 1986 with one condition— that the issuer's stock must be listed on the London Stock Exchange. The major characteristics of the complementary market are that business transaction is mostly by telephone (interbank market); loans are unsecured and need not be self-liquidating; there is no lender of last resort (CD market); and borrowers and lenders have more alternatives to achieve their purposes. The recent growth of the complementary market has been tremendous under more liberal conditions.

Exhibit 8.16 indicates that the growth of Treasury bills, commercial paper, and sterling CDs from 1991 to 1995 was at a much higher rate than that of local authority securities and sterling acceptances. However, the total money market size as a percentage of GDP has remained virtually unchanged over this period. (about 39%.)

London Foreign Exchange Market

The foreign exchange market in London is the largest in the world. Its average daily turnover was $464 billion in 1995. At the center of the market are more than 500 banks—domestic and foreign—and other financial institutions. Some buy and sell foreign exchange for their own account. In the case of large transactions, foreign exchange brokers may act as intermediaries. All brokers are members of the Foreign Exchange and Currency Deposit Brokers Association. As stated previously, the Bank of England closely supervises trading arrangements and also deals actively in the market on behalf of its own customers—chiefly, government departments and central banks of other countries. The Bank of England buys and sells foreign exchange to maintain the stability of sterling in the exchange market.

The activities in the London foreign exchange market are similar to those in other markets, including spot, forward, futures, options, arbitrage, and currency

EXHIBIT 8.16	**Selected Money Market Instruments in the United Kingdom**		
	1991–1995		
(£ Millions)	**1991**	**1995**	**Growth Rate**
Treasury Bills Outstanding	10,054	18,037	79%
Sterling Acceptances	24,632	18,721	−24
Certificates of Deposit and Other Short Term Paper	52,307	73,691	41
Other Currencies CDs and Other Short Term Paper	65,648	89,217	36
Commercial Paper	11,554	21,038	82
Local Authority Securities	52,157	47,599	−9
Call and Overnight	8,956	7,421	−17
Total Money Market Size	225,308	275,724	22
Gross Domestic Product	574,146	699,573	22
Total Money Market Size as Percentage of GDP	39.24%	39.40%	

SOURCES: Central Statistical Office, Financial Statistics, Bank of England *Quarterly Bulletin*, (February 1996.)

swaps. London's foreign exchange market is closely related to its money market due to the huge volume of Eurocurrency transactions and foreign currency CDs.

INTERNATIONAL LINKAGE

London has long served as an international financial center. The pound sterling, backed by the gold standard, was the cornerstone of international finance in the nineteenth century. London was the leading center for international trade financing before the Second World War. Since the war, London has continued to attract foreign commercial banks and other financial institutions to participate in the dynamic development of financial markets. According to the *Bank of England Quarterly Bulletin,* August 1995, 268 foreign banks were located in London with more than 400 branches, subsidiaries, and representative offices. After the Big Bang in 1986 foreign securities houses flocked to London to participate in the growing international capital market, especially trading in Eurobonds and international stocks. London continues to hold a strategic position for international financial activities.

The presence of British banks, insurance companies, and securities houses in all major financial centers (such as New York, Tokyo, Europe, Singapore, Australia, Brazil, Mexico, and Hong Kong) reflects a new strength in international finance. The United Kingdom has become a creditor nation second only to Japan. British pension fund investments overseas and British direct investment in the United States and other countries have increased markedly. Conversely, foreign portfolio and direct investment in the United Kingdom also have increased in recent years due to prospective economic and financial opportunities in the changing Europe.

Tokyo as a Financial Center

Meiji Restoration

A new era started by the Emperor of Japan in 1868 to make Japan a modern nation.

Japan had borrowed foreign capital and technology from London and western European countries from the time of the Meiji Restoration in 1868 until the First World War. Once again, after the Second World War, Japan obtained foreign capital and technology, primarily from the United States to build its war-torn economy. The Tokyo Stock Exchange was established in 1878. However, the Exchange did not enjoy international status until the 1970s when Japan emerged as an economic power second only to the United States, and as a financial power in the 1980s when Japan became the largest foreign exchange holding nation. Tokyo has evolved into a formidable competitive center for international financial business as a result of its "miracle" economy, its huge financial reservoir, the strong yen, and efficient financial institutions.

Before 1970 Tokyo was not considered an international financial center for several reasons. First, financial markets in Japan were not influenced by market forces but rather by government policy directed toward national economic objectives. The government planned but did not control the national economy. Allocations of financial and nonfinancial resources were based on national priorities. The financial system and financial markets were considered instrumental in achieving national economic purposes. Second, Japan was a capital-importing country in the 1950s and 1960s, shifting its financing sources from the United States to Europe after the United States imposed the Interest Equalization Tax in 1963. Third, strict government regulation of the securities market in Japan discouraged foreign financial institutions from participating in market activities. Fourth, foreign exchange control in Japan limited the flexibility of foreign borrowers and investors.

However, conditions favorable to Tokyo as an international financial center developed gradually and were reinforced by national and international developments after 1970. The "oil shock" in 1974 forced the Japanese government to increase aggregate spending in order to lift the national economy from recession. An increase in government bond issues encouraged the development of a large secondary market in government bonds and a bond repurchase market called the Gensaki market. The Gensaki market allowed outflows of funds from regulated bank deposits, because business and institutional depositors had withdrawn their funds from banks to the more lucrative bond repurchase market. This action prompted the monetary authorities to permit banks to issue negotiable certificates of deposit (NCDs) at market rates in 1979. Increasing issues of yen-denominated bonds to foreign borrowers in Tokyo also stimulated growth of the international capital market in the 1970s. The huge financial reservoir in Japan that resulted from trade surpluses and high personal saving rates attracted foreign borrowers (such as U.S. corporations) and international fund raisers (such as the World Bank and Asian Development Bank).

In the 1980s with the liberalization of the yen, the Japanese government and the Tokyo capital market opened the door to foreign banks and securities houses. According to reports published by Japan's Securities Research Institute in 1988 and 1992, the net increase in foreign purchases of Japanese stocks surged from about $4 billion in 1981 to $48 billion in 1987, but declined to $16 billion in 1990 due to the Tokyo stock market crash. To meet the growing domestic and international demand, a computerized system for transactions was put into full operation by the Tokyo Stock Exchange in 1983, more foreign firms were admitted to the TSE after 1986, an offshore banking market was established in 1986, and financial futures trading started in 1987. As a leading financial center, however, Tokyo has been facing many challenges in the 1990s primarily due to the economic recession in 1993 and slow recovery in 1994-1995. Financial scandal in the real estate and banking sectors have also damaged the financial system that is in need of immediate and effective reform.

Gensaki

Gensaki is a market for repurchase agreements with government securities as collateral; it liberalized the Japanese money market in 1974 and in the years after.

THE JAPANESE ECONOMY

Japan has turned itself from a poor country after World War II to a powerful economic nation second only to the United States. Japan enjoyed its GDP growth rate at an annual average of 11% in the 1960s, 5% in the 1970s, and 4% in the 1980s. Its per capita income in 1991 was about $26,900. Japan—even with its lack of natural resources—has managed its economy successfully due to several major factors. First, it allocated the productive sectors effectively on the basis of national priorities (for example, manufacturing and exports). Second, Japan successfully commercialized technology, as developed in America. Third, it has had a high savings rate, high investment rate, and high growth in productivity. Fourth, in the 1980s it enjoyed high export prices for manufacturing goods but low prices of goods for imports. Fifth, appreciation of the Japanese yen against the U.S. dollar since 1986 has pushed up the value of Japanese financial assets, providing a powerful competitive edge to Japanese financial institutions in the international arena.

From 1945 to 1955 Japan methodically reorganized the national economy that had been devastated by the Second World War. From 1955–1970 the Japanese economy enjoyed a "take-off," supported by technology primarily in the form of joint ventures and by official and private foreign loans. During this period, Japan enjoyed export-led economic growth. The oil shock in 1974 led to a recession, but Japan recovered quickly due in part to increased government spending. Japan was also successful in bringing the inflation rate down from 24% in 1974 to 0.7% in 1983.

As Exhibit 8.17 shows, in the period 1980–1991 Japan enjoyed steady GDP growth with a declining price level and low unemployment. Japan's economic performance in this period was above average for OECD countries. Government deficits gradually decreased due to buoyant tax revenues. Since 1983 the huge current account surplus has had a significant impact on the domestic and world economy. Domestically a strong yen has led the Bank of Japan, under pressure from the United States, to buy dollars in the open market. The increased yen supply has caused lower interest rates that have stimulated housing construction and purchase of stocks, as well as investment by small businesses.

Since 1987 the Japanese government has introduced a series of economic reform measures. These reforms include income tax cuts, consumption tax increases, promotion of imports, increased financial assistance to developing countries, and privatization of government-controlled companies (for example, sale of Nippon Telegraph and Telephone shares to the public). The government addressed these reforms in the design of the five-year plan (1988–1992). However, a sluggish Japanese economy in 1992–1995 has forced the government to increase spending, and budget deficits rose during this period. On the international front, Japan still managed its current account surpluses. However, its patterns of foreign trade and investment have changed.*

THE JAPANESE FINANCIAL SYSTEM

Historically the Japanese financial system has been designed to serve the Japanese economy. The segmentation of its banking system and the slow development of its capital and money markets until the 1980s reflect an imbalance in the financial

---

* OECD, *Economic Surveys: Japan* (1995).

EXHIBIT 8.17 **Selected Japanese Economic and Financial Statistics**

1980–1995

	1980	1981	1982	1983	1984	1985	1986	1987	1988	1989	1990	1991	1992	1994	1995
Gross Domestic Product	4.3	3.7	3.1	3.2	5.1	4.9	2.5	4.6	5.7	4.9	4.8	4.1	1.5	0.5	0.9
Consumer Price Index	3.8	3.2	1.9	0.7	1.2	1.4	1.9	-0.1	0.6	2.3	3.3	3.3	1.7	0.3	-0.5
Unemployment Rate	2.0	2.2	2.4	2.7	2.7	2.6	2.8	2.8	2.6	2.3	3.3	2.1	2.2	2.9	3.1
Yen Exchange Rate (Currency Units per U.S. Dollar)	226.63	220.63	249.06	237.55	237.45	238.47	168.35	144.60	128.17	138	129	134	126	102.1	94
Government Surplus or Deficit (−) (in Billions of Dollars)	-6.2	-5.9	-5.9	-5.6	-4.7	-4.0	-3.3	-3.8	-3.4	-3.2	-3.3	-3.9	-4.1	-3.2	-6.0
Current Account Surplus or Deficit (−) (in Billions of Dollars)	-10.7	4.8	6.9	20.8	35.0	49.2	85.8	86.7	77.8	57.0	35.8	72.6	117.6	130	111
Short-Term Gensaki	11.45	7.58	6.84	6.49	6.32	6.47	6.96	3.87	4.22	4.73	6.62	5.61	3.86	2.1	1.1
Rate 10-Year Government Bond Yields	8.9	8.4	8.3	7.8	7.3	6.5	5.2	5.0	4.83	5.64	7.20	55.3	6.00	4.2	3.3
Money Supply M1	2.6	3.3	5.8	3.6	2.8	5.0	6.9	10.5	8.4	4.1	2.0	3.0	4.8	5.4	8.2
Saving Ratio (% Disposable Income)	17.9	18.2	16.5	16.3	16.0	16.0	16.4	16.1	15.6	15.4	15.0	16.0	18.0	16.0	16.1
Flow of Long-Term Capital (in Billions of Dollars)	2.3	-9.7	-15.0	-17.7	-49.6	-64.5	-131.5	-137.1	-130.9	-87.9	-43.5	37.1	2.6	-82.0	-84.5

NOTE: All figures are in percentages over the previous year except in yen and dollar as indicated.

SOURCES: *IMF Economic Outlook* (1996); *Bank of Japan Monthly Statistics*; and *Federal Reserve Bulletin*, various issues.

EXHIBIT 8.18   **Financial Institutions in Japan**

1. The Bank of Japan
2. All Banks (87) Member banks of the Federation of Bankers Associations of Japan
   A. Banking Accounts
      (1) City Banks (13)
      (2) Regional Banks (64)
      (3) Trust Banks (7)
      (4) Long-term Credit Banks (3)
   B. Trust Accounts (9) Trust accounts of the one city bank, two regional banks and seven trust banks
3. Foreign Banks in Japan (81)
4. Financial Institutions for Small Business
   (1) Sogo Banks (68)
   (2) The Zenshinren Bank
   (3) Shinkin Banks (455)
   (4) The Shoko Chukin Bank
   (5) National Federation of Credit Cooperatives
   (6) Credit Cooperatives (422)
   (7) National Federation of Labor Credit Associations
   (8) Labor Credit Associations (47)
5. Financial Institutions for Agriculture, Forestry, and Fishery
   (1) The Norinchukin Bank
   (2) Credit Federations of Agricultural Cooperatives (47)
   (3) National Mutual Insurance Federation of Agricultural Cooperatives
   (4) Mutual Insurance Federations of Agricultural Cooperatives (47)
   (5) Agricultural Cooperatives (4,028)

   (6) Credit Federations of Fishery Cooperatives (35)
   (7) Fishery Cooperatives (1,737)
6. Securities Finance Institutions
   (1) Securities Finance Companies (3)
   (2) Securities Companies (210)
7. Insurance Companies
   (1) Life Insurance Companies (24)
   (2) Non-Life Insurance Companies (23)
8. Government Financial Institutions
   (1) The Japan Development Bank
   (2) The Export-Import Bank of Japan
   (3) The People's Finance Corporation
   (4) The Housing Loan Corporation
   (5) The Agriculture, Forestry, and Fisheries Corporation
   (6) The Small Business Finance Corporation
   (7) The Hokkaido and Tohoku Development Corporation
   (8) The Japan Finance Corporation for Municipal Enterprises
   (9) The Small Business Credit Insurance Corporation
   (10) The Environmental Sanitation Business Finance Corporation
   (11) The Okinawa Development Finance Corporation
9. Governments
   (1) Trust Fund Bureau
   (2) Postal Savings
   (3) Postal Life Insurance and Postal Annuity

system. The liberalization of Japanese financial markets since 1975 has strengthened the Japanese financial system, but it needs more thorough review and reform in view of the stock market scandal in 1991–1992. The following is a brief discussion of the changes in financial institutions, flow of funds, and financial market liberalization.

Exhibit 8.18 indicates that the Bank of Japan—the central bank—is the lender of last resort, government fiscal agent, and is responsible for monetary policy. The Bank was established in 1885 and modeled on the Bank of England. Traditionally it has relied on the discount rate to influence the money supply and interest rates. After the Second World War the Bank of Japan began to use reserve requirements and open market operations as additional instruments of monetary control. Normally city banks and long-term credit banks have played an important role in Japanese

EXHIBIT 8.19	Japan's Flow of Funds (¥ Billion)			
	1993		**1994**	
	Surplus	**Deficit (−)**	**Surplus**	**Deficit (−)**
Household Sector	48,079		43,327	
Corporate Sector		−15,153	4,925	
Public Sector Total		−16,756		−26,188
Central Government		−4,167		−7,617
Public Corporations and				
Local Authorities		−12,589		−18,571
Financial Institutions				
Sector		−1,564		−8,812
Rest of the World				
Sector		−14,615		−13,200
Total	48,079	−48,088	48,252	−48,260

SOURCE: Bank of Japan, *Economic Statistics Monthly,* Summarized by OECD Financial Statistics (June 1996):43.

economic growth and development. The 13 city banks, with their head offices in Tokyo and branches in major population centers, are a prime source of short-term funds to the corporate sector, while the long-term credit banks, such as the Industrial Bank of Japan established in 1902, supply long-term funds to capital intensive industry. While regional banks serve the short-term borrowing needs of small- and medium-sized corporations, mutual loans and savings (Sogo) banks generally serve small business. Specialized financial institutions for agriculture, forestry, and fishery serve these special parts of the national economy. Securities companies including "the big four" (Nomura, Yamaichi, Nikko, and Daiwa) are important to the securities markets. Government financial institutions are instrumental in directly influencing the specific areas of the economy and finance. Postal savings are the most important means to absorb personal savings for financing the public sector. Since the 1970s and the 1980s foreign banks and securities firms have increased their presence in Tokyo. The supervision of financial institutions is the responsibility of the Ministry of Finance (MoF).

In Japan, financial institutions have heavy responsibilities in the flow of funds from savers to borrowers, the so-called "indirect financing." Exhibit 8.19 indicates that the household sector serves as the primary source of funds. The corporate sector, public sector, financial institutions, and rest-of-the-world sector tend to be funds users. Trends clearly show that public corporate and financial sectors as well as rest of the world have continued to increase their demand for funds.

Since 1970 financial liberalization has exerted profound effects on Japanese financial markets, financial instruments, structure of portfolio investment, and conduct of monetary policy as we will discuss later. The major changes relative to liberalization and regulatory reform are:

1970—Permission was given by the government to establish yen-denominated foreign bonds (samurai).

1972—Bill discount market was approved by the Bank of Japan.

1976—Gensaki (repurchase of government bonds) market was formally recognized.

1979—CDs were introduced to the money market.

1982—Foreign banks were allowed to trade short-term bonds and participate in repurchase agreements.

1984—Permission was given for residents and nonresidents to issue Euroyen bonds and CDs. Japanese can buy foreign CDs and commercial paper. Bankers acceptance market was established.

1985—Ceiling on interest on deposit yields was abolished. Permission for foreign banks to deal in national bonds was granted.

1986—Offshore banking was established.

1987—More foreign securities companies were approved as members of the Tokyo Stock Exchange.

1988—The Tokyo Stock Exchange signed with the Chicago Board of Trade (CBT) and the Chicago Mercantile Exchange (CME) an accord for the exchange of market surveillance information.

1989—Tokyo International Financial Futures Exchange (TIFFE) was established.

1992—Securities and Exchange Surveillance Commission was established.

1996—Pension funds no longer have to invest at least half of their funds in government bonds or other safe assets—they can increase investment in domestic and foreign securities.

THE JAPANESE CAPITAL MARKET

Zaibatsu

A great industrial or financial combination in Japan between the First and Second World Wars.

"Samurai"bonds

Samurai bonds are yen-denominated bonds issued by foreign governments and corporations in Japan.

"Shogun"bonds

Shogun bonds are foreign-currency-denominated bonds issued by foreign governments and companies in Japan.

After the Meiji Restoration the Tokyo and Osaka Stock Exchanges were established in 1878. The rapid industrialization in Japan required long-term capital, and Japan was forced to borrow from London. Between the two world wars, Japanese industries were mainly financed by Zaibatsu companies (the industrial families of Japan who controlled major banks and industries). The Securities and Exchange Law, patterned after the American law, was enacted in 1948. The need for capital to rebuild the country was met primarily by borrowing from the United States. From 1950–1970, the Japanese capital market was basically a local market that exhibited cyclical development. Beginning in 1970, foreign borrowers issuance of yen-denominated (samurai) and foreign currency-denominated (shogun) bonds marked the emergence of Tokyo as an international financial center. Tokyo became recognized as a major international financial center in the 1980s with the growing Japanese economy, trade surplus, and high personal savings. Since 1979 market forces have played a more important role in corporate external financing, although bank loans still account for a significant amount of financing.[*]

Exhibit 8.20 indicates that corporate funds raised through equity financing by listed companies in Japan increased from ¥3,013 billion in 1987 to ¥3,792 billion in 1990, of which public offerings, rights offerings, and warrants accounted for 40% of total issues. Most of this increase was attributable to financial institutions, especially city banks, that sought to increase their capital base. However, equity financing in 1991–1995 decreased substantially due to a bearish Tokyo stock market. In the bond market (see Exhibit 8.21) new issues occurred mostly in the government sector, especially discount government notes and bills purchased by individuals. Public offering of convertible bonds recorded a growth from ¥5,256 billion in 1987 to ¥6,867 billion in 1989, reflecting investor optimism concerning the stock market. Public offerings in the market declined sharply in 1990 and 1991–1995 due to a bearish stock market. Generally Japanese corporations issue Euroyen bonds in Europe to avoid the restrictive domestic capital market and to raise funds abroad for financing international and domestic needs at lower cost.

---

[*] For detailed analysis, see *Securities Market in Japan 1988 and 1996*. Tokyo: Japan Securities Research Institute.

EXHIBIT 8.20 — Equity Financing, Listed Companies

	RIGHTS OFFERINGS		PUBLIC OFFERINGS		PRIVATE PLACEMENTS		EXERCISE OF WARRANTS		TOTAL		STOCK SPLITS	
	No. of Cases	Amount Raised (Yen Bils.)	No. of Cases	Amount Raised (Yen Bils.)	No. of Cases	Amount Raised (Yen Bils.)	No. of Cases	Amount Raised (Yen Bils.)	No. of Cases	Amount Raised (Yen Bils.)	No. of Cases	Shares Granted
1987	26	436	99	1,394	22	109	241	1,074	388	3,013	351	3,278
1988	40	787	157	2,582	23	104	316	1,309	536	4,782	373	3,945
1989	32	726	227	5,830	22	102	435	2,190	716	8,849	425	5,550
1990	39	825	121	1,975	21	315	397	678	578	3,792	400	4,432
1991	40	218	27	126	19	104	309	360	395	808	372	3,451
1995	12	96	8	33	19	160	118	299	157	588	189	1,015

NOTE: The old term "bonus issues" has been replaced by the new term "stock splits" since 1990.

SOURCE: Tokyo Stock Exchange (1996):36

EXHIBIT 8.21 — Public Offerings of New Securities (¥ Billions)

	INTEREST-BEARING GOVERNMENT BONDS		Discount Government Notes and Bills	Municipal Bonds	Government Guaranteed Bonds	CORPORATE BONDS			Yen-Based Foreign Bonds	Total
	Long-Term	Medium-Term				Elec. Power	NTT	Others		
1987	17,986	3,027	5,366	846	2,202	530	385	28	448	30,817
1988	17,557	2,506	4,709	1,101	2,513	688	150	72	635	29,931
1989	14,541	1,620	9,016	791	2,033	520	60	4	1,101	29,685
1990	9,716	1,845	20,654	996	1,774	1,678	150	6	1,203	38,023
1991	11,263	1,870	19,231	903	1,952	1,765	200	417	68	38,282
1995	18,560	5,480	30,624	1,967	2,953	1,625	155	3,271	1,617	66,247

NOTES: 1. Those bonds issued in foreign countries are excluded.
2. Convertible bonds and bonds with stock subscription warrants are excluded.

SOURCE: Tokyo Stock Exchange (1996):37

EXHIBIT 8.22	**Stock Trading Volume on Stock Exchanges 1990–1995**

(Millions of Shares, ¥ Billions)

	ALL EXCHANGES	TOKYO	
	Volume	Volume	(%)
1990	145,837	123,099	84.4
1991	107,844	93,606	86.4
1992	82,563	66,408	80.4
1993	101,173	86,935	85.9
1994	105,937	84,514	79.8
1995	120,149	92,034	76.6

NOTE: Trading volume and value of foreign stocks are not included. Besides Tokyo Stock Exchange, other Stock Exchanges are Osaka, Nagoya, Kyoto, Hiroshima, Fukuoka, Niigata, and Sapporo.

SOURCE: Tokyo Stock Exchange (1996):100.

In the secondary market, trust banks and investment trusts are big buyers of bonds. City banks, business corporations, and foreign investors are selective bond buyers depending on profitability. The Tokyo Stock Exchange demonstrates a large bond trading volume. As Exhibit 8.22 shows, in 1991 the Tokyo Stock Exchange accounted for about 86% of trading volume among the nine stock exchanges in Japan. The number of foreign stocks listed on the Tokyo Stock Exchange decreased from 88 in 1987 to 77 in 1995, according to the *Tokyo Stock Exchange Fact Book* 1992 and 1996.

In the period 1989–1995 share ownership by individuals was 23.0%, by institutions and corporations, 70%, and by foreigners 7%.

THE JAPANESE MONEY MARKET

Prior to 1975 the Japanese money market was controlled by the Bank of Japan. Gradually the money market gained greater openness. In the early period the major policy instruments of the BOJ were credit rationing at the discount window, discount rates variation, purchases and sales of commercial bills, and loan limits on city banks. The BOJ controlled the availability of bank funds to the corporate sector. The corporate sector had limited access to the securities market that was dominated by government bonds. Whenever the BOJ restricted funds at the discount window or through the open market (formally operating since 1971), the interbank rate played an important role in the transmission of BOJ policy. For example, the interbank rate affects the volume of call money from city banks, regional banks, and other financial institutions. In turn, the volume of call money affects the business loans of the institutions.

The oil price shock in 1974 accelerated open money market development and market liberalization. After the oil shock, business borrowings were sluggish, and in 1974 the government had to rescue the economy from recession by deficit spending. A rising volume of government debt led to the emergence of a growing secondary government bond market and the approval of the Gensaki market to establish repurchase agreements on government securities (equivalent to repos in the U.S. money market). At this juncture, market forces played a more important role in the allocation of funds.

To stimulate competition for loan funds, the BOJ approved issuance of additional types of money market instruments by banks: certificates of deposit (CDs) in

EXHIBIT 8.23	**Major Money Market Instruments in Japan**		
	1991–1995		
(¥ Trillion)	**1991**	**1995**	**Growth Rate(%)**
Call Money Market	35.3	38.6	9%
Treasury Bills	9.2	12.8	4
Bill Discount Market	16.5	9.9	−40
Certificates of Deposit (CDs)	17.3	24.3	41
Commercial Paper	12.4	10.5	15
Gensaki Market	6.0	11.1	83
Total Money Market Size	96.7	107.2	11
Gross Domestic Product	459.6	480.7	5
Total Money Market Size as Percent of GDP	21%	22%	

NOTE: Treasury bills were introduced in 1986; yen commercial paper was introduced in 1987.

SOURCE: Bank of Japan, *Economic Statistics Monthly*, May (1996):3

1979, foreign commercial paper in 1982, and Euroyen CDs in 1984. These actions have stimulated direct competition among financial institutions in Japan and have altered the practice of monetary control by the central bank. For example, the BOJ's open market operations now include large CDs. The BOJ regards open market operations as a more flexible instrument with which to influence interest rates than the discount window. The central bank also influences the bill discount market by changing one-month and two-month bill rates on the interbank market. Yen commercial paper has been popular, and even the BOJ is considering conducting operations in the CP market.

In Japan, the oldest money market instrument is the call money market, representing the borrowing of funds between banks. This transaction takes place when city banks borrow from regional banks and other financial institutions to adjust their liquidity positions. As mentioned previously, the interbank rate is influenced by the discount rate. The bill discount market with maturities ranging from one to four months is really an extension of the call money market that was established in 1971. The Gensaki market and CD market were the products of financial liberalization in the 1970s. The yen call money market and the dollar call money market developed simultaneously. Foreign and Japanese banks as well as brokerage firms participate in these markets, adjusting their foreign exchange positions in relation to the Eurocurrency market. Since 1972 the Minister of Finance has imposed regulations on these markets. As shown in Exhibit 8.23, the money market in Japan has grown tremendously in the period 1985–1991, especially the newly developed yen commercial paper market. It increased moderately in the 1991–1995 period, except the higher growth rates in the CDs and Gensaki markets.

INTERNATIONAL LINKAGE

Tokyo emerged as an international financial center only after 1970 when foreign borrowers issued samurai (yen denominated bonds) and later shogun (dollar denominated bonds) in Tokyo. Liberalization of the yen currency and capital markets further strengthened the position of Tokyo as a major center in the globalization of financial markets. As of 1988 approximately 81 foreign banks and 60 foreign securities houses had main offices or branches in Tokyo. Increased foreign investment in Japanese bonds and stocks reflects the importance of Tokyo's financial markets. Foreign participation has been more active in the Gensaki, call money, CD, and CP money markets.

The high daily foreign exchange turnover especially in yen/dollar transactions has made Tokyo the third largest foreign exchange market after London and New York.

Equally important is the presence of Japanese banks and securities houses in all major international centers including New York, London, Hong Kong, and continental Europe. These centers assist Japanese corporations in borrowing overseas and in channeling the outflow of surplus capital in the total amount of $800 billion during the period 1981–1995 (see Exhibit 8.17).

Comparisons of Three Major Financial Centers

ECONOMY

The United States, United Kingdom, and Japan made considerable progress in reducing the fluctuations of their national economies during the 1980s. GDP growth rates were steady in the range of 3–5% per annum, while inflation and unemployment rates were lower. Government spending and the saving ratio are quite different among these three industrial economies. While U.S. government deficits remained the highest among the three, its saving ratios have been the lowest. The United Kingdom is the only country of the three that has managed to reduce government deficits in recent years, whereas its saving ratios have also been lower (from 14% to 6% in the 1980–1988 period). As a ratio of GDP, Japanese government deficits have been reduced gradually. Japan's high saving ratios have fully offset government deficits. Japan's high saving rates plus the continued trade surplus have become major sources of funds used in part to finance the U.S. twin deficits. In the 1991–1995 period all three economies suffered recession in the early 1990s but the United States recovered quicker than others. Government deficits of all three countries remain high by historical standard.

FINANCIAL SYSTEMS AND MARKETS

The separation of commercial banking and investment banking apply to both the United States (under the Glass-Steagall Act) and Japan (under Article 65 of the Securities and Exchange Act). The U.S. financial system is considered flexible and innovatively oriented, while the Japanese financial system is a more complex one. The Big Bang revolutionized the British capital market, but the planned unification of the European markets may compel the British to change regulations that apply to the financial industry. In the 1980s many countries found that their financial systems were under pressure from the liberalization and internationalization of financial markets, and the rapidity of capital flows supported by telecommunications and computerized information. Worldwide recessions in 1991–1992 exposed the weaknesses of the financial systems in these countries. As a result, the current systems will require additional reform and adaptation. Restrictions on U.S. interstate banking should be abolished; U.K. banks and stock exchanges should be reshaped in light of the new European financial competition; and the Japanese financial system should become more market oriented instead of subject to government control.

Financial markets are mechanisms that channel the flow of funds from savers to users. Innovative financial instruments and a more flexible institutional framework assist in improving the allocation of funds toward various purposes. Generally, the three financial centers under discussion serve the national and international economies. As indicated in Exhibit 8.8, the U.S. money market is the largest in volume ($3,052 billion), and the Japanese money market is the second largest (yen 107 trillion). As a percent of GDP, the U.S. money market is the largest (42.1% of GDP) followed by the U.K. money market (39.4% of GDP).

INTERNATIONAL LINKAGE

This chapter primarily deals with flows of capital in the three financial centers. Among the three, London has enjoyed its international status the longest. At present the cornerstone of London's financial markets is the Eurodollar market, foreign stock listings, foreign exchange markets, and foreign bank representation in London. On the U.S. side, the dollar is still the most preferred currency for international transactions. U.S. financial institutions and multinational corporations have been highly active overseas. Japan is considered a new economic force in international trade and investment. Japanese international bank assets have increased dramatically in the short time period since 1985, while the U.S. and U.K. shares declined in the same period. The appreciation of the yen and the depreciation of the dollar have strengthened the competitive capacity of Japanese banks. The offshore banking markets in these three major financial centers are also important components of the centers' international functions (see Chapter 6).

SUMMARY

Globalization of financial markets started in the 1960s when world trade and multinational corporations began to prosper. This trend accelerated in the 1970s due in part to the need for petrodollar recycling. Economic prosperity among industrialized countries in the 1980s and the rapid growth in international capital flows transformed financial markets. These markets now conduct business on a global scale.

Based on the enormous size of the U.S. economy and the participation of domestic and foreign financial institutions, New York's capital and money markets are the largest in the world. Recent suggestions for U.S. banking reforms are designed to simplify supervision of U.S. commercial banks and improve their competitiveness at home and abroad. The adoption of SEC Rule 144A, effective as of April 1990, provides a safe haven to any domestic or foreign issuer offering securities to qualified institutional investors on an unregistered basis. This important step will enable the United States to compete more effectively with the Eurobond market.

London is a major financial center, largely due to its leading position in the Eurocurrency market, the size of its foreign exchange market, the international listing of foreign stocks, the excellent communications network, and its participants' financial expertise. The United Kingdom has adopted measures to strengthen London's position in light of the emerging European-wide competition after 1992 and European Monetary Union in 1999.

Tokyo became a major financial center in the 1980s, primarily as a result of the strong Japanese economy, high saving rates, continued trade surpluses, and the growth of direct and portfolio investment on a worldwide basis. Recent overspeculations on the Tokyo stock and real estate markets have forced the Japanese government to readjust its policy toward domestic and overseas markets. Moreover, it has compelled Japanese banks to restructure their balance sheets and other domestic financial reforms in the 1990s.

PART THREE

International Banking

*I*nternational banks carry out a wide range of activities. In Part III we examine the international bank in connection with its objectives and operating formats. Here we consider the changing role and importance of banks in different countries. We also study alternative organizational formats for conducting overseas banking. Finally, we analyze the primary service activities of banks including financing foreign trade, mobilizing funds through money market channels, and international lending. These four chapters provide an integrated analysis and description of the major trends and activities of international banking.

ENVIRONMENT OF GLOBAL FINANCE

INTERNATIONAL FINANCIAL MARKETS

INTERNATIONAL BANKING

INTERNATIONAL CORPORATE FINANCE

INTERNATIONAL PORTFOLIO MANAGEMENT

CHAPTER 9

Global Banking: Overview

INTRODUCTION

In this chapter we consider four basic aspects of global commercial banking, namely, 1) broad trends, 2) organization and operations, 3) regulation via capital requirements, and 4) changes in international competitiveness. From an American perspective, the past 30 years have witnessed significant changes in relative position with regard to global banking. During the 1960s American banks awakened to the opportunities and need to expand internationally. In this decade they grew and dominated international banking. The decade of the 1970s witnessed new competitive factors and a changing environment. Japanese and European banks began to chip away at the strong competitive position enjoyed by American banks. This decade could be characterized as one of new competition and environmental challenge. The decade of the 1980s witnessed a relative decline in the position of American banks, with European and especially Japanese banks displacing American banks in global as well as domestic banking markets in the United States.

This chapter describes how these shifts in competitive balance took place.

LEARNING OBJECTIVES IN THIS CHAPTER

1. To develop an awareness of how over the past several decades global banking has evolved and responded to new opportunities and problems.
2. To examine in detail the many activities and operational areas encompassed in global commercial banking including investment banking.
3. To appreciate the impact on the relative status of American banks as a result of growing international competition.
4. To understand the strategies and organizational formats utilized by international banks.
5. To realize the importance of adequately regulating international banking and the methods employed to accomplish proper regulation.
6. To consider the role of bank cost of capital as an underlying factor that influences international competition of banks based in different countries.

KEY TERMS AND CONCEPTS

- agency
- Basle Accord
- branch
- capital adequacy
- competitiveness
- correspondent bank
- cost of capital
- cost of equity
- Edge Act
- financial innovations
- Hausbank
- IBA Amendment of 1991

- international banking facility (IBF)
- keiretsu
- market share
- merchant bank
- national treatment
- petrodollar recycling
- price-earning ratio (PE)
- reciprocity
- representative office
- risk based capital
- safe haven
- universal bank

ACRONYMS

SLC Standby letter of credit
OBS Off-balance-sheet

BCCI Bank for Credit and
        Commerce International

Evolution of International Banking

TRENDS IN INTERNATIONAL BANKING

The origins of foreign branch banking can be traced back to the nineteenth century. By 1960 there was a significant foreign banking community in London. Early arrivals opened banking offices in London for several reasons:

1. to meet the needs of the foreign subsidiaries of domestic corporate customers,
2. to participate in the foreign exchange market, and,
3. to participate in the sterling bill market.

The past quarter century has witnessed a remarkable development in international banking, at first led by American banks and subsequently bolstered by European, Japanese, and other banks. American banks were quick to invent new approaches and techniques, and to create and conquer innovative market sectors. Eventually, banks from other countries joined in competition and have won back important shares of these new markets.

American problems and crises were turned into challenges and opportunities. When American banks were saddled with capital controls on foreign lending (1964–1965), they "discovered" overseas branches. Oil price escalation became an opportunity to recycle petrodollars. Even the debt crisis of the 1980s presented some banks with highly profitable opportunities to reschedule, make markets in debt paper, and service a high margin swaps program. In the 1990s many large banks have increased their focus on investment banking activities.

EXHIBIT 9.1	Trends and Developments in International Banking

Time Period	Major Developments
I. Early Expansion 1960s	1. Growth of Eurocurrency Market 2. Expansion in Number of Foreign Banking Offices
II. Oil Crisis and Growing Competition 1970s	3. First and Second Oil Price Shocks 4. Petrodollar Recycling 5. Growth of Syndicated Euroloan Market 6. Greater Competition Among International Banks, U.S. Bank Lead Diluted by Other Banks
III. Debt Crisis and Financial Innovations 1980s	7. Developing Nations Debt Crisis 8. Financial Innovations 9. Securitization and Portfolio Investment 10. Internationalization of Financial Markets Including the Big Bang of 1986 11. Shift Toward Investment Banking Activities 12. 24-Hour Trading in Foreign Exchange, U.S. Treasury Securities 13. International Agreement on Bank Capital Requirements
IV. Preparing for Financial Integration 1990s	14. Cross Border Bank Alliances 15. Single European Market in Financial Services

SOURCE: Compiled by authors

Early Expansion The 1960s was a period of early expansion for international banks. A surge in U.S. bank lending to affiliates of American companies operating in the Common Market prompted the establishment of many overseas bank branches of American and later non-American banks (Exhibit 9.1). The Eurocurrency market also had its early origins in the 1960s. During this period many American banks established branch offices, for example, in London to engage in Eurodollar activities, in the Bahamas to enjoy safe haven status* and on the European continent to service corporate affiliates.

Oil Crisis and Growing Competition The decision of the oil exporting (OPEC) countries to raise oil prices in 1973 set off a series of crises in international banking. First, the U.S. government had to suspend its capital control program to facilitate the recycling of petrodollars via the U.S. financial system. Inflation pressures that resulted from oil price increases destabilized foreign exchange markets. In addition, the newly introduced floating rate system met its first test of strength. Fortunately the system held up reasonably well.

Petrodollars

Dollar exchange earned by oil export nations. Increased rapidly in 1970s with petroleum price increases.

International banks experienced a rapid growth in loan demand in the 1970s. This demand came from the oil importing countries and also from the inflation of costs experienced during this period. The syndicated Euroloan market grew rapidly, as did bank profitability. High profit in this market attracted European, Japanese, Canadian, and other banks. The rising competition for Eurocurrency and Euroloan market share represented one of the first challenges to the dominant position of American banks in international banking.

Debt Crisis and Financial Innovation The two oil shocks (1974 and 1978–1979) and the interest rate shock (1979–1981) raised the borrowing and debt

_____

* Safe havens or tax havens may be defined as centers that attract substantial bank deposit and other type investment funds. This status is because they provide valuable business and financial advantages not available elsewhere. These include freedom from exchange controls, favorable tax climate, political stability, and adherence to privacy of information regarding customer activities.

| **EXHIBIT 9.2** | **Market Trading of U.S. Treasury Bond Futures** |

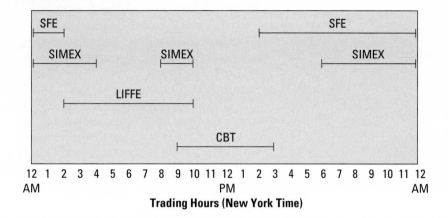

SFE   — Sydney Futures Exchange
SIMEX — Singapore International Monetary Exchange
LIFFE — London International Financial Futures Exchange
CBT   — Chicago Board of Trade

Source: Julian Walmsley, *The New Financial Instruments*, (New York:Wiley, 1988) 105.

service burdens faced by most developing countries. By 1982 many developing nations found that they were unable to carry out debt service from borrowing heavily in external markets. The 1982 announcement by Mexico and other large debtors that they were unable to meet such payments brought a transformation to the world of international finance. From that point on, many international banks curtailed lending to developing nations and sought ways to service customers without assuming direct balance sheet credit exposures.

Financial Innovations

Process and product changes in the use and type of financial instruments.

Financial innovations such as note issuance facilities (described in Chapter 6), interest rate swaps (described in Chapter 7), and currency swaps became leading growth markets. The securitization of international credit-making displaced direct lending by banks. Commercial banks shifted focus toward investment banking activities to support underwriting and distribution of medium-term credit instruments.

Banks began to focus on providing more complete market trading of securities. During the 1980s, for example, U.S. Treasury securities became eligible for trading in Tokyo and Europe, as well as in North American markets, both spot and futures (Exhibit 9.2). Similarly, leading international banks sought to develop 24-hour banking office systems that would permit them to trade foreign exchange, Eurocurrencies, and money market assets at any time of the day in all the leading world financial markets.

The 1980s also witnessed another "sea-change" development. The Basle Accord, an international agreement, was concluded in 1988, specifying uniform capital standards for commercial banks. This agreement is discussed in detail in a later section of the chapter. These risk-based capital requirements became necessary due to the increasing competition among international banks, the greater volatility in financial markets, and growing concerns that a banking crisis in one country could spread to other countries unless internationally agreed upon safeguards were put in place.

Financial Integration and Investment Banking   The 1990s brought a single European market in financial services. As a result, European banks are forming alliances with one another to withstand increased competition. In addition, non-European banks are seeking to protect existing market positions in Europe and to develop a European presence if they do not already operate there.

A first wave of cross-border banking alliances was initiated in the Big Bang of 1986 when the London Stock Exchange was reorganized and the British banking authorities sought to modernize the system of securities trading in London. American and European bank organizations acquired ownership of old-line British merchant banks and London stockbrokers. A second wave of cross-border banking alliances commenced in 1988–1989 with the Little Bang that took place in the Madrid Stock Exchange and with the preparations for a single market for financial services in Europe.

Broader financial integration has contributed to rapid growth in capital markets. In turn this has resulted in greater cross-border investment and a shift in emphasis by large banks to participate actively in investment banking.

The evolving scene of international banking has witnessed the modification of existing services and the addition of many new activities. The development of new activities has in turn generated growth for international banks. New activities can be grouped according to how long banking institutions have used particular techniques.

The first group includes traditional activities. Trade financing techniques used today can be traced back many centuries. We examine export-import finance in detail in Chapter 10. Foreign exchange and foreign loan also are traditional for banking institutions (Exhibit 9.3).

EXHIBIT 9.3	**Evolution of International Banking Activities**

Activity	Nature of Operation
I. Traditional Activities (1960s)	
1) Export-Import Finance	Letter of credit, collection, processing drafts and documents
2) Foreign Exchange	Buying/selling foreign currencies
3) Foreign Loan	Loans to customers located in other countries
II. New Activities (1970s and 1980s)	
1) Eurocurrency Market	Dealing, funding in Eurocurrencies
2) Syndicated Euroloans	Organizing and participating in syndicated Euroloans
3) Merchant Banking	Eurobond issue and secondary trading, corporate services including mergers
III. Innovative Activities (1980s and 1990s)	
1) Innovative Financing	Provide Note Issue Facilities (NIF), interest rate swaps, and exotic derivatives
2) Global Money Market	24-hour Dealing room operations
3) Manage LDC Loan Portfolio	Collection, rescheduling, secondary trading, swaps
4) Private Banking	Provide financial services to high wealth clients on global basis
IV. Investment Banking (1990s)	
1) Underwriting	Purchase new bond and equity issues for sale/distribution to investors
2) Securities Trading	Participating in stock exchange trading as dealers/brokers, making markets for securities
3) Corporate Finance	Advisory services for financing, mergers and acquisitions; providing support market services in these areas
4) Fund Management	Providing portfolio management services for institutional and high wealth investors

The second group includes activities that were new a decade or so ago. Here we focus on the Euromarkets and their development. We consider these activities in Chapter 6 (Eurocurrency Market and Offshore Banking), Chapter 7 (International Bond Market), and Chapter 11 (Bank Money Management).

The third group includes innovative activities, primarily developed in the last decade or currently in the process of development. Four distinct areas of activity are discussed. First, innovative financing includes note issuance facilities (NIFs), interest rate swaps, and other techniques developed in the 1980s. These instruments are discussed in Chapter 7 (International Bond Market) and Chapter 14 (Foreign Affiliate Financing). Global money market dealing stems from international banks searching for growth and the opportunities they perceive for developing round-the-clock trading facilities in certain money market instruments including U.S. Treasury securities, other central government issues, CDs, and other money market paper.

During the 1980s creditor banks faced the problem of managing their LDC loan portfolios under adverse conditions. There were repeated instances of moratoria on interest and principal payments or even complete suspension of payments. Banks had to respond by rescheduling loans, writing off uncollectible loans, or selling loans in the developing secondary market. Also banks were presented with opportunities to convert debt paper into more attractive investments. These activities are highlighted in Chapter 12.

Private banking is a new activity for international banks, although it has existed as a small part of domestic bank activities for a long time. Primarily, private banking seeks to service individuals of high wealth and income. This client base is huge and growing. Precise figures for the world wealth explosion do not exist, but the International Monetary Fund and other sources indicate that deposits in the world's four top tax havens (Switzerland, Singapore, Cayman Islands, and Luxembourg) exceed $900 billion. International private banking differs from its domestic counterpart. At Manufacturer's Hanover Trust Company, banking assets of U.S. clients are allocated as 80% loans, 10% deposits, and 10% managed portfolios. By contrast, the bank's international private banking assets consist of 80% deposits, 10% managed portfolios, and 10% loans.

Investment Banking

Banking activities that focus on securities issuance and trading.

Investment banking includes primary security issues via underwriting, providing securities trading services, corporate finance, and fund management. This area of activity is described in a later section of this chapter.

Change in Composition of Top 100 Banks 1956–1994   Over the four-decade period 1956–1994, sweeping competitive and structural changes took place in global banking. These changes are reflected in Exhibit 9.4 that provides details on the nationality of the world's largest banks during the period 1956–1994. The following observations are made with reference to these changes.

First, while U.S. banks enjoyed a wide lead in 1956, this margin narrowed and subsequently non-U.S. banks have become dominant. In 1956 five of the top ten banks were U.S. institutions, and 44 of the top 100 were U.S. banks. By 1989 none of the top ten banks were U.S. institutions, and only seven of the top 100 were U.S. banks. By 1994, 11 of the top 100 were U.S. banks. In the period 1956–1994, the U.S. bank share of deposits in the top 100 banks declined from 52.4% to 9.0%. Many factors can be used to explain this shift, including the fall in value of the U.S. dollar relative to other currencies, a weaker balance of payments position that impaired the ability of U.S. banks to provide international credits, and the expansion of non-U.S. economies to the point where their banking institutions assumed a relatively larger position in global credit.

EXHIBIT 9.4   **Nationality of World's Largest Banks**

	NUMBER OF BANKS IN TOP 10 BY DEPOSIT SIZE							NUMBER OF BANKS IN TOP 50 BY DEPOSIT SIZE						
	1956	1960	1970	1979	1989	1991	1994	1956	1960	1970	1979	1989	1991	1994
Japan	—	—	—	—	8	8	10	3	8	11	16	22	20	21
United States	5	6	4	2	—	—	—	25	19	13	6	2	1	5
Germany	—	—	1	2	1	—	—	—	3	4	7	8	8	9
Italy	—	—	1	—	—	—	—	3	5	4	2	3	4	1
Canada	2	1	1	—	—	—	—	6	5	5	4	1	1	—
United Kingdom	3	3	2	2	—	—	—	7	5	4	4	4	4	4
France	—	—	1	4	1	2	—	3	3	3	4	5	5	5
Netherlands	—	—	—	—	—	—	—	—	—	1	3	2	3	2
Spain	—	—	—	—	—	—	—	—	—	—	—	—	—	—
Switzerland	—	—	—	—	—	—	—	—	—	3	3	2	3	3
Belgium	—	—	—	—	—	—	—	—	—	—	1	—	—	—
Sweden	—	—	—	—	—	—	—	—	—	—	—	—	—	—
Australia	—	—	—	—	—	—	—	1	1	1	—	—	—	—
Austria														
Brazil														
Other	—	—	—	—	—	—	—	2	1	1	—	1	1	—

	NUMBER OF BANKS IN TOP 100 BY DEPOSIT SIZE							PERCENT OF TOP 100 DEPOSITS HELD BY NATIONAL GROUPS						
	1956	1960	1970	1979	1989	1991	1994	1956	1960	1970	1979	1989	1991	1994
Japan	9	12	24	24	31	28	31	5.1	9.7	19.4	23.6	46.0	44.6	46.1
United States	44	37	22	15	7	5	11	52.4	44.8	29.1	14.4	4.4	2.9	9.0
Germany	3	7	11	14	12	11	13	1.3	5.0	10.0	16.8	11.1	11.8	12.6
Italy	6	7	9	9	8	9	7	3.8	5.4	8.7	6.6	5.5	6.3	3.7
Canada	7	7	5	6	5	5	5	9.5	8.7	6.8	5.2	3.2	3.1	2.6
United Kingdom	10	10	5	5	6	6	6	14.9	13.6	7.6	6.9	6.2	6.3	5.8
France	5	4	3	4	7	8	8	4.0	4.1	4.8	10.4	9.1	8.9	8.7
Netherlands	1	1	3	4	4	3	3	0.4	0.5	2.1	4.5	3.1	2.6	2.9
Spain	2	1	3	4	2	6	4	0.9	0.5	1.3	1.9	0.9	2.7	1.9
Switzerland	5	4	3	3	3	3	3	2.2	2.4	3.2	3.3	2.8	3.3	2.9
Belgium	1	3	4	3	4	5	5	0.5	1.3	2.1	2.1	2.0	2.4	2.3
Sweden	2	2	2	2	1	3	0	1.1	1.2	1.0	0.9	0.4	1.3	—
Australia	2	2	3	2	3	4	2	1.2	1.1	2.1	0.9	1.3	1.8	0.7
Austria							1							0.3
Brazil							1							0.4
Other	3	3	3	5	7	4	0	2.2	2.0	1.8	2.5	4.0	2.0	—

Other includes Argentina, Australia, Denmark, India, Brazil, Hong Kong, Israel, Austria, Iran, and Iraq.

SOURCE: Comptroller of the Currency, *Foreign Acquisition of U.S. Banks* (1981); 194, and Moody's *Bank & Finance Manual,* various issues.

Second, Exhibit 9.4 reflects the growing importance of Japanese banks. Between 1956 and 1994 Japanese banks increased their representation among the top 50 banks from three to 21. In the same period Japanese banks' share of deposits in the top 100 banks increased from 5.1% to 46.1%.

Third, a more diverse representation developed among the top banks. More countries are represented among the top 50 and top 100 banks. This trend reflects a greater level of financial development in these countries, and in some cases a change in the structure of banking resulting from mergers and acquisitions.

Finally, the information in Exhibit 9.4 may reflect a declining international competitiveness of U.S. banks, as well as changes in the competitiveness of major banking institutions in other countries. This issue is discussed in detail in the final section of this chapter.

Global Organization and Operation

CROSS-BORDER BANKING

Bank management seeks to promote the maximum rate of earnings and growth consistent with maintaining a prudent risk exposure. The same guidelines used in bank policy formulation for domestic activities are applicable to international activities. U.S. banks conduct their cross-border business by means of several organizational formats and relationships. These include foreign correspondent banks, overseas branches, foreign affiliates, and international banking corporations. Banks employ a variety of strategies in developing and expanding their international operations. As one banker said, "No single route is the best for all countries and all conditions."

Most American banks rely at least in part on correspondent banks to develop their overseas business. Under this procedure a U.S. bank may have an agreement with a foreign bank in which the two banks act as agents for each other. In this respect they make and receive payments and negotiate and accept drafts for one another. Further, the banks may maintain deposit balances with one another to provide for payments and settlements transacted for the account of the correspondent bank. The two banks may refer business to one another on a reciprocal basis. Finally, they will provide other services for each other, such as obtaining credit and other information regarding prospective borrowers, as well as provide business information needed by customers. Alternative organizational forms are available to banks for the purpose of establishing an office in a host country, including the branch, agency, and subsidiary bank. These formats are discussed in a subsequent section.

NATIONAL SYSTEMS AND RECIPROCITY

National banking systems differ from each other in many respects. For this reason we consider some of the key differences among selected national systems. Our purpose is to understand the following:

1. Banking in one country may not be "banking" in another. The activities permitted banks may differ very much between any two countries. Some countries allow banks to deal in securities listed on the stock exchange, while other countries prohibit this activity. The appendix to this chapter describes the role and status of large German banks as holders of common stock in companies in that country.

2. As a host country each nation has its own views and policies regarding permitted cross-border banking activities. Some countries have severely limited foreign bank entry (Taiwan and Mexico).

3. The above described intercountry differences fundamentally affect the extent to which and the formats by which cross-border banking activities can take place.

National Systems   Two approaches can be discussed when comparing national banking systems in terms of the breadth of activities allowed to banking institutions. The *universal approach* is the most liberal and permits banks to carry out deposit and lending activities, securities dealing, and ownership activities. Countries that follow the universal banking approach include Germany and Switzerland. The

Universal Banking

Banks carry out deposit and securities trading activities.

appendix to this chapter provides details concerning German bank activities, especially ownership of industrial corporations. The *specialist approach* tends to separate deposit and lending activities from securities-related activities. Commercial banks operating under the specialist approach are allowed to carry out deposit and loan functions, but they may be prohibited from engaging in securities-related activities. Banks in the United States and the United Kingdom have been regulated according to the specialist approach.

Most other countries fall somewhere between these two approaches. Japan follows the specialist approach. Japanese commercial banks do not carry out new securities underwriting or stock exchange trading activities. However, the Japanese industrial structure traditionally has followed the group or circle-of-interest pattern. The leading city banks form the nuclei of enterprise groups that have succeeded the former *zaibatsu* family conglomerates. Therefore a number of keiretsu groups exist where stock cross-holdings represent a basic part of the pattern. Banks participate prominently in these *keiretsu* groups, holding shares in industrial companies. In turn bank shares are held by other companies in the group.

Reciprocity Two basic approaches are available to governments to guide their relationships with other countries with regard to inward and outward investment. These approaches are reciprocity and national treatment. In the case of reciprocity, inward investment is permitted when the home country of the investor permits equivalent investment by host country investors. In the case of national treatment, foreign investors are extended the rights of national (local) investors. The United States explicitly provided for national treatment of foreign banks in the International Banking Act of 1978. This issue is discussed in a later section.

The U.S. banking system differs markedly from others in two other important respects. First, the American system is splintered into 50 semi-compartmentalized state systems, operating on a dual supervisory basis (federal and state). Second, U.S. policy neither promotes nor discourages inward or outward investment by foreign banks or American banks. In the past, key states—California and New York—have employed reciprocity and continue to do so. By contrast many states prohibit foreign banks from establishing offices within their jurisdiction, with the exception of Edge Act offices. The federal government has embraced the principle of national treatment with regard to the establishment of foreign banks in the United States and to the acquisition of existing institutions by foreign banks. This principle represents a policy of nondiscrimination that accords equal opportunity to foreign and domestic banks.*

These conditions tend to facilitate foreign bank entry into the United States without necessarily opening foreign banking markets to American banks. Many nations with a large banking representation in the United States prohibit foreign acquisition of controlling interest in their banks. In addition, banking concentration can be very high in these countries, thus reducing the ability of foreign banks (particularly U.S. banks) to penetrate these markets. By contrast, U.S. laws have reduced banking concentration at the national level. They also have provided *potential* foreign acquirers of U.S. banks with many significant acquisition opportunities.

Banking structures in many foreign nations do not provide easy opportunities for American bank entry. In most industrialized nations a top tier of three to seven

Keiretsu
Group of companies where cross stock holdings reinforce cooperative behavior.

Reciprocity
Home country extends equivalent investment rights to foreign firms as are extended its own firms.

National Treatment
Home country extends foreign firms rights of national or local investors.

---

* Weiss, Steven J. "A Critical Evaluation of Reciprocity in Foreign Bank Acquisitions." *Foreign Acquisitions of U.S. Banks,* Comptroller of the Currency (1981):263.

banks controls 40% to 80% of total commercial bank assets. The fact that some of these banks are government owned further narrows the field of opportunity.

Branching has been the major method for U.S. banks to expand and diversify overseas. Flexibility, control, and low cost are the reasons it is the primary form of American bank entry into other countries. Several large U.S. banks have established specialized securities or capital market affiliates based in the United Kingdom and other countries to carry out investment banking functions.

INTERNATIONAL REPRESENTATIONAL FORMATS

In this section we consider the formats used by banks in developing and expanding their cross-border activities. The most extensively used formats are described in Exhibit 9.5. Representative offices are employed where the host government does not permit full branch or subsidiary banking offices, or as a first stage in the eventual development of a full branch. Representative offices are not authorized to conduct full banking operations, but many function as a contact point for local customers.

Overseas branches probably offer the greatest combination of flexibility and control. They generally are authorized to carry out a full range of banking activities. The overseas branch has been the major format used by American banks in developing their overseas banking. In a subsequent section we analyze their activities in detail.

The agency operates much like an overseas branch, with the exception that it generally cannot accept deposits. The agency is used in cases where full branches are prohibited, in cases where nondeposit activities (lending) are paramount, or in cases where reciprocity requirements may not be feasible. Foreign banks have used the agency format in New York, and in the past New York licensed agencies and branches of foreign banks. In the 1960s and 1970s Japanese banks used the agency as a lending base for loans to Japanese companies including large trading houses.

Representative Office
Office allowing contact with local customers, but with no operating privileges.

Branch
Office that can carry out full range of banking activities.

Agency
Banking office similar to a branch, except not permitted to accept deposits.

EXHIBIT 9.5	International Representational Formats Used by Commercial Banks		
Format	**Activities**	**Advantages**	**Disadvantages**
Overseas Branch	General banking	Flexible / Ease of control	Operating losses accrue to parent
Representative Office	Contacts with customers	Low cost / Easy to organize	Limited in activities
Agency	Wide range of activities	Not restricted in lending	Cannot accept deposits
Subsidiary Bank	General banking	Expansion via acquisition	Host may restrict use of subsidiary
International Banking Corporation	U.S. Edge Act Corporation	Flexible	Special regulatory provisions
Subsidiary Finance Company	Commercial loan, leasing, other	Used where bank prohibited	Cannot accept deposits
Merchant Bank or Investment Bank	Banking and corporate services	Flexible	Low capital base
Consortium Bank	Eurocurrency market	Separate Entity, Participate in Euroloans	Shared ownership and control
International Banking Facility	Eurodollar banking with U.S. office	Joint office facility, U.S. location and time zone	Cannot lend to U.S. borrowers

These concentrated loan exposures could not have satisfied bank examiners if deposit-taking branches had booked these loans.

The subsidiary bank can be reestablished or an existing bank can be acquired. For example, the Hong Kong-Shanghai Banking Corporation acquired the Marine Midland in New York that gave the Hong Kong parent a substantial position in the New York banking market. By contrast, the Bank of Tokyo established a *de novo* subsidiary bank in New York, chartered by the New York Superintendent of Banks. National Westminster Bank (U.K.) developed a large representation in the United States through its NatWest USA subsidiary; in 1988 this subsidiary held assets of $11.9 billion and ranked twenty-third in the United States. NatWest sold this subsidiary to an American bank in 1996.

Special international banking corporations have been used in various ways, depending on needs and opportunities as well as on regulatory provisions. In the United States, the Edge Act Corporation has been in use since 1919, when enabling legislation was put into place. In 1992 there were 125 Edge Act corporations in existence. Edge Act corporations are federally chartered, and their activities are supervised by the Board of Governors of the Federal Reserve System.

Edge Act Corporation

Special international banking corporation that carries out international banking operations.

Edge Act corporations carry out three basic types of activities: general international banking, equity investments, and specialty financing. Given the restrictions on interstate banking, many interior and West Coast banks established New York-based Edge Acts so that they could service their customers requiring foreign exchange, trade finance, and international money market services. Approximately 80% of Edge Act banking offices are concentrated in New York, Chicago, Los Angeles, Miami, Houston, and San Francisco.* Since passage of the International Banking Act of 1978, foreign banks are permitted to own and operate Edge Acts. Edge Acts can make equity investments in foreign banks, foreign financing companies, and companies providing a mix of financing and banking services. Also Edge Act units provide specialty financing services to overseas borrowers. These services may involve purchase of long-term notes and bonds issued by industrial company borrowers in developing nations.

Consortium banks are a product of the early development of the Eurocurrency market (1968–1975). These banks were organized by two or more large parent banks that wanted to have a subsidiary banking unit that could generate profit and independently develop its own special niche in the then rapidly growing Euromarket.

Subsidiary finance companies have been established and/or bought into in cases where bank entry is prohibited or severely limited by the host government (Australia, Taiwan, South America). Alternatively, specialized subsidiary finance companies are established to carry out activities not generally permitted to the banking company including leasing and securities brokerage. As a result, American and European banks have established leasing affiliates in many developing nations, have invested in investment banks in Latin America, and have acquired securities brokers and dealers in the United Kingdom, which lead to the Big Bang of 1986.

Merchant Bank

Carries out wide range of investment banking activities.

Merchant banks are not easily defined. Probably the best known merchant banks are those based in London that have carried out international banking, corporate services, and portfolio management activities. Names such as Hambros,

---

* Curtis, Carole, and James C. Baker, "The Evolution of the Super Edge: Regulation and Operations of Edge Act Banks." *Journal of World Trade Law,* Vol. 21 (December 1987):32.

EXHIBIT 9.6	**Comparison of Edge Act and International Banking Facility (IBF) Operating Formats**

EDGE ACT UNIT | **INTERNATIONAL BANKING FACILITY**

SIMILARITIES

1. Generally operate from banking offices located in United States
2. Both American and foreign banks can utilize this operating format
3. Generally restricted to servicing international clientele

DIFFERENCES

EDGE ACT UNIT	INTERNATIONAL BANKING FACILITY
1. Broad operating framework that includes general banking, specialty finance, and equity investments in foreign bank affiliates	1. Narrower operating framework, primarily related to Eurobanking activities
2. Treated as onshore operating entity, with responsibility to domestic (U.S.) reserve requirements and local taxes	2. Treated as offshore operating entity, with limited or no (U.S.) responsibility for domestic reserve requirements and local taxes

Rothschild, Kleinwort Benson, Schroders, and Morgan Grenfell have stood out in the past as representative merchant bankers. More recently, the term "merchant banking" has become associated with the shift to investment banking and securitization activities.

International Banking Facility

Conducts offshore banking activities in the United States.

International Banking Facilities (IBFs) were first established in the United States in 1981. U.S. and foreign banks may establish IBFs that accept time deposits from foreign customers without the deposits being subject to U.S. reserve requirements. Currently nearly 600 IBFs operate much like Eurodollar market intermediaries except they are located in the United States, primarily in New York, California, and Florida. IBFs increase the competitive position of U.S. banks and have been popular. U.S. banks own nearly half of the IBFs.

IBFs and Edge Acts enjoy various similarities and differences. Both organizational formats are available to American and foreign banks operating in the United States. These similarities and differences are outlined in Exhibit 9.6.

OVERSEAS BRANCHES OF AMERICAN BANKS

Overseas branches have played a leading role in the growth and diversification of international operations of American banks. In 1960 eight American banks operated only 124 overseas branches. These branches held $12 billion in assets.* By 1989, 126 banks were operating 819 overseas branches with total assets of $264 billion (Exhibit 9.7). In 1993 overseas branches held $560 billion in assets, equivalent to more than 16% of the assets in domestic offices of American banks.

Foreign branches of American banks are important for the following reasons:

1. They bring strong competitive forces into the local money and banking markets of the host country. In effect, they have transformed the money markets of London, Singapore, and Hong Kong.

---

* Lees, Francis A. *International Banking and Finance.* London: Macmillan, 1974.:8.

EXHIBIT 9.7	**Growth of Overseas Branches of American Banks, 1970–1993**						
	1970	**1975**	**1980**	**1985**	**1986**	**1989**	**1993**
Number Banks with Branches	79	126	159	162	158	126	153
Number of Overseas Branches	532	762	787	916	885	819	772
Assets of Branches	$50.0	$145.3	$310.5	$289.7	$290.0	$264.0	$560.5
Assets as % of Total Assets: All Insured Commercial Banks	7.3%	13.1%	16.3%	8.9%	8.3%	6.7%	16.7%
Assets of Branches in U.K.	$24.0	$66.7	$107.4	$93.9	$94.0	$72.0	$172.7
Assets of Branches in Bahamas and Cayman Islands	$4.0	$36.6	$93.3	$76.5	$76.0	$81.0	$140.1

Amounts are in billions of U.S. dollars

Source: *Statistical Abstract of the United States*

2. They have become a major factor in developing the Eurocurrency market, now one of the three largest international money markets.
3. They provide an integrating mechanism, linking the world's financial markets.
4. They facilitate the parent bank's carrying out financial services for customers, irrespective of geographic location or time zone of the bank customer.

Several basic points can be made concerning the branch operations, as reflected in these combined accounts.

1. Eurocurrency dealing is an important activity in many foreign branches.
2. Interbank claims dominate the balance sheet. These represent claims face to face with the parent bank, other branches of the parent, or other banks.
3. Corporate loan and deposit are actively sought after.
4. Interoffice servicing represents a substantial part of branch activity. These transactions are interoffice claims arising from performance of services by one unit of the system for another unit, transfer of funds via the system for customer account, and (to a smaller amount) intersystem fund transfers related to money arbitrage and international funding.

In Exhibit 9.8 we can visualize some of the activities of the branches and the role they play in the *branch system*. Note that emphasis is on the *branch system,* that gives the global bank the ability to carry on activities in a more efficient manner.

Four types of service activities are represented in Exhibit 9.8. First, the branch system can shift the money market dealing position from one time zone to another during the day. This action reduces the riskiness of money market dealing and increases the chances for taking advantage of opportunities provided by local news releases. For example, the Singapore or Hong Kong branches can deal in U.S. Treasury securities (futures market trading) and be in the market to respond to news releases from Tokyo (Japanese trade balance release or interest rate release).

Foreign branches can provide local financial services required by clientele of the system located anywhere in the world. Also, branches can advance funds for local

| EXHIBIT 9.8 | **Global Branch System—Major Uses** |

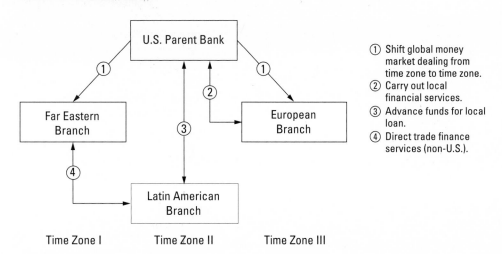

① Shift global money market dealing from time zone to time zone.
② Carry out local financial services.
③ Advance funds for local loan.
④ Direct trade finance services (non-U.S.).

lending. Finally, these branches can provide direct trade finance services when there are trade flows between two countries in which these branches are located (Exhibit 9.8, Far Eastern country and Latin American country).

Regional Characteristics of Overseas Branches   Overseas branches can be successful based on their ability to satisfy the parent banks' needs within limits imposed by the local environment. Operations of overseas branches reflect the unique environment of the host country, as well as the needs of the parent organization. In the following we describe the basic character of branches in different parts of the world.

The U.K. branches have enjoyed a distinct role. London is a leading world financial center and possesses a unique money market mechanism. In addition, the U.K. economy offers American multinationals favorable opportunities for investment. Consequently, two activities have dominated U.K. branches, namely, wholesale money market and services provided to multinational companies. Within the context of money market activities, Eurodollar dealing and dollar-sterling swaps play a prominent role.

Continental branches operate in a manner similar to that of U.K. branches. However, there are several differences. First, continental branches are smaller in size, explained by the fact that the London Eurodollar market dwarfs all other Eurocurrency market sectors. Second, continental branches tend to operate more on a multicurrency basis (a mix of Eurodollars, Eurosterling, and EuroFrench Francs).

While the European branches are basically wholesale in nature, the Latin American branches are essentially retail. On average, Latin American branches are no more than one-fifth the size of European branches. These branches carry on general financial services, carry out local collections between business firms (the practice in many Latin American countries), finance foreign trade, and manage the dollar book of the parent organization. The latter refers especially to the dollar denominated external loans in which the parent bank (United States) has participated. These assets can be converted into bonds, equity investments, or portfolio investments in the debtor (host) country.

Asian branches operate under diverse conditions. On average, these branches hold considerably larger amounts of assets than the Latin American branches but are not as large as the European branches. The branches in Japan are an exception. They are quite large and operate mainly in wholesale activities.

Asian Dollar Market
Offshore market for dollar deposits similar to Eurodollar market. Located in Singapore and Hong Kong.

The Hong Kong and Singapore branches benefit from direct access to the Asian Dollar Market. These branches can swap funds between the local currency market and the Asian Dollar Market. In addition, there are opportunities for providing diversified financial services in these two regional centers. These include trade financing, offshore deposit, syndicated loan, merchant banking, and innovative financing (note issuance facilities and interest rate swaps). Since the economic opening of mainland China, Hong Kong branches participate in financing rapidly growing trade and investment between China and Hong Kong.

African branches reflect larger branch assets than Latin American branches. This difference is due in part to the mix of oil-exporting African nations, where incomes and liquid funds are higher. African branches provide a mix of development financing services, general retail bank services, trade finance, and services to local affiliates of multinational companies.

Middle East branches can tap the oil wealth of oil-exporting nations. However, in periods of falling or low petroleum prices this source of liquidity tends to dry up. Branches in Oceania are of relatively recent origin, due to the fact that Australia only opened its banking market to foreign banks in the late 1980s.

FOREIGN BANKING IN THE UNITED STATES

In this section we consider the current situation with respect to the operations of foreign banks in the United States; we analyze the reasons for the rapid expansion of foreign banking in America since the early 1970s; and we describe the strategies that foreign banks employ to develop a banking operation in the United States.

In part this section is intended to be illustrative of the growing importance of global banking to the host country. In this example the United States is the host country, receiving foreign investment inflows directed at the banking sector. In the next several pages we follow the growth and pattern of foreign bank entry into the United States, consider the specific objectives of foreign banks in establishing a U.S. presence, and the regulatory response of the U.S. government.

Growth and Format   Foreign interest and ownership of U.S. banks has increased dramatically since the early 1970s. In 1972 assets of foreign banks operating in the United States represented about 3.3% of total domestic assets of all U.S. banks ($26.1 billion). In 1994, 291 foreign banks were operating 725 U.S. banking offices, representing 18% of domestic banking assets. These offices held $859 billion in assets (Exhibit 9.9). The leading banks in terms of home country nationality were Japan, United Kingdom, Canada, Italy, and France.

Foreign banks have used a variety of organizational formats in the United States including agency, bank subsidiary, representative office, Edge Act corporation, investment company, and international banking facilities. The major difference between an agency and a branch is that an agency does not accept deposits. Canadian banks have used the agency format in New York, in part to manage U.S. dollar funds invested in the New York money market. By contrast Japanese banks have used their New York agencies to book large dollar loans.

EXHIBIT 9.9	Foreign Banking Offices and Assets in the United States 1986–1994								
Nationality of bank	**NUMBER OF BANKS WITH U.S. OFFICES**			**NUMBER OF U.S. OFFICES**			**ASSETS IN U.S. OFFICES**		
	1986	**1990**	**1994**	**1986**	**1990**	**1994**	**1986**	**1990**	**1994**
Total	263	288	231	638	718	725	$468.1	$757.4	859.2
Japan	27	45	52	91	137	142	$201.8	$408.9	392.6
U.K.	14	11	9	52	42	32	$44.3	$38.6	61.9
Canada	9	6	6	53	49	42	$42.0	$42.8	61.0
Italy	12	13	12	26	27	24	$28.1	$46.6	35.6
Hong Kong	11	10	10	30	30	33	$24.1	$25.9	22.9
Switzerland	7	6	6	17	17	15	$21.9	$22.4	44.6
France	15	15	12	42	37	32	$20.2	$33.2	88.7
Germany	12	12	12	21	21	21	$7.5	19.2	36.1
Netherlands	4	4	3	17	27	22	$6.5	$15.7	48.8
S. Korea	—	—	8	—	—	30	—	—	12.1

Assets in billions of U.S. dollars

SOURCE: *Statistical Abstract of the United States*

Subsidiary banks are oriented toward the domestic market and retail banking. British and Japanese banks operate a number of large subsidiary banks in the United States. Representative offices do not perform banking functions, but provide information and serve as points of contact for the parent bank. Edge Act corporations engage in international trade finance and carry out other international banking operations.

Investment companies are located in New York and engage in investment and financial activities on a limited regional basis. International Banking Facilities (IBFs) are involved in Eurodollar type money market operations and generally must confine their clientele to nonresidents of the United States.

Strategies—Extension of Parent   Foreign banking offices in the United States may be considered as an extension of the parent bank. In this regard the organizational format and the operations of the American banking offices will be such that the foreign bank can bring its activities to the United States. This operation can be understood if we consider the activities of specific groups of banks, especially prior to 1978, the year the International Banking Act was adopted.

In the period before 1978 German and Swiss banks employed the strategy of using U.S. branches and New York-based securities affiliates. This strategy permitted these banks to operate in the United States as they did at home—as universal banks. They enjoyed the advantage over American banks of being able to simultaneously carry on commercial banking and investment banking business. Since there was no federal supervision of foreign banks in the United States until the International Banking Act of 1978, the Glass-Steagall separation of commercial and investment banking had no application.

Canadian banks have been able to service their home country clientele effectively from the operating bases established in New York and elsewhere in the United States. In the case of their New York representation, the Canadian banks use the agency and New York trust company. The agency manages New York money market operations, as well as provides general banking (except deposit) services. The New York trust company operates a corporate trust service for the U.S. dollar bonds sold in the New York capital market. It services the bond investors and the

Canadian borrowing entities by paying interest on these bonds to U.S.-based investors and by redeeming bonds at maturity or at call.

Japanese banks combined the New York agency, California and New York subsidiary banks, and a Chicago-based branch to best service their needs. The New York agency can make large loans with substantial concentrations (not permitted to deposit-taking banking institutions). These loans can be funded with money market or other borrowings. The combination of New York and California-based subsidiary banks and the Chicago branch permitted Japanese banks to operate deposit-taking offices on a multistate basis, generally not available to domestic banks in the period prior to 1978.

Diversified Objectives   Foreign banks have had diverse reasons and objectives in establishing direct representation in the United States. Most of the largest banks in the world have established banking offices in the United States.

An important specific reason for foreign bank expansion in the United States is to service corporate customers. There have been several "waves" of foreign business investment into the United States in recent decades by German, Dutch, British, Japanese, French, and other investors. Closely related to this trend has been the opening of strategically located banking offices of foreign banks from the same countries. This strategy aims at retaining the lead bank relationship with home country industrial corporations and other companies that have investments in the United States.

In 1987 it was reported that 500 subsidiaries of Swedish companies were operating in the United States.* Effective January 1, 1987, Swedish banks were allowed to open branches abroad, in part explaining the rush of Swedish banks to the United States.

Foreign banks are attracted to New York to participate in the large and flexible money market for funding and investing, and to generate profit from money market dealing operations. A New York location provides time zone advantages over European and other locations. Easier access to dollar funds can provide a bank with strategic funding advantages.

Several foreign banks have established a U.S. presence, especially for the purpose of developing corporate services activities. Non-American banks have not been especially successful in penetrating this area of activity.

Banks from developing countries benefit from a U.S. (particularly a New York) office. First, a New York office can effectively manage dollar funds. Second, if the bank has a relatively high credit rating, it is able to borrow local dollar funds for short-term needs (trade finance, dollar settlements). Third, a certain measure of prestige is associated with a New York or London office. These are the two largest centers for foreign banking offices. Also, there is more direct access from New York to develop business contacts, correspondent relations, and information regarding new developments in global finance.

INTERNATIONAL BANKING ACT OF 1978

In this section we consider the broad issue of how host governments treat foreign banks that seek to establish operating offices in their respective countries. Reference has been made already in this chapter to restrictions, formal and informal, that host

---

* Cohen, E. "Japanese and Swedes Wade In." *The Banker* (March 1987):92.

governments exercise, and the responses of banking institutions in their efforts to expand internationally.

International Banking Act

Federal legislation in 1978 that first placed foreign banks under central government regulation.

The International Banking Act of 1978 was put in place in response to the regulatory problems and inequities that were developing as foreign banks expanded their operations and banking offices in the United States. We should remember that the IBA was the first effort in the United States to place foreign banks under federal regulation. Until 1978 only state regulation applied to foreign banks, and this regulation permitted these institutions to select states of entry and entry formats (branch or subsidiary) that maximized their flexibility and competitiveness.

The following summarizes the major regulatory problems perceived in 1978:

1. Foreign banks could operate deposit-taking units on an interstate basis with a branch or subsidiary in New York, a branch in Chicago, and a branch or subsidiary in California. On the other hand, American banks generally were restricted from interstate deposit activities.

2. Some foreign banks established securities affiliates in the United States thus transferring their universal banking approach from home. Meanwhile American banks were restricted under the Glass-Steagall Act from investment banking-type activities.

3. Foreign banks generally were not subject to Federal Reserve reserve requirements. Many foreign banks operating in the United States were subject to state imposed reserve requirements that in many cases permitted use of government securities or interbank time deposits to satisfy these requirements. This policy tended to give these operating units an advantage over large U.S. banks subject to Federal Reserve cash reserve requirements.

The IBA sought to narrow or remove these competitive inequalities, but at the same time adopted an open approach toward foreign banks. In this regard the IBA incorporated a national treatment rather than a reciprocity approach. Under national treatment detailed bilateral negotiations generally are not required. To insure that American banks are given fair and equal access in host countries, the IBA requires that the U.S. Treasury generate periodic reports concerning "Foreign Government Treatment of U.S. Banking Organizations." Several of these reports have been made since the IBA was enacted.

The most important provisions of the International Banking Act of 1978 are:

1. Established federal supervision over foreign banks operating in the United States. Provided for federal licensing of foreign bank branches and agencies in the United States as an alternative to state licensing.

2. Limited the interstate deposit operations of foreign banks, based on practices applicable to U.S. banks. Foreign banks were required to select a home state where deposit-taking activities were permitted. Existing interstate deposit activities were frozen with grandfather protection.

3. Large foreign banks with operating offices in the United States were made members of the Federal Reserve System with reserve requirements applicable to deposits in U.S. banking offices. These banks were given benefits of Federal Reserve membership including access to the discount window.

4. New securities affiliate activities were frozen, but existing activities were given grandfather protection.

5. U.S. banks were provided access to more flexible interstate international banking operations via Edge Act affiliates. Edge Acts were permitted to branch interstate.

EXHIBIT 9.10	Foreign Bank Activities as Percent of Domestic Banks March 1996
Ownership of U.S. Treasury Securities	14.9%
Ownership of Other Securities	37.6
Holdings of Commercial and Industrial Loans	33.8
Total Assets	19.0
Transaction Accounts	11.1
Federal Funds Purchased/Sold	43.2
Total Loans	17.1

SOURCE: *Federal Reserve Bulletin*

At the same time foreign banks were also given the opportunity to invest in Edge Act affiliates.

Since passage of the International Banking Act in 1978, foreign banks have continued to expand aggressively in the U.S. banking markets. However, they now operate on more equal terms with domestic banks than before 1978.

IMPORTANCE OF FOREIGN BANKS

The operations of foreign bank branches and agencies in the United States continues to expand. Their importance can be seen by considering their share of various aspects of the U.S. banking business. This analysis is not complete since it excludes foreign owned banking subsidiaries in the United States. Also, it makes the comparison based on assets and liabilities of large weekly reporting banks that represent less than half of the total resources of U.S. domestic banks.

The following comparisons are significant:

1. Combined assets of weekly reporting foreign bank branches and agencies represent 19.0% of those of large weekly reporting U.S. commercial banks (Exhibit 9.10).
2. Asset-creating activities of foreign banks are of greatest relative importance in the following areas:
   a. foreign bank commercial and industrial loans are 33.8% as large as those of domestic banks.
   b. foreign bank holdings of U.S. Treasury and other securities are 14.9% and 37.6% as large as those of domestic banks.
3. Funding of foreign bank branches and agencies is more dependent on purchased funds, especially federal funds. Foreign bank branches and agencies are heavy borrowers in the federal funds market, taking more than half of the funds sold by large weekly reporting banks.

Between 1992 and 1996 foreign bank assets have held relatively steady at 19 percent of the assets held by domestic banks.

Trend to Investment Banking

BASIC RATIONALE

As large banks in America, Europe, and Asia prepare themselves for competing on a global playing field, they inevitably look in the direction of investment banking. Many large American banks have increased their focus on investment banking, beginning in the 1980s when regulators indicated willingness to make exceptions to the Glass-Steagall separation of investment and commercial banking. As a result, large American banks purchased discount stock brokerage firms, created affiliates to trade and underwrite corporate securities, widened the scope of their derivatives trading and services, and expanded their corporate advisory services in mergers and acquisitions.

American banks extended their services overseas, aiming at global market sectors that were increasing due to deregulation, economic integration, and privatization activities. Banks in other countries similarly set targets for capturing investment banking business on a cross border basis. The factors propelling banks in this direction included:

1. Desire to obtain revenues and profits not dependent on volatile and risky interest rate spreads (cost of funds versus interest rate charge on loans).
2. Need to diversify revenues and profits to achieve a more stable base of earnings.
3. Inherent stability of some components of investment banking revenues (fund management fees).
4. Desire to expand business and earnings growth.
5. Maximize prospects for long range survival, based on projections that in early twenty-first century there will be only a few dozen major investment banking firms operating as global players.

FOCUS ON LONDON

During the 1990s London and New York have emerged as strategic locations for representation by large banks seeking to strengthen global competitiveness. In some respects London enjoys an edge based on its flexible regulatory posture, traditionally greater global focus, and dual currency financial market.

London has been an attractive center for leading banks from many countries that are seeking to develop a strong investment banking organization. Large U.K. clearing banks have developed investment banking units through a mix of internal growth and acquisitions of smaller securities houses. American banks have established new capital market affiliates in London that have achieved high internal growth.

Continental European banks have acquired many of the formerly independent U.K. merchant banks. German banks in particular have invested in London based merchant banks (Exhibit 9.11). As reflected in the table, the year 1995 was a particularly active one for such acquisitions.

Specific advantages gained by Deutsche Bank, Hypo Bank, ING, SBC, and Merrill Lynch are that they have instant benefit of the specialized investment banking functions carried on by the acquired London institution. This includes fund management (Foreign & Colonial), corporate advisory (Warburg), emerging market equity analysis (Barings), emerging debt strategy (Morgan Grenfell), and a large share of London stock market trading and market making capacity (Smith & New Court).

More general advantages include:

1. direct access to London's new issue and secondary market trading operations.
2. participation in London's dual currency money market.
3. expectation that London's role will grow as financial center for a more integrated European market in financial services.
4. time zone advantage since London is the closest link to New York of all the European financial centers.

EXHIBIT 9.11	Selected Acquisitions of London Banks-Securities Houses by Non-U.K. Banking Firms	

Acquirer and Home Country	Acquired London Institution	Year Acquired
Deutsche Bank, Germany	Morgan Grenfell	1989
Berliner Handels und Frankfurter Bank and Credit Commercial de France Germany, France	Charterhouse	1993
Hong Kong Shanghai Banking Corp. Hong Kong, U.K.	James Capel	1990
Bayerische Hypotheken und Wechsel Bank Germany	Foreign & Colonial	1989
ING, Netherlands	Barings	1995
Commerzbank, Germany	Jupiter Tyndall	1995
Swiss Bank Corp. Switzerland	S. G. Warburg	1995
Dresdner Bank, Germany	Kleinwort Benson	1995
Merrill Lynch, U.S.	Smith New Court	1995

5. externalities offered in London, including professional workforce skilled in investment banking operations and related services such as clearing and settlements, securities custody, and information flow.

Increased Competition

CROSS BORDER COMPETITION

The past two decades have witnessed a growing tendency toward the globalization of finance. This takes the form of banks seeking cross border alliances, developing more complete global systems, a shift toward investment banking, and the development of new financial products and services. In the previous section we noted that cross border alliances in the form of acquisitions have permitted banks in Germany, the Netherlands, and other countries to develop stronger investment banking units and to move in the direction of completing a global banking system. For example, through its acquisition of Barings in 1995, ING Bank can provide a wide range of investment services in 30 countries around the world.

The Hong Kong & Shanghai Banking Corporation operates strategic bases in Hong Kong, its original headquarters, in New York through its ownership of Marine Midland Banks, and in London where it has located a new headquarters as well as acquired Midland Bank, James Capel stockbrokers, and other merchant banking offices. In 1997 HSBC acquired ownership in a leading Brazilian bank.

JP Morgan now has the capacity to trade U.S. Treasury securities around the clock, based on its Tokyo and London offices complementing the New York trading of these securities. Similarly, large Japanese banks have established bond trading units in New York and London to service home and overseas clients on a 24-hour basis.

Large banks have worked aggressively to develop new products and services, offering them to customers through specialized trading and service units located where markets for these products exist. An important aspect of this is the exchange trading and over-the-counter distribution of derivative instruments in London,

New York, Chicago, Osaka, Singapore, and several other locations. For example, the London International Financial Futures Exchange (LIFFE) has numerous members representing parent banks and financial institutions based in nearly all OECD countries.

RELATED PROBLEMS

The growth in cross border competition has produced related problems. These fall into several categories:

1. Greater difficulty for regulatory surveillance and control.
2. Increased exposure of banking institutions and markets to risk.
3. Internal control problems within banking organizations.

As the scope and complexity of cross border banking increases, it becomes more difficult for regulatory agencies and central banks to keep up with the changes. This problem manifested itself in the 1991 case of the Bank for Credit and Commerce International (BCCI). This case and the resulting 1991 amendment to the IBA are discussed in a following section.

Another area of regulatory difficulty is that banks based in different countries may enjoy lower nominal or real cost of capital. This is alleged to result from differences in monetary exchange rate systems and from differences in capital requirements (leverage opportunities). To provide a more level playing field in this respect and to assure adequate capital for bank solvency, the central banks of major industrial countries agreed to establish standard or uniform capital requirements for their respective banks. These are described in detail in a subsequent section of this chapter.

REGULATORY RISK IN DERIVATIVES MARKETS

The decade of the 1990s has seen numerous accounts of derivatives-related losses on the part of established firms. These incidents have precipitated concern over the rapid growth of derivatives markets, the possible dangers to banks and other participants in derivative instrument transactions, and the possible impairment of confidence in the derivatives markets themselves.

A 1993 report of the risks associated with derivatives was published by the Group of Thirty. This report identified four basic risks:

Market Risk	—	risk to earnings from adverse movements in market prices.
Operational Risk	—	risk of losses occurring as a result of inadequate systems and control, human error, or failure of management.
Counterparty Credit Risk	—	risk that a party to a derivative contract will fail to perform its obligation. This exposure is estimated as the cost of replacing a contract if a counterparty to a contract defaults.
Legal Risk	—	risk of loss should a contract be found to be legally unenforceable. As legal contracts, derivatives require a legal infrastructure to provide for resolution of conflicts and enforcement.

EXHIBIT 9.12	Three Cases of Substantial Losses on Derivatives	
Principal Players	**Brief Description of Case**	**Amount of Loss**
1. Metallgesellschaft AG	U.S. oil subsidiary of German parent company adopted hedging strategy for long-term fixed price delivery contracts. Purchased oil swaps and futures contracts for hedge. Precipitous decline in oil prices caused funding problems, and NYMEX removed hedging exemption.	More than $1 billion
2. Barings PLC	Singapore based trader wrote options and straddles on NIKKEI-225 futures contracts, with expectation market would have low volatility. Kobe earthquake early in 1995 sent Japanese stock market into tailspin.	$927 million
3. Bankers Trust - Proctor & Gamble	Bank sold leveraged interest rate swaps to P&G. The 1994 rise in U.S. interest rates led to losses on these complex swap positions and lawsuit by P&G, subsequently settled out of court.	Close to $200 million

These risks are not unique to derivative instruments, and similar types of risks manifest themselves in traditional areas of financial intermediation, such as banking and underwriting securities. Nevertheless, there appears to be a popular perception that rapid growth of derivatives trading can pose special problems for financial markets. Most of these concerns center on the expansion of the over the counter (OTC) derivatives market. This is because these instruments are nonstandard contracts, without secondary trading, and with only limited public price information. OTC markets lack some of the financial safeguards used by futures and options exchanges, such as margin requirements and daily marking to market of contracts, which insure that all market participants settle losses promptly. Absence of these safeguards, together with the complexity of new generation financial derivatives and growing market size, give rise to concerns that continued growth of derivatives trading might somehow contribute to financial instability. Finally, there is concern that federal regulatory agencies in the United States and their counterparts in other countries have failed to keep pace with rapid innovations in OTC derivatives markets. These concerns are reinforced by frequent reports of derivatives-related losses among banks and large corporations (Exhibit 9.12).

The traditional rationale for regulating financial markets is based on concern that events in these markets can have a significant impact on the economy. Recent interest in regulating derivatives markets in a more comprehensive way stems from concern that these markets expose banks and the financial system to greater risk and instability.

Risk is inherent in all financial activity. Financial intermediaries, including commercial and investment banks, specialize in managing financial risks. Regulation seeks to encourage these institutions to manage risks in a prudent manner, but it cannot eliminate risks inherent in financial intermediation. Business firms (including banks) cannot earn profits without taking risks. Regulators seek to reduce risks taken on by regulated institutions, but if overzealous in this direction may make it too difficult or impossible for enterprises to earn profits.

The conventional wisdom holds that derivatives markets operate to facilitate risk transfer. Derivatives markets exist to facilitate this transfer of risk from firms that wish to avoid such risks to others willing to or suited to manage these risks. In this regard, rapid growth of derivatives markets in recent years simply reflects technology advances in risk management.

The collapse of Barings provides an example of how excessive speculation by a bank participating in securities and derivatives market transactions experienced large losses, resulting in insolvency and fear of disruption of financial markets. In this particular case the bank's management was overly complacent in the face of a large number of warning signs. Exhibit 9.12 outlines the nature of this case and Exhibit 9.13 provides a graphic account and analysis of the positions taken.

The Barings case brought calls for more comprehensive regulation of derivatives markets. However, exchange-traded derivatives such as futures contracts have long been subject to comprehensive government regulation. In the United States the SEC regulates securities and options exchanges, while the Commodity Futures Trading Commission (CFTC) regulates futures exchanges and futures brokers. OTC derivatives markets are not regulated by any single federal agency, but most OTC dealers (banks and brokerage firms) are subject to federal regulation. Also, large brokerage firms in the United States have agreed to conform to regulatory guidelines and to make regular disclosures to the SEC and CFTC concerning derivatives-related risks.

The Barings case involved exchange traded derivatives contracts. Senior management was criticized for insufficient effort to adequately monitor and supervise the activities of subsidiaries. The Barings debacle involved a regulated U.K. merchant bank trading in regulated futures markets, and illustrates the limits of regulation. Rules and regulations already in place should have prevented a single trader from accumulating catastrophic losses. But the Singapore and U.K. regulators granted exemptions that made it possible for the so-called "rogue trader" to continue his activities without detection. The instruments traded were not complex or exotic instruments. In the case of Barings, the Bank of England concluded it was not the complexity of the transaction, but the failure of a number of individuals to do their jobs properly that made the bank susceptible to large losses.

The Barings disaster made certain issues clear with respect to the regulatory framework and risks in the derivatives markets:

1. There was a need for some legal and regulatory reforms and for increased international cooperation among exchanges and their regulators.
2. Market discipline is a necessary aspect of regulation. The much publicized accounts of derivatives-related losses led many firms to review and improve their risk management practices.
3. Regulation cannot substitute for sound management practices. The risk monitoring function within a bank entails independence from bank profit centers where risks are being analyzed.

In January 1996 the Federal Reserve Board announced it would examine and rate the risk management systems of national banks. These examinations will focus on active board and senior management oversight, adequate procedures and limits, adequate risk management information systems, and comprehensive internal controls. In addition, the board has created a rating system to be factored into overall

EXHIBIT 9.13   Unauthorized Derivatives Trading Generates Big Losses

In 1992 Barings sent Nicholas Leeson, a clerk in the London office, to manage the accounting and settlement operations at its Singapore futures subsidiary. Barings Futures Singapore (BFS) was established to enable Barings to execute trades on the Singapore International Monetary Exchange (SIMEX). Most of the BFS business was concentrated in executing trades for a limited number of financial futures and options contracts, including the NIKKEI-225 contract, the 10-year Japanese Government Bond (JGB) contract, the three-month Euroyen contract, and options on these contracts (futures options).

Early in 1992 Leeson asked permission to take the SIMEX examinations that would permit him to trade on the floor of the exchange. He passed these and began trading that year. Subsequently, Leeson was named general manager and head trader. Normally the functions of trading and settlements are kept separated to provide independent verification of trading records. Leeson was not relieved of his authority over back-office operations when he was given responsibilities to manage trading.

Soon Leeson was conducting proprietary trading in the NIKKEI-225 stock index futures and 10-year Japanese Government Bond futures. Both contracts trade on SIMEX and the Osaka Securities Exchange (OSE). His authority extended to arbitrage price discrepancies on these contracts on the two exchanges. This involved buying the lower priced contract on one exchange while selling the higher priced contract on the other. This arbitrage involves only perfectly hedged positions, a low risk activity. Unknown to Barings management in London, Leeson undertook a riskier trading strategy, placing bets on the direction of price movements on the Tokyo stock exchange. He reported spectacular trading profits, which accounted for a significant share of Barings aggregate profits. Leeson was able to manufacture fictitious reports concerning trading activities. He had set up a special account, and by manipulating information on his trading was able to conceal trading losses and report large profits. In the four years 1992–1995 Leeson concealed trading losses of £$2 million, £$21 million, £$185 million, and £$619 million, respectively.

A major part of his trading strategy was the sale of options on NIKKEI-225 futures contracts. The seller earns a premium, and if the option expires out-of-the-money, the premium becomes a profit. If prices become more volatile than expected, an option seller's losses are unlimited. In 1994 Leeson began selling option straddles, the simultaneous sale of both calls and puts on NIKKEI-225 futures. Figure C shows the payoff at expiration to the seller of an option straddle. In this case the seller of an option straddle earns profit only if the market proves less volatile than predicted. Leeson's strategy, a bet that the Japanese stock market would neither fall nor increase by any large amount, could be successful only if stock prices remained stable.

By January 1995 Leeson was short over 37,000 NIKKEI calls, and almost 33,000 NIKKEI puts. Also, he held a long position of more than 1,000 contracts in NIKKEI stock index futures. On January 17 disaster struck when a violent earthquake in Kobe, Japan, brought the Japanese stock market to a tailspin. The NIKKEI index fell over 1,500 points. Further volatility in the markets resulted in greater losses, and Leeson continued to increase his exposure. By February 23, 1995, he had bought more than 61,000 NIKKEI futures contracts, representing 49 percent of total open interest in the March futures contract and 24 percent of the open interest in the June contract. Further, his position in Japanese government bond futures of more than 26,000 contracts represented 88 percent of the open interest in the June 1995 contract. Leeson also began to deal in Euroyen contracts, betting that Japanese interest rates would fall.

Leeson's trading exposed Barings to massive margin calls as losses mounted. Over £$740 million was committed to finance margin calls. When a London-based Barings settlements specialist visited Singapore in late February to review a discrepancy in one of the accounts, Leeson and his wife left Singapore. Investigation of Leeson's private records revealed he had lost astronomical sums of money, at which point the London office contacted the Bank of England for assistance. The Bank of England's Board of Banking Supervision investigated the case, and reported total losses attributable to Leeson's actions at £$927 million, far in excess of Baring's total equity of £$440 million. Most of the cost of the Barings debacle was borne by its shareholders and by ING, the Netherlands-based banking group that bought Barings. ING had to pay £$660 million to recapitalize the firm.

Continued

| EXHIBIT 9.13 | **Payoffs to Selected Options Trading Strategies** |

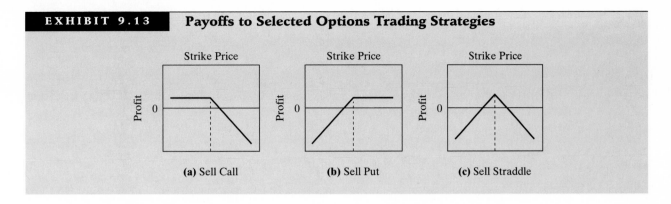

(a) Sell Call   (b) Sell Put   (c) Sell Straddle

---

assessment of management. The rating system to be introduced contains five grade levels.

Rating 1 (Strong)	—	Management effectively identifies and controls all major types of risk.
Rating 2 (Satisfactory)	—	The institution's management is largely effective, but lacking to some modest degree.
Rating 3 (Fair)	—	Management practices are lacking in some important ways, and require more than normal supervisory attention.
Rating 4 (Marginal)	—	Risk management practices generally fail to identify, monitor, or control significant risk exposures in many material respects.
Rating 5 (Unsatisfactory)	—	There is a critical absence of effective risk management practices.

Clearly, a rating less than 2 could be catastrophic to an individual bank status in the derivatives market. The nature of new business lines developed by leading derivatives trading and dealing banks permits them to change their risk profiles very quickly. Therefore more frequent examinations and monitoring will be necessary. Also, regulatory agencies will need to recruit examiners capable of understanding the complexities of risk-taking in the derivatives markets.

Regulatory Responses to Increased Competition

The preceding section focused on the effect of increased banking competition, specific problems encountered, and need for improved regulatory response. Also, we noted that the FRB has moved toward examining banks with a new focus on the effectiveness of their risk management controls. In the following sections we focus on the BCCI case and the resulting 1991 amendment to IBA, efforts to deal with Herstatt risk, and the adoption of standard bank capital requirements.

THE BCCI CASE

In 1991 the government of the United Kingdom closed the Bank for Credit and Commerce International (BCCI) operation in London and took control of its assets. Banking authorities in the United States and other countries also closed down BCCI's operations in their countries. Since these closings, it has become evident that depositors in many countries where BCCI operated may recover little from liquidation of the bank's assets.

BCCI had never been authorized to engage in deposit banking in the United States. However, it indirectly gained control of First American Bankshares (originally known as Financial General Bankshares) that operates banks in the District of Columbia and several states. Prior to the U.K. action toward BCCI, this institution was indicted in the United States for money laundering and in 1989 pleaded guilty in a federal court.

The BCCI case raised a number of questions concerning effective regulation of international banking. BCCI operated around the world in a manner that made it difficult for regulatory authorities in key banking markets (United Kingdom and United States) to gain effective supervisory authority over its activities. BCCI operated as a Luxembourg corporation with headquarters in London. Stockholders were mostly from the Middle East, and operations extended to most parts of the world.

Effective supervision of BCCI was difficult for the following reasons:

1. Supervisory agencies in one country lacked access to information held by counterpart agencies in other countries.
2. Legal maneuvers of BCCI could prevent disclosure of documents and other information of interest to bank authorities.
3. Laws that govern international banks often do not require maintenance of consolidated records about their operations.

In 1991 new federal banking legislation strengthened Federal Reserve Board authority over foreign banking activities in the United States. This legislation was in large part a response to the problems and dangers made apparent in the BCCI case.

IBA Amendment of 1991

In December 1991 federal legislation (Foreign Bank Supervision Enhancement Act) amended the IBA. This amendment aimed at strengthening federal supervision and examination of foreign bank operations in the United States. This amendment provided the following:

1. Under the IBA a foreign bank must obtain approval of the Federal Reserve Board before establishing a branch or agency or before acquiring ownership or control of a commercial banking company.
2. In approving an application, the Federal Reserve Board must determine that the foreign bank engages directly in the business of banking outside the United States, that it is subject to comprehensive supervision or regulation on a consolidated basis in its home country, and that the foreign bank has provided adequate information to assess the application.
3. The Federal Reserve Board is given authority to terminate the activities of a state chartered branch, agency, or commercial lending subsidiary of a foreign bank if the foreign bank is not subject to comprehensive supervision or regulation in its home country or if it is operated in an unsafe and unsound manner.
4. The Federal Reserve Board must develop and publish criteria to be used in evaluating the operation of any foreign bank in the United States that the board has determined is not subject to comprehensive supervision or regulation.

5. State chartered branches and agencies of foreign banks are limited to the same activities and lending limits as those given to federally chartered branches and agencies, unless the Federal Reserve Board and the FDIC approve exceptions.

6. The Federal Reserve Board is authorized to impose conditions on the approval of federal branches and agencies by the office of the Comptroller of the Currency.

7. The Federal Reserve Board is authorized to examine branches and agencies by the office of the Comptroller of the Currency.

8. Other provisions of the 1991 legislation require approval by the Federal Reserve Board for foreign banks to establish representative offices, require foreign banks that maintain retail accounts (balance under $100,000) to establish a banking subsidiary and obtain deposit insurance from the FDIC, and require the board to report to Congress on the regulatory capital standards that apply to foreign banks operating in the United States.

DEALING WITH HERSTATT RISK

In June 1974 Germany's Bankhaus I.D. Herstatt collapsed. In this case banks in other countries suffered losses when Herstatt was unable to cover its settlements obligations at the close of the business day. Since this event central bankers have been struggling to ensure that a similar incident will not be repeated. The collapse of BCCI in 1991 caused currency settlements and losses for several banks, renewing concern over what has come to be referred to as Herstatt risk.

Herstatt Risk

Related to inability of a bank to make cash settlements at end of day's clearings.

Since 1991 central banks have been pushing commercial and investment banks harder than ever to come up with ways to reduce the risks associated with end-of-day settlements in the $1.3 trillion a day global foreign exchange market. Currency trading is more complex than two decades ago, and includes many types of participants such as hedge funds, corporations, and institutional investors.

Central banks fear that one of their banks will suffer major losses, high systemic risks associated with bungled currency trades, or a chain reaction where banks that do not get paid refuse to pay their creditors.

If one of these occurred, at the least there could develop payments gridlock. At the worst there could develop sizeable credit losses. The basic risk, or "Herstatt risk", is that the bank pays the currency it owes on a foreign exchange trade to another bank but doesn't collect. In the 1974 Herstatt episode, American banks lost approximately $200 million.

An October 1994 study by a task force of bankers and the Federal Reserve Bank of New York noted that risks involved in settling a single day's trades can last up to three days. The study faults banks for not clearly understanding the causes of risk, and for not implementing modern back-office procedures. A market participant might unwittingly increase its exposure to high levels by paying out funds on subsequent transactions without having received payment on the initial transaction.

Some partial solutions to Herstatt risk that have been recommended or implemented include:

1. banks tighten their internal money transfer systems.

2. banks promote sound risk management practices with contingency plans for crisis management.

3. banks establish netting arrangements (multilateral and bilateral) for single payment settlement at the end of trading day in each currency.

Unfortunately, netting does not entirely remove the Herstatt risk, but it does reduce it significantly (often only up to about 90 percent). Also, some netting systems do not handle all currencies. Some countries do not permit netting.

CAPITAL ADEQUACY AND BANK CAPITAL REQUIREMENTS

The rapid growth of international banking in the 1960s and 1970s brought numerous problems. Among these were significant bank failures, including the Intra Bank of Lebanon (1967) due to weakening confidence and substantial withdrawals, the Herstatt Bank in Germany (1974) due to foreign exchange losses, and the Franklin National Bank of New York (1974) as a result of weak management and overextended foreign exchange trading.[*]

According to Professor James C. Baker of Kent State University, expanded overseas operations give emphasis to the problem of bank capital adequacy. Loan limits imposed on American banks generally have been based on the parent bank's capital.

"Since overseas branches do not have capital, their loan limits are based on the parent's capital; this gives branches of major banks a competitive edge vis-a-vis local home country banks. It also permits branches to operate at a higher level of loan activity than might be safe. The higher risk inherent in some operations permitted overseas branches (but disallowed the parent) also points toward imposition of some type of capital adequacy regulation on overseas branch operations."[†] Baker seems to have been aware of impending problems some years before the major central banks came to grips with these issues.

Bank capital plays an important role in assuring bank solvency. During the two decade period 1970–1990 international and domestic developments drew the attention of bank regulatory agencies in the United States and other countries to the need for stronger and more uniform bank capital requirements. Negotiations led to the Basle Accord, notable in that it is the first multilateral agreement in history to provide for mutually agreed upon and enforced bank capital standards. The implementation of this agreement in the 1990s has been and will continue to be an interesting development. Even more interesting is the question of what the Basle Accord might lead to in the way of further international agreements concerning conditions for competition in global banking and financial markets.

RISK-BASED CAPITAL REQUIREMENTS

Early capital requirements in the United States were related to deposits with the objectives of assuring bank solvency and depositor protection. The banking crisis of the 1930s altered views in this regard and shifted attention to the relationship between capital and the level of related assets. The risk-asset approach evolved in the 1950s and related bank capital to the composition of bank assets. The Basle Concordats of 1975 and 1983 were the first international efforts to advance international regulation of banks. These established that in the event of a solvency crisis involving a Eurobank, the central bank in the country of the Eurobank's headquarters will act as lender of last resort if the affected unit is a foreign branch.

---

[*] This episode of bank failures is described in James C. Baker, *International Bank Regulation.* New York: Praeger, 1978, Chapter 1.

[†] Baker, p. 37.

In 1981 U.S. bank regulatory agencies announced minimum primary capital-asset ratios. In 1983 the International Lending Supervision Act was put into place. This act gave regulatory agencies authority to enforce compliance with regard to capital requirements that these agencies established. During the 1980s average primary capital-to-asset ratios for commercial banks began rising steadily. In this period several developments made it imperative that regulators enforce higher capital adequacy standards, including the international debt crisis, a rising level of off-balance-sheet activities of banks, increased volatility in financial markets, increased bank participation in volatile markets, and more intense competition among international banks.

During the 1980s U.S. bank regulators made an effort to develop risk-based capital standards. The reasons for this were:

1. to remove disincentives to hold low risk assets (U.S. Treasury bills);
2. to relate capital requirements in part to off-balance-sheet activities;
3. to bring American capital standards in line with other countries where banks were major competitors in international markets; and
4. to lower the overall risk profile of the U.S. banking industry.

Initially, U.S. bank regulators did not expect to develop an international agreement or to achieve an internationally converging bank capital standard.

In 1986 U.S. regulatory agencies began collaborative discussions with the Bank of England to develop a common risk-based system. A significant obstacle that slowed down U.S. and U.K. progress was the lack of agreement on defining what constitutes bank capital. Discussions led to a two-tier definition of capital, the forerunner of the approach followed in the Basle Accord. In January 1987 a joint agreement was announced by the United States and United Kingdom to establish a minimum capital standard related to the level of bank risk including off-balance-sheet items. Further, they proposed that other countries adopt a minimum capital requirement. In March 1987 the Federal Reserve and Bank of England proposed specific risk-based capital requirements.

Even before the conclusion of the U.S.-U.K. agreement, Japanese banking authorities had joined the discussion. In October 1987 a draft accord was worked out setting new capital requirements for 17 industrial nations. Earlier in the year the Cooke Committee had proposed that the U.S.-U.K. agreement be expanded to include a number of industrial countries. By December 1987 a committee of central bank officials published specific proposals for risk-based capital requirements with minimum capital standards to take effect in 1992 and with interim standards to begin in 1990. The Basle Accord was announced in July 1988. The provisions of the Basle Agreement were binding for multinational banks only. Several nations including the United States began to apply these provisions to all of their commercial banks.

Risk-Based Capital

Capital requirement imposed by bank, weighted according to risk of assets.

Basle Accord

International agreement to impose minimum capital requirements for banks—related to riskiness of assets.

DETAILS OF THE BASLE ACCORD

The Basle Agreement became fully effective at year-end 1992, with transitional rules to be applied until that date. The risk-based capital system described in the Basle Accord includes the following guidelines:

1. a definition of capital for measurement reasons,
2. a system for calculating risk-based assets according to four broad risk categories, and
3. a schedule for achieving a minimum ratio of capital to risk-weighted assets.

Primary Capital

Under Basle Accord, Tier 1 capital, or the initial four percent capital, satisfied only with certain types of capital.

Supplementary Capital

Under Basle Accord, Tier 2 capital, or the second four percent of capital, satisfied with a wide range of types of capital.

Capital is divided into two components. Tier I primary capital includes common stock issued and fully paid, retained earnings, disclosed reserves (primarily allocations of retained earnings), and perpetual noncumulative preferred stock minus goodwill (excess of purchase price of any acquisitions over book value). Tier II supplementary capital includes limited life and cumulative preferred stock, undisclosed reserves, 45% of reevaluation reserves, general loan loss reserves (unrelated to specific assets), hybrid debt-capital instruments, and subordinated debt. By 1992, banking organizations were required to have Tier I capital in an amount equivalent to at least 4% of risk-weighted assets, and total capital (Tier I plus Tier II capital) equivalent to at least 8% of risk-weighted assets.

Four weight categories were the risk-weighting framework adopted by the Basle Committee. The lowest weight category (zero percent) applies to central government securities and cash. A 20% weight applies to short-term interbank claims and to general obligation securities of municipal governments. Residential mortgages carry a weight of 50%. Risk assets (commercial loans, claims on foreign governments, and certain other assets) fall in the 100% weight category.

The calculation of credit equivalent amounts and the resulting capital ratio is illustrated in Exhibit 9.14.

Capital requirements for off-balance-sheet instruments involves a two-step process. These are converted to credit-risk equivalents by multiplying the nominal amounts by a credit conversion factor. The resulting amount is weighted, depending on the risk (counterparty). Off-balance-sheet instruments that are essentially substitutes for loans (standby letters of credit) carry a 100% factor. A 50% conversion factor is used for performance bonds, note issuance facilities (NIFs) and revolving underwriting facilities (RUFs). A 20% conversion factor is used for short-term, trade-related contingent liabilities.

Regulation H and Y Amendments   The Board of Governors of the Federal Reserve System amended its risk-based capital guidelines in 1994 with respect to:

1. qualifying bilateral netting contracts,
2. treatment of net unrealized holdings gains (losses) on securities available for sale, and
3. concentrations of credit risk and the risks of nontraditional activities.

The original Basle Accord and Federal Reserve Board guidelines provided that off-balance-sheet interest rate and exchange rate contracts be incorporated into risk weighted assets by converting each contract into a credit equivalent amount. Exposure would be determined individually for each rate contract entered into by a banking organization. The new 1994 treatment permits banking institutions to net positive and negative market values of rate contracts.

On May 31, 1993, the Financial Accounting Standards Board issued FAS 115, which established "net unrealized holding gains (losses) on securities available for sale" as a new element of common stockholder equity. All banking organizations were required to adopt FAS 115 for generally accepted accounting principles and regulatory reporting.

FAS 115 divides securities held by banking organizations into three categories:

1. securities held to maturity
2. trading account securities
3. securities available for sale

EXHIBIT 9.14	**Sample Calculation of Risk-Based Capital Ratio**
Regulation Y, Appendix A	Capital Adequacy Guidelines

ATTACHMENT I—SAMPLE CALCULATION OF RISK-BASED CAPITAL RATIO FOR BANK HOLDING COMPANIES

EXAMPLE OF A BANKING ORGANIZATION WITH $6,000 IN TOTAL CAPITAL AND THE FOLLOWING ASSETS AND OFF-BALANCE-SHEET ITEMS:

Balance Sheet Assets

Cash	$5,000
U.S. Treasuries	$20,000
Balances at domestic banks	$5,000
Loans secured by first liens on 1- to 4-family residential properties	$5,000
Loans to private corporations	$65,000
Total Balance-Sheet Assets	$100,000

Off-Balance-Sheet Items

Standby letters of credit (SLCs) backing general-obligation debt issues of U.S. municipalities (GOs)	$10,000
Long-term legally binding commitments to private corporations	$20,000
Total Off-Balance-Sheet Items	$30,000

This bank holding company's total capital to *total* assets (leverage ratio) would be:

$$(\$6,000/\$100,000) = 6.00\%)$$

To compute the bank holding company's weighted-risk assets:
1. Compute the credit-equivalent amount of each off-balance-sheet (OBS) item.

OBS Item	Face Value	Conversion Factor		Credit-Equivalent Amount
SLCs backing municipal GOs	$10,000	× 1.00	=	$10,000
Long-term commitments to private corporations	$20,000	× 0.50	=	$10,000

Capital Adequacy Guidelines	**Regulation Y, Appendix A**

2. Multiply each balance-sheet asset and the credit-equivalent amount of each OBS item by the appropriate risk weight.

OBS Item 0% Category	Face Value	Conversion Factor		Credit-Equivalent Amount
Cash	$5,000			
U.S. Treasuries	$20,000			
	$25,000	× 0	=	0
20% Category				
Balances at domestic banks	$5,000			
Credit-equivalent amounts of SLCs backing GOs of U.S. municipalities	$10,000			
	$15,000	× 0.20	=	$3,000
50% Category				
Loans secured by first liens on 1–4 family residential properties	$5,000	× 0.50	=	$2,500
100% Category				
Loans to private corporations	$65,000			
Credit-equivalent amounts of long-term commitments to private corporations	$10,000			
	$75,000	× 1.00	=	$75,000
Total Risk-Weighted Assets				$80,500

This bank holding company's ratio of total capital to weighted-risk assets (risk-based capital ratio) would be:

$$(\$6,000/\$80,500) = 7.45\%$$

SOURCE: Board of Governors, Federal Reserve System, Regulation Y, Appendix A, March 15, 1989.

Trading securities are reported at fair value (generally market value) with net unrealized changes in value reported directly on the income statement. Under FAS 115 securities held to maturity are recorded at amortized cost. Securities meeting the definition of the "available for sale" category are reported at fair value. Changes in fair value are to be reported, net of tax effects, directly in a separate component of common stockholders equity. Any unrealized change in value has no impact on reported earnings, but affects the equity capital position.

In 1994 the Federal Reserve Board ruled that net unrealized gains and losses on available for sale securities generally are not to be included in capital. However, unrealized losses on marketable equity securities will continue to be deducted from Tier I capital.

Institutions that are identified through examination as having significant exposure to concentrations of credit risk or that are not adequately managing concentration risk should hold capital in excess of the regulatory minimums. Further, as banking institutions begin to engage in nontraditional activity, the risks of that activity will be analyzed and given appropriate capital treatment.

IMPLICATIONS

There are several implications from adoption of risk-based capital requirements. They are:

1. Bank portfolios will shift to some degree. The substantially lower weighting given to government securities as contrasted with loans (zero percent versus 100%) offers opportunities for banks to make holdings of such securities a larger part of their balance sheets. Exhibit 9.15 illustrates the comparative earnings generating power of selected risk assets.

2. The price of some off-balance-sheet services may rise, and the quantity made available may decline.

3. Some banks based in several countries will have to raise capital or reduce their assets. In some cases both actions may be required. Some banks may have difficulty in meeting the new set of capital requirements. Non-U.S. banks also will have to raise additional capital. Exhibit 9.16 illustrates the extent to which the U.S. preferred stock market has been used to generate Tier I capital.

4. In the future we can expect greater emphasis on evaluating bank strength and bank creditworthiness from the viewpoint of capital adequacy.

5. The measurement and evaluation of bank profitability will shift toward capital-oriented measures as contrasted with asset-oriented measures.

6. Pressures will increase for commercial banks to move toward investment banking type activities. This strategy had been pursued by Bankers Trust and J. P. Morgan prior to 1988. These banks have given less emphasis to long-term lending, have the most liquid balance sheets, and enjoy the strongest risk-based capital position, showing a total ratio of capital to risk adjusted assets of more than 12%—comfortably ahead of the 1992 requirements.

BANK COST OF CAPITAL AND INTERNATIONAL COMPETITION

We now consider how bank capital costs are defined and measured, compare capital costs facing banks in different countries, and analyze the role played by cost of equity.

EXHIBIT 9.15	**Comparative Earning Power of Selected Commercial Bank Asset Categories Relative to Bank Capital**

Given the asset conversion factors under the Basle Accord, international banks will find that each risk asset category will have a different earnings generating power. To illustrate this relationship, in the following table we estimate the dollars of earning assets that can be supported. This number is stated in Column 1. It is calculated as follows:

$$\text{Multiplier} = \frac{1}{\text{Conversion Factor}} = \frac{1}{.20} = 5.0$$

$$\frac{\text{Multiplier} \times \text{Amount Capital}}{\text{Required Capital Ratio}} = \frac{5 \times \$80}{0.08} = \$5,000$$

These calculations are applicable to municipal bonds. In the case of residential mortgage loans, substitute 0.50 for 0.20 to arrive at multiplier of 2.

EARNING POWER PER $80 OF BANK CAPITAL

	Amount Assets Supported Per $80 of Bank Capital[1]	Gross Interest Income[2]	After-Tax Earnings[3]	Earnings as Percent Bank Capital[4]
U.S. Treasury Securities	$20,000[4]	$1,600	$240	300.0%
Municipal Bonds	$5,000	$360	$90	112.5%
Interbank Claims	$5,000	$400	$60	75.0%
Residential Mortgages	$2,000	$200	$30	37.5%
Business Loans	$1,000	$110	$16.50	20.6%

[1] The amounts indicated are based on an assumed 8% required capital and use the risk-adjusted weights embodied in recently enacted capital adequacy requirements as administered by the Federal Reserve. This requirement calls for a zero percent weight for U.S. Treasury securities, a 20% weight for general obligation municipal bonds and interbank claims, a 50% weight for residential mortgages, and a 100% weight for business loans.

[2] Interest rates assumed are 8.0% for U.S. Treasuries, 7.2% on municipal bonds, 8.0% on interbank claims, 10.0% on mortgages, and 11.0% on business loans.

[3] After-tax earnings assume a 75% gross expense ratio and a 40% effective tax rate. This leaves 15% of gross interest income as after-tax earnings, except in the case of municipal bond interest income, where after-tax earnings represent 25% of gross interest.

[4] While the asset category U.S. Treasury securities carries a zero percent weight, we assume a 5% weight and a multiple of 20 in calculating the total amount that can be supported by a given amount of bank capital.

IS THERE AN OPTIMAL EARNINGS GENERATING ASSET MIX?

This question can be answered when we consider operating risks and operating constraints faced by banks. If we can work with the constraint that no single asset category can represent more than 25% of assets, and that interbank claims are further restricted to 10% of assets, we have the following asset allocation: U.S. Treasury securities 25%, residential mortgages 25%, municipal bonds 25%, loans 15%. The weighted earnings as percent of capital funds will be calculated as follows:

$$(300 \times .25) + (112.5 \times .25) + (37.5 \times .25)$$

$$+(75 \times .10) + (20.6 \times .15) = 123.090\%$$

In a 1991 study the New York Federal Reserve Bank reported on the declining market share of U.S. banks in commercial lending to domestic firms.* The comparison of U.S. banks and banks from five other countries demonstrated that in the period 1984–1989, changes in market share of U.S. commercial lending conformed closely with bank cost of capital (Exhibit 9.17). In the period reviewed, Japanese banks almost tripled their banking market share while enjoying the lowest cost

---

* Zimmer, Steven R., and Robert N. McCauley, "Bank Cost of Capital and International Competitiveness," FRBNY *Quarterly Review.* (Winter 1991).

EXHIBIT 9.16   **U.K. and Other Banks Tap into Low Cost Source of Capital—the U.S. Preferred Stock Market**

British banks, constantly on the prowl for new capital, have found a new source of supply in the U.S. preferred share market. In the five-month period ending November 1989 British and other non-U.S. banks have raised close to $1 billion in capital funds in the U.S. preferred stock market. The cost of capital has been approximately half of that for new equity (common stock).

Despite their low cost, the preferred shares rank on a par with equity as Tier I or core capital under the rules of the Basle Accord. This market for preferred shares was born out of an exception made to the Basle rules when they were formulated. Banking supervisors agreed to extend the definition of Tier I capital to include preferred shares, provided they were permanent and their dividends could be interrupted like dividends on common

shares. The shares were known as noncumulative permanent preferred. The exception was made largely to accommodate U.S. banks that are heavy users of preferred shares. A U.S. corporation is responsible for making the substantial payment. The receiving corporate investor enjoys a dividend exclusion, which is built into the U.S. tax structure to minimize double taxation of intercorporate dividends.

A $184 million preferred issue by Barclays provides for a gross dividend of 10.875% (see table), equivalent to a net cost of 8.156%, roughly half of Barclays' cost of equity capital. Since the Barclays issue, other banks such as Allied Irish, Midland, and Royal Bank of Scotland have issued preferred shares in the United States or have developed plans to do so.

ISSUES OF U.S. DOLLAR PREFERENCE SHARES BY NON-U.S. BANKS

Issuer	Amount ($ mill)	Gross Dividend	Lead Bank Manager	Co-Lead
Barclays Series A	316	11.12	Shearson	Merrill Goldman
Barclays Series B	184	10.875	Merrill Lynch	Shearson Goldman
Allied Irish Banks	180	11.875	Merrill Lynch	None
Royal Bank of Scotland	200	11.25	Merrill Lynch	Shearson
Westpac	100	12.000	Merrill Lynch	Shearson PruBache

Filed with SEC	Amount ($ mill)	Advisor		
Midland	500	Merrill		
Barclays	500	n/a		

SOURCE: *Financial Times,* November 7, 1989, p. 31.

capital. American and U.K. banks lost market share and experienced the highest cost of capital. In between were Swiss, German, and Canadian banks, whose changes in market share appeared to vary inversely with cost of capital.

In a subsequent analysis the FRBNY study noted that foreign banks gained even more market share in the standby letter of credit (SLC) market than in commercial lending. In the standby letter of credit market a bank sells a contract to pay a maturing obligation of a company or municipal government unit in the event the issuer fails to pay. In 1985 U.S. banks wrote an estimated one-third of the standby letters of credit backing U.S. commercial paper, but only 7% in 1989. By contrast Japanese banks raised their market share from 18% in 1985 to 42% in 1989. The FRBNY report observes that the Japanese banks' cost of equity advantage helped raise their market share.

The study further notes that U.S. banks have withdrawn from foreign lending. Over the period 1983–1989 the U.S. bank share of cross border loans to nonbanks fell from 28% to 17%.* This trend extended beyond 1989.

---

* FRBNY, page 34.

EXHIBIT 9.17	**Change in Market Share in Commercial Lending to Firms in the United States, 1984–1989, and Cost of Capital for U.S. Loans**

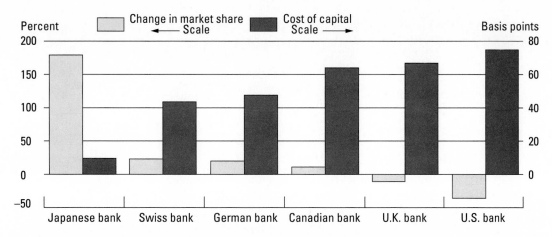

NOTE: Cost of capital bars show weighted average of the required spread for branch and subsidiary: commercial loans, where weights reflect shares of commercial loans booked in branches and subsidiaries by each country's banks in 1989.

Sources: Frbny Quarterly Review, (Winter) 1991, 54 and Federal Financial Institutions Examination Council. *Reports of Condition* as analyzed by George Budzeika. "Competitiveness in Commercial Lending in the United States," Federal Reserve Bank of New York working paper, appendix.

Cost of Capital

Return required on capital or bank funds, as determined by the capital market.

Defining and Measuring Bank Cost of Capital   We define the cost of capital for banks as the net spread between bank borrowing and lending rates that a financial product must generate to increase the market value of the bank. In an earlier section we described the risk-based capital standards agreed to under the Basle Accord. An international standard on bank capital places a limit on the bank's ability to use leverage. Therefore the stock market determines a bank's cost of capital, giving a valuation to earnings adjusted for any risk premium considered necessary.

This definition of cost of capital differs from cost of capital applied to industrial corporations. First, bank cost of equity is crucially important; banks employ considerably more leverage than industrial corporations, and this leverage imposes a heavy burden on the need to earn a satisfactory return on capital. Second, with international capital standards applicable, the equity required is a determined quantity. While regulators may set minimum equity levels, the market largely determines the cost of the equity.

Bank managers must issue new equity that is sufficient to support new loans, providing that the market value of outstanding shares can be maintained. The return on new equity needed to support increased loans must be as high as the profit rate on the bank's outstanding equity. The appropriate profit rate is after-tax earnings divided by market value of equity.

Price-Earnings Multiple

Ratio of price of bank common stock to earnings per share of common stock.

If the stock market assigns a bank a share price that is 25 times earnings (price-earnings multiple), the bank management would have to impose a minimum loan profit of 4% on the equity allocated to this loan (obtained by dividing 25 into 1). This is equivalent to a 16 basis point after-tax return (using a 4% Tier 1 equity amount).

$$\text{After Tax Return} = \%\ \text{Equity Capital} \times \text{Profit Rate Required}$$

$$= .04 \times 4\%$$

$$= .16\ (16\ \text{basis points})$$

EXHIBIT 9.18	**Relative Size of Financial Product, Allocated Equity, and Gross and Net Spreads**

Balance Sheet (dollars):

Loan	$1,000
Equity	40

Profit Statement (basis points):

Gross Spread	50[1]
Net Pretax Spread	26.7
Net After-Tax Spread	16[2]

Costs and Returns:

Return on Equity	4%[3]
PE Multiple	25

[1] Amount required to cover operating costs and taxes and to leave adequate after-tax return.

[2] Assume tax rate of 40%. This leaves $1.60 per $1,000 of loan or 4% relative to equity.

[3] Use 1/PE = return on equity.

If taxes take 40% of earnings, the bank requires a pretax net spread of 26.7 basis points.[†]

$$\text{Pretax Net Spread} = \frac{\text{Basis Points Required of after-Tax Return}}{(1 - \text{Tax Rate})}$$

$$= \frac{16}{.60}$$

$$= 26.7 \text{ basis points}$$

Cost of Equity   How does the bank cost of capital relate to the cost of equity? We can see this clearly in Exhibit 9.18. The return on a financial product (e.g., bank loan) must cover the required profit rate on the equity allocated to support this product. This return is equivalent to the long-term profit rate of the bank. Current profit rates can be used as proxies for long-term profit rates, understanding that profit levels may be growing over time subject to cyclical influences, and that at times a bank can become undercapitalized. When a bank is undercapitalized, cost of equity is likely to be overstated. For example, if a bank's equity level is below international capital standards, the bank must either reduce assets or issue new equity shares. In either case there will be reduced earnings (with fewer assets) or dilution of shareholder earnings as new shares are issued. Current earnings of the undercapitalized bank will overstate cost of equity (the ratio of profits to equity will be relatively high due to the depressed total in the equity part of the balance sheet).

Certain problems emerge when we attempt to compare reported bank profits across countries. These issues relate to use of different accounting practices and the existence of different economic conditions. The FRBNY study makes four adjustments to the reported profits of banks in six countries to arrive at comparable cost of equity estimates:

1. adjustment for differential treatment of developing country debt,

---

[†] The gross spread on the loan must cover expenses (labor and capital costs, loan default losses, and other expenses). The net after tax spread needed to generate the required equity return is the bank's cost of capital for the loan.

2. adjustment to impose equity accounting on shares held by Japanese and German banks,

3. adjustment for interaction of growth and inflation with bank net nominal asset positions, and

4. adjustment for discrepancies between stated depreciation and economic depreciation.

U.S. banks experience the only sizeable upward adjustment relative to developing country debt. German and Japanese banks experience a sizeable adjustment (upward) for share cross holdings. Banks in all countries experience a downward adjustment to cost of equity relative to their depreciation practices and inflation-related adjustments.

COST OF CAPITAL FOR FINANCIAL PRODUCTS

The preceding discussion suggests a two-step procedure for bank managers in "pricing" individual financial products.

1. Estimate cost of equity.
2. Calculate spread or fee required on the financial product to cover equity costs. (Equity costs relate to Tier 1 capital under the Basle Accord. In addition it is necessary to cover Tier 2 capital costs that are not included here for purposes of keeping the discussion uncomplicated).

The Basle Agreement sets the risk weight on corporate loans at 100%,* and the required shareholder equity at 4% of loan amount. The bank manager must estimate the spread required. To estimate the spread, the following information is needed.

Information	Assumed Value
1) Cost of equity	12%
2) Percent equity required	4%
3) Basle risk weight	100% (corporate loan)
4) Corporate income tax rate	34%

The spread charged must be sufficient so that the bank covers the required return on equity after tax. Using the values indicated above we have:

$$\text{Spread} \times (1 - \text{Tax Rate}) = \text{Cost of Equity} \times \text{Risk Weight} \times \% \text{ Equity Required}$$

$$S \times (1-T) = 12 \times 1 \times .04$$

$$S = \frac{.48}{.66}$$

The required spread for the corporate loan is 0.727 percent, or 72.7 basis points.[†]

The FRBNY study considers the spread or fee required to cover cost of equity for three different financial products: a standard corporate loan, a commitment to lend (extending beyond one year), and a ten year dollar interest rate swap. The estimates published in the Federal Reserve Bank of New York study are presented

---

* By comparison, the Basle Agreement sets the risk weight on commitments to lend at 50%, and on interest rate swaps at 5% of notional amount plus 100% of positive market-to-market value.

† Determination of the cost of capital may be more complex. This factor is because inflation may influence the real after-tax return earned by equity.

EXHIBIT 9.19   **Spread or Fee Required to Cover Cost of Equity**

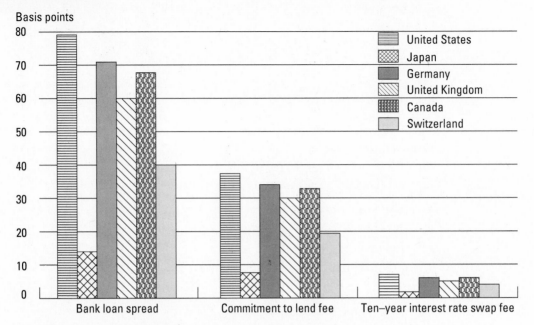

Source: Federal Reserve Bank of New York staff estimates.
Note: Interest rate swap fee should be compared with one–half of swap spread as quoted in the market.
Source: FRBNY Quarterly Review, (Winter 1991) : 47.

in Exhibit 9.19 . There is substantial variation across countries. U.S., Canadian, or U.K. banks need net spreads of 60–80 basis points. Japanese banks need net spreads somewhat above 10 basis points. These spreads are net of all expenses. The required fees on a commitment to lend generally follow that on spreads for corporate loans. U.S., U.K., and Canadian banks require considerably higher net fees than Japanese banks.

The required annual net fee on interest rate swaps should be considered. This fee is between 5 and 10 basis points for banks in the United States, United Kingdom, and Canada, which means they may not be able to earn enough on swaps to cover the cost of equity (Tier 1).

INTERNATIONAL DIFFERENCES IN BANK COST OF CAPITAL

In general, international differences in bank cost of capital appear to be consistent with country differences in household savings levels, macroeconomic stability, and relations among banks and corporations.

Low equity costs for Japanese banks is related to the national policy of smoothing economic growth. Until 1991 Japan was more successful than other leading industrial economies in achieving steady growth. Japanese banks are heavily exposed to equity prices and benefit in particular from an effective stabilization policy.

Higher household savings (for example, in Japan and Germany) and lower household access to bank credit tend to lower equity costs. While the mobility of capital across national borders has integrated financial markets, equity markets remain relatively segmented. This factor permits differences in national savings to influence the valuation of equity income streams somewhat differently on a country-to-country basis.

Close links operate in Germany and Japan between bankers and business borrowers. Industrial organization in Germany and Japan can lower risk premiums on debt of industrial firms, and simultaneously permit higher leverage than could take place in the United States or United Kingdom. The mix of debt and equity claims banks have on customers in Germany and Japan may spread risks and facilitate information flow. Close links with corporations have served Japanese banks well. Reciprocal shareholdings may facilitate lower capital costs for Japanese banks.

SUMMARY

Cross border banking takes several organizational formats including correspondent banks, foreign branches and agencies, and other types of offices overseas (representative offices and subsidiaries).

National banking systems differ from one another in many respects. These differences include the range of activities permitted banks and government policies toward entry of foreign banking institutions. Governments can follow a policy of reciprocity or national treatment in their relationships with other countries whose banks seek to establish offices in their jurisdiction. In the case of national treatment, foreign investors are extended the rights of national (domestic) investors.

U.S. banks have used foreign branches as their key organizational format in developing overseas representation. Other organizational formats used include the Edge Act corporation, subsidiary banks, and representative offices.

Rapid growth of foreign banking in the United States in the 1970s led to enactment of legislation to regulate this activity. The International Banking Act of 1978 sought to equalize the competitive position of foreign banks operating in the United States with American banks. Foreign banks were given national treatment.

The Basle Accord of 1988 sought to establish uniform bank capital requirements for international banks. This agreement was motivated by the need to lower the risk profile of banks, to equalize competitive position, and to remove disincentives for banks to hold low risk assets (government securities).

Since 1988 increased investment banking activities of banks have caused regulators to consider additional measures to ensure that bank risk exposures are not excessive, and that banks are implementing appropriate internal controls. Changes in market share of U.S. commercial lending conform closely with bank cost of capital. When compared with banks from six leading countries, banks with high cost of capital were the most susceptible to market share loss. Given the high cost of capital, banks must charge (earn) high net profit spreads on the various financial products they provide.

APPENDIX

"THE POLITICS OF POWER: THE INFLUENCE OF GERMANY'S BIG BANKS."
THE FINANCIAL TIMES, (JULY 20, 1989): 17

Deutsche Bank, Dresdner Bank, and Commerzbank all own huge equity stakes in the country's best-known companies, particularly in retailing and building. And as befits Germany's most powerful financial institution, Deutsche Bank holds the pearl—a 28% share in Daimler-Benz, Germany's biggest industrial group (Exhibit 9.20).

EXHIBIT 9.20	**West German Industrial Stakes**	
Bank	**Stake In**	**Size %**
DEUTSCHE BANK		
(directly)	Daimler Benz	28.24%
	Philipp Holzmann	30.00%
	Karstadt	25.08%
	Klockner	
	Humboldt-Deutz	40.00%
	Sudzucker	23.05%
	Fiat	2.50%
(indirectly)	Metallgesellschaft	10.90%
	Horten	18.75%
DRESDNER BANK		
(directly)	Brau und Brunnen	27.20%
	Heidelberger Zement	25.10%
(indirectly)	Bilfinger and Berger	25.00%
	Metallgesellschaft	23.10%
COMMERZBANK		
(directly)	Karstadt	25.00%
(indirectly)	Heidelberger	
	Druckmaschinen	25.00%
	Hochtief	25.00%
	Horten	6.25%
	Linotype	25.00%

Some bankers claim relations with businesses are now less intimate than in the past. The "Hausbank" relationship that manacled a corporation to one bank has loosened as companies have become more liquid, have diversified their borrowing, and have turned more to securitized instruments.

The European Community's new Second Banking Directive will require EC banks with holdings of outside companies to adopt two important new criteria in assessing their stakes.

1. No single participation in a company can exceed 15% of a bank's shareholder funds.
2. A bank's total equity stakes must not be worth more than 60% of its shareholders' funds.

On the face of it, Deutsche Bank, owner of the most glittering portfolio, will be most affected. The market value of its stakes in quoted companies in which it had a 20% share or more amounted to DM 9.2 billion at the end of 1988, equivalent to about 40% of its current share price.

While the new EC directive may not be causing German bankers any sleepless nights, the growing domestic debate over the banks' "power" has started to rankle. Dozens of politicians are taking aim at the big banks. Few are more critical than the Liberal Free Democrats (FDP). According to the FDP, equity participation should be limited to 15%. The socialist SPD wants a 5% ceiling.

The SPD has also called for limits on the number of supervisory board posts leading bankers may hold. It wants individual members of a bank's managing board to be limited to five supervisory board posts at nonassociated companies. That ratio would hit Deutsche Bank particularly hard; its 12 management board members share just under 100 supervisory board jobs between them. The Federated Cartel Office shares this concern and wants representatives from a bank to be barred from sitting on the supervisory boards of companies that compete with one another.

According to Wolfgang Roller, chief executive of Dresdner Bank and the current president of the German Banker's Federation, only 114 of the 1,446 supervisory board seats on Germany's biggest companies are occupied by private sector bankers. Mr. Herrhausen, chief executive of Deutsche Bank said that there are only 86 cases of industrial stakes where the banks hold more than 10% of the shares.

The banks emphasize that many of their industrial stakes are the legacy of earlier rescue packages, where debt was converted into equity.

REVIEW QUESTIONS

1. Explain how international financial problems led international banks to adopt new initiatives. Give examples.
2. How did the development and expansion of international banking differ in the decades of the 1960s, 1970s, and 1980s? Is it likely that a similar pattern will prevail in the 1990s?
3. In what ways does 24-hour operation of financial markets affect international banks, borrowers, and investors?
4. What is private banking, and why might it prove to be an avenue for international expansion for banks in the future?
5. Over the period 1956–1986 the composition of the top 100 banks around the world changed. How did it change? Why did these changes take place?
6. What is the importance of correspondent banking internationally?
7. Compare and contrast national treatment and sovereignty as a means of facilitating or permitting cross border banking.
8. How does universal banking compare with the U.S. model of banking?
9. Outline the advantages and disadvantages of the following formats used in cross border banking:

   representative office   consortium banking   international banking facility
   overseas branch   merchant bank
   Edge Act Corporation
10. Describe the importance of overseas branches as a means for U.S. banks to expand internationally.
11. How important is foreign banking in the United States? Are there significant differences between the strategies used by foreign banks from different countries in expanding in the United States?
12. What was the reason for enactment of the International Banking Act of 1978?
13. Why is capital adequacy important?
14. What is the Basle Accord? What are the likely implications of the Basle Accord?
15. An international bank has the following assets: central government securities $136 million, mortgage loans on residences $540 million, business loans $621 million, and interbank claims $149 million. The same bank has the following capital: common stock $25 million, retained earnings $17 million, cumulative preferred stock $10 million, general loan loss reserves $12 million, and subordinated debt $5 million.
    a. Calculate the bank's risk-weighted assets.
    b. Calculate the bank's total capital to total assets ratio, according to the Basle risk weighted assets method.

16. Explain how each of the following might influence the cost of bank capital in Helgoland.
    a. The personal savings rate shifts up.
    b. The government initiates a new fiscal policy mix that lowers the amplitude of business cycles.
    c. The government institutes an insurance program for bank deposits.
    d. New rulings concerning corporate governance allow banks to join "industrial groups" in which share cross holdings are permitted.

17. The stock market assigns a European bank a share price 15 times earnings. The tax rate on bank profits is 35%. Tier 1 capital requirements are standard. What is the bank's cost of capital?

18. A Japanese bank is negotiating a corporate loan with a Canadian borrower. The cost of equity is 9%, Tier 1 capital is standard, the Basle risk weight is 100%, and the corporate income tax rate on banks is 34%. What is the required spread?

SELECTED BIBLIOGRAPHY

Bank for International Settlements, *Annual Reports,* Basle.

Baker, James C. *International Bank Regulation.* New York: Praeger, 1978.

Baker, James C., and M. G. Bradford. *American Banks Abroad: Edge Act Companies and Multinational Banking.* New York: Praeger, 1974.

Bardos, Jeffrey. "The Risk-Based Capital Agreement: A Further Step Towards Policy Convergence." *Quarterly Review,* Federal Reserve Bank of New York, (Winter 1987–1988).

Board of Governors of Federal Reserve System, *Rush Based Capital Guidelines,* Regulations H and Y, December 7, 8, 15, 1994.

Curtis, Carole, and James C. Baker. "The Evolution of the Edge Act: Regulation and Operations of Edge Act Banks." *Journal of World Trade Law,* Vol. 21, (December 1987). Comptroller of the Currency. *Foreign Acquisition of U.S. Banks,* Washington, D.C., 1981.

DeLong, Gayle L. "The Challenge of Operating under a Foreign Regulatory System." *The Banker's Magazine,* (November-December 1992). "International Banking Survey." *The Economist,* (April 10, 1993).

Financial Times, German Banking and Finance, Supplement, (May 29, 1996).

Hultman, C.W., and I. Vertinsky. "Choice of Entry Timing and Scale by Foreign Banks in Japan and Korea." *Journal of Banking and Finance,* (April 1992).

Kambhu, John, Frank Keane, and Catherine Benadon. "Price Risk Intermediation in the Over the Counter Derivatives Markets." *Economic Policy Review,* Federal Reserve Bank of New York, (April 1996): 1–16.

Key, Sydney J. "Mutual Recognition: Integration of the Financial Sector in the European Community." *Federal Reserve Bulletin,* (September 1989).

Kuprianov, Anatoli. "Derivatives Debacles: Case Study of Large Losses in Derivatives Market." Federal Reserve Bank of Richmond *Economic Quarterly,* (Fall 1995).

Lamfalussy, A. "Globalization of Financial Markets: Supervisory and Regulatory Issues." Federal Reserve Bank of Kansas City, *Economic Review,* (January 1988).

Lees, Francis A. *International Banking and Finance.* New York: Macmillan, 1974.

Lewis, Alfred. *EU and US Banking in the 1990s.* London: Academic Press, 1996.

Molyneux, P., and J. Thornton. "Determinants of European Bank Profitability: A Note." *Journal of Banking and Finance,* (December 1992).

Quinn, Brian Scott. *The New Euromarkets.* New York: Halsted-Wiley, 1975.

Rochet, Jean-Charles. "Capital Requirements and the Behavior of Commercial Banks." *European Economic Review,* (June 1992).

Rivera, Luis Eduardo. "The Influence of Multinational Bank Entry on Net Interest Margins—Case Study Spain." Paper presented at meeting of Eastern Economic Association, March 1992, New York.

Rose, Peter S. *Japanese Banking and Investments in the United States: An Assessment of Their Impact upon U.S. Markets and Institutions.* New York: Quorom Books, 1991.

Sesit, Michael. "Banks Seek to Curtail Growing Risks in Settling Foreign Exchange Trades." *Wall Street Journal,* (March 15, 1995): 5A.

Seth, Rama. "Profitability of Foreign Banks in the United States." *Federal Reserve Bank of New York Research Paper,* December 1992.

Walmsley, Julian. *The New Financial Instruments.* New York: Wiley, 1988.

Waters, Richard. "Putting Back the Trust into Bankers Trust." *Financial Times,* (May 3, 1996): 19.

CHAPTER 10

Financing Foreign Trade

INTRODUCTION

Continued growth of the world economy since 1988 pushed the volume of world exports to a new level of $4,908 billion in 1995. According to the *IMF Economic Outlook 1996,* in the period 1988–1995, the average annual growth rate of the world economy was 3.05%, and the average annual growth rate of world exports and imports was 6.90%. The growth of international trade during this period was attributed to the increased volume of trade among all countries. While industrial countries reduced their shares of trade from 70% to 66.6%, the developing countries increased their shares from 30% to 33.4%.

Foreign trade as "an engine of economic growth"
Economic growth of a nation is primarily stimulated by exports that generate trade surplus that in turn stimulates domestic production, investment, employment, and economic growth.

Every nation is concerned with expanding trade via favorable terms on trade finance. First, national governments are concerned with financing foreign trade because rising levels of exports and imports generate jobs and income. For this reason many countries consider foreign trade as "an engine of economic growth." International trade (imports and exports) accounted for about 40% of the GDP in the United Kingdom, 47% in West Germany, 16% in Japan, and 16% in the United States. Government policies that assist and encourage foreign trade will be discussed later in this chapter. Second, in the private sector exporters are concerned with being paid by foreign buyers. They must actively control production costs, the risk of shipment to the foreign market places, and manage profit positions. Third, under conditions of free trade, consumers benefit from having a wider choice of products at lower prices. Methods of financing imports influence the importer's decision on what to import, what country to import from, and how to import goods to best meet domestic demand. Fourth, trade financing is an important activity for international banking. Traditionally trade financing and foreign exchange have been the major activities of international banking. But recent changes in trade patterns, the economic environment, and trade financing methods compel bankers to look for new ways and instruments to generate profits. Even a national central bank has to consider the impact of its monetary policy on interest rates, the value of its national currency, and the nation's international trade position.

This chapter analyzes foreign trade financing from a practical standpoint. The first section examines risks in foreign trade related to trade financing. The second section discusses traditional trade financing—letters of credit and the modern technology that has improved the efficiency of the letter of credit. The third section explains other trade financing methods—ranging from simple to complex—currently employed on a worldwide basis by importers and exporters. The fourth section reviews various types of institutions, private and official, that have been promoting and financing foreign trade, and that are key players in international trade. The final section discusses recent trends in international trade, sources of information on trade financing, and selection of trade financing strategies and methods to reduce costs and risks.

LEARNING OBJECTIVES IN THIS CHAPTER

1. To understand the common risks—geographic, foreign exchange, political, inflation and interest rate, market, and payment—in foreign trade of which all concerned parties should be aware.
2. To analyze the traditional foreign trade financing instruments—letters of credit—in detail, including modern "electronic letters of credit" technology.
3. To explain other foreign trade financing methods such as open account, consignment, factoring, forfaiting, countertrade, and international leasing as flexible tools for importers and exporters to meet their changing conditions.
4. To examine many important roles played by national and international institutions in promoting and financing foreign trade.
5. To collect and analyze relevant information on foreign trade in order to map out a strategy for minimizing costs and risks in the trade financing process including trade dispute settlement.

KEY TERMS AND CONCEPTS

- Confirmed Irrevocable Letter of Credit
- Countertrade
- Edge Act Corporation
- Factoring
- Forfaiting
- Real Profit Pricing
- Revolving Letter of Credit
- Revocable Letter of Credit
- Sight Draft
- Standby Letter of Credit
- Syndicated Lease
- Time Draft—Bankers Acceptance
- Trade Bloc

ACRONYMS

L/C	Letter of Credit	**EXIM-**	Export and Import
D/P	Document Against Payment Draft	**BANK**	Bank of the United States
		FCIA	Foreign Credit Insurance Association
D/S	Days After Sight		
D/A	Document Against Acceptance Draft	**PEFCO**	Private Export Funding Corporation
ICC	International Chamber of Commerce	**CCC**	Commodity Credit Corporation

OPIC	Overseas Private Investment Corporation	**COFACE**	Compagnie Francaise pour L'Assurance du Commerce Exterieur
ECGD	The U.K. Export Credit Guarantee Department	**BFCE**	Banque Francaise pour le Commerce Exterieur
MITI	Japan's Ministry of International Trade and Industry	**AKA**	Ausfuhr Kredit
		KFW	Kreditanstalt fur Wiederaufbau
IFC	International Finance Corporation	**IDA**	International Development Agency
EXIM	Export-Import Bank of Japan	**FCS**	Foreign Commercial Service
GATT	General Agreement on Tariffs and Trade	**WTO**	World Trade Organization

Risks in Foreign Trade

Foreign trade is the movement of goods, but also encompasses flows of service and capital between trading partners and financial institutions. Given that different countries have their own government regulations, currencies, cultures, and languages, there are problems and risks in international trade. Importers and exporters as well as financial institutions participating in trade financing must recognize and deal with these risks. The risks are not mutually exclusive. For example, the lack of communication between buyer and seller in different countries may result in ignorance of the foreign market, where the seller may sell his or her product at an incorrect price. A sudden change in political relations between two countries may be detrimental to the interests of importers and exporters. Exporters may face restrictions on shipping merchandise to importers in another country, even though they previously signed binding contracts. Importers also may experience difficulties in making payments to sellers in another country, due to their government's imposition of foreign exchange controls. A comprehensive analysis of risks must include:

- Geographic risk
- Foreign exchange risk
- Political risk
- Inflation and interest rate risk
- Market risk
- Payment risk

GEOGRAPHIC RISK

A common problem confronting foreign traders is geographic or distance risk. This risk occurs in the transportation of goods by sea, land or air. Shipment by sea requires a long period of time with risks such as spoilage, fire, collision, and delay due to weather. Shipment by land may be more convenient but still may involve risk related to different transportation systems and customs regulations. Shipment by air is faster but costlier. Modern shipping methods such as use of containers, air freight, and train cargo economize on transportation costs, but there are residual risks. Fortunately, many risks such as fire, storm, spoilage, water damage, and labor strikes are insurable. In addition to transportation problems, miscommunications between buyer and seller in different countries can also present problems. Incomplete information on the part of the importer or exporter may lead to misunderstandings. For these reasons foreign traders and financial institutions must be aware of the risks associated with geographic location. Modern technology such as fax provides faster communication and exchange of information between importer and exporter than traditional letter writing methods. Thus geographic risk associated with miscommunication and incomplete information can be reduced.

FOREIGN EXCHANGE RISK

There may be less foreign exchange risk under a fixed exchange system than under a floating rate system. Nevertheless, fixed exchange rates change when balance of payments conditions warrant a change. Since 1973 under the floating exchange rate system, currency values are determined by supply and demand. Basically the supply and demand for a currency depends on the flow of imports and exports of the country, as well as the inflow and outflow of capital to and from that country. Both importer and exporter face foreign exchange risk. Fluctuations in currency value affect costs and profits of their transactions. Prices of imported raw materials may change if the exporter's currency appreciates or depreciates in comparison with the currency of the importer. Changes in raw materials prices affect the selling price and profit earned by the exporter, as well as the profit the importer could earn on the product.

In order to minimize the adverse effect of currency fluctuations, international traders may hedge their currency risk by purchasing forward contracts, or utilize other hedging techniques discussed in Chapter 5.

To avoid foreign exchange risk, many importers and exporters prefer to invoice the transaction with a currency of stable value, even if it is not their currency. Prior to World War II, traders preferred the British pound sterling because of its stability. The U.S. dollar has been popular in foreign trade financing in the postwar era. The Japanese yen and deutsche mark also have been used by international traders due to the relative stability of their values.

POLITICAL RISK

Political risk in foreign trade can take many forms. In severe cases such as war between nations, trade between belligerent countries is impossible. A revolution may temporarily halt a nation's foreign trade activities with other nations. Nationalization of banks by the government may shift trade financing from private commercial banks to government agencies. Foreign exchange and capital controls imposed by the British government in 1957 was a classic case, where trade financing demand shifted from the pound sterling to the U.S. dollar almost overnight.

Even under normal circumstances foreign traders face political risk when a country changes its trade policies on tariffs or quotas, restricts imports and exports, or imposes special taxes. There have been many special cases of political risk in foreign trade. In the 1930s most industrial countries adopted trade protection measures such as imposing trade restrictions and foreign exchange controls. The reduction in international trade in the 1930s was hampered not only to foreign traders, but also to the world economy. In the 1970s OPEC (Organization of Petroleum Exporting Countries) imposed a cartel price on oil that exerted profound effects on the structure of world trade.

INFLATION AND INTEREST RATE RISKS

Inflation can have favorable or unfavorable effects on the profitability of firms engaged in foreign trade. If inflation occurs in the exporting country, importers must determine how price changes of imported goods in home currency will influence the real profit margin. If inflation occurs in the importing country, the importer must price the imported goods according to the domestic price index plus a margin for profit. Otherwise the importer may end up with a loss. This procedure is called real profit pricing. Sometimes importers operating under an inflationary environment use an "inflation expectation" approach to mark up the price of merchandise. This practice can discourage consumer purchases, reinforce and at times accelerate inflationary expectations, and discourage foreign trade.

Real profit pricing

An exporter must price his or her product according to the domestic price index plus a margin for profit. This is intended to maintain a real profit margin, especially under inflation conditions.

Inflation also affects interest rates that in turn, affect the cost of financing foreign trade. According to the *U.N. World Economic Outlook 1988,* when inflation and high interest rates prevailed in the period 1980–1982, the value of world exports decreased from $1,989 billion to $1,830 billion.

MARKET RISK

Among the risks analyzed in this section, market risk can exert the most direct and immediate impacts on exporters and importers. Market risk normally refers to problems in relation to product, price, competition, and ultimate buyer acceptability. From an exporter's standpoint, considerable analysis may be required to market a product successfully in a foreign country. Testing the acceptability of new products in a competitive market requires a great deal of time. Export of high quality products may be affected adversely by counterfeit products in international markets. Even under normal circumstances exporters face the risk of importers rejecting a product, not because of product defects but purely due to sudden change in consumer demand. This change may force the importer to sell the product at a loss.

From an importer's standpoint, market risk is always present. It is necessary for the importer to select the right product at the right time, and to offer that product at a competitive price to meet consumer demand. Any unexpected developments along this process could adversely affect the importer's profit. Untimely arrival of goods ordered from foreign sources—direct or in transit—could affect merchandise marketability. Seasonable or perishable products are particularly vulnerable in the importer's market. Inferior foreign workmanship, improper style selection, or incorrect size of merchandise are typical problems often encountered in the importing business.

PAYMENT RISK

Exporters face payment risk under various circumstances. If the exporter ships the merchandise to an importer on a consignment basis, he or she will receive payment only after the importer sells the merchandise. The final amount will be based on market conditions. Even under a letter of credit the exporter may ship the merchandise and obtain the proceeds from discounting the draft from his (exporter's) bank. If the letter of credit (L/C) contains the "recourse" clause, the exporter still faces the payment risk should the exporter's bank not receive payment from the importer for one reason or another (for example, financial difficulty may prevent the importer from carrying out his or her contractual obligation). The government in the importing country can also be a source of payment risk to exporters. Pressed by balance of payments and foreign exchange problems, a government may block outward payments to foreigners. Exporters may not receive payment if their products are disapproved by the importers' government agencies (such as the U.S. Food and Drug Administration).

To a lesser extent, importers also face payment risk. Payments in advance present risks to importers if exporters do not comply with the terms of the contract. Under a letter of credit, the financing bank faces a payment risk. The importer's bank has the obligation to pay the exporter if the presentation of documents by the latter is in compliance with the terms of the L/C. If the importer refuses to pay because of defective merchandise, the paying bank cannot take title to the goods. To avoid this risk, many commercial banks have created trading companies that under law can take title to the goods.

To avoid payment risks, the exporter may arrange trade financing through "forfaiting" with the importer. This will be explained in detail later in this chapter under the section "other foreign trade financing".

Traditional Foreign Trade Financing: Letter of Credit

International trade risks are inevitable. International traders try to minimize or eliminate these risks. From a historical perspective the practical method that many international traders use for this purpose is the letter of credit (L/C). The most important function of the L/C is to give confidence to both exporter and importer through an impartial mechanism that commercial banks with international banking experience have developed. The letter of credit assures the exporter that a bank will make payment for goods shipped. It assures the importer that the exporter will not be paid unless the documentation submitted by the exporter conforms to the terms and conditions of the letter of credit. An L/C issued by a commercial bank with worldwide banking facilities solves the financing problem. In addition it assures that banks involved in the transaction will control the documents. The issuing and paying commercial banks perform various services for which they receive fees. Foreign trade financing by letter of credit is usually under the guidelines known as "Uniform Customs and Practice for Documentary Credits" issued by the International Chamber of Commerce (ICC) Publications No. 500 in May 1993.

THE FINANCING PROCESS

The basic purpose of international trade is for the exporter to get paid according to invoice values and for the importer to obtain the goods as ordered. To achieve this purpose several steps must be taken as shown in Exhibit 10.1.

Step 1   The importer and exporter must sign a contract agreeing on certain terms that include the kinds of merchandise, the quantity and quality required, the price of each kind or type, the method and time of shipment, the packing method, a list

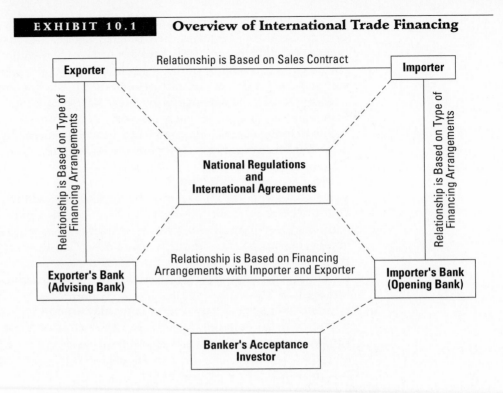

EXHIBIT 10.1   **Overview of International Trade Financing**

of size and specifications, and certificates of inspection or analysis. In some special cases certificate of origin is required, usually if goods are assembled or transhipped in a third country involved in the transaction.

Step 2   If trade financing by bank is preferred as in many cases, the importer has to apply for a letter of credit (L/C) from a commercial bank (opening bank). After checking the application and the credit standing of the importer, the commercial bank issues an L/C and sends it to the exporter (beneficiary) through an advising bank in the foreign country that is usually a correspondent bank or its own branch in that country.

Step 3   After receiving the L/C from the advising (exporter's) bank, the exporter is sure about the payment in accordance with the L/C, based on the signed contract with the importer. The exporter will ship the merchandise and present all required documents under the L/C to the advising bank. If it is a confirmed and irrevocable L/C, the exporter may get the proceeds, or discount the time draft from the advising bank for a fee. The advising bank then forwards all documents to the opening bank for examination against the L/C and for reimbursement.

Step 4   If the documents are in good order, the opening bank credits the advising bank. If it is a time draft, the importer's bank accepts the draft and guarantees to pay the presenter on maturity. This becomes a "banker's acceptance" that can be sold to investors in the money market.

Step 5   The importer's bank forwards all required documents to the importer as stipulated in the L/C with a debit note (for example, charges the importer's account the full amount plus commission).

Step 6   The importer takes the bill of lading to the shipping company, picks up the merchandise, and clears all imported merchandise at the custom.

Finally, all parties concerned must keep in mind national regulations and international agreements. For example, the importer must be aware of changes in tariffs and quotas, and the exporter must know what export licenses may be required. Banks should advise their customers about pertinent government regulations. Even investors that purchase banker's acceptances should understand the regulations governing this instrument, such as the maturity of banker's acceptance in the United States is limited to not more than six months or 180 days.

Types of Letters of Credit

Several types of letters of credit are commonly used in import and export financing. They are described as follows.

Confirmed Irrevocable Letter of Credit   The importer's bank issues this type of L/C, and a bank in the exporter's country confirms the L/C. The importer's bank irrevocably commits itself to pay against the exporter's draft, and the confirming bank (usually the advising bank) adds its commitment and assumes the responsibility to pay the exporter's draft if the presentation of the required documents is in good order. This type of letter of credit gives the exporter the greatest protection, with the commitment of two banks to make payment should one of the banks not honor the draft for any reason.

Unconfirmed Irrevocable Letter of Credit   This type of credit differs from the one just mentioned in one important aspect: the advising bank (the exporter's bank) is under no obligation to pay such a draft. Payment is the sole responsibility of the opening bank (the importer's bank).

Revocable letter of credit

The importer's bank may amend or cancel the letter of credit at any time without approval by the exporter (beneficiary).

Revolving letter of credit

One letter of credit to handle multiple shipments on a continuing basis instead of establishing an individual letter of credit for each shipment.

Revocable Letter of Credit   The importer's bank issues this type of credit, and the exporter's bank advises but may or may not add its confirmation of this L/C. The importer's bank may amend or cancel the credit at any time without approval by the exporter (beneficiary). Obviously this type of credit gives the exporter no protection prior to negotiation of his or her draft.

Revolving Letter of Credit   When an exporter and importer agree that goods will be shipped on a continuing basis, it may be desirable to establish one letter of credit to handle the multiple shipments, rather than to establish an individual letter of credit for each shipment. This type of credit is convenient and economical for both importer and exporter over an extended period of time.

Transferrable/Assignable Letter of Credit   Under this type of credit the beneficiary (exporter) may request the opening bank through the advising bank to make the credit available to one or more secondary beneficiaries up to the total value of the original credit instrument. This type of credit is issued mostly when the exporter acts as a middleman. Here the exporter can generate a profit, based on the difference between the original amount of the credit and the total amount he or she assigns to the secondary beneficiaries. In other cases the exporter may not have enough goods in supply to meet his or her credit requirements and must shift part of the order to other manufacturer(s). In any case, the advising bank and the opening bank must execute the negotiation of draft and documents on the basis of the original letter of credit.

Standby Letter of Credit   This type of credit does not typically involve direct purchase of goods or presentation of shipping documents. In international trade, especially when conducted by multinational corporations, the seller may prefer to ship the goods to the buyer in another country and to invoice on an open account basis. If the buyer fails to pay, the issuing bank (buyer's bank) will pay the seller. A seller or exporter pays the bank a small fee in return for the bank's promise to pay if the buyer or importer defaults on the obligation covered by the standby letter of credit. This type of credit instrument is also used for short-term borrowing. During a period of volatile economic conditions such as in the 1980s, many business firms issued commercial paper (C/P) and at the same time obtained standby L/Cs for two purposes. First, to strengthen the borrowers' credit standing in the C/P market, because the borrowings are backed by commercial banks. Second, to lower the cost of borrowing since the fee the borrower pays to the bank for a standby L/C is usually lower than the interest payment on the commercial paper without the backing of the standby L/C. For example, the borrower may pay only 10.5% instead of 12.0%. The reduction in interest of 1.5% will be more than sufficient to offset the bank's charge of 1% for the standby L/C. With certain conditions, commercial banks like to issue standby L/Cs, due to the fact that they increase income without being considered as direct lending by monetary authorities.

Standby letter of credit

A seller or exporter pays a fee to the bank in turn for the bank's promise to pay if the buyer or importer defaults on the obligation covered by the standby L/C.

IMPORT LETTER OF CREDIT

In foreign trade the most popular type of letter of credit is the irrevocable letter of credit. The import letter of credit is illustrated in Exhibits 10.1, 10.2 and 10.3. The procedures followed under an import L/C are essentially as follows.

Application for Letter of Credit   As shown in Exhibit 10.2, U.S. Importer Company in New York requests Citibank to open a letter of credit for H.K. Exporter Company, located in Hong Kong, in the amount of $1,000,000.00 covering a shipment of widgets from Hong Kong to New York. The draft will be paid at sight in New York. Upon receiving the application, the opening bank must examine it carefully and check the credit line and credit status of the applicant. If the application is consistent with national and international legal requirements and satisfactory to both sides, the importer and the opening bank sign an agreement to open an L/C.

Contents of a Letter of Credit   As shown in Exhibit 10.3, the import letter of credit contains all required information including: the names of the importer (account party) and exporter (beneficiary); place and date of issuance; the tenor of the draft (sight or time); name and address of advising bank; general description of merchandise; a list of documents that must accompany the draft; the maximum amount up to which the beneficiary may draw; the latest shipping date; the expiration of the credit; the type of credit (irrevocable or other); statement about charges such as ocean freight and insurance; and authorized signature of the issuing bank.

Advising Bank and Amendments   The advising bank may or may not add its confirmation to the credit depending on the request of the opening bank. After the

EXHIBIT 10.2	**Application for Letter of Credit**

Application and Agreement For Documentary Letter of Credit

Citibank, N.A. 111 Wall Street North American Trade Finance	16th Floor, New York, N.Y. 10005 Credit Number:

Advising Bank (Name and Address) Citibank, N.A. P.O. Box 18 Hong Kong, Hong Kong	Applicant (Name and Address) U.S. Importer Co., Ltd. Importer Street New York, N.Y. 11111
Beneficiary (Name and Address) H.K. Exporter Co., Ltd. Exporter Road Hong Kong, Hong Kong	Amount US$1,000,000.00 (in specific currency of Credit)
	Expiry Date and Place October 16, 19xx (for negotiation) Hong Kong

Subject to the following terms and conditions, please issue your Irrevocable Letter of Credit (hereinafter called the ''Credit'') to be available by the beneficiary's draft(s):

Drawn at ☒ Sight, ☐ _____ Days Sight, ☐ _____ Days Date, ☐ other _____ .

Drawn on ☒ Citibank, N.A. New York, N.Y. for __100__ % invoice cost.

Drawn on ☐ _____ for _____ % invoice cost.
    (Name and Address of paying bank if any).

Accompanied by the following documents which are indicated by an ''X''.

☒ Commercial Invoice(s) ___1___ original(s) and ___2___ copies.

☐ Customs Invoice(s) _____ original(s) and _____ copies.

☐ Insurance Policy and/or Certificate (to be effected by shipper, unless otherwise indicated below)

☐ Insurance to include: (list coverage) _____

☒ Transport Document: ☒ Marine, ☐ Multimodal, ☐ Air, ☐ Other (define) _____

  issued in full set consigned: ☐ to, or ☒ to the order of U.S. Importer Co., Ltd. _____

  marked Freight ☐ Collect or ☒ Paid and notify U.S. Importer Co., Ltd. Importer Street,
New York, N.Y. 11111 _____ Dated Latest: October 10, 19xx

☐ Other documents _____

Covering: Merchandise described in the invoice(s) as: (Brief Description)
  Widgets

Terms:

☐ FAS _____ , ☐ FOB _____ , ☒ CFR New York , ☐ CIF _____ .

☐ CPT _____ , ☐ CIP _____ , ☐ Other _____ .

Shipment from ____Hong Kong____ to ____New York____

For Multimodal Transport Document only:
Place of Receipt / Taking in Charge _____ Place of Final Destination _____

Partial Shipment ☐ Permitted, ☒ Prohibited   Transhipment ☐ Permitted, ☒ Prohibited

Draft(s) and documents must be presented to the negotiating or paying bank within __15__ days after the date of issuance of the Bill(s) of Lading or other shipping documents, but not later than the expiry date of the Credit.

☒ All banking charges other than issuing bank's charges are for account ☒ Beneficiary, ☐ Applicant.

☐ Negotiation fees are for account ☐ Beneficiary, ☐ Applicant.

☐ Discount charges are for account ☐ Beneficiary, ☐ Applicant.

☐ Acceptance fees are for account ☐ Beneficiary, ☐ Applicant.

☒ Insurance effected by the Applicant.

Attachments hereto impose additional terms and conditions on Applicant and/or Citibank and are incorporated into this Application and Agreement as if fully set forth herein.

Transmit the Credit through your correspondent, or directly to the beneficiary, or to: the Advising Bank

_____ , by ☐ Cable/Swift, ☒ Airmail, ☐ Courier Service, ☐ Pre-Advice by Cable/Swift.

All drafts and documents called for under the Credit are to be delivered by the negotiating or paying bank to Citibank, N.A., New York by Airmail in a single mailing.

Shipping documents for custom house entry are to be sent by you to Applicant

To induce the establishment of the Credit, Applicant agrees to the terms and conditions of the Agreement as set forth hereinafter.

SOURCE: Citibank N.A. Citicorp

EXHIBIT 10.3 **Import Letter of Credit**

Citibank, N.A.
North American Trade Finance
111 Wall Street
New York, New York 10005

September 16, 19xx

BENEFICIARY:

H.K. Exporter Co., Ltd.
Exporter Road
Hong Kong, Hong Kong

MAIL TO:

Citibank, N.A.
P.O. Box 18
Hong Kong, Hong Kong

Dear Sirs:

By order and for account of our client, U.S. Importer Co., Ltd., Importer Street, New York, N.Y. 11111, we hereby issued our Irrevocable Letter of Credit No.0000000 in your favor for an amount not to exceed the aggregate US$1,000,000.00 (One Million United States Dollars) available by your draft(s) at sight drawn on us for 100% invoice value marked "Drawn under Citibank, N.A. Letter of Credit No.0000000" accompanied by the following documents to be negotiated in Hong Kong on or before October 16, 19xx.

1. One original and two copies of commercial invoice stating that it covers widgets, CFR New York.
2. Full set clean on board ocean bills of lading evidencing shipment from Hong Kong to New York consigned to the order of and notify U.S. Importer Co., Ltd., Importer Street, New York, New York 11111, marked freight prepaid and dated not later than October 10, 19xx.

Partial shipment prohibited.　　　　　　Transshipment prohibited.
Insurance effected by the buyer.
All banking charges other than issuing bank's charges are for account of beneficiary.

Draft(s) and documents must be presented to negotiating or paying bank within 15 days after the date of issuance of the bill(s) of lading or other shipping documents but prior to expiry of the letter of credit.

We hereby engage with drawers and/or bona fide holders that drafts drawn and negotiated in conformity with the terms and conditions of this letter of credit will be duly honored on presentation. The amount of each draft drawn hereunder must be endorsed on the reverse side of this letter of credit by the negotiating bank.

Except as far as otherwise expressly stated, this credit is subject to the Uniform Customs and Practice for Documentary Credits (1993 Revision) International Chamber of Commerce Publication No. 500.

Very truly yours,

Signature
Authorized Signature

SPECIMEN

Source: Citibank N.A. Citicorp

advising bank delivers the irrevocable L/C to the beneficiary, the liability of the issuing bank to pay when the required documents are properly presented is established.

It is not unusual for the beneficiary to request that the buyer (importer) amend the letter of credit for certain reasons. These reasons can include provisions for delays due to bad weather or labor strikes, delay in shipment of the merchandise by the shipping firm, sudden changes in prices of raw materials or fuel used in the manufacturing process, or need to adjust the price of the final product. The buyer

---

EXHIBIT 10.4   **Sight Draft**

Item 160499 (SF 1468(L) Re.10-77)

Hong Kong, Hong Kong, October 1, 19 XX

1-8
210

At sight

PAY TO THE
ORDER OF H.K. Exporter Co., Ltd.

$ 1,000,000.00

One Million and 00/100 - **DOLLARS**

FOR VALUE RECEIVED AND CHARGE TO ACCOUNT OF CITIBANK LETTER OF CREDIT NO. 0000000

Citibank, N.A.
111 WALL STREET
NEW YORK, N. Y. 10043

SPECIMEN

Signature

H.K. Exporter Co., Ltd.

⑆0210⑈0008⑇ 03152325⑉

SOURCE: Citibank N.A. Citicorp

must authorize amendment of the L/C, and the issuing bank communicates this amendment to the beneficiary through the advising bank.

Presentation and Examination of Documents   After the exporter ships the goods, he or she presents all required documents with the draft to the advising bank that, except for a confirming credit, forwards all documents and the draft to the opening bank for payment. If the opening bank finds all required documents in good order, the amount of the sight draft (see Exhibit 10.4) is paid immediately to the advising bank for the exporter's account. If discrepancies occur between the documents and the L/C (for example, the bill of lading shows five cartons are broken), the opening bank must inform the buyer that corrective action must be taken before payment is made. Under this circumstance, the buyer usually communicates with the exporter to obtain a reasonable adjustment.

Payment and Refinancing   When the issuing bank finally pays the amount stipulated in the credit to the exporter, it charges the importer's account and sends the documents to the importer who will obtain the goods from the carrier as indicated in the bill of lading (see Exhibit 10.5). Should the importer not have sufficient funds on deposit in the opening bank, he or she may request the bank to make a loan to cover the entire amount using the newly received merchandise as collateral. The importer will pay back the bank with interest when the merchandise is sold.

EXPORT LETTER OF CREDIT

Procedurally, there is a difference between the import letter of credit and the export letter of credit. Upon the application of the importer, a commercial bank may issue a commercial letter of credit in favor of an exporter located abroad. This document is called an import letter of credit. The issuing bank carries the main responsibility for payment to the exporter in accordance with the terms in the credit. By contrast, a foreign bank issues an export letter of credit in favor of a domestic exporter for the account of an importer abroad (see Exhibit 10.6). In the export credit, the exporter's (seller's) bank performs the functions of advising, confirming, and negotiating the letter of credit and carries the main responsibility for payment to the exporter.

| EXHIBIT 10.5 | **Hypothetical Bill of Lading** |

BILL OF LADING

Shipper H.K. Exporter Co., Ltd. Hong Kong, Hong Kong		B/L No. HK 1
Consignee (if 'To Order' so indicate) To Order Of: U.S. Importer Co., Ltd.		
Notify Party (No claim shall attach for failure to notify) U.S. Importer Co., Ltd. Importer Street New York, N.Y. 11111	For delivery of goods please apply to:	
Place of receipt	**Port of loading** Hong Kong	
Ocean vessel/Voy. No. H.K. Maru/Voy.9		
Port of discharge New York	**Place of delivery**	

—Particulars furnished by shipper —

Container No. Seal No. Marks and Numbers	Number of Containers or packages	Kind of packages; description of goods	Gross weight	Measurement
USIC 1/500	500 Ctns	Widgets	25,000 Lbs	

SPECIMEN

* Total number of Containers or other packages or units received by the Carrier (in words)

Freight and charges	Prepaid	Collect	RECEIVED by the Carrier the Goods as specified above in apparent good order and condition unless otherwise stated, to be transported to such place as agreed, authorised or permitted herein and subject to all the terms and conditions appearing on the front and reverse of this Bill of Lading to which the Merchant agrees by accepting this Bill of Lading, and local privileges and customes notwithstanding.
	$1,000.00		This particulars given above as stated by the shipper and the weight, measure, quantity, condition, contents and value of the Goods are unknown to the Carrier.
			In WITNESS whereof one (1) original Bill of Lading has been signed if not otherwise stated above, the same being accomplished the other(s), if any, to be void. If required by the Carrier one (1) original Bill of Lading must be surrendered duly endorsed in exchange for the Goods or delivery order.
			Number of Original B/L (s)
Total: $1,000.00			Place and date of issue Hong Kong, September 28, 19xx
Freight payable at			Signed on behalf of the Carrier
LADEN ON BOARD THE VESSEL H.K.Maru/Voy.9 Date September 28, 19xx			
ORIGINAL			

SOURCE: Citibank N.A. Citicorp

The letter of credit and draft used both for import and export credits are essentially the same, depending on the terms used in the credit.

Export Letter of Credit   As Exhibit 10.6 illustrates, H.K. Importer Company, Ltd., Importer Road, Hong Kong arranges to purchase 10,000 television sets from U.S. Exporter Company, Ltd. in New York City. In accordance with the contract, both importer and exporter agree that the shipment will be financed by a letter of

EXHIBIT 10.6	Export Letter of Credit

Citibank, N.A.
North American Trade Finance
111 Wall Street
New York, New York 10005

September 16, 19xx

U.S. Exporter Co., Ltd.
Exporter Street
New York, New York 11111

Gentlemen:

We are instructed by Hong Kong Bank, Bank Road, Hong Kong, Hong Kong to advise you that it has opened its Irrevocable Letter of Credit No. 000000 in your favor for account of the H.K. Importer Co., Ltd., Importer Road, Hong Kong, Hong Kong for an amount not to exceed in the aggregate US$1,000,000.00 (One Million United States Dollars) available by your drafts at 90 days sight drawn on us for 100% invoice value marked "Drawn under Hong Kong Bank Letter of Credit No. 000000" to be accompanied by the following documents:

1. Commercial invoice in triplicate stating that it covers 10,000 television sets.

2. Full set clean on board ocean bills of lading evidencing shipment from New York to Hong Kong drawn to the order of the H.K. Importer Co., Ltd. notify H.K. Importer Co., Ltd. Importer Road, Hong Kong, Hong Kong marked freight prepaid and dated not later than November 30, 19xx.

3. Packing list.

Partial shipments prohibited.   Transshipment prohibited.

The above-named opener of the credit engages with you that each draft drawn under and in compliance with the terms and conditions of this letter of credit will be duly honored on delivery of documents specified above if presented at this office on or before December 31, 19xx.

Except as far as otherwise expressly stated, this credit is subject to the Uniform Customs and Practice for Documentary Credits (1993 Revision) International Chamber of Commerce Publication No. 500.

Kindly address all your correspondences to the attention of the Letter of Credit Department at the above mentioned address mentioning thereon specifically our Ref. No. 999999.

Very truly yours,

Authorized Signature

SPECIMEN

SOURCE: Citibank N.A. Citicorp

credit confirmed and payable at 90 days after sight in the amount of $1,000,000.00. H.K. Importer Company asks its bank, Hong Kong Bank, Hong Kong to open an irrevocable credit payable at Citibank, N.A., New York with credit confirmed by that bank. Upon receiving instruction from the Hong Kong Bank, Hong Kong, Citibank issues a confirmed irrevocable credit to the beneficiary, U.S. Exporter Company, Ltd.

| EXHIBIT 10.7 | Time Draft—Bankers Acceptance |

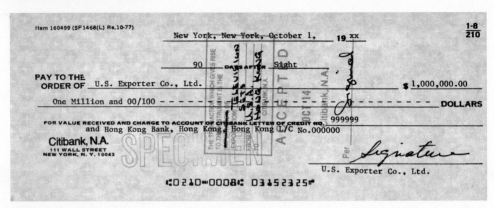

Source: Citibank N.A. Citicorp

Banker's Acceptance and Release of Documents   As soon as the U.S. Exporter Co. ships the goods, it presents the documents and the time draft to Citibank, N.A., New York for acceptance (not payable at sight). If Citibank finds the documents presented in good order, it accepts the time draft and an authorized officer signs it. This time draft becomes a banker's acceptance (see Exhibit 10.7) that is discounted by Citibank, crediting the proceeds to the U.S. Exporter Company, if the latter requests Citibank to do so. In this case, Citibank can petition the Federal Reserve Bank of New York for rediscount through the discount window at the current discount rate. In this process, the banker's acceptance is a money market instrument related to the central bank's monetary policy. If the U.S. exporter does not want its draft discounted, it can hold the accepted draft and present it to Citibank on maturity for payment of the face amount. More frequently, exporters choose to be paid the discounted amount at the time they present documents, and the draft is discounted.

> **Bankers acceptances** are negotiable instruments (time draft) drawn to finance export, import, and domestic shipments. The phrase comes from when a bank writes, the word "accepted" on the draft certifying its agreement to pay it at maturity.

Once Citibank accepts the time draft, it is a banker's acceptance with Citibank's guarantees to pay on maturity. Citibank immediately releases the documents to the H.K. Importer Company, Hong Kong through its opening bank, the Hong Kong Bank, Hong Kong. Citibank will debit the Hong Kong Bank's account at maturity for the face value of the draft plus commission.

MODERN TECHNOLOGY AND COMMERCIAL LETTERS OF CREDIT

Many large commercial banks have reorganized to improve their competitiveness in foreign trade financing. This reorganization includes establishment of Edge Act Corporations that can service all international banking and investment activities including foreign trade financing. Commercial banks have improved their efficiency in international trade financing with modern technology such as computers and telecommunications. For example Citibank has established a special affiliate, Citicorp Trade Services Ltd. (CTSL) that is a dedicated letter of credit (L/C) processing facility located in Hong Kong. CTSL is capable of providing L/C processing services for any Citibank branch worldwide. The growth of trade in the Far East and in trade between this region and other parts of the world, especially with the United States, necessitated the creation of this special unit. Customers in any geographic location are able to dial in to CTSL and transmit their application for letter of credit issuance or assignment. Issuance/assignment takes place automatically—with, of

> **Edge Act Corporations**
>
> These corporations are allowed under the Edge Act of 1919 to do international (not domestic) banking business such as trade financing, foreign exchange, and equity investment in foreign countries.

course, the necessary manual checking for control purposes—and the L/C is advised through the Citibank network to the beneficiary in the appropriate country. If required, advising can also be carried out via telex to other banks. This innovative "electronic letter of credit" is intended to reduce turnaround time, provide rapid transmission, reduce cost, increase control, improve back office operations, and increase interactive message capacity. It improves efficiency and reduces cost in processing the application for L/C. Nevertheless, the examination of required documents and payment to the exporter still remain the responsibility of the bank issuing the L/C.

Other Foreign Trade Financing

In addition to traditional foreign trade financing with letters of credit by commercial banks, there are many other financing methods that international traders commonly use. These methods are as follows.

PAYMENT IN ADVANCE

Payment in advance to the exporter could be made by the importer, the importer's bank, or the exporter's bank. In the first case, the importer pays for the goods at the time he or she places the order with the exporter. This method is used only when the importer's credit standing is unsatisfactory, or when the exporter has difficulty in raising capital to produce the goods ordered by the importer. In this case the importer assumes all risks. In the second case, usually at the request of the importer, the importer's bank makes payment to the exporter through the advising bank in accordance with the letter of credit. In the third case the exporter obtains funds from his or her bank upon presentation of documents evidencing shipment of the merchandise. In each case final settlement will depend on the importer bank's examination of all documents to ensure that the exporter has met his or her contractual obligation.

OPEN ACCOUNT

Selling on open account means selling on credit terms arranged between exporter and importer. Such an arrangement is extremely advantageous to the importer because it permits the importer to receive the goods and even to sell them before making payment. The exporter runs the risk that the importer may default. Legal procedures to collect under this method can prove difficult and expensive. For this reason open account settlements are used in cases where there are established relationships between sellers and buyers. Multinational corporation sales to foreign branches and affiliates as well as sales to high credit status buyers in stable business (German department store or Dutch food retail chain) are generally made on open account. Open account saves the two parties any fees that otherwise would be payable to banks under letter of credit, or documentary collection.

CONSIGNMENT

Under a consignment agreement the exporter ships the goods to the importer, but the exporter still retains the title of the goods until the importer has sold them and paid the exporter (consignor). The exporter finances his own products and runs considerable risk. This arrangement is usually made under the circumstances that either the exporter trusts the importer, or the marketability of the goods such as a new product is uncertain. Banks are reluctant to finance consignment, since laws in foreign countries make it difficult to enforce payment should the importer (consignee) default.

DOCUMENTARY DRAFT FOR COLLECTION

Under this arrangement, after shipping the merchandise to the importer the exporter presents a draft and documents to his or her bank. In turn the bank forwards documents to the importer's bank for collection. The exporter is guaranteed that payments will be made before the documents are released to the importer. Also, the importer is guaranteed that the documents are in order, and that they indicate the goods have been shipped in the designated manner. This form of payment is popular because it satisfies both exporter and importer; it is also less expensive than a letter of credit. Commercial banks servicing collections earn commissions and fees, even though they do not provide financing.

Documentary draft collections may take the form of a document against payment draft (D/P) or a document against acceptance draft (D/A). Under a D/P the exporter retains control of the goods until the importer pays. Under a D/A documents are delivered to the importer upon acceptance only. The importer obtains control of goods but is not required to pay until the maturity of the acceptance.

Uniform Rules for Collection were spelled out by ICC Publication No. 522 in 1995.

Factoring

An exporter sells his or her invoices to a factoring company at a discount on a with or without recourse basis. The factoring company will collect the face amount of the invoices from the importer.

Factoring   Factoring has been used in domestic trade financing for many years, and in recent years it has spread rapidly to many countries as a method of financing export sales. Factoring companies (many of them are bank owned) buy invoices from exporters at a discount. They can provide immediate cash up to 85% of the value of the exporters' invoices. The remaining amount, less a fee, is paid when the importer makes payment. The importer benefits from not having to deal with a draft or letter of credit. The exporter does not have to take the credit risk or currency risk. He does not have to wait for the overseas customer (importer) to pay. The service charge for export factoring is likely to be a little higher than domestic factoring. In order to obtain reliable credit information on foreign customers, export factors normally have good connections with foreign (local) factors on a reciprocal basis. Factoring is usually conducted under nonrecourse agreement with exporters.

FORFAITING

"Forfaiting" is a short- and medium-term trade financing technique used by financial institutions for facilitating exports from industrial countries to transitional and developing countries. Exporters can sell the promissory notes guaranteed by the importer's bank to forfaiters at a discount and without recourse.

This technique has developed since the 1960s when it was employed in trade between Western exporters—especially in West Germany, Italy, and Switzerland—and the Comecon countries in Eastern Europe. Forfaiting means that the purchase of trade obligations is due at some future date without recourse to any previous holder of the obligation. The word comes from the French *à forfait*—to forfait or surrender a right. Under a typical forfeiting arrangement, a forfaiter provides a source of finance to buyers in foreign countries and permits immediate payment to the exporter on nonrecourse terms. Basically the importer has to issue a promissory note, bill, or exchange that a bank in his or her country has endorsed (guaranteed or "aval"). The exporter sells the promissory note to a bank (the forfaiting bank) at a

EXHIBIT 10.8	**Basic Forfaiting**

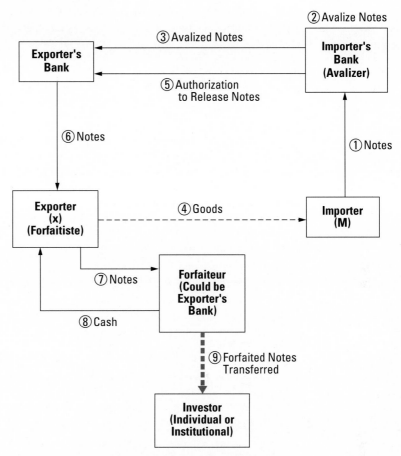

Courtesy of Professor James C. Baker, Kent State University

discount normally based on the prevailing interest rate. The forfaiter carries all political and commercial risk (see Exhibits 10.8 and 10.9).

The technique is particularly appropriate to medium-term financing of capital goods. It has helped stimulate foreign trade in Eastern Europe and in many developing countries in Asia and Latin America.

Conceptually, financing exports by forfaiting is similar to financing export with the banker's acceptance. Both methods are designed to provide payments to exporters and sources of finance for importers. However, there are many differences between these methods. First, under the banker's acceptance agreement, the accepting bank endorses the bill of exchange and pays the exporter cash by selling the bill as a money market instrument. The bank guarantees payment to the holder. The exporter is still bound to pursue a defaulting customer (for example, an Eastern European importer), and can still be held liable for the debt by the purchaser of the bill. In forfaiting, the exporter is not responsible for the bill once it is sold.

Second, in a free market economy such as the United States, a bank can present banker's acceptances to the central bank, such as the Federal Reserve Bank, as collateral for rediscount. In forfaiting, only private sector financial institutions take

---

EXHIBIT 10.9 **Hungarian International Bank's Forfaiting Techniques**

Hungarian International Bank entered the forfaiting market in London in 1974. In recent months it is integrating its specialist forfaiting service into a more holistic trade finance package designed to offer a more comprehensive package for exporters.

Innovatively, Hungarian International Bank is now offering clients a package that combines not only the traditional forfaiting of trade paper at fixed rates, but also preshipment finance to fund production. This financing can involve HIB providing an exporter with funds during the manufacturing period secured by the exporter assigning an irrevocable letter of credit opened by the importer to HIB.

In a way the process involves the bringing forward of the forfaiting transaction in terms of fund provision from the time when payments may normally be made on a stage basis after delivery of goods. Aside from the cash flow advantages that the overall preshipment and postshipment package offers to the exporter, it also puts the latter in a position to offer its client 100% finance terms at the outset compared with an up-front deposit and subsequent stage payments requested of the same potential client by a competitor.

In a similar innovative mode, HIB is now recommending appropriate foreign exchange funding to access the lowest available interest rates allied with foreign exchange rate guarantees to convert the received funds into the currency of the exporter's choice. The bank now offers exporters fixed rate, nonrecourse funding at the most appropriate rate with a locked in foreign exchange rate guarantee.

SOURCE: *Financial Times*, June (1, 1989), Export Finance 6 and 7.

---

part in the export-import financing process, and there is no lender of last resort. The forfaiter can either hold the instruments until maturity and collect the debt, or resell the instrument into a secondary market.

Third, forfaiters must be concerned when interest rates are rising, since their profits rely on their investment portfolios that consist mainly of fixed-interest forfait notes and bills of exchange. Rising interest rates mean less profit for the forfaiters.

In recent years, forfaiting has been used not only in Europe but also in Asia and the United States. For example, the sale of electrical turbines to Mexico financed through, Eximbank, which required 15% in down payment. A forfait house in the United States financed the down payment in cash through forfaiting. So the Mexican importer was able to finance 100% of the transaction.

COUNTERTRADE

Countertrade

Countertrade generally refers to barter trade, counterpurchases, buyback agreements, and switch trade that can be flexibly used by traders in different countries for avoiding tariffs and quotas, and possibly can conserve foreign exchange.

The concept of countertrade is based primarily on the ancient practice of barter. It has developed into a sophisticated branch of trade finance. Countertrade may take different forms, but the most popular types are barter trade, counterpurchase, buyback agreements, and switch trade. One example of barter trade was Saudi Arabia's payment for ten Boeing jumbo jets with $1 billion worth of oil in 1984. At present, counterpurchase is the most widely used of all countertrade techniques. This popularity is due to the fact that it helps many developed countries sell their high value product or capital goods. Developing countries that want to conserve foreign exchange and develop an industrial infrastructure welcome counterpurchase as a method of trade finance.

The arrangement made in 1989 between Tunisia and a group of automobile makers is a case in point. The deal involved car suppliers—including Peugeot and

Volkswagen—agreeing to purchase Tunisian made electronic and mechanical components. Tunisia saved foreign exchange and also benefited from the car suppliers' obligation to source technical product from it. Hopefully this agreement will have a favorable long-term effect on Tunisia's industrial base.

The classic example of buy-back agreements was the deal made by Western European companies and Russia in the early 1980s. Under this agreement, Western European companies supplied plant, equipment, technology, and technical assistance to Soviet Russia to build a gas pipeline. In turn Russia promised to ship gas to these countries at agreed prices after the project was completed.

Switch trade involves the transfer of a bilateral surplus to a third party. For instance, Colombia bought oil from Libya and paid for it in dollars. In turn, Colombia used its trade surplus of coffee with Hungary and therefore made dollar funds available to Libya. Some specialist countertraders located in London and Vienna assist importers and exporters from many countries in arranging this type of trade transaction.

Countertrade has been used by European, Asian, and Latin American firms, but it raises some questions on international regulations and obligations. The General Agreement on Tariffs and Trade (GATT) opposes this type of transaction on the grounds that it is used to circumvent GATT provisions, especially those dealing with nondiscriminatory trading practices, tariffs, and quotas. The IMF also has expressed its dissatisfaction with countertrade because this option (for example, barter trade) may help some debtor countries avoid making foreign exchange payments due to the IMF in accordance with original borrowing commitments.

INTERNATIONAL LEASING

International leasing has been considered important in developing countries because it can reduce foreign exchange outflows for imports of expensive capital goods, reduce balance of payments deficits, and introduce new technology to the national economy. Capital equipment including aircraft, ships, buses, and trucks can be leased from foreign leasing firms, thus avoiding the expenses of trade financing and immediate expenditure of foreign exchange. Many international banks and overseas subsidiaries of national leasing companies assist importing countries to structure the more complicated types of leasing. These types include operating, financial, and leveraged leases, all commonly used in domestic situations. The lessors, such as banks, usually enjoy tax advantages in their own countries (United States, United Kingdom, and Japan), since their respective governments encourage exports. For example, IBM has leased computers to firms in foreign countries (cross-border operating lease); GE has leased equipment to Asian countries (financing lease); the Australian airline, Quantas, has obtained aircraft from the combined financing efforts of Japanese banks, U.K. banks, and Australian companies (syndicated or leveraged lease).

Syndicated lease

Two or more international banks jointly purchase the equipment (such as an aircraft) from an exporter and lease to a user in another country.

Institutions Promoting and Financing Foreign Trade

In general, institutions promoting and financing foreign trade can be classified into four groups: private institutions, U.S. official agencies, foreign countries' official agencies, and world organizations.

Private Institutions

Business Corporations, Trade Associations, and Other Concerned Parties
Business corporations advertise their products in domestic and international magazines and periodicals. They inform customers how to order and finance their products in export channels. They also directly participate in foreign trade fairs. Trade associations normally represent their respective industries, promoting international trade and trade financing.

Commercial Banks

Commercial banks constitute the backbone of foreign trade financing. Commercial banks provide virtually all types of trade financing, ranging from letters of credit to countertrade. Large international banks such as Citicorp, Barclay's Bank, Mitsubishi Bank, and Deutsche Bank have comprehensive worldwide networks and strategies for dealing with international trade. Modern technology including telecommunications and computers has helped them to handle the increasing volume and complex problems encountered in trade financing. They provide specialist personnel to assist firms in the growing, competitive, and profitable trade financing world. To cope with the rapidly changing environment and growing volume of international trade (for example, increasing trade with ex-Communist countries, newly industrialized nations, and the European Uniform Market in 1992), many large commercial banks have established special units to service international trade needs such as trade service groups and trading companies that can take title to goods. Collectively, commercial banks in the United States have formed a national association to promote foreign trade. This is the Bankers' Association for Foreign Trade in the United States that holds an annual conference to discuss trade issues. Interested persons from business, academic, and government circles are invited to attend. Some large commercial banks even send specialists to their overseas branches as a way to train their local branch personnel as well as local traders who want to update their modern trade financing knowledge.

International Chamber of Commerce

This organization was founded in 1919. It acts to promote greater freedom of world trade, to harmonize and facilitate business and trade practices, and to represent the business community at the international level. It has a membership from more than 75 countries with its head office in Paris, and operates international offices in many major cities such as New York, Tokyo, and Vienna. The most important service that the ICC renders concerns the rules governing international trade credit. Its *Uniform Customs and Practice for Documentary Credit* is the "bible" for commercial banks in financing foreign trade—the issuance of letters of credit, examination of documents, negotiation of drafts, and foreign collections. The ICC also runs seminars on topics relating to international commerce and operates a court of arbitration.

U.S. Official Agencies

U.S. Department of Commerce   The U.S. Department of Commerce is vigorously promoting, but not financing, U.S. foreign trade mainly through its Trade Information Center, especially through its monthly publication of *Business America*.

The Export-Import Bank of the United States   The Export-Import Bank (Eximbank) is a corporation wholly owned by the U.S. government. It was created in 1934 by presidential executive order. The bank was established on a statutory basis in 1945 with the passage of the Export-Import Bank Act, and its charter has been renewed periodically.

The bank has three major functions: 1) provide direct loans to exporters and importers, 2) offer assistance to commercial banks and other financial institutions that are supporting export sales, and 3) provide export credit insurance and guarantees. The Eximbank's support for short-term (up to 180 days) export sales rests exclusively with the export insurance program that it operates jointly with the Foreign Credit Insurance Association (FCIA) that includes about 50 leading American insurance companies. FCIA was founded in 1961 and provides short-and medium-term policies covering commercial and political risks. Insurance coverage is provided for up to 90% to 100% of the exporter's or lender's credit exposure.

Closely associated with the Eximbank in some of its direct loan operations is the Private Export Funding Corporation (PEFCO). PEFCO was established in 1970 on the initiative of the Bankers' Association for Foreign Trade and is a private company owned by U.S. commercial banks and some industrial corporations. It extends medium- and long-term loans to finance foreign purchases of goods and services produced or originating from the United States such as power plants, aircraft, industrial installations, and railroad equipment. All PEFCO loans are unconditionally guaranteed by Eximbank on both principal and interest.

Commodity Credit Corporation   The Commodity Credit Corporation (CCC) is under the administration of the U.S. Department of Agriculture. It conducts four programs in connection with foreign trade. 1) Dollar financing is generally up to 12 months, sometimes up to 36 months. 2) Sales of surplus agricultural commodities may be paid for by foreign importers in local currencies. 3) Sales of surplus commodities may be under long-term contracts. 4) Barter transactions can be used. Goods eligible for financing under these programs must come from private stocks of surplus agricultural commodities in accordance with the list of commodities announced by the CCC on a monthly basis. All sales under the programs are made through private U.S. exporters.

Overseas Private Investment Corporation (OPIC)   OPIC was formed in 1971 and is wholly owned by the U.S. Department of Treasury with the objective of assisting U.S. private equity and loan investment in friendly developing countries. Its programs also promote world trade, since U.S. private investment abroad involves U.S. exports of capital goods, especially in cases of project financing in those countries. OPIC provides investment guarantee programs covering inconvertibility of currency, expropriation of property, and other political risks such as war and revolution. It charges relatively low fees for this insurance coverage.

Foreign Countries' Official Agencies

Over the past 70 years, many countries have established government agencies to stimulate and facilitate international trade. The major purpose of these agencies is to assist exports as a means of gaining domestic employment and earning foreign exchange. Some of the well-known official agencies in foreign countries are described briefly as follows.

United Kingdom The U.K. Export Credit Guarantee Department (ECGD), formed in 1919, offers a variety of trade financing services and credit insurance to any national export credit organization, including credit support to commercial banks. The credit term can be up to 12 years. ECGD provides broad coverage to exporters and lending banks for up to 95% of both political and commercial risk, including insurance against exchange risk.

France In 1946 France established the Compagnie Francaise pour l'Assurance du Commerce Exterieur (COFACE), which provides exporter credit insurance for commercial and political risks up to 90%. It also provides insurance against exchange and inflation risks. Another government agency, the Banque Francaise pour le Commerce Exterieur (BFCE) plays a central role in mobilizing necessary trade financing. It provides export credit and refinancing up to ten years. It discounts bills of exchange based on rediscounting at the bank of France.

Federal Republic of Germany In 1952 West Germany formed the Ausfuhrkredit (AKA) that is a consortium of German commercial banks, providing medium- and long-term export financing. AKA operates a special rediscount facility provided by the Bundesbank. Another government agency, the KFW (Kreditanstalt fur Wiederaufbau) provides funds at cheap rates to finance exports to developing countries. In 1962 the West German government commissioned two private firms, Hermes and Treuarbeit, to provide export credit insurance. Hermes also provides financing for exporters during the manufacturing period and insurance against foreign exchange risk.

Japan The Export-Import Bank of Japan (EXIM) modeled after its namesake in the United States was formed in 1952. It is the principal agency to finance Japanese exports. Its objective is to promote Japanese exports by supplementing and encouraging commercial bank financing. In the past few years, EXIM also has provided financing for imports in response to a large balance of payments surplus and need for domestic economic development. For export insurance covering commercial and political risks, the Export Insurance Division of the Ministry of International Trade and Industry (MITI) provides low-cost financing, and guarantee and exchange risk insurance.

In addition to the major trading countries, many other developed countries such as Italy, Holland, and the newly industrialized countries (South Korea and Taiwan) have established official agencies to finance and insure exports. Many developing and communist countries have also formed export agencies or state trading companies to strengthen their international trade financing positions.

World Organizations

World organizations that have indirectly helped international trade financing include the International Monetary Fund (IMF) and the International Bank for Reconstruction and Development (World Bank). The IMF was established in 1944. One of its responsibilities is to work toward the stabilization of exchange rates of member country currencies. Also, it extends loans to member nations, if they have a "temporary payments disequilibrium." These institutions definitely help the credit standing of member nations. Further, they encourage trade financing for the countries concerned. The World Bank was formed in 1945, and its major function is to finance the economic development requirements of member developing countries. It provides built-in export financing, where goods are imported for infrastructure projects. The World Bank also has cofinanced loans with government official credit agencies and commercial banks, covering imports of equipment needed in development projects such as power facilities.

Two other organizations belonging to the World Bank group play supplemental roles in financing the economic growth of developing nations. One is the International Development Agency, which makes low-interest, long-term loans to the poorest nations. IDA participates in the cofinancing of projects with government export credit agencies and private financial institutions similar to that of the World Bank. Exports related to these projects can receive trade financing. Another organization is the International Finance Corporation (IFC) that makes direct investments and loans to "productive private enterprises" in developing countries. These private businesses may use IFC financing for new ventures and resource exploration that stimulate international trade.

The establishment of World Trade Organization (WTO) in 1995 was designed to promote world trade and to improve trade dispute settlements. These will be discussed in a later section.

Minimizing Risks and Costs in Foreign Trade Financing

Like any business, international trade has its risk dimensions. In some respects it can be more risky than domestic business. Profitability of international trade depends on the costs involved. These costs are difficult to predict due to the fact that each transaction may have different risks and financing methods. However, international traders look for ways to reduce risks and costs in the short run as well as in the long run. The following steps are important to exporters and importers for achieving these objectives.

ANALYSIS OF CURRENT AND FUTURE TRENDS IN INTERNATIONAL TRADE

Analysis of current trends in international trade helps traders understand the patterns and trends. Traders must anticipate what products will be in demand among nations, and how these products can be best financed. For example, during the 1970s petroleum was the key product in international trade. Petrodollar recycling through large international commercial banks was a special phenomenon affecting trade financing. This situation changed in the 1980s. Economic recession in the industrial countries in 1980–1982 brought a reduced demand for oil. In the same period many developing countries that had borrowed heavily during the 1970s experienced difficulty in servicing their debts to commercial banks.

In the period 1983–1990 the pattern of trade and finance changed. The United States incurred major trade deficits, while Japan, West Germany, and Taiwan became trade surplus countries. The economic prosperity in the United States during most of the 1980s not only led to increased imports, but also stimulated world trade. In this period, Japan and West Germany became key suppliers of funds in international trade financing.

The ultimate purpose of current analysis is to look for opportunities for profit in international trade. Another purpose is to avoid any possible pitfalls in trade financing. There are many publications that help international traders to understand the current trends in trade. Statistics published by foreign trade journals, the U.S. Department of Commerce, and the *U.N. Monthly Bulletin of Statistics* as well as the *OECD Monthly Statistics* present the trends in international trade with regard to countries, products, regional trade, volume, prices, and terms of trade. Details concerning government policies on tariffs and trade financing can be obtained from many trade journals.

It is difficult to predict future trends in foreign trade due to the complexities involved. However, there are many sources of information that give certain clues to future activities in international trade. For example, the liberal political and economic movements in the Communist countries in the late 1980s has encouraged the growth of East-West trade in the 1990s. The planned European Uniform Market in 1992 has prompted many multinational firms and international traders to map out their strategies based on this new initiative toward European economic integration. The problems of a large debt service burden facing many developing countries will continue to reduce their capacity to import in the near future, but there are new opportunities for trade expansion in the newly industrialized countries (NICs). Many of those nations, such as South Korea and Taiwan, are trade-oriented economies. The globalization of international financial markets in the 1980s will help to promote mobilization of international capital. This trend will continue to facilitate trade financing in the 1990s. Those active in foreign trade will make use of publications by WTO, IMF, UN, OECD, and regional development banks, as well as trade banking and other specialized subject journals to obtain valuable information on future trends in international trade and trade financing.

ANALYSIS OF AVAILABLE INFORMATION ON GOODS TO BE IMPORTED AND EXPORTED

While analysis of current and future trends in international trade is helpful to foreign traders in charting their present and future courses of action, exporters and importers can have very specific information needs. For traders interested in the free-market economies, foreign trade, and trade financing information on countries, products for import and export, general price levels and price trends in those products, and regulations governing their import and export can be obtained from various sources. These sources include the trader's customers, the trader's overseas affiliates, the trader's own trade association, and foreign embassies and consulates. Information provided by customers and trade associations is useful but may not be adequate due to the competitive position of the customers who are in the same line of business. Information on trade provided by foreign consulates may tend to promote home country products rather than the real needs of the trader. Information provided by the trader's overseas affiliates will be oriented toward the trader's needs but may not be comprehensive on a global basis.

Valuable information on trade and trade financing may be obtained on a fee basis from large international, commercial banks that have world-banking networks. Banks collect and compile this information from formal and informal sources in foreign countries in which their branches and subsidiaries are located. The personal contacts and long-time observations of bank officers in various trading centers make this type of information highly valuable to importers and exporters, whom the banks are eager to serve. Special analyses published in magazines and newspapers such as *East West Trade, Business America, Financial Times, Euromoney, Asian Finance,* the *New York Times,* and the *Wall Street Journal* also provide valuable information on innovative methods of trade financing.

The U.S. Department of Commerce also provides practical and comprehensive trade and trade financing information. Their country-by-country analyses are contained in a regular monthly publication called *Overseas Business Conditions.* This publication describes the opportunities and risks in each respective country. The broad picture of international trade—especially the comparative analysis of bloc trading, state trading, trade protection, and trade discrimination and dumping—is provided by international organizations such as WTO and IMF.

CONSIDERATIONS FOR MINIMIZING COSTS AND RISKS IN TRADE FINANCING

Trade bloc

Trade blocs such as European Community (EC) and North American Free Trade Agreement (NAFTA) are generally designed to protect (through a common external tariff) their internal trade from countries outside the blocs.

Exporters and importers must develop a broad perspective on international trade and trade financing, and an understanding of the risks and financing techniques available to them. International traders must analyze, evaluate, and compare the hard facts to arrive at their final decisions on trade and trade financing. The following discussion outlines approaches to minimizing costs and risks, as depicted in Exhibit 10.10.

Regulations in Countries of Exporters and Importers   Exporters and importers need to be aware of the country risks on both sides because these risks affect costs and profits. Broadly speaking, country risk analysis involves: political risks such as changes in governments and policies; economic risks such as changes in economic conditions and balance of payments position; financial risks such as changes in interest rates and foreign exchange rates; and social risks such as civil disturbances. Exporters must be concerned with export regulations such as the export tax (see Exhibit 10.11), export insurance, financing institutions, final payments, and changing foreign exchange rates. Fluctuations in the value of the importer's currency may force the exporter to insist on using a stable currency for payment of goods (for example, a Japanese exporter may ship goods to Mexico, but may insist on settling the payment in U.S. dollars in the United States). Country risks can also affect importers' costs and profits. Social unrest and labor strikes in either country can delay arrival of the merchandise, thus affecting the price of the product. At times importers prefer to change suppliers, shifting from one country to another in order to avoid certain risks and reduce insurance costs.

Goods and Costs in Trade   International traders aim at utilizing competitive advantages to the fullest extent possible. To generate profits in a highly competitive world, traders must be aware of basic conditions and trends in trade financing: the nature of goods to be traded, supply and demand conditions for specific goods traded in international markets, market structures (such as monopoly, oligopoly, free competition), and the availability of specialized financing institutions. To minimize costs and risks, exporters may use various strategies. For example, GE leased nuclear reactors to Nigeria in the 1970s through its own export credit arrangements. GM sold buses to Brazil financed by a factoring firm of a bank that knew the credit status of exporter and importer. To circumvent an importing country's high tariffs, a multinational corporation may establish a factory in the importer's country. Also

EXHIBIT 10.10	**Major Elements in Consideration of Minimizing Risks and Costs in Foreign Trade Financing**

Regulation and Country of Exporter	Regulation and Country Importer	Goods and Costs in Trade	Risks and Insurance	Methods of Financing	International Regulations Institutions for Financing Foreign Trade
Developed Countries 7 Major Industrial Countries	Developed Countries 7 Major Industrial Countries	Manufacturers Capital Consumer	Transportation	Letter of Credit (L/C)	Private Commercial Banks Finance Companies Factoring Firms Edge Act Corporations
Others	Others	Primary Products Agricultural Minerals	Political	Payment in Advance	Government Credit Agencies
Newly Industrialized Countries	Newly Industrialized Countries	Fuel Oil Nonoil	Commercial	Open Account	International Financial Institutions IMF, World Bank IDA IFC Regional Development Banks (Financing Alternatives, Quality Services, and Guarantees)
Developing Countries Fuel Exporters	Developing Countries Fuel Importers	Others (Comparative Advantage Analysis and Economies of Scale)	Foreign Exchange	Consignment	
Nonfuel Exporters	Nonfuel Importers		Inflation Interest Rates	Collection	
Centrally Planned Economies Eastern Europe	Centrally Planned Economies Eastern Europe		Natural Fire Storm Flood Earthquake	Factoring	
Russian Federation China Others (Country Risk Analysis)	Russian Federation China Others (Country Risk Analysis)		Insurance Private Government	Countertrading	
			(Risk Management)	Forfaiting Cross-border Leasing (Analysis of Financing Costs and Payments Risks)	

the MNC can use open account for facilitating the trading of goods between its overseas affiliates.

Importers can also employ different techniques to handle trade financing of merchandise on a low-risk and low-cost basis. For example, in the case of importing capital goods under project financing in a developing nation, the host country

| EXHIBIT 10.11 | **Export Taxes and Agriculture** |

Export taxes are commonly used in agriculture because traditional taxes on income and profit are difficult to administer in this sector. In principle, land taxes are an attractive alternative. Where land is in fixed supply, a land tax is collected from economic rent and leaves production decisions unchanged. However, with a few exceptions such as Ethiopia, Kenya, Paraguay, Peru, and Somalia, land taxes generate less than 1 or 2% of total revenue. The low yield reflects the inadequacy of land registration and valuation. In many African countries and the Pacific Islands it is difficult to establish ownership because land tenure is based on customary arrangements. In other countries rural land transactions are infrequent. This infrequency restricts the use of market prices to determine the value of land. There are limitations on the use of presumptive measures to link land values to the productivity of land, because data on land quality and the variations in productivity between seasons are generally inadequate.

Some export taxes are implicit and result, for example, from the price-setting activities of marketing boards such as the Cocoa Board in Ghana and the Agricultural Development and Marketing Corporation in Malawi. These boards act as distributor and exporter for a few important smallholder crops and usually set farmgate prices below border prices, thereby implicitly taxing smallholders.

Evidence on the level of taxation suggests that in some countries producers of agricultural exports may be overtaxed. If export taxes substitute for income taxes, it is possible to compute a rate of tax on exports that will generate the same amount of revenue as a tax on the smallholder's income. A simple calculation for a typical cocoa farmer in Ghana in the early 1980s reveals that an export tax of 4% of the farmgate price would have yielded as much revenue as if the farmer's profits had been subject to income tax. The prevailing export tax was more than 100%. That suggests to the extent export taxes are substituted for income taxes, rates could have been reduced substantially. If used as a tax to capture excess profits, the export tax would be only 12%.

More importantly, export taxes create an incentive to shift production to other crops. Given the ample empirical evidence that smallholders respond to prices, the economic costs of export taxes are likely to be substantial. Where feasible, presumptive taxes on agricultural income may be preferable as in Uruguay.

Other arguments favoring export taxes include the desire to manipulate the terms of trade and the need for revenue. The former should be treated with caution.

Inelasticity of world demand in the short run can lead quickly to loss of markets in the long run because of changes in both world demand and supply. This situation happened to Ghana and Nigeria's world market share of cocoa and to Nigeria's and Zaire's share of palm oil in 1961–1963. The need for revenue cannot be ignored in the short run given the large budget deficits in many countries, especially if there is a case for export taxes as access or proxy user charge. In the long run extending broadly based commodity and income taxes to include the agricultural sector is necessary to reduce and eventually eliminate agricultural export taxes.

may attain favorable support from the World Bank and national credit agencies (see Exhibit 10.12). Importers of consumer goods generally look for alternative sources of supply and evaluate the competitive advantage. A revolving letter of credit may lower the costs of multiple shipments. Oil shipment may require more documents (such as certificates of origin, inspection, and chemical analysis) and consortium financing by a group of commercial banks. The U.S. Department of Agriculture and the Food and Drug Administration must carefully inspect and approve imports of agricultural products to the United States. This requirement usually involves deferred payment, subject to the respective government agency's approval.

Risks and Insurance Risk management is a complex and specialized subject. International traders must consult with their private and government insurance agencies regarding risks inherent in the shipment of goods and the costs of insur-

---

EXHIBIT 10.12   **Recycling Japan's Funds**

In 1987 the Japanese government pledged to recycle payment surpluses up to $30 billion in the form of completely untied public and private funds to developing countries in two tranches of $10 and $20 billion, respectively.

The first tranche consists of three parts: the creation of the Japan Special Fund of about $2 billion in the World Bank; the Japanese government lending to the IMF of 3 billion SDR; and the Japanese government's $2.6 billion contribution to IDA-8* and $1.3 billion contribution to the Asian Development Fund. The Japan Special Fund will comprise grants of ¥30 billion primarily for technical assistance in connection with World Bank-supported projects and programs, as well as for cofinancing World Bank-supported sectoral and structural adjustment loans. The fund also provides for expanded access to World Bank borrowings in the Japanese capital market, in an amount of ¥300 billion (a total of about $2 billion) to be spread over three years.

The second tranche was provided to the developing countries during a three-year period ending in 1990. Of this $20 billion, about $8 billion represents additional fund raising of the World Bank in the Tokyo market in accordance with the agreement between the Japanese government and the World Bank; the establishment of the Japan

Special Fund for the Asian Development Bank and the Inter-American Development Bank similar to that already established in the World Bank; and contributions to multilateral development banks. More than $9 billion represents expanded cofinancing in support of developing countries adjustment programs. The institutions backing this cofinancing with the World Bank and other multilateral development banks include the Export-Import Bank of Japan, the Overseas Economic Cooperation Fund (OECF), and Japanese commercial banks. Additional OECF direct loans may be provided for these programs. The remaining $3 billion is for expanded direct loans to the developing countries through the untied-loan scheme of the Export-Import Bank of Japan.

Finally, Japan also intends to advance by at least two years its target to double its official development assistance (ODA) to developing countries under its Third Medium-Term ODA Expansion Program and to have ODA disbursements exceed $7.6 billion in 1990. In 1986 Japan's ODA rose to $5.6 billion. Japan replaced France as the second largest provider of ODA after the United States. Japan has traditionally extended much of its aid to developing countries in Asia, but in recent years has increased its grants to Sub-Saharan Africa.

---

* IDA-8 refers to the eighth replenishment of funds to the International Development Association, an affiliate of the World Bank. This replenishment is provided by two dozen donor countries.

ance. In general, insurance covering export of capital goods can be covered by government agencies, as discussed previously. Private insurance generally covers consumer products. High-risk products such as chemicals involve large insurance premiums. If the terms of the trade are C.I.F. (cost, insurance and freight included in the price quoted), the exporter takes full responsibility for the shipment until the importer receives the goods from the carrier. If the terms are F.O.B (free on board), the importer takes full responsibility for the shipment after the exporter delivers the goods to the ship "on board."

METHODS OF FINANCING

In previous sections we examined various methods of financing. Here we analyze the comparative financing costs and payment risks associated with these methods. Letters of credit have been an important instrument in foreign trade financing for a long time and will remain important in the future. The major advantages of the L/C are that the issuing bank reduces risks for both importer and exporter. Exhibit 10.13

EXHIBIT 10.13	**Major Risks and Risk Reduction Measures in Foreign Trade**		
Risk	**1. Credit Risk**	**2. Currency Risk**	**3. Country Risk**
DEFINITION	Inability or unwillingness of buyer to make payment	Change in foreign exchange rate that is adverse to exporter or importer.	Political or economic development in importer's country that causes permanent or temporary delay in payments to seller.
RISK-REDUCING MEASURE	a. Use letter of credit b. Obtain cash deposit c. Obtain export credit insurance cover	a. Employ forward hedge currency b. Use futures on options market c. Invoice in own currency d. Contractual provision*	a. Have L/C confirmed b. Obtain export credit insurance cover

* Price adjusted, based on stipulated change in currency rate.

outlines the nature of these risks and some of the more frequently used risk reducing measures. Moreover, with financial backing and trade expertise on a worldwide basis, a L/C issued by a large commercial bank will facilitate large international trade transactions. A possible disadvantage is the higher financing cost and at times delays in the processing of documents. On the other hand, modern technology has helped reduce the costs and expedite the payment process. At present the L/C is more popular in Asia and Latin America than in Europe. Financing costs would be lower if collections and open accounts were employed. Forfaiting is relatively safe and efficient, but the cost (discount on draft) depends on interest rates in the money market. This method is particularly popular in Eastern and Western Europe where financial and trading systems are different. Forfaiting has become a more sophisticated trade financing instrument (Exhibit 10.9). Countertrade is an innovative trade financing method due to its flexibility. It fits into complicated situations such as trade restrictions or lack of foreign exchange. Furthermore, countertrade allows international traders to swap goods for services. Costs and risks depend on the specific circumstances of goods and countries involved in the trade.

International Regulations and Institutions for Foreign Trade Financing

There are many regulations and rules governing international trade. Formally they include national regulation, bilateral and regional regulations, and multinational agreements (WTO). Informally they include the efforts of trade associations and the International Chamber of Commerce. This complex regulatory network usually determines the method of trade financing. International traders can utilize alternative techniques and different types of institutions to finance their trade. Private financial institutions generally are the most convenient channels for importers and exporters. These institutions provide a wider range of services with flexibility, but they can be more expensive. Financing and insurance provided by government credit agencies and world organizations may be cheaper but less flexible because their financing schemes are restricted to certain designated functions. For example, Eximbank is intended to promote national exports; world organizations are mainly interested in helping economic development in developing countries. In the case of project cofinancing, trade financing may be jointly sponsored by commercial banks, government credit agencies and world organizations. In any financing it is the traders' decision concerning where to cut costs and risks.

DISPUTE SETTLEMENT

Dispute settlement may become the last resort for international traders anxious to settle any disagreement. At present, no international legal body serves as an arbiter in settling serious trade disputes. However, there are some channels through which disputes can be settled.

INTERNATIONAL CHAMBER OF COMMERCE

In all commercial letters of credit recently issued by commercial banks there is a clause that reads: "This credit is subject to the Uniform Customs and Practice for Documentary Credits (1993 revision) International Chamber of Commerce, Publication No. 500". The ICC sets all rules on documentary credits for international trade. Minor discrepancies in documentation may be straightened out by the issuing commercial bank with the consent of both exporter and importer. Based on the rules, issuing banks are not responsible for the goods themselves in trade. However, they are responsible for examining the required documents and determining that the terms stipulated in the L/C have been satisfied.

Serious trade disputes between importer and exporter—or their issuing bank and advising bank—may be settled in a court of national jurisdiction. In this case, all parties concerned and their legal counselors must appear in court. Final settlement requires the presentation of pertinent evidence. Expert witnesses may be used to give their interpretation of the ICC Articles contained in the Uniform Customs and Practice for Documentary Credits.

FOREIGN COMMERCIAL SERVICE

The FCS is a part of the U.S. Department of Commerce. It serves U.S. international trade in more than 65 countries. Besides the promotion of U.S. international business overseas, one of its major functions is to help U.S. exporters and importers settle their trade disputes with foreign clients on a fact finding and conciliatory basis.

WORLD TRADE ORGANIZATION

From 1948–1994, the GATT did not have the function of helping exporters and importers settle their disputes. Its responsibility was to enforce international agreements on trade. Its primary concern was to examine claims of unfair practices by its members. Unfair practices usually referred to the use of trade barriers such as special applications of tariffs and quotas, price discrimination and dumping (sales below the full cost of production, including reasonable profit). Even though GATT had no power to sanction the member nations that violated its rules, most major trading nations adhered to the rules. Thus the GATT's rules and suggestions influenced national policies on trade, and indirectly influenced the trade practices of importers and exporters in member nations.

In 1995, the GATT was replaced by the World Trade Organization (WTO). In addition to the functions of the GATT, the WTO provides a single umbrella for trade agreements in goods, services, intellectual property, and other areas. Furthermore, disputes involving all WTO matters are subject to a single dispute settlement process. Thus the WTO ends the ambiguous foundation for world trade that GATT had provided since its inception in 1948.

SUMMARY

Historically, foreign trade has made an important economic contribution to society. International trade increases the flow of goods and services, benefits consumers, provides profits to traders, and contributes to national welfare. Since 1960 international trade has grown rapidly. Foreign trade and trade financing have become more important in areas of business policy, financial competition, national trade policy, and international trade agreements. Foreign trade and trade financing have significant influences on national production, prices, employment, income, consumption, saving, and investment.

Traditionally, importers and exporters have used letters of credit issued by commercial banks to finance international trade. However, the complexity of modern international trade requires more sophisticated trade financing methods. For example, importers and exporters may use a fax to quicken their information exchanges to achieve better financing agreements; commercial banks may use their worldwide telecommunication network to help their multinational firms develop a "package" trade financing; forfait financing may be appropriate if political and payment risks are present; countertrade is chosen when the trade involves both goods and services, foreign exchange controls, or more than two countries.

Basically, financing foreign trade requires risk management and cost management. Importers and exporters must analyze all pertinent information from local, national, and global sources concerning the goods and services to be traded. At the same time they must flexibly employ favorable trade financing methods that minimize risk and cost but yield reasonable profits.

REVIEW QUESTIONS

1. Explain the importance of foreign trade financing in relation to:
   a. National economic growth and development
   b. International banking and finance
2. Distinguish the foreign exchange risk from inflation and interest rate risk. Are these types of risk interrelated? How?
3. What is the basic difference between a letter of credit and a standby letter of credit?
4. What is the basic difference between an import letter of credit and an export letter of credit?

5. Explain the functions of the importer's bank and the exporter's bank, respectively, in the financing process under letter of credit. How could government policies of their respective countries affect their functions?

6. From an exporter's standpoint, what are the advantages and disadvantages of using forfaiting instead of letter of credit to finance his or her international trade?

7. From an importer's standpoint, what are the advantages and disadvantages of opening a confirmed letter of credit in the exporter's bank with a time draft (for example, 60 days after sight) denominated in the currency of the exporter's country?

8. Why do multinational firms tend to use "open account" or "documentary draft for collection" instead of letter of credit in their intracompany trade?

9. What are the most important reasons for some international financial institutions such as IMF and GATT or WTO to oppose countertrade as a method of international trade financing?

10. Why are importers and exporters concerned about market risk in international trade?

CASE 1

Cost and Risk in Trade Financing

A large New York department store opens an unconfirmed irrevocable letter of credit to a medium-size producer of wool products in London. The terms of the trade are: F.O.B. London; 90 days sight draft in the amount of £2,500; shipping date not later than September 15, 19xx.

The British exporter, through his or her advising bank in London, presents all required documents and a 90-day sight draft in the amount of £2,500 to the importer's bank (issuing bank) in New York. The exporter petitions the issuing bank to accept the draft, discount the draft immediately, and remit the net proceed in U.S. dollars to the exporter's account with a British branch bank in New York.

After examining the documents presented, the issuing bank found that they are in compliance with the terms of the L/C. The issuing bank follows the exporter's instructions and sends a credit advice to the exporter's bank in New York on the basis of the following information:

The face amount of the draft: £2,500
Current exchange rate as of September 10, 19xx:
£1 = $1.5870

Annual discount rate (365 days) for 90 days after sight draft bankers acceptance in New York: 8.60%
Bank commission on the face amount of draft: 1/2%

QUESTIONS:

1. What is the net amount in U.S. dollars that the issuing bank sends to the exporter's bank in New York?

2. What are the risks and cost involved in this trade financing to the British exporter?

3. What are the risks and cost involved in this trade financing to the British exporter, if the terms are changed from the 90 D/S draft to a sight draft, and from pound sterling to U.S. dollar on the invoice as well as on the draft?

4. If this trade is not financed by a letter of credit but conducted on a consignment-commission basis,
   a. what are the risks and costs to the exporter?
   b. what are the risks and costs to the importer?

CASE 2

Cost, Risk, and Profit in Trade Financing

Mr. Jamison is employed as an account representative at a London clearing bank. One of his customers, Worldwide Industries, exports its products to European countries and to the United States. Recently Worldwide Industries made an agreement with their buyers in the Netherlands that enables them to draw 90-day bills with denomination in Netherlands guilders. Documents are processed in the London office of Mr. Jamison's bank.

Worldwide has experienced narrower profit margins in recent months. Also, it has experienced a tight cash and working capital position and has requested that Mr. Jamison provide some help. Worldwide wants to protect profit margins on forthcoming shipments to the Netherlands. Three shipments are planned for April 1, May 1, and June 1, in each case for Netherlands guilder 1.0 million.

Current Rate on Netherlands guilder: March 25, 19xx

Spot (Guilder/£) 3.5010–3.5020

1 Month Forward 3.4920–3.4930
3 Month Forward 3.4740–3.4750
UK Base Rate = 11.0%
US $ 3 Month Libor Rate = 10.0%
Discount Rate on Export = 8.5%
Drafts in Amsterdam

Worldwide can borrow sterling from Mr. Jamison's bank at 1.5% over bank base rate, and alternately will charge 1.0% over the U.S. Libor rate.

QUESTIONS:

1. By what methods can Mr. Jamison suggest that Worldwide be protected from foreign exchange risks, while preserving profit margins?

2. Would any contractual foreign exchange obligations be required?

3. Show the costs of each method suggested, and any sterling cash flows each might produce.

SELECTED BIBLIOGRAPHY

Citibank. *An Introduction to Letters of Credit*. New York: 1991.

Cook, Timothy Q., and Robert K. LaRoche (ed). "Bankers Acceptances," *Instruments of the Money Market*. 7th ed. Federal Reserve Bank of Richmond, 1993.

Eng, Maximo. "Financing International Trade," Chapter 16 in Ingo Walter (ed) *Handbook of International Business*. New York: Wiley, 1988.

Eng, Maximo, and Francis Lees. "Export Financing and Risk," *National Development,* (June/July, 1986).

Eiteman, David K., Arthur I. Stonehill and Michael Moffit. *Multinational Business Finance*. Reading, MA: Addison-Wesley, 1992.

Euromoney. *Trade Financing*. (A Supplement to Euromoney) London: Euromoney Publications, February 1989.

Export-Import Bank of the United States: tied aid credits and other issues: before the subcommittee on International Development, Finance, Trade, and Monetary Policy of the Committee on Banking, Finance, and Urban Affairs, House of Representatives, May 10, 1990.

Francis, Dick. *The Countertrade Handbook*. Westport, CT: Quorum Books, 1987.

General Agreements on Tariffs and Trade. *Review of Development in the Trading System*. GATT, (April-September 1988).

Lecraw, Donald. "The Management of Countertrade: Factors Influencing Success," *Journal of International Business Studies,* (Spring 1989).

Mapi, A. *Handbook of Financing U.S. Exports.* 5th ed. Washington, D.C.: Machinery and Allied Products Institute, 1988.

International Chamber of Commerce. *Uniform Customs and Practice for Documentary Credits.* Publication No. 500, New York: ICC, 1993.

International Monetary Fund. *Foreign Exchange Regulations.* Washington, DC: IMF, 1996.

Khoury, Sarkis J. "Countertrade: Forms, Motives, Pitfalls, and Negotiation Requisites," *Journal of Business Research,* (June 1984).

Martin, Dalia, and Monika Schnitzer. "Tying Trade Flows: A Theory of Countertrade with Evidence," *American Economic Review,* (December 1995).

Matty, Thomas D. "Export Factoring Moves into the Spot Light," *Globe Trade,* (July 1989).

OECD. *Export Credit Financing System in OECD Member and Non-Member Countries.* Paris: Organization for Economic Cooperation and Development, 1995.

OECD. *Regional Integration and the Multilateral Trading System: Synergy and Divergence.* Paris: Organization for Economic Cooperation and Development, 1995.

United Nations. *World Economic and Social Survey.* New York: United Nations, 1995.

U.S. Department of Commerce. "Forfaiting Should Not Be Overlooked as an Innovative Means of Export Financing," and "Sources of Export Financing," *Business America.* Washington, D.C.: (February 1995).

World Trade Organization. *International Trade 1995: Trends and Statistics.* Geneve, Switzerland: WTO, 1995.

CHAPTER 11

Bank Money Management

INTRODUCTION

Eurocurrency and money market operations have become a key aspect of the global activities of international banks. This trend is attributable to the enormous size of international money markets, their efficiency and low transaction cost, and the complementary role of operations in these market sectors vis-a-vis global foreign exchange and lending. The Eurobank is situated at the center of trading activities in these markets (discussed in detail in Chapter 6). Many types of institutions function as Eurobanks, and these banking units conduct a wide range of funding, lending, and arbitrage activities. However, characteristics common to all Eurobanks are that they operate both a banking office located in an offshore banking center and an international money trading desk that functions as a managerial control center for Eurocurrency dealing.

Banking has become global, and today's commercial banks seek liquid funds for loan and investment in all corners of the world. As a result, commercial bank treasury management activities have become elevated in importance. In this chapter we analyze international treasury management, examine the various components of the international money markets, consider the objectives and operational aspects of treasury activities, consider the scope of Eurocurrency arbitrage, review the importance of forward yield curves as an analytical tool, and examine the various uses of the international treasury report.

We shall note that the various components of the international money markets provide a global finance system with very strong linkages. The strong links between money market sectors are the result of the important players in this global finance system: the large international banks, the specialized merchant and consortium banks, financial institutions, multinational corporations, governments, and international organizations such as the World Bank.

LEARNING OBJECTIVES IN THIS CHAPTER

1. To appreciate the size and scope of international money markets that are used by banks in their global operations.
2. To discover the sources of bank profits from Eurocurrency and related activities and risks.

3. To develop an awareness of the dynamic aspects of international money management and how banks develop strategies for use under these changing conditions.

4. To understand the importance and use of technical and analytical tools by banks engaged in international money management.

KEY TERMS AND CONCEPTS

- Currency arbitrage
- currency mismatch
- dealing room
- double swap
- effective cost
- Eurodollar arbitrage
- Eurosterling arbitrage
- forward yield curve
- funding
- International Treasury Report

- inward and outward arbitrage
- maturity gap
- maturity mismatch
- maturity transformation
- nominal cost
- offshore banking market
- positioning
- term structure
- treasury operations

The Market Sectors

In this section we outline the role of local money markets and the Eurocurrency market, and the nature of their activities. Further we consider their linkages, and how they perform together to provide a global finance system.

LOCAL MONEY MARKETS

money market

financial market in which short term funds are bought (borrowed) and sold (loaned).

Early after the Second World War, two major money markets played an important role in providing international financial services—New York and London. In the 1970s additional local money markets took on an increasingly international role, including Paris, Tokyo, Frankfurt, and Zurich.

In the period 1946–1965 New York provided liquid funds to the rest of the world in the form of dollar loans. Provision of dollar loans at relatively low interest rates was important in accommodating trade expansion, economic development, and foreign business investment. After 1965 New York was less able to carry out this function due to the capital controls program that limited offshore lending. Nevertheless, New York grew in importance as a depository for the official reserves of foreign central banks. Moreover, New York served importantly as an international payments and clearing center for dollar denominated payments and settlements. Finally, rapid growth of foreign exchange trading in New York has provided an important means of maintaining foreign exchange trading without interruption throughout the day. The New York market serves as the principal link between the European and Far Eastern foreign exchange markets, and facilitates continuous 24-hour trading. London has also played an important role as an international money market. As is explained in a later section of this chapter, London provides a dual currency money market with sterling and Eurodollar deposit, loan, and money market operations. Like New York, London has attracted several hundred foreign banking offices, and these foreign banking units are important players in the local money market. The Eurodollar market in London offers a financing base for international securities dealers and Eurobond underwriters, permitting these intermediaries to obtain dollar financing for their dealings in dollar denominated bonds and securities.

EUROCURRENCY MARKETS

Eurocurrency market

offshore money market in which term deposits denominated in several currencies are traded.

dealer bank

bank that makes a market in a financial asset, buying and selling at price differential (spread) that provides a profit margin.

The Eurocurrency market is a global money market. This market easily rivals New York in overall size and in its capacity to provide efficient liquidity adjustment to participants with large asset positions. The core of the market consists of several hundred dealer banks, all willing to buy (take deposits) and sell (place deposits) with other banks. In this case the commodity traded is time deposit claims of short- to medium-term maturities. Eurodollars account for close to three-fourths of the market total, with other Eurocurrencies (Eurosterling, EuroDMarks, EuroYen, etc.) making up the remaining part of the market.

Each currency sector of the Euromarket has its own interest rate pattern that is usually tied to the interest rates prevailing in the country of origin of the currency. Eurosterling interest rates tend to follow interest rate movements in London. There are close links between Eurodollar interest rates and New York interest rates, as there are between EuroFrench franc interest rates and Paris interest rates. Interest rates in a given local market and the relevant Euromarkets are closely linked because these rates can be arbitraged without any foreign exchange risk. Money market participants, while arbitraging funds between the local market and the same Eurocurrency sector, create a global system of money market interest rates. Commercial banks especially have strong incentives to carry on the arbitrage process, thus reinforcing this linkage.

A Global Finance System

swaps

simultaneous purchase and sale of financial claim at different maturities.

dealing room

bank or securities firm service facility for trading a number of financial claims, equipped with advanced communication and computer facilities for rapid execution of transactions.

The Eurocurrency market can be viewed as an integrated market system with strong linkages between its various currency sectors. These linkages operate through the ability of bank and other participants to shift funds from one currency sector to another via swaps that link Eurocurrency market sectors (Exhibit 11.1, Item A). Additional linkage channels connect the local money markets with the Eurocurrency market (Exhibit 11.1, Items B and C). In London, swaps between Eurodollar and sterling provide an important channel linking together the Eurocurrency and London money market sectors (Exhibit 11.1, Item D). Interest arbitrage (described in earlier chapters) between New York and London provides a useful and flexible link between two of the most important local money market sectors (Exhibit 11.1, Item E). Finally, Eurodollar/dollar interest arbitrage operates between those two dollar denominated sectors (Exhibit 11.1, Item F).

All of these linkages provide a global finance system that carries out the following basic operations:

1. Large banks can centralize the trading of assets in the interconnected money markets. Their dealing room operations bring together the trading of many types of international money market assets.

| EXHIBIT 11.1 | **The International Money Markets, Global Financial System** |

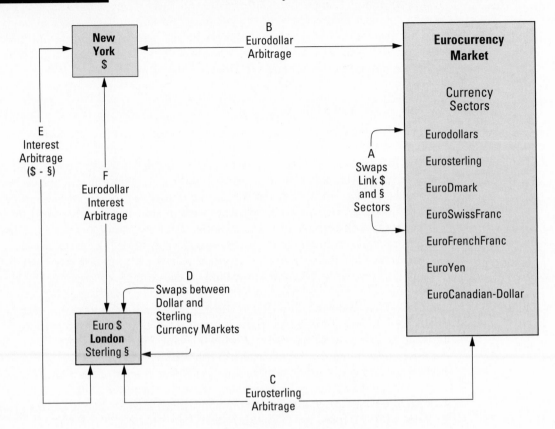

2. Dealer banks facilitate arbitrage flows of funds from one sector to another.

3. Borrowers and lenders enjoy greater flexibility and freedom to participate in international money market activities at a more efficient cost level.

Bank Treasury Operations

treasury management

sourcing and allocation of use of short-term funds, to achieve optimal cost-risk position.

funding

securing funds for short- and medium-term lending, managing foreign currency balances, dealing in money market, and obtaining international deposits.

International treasury management focuses on the sourcing of short-term funds and their profitable investment, with a view toward balancing cost of funds with risk and return. The dimension of risk encompasses liability management as well as asset management.

On the funding side international treasury management concerns itself with securing the funds required for short- and medium-term lending, carrying foreign currency balances related to foreign exchange trading activities, money market dealing, and obtaining international deposits. Obstacles abound in obtaining international deposits. For example, many countries maintain legislative or regulatory restrictions on foreign bank access to local deposit markets.

The mechanics of international treasury activities include: 1) sourcing funds, 2) allocating funds to alternative loan and investment sectors, 3) converting funds into currencies in which loans are to be denominated, and 4) providing for the reconversions of funds to the currency in which liabilities are denominated. These activities require the participation and decision making of bank personnel at all levels in the organizational structure.

FUNDING

At the center of banking activities is the treasury operation. The treasury typically focuses on the sourcing, allocation, and utilization of cash. The basic commodity of banking is cash, and one important requirement for an effective treasury operation is the low cost sourcing of these cash requirements. International banks face special difficulties in sourcing cash due to the greater volatility of international money flows, the sharp competition among banks and other types of borrowers for international funds, and the generally greater awareness and sophistication of international depositors. These difficulties are multiplied when international banks seek to obtain low cost funds in domestic money markets, since local banks tend to enjoy competitive advantages in bidding for and attracting local currency funds.

International banks tend to adopt comprehensive funding programs in their efforts to supply cash needs. A number of basic questions must be considered when a bank develops an international funding program:

1. What is the cost of funds?
2. How much risk assumption is necessary?
3. What are the mechanics of trading?
4. How do we use the funds obtained?

COST OF FUNDS

nominal interest

cost of funds expressed as annual percent rate. Ignores cost of funds components that may influence real or effective cost such as reserve requirements.

The cost of funds to an international bank can be affected by a number of factors, including the nominal interest (expressed as an annual percentage), applicable reserve requirements on deposit funds, administrative and operational costs, and deposit insurance costs. In the case of funding Eurocurrencies, only one of the four cost elements is significant, nominal interest. In effect, the nominal interest cost becomes the effective cost of funds. By contrast, in local money markets all four cost elements may be important, although where large amounts ($1 million or more) are traded, administrative and operational costs tend to become relatively insignificant. Deposit insurance costs vary from country to country, depending on the level of insurance premiums assessed by the relevant government insurance agency. In the discussion that follows we will consider only the reserve requirements in the adjustment of nominal interest costs to obtain the effective cost of funds.

Assume a large British bank operating a subsidiary in New York requires the use of U.S. dollar funds for a period of three months. These funds can be obtained from issuing negotiable certificates of deposit at 6.75% or borrowing via Eurodollar time deposits at 7.00%. The reserve requirement on certificates of deposit issued from the New York office is 8.0%. To compare the effective cost of funds, we must convert the nominal cost of certificates of deposit as follows:

$$\text{Effective Cost of Certificate of Deposit} = \frac{\text{Nominal Cost}}{1.00 \, \text{Reserve Requirement}} = \frac{6.75\%}{1.00 - .08} = \frac{6.75\%}{0.92} = 7.34\%$$

The effective cost of CD funds (7.34%) exceeds the effective cost of Eurodollar time deposits (7.0%). Remember, there is no reserve requirement applied to

effective cost

includes nominal interest adjusted for factors (reserve requirements, deposit insurance) that also may influence basic cost of funds.

"Treasury risk is a significant constraint on bank product development."—senior vice president, major money center bank

maturity mismatch

arises when bank borrows and lends funds at different maturities.

Eurocurrency deposits. The important advantage in funding cash requirements with Eurocurrency deposits is that these deposits escape reserve requirements and thus provide a lower effective cost, though arbitrage forces will tend to limit this source of cost advantage.

RISK ASSUMPTION

When seeking to fund their cash needs, international banks may be subject to three risk dimensions: currency risk, the risk from maturity mismatch, and counterparty risks. Currency risk could arise if a bank borrows Eurodollars, converts to another lending currency (e.g., French franc), and lends to a customer denominated in French francs. A depreciation of the franc in comparision with the dollar during the lifetime of the loan would leave the bank with a currency loss. For this reason banks generally swap funding currencies into loan currencies, which removes the open position or currency mismatch position.

The risk from maturity mismatch can arise when the bank borrows and lends at different maturities. For example, a bank could borrow one-month Eurodollars and lend six-month Eurodollars. For the next 30-day period, the bank has a maturity mismatch (a gap of five months). The larger the maturity gap, the larger the potential risk. The increased risk is because an adverse change in interest rate levels in the first 30-day period can lock in a negative return for a relatively long period (five months). For example, let us say that on day 0, Swiss Credit Bank borrows one-month Eurodollars at 5.70% and onlends these funds at 6.50% for 6-month maturity (Exhibit 11.2). If Eurodollar interest rates shift upward before the maturity of the borrowed position, as indicated in Exhibit 11.2, then on day 30 the Swiss Credit Bank must renew its borrowing at higher cost. If that bank chooses to do so at one-month maturity, the annualized cost will be 6.70%, in excess of the locked-in lending rate of 6.50%, generating a monthly loss of 0.20% (6.50%–6.70%) annual rate. If Swiss Credit Bank expects that on day 60 and day 90 the cost of one-month borrowing will be 7.10% and 7.70%, respectively, it will be thinking of borrowing at a longer term to

EXHIBIT 11.2   **Illustration of Upward Shift in Eurodollar Yield Curve**

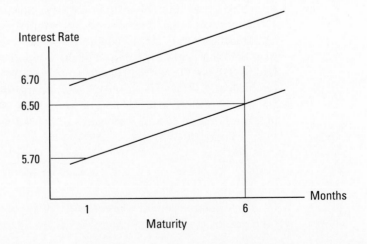

prevent any further expansion of the negative return on its borrowing-lending position. The preceding analysis applies to a single borrowing and lending position in the total portfolio of the Eurobank. We should remember that on an overall basis the Eurobank may benefit from an upward shift in interest rates, since interest income and interest expense will tend to shift upward together.

Finally, the international bank must integrate individual credit judgments to limit the possibility that the counterparty in money market transactions may not meet its transaction commitments. Regarding deposit exposure to other banks in the interbank market, such limits take into consideration the counterparty bank's credit quality, the duration of the exposure, and ancillary business relationships with the other bank. Foreign exchange lines are generally set at a multiple of the deposit line. Counterparty risk containment also requires monitoring daily settlement exposures, the total amount due from a counterparty on a given day. This latter risk dimension is sometimes called Herstatt risk, after the failure in 1974 of Bankhaus Herstatt. Substantial losses occurred as other banks delivered deutsche marks but did not receive the corresponding dollar amount of the foreign exchange transactions due to the bank's closure late in the settlement day.

Mechanics of Trading

Dealing in Eurocurrencies and other money market assets requires that the international bank operate an international money trading desk. In most banks this facility is a full-fledged money market dealing room with dozens of dealers, each specializing in some particular type of money market investment. The specialties may focus on such money market instruments as Treasury bills, certificates of deposit, short-term notes or foreign currencies, Eurocurrencies, and financial futures and options. Some large international banks advertise that they operate as many as a dozen full service dealing rooms around the world. This structure tends to provide around-the-clock service for bank customers. Banks make substantial investments in dealing room operations due to the need for computer and telecommunications hardware and software required for each dealing position.

Funding Costs and End Use

In its international money market operations a bank will estimate its cash needs, fund this need at lowest possible cost, and pass funds on to the various departments (corporate lending, Eurobond trading, and money market dealing sections). In this regard, daily and weekly treasury projections of cash needs represent a basic information input. Bank profitability will be enhanced by the spreads that can be maintained between funding costs and loan and investment returns generated by the various using departments. In this connection, profits are generated for the bank as the dealing room operation generates cash at low cost. Other divisions of the bank employ these funds at interest rate returns that are higher than the basic cost of funds. End uses might include the following:

- investment in money market assets (CDs, Treasury bills)
- participation in Euroloans
- operation of secondary trading market in Eurobonds and other securities
- original underwriting of Eurobonds

A second and important source of profit comes from operations carried out exclusively within the dealing room (discussed later in this chapter) that generate bank profits.

Term Structure and Forward Yield Curve

The international money market provides opportunities for international banks to carry out a wide range of dealing, arbitrage, and speculative financing activities. These activities provide an opportunity to develop more integrated financial vehicles for the bank, as well as to accommodate basic customer financial service requirements.

Access to several different Eurocurrency sectors at alternative maturities injects considerable flexibility and choice into international money market operations. The term structure of interest rates controls these choices. This flexibility can be best appreciated by means of an illustration. Let us assume an international bank must provide a corporate customer with a deutsche mark financing for six-month maturity. Given the market conditions reflected in Exhibit 11.3 and Exhibit 11.4, the bank has several ways of funding this credit. A first set of possibilities is to borrow EuroDmarks at various possible maturities (overnight, one-month, three-month, six-month). A second set of possibilities is to borrow Eurodollars at various possible maturities and to swap the dollars to deutsche marks. The first

term structure

shape and configuration of interest rate at different maturities within a given currency sector.

EXHIBIT 11.3	**Term Structure and Forward Yield Curve, Based on Eurodollar and EuroDmark Interest Rates**

Maturity	(1) Cost of Eurodollars	(2) Cost of EuroDmarks	(3) Forward Yield Curve	(4) Actual Forward Premium on Dmark	(5) Advantage of Dollar Funding
Overnight	5.92%	4.00%	1.92	1.85%	−0.07
1-Month	6.00	4.20	1.80	2.05	0.25
3-Month	6.30	4.40	1.90	2.10	0.20
6-Month	6.70	4.60	2.10	1.95	−0.15

NOTE: The cost advantages reflected in column 5 are not necessarily a product of failure of interest rate parity conditions to be applicable. Rather, they result from differential taxation in countries, possible government restrictions on certain types of cross-border capital transactions, and differences in risk perceptions and risk premia for investors operating from diverse currency bases.

EXHIBIT 11.4	**Eurodollar and EuroDmark Yield Curves and Forward Yield Curve**

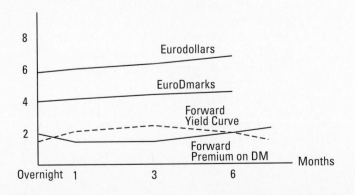

alternative—borrowing deutsche marks at different possible maturities—involves selecting the level of interest rate risk (based on the maturity gap). The second set of possibilities—borrowing Eurodollars—involves taking on currency risk, unless a swap is used to eliminate currency risk.

forward yield curve

based on differential between cost of funds denominated in one currency at given maturity, and cost of funds denominated in a second currency at the same maturity.

The cost of each of these funding alternatives is reflected in Exhibit 11.3, columns 1, 2 and 4. Column 3 is derived by subtracting Column 2 from Column 1, and presents us with a forward yield curve. This forward yield curve is the differential between the cost of Eurodollars at a given maturity and the cost of EuroDmarks at the same maturity. The plotted forward yield curve indicates how much more expensive dollar funding is as compared with deutsche mark funding, without considering the profit from swapping dollars into deutsche marks. The cost discrepancies do not necessarily reflect failure of interest parity conditions (see note to Exhibit 11.3).

This information is valuable to the bank in establishing a funding strategy, as it shows the cost differential in using alternate sources of funds. If we combine our information in Exhibit 11.4 with a forecast of yield curves, we have a better understanding of the possible effects of the risk and cost implications from alternate funding strategies. For example, suppose we expect the dollar yield curve to shift upward by approximately 1% at all maturities. This shift presents a potential risk in the case of dollar funding, in addition to the direct effect of the cost of funds. If we believe there is a strong probability of the Eurodollar yield curve shifting upward, we can adopt alternate funding strategies based on EuroDmark funding.

The data in Exhibit 11.3, Column 4 reflects the swap profit from dollars to deutsche marks. Column 5 tells us whether Eurodollar or EuroDmark funding is more advantageous for the bank. At overnight and six-month maturities, arbitrage of dollars to deutsche marks is unprofitable, indicating that deutsche mark funding is preferable. At one-month and three-month maturities, arbitrage of dollars to deutsche marks is profitable; however, the bank lender faces a maturity gap. At the end of one month or three months the Eurodollar borrowing cost must be rolled over, along with the swap of dollars into deutsche marks. Since these costs are unpredictable the bank faces a dollar refunding risk, even though the loan is denominated in deutsche marks. The dollar refunding risk may be reduced or avoided by the following courses of action:

1. Borrow Eurodollars at three months rather than one month to lessen the dollar refunding risk.
2. Shift to deutsche mark funding at six months, even though it reduces profit and the competitive position of the bank.
3. Shift to the deutsche mark funding at three months, even though more costly, if there is lower probability of the deutsche mark interest rate shifting up than the dollar interest rate.

Generating Bank Profits

profit center

operating unit of a bank (money market dealing room) that seeks to generate profit based on overall operations.

The bank's money market dealing room serves two primary functions. These are to service the general needs of the bank including the needs of customers and to operate as a profit center in its own right. In the latter function the dealing room does not necessarily service other departments of the bank or the bank customers. Rather, the desk seeks in a direct way to earn profits by generating market transactions.

We will explore four basic sources of profit generation in Eurocurrency operations including basic dealing, maturity transformation, currency arbitrage, and fund positioning (Exhibit 11.5). Before describing these four activities we should note the following. Due to capital constraints during the latter 1980s, a number of banks have restricted the volume of their activities. Capital constraints require banks to hold capital relative to specific risk asset categories. Since profit margins tend to be quite low on Eurocurrency asset-liabilities booked, it may become relatively unattractive for banks to increase their asset holdings and related capital. The reader may consult Chapter 9, *Capital Requirements* section for additional discussion.

BASIC DEALING

The core of Eurocurrency activities tends to be the deposit and redeposit of currencies in offshore banking markets. The term offshore refers to the location of banking units outside the country whose currency is being traded. For example, Eurodollars are normally traded offshore from the United States, Eurosterling is traded in Paris offshore from London, and Euro Swiss franc is traded in Paris and Luxembourg offshore from Zurich. Offshore money markets, unlike domestic markets, are unregulated and are not subject to reserve requirements imposed by a central bank. This lack of regulation allows offshore markets to have lower costs and to be more efficient than domestic markets. For instance, dollar deposits in New York banks are subject to Federal Reserve cash reserve requirements, whereas Eurodollar deposits in London and Paris banking offices are not subject to these reserve requirements. Therefore basic dealing in the Eurocurrency market can be more profitable than dealing in the home country banking market.

Each Eurodollar taken by a dealer bank can be fully redeposited in another bank or loaned to a borrower. The redeposit chain of Eurodollars going from one bank to another is complete. Eventually, the redeposit chain is broken when a Eurobank finds an opportunity to lend to a nonbank at a favorable profit margin. Basic dealing

EXHIBIT 11.5	Four Sources of Profit in Eurocurrency Dealing		
Source of Profit	**Type of Activity**	**Return**	**Risk**
1. Basic Dealing	Interbank buying and selling of relatively short-dated Eurocurrency time deposits.	Low return, based on narrow interbank trading spread.	Low risk, depending on credit status of counterbank.
2. Maturity Transformation	Transforming given maturity funds purchased on bid side of market into different maturity funds sold on ask side.	Moderate return, depending on steepness of yield curve.	Moderate risk, depending on size of maturity gap.
3. Currency Arbitrage	Standard interest arbitrage. Moving funds from one currency sector of the money markets to another currency section.	Low return, based on combination of interest spread and forward spread.	Low risk, depending on credit from status of counter part bank.
4. Funds Positioning	Taking a speculative position on the expectation that a given interest rate or foreign exchange rate will change in a predetermined direction in the near future.	High return, based on successful projection of rate change.	High risk, given possibility that rate may move in opposite direction than expected.

involves a bank offering to buy and sell a given Eurocurrency (e.g., Eurodollars) at a given maturity. Under these conditions the bank is operating on both sides of the market by offering to buy (bid) a given maturity deposit (e.g. one-month) at one interest rate (6%), and offering to sell (ask) at a somewhat higher rate (say 6.13%). The interest rate spread between bid and ask constitutes the gross profit of the dealer bank. The spread will be narrow in cases of actively traded currencies such as the Eurodollar and Eurosterling, and wider in cases of less actively traded currencies such as the Eurolira and Euroguilder.

MATURITY TRANSFORMATION

> For lending Eurocurrancies, competition typically leads to bid/ask spreads with extremely narrow margins of profit.

Eurobanks will find it difficult to survive on a diet of basic dealing, since spreads tend to be quite narrow. Larger spreads can be generated by maturity transformation. With an upward sloping yield curve as indicated in Exhibit 11.6, a dealer bank can bid for one-month Eurodollars at 6.40% and place a two-month Eurodollar time deposit at 6.80% (ignoring the bid-ask spread that reduces the profit somewhat). This transaction introduces a maturity gap between the liabilities (one-month maturity) and assets (two-month maturity) of the Eurobank. The maturity gap creates a risk position for which the bank hopefully receives an increased return in the form of a wider interest spread. At the end of one month the bank will have to refund its two-month deposit liability. If interest rates shift up before the refunding takes place, the increase in interest cost could wipe out the entire profit, and even create a loss on that part of the bank's balance sheet. Banks can manage maturity gaps (interest rate exposures) in the derivatives market. Increasingly, they utilize interest rate futures and swaps for such purposes. There is a tradeoff between risk (measured by the maturity gap) and profit (the spread in interest rates at the borrowing and lending points on the Eurodollar yield curve).

> **maturity gap**
>
> borrowing and lending funds at different maturities, leaving bank exposed to risks from shift in level of interest rates.

Greater potential return (and greater risk) is created by widening the maturity gap. Initially the bank could have bid for one-month Eurodollars at 6.4% and placed a time deposit for four months at 7.6%, generating a gross interest spread of 1.2%. Increased risk operates from the longer maturity gap, three months in this case. The need to refund the four-month deposit leaves the bank exposed to the risk of rising interest rates over a period three times as long as the former case (placing a two-month time deposit).

| **EXHIBIT 11.6** | **Eurodollar Yield Curve** |

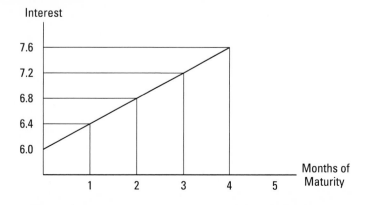

Dynamics of Maturity Transformation   The preceding analysis of profit generation from maturity transformation considers static conditions in the Eurocurrency market (absence of changes in interest rate levels). We now consider more realistic dynamic conditions. Four scenarios or comparisons are considered and outlined in Exhibit 11.7:

1. Small versus substantial upswing in Eurodollar interest rates
2. Steeper slope in yield curve with lower interest rates
3. Upward interest rate shift
4. Downward interest rate shift

Small versus Substantial Upswing   In this scenario one-month and six-month Eurodollar interest rates are 6.0% and 7.0%, respectively. Given the expectation of a small interest rate change, Eurobanks may be expected to continue to borrow short and lend long, maintaining the existing maturity gap. Given the expectation of a substantial rate change, a different picture should emerge. Eurobanks should borrow long (six-month) and lend short (one-month). After the interest rate shift is completed, they can revert to a positive (borrow short-lend long) gap status (Exhibit 11.7).

Steeper Slope in Yield Curve with Lower Rates   In this scenario the Eurobank can earn higher profit by maintaining a positive gap due to the steeper slope (wider differences in rates at different maturities) in yield curve. In that instance it is

| EXHIBIT 11.7 | Dynamics of Maturity Transformation in the Eurocurrency Market |

EURODOLLAR INTEREST RATES | | | **ALTERNATIVE SCENARIOS AND MONEY MARKET ACTIVITY** | |

Market Now	Later Scenario I	Later Scenario II	Scenario I	Scenario II
1. Small Versus Substantial Upswing				
1 Month 6.0%	7.0%	9.0%	Borrow short	Borrow long lend
6 Month 7.0%	8.0%	10.0%	Lend long	short, temporarily
			Maintain gap.	reverse gap. Later revert to positive gap.
2. Steeper Slope with Lower Rates				
1 Month 6.0%	4.5%	NA	Maintain gap for	NA
6 Month 7.0%	6.0%	NA	greater profit or reduce gap and related risk to maintain profit level.	
3. Upward Interest Rate Shift				
1 Month 6.0%	8.0%	NA	Borrow long and	NA
6 Month 7.0%	9.0%	NA	lend short until rate change is completed. Then return to a positive gap.	
4. Downward Interest Rate Shift				
1 Month 6.0%	NA	5.0%	NA	Borrow short and lend
6 Month 7.0%	NA	6.0%		long until rate change is completed. If possible shorten borrowing maturities to overnight and one week.

possible to maintain the gap (one-month to six-month) for increased profit, or reduce the gap (and related risk) to maintain the profit level.

Upward Interest Rate Shift   In this scenario the Eurobank expects interest rates to shift upward. An appropriate action would be to borrow long (locking in low cost funds for six months) and lending short (to rollover as rates shift up).

Downward Interest Rate Shift   In this scenario the Eurobank expects interest rates to shift down. It is appropriate to continue to borrow short and lend long. However, in the time period over which rates are falling, the Eurobank could profitably shorten borrowing maturities to more quickly benefit from declining rates.

CURRENCY ARBITRAGE

interest arbitrage

borrowing one currency at a given interest rate, exchanging into a second currency for investment at a different interest rate. Can be on a covered (swapped) basis, or uncovered basis.

Currency arbitrage constitutes a third source of profit generation. We have discussed the mechanics of currency or interest arbitrage in an earlier chapter. That discussion focused mainly on the static aspects of the situation, namely, when interest rates and spot-forward exchange rates are fixed. Realistically, these rates are constantly subject to change, and these changes open up new opportunities for profitable interest arbitrage.

We can illustrate how interest rate changes can open up a "temporary window of opportunity" for profitable currency or interest rate arbitrage. In Exhibit 11.8 we present an initial equilibrium money market, where on Day I interest rate parity conditions prevail. There is no profit to be earned from covered interest arbitrage. The interest rate spread (Eurosterling rate minus the Eurodollar rate) is equal to the spot-forward spread (annualized cost of swap of dollars into sterling).

Early on Day II Eurosterling interest rates rise by a full percentage point. This rise results from action taken by the Bank of England that elevates interest rates in the sterling (London) money market and that quickly becomes transmitted to the Eurosterling sector. The effect of this action is to create opportunities for profitable, covered interest arbitrage from Eurodollars to Eurosterling. The data in Exhibit 11.8 indicate a net advantage from this arbitrage.

$$\text{Net Advantage} = \text{Interest Rate Spread} - \text{FX Spread}$$
$$(\$ \times £) = (10.5 - 7.50) - (2.0\%)$$
$$= 1.0\%$$

EXHIBIT 11.8	**Covered Interest Arbitrage and the Adjustment of Markets Toward Interest Rate Parity**		
Market Sector	Day I Initial Equilibrium Market	Day II Market Rates Prior to Arbitrage Flows	Day III Market Rates After Interest Arbitrage Flows
Spot Pound	$2.0000	$2.0000	$2.00500
180-Day Pound	1.9800	1.9800	1.9799
Eurodollar Rate	7.50%	7.50%	7.75%
Eurosterling Rate	9.50%	10.50%	10.25%
Annualized Cost of Swap $ to f	2.0%	2.0%	2.50%
Interest Rate Spread	2.0%	3.0%	2.50%
Net Advantage of Arbitrage ($ to f)	0	1.0%	0

Covered interest arbitrage goes on during Day II. By Day III this arbitrage has had the following effects:

1. Funds shifted into Eurosterling deposits have brought rates down to 10.25%.
2. Funds pulled away from Eurodollar deposits have pushed Eurodollar rates up to 7.75%.
3. Upward pressure from swap transactions has pushed spot sterling to $2.00500.
4. Downward pressures from swap transactions have pushed forward sterling to $1.9799.

Therefore on Day III we have a new equilibrium in the financial markets with the interest rate parity condition restored. The interest rate spread (2.50%) equals the spot-forward rate spread.

On the interest rate side these changes can result from a change in the demand for loan funds. For example, in Great Britain business loan demand may increase, pushing interest rates up in the sterling (London) and Eurosterling money market sectors. These changes are reflected in Exhibit 11.9 where credit conditions on Day 1 and Day 8 (a week later) are shown. The upward pressure on interest rates are fully reflected in the Day 8 market conditions in Exhibit 11.9. The important point is that while the markets tend to return back to near equilibrium, changes do take place in Eurosterling interest rates and in forward discounts on sterling. Dealing banks in a position to see this happening could take appropriate action to benefit as follows:

1. Sell forward sterling aggressively.
2. Buy forward dollars aggressively.
3. Borrow Eurosterling for long maturities.
4. Lend Eurosterling for short maturities.

FUNDS POSITIONING

"The less traveled foreign currency avenues are the more profitable."—senior FX dealer

When we examine the dynamics of currency arbitrage, we begin to consider how bank dealers in the international money market fortuitously find themselves in a position to take advantage of changes in interest rate and foreign exchange spreads. In many cases, these same banks are attempting to forecast interest rate and foreign exchange rate changes. The purpose in doing so is to be able to position the bank to benefit from such changes. For example, in a situation where a dealer bank can

EXHIBIT 11.9 **Interest Rates and Foreign Exchange Rates— Three-Month Maturities**

Market Conditions	Equilibrium (Interest Rate Parity)	Disequilibrium (Profitable Arbitrage) Day 1	Equilibrium (Interest Rate Parity) Day 8
Eurodollars	6.00%	6.00%	6.00%
Eurosterling	9.75%	10.75%	10.75%
Spot Sterling	1.5000	$1.5000	$1.5000
Forward Sterling	1.4859	1.4859	$1.4822
Percent Discount on Sterling	3.75%	3.75%	4.75%
Profit in Swap of Dollars to Sterling	0	+1.0%	0

anticipate a rise in Eurosterling interest rates (Exhibit 11.10), a speculative position could be taken as follows:

Day 1:   Buy one-month sterling at $1.9933—Sell 12-month sterling at 1.9200
Day 31: Sell spot sterling at $2.0000—Buy 11-month sterling at 1.9083

At all times there is a balanced currency position, with no exposure long or short. In closing out the one-month purchase of sterling with a spot sell on Day 31, a profit is generated of $0.0067 per pound sterling positioned. In closing out the 12-month sell position at its maturity, a profit is generated of $0.0117 per pound sterling positioned. In this case, the gross profit could be $0.0184 per pound sterling position taken (Exhibit 11.11).

We can better understand this fund positioning by referring to Exhibit 11.12. Initially we are on the upper forward curve, and can swap (points A and B) on that curve. After the interest rate rise in London we are on the lower forward curve, where we enter into a second swap (points C and D). The calculated forward rates of exchange are presented in Exhibit 11.11.

There are several risks in this type of fund positioning. One risk is that interest rates in London on sterling securities will decline, not rise. If this should happen, the fund positioner would take losses. Similarly, if interest rates on dollar money market instruments rose, the interest differential would narrow, and the fund positioner

fund positioning

taking long or short position in the money market or currency market to realize a profit. Based on expected change in interest rate and/or exchange rate.

forward curve

trading curve on which one can buy/sell currency at various forward maturities.

EXHIBIT 11.10	**Forward Discount on Sterling Given Four and Five Percent Interest Rate Differentials, Assuming Perfect Market Equilibrium**	
	Market Conditions before Rise in Sterling Interest Rates	**Market Conditions after Rise in Sterling Interest Rates**
Money Market:		
Sterling Interest Rate	10.0%	11.0%
Dollar Interest Rate	6.0%	6.0%
Foreign Exchange Market:		
Spot Sterling	$2.0000	$2.0000
1-Month Sterling	1.9933	1.9917
11-Month Sterling	1.9267	1.9083
12-Month Sterling	1.9200	1.9000
Monthly Change	0.0067	0.0083

NOTE: The monthly change is based on the assumption that the interest differential is the same at all maturities. Therefore the forward discount on sterling is stepped in equal amounts each month.

EXHIBIT 11.11	**Profit Calculation—Speculating on Rise in Eurosterling Interest Rate**

Profit Taken End of Month 1:	
1. First Swap Position—Buy One-month Sterling at	$1.9933
2. Second Swap Position—Sell Spot Sterling at	$2.0000
3. Profit Per Pound	$0.0067
Profit Taken End of Month 12:	
4. First Swap Position—Sell 12-month Sterling at	$1.9200
5. Second Swap Position—Buy 11-month Sterling at	$1.9083
6. Profit Per Pound	$0.0117
Overall Profit Per Pound (Lines 3 + 6)	$0.0184

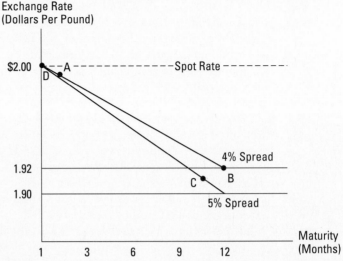

EXHIBIT 11.12	Illustration of Forward Trading Curves Given Different Interest Spreads between Dollar and Sterling

Note: Points A and B indicate initial swap position. Points C and D indicate second swap position. First swap consists of 1-month buy sterling and 12-month sell sterling. Second swap consists of spot sell sterling and 11-month buy sterling.

would incur losses. If interest rates do not change after the position is taken, the speculator will not be affected since there is a balanced (nonexposed) position. However, if the speculator rolls over the position, there will be a small loss at each roll over.*

Single, Dual, and Multicurrency Operations

International money market activities of large banks can focus on single currency operations, dual currency operations, and multicurrency operations. In each case the problems encountered and solutions adopted will differ. To illustrate the single currency case we consider Eurodollar arbitrage between New York and offshore markets. To illustrate the dual currency case we consider the London money market and the possibilities for arbitrage between sterling and Eurodollars. The more complicated situation of multicurrency arbitrage is developed around the International Treasury Report.

EURODOLLAR ARBITRAGE

General Overview of Arbitrage   Since the removal of U.S. capital controls in 1974, Eurodollar and domestic interest rates in the United States have exhibited a close correlation. Eurodollar interest rates are largely determined by domestic dollar rates. Two-way arbitrage maintains close links between the Eurodollar market and the U.S. banking system. It is safe to say that the Eurodollar market and the U.S.

---

* The roll over swap with no change in interest rates will be: buy one-month sterling at $1.9933 and sell spot sterling at $2.000.

money market are closely integrated sectors of the global financial markets. The U.S. and Eurodollar money markets are linked together by the arbitrage activities of large money center banks and nonbank borrowers and lenders. Financial transactions undertaken by these money market participants as a result of interest rate differentials tend to narrow those differentials. When it is profitable to shift or arbitrage funds between markets, the shifts tend to narrow the gap so that eventually any further arbitrage may become unprofitable.

Bank Regulatory Practices   Bank regulatory practices and market pricing practices differ from country to country and generate different interest cost and profit perceptions among money market participants. Nonbank borrowers must consider different compensating balance requirements and varying loan spreads in comparing effective loan costs. Banks must consider the influence of reserve requirements and deposit insurance assessments on cost of funds. As a result, arbitrage incentives may differ for different groups of money market participants. This difference may produce conditions where bank participants may have an incentive to move funds into the U.S. money market, while at the same time nonbank participants face the incentive to shift funds from the United States to offshore dollar markets. Several factors limit commercial bank exploitation of arbitrage opportunities.

1. Bank management and investors in bank stocks are more sensitive to the rate of return earned on total assets and the possible adverse effects arbitrage can have on the rate of return on assets.
2. Bank regulators have focused attention on the adequacy of bank capital and the trend toward lower capital-to-asset ratios that has taken place from 1978 to 1989.
3. More recently U.S. banks have grown more concerned about the riskiness of interbank placements, due to the problems encountered by bank lenders with loans to developing countries and Eastern Europe.

We may distinguish between two categories of bank arbitrage. In some types of arbitrage operations the bank issues new liabilities and acquires new assets, thus expanding its balance sheet. In other types of arbitrage operations, the size of the bank's balance sheet remains unchanged. In the second case the bank is shifting funding among various liability categories.

London and Dual Currency Operations

dual currency market

market in which two currencies play important roles as borrowing and lending vehicles.

London offers the advantages of a dual currency money market to banks and corporations that are headquartered in that city. Local currency (sterling) money market facilities are well developed, and at the same time banks have the sizeable Eurodollar market facility with which to work. In London, banks and corporations have access to dollar as well as sterling CD trading, dollar and sterling time deposits, and a highly efficient foreign exchange market—the world's largest—to facilitate shifting between the two major currency sectors.

Due to these advantages, several hundred foreign banks have established money management offices in London. In addition, multinational corporations use London as a regional financing headquarters. The London banking offices can carry out the following activities: bid for Eurodollars as well as sterling deposits, hold liquid assets in the form of short-term Eurodollar or sterling deposits with banks, issue and deal in sterling and dollar certificates of deposit, fund Eurodollar and sterling loans, participate in offshore loans, and obtain financing to support holding of dollar or sterling investment assets with no currency exposure.

The existence of two different currency yield curves in the London market affords money market participants additional dimensions of profit-generating activity and greater flexibility in carrying out liquidity adjustments. Participants can take a position to benefit from an interest rate change or exchange rate change.

Large international banks find the London market particularly useful for the following reasons:

1. funding dollar or sterling loans;
2. developing a profitable and active foreign exchange and Eurocurrency dealing operation; and
3. carrying out profitable money market trading activities in CDs, notes, bills of exchange, and other short-term and financial assets.

INTERNATIONAL TREASURY REPORT

Wide opportunities for profitable international money arbitrage exist, considering that international banks may use major Eurocurrency market sectors as well as domestic currency market counterparts in their international treasury activities. What is needed is a means of combining the information available on domestic and Eurocurrency interest rates, and the cost of currency swaps needed to carry out arbitrage transactions. In most banks this information is presented in the International Treasury Report, considered in detail in the following discussion.

International Treasury Report
report that provides banks with data helpful in carrying out a range of global money market transactions.

General Uses of International Treasury Report   The International Treasury Report provides the international banker with statistical data that is helpful in carrying out a wide range of money market activities. The information contained in the International Treasury Report includes the following (see Exhibit 11.13):

1. Local money market and bank deposit interest rates
2. Cost of foreign exchange swaps
3. Eurocurrency deposit (bid-ask) rates
4. Interest rates and swap rates at various maturities

From the International Treasury Report the international banker can 1) search out lower cost sources of funds, 2) locate higher return outlets for funds, 3) calculate possible arbitrage paths for moving funds based on location or maturity, or both, and 4) compare interest arbitrage differentials with swap costs. This information can be utilized by the bank in its own operations, or be made available to customers so that their international financial needs can be planned more carefully.

We should remember that where reserve requirements and deposit insurance costs apply, these factors generally must be used to adjust costs of funds and net profit calculations derived from using any particular arbitrage channel. These adjustments were described in the previous section on Eurocurrency arbitrage.

outward arbitrage
U.S. bank borrows domestic funds and redeposits them in overseas branches.

Inward and Outward Arbitrage   Large U.S. banks make use of their foreign branches in balancing off credit fund availability between domestic and offshore markets. Depending on the direction that funds flow, arbitrage activities can be classified as inward or outward. In the case of outward arbitrage a U.S. bank obtains domestic funds by issuing large certificates of deposit (CDs) and redepositing these

EXHIBIT 11.13	**International Treasury Report (Cost of Funds/Return on Funds) December 1981**					

Domestic Interest Rates		**Cost of FX Swap from $**		**Eurocurrency Deposit Rates Bid Asked**		
U.S. Dollar				**Eurodollar**		
				Overnight	12.87-13.00	
Bank deposit rate	12.62	One-month	0	One-month	13.31-13.44	
Prime bank loan	15.75	Three-month	0	Three-month	13.75-13.88	
T-Bill	11.90	Six-month	0	Six-month	14.81-14.94	
Deutsche mark				**Euro Dmark**		
Bank deposit rate	9.50	One-month	−2.71	One-month	10.44-10.57	
Prime bank loan	13.00	Three-month	−3.18	Three-month	10.50-10.63	
Money mkt rate	10.50	Six-month	−3.96	Six-month	10.56-10.69	
Swiss Franc				**Euro Swiss franc**		
Bank deposit rate	7.75	One-month	−3.24	One-month	8.87-9.00	
Prime bank loan	8.00	Three-month	−4.04	Three-month	9.25-9.38	
Money mkt rate	10.12	Six-month	−5.06	Six-month	9.25-9.38	
Pound Sterling				**Eurosterling**		
Bank deposit rate	14.25	One-month	+1.78	One-month	15.37-15.50	
Prime bank loan	14.50	Three-month	+1.67	Three-month	15.69-15.82	
T-Bill	15.31	Six-month	+0.97	Six-month	15.69-15.812	
French Franc				**Euro French Franc**		
Bank deposit rate	9.16	One-month	+2.06	One-month	15.75-15.88	
Prime bank loan	14.00	Three-month	+2.75	Three-month	17.00-17.13	
Money mkt rate	15.25	Six-month	+3.44	Six-month	18.00-18.13	
Yen				**Euroyen**		
Bank deposit rate	6.50	One-month	−7.08	One-month	6.12-6.25	
Prime bank loan	7.00	Three-month	−6.92	Three-month	6.12-6.25	
T-Bill	5.68	Six-month	−7.54	Six-month	6.87-7.00	

NOTE: Minus sign indicates negative swap cost (profit). Therefore a swap of dollars to deutsche mark generates a profit. A swap from dollars to French franc incurs a cost. If we reverse direction, a cost becomes a profit. A swap from French franc to dollars generates a profit.

SOURCE: Morgan Guaranty Trust Co., "World Financial Markets," *Wall Street Journal.*

funds in its overseas branches. When the overseas branch places (redeposits) the funds in the Eurocurrency market or makes a new loan to a corporate customer, outward arbitrage increases the bank's global balance sheet. While outward arbitrage generally is evaluated on the basis of cost of funds in the domestic CD market, other domestic funding sources can be used. If rates are favorable, outward arbitrage may be funded by new issues of banks holding company commercial paper. However, the CD market is larger, more liquid, and more flexible for use in raising arbitrage funds.

While in the previous illustration outward arbitrage added to the bank's balance sheet, a bank could engage in outward arbitrage with no net increase in the balance sheet. A bank could use new CD domestic funds to replace existing Eurodollar funds. In actual practice, this type of liability switching is a less important aspect of international arbitrage operations because of the need of integrating international branch operations with domestic office money market activities.

Inward arbitrage takes place when U.S. banks shift their funding from domestic to foreign sources. This shift is likely to occur when U.S. banks bid aggressively for funds in the domestic money market sectors. More active international banks turn to the Eurodollar interbank market for lower cost funds. A U.S. bank raising funds in the Euromarket must compare the effective cost of external funds with the effective cost of domestic funds. The effective cost of external funds is equal to the nominal interest rate on Eurodollar deposits adjusted for any reserve requirement that is

inward arbitrage

U.S. bank bids for Eurocurrency funds and moves them onshore for domestic use.

The German central bank has been active (and effective) in adjusting reserve requirements on bank borrowings from the Euro markets, as a way to regulate net capital inflows to Germany.

EXHIBIT 11.14	Arbitrage Advantage With Outward Flow

OUTWARD ARBITRAGE

Given the following information:

Three-month secondary certificate of deposit (CD) rate	9.00%
Three-month Eurodollar bid rate	12.00%
Federal Deposit Insurance Corporation FDIC) insurance premium CD reserve requirement	0.037%
	6%(0.06)

Effective cost of domestic funds calculated as follows:

$$\text{Effective cost of domestic funds} = \frac{9.00\% + 0.037\%}{(1 - 0.06)} = 9.61\%$$

This outcome indicates a bank can make a profit of 239 basis points (12.00% − 9.61%) on an outward arbitrage transaction.

As banks take advantage of this opportunity, they bid up CD rates and push down Eurodollar rates until the incentive is eliminated. If the rates are bid to the following levels, the arbitrage incentive is eliminated.

Three-month secondary CD rate = 10.40

Three-month Eurodollar bid rate = 11.10%

Based upon the same type of calculation, the effective cost of domestic CD funds is now 11.10%.

$$\frac{10.40\% + 0.037\%}{(1 - .06)} = 11.10\%$$

The effective cost of domestic funds equals the external value of these funds to the U.S. bank. Note that the Eurodollar/domestic rate differential has been narrowed from 300 basis points to 70 basis points by bank arbitrage.

applicable. U.S. banks will move funds onshore when the effective cost of external funds (Eurodollar) is lower than the effective cost of domestic funds (CD). In effect this arbitrage activity places a floor on the cost of funds in the offshore market. Whenever the Eurodollar interest rate falls below this level, U.S. banks will borrow funds offshore and bid up the Eurodollar rate until the lower limit is restored.

There is a practical limit to inward arbitrage. This limit works through the absence of a well-developed domestic interbank market for term funds. Rates in the term repurchase agreement market are usually unattractive. Participation by banks in the term federal funds market is subject to regulations that limit a bank's indebtedness relative to its capital and surplus.

The following are cost factors that control arbitrage incentives:

1. level of interest rate on borrowed funds;
2. reserve requirements on domestic liabilities or net positive Eurodollar borrowings;
3. required insurance on bank deposits; and
4. risk premium on Eurodollar interbank placements.

Other factors are important in determining the size of a bank's arbitrage transactions. Capital controls can prevent a bank from engaging in external lending, external borrowing, or both. Bank arbitrage activities may be limited by internal constraints governed by balance sheet relationships. Bank management perceptions of risk may translate into specific limits on balance sheet ratios. This perception of risk applies most specifically to ratios of bank capital adequacy and profitability.

In Exhibit 11.14 outward arbitrage takes place when the domestic CD rate is 9.00%, and the Eurodollar bid rate is 12.00%. Given these rates, the effective cost

EXHIBIT 11.15	**Arbitrage Advantage with Inward Flow**

INWARD ARBITRAGE

Given the following information:

Three-month secondary CD rate	9.90%
Three-month Eurodollar rate	10.30%
FDIC insurance premium	0.037%
CD reserve requirement	12% or 0.12
Eurodollar reserve requirement	6% or 0.06

To determine if an inward arbitrage incentive exists, calculate effective cost of both domestic and external funds as follows:

Effective cost of domestic

$$\text{funds} = \frac{9.90\% + 0.037\%}{(1 - 0.12)} = 11.29\%$$

Effective cost of external

$$\text{funds} = \frac{10.30\%}{(1 - 0.06)} = 10.96\%$$

While the nominal cost of Eurodollar funds is 40 basis points higher than the nominal cost of domestic funds, the effective cost of Eurodollar funds is actually 33 basis points lower than the effective cost of domestic funds. U.S. banks will have an incentive to obtain Eurodollars from their offshore branches in lieu of issuing new CDs. This incentive will place upward pressure on the Eurodollar rate and downward pressure on the CD rate until effective costs are equalized as follows:

Three-month secondary CD rate = 9.80%

Three-month Eurodollar offer rate = 10.51%

The effective cost of domestic funds equals the effective cost of Eurodollar funding (11.18%). No incentive for inward arbitrage remains.

of domestic funds is 9.61%, and there is a 239 basis point incentive for outward arbitrage. The flow of arbitrage funds pushes the domestic CD rate to 10.40% and the Eurodollar bid rate to 11.10%, at which point there is no longer any arbitrage incentive.

In Exhibit 11.15 inward arbitrage takes place when the domestic CD rate is 9.90%, and the Eurodollar offer rate is 10.30%. Given these rates, the effective cost of domestic funds is 11.29%, and the effective cost of external funds is 10.96%. Consequently, inward arbitrage takes place. The flow of arbitrage funds pushes the domestic CD rate down to 9.80% and the Eurodollar offer rate up to 10.51%. At these levels the effective cost of internal funds is equal to the effective cost of external funds, at which point there is no longer any arbitrage incentive.

International Treasury Report in Detail

The International Treasury Report (Exhibit 11.13) presents us with a comprehensive view of the global money market system. The report includes the basic costs and returns from money arbitrage across all important money market sectors.

In the discussion that follows we consider arbitrage between different sources and uses of funds involving two different currencies. The International Treasury Report includes opportunities for arbitrage between six currency sectors. This provides 15 bilateral combinations of currencies for arbitrage purposes.

In the right column the ITR provides information on Eurocurrency borrowing and lending opportunities. We should note that interest rate levels in some sectors (Euroyen, Euro Swiss franc) are low, while in other sectors (Euro French franc,

Eurosterling) interest rate levels are high. There are several explanations for this difference.

1. Interest rates in the Eurocurrency market tend to follow interest rates in the home currency. Therefore high rates in the United Kingdom and France will tend to generate high rates in the Euromarket for the related currencies (Eurosterling and Euro French francs). Low rates in Germany and Switzerland will tend to cause lower rates in the Euromarket for the related currencies (Euro Dmark and Euro Swiss franc).*

2. Strong currencies tend to exhibit low interest rates in their domestic money markets as well as in the Euromarkets. Weak currencies tend to exhibit higher interest rates in these markets.

DOLLAR-STERLING ARBITRAGE

The center column of the ITR provides information on the cost of swaps *from dollars*. This is in the form of annualized rates that are comparable to interest rates. We can use this information to calculate the incentives for arbitrage between money market sectors. For example, an international bank dealing in Eurocurrencies can bid for one month Eurodollars at 13.31%, swap these funds into sterling at a cost of 1.78%, and place one-month Eurosterling on deposit with another Eurobank at 15.50%. The annualized net advantage in this case is 0.41%, calculated as follows:

Cost of Eurodollars	13.31%
Cost of Swap	1.78
Total Cost	15.09%
Return on Eurosterling	15.50
Net Incentive into Sterling	+0.41%

Since there are six currencies that can be transacted, there are 15 pairs of currencies for arbitrage purposes. In some cases the net incentive will be high, and in other cases the net incentive will be low. In part this incentive depends on the Eurocurrency combinations involved. Eurodollar, Euro Dmark, and Eurosterling market sectors are large, and the markets have depth. In such cases arbitrage volume between these sectors is substantial and rates are competitively narrowed down. For example, taking the possibility of borrowing three-month Euro Dmarks and swapping into three-month Eurodollars, the net incentive is 0.20, or 20 basis points, calculated as follows:

$$\text{Return on Funds} - \text{Cost of Fund} = \text{Net Incentive}$$
$$13.88\% - (10.50\% + 3.18\%) = 0.20\%$$

The cost of Euro Dmark funds is the sum of the Euro Dmark bid rate (10.50%) and swap cost (3.18%).

YEN-FRENCH FRANC ARBITRAGE

Taking Eurocurrency market sectors where volume is lower and markets are thinner, the net incentives may be higher, in the range of 40–80 basis points or more. Higher incentives would tend to be the case in the Euro Swiss franc and Euro French

---

* Most of the arbitrage in the dollar sector occurs between the Federal funds and overnight Eurodollar rate. Arbitrage between longer maturity deposits is less common.

franc sectors. Taking the possibility of borrowing three-month Euroyen and swapping it into three-month Euro French francs, the net incentive is 1.34%, or 134 basis points. In this situation a double swap may be necessary.* The double swap involves two separate swaps back to back. The first swap is from yen into dollars. The second swap is from dollars into French francs.

double swap

Involves two separate swaps, back to back.

The first swap involves:	The second swap involves:
Sell Yen spot (for dollars)	Buy French francs spot (for dollars)
Buy Yen forward (premium)	Sell French francs forward (discount)
Cost = 6.92%	Cost = 2.75%

Note that dollars play the role of an intermediary currency, linking together the two swaps.

$$\text{Profit} - \text{Cost} = \text{Incentive into francs}$$
$$(17.13\%) - (6.12 + 6.92 + 2.75) = 1.34\%$$

The left column in the ITR indicates interest rates in domestic financial markets. We should note that nominal profit margins between bank deposit rates and rates on U.S. prime bank loans vary considerably. Profit margins are lowest in the cases of Japan, the United Kingdom, and Switzerland. Profit margins are quite high in France and Germany, and the money market arbitrage opportunities are widened considerably when we take all three columns into consideration. Funds can be sourced in the Euro Dmark market and swapped into dollar loans at the prime bank lending market. Euroyen can be swapped into sterling for investment in sterling Treasury bills. French franc bank deposits can be obtained locally and swapped into Eurodollar deposit placements.

DEUTSCHE MARK—DOLLAR ARBITRAGE

Taking another illustration, where an international bank bids for three-month Euro Dmark deposits, and swaps them into dollars for loan in the corporate lending market, with a 3% reserve requirement on U.S. bank Eurocurrency borrowings, we have:

$$\text{Cost of External Funds } \frac{10.50\%}{1.00 - 0.3} = 10.83\%$$

The cost of funds is 10.83% Euro Dmark rate adjusted for reserve requirement in U.S.

3.18%	Cost of swap
14.01%	Total cost of funds
15.75%	Prime Rate in U.S.
1.74%	Incentive into dollars

The preceding indicates that there is a very strong incentive to swap Euro Dmarks into dollars. There is one difficulty with this swap. Prime loan rates reflect

---

* A double swap may be more efficient and lower cost when the dollar sector is more active and offers a greater depth and stability of quotations.

what can be obtained by bank lenders at times when there is plentiful loan demand. It is rarely the case that bank lenders can book all the commercial and industrial loans that they would like. Therefore another constraint in international money arbitrage based on the ITR is that the various end uses may have only limited capacity to absorb funds.

SHORT-DATED INTEREST RATE FUTURES

Bank management of short-dated funds has taken on added complexities, if only because of the many financial instruments and contracts available for use. In this section we consider the use of short-dated interest rate futures contracts. A number of short-term (three-month) Eurocurrency futures are traded on the Chicago Mercantile Exchange (CME), London International Financial Futures Exchange (LIFFE), and other exchanges in Singapore, Tokyo, and Paris.

Probably the most liquid of the Eurocurrency futures is the three-month Eurodollar future traded on the IMM of the Chicago Mercantile Exchange. Eurodollar futures contracts are like currency and other futures contracts (Chapter 5) in that the contract is a bet on the direction of short-term interest rates. The Eurodollar futures price is based on three-month LIBOR, with face value of $1 million. The interest rate is quoted as an annual rate.

The Eurodollar futures price is defined as

100   minus   (interest rate, stated in percent, on a three-month Eurodollar deposit for forward delivery).

Thus if the interest rate on the forward three-month deposit is 6.26%, the Eurodollar futures price is

$$100 - 6.26 = 93.74$$

Therefore if interest rates go up, the Eurodollar futures price goes down, and the short positioned investor makes money. If interest rates go down, the Eurodollar futures price goes up, and the long positioned investor makes money. A speculator would go with short futures if he believes that interest rates will rise, but will go long if he believes interest rates will fall.

The face value of the contract is $1 million. One basis point (equal to 0.01%) has a value of $100 (assuming a 360-day deposit). Given a three-month deposit, the value of one basis point is $25 ($100/4). The futures exchange defines a one basis point move in the price as a transfer of $25 between the long and short position. As an example, suppose the futures price drops from 93.74 to 93.71. The short side gains $75 (3 × $25), and the long side loses $75. The futures price is determined in the market on a minute-to-minute basis, and the number of long and short contracts exchanged is equal at the price prevailing at that time.

LIFFE SHORT STERLING FUTURES

In 1996 the LIFFE provided six short-term interest rate futures contracts, based on three month money market rates. These include sterling, Euromark, Eurolira, Euroswiss, ECU, and Euroyen.

The short sterling contract is based on the three-month sterling interbank rate for a £500,000 deposit. Like other short-term interest rate future contracts, short

EXHIBIT 11.16	**Three-Month Sterling Futures (LIFFE)** **£500,000 Points of 100%**						
	Open	**Sett price**	**Change**	**High**	**Low**	**Est. Vol**	**Open Int.**
Jun	93.90	93.91	+0.01	93.91	93.90	2,741	66,228
Sep	93.84	93.83	−0.01	93.84	93.81	8,868	60,338
Dec	93.62	93.62	—	93.62	93.59	6,682	69,733
Mar	93.31	93.32	+0.01	93.32	93.28	2,738	48,824
Jun	92.92	92.94	+0.02	92.94	92.89	1,667	37,318

SOURCE: *Financial Times,* 30 May, 1996.

sterling futures effectively fix the cost of borrowing or lending money for the three-month sterling on the expiration date of the futures contract. This makes the futures contract equivalent to an exchange traded forward agreement to borrow or lend money for a future three month period at an interest rate fixed now. For example, a September short sterling futures contract purchased in June fixes at time of purchase a three month interest rate commencing in September. The futures price reflects the forward interest rate for the period of the loan.

In Exhibit 11.16 we have information provided by the LIFFE for short sterling futures contracts covering the period 1996–1997. The open interest for each contract is the total number of financial futures contracts outstanding, long (purchases) equal to short (sales) positions. This does not include contracts purchased/sold in "day trading" which are not held over night. We can see that the September 1996 contract closed at 93.83 and the December contract at 93.62 (settle price).

The forward rate implied by the September contract is $100 - 93.83 = 6.17\%$, and the forward rate implied by the December contract is $100 - 93.62 = 6.38\%$. The smallest price move permitted by the exchange on a futures contract is known as the tick size. The tick size of the short sterling contract is 0.01% or 1 basis point out of 1.00%. Therefore the minimum price change the September contract could experience in trading would be from 93.83 to 93.82 or 93.84. In the short sterling contract the nominal value per contract is £500,000, and 1 basis point is worth £50. The contract is for three months, which means value per tick is £50/4 = £12.50. If price moves up two ticks, the buyer of eight short sterling contracts will make a gain of $8 \times 2 \times £12.50 = £200$.

There are more contract expiration months for the short sterling than other LIFFE futures contracts. In the exhibit, hedgers and traders can use this contract in May 1996 (when the data was published) to buy/sell short sterling futures for a June 1997 date. The exhibit provides illustrations of how market participants may utilize the short sterling futures contracts.

Eurocurrency-Eurobond Arbitrage

The Eurocurrency market provides opportunities for arbitrage against other financial markets. This is applicable to Eurobonds, which are intermediate to long-term assets. Eurobond arbitrage depends upon the relationship between short-term interest rates and bond coupon interest rates.

As Eurobonds approach maturity, opportunities may arise to generate profits by borrowing short-term and buying bonds. Depending on the currencies through which this arbitrage works, profits may be enlarged or diminished from the arbitrage. The following illustrates the operation of arbitrage between the Eurocurrency and Eurobond sectors.

A London-based trader notes that a deutsche mark denominated Eurobond with a 5.0% coupon and one year to maturity is quoted at 95.5%–96%. The trader can deal in the Eurodollar interbank market with 12-month deposits quoted at 9 3/8%–9 1/2%. Further, a one-year swap of dollars into deutsche marks can be negotiated at a spot buying rate of DM 1.8020/$ and a 12-month forward selling rate of DM 1.7860/$. Will the arbitrage be profitable?

At the completion of one year the bond will pay DM 1,000 face value plus a coupon of DM 50. The deutsche mark return on the bond is

$$\frac{1050}{960} = 1.0937 \ (9.37\%).$$

The dollar return on the bond is

$$1.0937 \times \frac{1.8020}{1.7860} = 1.1035 \ (10.35\%)$$

The dollar return of 10.35% exceeds the trader's cost of funds (9.5%). Therefore the trader will buy the bond for arbitrage. In this illustration we ignore transaction costs that are relatively low in the Eurobond market.

SUMMARY

Money market operations of international banks focus on leading national money market sectors—New York and London—and the Eurocurrency market. Taken together, these markets make up a global finance system.

Commercial bank international treasury operations include securing required funds, carrying foreign currency balances related to foreign exchange trading, and money market dealing (buying-selling instruments including deposits). Fund costs must be adjusted for reserve requirements, deposit insurance premiums, and risk factors.

Banks can generate profits from money market (Eurocurrency) activities in several ways, including straight dealing (market making), maturity transformation, currency (interest) arbitrage, and funds positioning. In the most complex case these can involve multicurrency operations, usually developed around the International Treasury Report. In each case the return from the activity varies directly with the degree of risk assumed by the bank.

REVIEW QUESTIONS

1. What do we mean when we say London is a dual currency money market? How does this affect bank money market operations?

   Use the International Treasury Report in Chapter 11 (Exhibit 11.13) to answer questions 2–7.

2. What is the net advantage from arbitraging three-month Eurosterling to Euro French franc?

3. What is the net advantage from arbitraging six-month Euroyen to Euro Swiss franc?

4. What is the net advantage from arbitraging Euro French franc to Eurosterling? Does this answer in any way reflect the ability of the money market and foreign exchange market to equilibriate together?

5. A corporate treasurer in Paris wants to borrow 150 million French franc at three-month maturity. Which Eurocurrency funding would provide the bank with the largest profit on interest rate spreads?

6. A German corporation has idle funds (deutsche mark) to invest for one month on a covered basis. Which of the six Eurocurrency sectors is the most attractive?

7. A London bank has excess funds from bank deposits (no reserve requirement) to invest. Should it invest in local T bills, or in another money market?

8. Given the following information:

three-month New York CD rate	7.0%
three-month Eurodollar bid rate	9.2%
FDIC insurance premium	0.037%
Federal Reserve reserve requirements on CDs	3% (.03)

   a. What is the effective cost of domestic CD funds?
   b. How much profit can a bank make in an outward arbitrage transaction?
   c. Market equilibrium will be reached when the effective interest cost of domestic CD funds equals the three-month Eurodollar interest rate. When the CD rate reaches 7.25%, and markets are in equilibrium, what will be the related Eurodollar interest rate?

9. Given the following information:

three-month New York CD rate	8.20%
three-month Eurodollar bid rate	8.50%
FDIC insurance premium	0.037%
Federal Reserve reserve requirement on CDs	8% (.08)
Federal Reserve Eurodollar reserve requirement	3% (.03)

   a. What is the effective cost of domestic CD funds?
   b. What is the effective cost of Eurodollar funds in the case of inward arbitrage?
   c. How much profit can a bank make in an inward arbitrage transaction?

10. A Zurich banker can purchase dollar Eurobonds maturing in exactly one year. They pay an 8.0% coupon and are quoted 98.5–99. The Zurich banker finds Eurosterling one-year deposits quoted at 9 1/8%–9 1/4%. The banker can enter into a one-year swap of sterling into dollars at a spot buying rate of $1.7830, and a forward selling rate (one-year maturity) of $1.7658.
    a. What is the current yield on the dollar Eurobond? Yield to maturity?
    b. What is the sterling return on the bond?
    c. Will the Zurich banker go ahead with this arbitrage transaction?

11. Outline the international role of the New York money market from 1946 to the present.

12. How is the London money market similar and different compared to the New York money market?

13. What are the most important instruments traded respectively, in the New York, London, and Eurocurrency markets?

14. You buy a September Eurodollar IMM contract at 92.45 and two weeks later close out the contract when the price is 93.16. Explain the cash flow outcome in this futures contract transaction.

15. You buy a December LIFFE short sterling contract at 91.68 and ten days later close out the contract when the price is 91.02. Explain your cash flow in the futures contract.

16. A U.S. corporate affiliate operating in the United Kingdom borrows £ 10 million from a bank at a 0.750 percent margin over the three month interbank rate, and sells 20 LIFFE short sterling futures contracts at a price of 92.05. The loan is drawn down immediately. The loan maturity is six months and the sterling interbank interest rate is reset at the three-month interval for the second period (three month) of the loan at 1.25% higher rate than for the first period. At the three-month interval the borrower closes out the futures contracts at a price of 90.40. What is the increased borrowing cost from the higher reset rate? What is the futures profit? Was the futures hedge worthwhile?

SELECTED BIBLIOGRAPHY

Aliber, Robert Z. "International Banking: A Survey," *Journal of Money, Credit, and Banking,* (November 1984).

Bank for International Settlements. *Annual Report,* Basle.

Brady, Simon. "Rise of the Forex Powerhouses," *Corporate Finance,* (September 1995): 25–28.

Coulbeck, Neil. *The Multinational Banking Industry*. New York: New York University Press, 1984.

Davis, Steven I. *The Management of International Banks*. Surrey, England: MacMillan Publishers Ltd, 1983.

Dufey, Gunter, and Ian Giddy. *The International Money Market*. 2d ed. Englewood Cliffs, NJ: Prentice Hall International, Inc., 1995.

Grabbe, J. Orlin. *International Financial Markets*. New York: Elsevier, 1996.

Hultman, Charles W. *The Environment of International Banking*. Englewood Cliffs, NJ: Prentice Hall, 1990.

International Monetary Fund. *International Capital Markets: Developments Prospects and Key Policy Issues*. Washington, D.C., September 1996.

Khoury, S.J. *The Deregulation of the World Financial Markets: Realities, and Impact*. Westport, CT: Quorum Books, 1990.

Meese, R., and K. Rogoff. "Was It Real? The Exchange Rate—Interest Differential over the Modern Floating Rate Period," *Journal of Finance,* (September 1988.)

Mishkin, Frederick S. "Are Real Interest Rates Equal Across Countries? An Empirical Investigation of International Parity Conditions," *Journal of Finance,* (December 1984).

OECD. *Financial Market Trends,* 1992, 1996.

Revell, Jack. (ed). *The Changing Face of European Banks and Securities Market*. New York: St. Martin's Press, 1994.

Sarver, Eugene. *The Eurocurrency Market Handbook*. New York: New York Institute of Finance, 1990.

Schmerken, Ivy. "A Boston Superregional Rightsizes for the Global Track," *Wall Street & Technology,* (March 1994): 38–44.

Shirreff, David. "Bankers' Feeding Frenzy," *Euromoney,* (September 1995): 62–68.

Stigum, Marcia. *The Money Market*. 3d ed. Homewood, IL: Dow-Jones-Irwin, 1990.

Taylor, Mark. "Covered Interest Parity: A High Frequency High Quality Data Study," *Economica,* (November 1987).

_____.*Trading Activities at Commercial Banking:* a paper prepared by the staffs of the office of the Comptroller of the Currency, Federal Deposit Insurance Corporation, and the Board of Governors of the Federal Reserve System. Washington, D.C., 1995.

_____. "The Trading Bank," *Euromoney,* (June 1993): 34–35.

Thurston, Charles. "The Big Get Bigger," *Global Finance,* (December 1995): 91–94.

Walton, Anthony. "What Next for Foreign Banks," *Bankers Magazine,* (January/February 1994): 29–33.

CHAPTER 12

Bank Lending, Euroloans, and Country Risk Analysis

PAST TRENDS AND CURRENT SITUATION

Since the postwar period foreign lending by international banks has played a key role in financing expansion of the world economy. In the past, American bank loans supported the growth of world trade between the United States and its trading partners as well as between second and third countries. Moreover, such loans have supported overseas investment by U.S.-based multinational companies. Foreign loans have provided foreign exchange to governments attempting to stabilize their economies, strengthened foreign banks needing "lender of last resort" support, and provided credit in countries where banking facilities and loan funds were inadequate relative to need. Finally, foreign bank loans often have played an important role in refunding existing loans, at times in connection with multilateral debt rescheduling essential to prevent default of loans by debtor nations.

In the sections that follow we consider the past growth and importance of foreign lending, analyze bank credit control, evaluate country risk analysis and syndicated lending, and consider the growing importance of loan securitization and new credits issued in the emerging debt market.

LEARNING OBJECTIVES IN THIS CHAPTER

1. To understand the role and importance of bank lending to the global economy.
2. To appreciate the nature of bank lending and the importance of this activity, to be aware of the risks related to international lending, and to understand methods used by banks and supervisory agencies to control these risks.
3. To understand the growing role of securitization and underwriting of debt securities, as interrelated aspects of how major banks intermediate loan capital on a global basis.
4. To develop an understanding of the concept, measurement, evolution, and use of country risk analysis from the bank lenders' and other investors' point of view.
5. To perceive the history and evolution of the syndicated Euroloan market, the risks peculiar to it, and the role it plays.

6. To discern the origins and causes of the international debt crisis and the role played by the Brady Plan in dealing with the debt crisis.

7. To grasp the origins, development, and growing importance of the market for emerging debt.

KEY TERMS AND CONCEPTS

- Baker Plan
- Brady bonds
- Brady Plan
- country exposure
- country risk
- country risk analysis
- credit limit
- cross default
- debt capacity
- debt crisis
- debt-equity swap
- Four Cs

- loan classification
- negative pledge
- Paris Club
- participation fee
- political risk analysis
- reference interest rate
- rescheduling
- sovereign immunity
- syndicated loan
- systematic risk
- transfer risk

ACRONYMS

CAMEL   Capital Asset Management Earning Liquidity

EBRD   European Bank for Reconstruction and Development

FFIEC   Federal Financial Institutions Examination Council

ICERC   Interagency Country Exposure Review Committee

ILSA   International Lending Supervision Act (1983)

Global Sources and Uses of Funds

Each year the Bank for International Settlements (BIS) provides comprehensive estimates of international banking activity in its *Annual Report.* This information includes estimates of the sources and uses of international banking funds, and changes in international bank assets and liabilities by nationality of banks. This information is useful in the analysis of the role of international banks as intermediaries and providers of funds.

The BIS data on sources and uses of bank funds considers banks' international lending as one important activity that is part of a broader total. This broader total includes the following specific activities:

1. borrowing/lending funds *between banks,* across borders based on domestic surpluses and shortages of funds

2. borrowing/lending funds to *nonbanks,* across borders

3. interbank redepositing

According to data provided in the *Annual Report of the Bank for International Settlements,* at year-end 1991 the aggregate amount of international bank credit outstanding approached $7.5 trillion. Of this total, more than 59% represented interbank redepositing (Eurocurrency and offshore banking activities). Another 24% represented international bank borrowing from and lending to *nonbank* entities. Finally, 16% represented banks' own domestic use (or supply) of international funds for domestic lending. These funds are derived from domestic surplus funds and channeled by interbank activities.

This large stock of interbank claims increased steadily during the 1980s. In the first half of the decade growth was relatively slow, averaging $110 billion a year. This slow growth was due to the onset of the international debt crisis, the increasing concern of bank lenders over repayment prospects, the more critical viewpoint of national bank regulators toward international lending, and the availability of alternative sources of financing including international bonds and commercial paper. In the second half of the 1980s the stock of interbank claims grew more rapidly, averaging $205 billion a year. This more rapid growth reflected the need of banks to finance a wider range of activities. Those activities include cross border mergers and acquisitions. Also, more countries became eligible for credits. In the 1990s emerging debt markets became a new source of funds for countries with improved credit worthiness.

Over the period 1970–1996 banks from many leading creditor countries participated in international lending. In the 1970s American banks took the lead, based on their ability to mobilize funds efficiently and at relatively low cost in the Eurocurrency market. Gradually, banks from other countries began to play a more important role. During the 1980s and 1990s Japanese and German banks became highly competitive in international lending, supported by strong currency positions and large current account payments surpluses. Exhibit 12.1 provides an overview of the position of banks residing in key financial centers. United Kingdom, Asian center, and Japanese banks lead in cross border claims, followed by U.S., French, and German banks.

PAST GROWTH AND IMPORTANCE OF FOREIGN LENDING

If we were to examine the loan portfolios of large American banks in 1960 we would come to the following conclusions. First, at that time the total amount of

EXHIBIT 12.1	Cross Border Bank Claims, by Residence of Banks (Billions of U.S. Dollars) Year-End 1994	
Nationality of Banks	**Amount of Bank Claims**	**Percent of Total**
Japanese Banks	1607	14.2
German Banks	469	6.6
French Banks	527	7.4
U.S. Banks	532	7.5
Italian Banks	137	1.9
Swiss Banks	404	5.7
U.K. Banks	1200	16.9
Dutch Banks	177	2.5
Spanish Banks	110	1.5
Caribbean Centers	640	9.0
Asian Centers	1038	14.6
Other	861	12.2
	7103	100.0

NOTE: Includes cross border positions in all currencies plus foreign currency positions.

SOURCE: Bank for International Settlements, *Annual Report* 1995, p. 170.

foreign lending was small in dollar volume, amounting to $5.3 billion of claims and representing only 2% of total U.S. bank assets (Exhibit 12.2). Second, close to half of the claims outstanding were concentrated in 12 countries including Germany, United Kingdom, Switzerland, Canada, Japan, Mexico, Brazil, Argentina, Chile, Colombia, Venezuela, and the Philippines. Finally, the major share of loans and credits extended overseas was short-term (70%) rather than long-term (30%). Claims on Latin America represented the largest single regional subtotal, reflecting the long standing special linkages of U.S. business and commercial firms, and the extent to which Latin America gravitated into the "dollar bloc."

In the three decades since 1960, U.S. banks have reported an unprecedented growth of claims on foreigners. In the five-year period 1960–1965 claims on foreigners increased by 130%. Growth slackened in the subsequent five-year period in response to the foreign credit restraint imposed by the Board of Governors of the Federal Reserve System. This restraint imposed ceilings on American banks' loans to borrowers located in developed nations. LDC borrowers were exempt from these limits, as evidenced by the significant increases in loans to Latin America (17%), Asia (31%), and Africa (66%) in the period 1965–1970.

In 1974 the OPEC countries quadrupled the price of oil. This created an enormous payments surplus for oil export countries, and the necessity to recycle these surplus petrodollars to oil importing countries so they could maintain oil and other imports at levels assuring sustainable production and economic activity.

The U.S. financial system played a major role in recycling petrodollars. Oil exporter countries increased dollar investments in the U.S. money market. These inflows led to an increase in deposits in American banks. In turn, American banks utilized the enlarged deposit base to fund loans to oil importing nations.

After 1975, U.S. bank claims on foreign borrowers experienced accelerated growth. Reasons for this growth include the following:

1. Mounting oil deficits compelled petroleum importing nations to borrow to balance foreign exchange budgets.
2. Inflation made it difficult for international borrowers to manage their budgetary positions on a balanced basis. In many cases, these borrowers (national governments and multinational companies) had to increase the amount of borrowing to be able to continue production, imports, and investment activities.
3. Expansion of multinational companies continued, along with cross border mergers and acquisitions and related borrowing needs.
4. Since 1982 considerable borrowing has occurred to take advantage of declining interest rates and smaller lending margins. In part this borrowing has been associated with efforts of debtors to reschedule loans, to refund debt at lower cost, and to generate lower cost-floating rate debt against which borrowers could carry out interest rate and currency swaps.
5. Since 1989 Brady debt restructurings have brought emerging country borrowers into the picture.

As of 1995 head offices of American banks had international loans and credits on their books aggregating $526 billion (Exhibit 12.2). More than 48% or $257 billion of this amount represents claims on Latin American countries. Another $115 billion or nearly 22% represents claims on Asian economies. Claims on European countries comprised another $130 billion of claims, or 25% of the total.

Foreign branches of American banks have come to play a more important role in overseas lending than their domestic offices. U.S. banks enjoy advantages in

| EXHIBIT 12.2 | | Claims on Foreigners Reported by Banks in the United States—by Region, 1960–1992 | | | | |

Year	Total	Europe	Latin America	Asia	Africa	Claims on foreigners as % Total Bank Assets
1960	5.3	1.1	2.3	1.2	—	2.0%
1965	12.2	2.8	3.6	4.2	0.3	2.3
1970	13.9	2.4	4.2	5.4	0.5	2.4
1975	58.3	11.1	23.8	17.7	1.9	6.0
1980	172.5	32.1	92.9	39.1	2.4	10.2
1982[1]	314.4	64.1	173.2	57.3	4.8	16.9
1985	401.6	106.4	202.6	66.2	5.4	16.4
1990	506.7	113.1	231.5	138.7	5.4	16.0
1995	526.2	130.3	257.3	115.3	2.7	13.7

Amounts in billions of dollars

[1] Commencement of international debt crisis

SOURCE: Board of Governors, Federal Reserve System.

booking certain types of loans in foreign branches. This policy fits in with operation of Eurocurrency money desk operations in the foreign branches. In 1979 U.S. banks booked approximately three-fourths of the claims and credits on non-U.S. entities in foreign branches. By 1982 this had declined to 57% of claims and by 1990, to 44%. As foreign branch claims became relatively less important, domestic office claims increased in importance.

CURRENT LOAN PORTFOLIO

In the discussion that follows we examine the loan portfolio in U.S. offices of American banks, as well as loans and credits in foreign branches. In a subsequent part of this discussion we consider the country exposure of American banks, including all loans whether booked in the head office or in a foreign branch.

The major features or distinguishing characteristics of U.S. bank lending overseas are:

1. Lending from U.S. banking offices is carried out largely in U.S. dollars. This policy shifts exchange risk to the borrower.
2. U.S. head office lending is heavily weighted with credits to foreign banks. In 1992 almost 23% of banks' claims on foreigners were on unaffiliated banks. Direct credits to banks are usually concentrated in developing countries.
3. Foreign lending is heavily oriented toward provision of short-term credits. At mid-year 1992 more than 82% of bank claims on unaffiliated foreigners was short-term (one year or less).
4. Short-term lending is more diversified by geographic area than long-term lending. In 1992 almost 50% of long-term lending was directed toward Latin American and Caribbean borrowers, whereas the largest geographic concentration in short-term lending was to Europe; this lending represented 36% of the total.

According to the federal regulatory agencies, over the past several decades foreign loans and credits of American banks have become more diversified. In 1960 virtually all of the overseas claims of American banks were booked at the head office. Foreign branch operations were minimal. At mid-year 1982 foreign branches represented nearly 57% of claims outstanding. This shift was an important structural change, since the credits and claims booked in foreign branches tend to be more diversified than those in head offices. For example, they include Eurocurrency deposit placements, local currency loans to borrowers residing in the country of location of the branch, medium-term Eurocurrency loan syndications, credits to local affiliates of multinational companies, and development credits. By 1990 a shift had taken place where 44% of aggregate bank claims were in foreign branches.

As of 1992 there was a fairly broad country distribution of U.S. bank exposures. The largest were against borrowers in the United Kingdom, Mexico, and Japan. Since the onset of the international debt crisis, U.S. banks have sought to reduce country exposures where loan servicing difficulties were experienced or considered to be a potential problem. In some cases these reductions were at the urging of bank regulatory agencies.

Loans to less developed countries comprise a large part of aggregate exposures. Credits to less developed countries satisfy a number of basic needs including:

1. loan reschedulings where the debtor country is unable to cover debt service requirements;
2. provision of foreign exchange to governments and central banks, especially where financial stabilization programs are under way;
3. provision of development loans to government owned industrial corporations;
4. provision of development loans to national development banks or similar finance institutions for subsequent relending;
5. provision of commercial credits to banks and exporters; and,
6. provision of term loans to corporate borrowers to finance capital spending.

In many cases, U.S. banks have sizeable exposure positions in countries that operate offshore banking markets. This situation is particularly true of the United Kingdom, Bahamas, Cayman Islands, Hong Kong, and Singapore, as analyzed in Chapter 6.

Bank Credit Control and Supervision   As international banks experienced an increase in the absolute and relative importance of their international loan portfolios, they sought to improve their organizational structures and credit risk evaluation procedures. In some cases banks introduced new organizational structures to provide more effective review and control over foreign lending. These operations include regional loan review committees, centralized files and records of multinational borrowers, special economic analysis and review units, and special account review officers to estimate the overall value of the account relationship. In other cases banks have reallocated work functions and responsibilities between units. In some instances new territorial officers and country desks were established, overseas branches were delegated increased latitude and loan limits, loan credit review and accounting files were centralized, and head office staff support facilities were enlarged.

Credit Analysis and Control   While large commercial banks have carried out substantial changes in their organizational structures, personnel staffing, and methods of centralizing and decentralizing international loan operations, basic or essential components of their credit analysis and loan review procedures remain relatively unchanged. These procedures include:

1. application of the four Cs of international credit making—namely, analysis of customer, credit, country, and currency risk factors;
2. establishment of loan limits for each lending officer assigned to the head office or foreign branch;
3. setting procedures for centralized record keeping and credit review; and,
4. periodic evaluation and reassessment of the banks' overall system of loan review procedures.

Application of the four Cs of international credit making constitutes an integral part of bank lending overseas. These include limits on credits to individual customers, evaluation of credit status of individual borrowers and application of loan limits in keeping with that borrower's borrowing capacity, limits on total credits in any one country, and limits on the amounts of assets and liabilities—actual and contingent—denominated in specific currencies. Foreign branches are generally subject to specific limits on the amount of loans, overdrafts, and other type credits permitted to any single account, and centralized record keeping procedures ensure that a customer's liabilities to branches and head office do not exceed agreed upon credit lines. In connection with the application of these procedures, there are limits on the amount an overseas branch may place on deposit with a given bank and on overnight foreign exchange positions.

Country loan limits involve ceilings on aggregate credits extended to borrowers located in specific countries. These country limits are important for several reasons. First, they facilitate needed geographic diversification of loan risk. Second, they facilitate the allocation of some part of bank funds to new borrowing countries where business development opportunities seem favorable. Finally, they represent an integral part of the bank's systematic approach toward risk reduction and control. More is said about country loan limits later in this chapter.

A second component of the credit analysis and control procedures is the establishment of loan limits for each lending officer. Each loan officer in a foreign branch or at head office is given a lending limit based upon the following considerations:

1. prior lending experience;
2. rank and level of responsibility;
3. type clientele; and
4. size of international loan portfolio relative to size of bank.

The officer limit may be $200,000 or $500,000 or some other figure. The limit governs the amount of the loan the officer may sponsor or authorize on his or her own responsibility. The officer may join another loan officer to jointly sponsor a loan of an amount exceeding their individual spending limits. The lending authority of a number of officers may have to be assembled to push through a large loan. In such cases the bank may also require the combined lending authority of territorial loan officers and senior officers at head office. In cases of large amounts, the loan approval of the board of directors may be required. Finally we should note that banking legislation in the United States imposes a percentage limit on lending to any one customer. In most cases an individual bank may not lend any more than

15% of its capital and surplus to a single borrower.* This policy means that a bank with $20 billion in total assets and $1.5 billion in capital funds may not lend in excess of $225 million to any single borrower.

A third component of credit analysis and control is the establishment of procedures for centralized record keeping and credit review. Individual bank procedures vary considerably. In some situations banks use a single loan and discount review committee. Some banks use separate committees to review domestic and international credits. In a few cases banks use regional or territorial committees. Where a bank uses a single committee, it generally consists of the senior credit officers of the bank. An executive level officer generally heads this committee and ordinarily reviews new loans exceeding specified amount limits.

Most international banks have adopted elaborate arrangements for centralized record keeping and auditing of overseas loans. Due to the need to maintain favorable customer relationships and because of legal requirements, American banks maintain a close overview of their aggregate credits to individual customers. Given the expanded operations of multinational corporations, American banks find it necessary to have available a summary, up-to-the-minute record of the global relationship with large corporate customers.

A final aspect of a bank's credit analysis and control procedures is to evaluate and reassess its system of international loan review periodically. This assessment must consider a) the changing relationship and importance of international customers, b) the possible need for new or revised procedures for credit evaluation and review, c) the possible development of weaknesses in the existing system, d) an appropriate diagnosis and prescription for strengthening loan review and credit control procedures, and e) approaches toward improvement in the auditing of the bank's loan portfolio where needed.

Supervisory Agencies and Foreign Loans

As American banks became increasingly active in international lending, U.S. banking regulators had to adapt to the need for increased and more comprehensive surveillance. An effective supervisory program consists of regular evaluations of banks through on-site inspections, examinations of operating reports that banks submit to regulatory authorities, and the constant monitoring of overall exposures to evaluate changes in level of risk in countries with high concentrations of loans.

Over the past two decades the federal regulatory agencies and Congress have introduced a number of measures aimed at improving supervision of overseas lending by U.S. banks. These measures have been motivated by events such as the Herstatt Bank failure of 1974, the international debt crisis of 1982, and difficulties experienced during bank examinations where examiners in different regions of the U.S. classify the same international loans differently. The measures adopted have improved U.S. banking supervision as well as increased the degree of cooperation taking place between countries.

---

* Exceptions to this rule exist where the loan is secured with U.S. Treasury securities or where the loan collateral is in the form of a staple marketable commodity.

| EXHIBIT 12.3 | Chronology of Measures Taken to Improve Supervision of Overseas Lending by U.S. Banks |

Year	Measure	Description
1965	U.S. banking authorities establish international divisions and overseas examination programs.	provide for on-site examinations of foreign branches of U.S. banks.
1972	U.S. regulators open London offices.	Comptroller of Currency and New York Banking Superintendent establish London offices to carry out on-site examinations.
1974	Comptroller establishes a structured approach for assessing foreign government loans in bank portfolios.	Comptroller established a Foreign Public Sector Credit Review Committee that evaluates credit facilities national banks make available to foreign governments.
1974	Recognition given to need to establish a framework for multilateral bank supervision by Governors of BIS.	Governors of Bank for International Settlements forms Committee on Banking Regulation and Supervisory Practices.
1977	U.S. banking authorities begin semiannual country exposure survey.	U.S. Banks must provide comprehensive data on foreign loan and credit exposures that can be disaggregated to evaluate risks.
1979	Three federal agencies join to establish the Interagency Country Exposure Review Committee.	This move improved interagency coordination of loan supervision. Also this agency shifted focus from classifying only banks' specific foreign public sector borrowers to evaluating bank transfer risk.
1980	Federal Financial Institutions Council (FFIEC) issued guidelines for U.S. banks to follow relative to foreign exchange dealing.	U.S. banks must develop written goals and policies for foreign exchange activities. These must describe the scope of the authorized dealing, delegation of responsibilities, and types of services offered.
1983	Congress enacts International Lending Supervision Act of 1983.	Requires banks to provide periodic reports on foreign country exposure. Requires transfers to Allocated Transfer Risk Reserves against assets impaired by transfer problems.
1984	Federal supervisors issue accounting regulations on accounting for international loan fees.	Establishes uniform requirements for accounting for fees from restructuring lending arrangements and fees charged and accrued in income.

MEASURES TO IMPROVE LOAN SUPERVISION

Congress and U.S. bank supervisory agencies responded quickly to the expansion in overseas lending. A brief chronology of significant measures taken is presented in Exhibit 12.3. In 1965 the banking authorities established international divisions and overseas examinations programs (Comptroller of Currency). In 1972 the Comptroller and New York State Banking Department opened a London office for the purpose of conducting on-site examinations of overseas branches. In 1974 the Comptroller of Currency established a structured approach for assessing foreign government loans. In 1977 U.S. banking authorities initiated a semiannual country exposure survey. Two years later the three federal agencies—Federal Reserve, Comptroller of Currency, and FDIC—joined to establish the Interagency Country Exposure Review Committee (ICERC). This committee improved coordination between federal agencies in monitoring and evaluating loan exposures and risks. In 1980 the Federal Financial Institutions Examination Council (FFIEC) issued guidelines aimed at tightening the way banks manage risk within their own foreign exchange dealing operations.

In 1983 Congress enacted the International Lending Supervision Act of 1983 (ILSA). This law outlines steps that regulators and banks must take to strengthen international lending procedures. Two important parts of the 1983 Act are discussed here. These relate to new uniform categories for identifying credits adversely affected by transfer risk problems, and the requirement that U.S. banks establish special reserves against certain loan assets whose value has been significantly impaired by protracted transfer problems.

Transfer risk

Inability of country to service external loan due to scarcity of foreign exchange.

Changes under ILSA include new definitions for transfer risk. A category called "Other Transfer Risk Problems" is used to highlight credits that do not warrant classification. It includes all or a portion of credits to a country not complying with external debt service obligations but taking positive steps to restore debt service.

Credits that have been classified due to transfer risk problems are combined with commercial loan classifications used in the standard evaluation of a bank's asset quality.

Supervisory agencies maintain that the bank's management and its auditors have responsibility for recognizing and accounting for any deterioration in the value of bank assets. Supervisory agencies have responsibility to assure that banks are following reasonable and prudent policies in this regard. To assure this policy, regulatory agencies pursuant to the ILSA require U.S. banks to establish special reserves against assets whose value has been significantly impaired by transfer risk problems. This Allocated Transfer Risk Reserve is established as a charge against income and will not be considered as bank capital.

Interagency Country Exposure Review Committee (ICERC)   In 1979 three federal agencies joined in establishing the ICERC. With this change the supervisory focus shifted from classifying only specific foreign public sector borrowers to evaluating foreign transfer risk, both public and private. The ICERC is comprised of nine federal bank examiners, three each from the Office of the Comptroller of the Currency, Federal Reserve, and FDIC. These examiners make assessments and classifications of country risk, based on a wide range of data. First, ICERC receives country studies prepared by the Federal Reserve. These studies cover economic, social, and political risk factors in the country and include information concerning a country's external debt and balance of payments. Second, the Federal Reserve Bank of New York prepares and sends ICERC a list of countries ranked by ability to service external obligations.

Rankings are based on five basic ratios:

1. current account deficit/exports
2. cumulative current account/exports
3. net external interest payments/exports
4. net external interest payments/international reserves
5. total current debt service requirement/international reserves

These rankings permit initial screening to categorize countries as a) strong b) moderately strong, or c) weak in their ability to service external debts.

Third, ICERC members visit money center banks to review country files and discuss country conditions with senior international officers. Bank analyses of countries are examined.

ICERC meets periodically in Washington to assess country risk.[*] The committee evaluates information gathered, categorizes countries on the basis of conditions reported, and determines the category that applies to U.S. bank loans in that country.

ICERC measures transfer risk as follows. First, external economic information is considered, such as balance of payments trends, external debt structure and debt service requirements. Short-term loans and credits are considered relative to IMF facilities and international reserve levels. Analysis of medium-term and long-term loans require greater emphasis on socio-political conditions and economic trends and their impact on cash flow available for debt service.

ICERC then distributes its country evaluations to federal bank examiners who regularly examine the international activities of U.S. banks. Also, it distributes findings relative to other "transfer risk problems," "substandard," "value impaired," and "loss" categorizations to banks with exposures to these countries so designated.

Examinations and Transfer Risk Classifications   U.S. supervisory agencies conduct examinations to evaluate a bank's condition and performance. This test provides banking authorities with guidelines for establishing composite ratings for all banks and for the entire banking system. U.S. banking regulators use the acronym CAMEL to identify their composite prudential ratings. This refers to bank examiner evaluations about a bank's *C*apital adequacy, *A*sset quality, *M*anagement depth and competence, *E*arnings level, and *L*iquidity. Examiners establish a performance rating for each of the elements in CAMEL and develop a composite rating from all separate performance ratings.

In 1983 the federal agencies implemented new examination categories for loans and credits adversely affected by transfer risk problems. Changes include new definitions for transfer risk classifications. Credits classified due to transfer risk problems are combined with commercial loan classifications used in the evaluation of a bank's asset quality.

Evaluation and Control Over Risk

TYPES OF RISK AND CONTROL PROCEDURES

Credit risk

Inability of borrower to service loan due to financial situation or status.

International banks must deal with several types of risks in the management of their international loan portfolios, including two types not generally encountered in domestic lending: country risk and currency risk. A third type of risk, credit risk, is encountered domestically as well as in international lending. A fourth type, systematic risk, is discussed in a later section of this chapter in connection with the expansion of the Euroloan market (Exhibit 12.4).

Foreign lending is not necessarily regarded as exposing commercial banks to a higher degree of credit risk. We define credit risk to include the risk of nonpayment

---

[*] Stokes, Bruce. "Mystery Surrounds Agenda, Decisions of Foreign Loan Review Committee." *National Journal.* (September 21, 1985): 2136–2139.

| **EXHIBIT 12.4** | **International Lending Risks, Bank Practices, and Risk Reduction Measures** | | | |

Type Risk	Short Definition	Severity of Risk	Bank Practice	Risk Reduction Measure
Credit	Inability or unwillingness of borrower to make debt service payment	Low	Lend to upper tier borrowers, in top quality levels	Exposure limit Diversity risks
Currency	Currency rate fluctuations	High	Avoid exposures Fund loans in same currency loaned or on hedged basis	Exposure limit
Country	Change in political or economic conditions that impairs ability of borrower to make hard currency payment	Wide variation from country to country	[1]Some banks pull out of high risk countries entirely [1]Some banks seek to further develop broad, locally based business in country	Exposure limit Diversify risks
Systematic	Credit quality in entire market sector deteriorates due to broad (systemic) factors	Euroloan market severely impacted by series of shocks	[1]Keep exposure in broad market sectors under control [1]Substitute credit services for direct lending	Minimize exposure in market sector subject to risk

[1] U.S. Bank regulatory agencies use the term transfer risk. This includes the possibility the government will take action to prevent paying foreign currency to lenders abroad.

relating to the inability or unwillingness of the borrower to generate cash or liquidate other assets to service the loan. In fact, it could be argued that in some ways credit risk tends to be reasonably controlled, where international lending is concerned. Early in this chapter we noted that a major part of claims on foreigners reported by banks in the United State consists of claims on foreign public borrowers where there is no credit risk, claims on the banks' own foreign offices, and claims on unaffiliated foreign banks where very low credit risk is perceived. Most of the credit risk is concentrated in corporate borrowers. But here also banks selectively lend to the larger corporate borrowers, where credit risk can be judged to be lower than in the case of domestic lending. The composition of foreign branch credits is similar, with a heavy concentration of claims on other branches of the parent bank, nonaffiliated banks, and public borrowers.

Currency risk is kept at a relatively low level insofar as international loan portfolios are concerned. While the severity of currency risk is high, bank practice is to avoid heavy exposures. U.S. bank head offices lend primarily in dollars, which results in shifting the foreign currency risk to the overseas borrower. Similarly, foreign branches maintain a fairly close balancing of their assets and liabilities by currency.

Country risk

Possibility that country will be unable to service external loan due to political and economic conditions.

Country risk is related to political and economic conditions in the borrower country. There are several elements to country risk. On the political side government action may prevent borrowers from paying foreign currency abroad. On the economic side the country of the debtor may experience deterioration in balance of payments conditions, creating a scarcity of foreign currency to make debt service payments. There are wide variations between nations in the severity of country risk. The possibility always exists that these conditions will change in such a way and to a degree that impairs the ability of a borrower in that country to make repayment in *hard currency*. Often country risk is confused with sovereign risk. Sovereign risk is a special type of hazard that bank lenders may face when providing credits to governments or parastatal borrowers. This risk occurs because under international law foreign governments are sovereign and cannot be sued without consent. Moreover, courts of one country cannot sit in judgment on the acts of another country. Finally, generally the property of a government and its agencies is immune from legal process resulting from court decision.

Systematic risk

Possible changes in market conditions across an entire financial market sector.

Systematic risk is related to changes in market conditions or credit quality in an entire financial market sector (Exhibit 12.4). As we describe in a later section of this chapter, the syndicated Euroloan market was severely impacted by a series of oil and interest rate shocks during the 1970s and 1980s. Banks with exposures concentrated in this market sector were adversely affected. As a result, banks have followed two approaches. They have substituted credit services for direct lending and have sought to keep exposures under control.

COUNTRY RISK ANALYSIS

Analysis of country risk can be broken down into three components. These are:

1. evaluation and forecast of country risk;
2. designation of country loan limits; and
3. pricing international loans based on country risk evaluation.

In this section we consider the first and second aspects of country risk analysis. In a following section we consider the pricing of international loans based on country risk evaluation and consider the overall risk-return relationship.

Country exposure

Amount of hard currency lending of bank concentrated in a particular country.

Evaluation of country risk can be broken down into a two-step procedure. First, we define and measure the banks' country exposure. Second, we consider the risk factors in specific countries. Measurement of country risk factors are subject to broad political and economic conditions in that country. The country risk factors may be totally independent of credit risk or changes in credit risk. Country risk exposure exists where servicing hard currency loans in a particular country could be threatened by the inability of that country to generate a sufficient amount of hard currency or foreign exchange to meet its requirements. In this sense country risk overlaps transfer risk; that is, the inability to generate foreign exchange required to meet obligations. (see Exhibit 12.4).

Here is an example of how country risk exposure is measured. A bank lender may have $14.5 million in credits outstanding in a given country. However, only a part of this amount might count as a country exposure. In Exhibit 12.5, only $6.2 million or less than half of the credits outstanding in Hyderabad represent country exposure. This difference is because we do not count local currency loans funded with

EXHIBIT 12.5	**Measurement of Country Exposure of Fourth National Bank of Buffalo in Hyderabad**			
	MILLIONS OF DOLLAR EQUIVALENT			
	U.S. $	**Deutsche Mark**	**Hyderabad Dinars**	**Country Exposure**
1. Head office credits in Hyderabad	3.6	—	—	3.6
2. Less Interbank placements	−0.4	—	—	−0.4
3. Less dollar advance to local branch	−1.0	—	—	−1.0
4. Eurocurrency branch, credits in Hyderabad	2.0	1.0	—	3.0
5. Hyderabad branch, credits Hyderabad	1.0	—	6.9	1.0
6. Gross total of credits outstanding	6.6	1.0	6.9	14.5
7. Country exposure	5.2	1.0	0.0	6.2

EXHIBIT 12.6	**Illustration of Country Exposure of Fourth National Bank in Hyderabad**

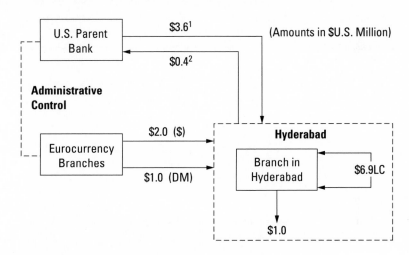

[1] Of which $1.0 is an advance to branch for local lending.

[2] Represents interbank placements where central bank and/or other banks in Hyderabad place dollar deposits with Fourth National.

local currency liabilities as part of country exposure. In addition, interbank placements in the form of cash assets held as deposits in correspondent banks would not count in the measurement of country exposure. This factor is because reciprocal deposits, or interbank placements, representing cash deposits of the central bank of Hyderabad are placed in Fourth National Bank of Buffalo, which reduces the country exposure accordingly. The $1.0 million head office advance to the branch in Hyderabad also is deducted, otherwise it would be counted twice.* Branches of the U.S. parent that provide Eurocurrency loans also contribute to the country exposure of the parent branch.

The same illustration is presented in Exhibit 12.6, where the parent bank, Eurocurrency branches, and local branch in Hyderabad are included in the figure.

---

* The dollar advance was loaned in dollars by the local branch in that country.

EXHIBIT 12.7	**Assessing Political Risk**

International lenders and investors recognize that political risk must be addressed. The difficulty is in defining and measuring it. Here we describe two different approaches toward assessing political risk.

One approach that attempts to include economic, social, and political factors into an assessment of the business climate is the Business Environment Risk Index (BERI). A panel of experts provides countries with subjective assessments, the highest possible value being equal to 100. The BERI model is useful in providing an indication of the general level of political risk in a given country. The panel of experts considers a wide range of factors in making these assessments. These factors include government actions that might affect company cash flows and valuation of property in that country, economic factors such as inflation and income growth, and the attitude in the foreign country toward private enterprise.

In contrast, *Institutional Investor* magazine surveys international bankers periodically to seek their assessment of country creditworthiness. Bankers are asked to rank each country on a scale from 100 (most creditworthy) to 0 (least creditworthy). Countries at the top of the list are considered good risks and can obtain loans from banks readily. Countries at the bottom of the list find it very difficult or impossible to obtain loan funds from commercial banks.

These two approaches share similarities and differences. They are similar in that a panel of specialists of experts provides the basic assessment input. Also, they are alike in that the assessments are subjective estimates. The difference is in their concept of risk. BERI considers risk from a broad, political perspective. The *Institutional Investor* survey is strictly from a bank lender's perspective, and therefore more narrowly defines risk.

The $3.6 million head office credits in Hyderabad include the $1.0 million advance to the local branch.

In general, American banks carry out their country evaluation at the head office. Staff economists have the responsibility of this function. Country evaluations are reviewed and updated frequently.

QUANTITATIVE COUNTRY RISK ANALYSIS

The quantitative analysis of country risk can be considered as analogous to the rating of debt issued by corporate borrowers. A major objective is to develop an overall estimate of the quality of debt paper issued by borrowers in the country. This overall estimate can be based upon a series of tests aimed at evaluating specific dimensions of debt-bearing capacity. Quantitative analysis does not replace or reduce the need for political risk analysis. Political risk analysis may be required to show that the government concerned has the political will and ability to take measures needed to facilitate debt servicing. Several political risk assessment indices are described in Exhibit 12.7.

Quantitative analysis of country risk can be carried out, using objective data provided on a fairly consistent basis for all countries entering into the comparative assessment.

To illustrate this approach, we analyze country risk for seven Latin American debtor countries. Six distinct dimensions of debt-bearing capacity are measured in this approach: liquidity, stability, balance of payments, incentives, and debt burden (Exhibit 12.8). Liquidity reflects current debt-servicing capacity. Stability measures the continuing and consistent ability to service debt over longer periods of time. Balance of payments analysis evaluates broader cash flow and financial relationships. The existence of favorable financial incentives relates to the ability of the

EXHIBIT 12.8	**Quantitative Country Risk Analysis (Completed September 1989)**						
	Weight	Argentina	Brazil	Chile	Colombia	Mexico	Peru	Venezuela
I. Liquidity:								
1. Reserves as % of Current Account Deficit	8	5	8	8	8	5	2	3
2. Reserves (Months) of Import Cover	8	3	3	5	5	6	3	8
II. Economic and Social Stability:								
3. GDP per Capita Growth	6	1	6	1	4	3	1	0
4. Real GDP Growth	4	0	3	1	2	1	1	1
5. Energy Consumption Per Captia	6	4	3	3	3	4	2	6
6. Percent Attending Secondary School	4	3	2	3	3	3	3	2
III. Financial Stability:								
7. Consumer Prices	10	0	0	5	5	1	0	5
8. Monetary Holdings as Percent GDP	8	6	0	0	0	6	0	8
IV. Balance of Payments:								
9. Export Growth Rate	10	0	6	4	10	8	0	0
10. Change in Terms of Trade								
11. Net Direct Investment as % Current Account Deficit	8	0	6	4	8	8	1	1
V. Financial Incentives:								
12. Real Interest Rate Level	6	0	5	6	0	5	—	0
VI. Debt Burden and Debt Service:								
13. External Debt as % GNP	8	4	6	3	6	5	6	5
14. Debt Service Ratio	8	4	6	6	5	5	7	6
Total	100	30	58	49	59	60	26	45

Sources: World Bank, *World Development Report 1989;* IMF, *International Financial Statistics* (August 1989); Barclays Bank, *Barclays Economic Review* (August 1989).

country to channel foreign exchange resources into productive markets (as contrasted with capital flight). The measure of debt burden and debt service indicates how substantial existing debt is relative to current income and foreign exchange resources.

The comparison of seven countries in Latin America will be reminiscent of bond analysis, where we compare companies in a given industry. For example, we compare utility bond interest coverage with the norm for utility companies, and financial company bond coverage with the norm for financial companies. In Exhibit 12.8 we obtain clear distinctions between low ratings (Peru and Argentina) suggesting high country risk for bank lenders, and high ratings (Mexico and Colombia) suggesting lower country risk.

Using the Results of Country Risk Evaluation   Commercial banks employ the results of their country evaluation systems in a variety of ways. At least four important uses should be considered:

1. analyzing loan portfolio quality;
2. satisfying regulatory authorities;

EXHIBIT 12.9	Matrix Technique for Assigning Country Loan Limits

3. establishing country loan limits; and
4. pricing international loans.

Bank loan and credit evaluation involves a two-step analysis. First, banks evaluate the quality of individual loans. Second, they evaluate the quality of the loan portfolio. As discussed in the following section that focuses on syndicated lending, the loan portfolio may take on a systematic risk that is not apparent when examining individual loans.

Establishing Country Loan Limits   Country analysis can be used to establish country loan exposure limits. The First National Bank of Chicago has used a system where risk ratings were made on a five-point scale ranging from A (very safe) to E (very risky) (see Exhibit 12.9). Determination of loan limits involves combining risk ratings with measurement of country size. These five categories are based on GNP with a size "V" country being the smallest. A size "I" country would be among the largest in the world.

Assignment of loan limits depends on the position of the country in the loan evaluation matrix (Exhibit 12.9). Twenty-five possible cells exist. Seven categories or cells (All E and D-IV and D-V) are allotted no loan limits.

In Exhibit 12.10 we present the country ratings established for the seven Latin American nations obtained in Exhibit 12.8. In addition, we review the GDP for these countries. The GDP ranges for categories A through E are also indicated in Exhibit 12.10. As indicated, Argentina and Peru obtain the lowest country loan limits, and Brazil and Mexico receive the highest limits. In Exhibit 12.9 four loan limit groups can be identified, with the highest loan limits to countries in cells numbered 1, 2, 6, 11, and 16.

Pricing International Loans   Interest rates on bank loans are influenced by a combination of risk evaluation, market conditions, and shifts in demand and supply for loan funds. In this section we consider the general factors that influence international loan spreads and explain why specific borrowers are assessed higher or lower loan spreads.

EXHIBIT 12.10	**Basic Data for Assignment of Country Loan Exposure Limits**

Country	Size (GDP)	Country Risk Rating	Matrix Position
Argentina	$71.5 billion	30	II D
Brazil	$299.2 billion	58	I C
Chile	$18.9 billion	49	IV C
Colombia	$31.9 billion	59	III C
Mexico	$141.9 billion	60	I C
Peru	$45.1 billion	26	III D
Venezuela	$ 49.6 billion	45	III C

Country size ratings are as follows:

I. $125 billion and higher;
II. $50–$124 billion;
III. $25–$49 billion;
IV. $10–$24 billion;
V. $9 billion and less.

SOURCE: *World Development Report 1989.*

In domestic bank lending interest rates allow for the narrowest loan spread in the case of central government borrowers (absence of credit risk) and larger loan spreads for nongovernmental borrowers. Where nongovernmental borrowers are involved, the loan spreads increase as a function of credit risk.

International bank lending is somewhat more complex. Central government borrowers pay varying interest rates because of differences in perceived country risk. In addition to this variance, other borrowers pay higher interest rates due to a) differences in country risk, b) differences in credit risk, and c) differences in currency of loan denomination.

There is very little published empirical work that analyzes and explains loan spreads in international lending. The small amount of literature available are from sources such as the World Bank and Bank for International Settlements. Our discussion summarizes loan spreads findings.

In a paper published in 1976 by the Federal Reserve Bank of San Francisco, N. P. Sargen* attempts to explain differences in the loan spreads that borrowing nations pay. He uses two estimating equations. The first equation shows how the loan spread varies between credits to developing countries and credits to developed countries. This equation uses 1) type of borrower (developed or developing), 2) date or year of loan commitment, and 3) length of the loan commitment. The findings indicate that borrowers from developing countries pay an average spread of about 140 basis points over LIBOR, while developed country borrowers on average pay about 25 basis points less.

The maturity of the loan exerts a relatively small influence on borrowing costs. The second equation developed by Sargen attempts to consider variations in loan spreads within the groups of developing countries. The variables used in this equation to explain loan spreads include 1) an income effect (higher income versus lower income LDCs), 2) a Mexico effect, in this case a dummy variable related to Mexico's long experience as an international borrower, 3) the debt-service ratio or ratio of debt-service payments to export receipts of the country, 4) inflation rate, 5) general increase in interest costs from 1974 to 1975, and 6) loan maturity. All six variables were statistically significant. The inflation and debt-service variables explain only a

---

* Sargen, N. P. "Commercial Bank Lending to Developing Countries." *Economic Review,* Federal Reserve Bank of San Francisco, (Spring 1976): 29.

small part of loan spreads, in each case adding about ten basis points to the spread on average. The income effect variable indicated that on average higher income LDCs paid a ten-basis point smaller spread than lower income LDCs. The Mexico effect suggested that this country enjoyed at least a 25-basis point advantage in loan spread over other higher income LDCs. The equation further indicated that on average developing country spreads increased 25 basis points between 1974 and 1975. It would appear that no single factor emerged in explaining variations in loan spreads among developing countries.

W. H. Bruce Britain carried out a similar analysis.* However, he made use of only a single independent variable to explain LIBOR spreads, the ratio of external debt to GNP. He found that LDC borrowers with higher debt to GNP ratios pay higher LIBOR spreads for medium-term funds.

In an analysis by Angelini, Eng, and Lees, the authors studied LIBOR spreads in the period 1975 and 1976. The analysis applied to developing country borrowers. Analyzing the syndicated Euroloan market during the second quarter of 1975, 13 developing country borrowers arranged loans with spreads ranging between 1.438% (Ecuador and Taiwan) and 2.50% (Guyana). Regression analysis produced an explanatory equation, wherein three country risk variables proved helpful in accounting for differences in LIBOR spreads. These variables were export growth, growth in per capita GNP, and ratio of GNP to external debt. Using the equation to calculate estimated spreads, there was a mean estimating error of 0.141% in LIBOR spreads. This should be compared with the actual LIBOR spreads that ranged between 1.438% and 2.500% in the period studied. This represents a 7% mean error when related to the midpoint of range of LIBOR spreads.

A similar analysis covering the fourth quarter of 1976 where 12 borrowers tapped the syndicated Eurocurrency market yielded somewhat different results. The two country risk variables most helpful in explaining LIBOR results are summarized in Exhibit 12.11. The equation indicates that the LIBOR spread increased by .048691 for each additional percentage of debt service ratio and by .03496 for every additional unit value in the ratio of imports to reserves.

The results of these two analyses are quite interesting, since no adjustment was made for loan fees. Front end loan fees permit bank lenders to obtain loan income up front, and at the same time permit borrowers to publicize lower LIBOR borrowing costs. In the analysis described, quarterly regressions yield different explanatory

EXHIBIT 12.11	**Regression of LIBOR Spread on Debt Service Ratio and Ratio Imports to Reserves (Fourth Quarter 1976)**		
	Debt Service		**Reserves to Imports**
Regression Coefficient	.03496		.04869
Standard Error	(.00852)		(.01134)
R Squared		0.8217	

SOURCE: A. Angelini, M. Eng, and F. Lees, *International Lending, Risk, and the Euromarkets,* London: Macmillan, 1979, 110.

---

* Britain, W. H. Bruce. "Developing Countries' External Debt and the Private Banks." *Quarterly Review,* Banca Nazionale del Laviro, (December 1977): 378–379.

variables, suggesting that banks are reevaluating country risk variables over the short run, and/or that different risk variables apply differently in influencing LIBOR spreads paid by different mixes of country borrowers.

Syndicated Euroloan Market

GROWTH OF EUROLOAN MARKET

The syndicated Euroloan market is highly efficient and low cost. As a result, loan volume has grown rapidly. As early as 1972 international lending through Euroloans had grown to $8.6 billion annually.

This market received its greatest growth impetus after 1972. When the OPEC countries quadrupled oil prices late in 1973, the supply of funds entering this market increased rapidly. The market achieved the unusually high growth rate of 38% annually in the period 1972–1976. This period was followed by almost equally high growth in 1977–1981 of 30%, stimulated by a second increase in oil prices and an upward trend in Eurodollar interest rates.

Loan syndication

Method by which banks diversify risks by allocating parts of a large loan to a number of participating banks.

Banks sought to diversify loan portfolios through a process of syndication. Banks diversified risks by subscribing for a modest proportion of any single loan. A bank that booked $100 million in new loans in a given year might distribute these credits over 20–30 different loans. As the loans increased in amount, larger bank syndicates became necessary.

Interest rate risks were shifted onto the borrower, since most loans were in floating rate form. Interest charged was based on a reference interest rate that correlated closely with the cost of funds. For Eurodollar deposits, this reference was the London Interbank Offer Rate (LIBOR), a cost of funds for banks funding loan portfolios by use of the London market. In this manner banks sought to take advantage of favorable interest margins over cost of funds (LIBOR), yet enjoyed a loan structure in which borrowers were more at risk relative to interest rate fluctuations than lender banks. In the period 1972–1981 market lending grew from $8.6 billion to $91.2 billion. Between 30% and 62% of the aggregate loan amount consisted of loans to developing countries. From 1982 to 1984 the market declined to approximately $52 billion in new loans.

Debt service ratio

Ratio of annual service payments on loan paid by country debtor, to its annual export receipts.

Between 1970 and 1982 debt indicators of developing countries advanced sharply. For example, the ratio of debt to GNP nearly doubled (to more than 26 percent for developing countries). In the same period the debt service ratio advanced from less than 15 percent to 20.5 percent. This ratio indicates the percentage of export revenues absorbed by interest and principal repayment.

After 1982, debt indicators stabilized and even improved for developing countries (Exhibit 12.12).

EXHIBIT 12.12	Debt Indicators for Low and Middle Income LDCs, Selected Years		
	1986	**1990**	**1991**
Ratio of Debt to GNP	37.9	32.1	29.5
Debt Service Ratio	30.0	19.8	21.2
Total Debt Outstanding and Disbursed	893.4	1047.0	1064.5
Private Debt as Percent of Total	58.7	49.9	48.6

SOURCE: World Bank, *Annual Report 1992*, 38.

Syndication   Syndicates of banks generally provide Eurocurrency credits. In this market short-dated Eurocurrency deposits finance longer term loans of relatively large amounts. A managing bank or several comanaging banks bring syndicates together. The following have been common features of the Eurocurrency loan syndication process:

1. Lead manager(s) assemble the syndicate by inviting a number of banks to participate in the loan.

2. One or more banks are designated reference banks. These banks are necessary to establish the LIBOR used as a reference interest rate. The loan spread is added to LIBOR to determine the floating rate paid by the borrower.

3. The manager designates an agent bank to take care of the treasury aspects of the loan. Treasury duties include receipt of loan interest, amortization, and distribution to participation banks.

4. Interest rates charged on Eurocurrency credits consist of a base rate (LIBOR) and a margin or spread over LIBOR. The interest rate is adjusted every three to six months, based on changes in market rates.

5. An elaborate fee structure is applied. Fees play an important role. In part they can be substituted for larger loan spreads. In this way borrowers advertise a nominally better credit status. Fees are paid at the outset of the loan, making the loan package more attractive to lenders. Fees influence the overall cost of a credit; this factor makes loan cost comparisons difficult. Several types of fees are utilized including a commitment fee where funds are available for the borrower to make drawings after the loan agreement has been signed. The commitment fee is charged on the portion of the loan not yet drawn. A management fee is paid to the lead bank or managing bank for arranging the loan. A participation fee is paid at the agreement date, or at the drawdown date to banks participating in the loan. The agent's fee is paid to the agent bank as compensation for services rendered. In total these fees can range between .50% to 1.25% of the face amount of the loan.

6. A large proportion of Eurocurrency credits is denominated in U.S. dollars. Other currencies of denomination have become more important, including the deutsche mark, pound sterling, Swiss franc, yen, and Netherlands guilder.

7. Syndicated Eurocurrency credits may take any of several forms. Revolving credits can be considered to be short-term facilities renewable for a specified number of years. Final repayment is in the form of a single payment. Fixed-term loans are most frequently encountered when applying a predetermined repayment schedule.

8. Changing market conditions can influence the maturity of Eurocurrency loans as well as loan spreads. In effect, there are cycles in bank lending with irregular timing. At times maturities have averaged ten years. At other times maturities have averaged three years. Generally, market disturbances and increasing concern over risk exposure result in shorter maturities and wider loan spreads.

Loan Costs and Loan Pricing   In an earlier section the pricing of syndicated loans was analyzed in connection with the role of key variables—country risk, credit risk, currency of loan denomination, and borrower status. We showed that LIBOR spreads could be reasonably well explained using variables such as debt service and the ratio of reserves to imports. In this analysis the primary focus is on factors influencing LIBOR spreads.

Loan pricing

Total interest charged to borrower, based on credit status, maturity, and other factors.

Loan costs represent an integral aspect of loan pricing. In examining loan costs, we are taking a broader view of the subject of loan pricing. Loan costs and the pricing of Euroloans carry our analysis several dimensions beyond the simple loan spread. In the case of floating rate Euroloans these dimensions of loan pricing may be considered to include:

1. spread
2. reference interest rate
3. front-end costs (fees)
4. currency of denomination factor
5. maturity factor

The first two dimensions represent periodic interest costs covering the basic cost of loan funds plus a spread reflecting necessary bank profits and lender risks. If the interest rate agreement is for six-month LIBOR plus a .75% margin (spread), the borrower will make periodic interest payments on the amount of the credit drawn, i.e., principal amount $\times$ (LIBOR + .75%).

In the case of a $100 million Euroloan, the division of the fees may be along the following lines:

Total fees 1.0% of loan amount	(Fees of $1 million)
To Lead Manager	20% or $200,000
To Managing Banks	20% or $200,000
To Participating Banks	60% or $600,000

The currency of denomination factor can influence loan costs in at least two ways. First, interest rates vary from one currency sector to another. Second, the potential gain/loss on a currency must be considered when the currency of loan denomination differs from the domestic operating currency of the borrower.

The maturity factor operates as follows: What the Euroloan market considers to be "standard" maturities changes from year to year, depending on Euroloan market conditions. In some years the market prefers shorter maturities (e.g., three years) and larger loan spreads may be required to induce bank lenders to provide longer maturity loan facilities.

Documentation   Loan agreements are important documents. A loan agreement gives a certain amount of protection to both parties. It specifies rights and obligations as lender and as borrower. The agreement specifies the conditions the borrower must meet throughout the life of the loan. Also it describes the method of operating the loan so that both sides can make it work over its lifetime. The agreement describes the timing, calculation and method of paying interest, principal, and fees where applicable. The agreement has important legal implications and must be legally flawless.

A number of specific clauses have been developed in Eurocurrency and international lending, and are included in the loan agreement. Some of the most important are described below:

1. Changes in circumstances. This clause provides that the loan becomes illegal if any law or regulation of any country with jurisdiction changes accordingly and the borrower must repay the loan. A second part of this clause is known as the increased cost clause, and it protects against a change in reserve requirements or taxes or any other factor that increases the bank's cost of funding the loan.

376 PART THREE   INTERNATIONAL BANKING

2. Sovereign Immunity. Under most laws a sovereign state has been immune from suit or seizure of assets. New York has been much more favorable to the banks since passage of the Foreign Sovereign Immunities Act of 1976, which limits sovereign immunity to contracts of governmental rather than commercial nature and provides that any waiver of immunity is irrevocable.

3. Governing Law and Jurisdiction. The former specifies by which law the contract shall be governed. Here there should be an established body of commercial law and a court system that is predictable and impartial. Jurisdiction to hear any case can be taken by courts in several countries.

4. Cross default. A default by the borrower under any other loan agreement constitutes an automatic default under the bank's agreement. This measure saves banks from helplessness if other banks are processing claims under other loans of the debtor that have been declared in default.

5. Negative Pledge. This clause forbids any further secured borrowing by the borrower unless the bank is secured "equally and rateably." It prevents a bank's position from deteriorating relative to other lenders.

Risk Sharing and Reduction   International banks have made use of the following techniques to reduce and shift risks involved in international lending:

1. Loan selection and structuring. Includes analysis of credits to screen out inferior loans, application of loan limits, emphasis on booking higher quality credits, and adherence to country, customer, and currency limits.

2. Participation in loans. Many banks participate in large loans, each taking a small portion of the total loan. This affords diversification of risk. Syndications have come to play a highly important role in overall lending.

3. Use of guarantees and insurance. Parent and affiliate companies, central governments, central banks, and commercial banks provide loan guarantees. A variety of agencies provide insurance on foreign loans and investments. The Export-Import Bank of the United States provides export credit insurance in conjunction with private insurance carriers (FCIA, or Foreign Credit Insurance Association). The Overseas Private Investment Corporation, a federal agency, writes insurance on foreign loans and investments by U.S. corporations as exporters or investors.

4. Floating rate loans. This type of loan protects the lender bank from interest rate fluctuations. The interest rate risk is shifted to the borrower.

Systematic Risk   Syndicated lending to developing countries accelerated during the 1970s. This acceleration in lending came about as a result of several factors. These include the continuing desire of developing countries to speed up economic development, the sudden expansion in the supply of loan capital through the syndicated Euroloan market, and the ability of banks to recycle petrodollars.

The decade of the 1970s was unique in several respects.

1. At no period in the past had expansion in international lending proceeded at as high a pace.

2. OPEC surpluses developed in amounts that could not have been anticipated or forecasted.

3. International banks were busily engaged in building and shaping a relatively new international money market—the Eurocurrency market.

4. The dollar-based Bretton Woods fixed exchange rate system was in large part replaced by a floating rate system.

In short, many aspects of the international financial order were being revised and restructured. During the decade of the 1970s it was difficult to anticipate an international credit crisis or a widespread loan repayment (transfer) problem. In 1977 one analyst of the developing country debt situation concluded that "The developing country borrowing problem may be temporary—that the high rate of developing-country government borrowing should subside by 1980, and that banks have acted to ensure themselves against the risk of default when that risk is high."[*] The decade of the 1970s was one in which a much revised international monetary system was implanted, where rapid changes were taking place in the structure and operation of international banking, and where Eurolending was accelerating. In this complex environment international loan and credit analysis was facing new challenges and problems.

In 1979 another analyst of international bank lending noted that "While the extent of country risk can be reduced in the loan portfolio by practicing diversification, it cannot be removed entirely."[†] Some part of this risk is nondiversifiable; that is, it is inherent in the structure and functioning of the Eurocurrency market itself. Two components of nondiversifiable or market (systematic) risk can be distinguished: 1) *market risk* or *nonpayment* related to the functioning of the Euromarket, and 2) risks faced by bank lenders when other bank lenders encounter difficulties in loan collection.

The growth of Euroloan lending to developing countries brought with it a *self-contained systematic risk* due to the following reasons:

1. Loan structure was based on floating rates. This structure left borrowers highly exposed to the risk of rising interest rates. The interest rate escalation in the period 1977–1981 imposed a shock on the market that many LDC borrowers neither could anticipate nor recover from.

2. A higher proportion of borrowers and loans became exposed to the risks of floating interest rate debt. According to the World Bank *World Development Report 1985,* the share of floating rate debt in total outstanding disbursed public debt rose from 16% in 1974 to 43% in 1983.[‡] The increase was concentrated among the middle income countries that borrowed heavily from private sources, located particularly in Latin America.

3. A large share of loans was going to LDC countries dependent on commodity product exports. The world recession of 1981–1982 reduced commodity prices and slowed the growth in the volume of developing-country exports.

4. A large share of loans was going to LDC countries that were oil importers. The escalation of oil prices in 1974 and 1978–1979 introduced two oil shocks that permanently impaired the debt service capacity of oil importer borrowing nations.

---

[*] Britain, W. H. Bruce. "Developing Countries, External Debt, and the Private Banks." *Quarterly Review* Banca Nazionale Del Lavoro (December 1977): 366.

[†] Angelini, A, M. Eng, and F. Lees. *International Lending, Risk and the Euromarkets.* London: Macmillan, 1979, 159.

[‡] *World Development Report 1985,* 20.

5. Bank lenders were finding their syndicated medium-term loans were highly concentrated among LDC borrowers. In the period 1978–1981 the five largest borrowers alone accounted for 53% of developing-country borrowing. Having shifted the interest rate risk onto the borrowers, banks were becoming aware that they had simply traded one risk for potentially greater transfer and commercial risks.

6. Lenders encountered difficulty in achieving efficient diversification of their international loan portfolios. In part this was due to the increase in average size of loans in the syndicated medium-term market. Also, this was the result of the increase in lending to public sector borrowers in LDC countries.

7. Incentives in the syndicated market were very strong for growth in loan volume. This is related to the front-end fee structure. Banks that increased loan portfolios by a smaller amount in a given year would experience a decline in fee income. This decline would take place even though total loans were increasing. The incentive was strong for larger loan participation each successive year, irrespective of the creditworthiness of loan applicants.

In analyzing the syndicated loan market (Exhibit 12.13), we can observe that the peak of *new* Euroloan lending to developing countries was 1979, whereas the peak in *total* Eurolending came several years later in 1982. Approximately the same pattern can be observed if we examine the percentage of Euroloans going to developing countries. A peak (62%) was reached in 1979, and a downtrend followed in the share of Euroloans directed to developing countries through the period 1979–1984.

EXHIBIT 12.13   **Syndicated Euroloans: Total and to LDCs**

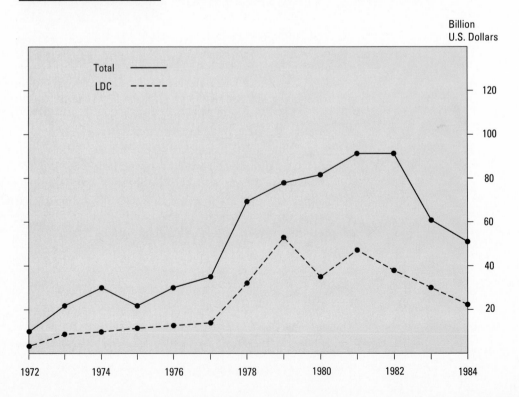

Bank lenders faced a growing tendency toward systematic risk as they expanded their lending to developing countries. This risk was due to two factors. First, the developing-country borrowers were similarly affected by global trends and developments. Rising interest rates, declining commodity prices, and a series of oil price shocks had an adverse effect on debt-service capacity. This affected practically all developing-country debtor nations in a similar way. The debt paper of LDC borrowers deteriorated in quality as a result of systemic factors. Second, through the loan syndication process, lending banks held a "market index" portfolio of developing debt paper. All of the lending banks were fully and equally exposed to a widespread deterioration in LDC debt paper.

As a result, when the debt crisis manifested itself in 1982, bank lenders found that there was no way to escape the problem. The entire market for developing-country debt paper faced an abrupt decline in value. Banks faced the prospect of holding uncollected loans, a rapidly escalating demand for debt reschedulings, and substantial and deepening discounts on developing-country debt paper.

The solutions sought by bank lenders fall under three broad categories:

1. Direct debt related activities. These include debt rescheduling, dealing in the secondary market for debt paper, and carrying out swaps or exchanges of debt paper for alternative assets (bonds, equity investments). These measures are discussed in a later section of this chapter.
2. Voluntary measures involving a shift toward off-balance-sheet operations and generation of fee income.
3. Involuntary measures that the supervisory authorities and central banks forced upon the banks.

The second and third of these solutions are discussed briefly in the following section.

New Directions

During the 1980s bank lenders revised their strategies for competing in the international financial markets. They sought to avoid or minimize the risks of direct lending and developed new sources of profit. This goal resulted in banks developing innovative financing techniques and shifting their focus toward fee-earning activities. In Chapter 6 we discussed the use of note issuance facilities (NIFs), whereby banks can generate fees but avoid participating in balance-sheet lending. Also in Chapter 7 we discussed the growth of interest rate and currency swaps, where banks can generate fees to arrange these swaps for counterparties, who are already servicing existing debt or who are in the process of taking on new indebtedness.

Finally, international banks from leading industrial countries have become subject to standard capital requirements. These requirements resulted from the Basle Accord of 1988 and were motivated by the concern of regulatory bodies and governments over increased volatility in financial markets and the consequent risks facing bank lenders. The Basle Accord calls for increased risk-based capital requirements.

International Debt Crisis and Securitization   In 1982 the government of Mexico announced that it could not continue to make scheduled interest payments on external debt. In the months following this announcement, other LDC debtor countries indicated they were unable to keep up with the dollar transfers required

Debt crisis

Refers to 1982 and following period when many developing country debtors were unable to make service payments on external loans.

for scheduled interest payments on external debt. From 1982 until 1987 the world financial system operated under the shadow of an international debt crisis. This crisis was at least partly responsible for the slowing down of world economic growth in the 1980s. With the Brady Plan initiated in 1989 major debtor countries appear to be enjoying restored creditworthiness. As a result, the emerging debt markets enjoy new life and provide opportunities for global financing.

Changing Perceptions   In the eight-year period following 1982, perceptions concerning the debt crisis evolved through several distinct phases. These changing perceptions influenced the attitudes of creditor banks, the initiatives by the U.S. government to deal with the debt crisis, as well as the mix of approaches taken toward solution of the debt crisis.

At the outset of the debt crisis, a widely accepted view was that this was no more than a temporary liquidity problem. According to this view, debtor countries were perceived as temporarily short of foreign exchange reserves. These shortages would be relieved, given an upturn in world commodities prices and as international capital markets resumed cycling mobile capital.

By 1985 it was clear that the debt crisis was more than a liquidity problem. In October of that year U.S. Treasury Secretary James Baker proposed a new initiative. This called for increased lending to 15 major debtor nations, including $20 billion from commercial banks and $9 billion from the IMF and World Bank. At the same time Baker called for new loans to the poorest countries. The IMF and World Bank were to work jointly to achieve free market reforms. The Baker Plan was significant as the first signal that recognized the severity of the debt problem.

In 1987 two developments indicated the extent to which perceptions had changed regarding the severity of the debt problem. Early that year Citibank wrote off $3 billion in LDC loans. The Citibank action represented one of the first major write-offs by a large bank. This came close on the heels of a debt moratorium, announced by the Brazilian government in February 1987.

A second development was the launching of a debt-for-debt conversion by Mexico, with the assistance of Morgan Guaranty Bank of New York. This conversion provided for the retirement (exchange) of $20 million of loan paper held by bank creditors (selling at 50 percent of face value) for every $10 million of face value bonds issued by Mexico. These new bonds would be collateralized by U.S. Treasury zero coupon bonds purchased by Mexico. In effect, Mexico could purchase $10 million maturity value of U.S. Treasury zero coupons with $4 million cash outlay, and retire $20 million in face value of bank debt. Unfortunately, the terms of this swap were not attractive, and only a modest amount of debt was retired.

By 1987–1988, analogies were being made between the Latin American debtors and the German postwar reparations (transfer) problem (1920–1928). At this time the debt crisis had become elevated in importance to the seriousness of a global transfer problem.

A fourth interpretation of the debt crisis came in 1989 when U.S. Secretary of Treasury Nicholas Brady opened an initiative toward debt reduction. The IMF and World Bank were to provide funding for debt and debt-service reduction through debt buybacks. In addition, banks could exchange old debt for new collateralized bonds, referred to as Brady Bonds. Creditor governments would continue to reschedule or restructure their own loans through the Paris Club, a format for government or official creditor loan negotiations. Debtor countries were asked to maintain growth-oriented adjustment programs and take measures to encourage repatriation of flight capital.

The response of banks to this initiative was mixed. A Mexican debt agreement was reached, whereby new funds could be provided to Mexico. A discussion of this agreement with Mexico (the Brady Plan) is provided later in this chapter.

Changing perceptions concerning seriousness of the debt crisis were reflected in the prices on debt paper traded in the secondary market, where creditor banks buy and sell debt paper. Favorable developments in the international financial position of debtor countries have been met with increases in the prices at which debt paper has traded, while unfavorable developments have been accompanied by a fall in price. We should note that individual banks may have their own specific motives for dealing in this secondary market. The more prevalent motivating factors include:*

1. desire to reduce overall developing-country debt exposure;
2. objective to achieve "portfolio recomposition" by selling some paper and buying other paper;
3. desire to generate trading profit; and
4. to make use of tax write-offs available to the bank.

Loan Rescheduling and Swaps

Loan reschedulings have functioned as a means of providing temporary relief to debtors and as an interim solution to the debt crisis. As a form of temporary relief, reschedulings have functioned to give debtor countries a breathing period in which they could achieve economic reforms and improve external payments relations. Reschedulings have not solved the debt problem, but do provide temporary relief.

Loan reschedulings are carried out under the Paris Club with respect to official credits (intergovernmental), and under negotiation with commercial bank creditor committees (London Club) with respect to bank credits. The frequency and dollar value of reschedulings increased year by year after 1982.

Loan reschedulings generally involve revising the original loan agreement with respect to loan maturities and the schedule of repayments of principal. They may also include new provisions for fees—especially where commercial bank credits are involved—as well as a new basis of interest charges. As a result of the ILSA (1983), restructuring fees are subject to limits and time constraints on their accrual to current income. Interest charges on a restructured loan may be revised upward or

Paris Club

Negotiation for loan rescheduling with respect to official creditors.

London Club

Negotiation for loan rescheduling with respect to commercial bank private credits.

EXHIBIT 12.14	**Comparison of Cash Flows of Principal Repayment Before and After Loan Rescheduling**						
	Year 1	Year 2	Year 3	Year 4	Year 5	Year 6	Year 7
Old Loan Agreement	$15	$15	$20				
Revised Loan Agreement	0	0	0	$10	$10	$15	$15

---

* Trading in country debt paper expanded when banks were prepared to admit that LDC loan assets were worth less than face value. By making provisions through loan write-downs and loan losses, banks accepted the impact on their own balance sheet and income statements.

EXHIBIT 12.15   **Debt Equity Swaps**

A few of the debtor countries whose liabilities are being traded at a discount have utilized the existence of the discount market to encourage a flow of private investments and to gain other advantages. The popular term for the conversion of discounted debt into local currency assets is a "debt-equity swap." "Debt conversion" would be a more appropriate term, since conversion of external debt instruments into domestic obligations can take place not only for foreign direct investment purposes, but also for more general purposes by residents or nonresidents of the debtor country. In essence a foreign investor wishing to buy assets in a debtor country can, through a debt-equity swap, obtain local currency at a discount.

Chile has a well-developed legal framework for the conversion of external debt into domestic assets. There is a similar procedure for the conversion of debt using foreign currency holdings by domestic investors.

The following graph explains the detailed steps involved in the debt conversion.

Debt-equity swaps are open only to nonresidents who intend to invest in fixed assets (equity) in Chile. The first step is to locate and buy a Chilean debt instrument denominated in foreign currency at the going discount. Next, with the intermediation of a Chilean bank, the foreign investor must obtain the consent of the local debtor to exchange the original debt instrument for one denominated in local currency, and the permission of the central bank to withdraw the debt. Finally, the foreign investor can sell the new debt instrument in the local financial market and acquire the fixed assets or equity with the cash proceeds of the sale.

The main difference between the debt-equity swap and the straight debt conversion is that the debt conversion is available to resident or nonresident investors with foreign currency holding abroad. In addition, once the conversion has taken place, the investor faces no restriction on the use of the local currency proceeds.

The debt conversion scheme allows the debtor country first to reduce the stock or the rate of growth of external debt. Second, it is a means to attract flight capital as well as foreign direct investment. Third, debt-equity swaps imply a switch from the outflow of interest and principal on debt obligations to the deferred and less certain outflows associated with private direct investment.

For commercial banks these swaps provide an exit instrument or a means to adjust the risk composition of their portfolio. For banks that wish to continue to be active internationally, losses on the outstanding portfolio can be realized at a time and on a scale of the bank's own choosing and by utilizing a market mechanism.

The emergence of an active market in debt instruments of developing countries offers opportunities to both debtors and lenders. There are, however, obstacles to its development. Debtor countries must ensure that transactions take place at an undistorted exchange rate, otherwise the discounts on the debt may be out-weighed by exchange rate considerations. In addition, long-term financial instruments in the domestic markets are needed to ensure that the conversion into domestic monetary assets does not increase monetary growth above established targets. The incentives for foreign investors will be nullified if the broader domestic policy environment is not conducive to inflows of foreign investment. Finally, a minimum regulatory framework is required. Documentation for debt restructuring must be adjusted to allow prepayment for debt conversion purposes. Clear rules facilitate the transactions. Overregulation, particularly in the form of administrative procedures for investment approval, are a deterrence.

Continued

---

downward, depending on conditions and circumstances of the borrower and on financial markets. As shown in Exhibit 12.14, the borrower is given a three-year grace period, annual principal payments are reduced, and a longer repayment period is provided. Several debtor countries have initiated programs to encourage the conversion (swapping) of debt claims for equity investments or for other debt instruments. Chile has enjoyed favorable success in this area. Exhibit 12.15 illustrates how the Chilean debt conversion process works. Subsequently other debtors including Mexico and Brazil initiated debt/equity swap programs. Basically the debt-for-equity swap works as follows:

EXHIBIT 12.15   *Continued*

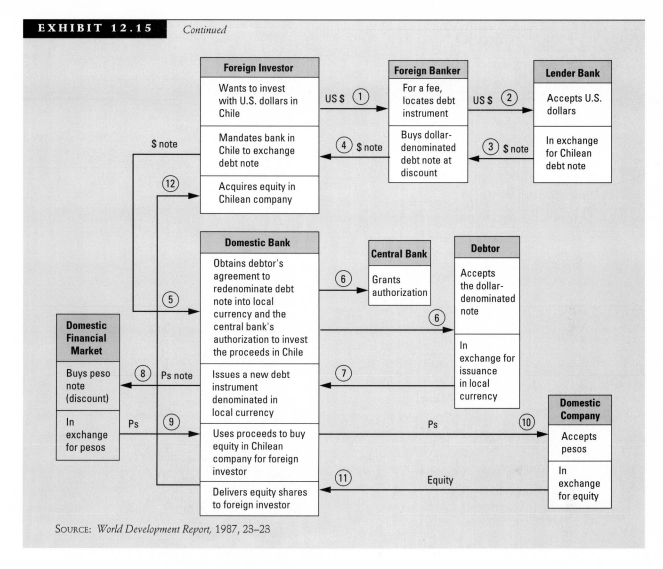

SOURCE: *World Development Report*, 1987, 23–23

Outside Debtor Country

1. Lender bank sells claim on debtor country, usually at a discount, in the secondary market to a foreign investor—often through an intermediary bank.
2. The foreign investor surrenders the claim to the central bank of the debtor country—often through an intermediary bank. In return the investor receives a local currency claim that may be used to pay an equity stake in a domestic company.

Inside Debtor Country

1. Debtor entity exchanges dollar debt for local currency debt held by domestic bank or investor.
2. Central bank grants authorization for transaction.
3. Foreign investor uses local currency claim in the capital market to acquire an equity stake in a local company.
4. Local currency is paid to the local company in exchange for the equity stake issued by the local company.

The equity stake can be an increased investment in an existing company affiliated with the foreign investor (multinational company); acquisition of an equity stake in an unaffiliated company; purchase of an interest in a venture capital company that invests in local companies; or purchase of shares listed on the local stock market. Each country regulates the type of capital market transactions that represent the local end of the swap.

Debt-equity swaps contain several disadvantages. First, debtor countries regard large amounts of conversions as potentially inflationary. Second, it can be debated concerning how much and what form of incremental investment may be induced. The overall level of inward investment may remain unaffected with the swaps simply facilitating lower-cost investment. Finally, debt-equity swaps may deflect investment from areas that the host government considers high priority.

From the preceding material we can see that international lender banks, foreign banks that participate in the buy-sell activity in developing-country debt paper, and banks operating as intermediaries in the debtor country can all participate in the debt conversion process.

DEBT REDUCTION

In March 1989 U.S. Treasury Secretary Nicholas Brady launched a new debt initiative. Brady proposed a shift in emphasis toward relief through market-based debt reduction. Banks would voluntarily reduce their claims on debtor countries in return for credit enhancements on their remaining exposure. These enhancements would include:

a. collateral accounts to guarantee principal or interest in a bond exchange.
b. cash payments in the context of debt buy backs.

Official creditors (including the World Bank) would provide cash up front for the debt operations. Countries actively reforming their policies would benefit from loans from the IMF and World Bank, Paris Club reschedulings, and loans from government agencies. Debtor countries would be expected to adopt strong policies to ensure that they would be able to service reduced debt obligations. This arrangement would include measures to promote domestic savings, and repatriation of flight capital. Banks would be offered incentives such as collateralized guarantees.

Brady Plan
Initiative to reduce debt by exchange of debt for a smaller amount of better quality and collateralized debt.

To implement the Brady Plan, countries and bank steering committees negotiated comprehensive packages that offered menus of debt and debt service reduction. These menus differed in details from case to case, and gave banks a range of choices. Some menus included buyback options—outright sales of bank claims at a discount for cash. Alternately, new money/debt conversion options permitted banks to exempt their existing exposure from debt and debt service reduction, provided they disbursed fresh money.

Discount and par exchanges combined elements of a buyback and restructuring, and proved to be the most popular options (Exhibit 12.16). Creditors swapped loans for new bonds with a lower principal amount (discount exchange) or with the same principal but lower-than-market fixed interest rates (par exchange). Creditors benefitted from the inclusion of irrevocable collateral accounts to the securities. Generally, the principal of Brady Bonds was fully secured by zero coupon U.S. Treasury bonds.

Brady Bond
Collateralized bonds issued in exchange for old debt under debt reduction/conversion plan initiated in 1989.

The menu approach encouraged nearly universal participation by bank creditors and helped maximize debt reduction. Banks could choose options that best fit their particular tax, regulatory, and accounting situations. These debt operations entailed

EXHIBIT 12.16   **Principal Restructuring Options in a Brady Menu**

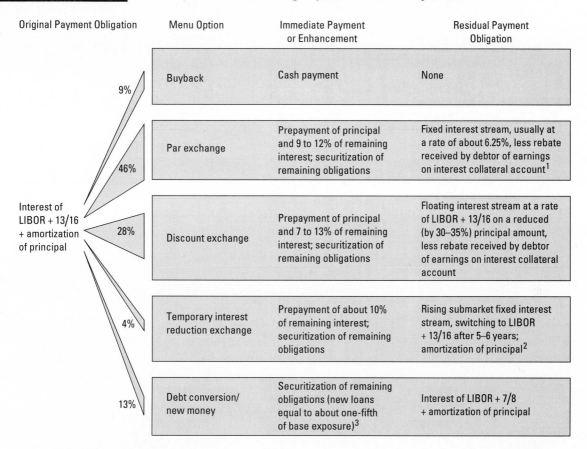

Original Payment Obligation	Menu Option	Immediate Payment or Enhancement	Residual Payment Obligation
9%	Buyback	Cash payment	None
46%	Par exchange	Prepayment of principal and 9 to 12% of remaining interest; securitization of remaining obligations	Fixed interest stream, usually at a rate of about 6.25%, less rebate received by debtor of earnings on interest collateral account[1]
Interest of LIBOR + 13/16 + amortization of principal 28%	Discount exchange	Prepayment of principal and 7 to 13% of remaining interest; securitization of remaining obligations	Floating interest stream at a rate of LIBOR + 13/16 on a reduced (by 30–35%) principal amount, less rebate received by debtor of earnings on interest collateral account
4%	Temporary interest reduction exchange	Prepayment of about 10% of remaining interest; securitization of remaining obligations	Rising submarket fixed interest stream, switching to LIBOR + 13/16 after 5–6 years; amortization of principal[2]
13%	Debt conversion/ new money	Securitization of remaining obligations (new loans equal to about one-fifth of base exposure)[3]	Interest of LIBOR + 7/8 + amortization of principal

[1] Initial interest rates were sometimes lower (for example, 4% for Argentina), reflecting the shape of the yield curve at the time of agreement in principle.

[2] Rates reflected term structure at time of agreement in principle.

[3] The Mexican new money option did not entail securitization of the base. The Brazilian agreement provides for an interest capitalization option in addition to a debt conversion/new money option.

NOTES: Most menus did not include the full range of options. Several packages provided for the refinancing of outstanding overdue interest at market rates following an initial cash down payment. Percentages show proportion of aggregate principal allocated to each menu option for agreements concluded by mid-1993. Countries also achieved debt relief through debt conversions. These conversions took place before and after the Brady operations but were not part of the menu in a Brady exchange.

SOURCE: Federal Reserve Bank of New York staff estimates.

large, up front cash outlays for buybacks, collateral purchases for the exchanges, and in some cases, payments on interest arrears. Official sources provided the bulk of the financing.

The new Brady strategy encouraged the maintenance of debt conversion schemes. The pace of conversions accelerated after 1989. Seven Brady Plan operations completed to 1993 achieved significant reductions in debt service obligations, and smaller reductions in debt outstanding. The Brady restructurings enhanced the quality of debt held by creditors, since it is now better collateralized and of longer maturity. The substitution of long maturity debt has broken the vicious cycle of continuous debt renegotiation. Brady countries are perceived to have improved debt servicing capacity and creditworthiness. As a result, these countries reentered the international capital markets on more favorable terms. There has been a virtual

EXHIBIT 12.17	**Capital Inflows and Increases in Reserves in the Developing World**						
	1975–82	1983–90	1990	1991	1992	1993	1994
	IN BILLIONS OF US DOLLARS						
	NET CAPITAL INFLOWS[1]						
Total Developing Countries[2]	22.5	37.7	37.2	152.8	142.1	151.3	135.7
Asian[3]	8.9	12.5	14.6	34.1	46.1	53.1	54.0
Mexico	6.2	0.6	9.8	22.9	26.6	30.6	10.0
Other Latin America[4]	14.1	3.9	1.6	6.1	26.2	26.3	22.9
	NET INCREASE IN RESERVES						
Total Developing Countries[2]	9.5	15.2	33.3	71.4	69.9	68.2	48.9
Asia[3]	3.7	16.0	16.5	37.4	45.4	41.8	49.7
Mexico	−0.1	0.3	2.3	8.0	1.7	7.2	−18.9
Other Latin America[4]	0.9	0.9	10.5	8.1	22.2	11.8	11.1

[1] Changes in the net official monetary position are excluded.

[2] Excluding Hong Kong, for which capital account data are unavailable.

[3] China, India, Indonesia, Korea, Malaysia, Singapore, Taiwan, and Thailand.

[4] Argentina, Brazil, Chile, Colombia and Venezuela.

explosion of private capital flows to borrowers, especially Brady countries that formerly were credit-constrained. The increase in capital inflows to restructuring countries and other developing countries is presented in Exhibit 12.17. The year 1990 represents a turning point, with significant net capital inflows to Mexico ($9.8 billion) and to other debt restructuring countries. Over the period 1991–1994 net capital inflows to developing countries averaged $146 billion. As can be observed in Exhibit 12.17, these countries experienced substantial increases in holdings of foreign exchange reserves after 1990.

Securitization

Transforming illiquid asset into a tradeable market security.

Debt Crisis and Securitization   Securitization is the transformation of an illiquid asset into a security that is market tradeable. Securitization tends to produce assets that are more liquid. Securitization has been adopted by banks as a means of competing more effectively with investment and securities firms, to alleviate problems associated with the debt crisis, as a way of developing emerging market operations, to generate income without taking on credit exposures, and to further the development of investment banking and related activities.

Securitization takes several forms, including

1. trading and sale of bank loans, including syndicated bank loans originally extended to developing country borrowers.
2. issues of securities that take the place of or substitute for loans (commercial paper, Euronotes). This topic is discussed in Chapters 6 and 8.
3. issue of asset-backed securities, in the form of pass through or pay through. A pass through allows the transaction to go off the issuer's balance sheet. Principal and interest are passed through to the security holders. A pay-through bond is a loan, not a sale of assets. Collateralized Mortgage Obligations (CMOs) are a commonly used form of pay-through financing.
4. credit enhancement. First used in U.S. municipal markets, via insured managed bond issues. Banks also provide credit enhancement by providing letters of credit to support new issues. The insured or guaranteed debt instrument can be sold to investors without updated financials.

In the early 1980s commercial banks turned to selling loans as a special stand-alone business. This resulted from increased competition (commercial paper), growing use of securitization in general, and the onset of debt crisis in the syndicated Euroloan market. Loan sales can be referred to as subparticipations; loans on one banker's balance sheet are sold on a nonrecourse basis to another bank or nonbank investor.

Loan sales allow banks to fight against loss of market share to securities houses as securitization proceeds. Buyers include institutional investors and thrift institutions. Loans are sold through assignment, subparticipation, and novation.

Novation creates a new loan and loan documentation, and the seller is replaced by the buyer with lender rights and obligations. Assignment leaves the original loan agreement undisturbed, but the right to receive interest and principal is transferred to a different lender. Generally participation is an agreement where the buyer or subparticipant puts the seller in funds for an agreed participation in the loan. The seller pays the buyer a share of the payments of principal and interest but the original credit relationship remains unchanged.

Asset-backed securities involves the repackaging of receivables (auto loan, credit card, lease receivables) into market tradeable securities. The asset-backed market for debt consists of two sectors. First, there are plain vanilla publicly traded issues, backed by auto loans or credit card receivables. Second, there are smaller issues, often with lower credit ratings or from countries that contain an added dimension of political and currency risk. Often these debt securities are placed in the costlier private placement market.

In Exhibit 12.18 we find examples of internationally issued asset-backed securities. These were the first cases of such offerings by borrowers based in these

EXHIBIT 12.18	**International Asset-Backed Securities**			
Issuer	**Amount**	**Features**	**Issue Date**	**Rating and Interest Rate**
GPA Group, Ireland	$4.05 bill.	Irish aircraft leasing for balance sheet restructuring. Backed by lease revenues or sale of aircraft.	March 1996	AA to BB Four tranches
Yacimentos Petroliferos Fiscales (YPF), Argentina	$440 mill.	Seven year bonds backed by revenue of petroleum sales to Chilean petroleum firm. Includes oil price hedge and fund to cover 3 months debt service.	Nov 1995	BBB 7.5%
Aracruz Celulose, Brazil	$200 mill.	World's largest producer of eucalyptus pulp. Security of trade receivables.	Feb 1996	BBB
Acominas, Brazil	$200 mill.	Brazilian semifinished steel producer. Backed by export receivables.	March 1996	Private placement.
Hong Kong Super Auto 1	HK$ 500 mill.	Backed by auto loans.	1995	N/A

SOURCE: Compiled by authors.

countries. In all cases, borrowers were able to use this type of structured finance to achieve a superior rating and/or lower financing cost through use of the asset-backed form of securitization. This is possible for the following reasons:

1. Generally these are overcollateralized to compensate for risk. Underlying assets have value in excess of the borrowing.
2. Securitized issues have inherently less event risk than comparable corporate obligations.

Emerging Debt Markets: A New Industry

The secondary market for LDC debt began in the year of the debt crisis. Up to that time banks swapped debt paper among themselves at face value, largely to achieve portfolio management objectives. From 1982 on, it was realized that loan repayment schedules were not likely to be met, and that the cutoff of new lending placed debtor countries in positions of severe financial constraint. As a result, we have the emergence of a market for discounted debt.

This secondary market has evolved steadily since 1983. While it began as a place for isolated one-on-one deals between banks, it has developed into a global market for bank and nonbank participants. It also has developed into an important mechanism for the valuation of debt that banks hold. This valuation is becoming more important as debtor countries enter into programs to buy back existing debt. Finally, the market has become more complex in terms of the variety of transaction types. While originally deals were confined to portfolio management activities, other types of transactions are becoming important, including speculation, brokerage, and market making. One transaction is the interest arbitrage buy and sell (Exhibit 12.19).

With implementation of the Brady Plan in 1989 the market for debt obligations of emerging countries have enjoyed explosive growth.

THE MARKETS AT A GLANCE

Emerging debt market
Market where debt of developing and transitional countries is issued and traded.

The emerging debt markets include the debt issued by country entitites held and traded by private international investors. We use a global definition, including the debt of all developing countries in Asia, Africa, and Latin America, and the debt of emerging European countries (including Eastern European countries formerly part of the communist bloc). Issuers of debt in emerging countries include the central government, other government units and agencies, state enterprises, private companies, and banks.

EXHIBIT 12.19	Annualized Return on LDC Debt Paper Held One Month
Purchase Price (% Face Value)	55.0%
Sales Price (% Face Value)	53.5%
Interest Received (Quarterly Interest Plus LIBOR Spread)	2.50%
Principal (Face Value)	$1,000,000
Payment for Paper	$550,000
Sales Price	$535,000
Interest Each Quarter	$25,000
Annualized Return	$21.8%

International investors include a wide range of types. These investors range from highly sophisticated traders in impaired debt who monitor country performance in detail, to very conservative institutional investors wishing to hold a small amount of relatively low risk claims to obtain a higher average yield. A number of professional fund managers who scrutinize risks and returns have become adept at identifying undervalued markets. Country and regional funds are a significant and more important new category for investors. Various types of special arbitrage, hedge, and speculative funds have been established to invest in emerging market debt and equity securities.

Trading Emerging Debt   The deepening involvement of international investors in emerging markets covers debt as well as equity markets. Opportunities in fixed income securities have grown impressively. Although trading debt of developing countries has been in existence for more than a decade, trading was very thin in this market through the mid-1980s. Since the Brady initiative, trading volume has increased as countries improved their economic performance and as market participants recognized that these countries could regain access to credit markets.

The growth in trading volume of emerging debt has been truly phenomenal. Over the period 1990–1993 trading volume reported by the top ten debt traders doubled each year. In 1994 and 1995 trading volume exceeded $2.7 trillion (Exhibit 12.20). In 1995 debt trading was dominated by Brady Bonds (57 percent), local instruments (15 percent), and loans (6 percent). Latin American and Caribbean debt trading dominates, accounting for more than 80 percent of reported trading each year.

The five top trading banks in 1993 were JP Morgan, Salomon, Chemical, Chase, and Citibank. The merger of Chase and Chemical in 1995 moved the new institution to first rank.

New Loans   The expansion that has taken place in new loans to emerging countries is based on the fact that debt restructuring is successful, and the expectation that restructuring will continue to take place. Market participants have become increasingly convinced that debt prices reflect risk with reasonable accuracy. As the market in debt has become more liquid, the new issue market has recovered strongly. This recovery can be seen in the international bond market, where new issues by developing and former socialist economies rose from $2 billion in 1985 to $7 billion in 1990 and to $15 billion in 1992. The volume in 1995 is estimated at close to $40 billion.

Emerging market countries have established a large number of contingent borrowing facilities, such as commercial paper, medium-term notes (MTNs), and other borrowing facilities. Many new issuing countries have regained access to these

EXHIBIT 12.20	Emerging Market Debt Trading Volume (U.S.$ Billions)		
1988	40	1992	730
1989	65	1993	1979
1990	95	1994	2766
1991	200	1995	2739
		1996	5296

SOURCE: Emerging Markets Traders Association.

EXHIBIT 12.21	International Capital Market Financing of Debt Restructuring Countries, 1990–1993 (U.S. $ Billions)				
Country	Gross International Bond Issues	International Equity Issues	Net EuroCD Issues	Net Euro Commercial Paper Issues	Total
Mexico	18.8	7.8	4.5	2.5	33.6
Venezuela	3.8	0.2	—	0.1	4.1
Uruguay	0.2	—	—	—	0.2
Philippines	0.3	0.6	—	—	0.9
Argentina	5.1	2.7	—	0.7	8.5
Brazil	10.1	0.1	—	0.3	10.5
Chile	0.5	0.3	—	—	0.8
Total	38.8	11.7	4.5	3.6	58.6

SOURCE: New York Federal Reserve Bank, *Quarterly Review,* Winter 1993–1994.

markets. In many cases the borrower is a private sector entity, not a government borrower.

We can gain some perspective on the country issuers and types of debt utilized from Exhibit 12.21. Here we present data on international capital market financing by debt restructuring countries, covering the period 1990–1993. These countries have either restructured their debts successfully in pre-Brady arrangements or entered or are approaching Brady status for debt exchange and debt reduction. Three types of debt issue are reflected in Exhibit 12.21: international bonds, Euro-CD issues, and Euro-commercial paper issues. International bonds account for approximately 60% of total capital market financing.

Why Success and High Growth   We maintain that the emerging debt market is becoming a permanent part of the international investment landscape. These reasons include:

1. debt restructuring, securitization, and wider variety of type instruments
2. policy reforms in emerging market countries
3. private sector institutional interest
4. official support by creditor governments and organizations

Private Sector Institutional Interest   The secondary market for impaired bank debt, Eurobonds, and debt of Latin American and other emerging market countries generates large profits for banks that facilitate new issues and trading of these securities.

Banks and financial institutions of various types have prospered in the emerging debt markets. This includes debt traders who in 1993 assisted in debt turnover of more than $1,000 billion. A broad range of institutional investors holds more than $200 billion in emerging debt that offers high yields (at least 3% over higher rated debt paper such as corporate and central government bonds).

Commercial bank creditors earn fees by rescheduling pre-Brady countries. Originating investment bankers earn underwriting fees on bond and note issues. Finally, fund management groups in the United States and United Kingdom earn fees on creating and launching investment funds that hold primarily emerging country debt. The estimated total profit generated from these activities in one year probably exceeds $15 billion. Banks, fund managers, and other financial institutions have strong motives for developing and supporting emerging debt markets.

Official Support   The successful expansion of the emerging debt markets has been helped by official support. Governments, particularly the United States, have taken a pro-advocacy position. The Bush administration changed the direction of U.S. policies regarding Third World indebtedness. The new initiative announced by Treasury Secretary Nicholas F. Brady in March 1989 called on banks to accept an orderly process of debt reduction and requested that international financial institutions (IMF and World Bank) support this process through changes in their lending policies. Finally, international and regional development banks such as the European Bank for Reconstruction and Development (EBRD) have worked to develop these debt markets. For example in 1994 the EBRD initiated a facility to issue up to Hungarian Florints (HUF) 5 billion. These bonds are rated AAA and the direct obligation of *EBRD*. The National Bank of Hungary issued a foreign exchange license that permits free exchange of convertible currency for and from HUF in connection with purchase and trading of bonds by foreign investors. Exhibit 12.22 reproduces the front page of the prospectus for this unique bond issue. EBRD's purpose in this transaction is to add to the range of securities denominated in HUF that are tradeable, to provide an AAA international benchmark bond for foreign investors that is issued and denominated in HUF, to facilitate inward/outward investment flows to and from Hungary, and to add to the liquidity of the local currency bond market in Hungary.

A Chronicle of the Emerging Debt Market   Some insight into qualitative improvement of the emerging debt market can be seen in Exhibit 12.23. This table depicts maturities of international bond issues for three debtor countries who at different times carried out Brady operations. Mexico was the first Brady country of the three in 1989. Argentina followed in 1992, and Brazil entered into a Brady operation in 1994. While other factors no doubt are important, the time variable plays a significant role. The maturity structure of Mexico's bond issues is quite satisfactory. All of these bonds were issued subsequent to achieving Brady status. Argentina is a different case. Most of the bond issues came before or concurrent to attaining Brady status. The maturity structure is not as favorable as in the case of Mexico. Finally, all of Brazil's bond issues came several years prior to achieving Brady status. We can see that the maturity structure is the least satisfactory.

We now turn to the secondary market for medium-term bank debt. Over the period 1986–1993 (Exhibit 12.24) this market exhibited high volatility. This volatility reflects changing perceptions and conditions in the market and economic trends in the debtor countries. The period 1987–1988 was a difficult period for this market, as economic trends in several debtor countries were less satisfactory. Several large U.S. banks wrote off large amounts of their loans, beginning in 1987. Over the period 1987–1992 leading U.S. banks charged off more than $25 billion of their loans, equivalent to one-third of their 1987 exposure. Announcement of the Brady Plan was followed by a short, up-down cycle in prices of debt. A series of Brady agreements in 1989–1990 set the stage for a 1990 recovery in market prices. The improvement in prices in 1990–1992 is well known, and reflects a revitalized interest in emerging debt market activities.

EXHIBIT 12.22 **Prospectus**

EUROPEAN BANK FOR RECONSTRUCTION AND DEVELOPMENT

ISSUE FROM TIME TO TIME OF UP TO **HUF 5,000,000,000** FLOATING RATE BONDS DUE 1999 SUBJECT TO A MINIMUM AGGREGATE AMOUNT OF **HUF 1,000,000,000**

The European Bank for Reconstruction and Development (the "Issuer") may issue from time to time up to HUF 5,000,000,000 Floating Rate Bonds due 1999 (the "Bonds") provided that the Issuer shall issue a minimum of HUF 1,000,000,000 aggregate principal amount of Bonds. Bonds issued at the same time will comprise a tranche (a "Tranche"). Each Tranche will have a minimum principal amount of HUF 100,000,000 and will be issued on the same terms as the first Tranche (the "First Tranche"), except that the management group, including lead manager, principal amount, issue price and interest commencement date may vary from Tranche to Tranche. The management group including lead manager, principal amount, issue price and interest commencement date for each Tranche, other than the First Tranche, will be set out in a supplement to this Prospectus (a "Supplement") which will be published in connection with such Tranche. Bonds comprising a Tranche will, on issue, be consolidated and form a single series with all other outstanding Bonds. See "Information relating to Tranches".

FIRST TRANCHE: **HUF 1,000,000,000** FLOATING RATE BONDS DUE 1999
FIRST TRANCHE ISSUE PRICE: 100 PER CENT.
FIRST TRANCHE INTEREST COMMENCEMENT DATE: 5TH AUGUST, 1994
RATE OF INTEREST: 27.75 PER CENT. FOR THE FIRST INTEREST PERIOD DWIX PLUS 1.75 PER CENT. FOR SUBSEQUENT INTEREST PERIODS

Application will be made to the Budapest Stock Exchange ("BSE") for Bonds comprising the First Tranche to be admitted to the "Traded" category

The Bonds will be issued in bearer form in the basic denomination of HUF 100,000 and multiple denominations of 10 × HUF 100,000 and 50 × HUF 100,000. Bonds will mature on the Interest Payment Date falling on, or nearest to, 5th August, 1999 and will be redeemed at their principal amount. Bonds may not be redeemed before such date.

Interest on the Bonds is payable semi-annually in arrear on the Interest Payment Dates falling on, or nearest to, 5th August and 5th February in each year at a rate based on the value of the Daiwa-MKB Hungarian Treasury Bill Yield Index (the "DWIX") plus a margin of 1.75 per cent., provided that the rate for the Interest Period ending on the Interest Payment Date falling on, or nearest to, 5th February, 1995 shall be 27.75 per cent.. See "Terms and Conditions of the Bonds—Interest", "Payment of Principal and Interest" and "Information relating to the Daiwa-MKB Treasury Bill Yield Index".

Each Tranche will be initially represented by a temporary global bond (without interest coupons) in bearer form (a "Global Bond") which will be deposited with The Central Depository and Clearing House (Budapest) Ltd. ("KELER") on or about the closing date for the Tranche (the "Closing Date") and will be exchanged for Bonds in definitive form on or after the fortieth day following such Closing Date.

The Bonds will be direct and unsecured obligations of the Issuer. Hungarian and foreign investors may apply for Bonds (see "Application Timetable and Procedures") but the purchase, holding and trading of HUF denominated securities by foreign investors is restricted under Hungarian foreign exchange regulations. The National Bank of Hungary (the "NBH") has issued a foreign exchange licence (the "Licence") which permits the exchange of freely convertible foreign currency for, and from, HUF in connection with the purchase, holding and trading of Bonds by foreign investors. To ensure that foreign investors have the benefit of the Licence, foreign investors may only purchase, hold and trade Bonds as set out under "Information relating to Foreign Investors", "Application Timetable and Procedures" and "Secondary Trading". Despite the general terms of the Licence, the only freely convertible foreign currencies that may be used are U.S. dollars, pounds sterling, Austrian schillings and Deutsche marks.

DAIWA-MKB (HUNGARY) INVESTMENT AND SECURITIES CO., LTD.
CREDITANSTALT SECURITIES LTD.
CS FIRST BOSTON (BUDAPEST) RT.
MKB SECURITIES AND INVESTMENT CO., LTD.
INTERNATIONALE NEDERLANDEN SECURITIES (HUNGARY) RT.
NATIONAL SAVINGS BANK SECURITIES AGENCY LTD.
POSTBANK SECURITIES SELLING AND INVESTMENT LTD.
ARANY-BROKER LTD.
CO-NEXUS SECURITIES LTD.
DUNAINVEST STOCK BROKER AGENCY LTD.
FIRST HUNGARIAN-ENGLISH BROKER INC.
INTER-EURÓPA INVESTMENT LTD.
K & H SECURITIES LTD.

15th July, 1994

EXHIBIT 12.23	**Maturity of International Bond Issues of Selected Debtor Countries, 1990–1992. Percent of Bond Issues**		
Maturity	**Mexico**	**Argentina**	**Brazil**
Over 5 Years	23.3%	—	—
5 Years	52.3	39.7%	8.3%
3–5 Years	12.0	21.3	25.7
2–3 Years	3.3	0.9	15.2
0–2 Years	9.0	38.1	50.8
	100.0%	100.0%	100.0%

SOURCE: Federal Reserve Bank of New York *Quarterly Review,* Winter 1993–1994.

EXHIBIT 12.24   **Average Secondary Market Prices for Medium-Term Bank Debt**

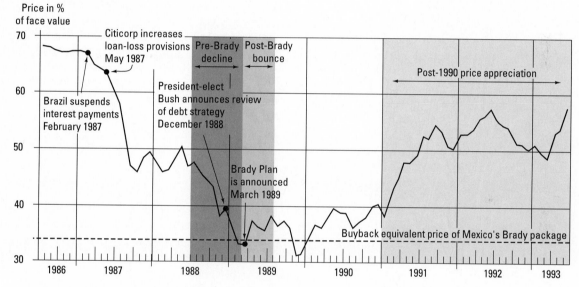

NOTE: Index weights countries' debt prices by their share in total debt at the start of the period. The countries included are Argentina, Bolivia, Brazil, Chile, Colombia, Cote d'Ivoire, Ecuador, Mexico, Morocco, Nigeria, Peru, the Philippines, Uruguay, Venezuela, and Yugoslavia. Index reflects stripped prices (that is, prices adjusted to remove the effects of partial collateralization and interest reduction) following Brady restructurings.

SOURCES: Salomon Brothers; Federal Reserve Bank of New York staff estimates.

SUMMARY

In recent decades foreign lending by international banks has played a key role in financing expansion of the world economy. These loans support foreign investment, provide credits in countries where banking facilities and capital are in short supply, and facilitate trade finance and loan reschedulings.

U.S. banks' international lending is carried out mostly in U.S. dollars. Lending procedures include analysis of risk factors, establishment of loan limits, centralized record keeping and credit review, and periodic examination of loan procedures. Country risk analysis has become an important role of bank control procedures.

Country evaluation is used to analyze loan portfolio quality, to satisfy regulatory agencies, to establish country loan limits, and to price international loans.

The syndicated Euroloan market has become a primary channel for lending. This market has proven to be exposed to systematic risk.

The international debt crisis brought a fundamental change in international lending. Bank creditors engaged in loan reschedulings to avoid default. Also they arranged debt/equity swaps to convert loans into more attractive assets. Bank creditors developed a secondary market for LDC debt paper.

The emerging debt markets have developed into a new sector of the global finance industry. They provide expanding opportunity for bank participants to trade and assist in the issuance of new debt securities.

APPENDIX

BANK EVALUATION OF EMERGING MARKETS DEBT
GENERAL APPROACH

As noted in this chapter, large banks such as JP Morgan, Chase, Salomon, Morgan Grenfell, Merrill Lynch, Lehman, and ING Bank are leading traders of emerging debt. Each has developed its own unique approach toward sovereign risk assessment. This appendix is based on the approach followed by banks such as Chase, as reflected in various publications and statements concerning this subject.

Assessment of sovereign risk uses a framework similar to what is employed for corporate bond analysis. Strong focus is on the sovereign's cash flow, balance sheet strength, and outlook for sustained economic growth. Broad guidelines followed in this analysis are:

1. Sovereign ability to pay is a primary determinant of relative value.
2. Management of central government fiscal accounts is the best lead indicator of ability to pay and probability of repayment, more so than balance of payments.
3. Foreign exchange and monetary policies determine the real interest rate and foreign exchange rate. Appropriate policies are needed in these areas to achieve sustained fiscal performance and growth.
4. Saving and investment performance is a primary determinant of future ability to achieve sustained economic growth, in turn the basis for a strong and well-balanced government budget and ability to pay.
5. Noneconomic factors are important, requiring political and institutional analysis.

The private sector is the primary source of foreign exchange flows, as well as foreign capital requirements. Debt ratios and debt service ratios must be used carefully in the analysis of ability to pay, since private sector and government sector debts and cash flows are mixed together. Erroneous conclusions can follow unless this is understood. In most emerging countries the greater part of foreign debt is owed by their sovereign, but most of the foreign exchange is earned by the private sector. For example, in 1995 in aggregate in 40 emerging nations the private sector foreign debt represents only 12 percent of aggregate debt, while public sector debt accounts for 88 percent. To service foreign debt, the sovereign must purchase needed foreign exchange from the private sector, paying with domestic money. A fundamental issue is how effectively the sovereign accomplishes the shift or transfer of foreign exchange resources from the private sector. Unfortunately, balance of payments data do not distinguish well between public and private sector cash flows.

Fiscal Austerity

A sovereign government can insure it will have resources needed to service foreign debt through fiscal austerity. The success of the Brady Plan from 1990 on was because Mexico, Argentina, and other countries adopted fiscal austerity measures, prior to restructuring external debt into Brady Bonds. The Brady Plan worked due to the fact that austerity measures provided the necessary financial economic equilibrium.

The value of sovereign assessment based on government fiscal performance can be demonstrated by comparing Venezuela and Thailand over the period 1989–1996. If we apply a balance of payments analytical approach, it appears that Venezuela has a stronger ability to pay than Thailand (Exhibit 12.25A). The current account cash flow before interest payments gives the impression that Venezuela (rated B+) ranks better than Thailand (rated A). Interestingly, the Venezuelan surplus reflects weakness in domestic investment. The balance of payments approach gives the wrong answer.

If we turn to the fiscal approach (Exhibit 12.25B), we can observe that the primary fiscal balance (before interest payments) of Thailand demonstrates a superior credit position in comparison with Venezuela. Thailand's current account deficit

EXHIBIT 12.25A   **Current Account before Interest Payments**

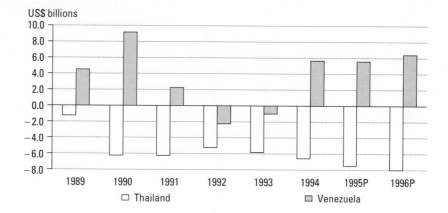

EXHIBIT 12.25B   **Primary Fiscal Balance**

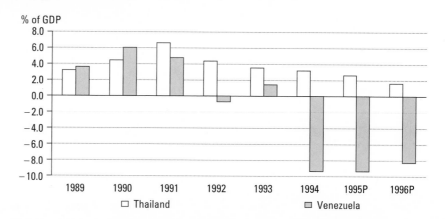

EXHIBIT 12.26   **Chase Sovereign Risk Framework**

1. Primary Budget Balance (percent of GDP). Balance of revenues and expenditures, excluding all interest payments on domestic and foreign debt. Analogous to corporate cash flow.

2. Nominal Budget Balance (percent of GDP). Primary balance as above, plus net interest expenditures, interest paid on domestic and foreign debt minus interest earned on the government's financial assets. Approximates change in total debt of the sovereign.

3. Import Cover (months of cover). Official international reserves in equivalent months of imports of goods and services including interest. Changes in cover reflect imbalances in the economy.

4. Public Debt Ratio. Total public debt, internal and external, divided by current GDP. Consistent cross country perspective on the size of sovereign's balance sheet liabilities.

5. Gross National Savings (percent of GDP). Savings ratio measures supply of domestic savings to support future growth. Low level is associated with stagnant growth or high dependence on foreign saving.

6. Real Fixed Investment (average annual growth rate). Provides measure of demand for savings for investment. Sustained positive rate of investment growth is essential for country's future growth.

---

reflects an energetic private sector financing growth through foreign direct investment and foreign borrowing. The sovereign is running a budget surplus. On the other hand, Venezuela's government lacks domestic currency to purchase dollars required for debt service, leading to debt arrears, increased money creation, and inflation.

The Chase sovereign risk analysis relies on six indicators that measure sovereign cash flow, balance sheet strength, and growth (Exhibit 12.26). This analysis allows cross country comparisons, sounds warnings when country conditions change, and relates closely to ability to pay.

ABILITY TO PAY

The 1990s have demonstrated that ability to pay is the primary determinant of market value of emerging debt instruments. This is supported by 1) growing political awareness in borrowing nations, 2) increased capital market linkages, and 3) the value orientation.

Political leaders in most emerging market countries realize they face a global competition for capital. To attract capital they must open their economies to foreign investment and implement needed economic reforms. Admittedly, there are cases of economic management failure as in Mexico in 1994–1995. Nevertheless, most emerging market countries maintain their commitment to carry through economic reforms.

Ability to pay continues to gain importance in the valuation of emerging market debt, because of the growing linkages between domestic and international capital markets. When an emerging market country converts bank debt into Brady Bonds, it has moved almost irreversibly toward the globalized financial markets in which such debt issues trade actively.

Year by year emerging debt is becoming more value oriented. Financial markets provide an instant feedback on economic trends and policies. Sensible policies are rewarded by greater access, narrower interest spreads over reference rates, and lower overall cost of borrowed funds. When Mexico allowed financial policies to regress in 1994, it was quickly penalized by falling prices in its stock and bond markets, rising interest costs, and lessened access to global sources of capital.

REVIEW QUESTIONS

1. Over the past three decades cross border claims of international banks have grown at an impressive rate. How can you explain this high growth?

2. What are the major characteristics of international lending by international banks?

3. Compare and contrast international lending to industrial countries and developing countries.

4. Describe the major credit and control measures used by international banks.

5. What are the major risks banks face in international lending? How do they control and minimize these risks?

6. Compare and contrast the analysis and rating of corporate bonds with the analysis and evaluation of country risk.

7. Explain how country risk evaluation is used.

8. Describe the role and purpose of the syndicated Euroloan market. How did this market become subject to systematic risk?

9. What have been the effects of the international debt crisis?

10. How do loan reschedulings work? Are they of benefit to banks, debtors, or other parties?

11. Trace the operation of a debt for equity swap. Who gains? Who loses?

12. How serious are the effects of the debt crisis on debtor countries?

13. A Latin American country intends to modernize its rail system with new rolling stock. The foreign exchange cost is estimated at $850 million. The modernization will increase value of output of the railway by $140 million annually. Two alternative financings are possible. Which should be used? Why?
    a. 20-year loan at 13% interest
    b. 10-year loan at 11% interest
    Principal is to be repaid in equal annual amounts.

14. Explain how the secondary market for LDC debt paper is organized. Would you expect prices in this market to be volatile or stable? For what reason?

15. A U.S. corporation is planning an investment in Ecuador. It is possible to undertake a debt/equity swap for this purpose. Debt can be purchased at 45% of face value. Currently the Ecuador peso is exchanged for dollars at 50 pesos per dollar. The central bank will permit an exchange of debt paper for pesos at a rate of 26 pesos per dollar of face value of debt paper exchanged. What is the effective cost of pesos in this case?

16. Explain the role played by Brady Bonds in solving the debt problem of developing countries. Is it likely that investment bankers will generate very much business and profit in this area in the future?

17. The country risk analysis section assesses seven Latin American nations as of 1989. Update this analysis and compare the relative rankings obtained.

18. A London bank syndicate manager sets up a $100 million term loan (3 years) with a margin of 1 percent over six month LIBOR. An American bank takes a

$5 million participation in the loan. The loan is fully drawn at the beginning of the first year. Principal repayments do not begin until the end of the second year. At that time 40 percent of the loan is repaid, with the balance of the principal repaid at the end of the third year. Participating banks earn a front-end fee of .0025%. The six month LIBOR reference rates for the six month periods are 9, 10, 10, 11, 10, and 8 percent. Assuming interest calculations are applicable to six month time periods, what are the amounts of interest, fees, and principal repayment the American bank receives on its loan participation for the three year period? How much gross profit does the bank report each year?

CASE 1

The Moroccan Debt Arbitrage

Merchant and investment banks advise clients regarding arbitrage opportunities in the emerging debt markets. Early in 1993 the following situation presented itself. Moroccan debt (Tranche A and Tranche B) was trading at substantial discount. The Tranche A benchmark asset was a yield play. What opportunity was there to diversify away from Tranche A debt into assets of similar quantity but better appreciation potential?

In 1990 Morocco and its bank creditors implemented a restructuring agreement on Tranche A and

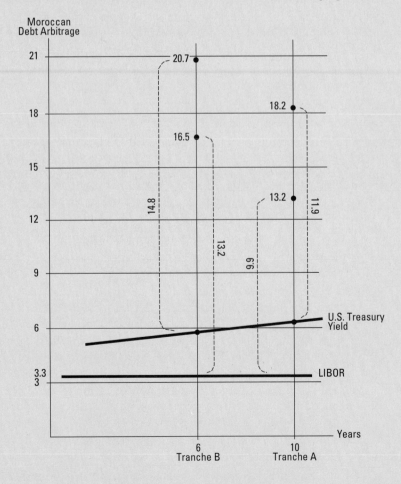

(Continued)

Case 1 (*Continued*)

MOROCCO: TRANCHE A AND TRANCHE B COMPARED

	Tranche A	Tranche B
Price (% of face)	49.375	52.0
Yield to maturity (% based on current LIBOR)	13.2	16.5
Discount margin (%)	9.9	13.2
Yield to maturity (%, based on swap rate)	18.2	20.7
Spread over swap rate (%)	11.9	14.8

Tranche B debt. Morocco was not seeking Brady debt forgiveness on either Tranche. Given its smaller size Tranche B is less liquid than Tranche A, and the latter is an attractive yield play with a longer average life (10 years). Tranche B has a superior yield and shorter average life (6 years). The higher yield suggests that the market is putting a low value on the early maturities. This action is probably inappropriate. Morocco was honoring Paris Club payments indicating intent to pay all commitments on Tranche B. Also the country has a strong commitment to make the currency convertible.

The advisory committee concluded that Tranche B is more attractive than Tranche A. An indication of this conclusion is to compare potential upside price of Tranche B if traded at the same discount margin as Tranche A. With Tranche A at 48.375, Tranche B would have to rise to more than 61 for the discount margins to equate. Given lower liquidity of Tranche B, it is unlikely that this gap in discount margins will be fully closed by the market. However, a reduction in the gap is almost inevitable.

NOTE: The discount margin equals the excess of yield to maturity over LIBOR for each tranche. Spread over swap rate equals yield based on swap rate minus U.S. Treasury yield (swap rate).

CASE 2

Secondary Market for LDC Debt Paper

A European based bank holds a developing country loan portfolio of $300 million, distributed between 18 different LDC countries. It is evaluating alternative strategies for managing and using its debt paper and for developing a new debt conversion service for corporate clientele.

Over two-thirds of its debt paper involves the following countries:

Argentina	Egypt	Philippines
Brazil	Mexico	Thailand
Chile	Nigeria	

Compare and contrast the following two strategies, using information in the chapter and sources of infor-

mation relating to the possible opportunities for investment and debt conversions in these countries.

Strategy I: Aggressive.

Develop a special department to actively trade debt paper for profit. Also establish a service facility for corporate clientele interested in finding profitable investments in developing countries. Establish a venture capital fund to make equity investments in LDCs.

Strategy II: Conservative.

Manage debt paper portfolio to minimize write offs. Use secondary market to lower overall exposure.

SELECTED BIBLIOGRAPHY

Angelini, A., M. Eng, and F. Lees. *International Lending, Risk, and the Euromarkets*. London: Macmillan, 1979.

Avery, William P. "The Origins of Debt Accumulation Among LDCs in the World Political Economy." *The Journal of Developing Areas,* (July 1990).

Bank for International Settlements. *Annual Reports,* various issues.

Bienen, Henry, and John Waterbury. "The Political Economy of Privatization in Developing Countries." *World Development,* (March 1991).

Borensztein, Eduardo. "Will Debt Reduction Increase Investment?" *Finance and Development,* (March 1991).

Britain, W.H. Bruce. "Developing Countries External Debt and the Private Banks." Banca Nazionale del Lavoro *Quarterly Review,* (December 1977).

Bulow, Jeremy, and Kenneth Rogoff. "Sovereign Debt: Is to Forgive to Forget?" *American Economic Review,* (March 1989).

Chase Manhattan Corporation. *The Emerging Markets Handbook,* (Fall 1995).

Clark, John. "Debt Reduction and Market Reentry under the Brady Plan." Federal Reserve Bank of New York *Quarterly Review,* (Winter 1993–1994).

Cuddington, John. *Capital Flight: Estimates, Issues, and Explanations.* Princeton: Princeton Studies in International Finance, No. 58, 1986.

Dooley, Michael P. "Buy-Backs and Market Valuation of External Debt." *IMF Staff Papers,* June 1988.

Durr, B., and S. Fidler. "Banks Snub Plan to Repurchase Chilean Debt." *Financial Times,* (November 24, 1989): 6.

French-Davis, Ricardo, and Stephany Griffith-Jones (eds). *Coping with Capital Surges.* London: Lynne Rienner, 1995.

Fridson, Martin S. "International Emerging Markets Debt in the Asset Allocation Process." *Journal of Emerging Markets,* (Spring 1996).

IMF. "Approaches to Debt Reduction." *Finance and Development,* (September 1989).

Journal of Emerging Markets, "Debt Trading Volume Stabilizes in Emerging Markets." (Summer 1996): 69–72.

Lees, F. "International Commercial Banking," Chapter 18 in Ingo Walter (ed.) *Handbook for International Management.* New York: Wiley, 1988.

Martinson, M., and J. Houpt. "Transfer Risk in U.S. Banks." *Federal Reserve Bulletin,* (April 1989).

Mathis, F. John (ed). *Offshore Lending by U.S. Commercial Banks.* Philadelphia: Robert Morris Associates, 1981.

Morgan, J.P. "LDC Debt Reduction: A Critical Appraisal." *World Financial Markets,* (December 1988).

Picher, Ida. "The Outer Limits." *Institutional Investor,* (April 1996): 89–93.

Rivera, Luis E. "The Influence of Multinational Bank Entry on Net Interest Margins—Case Study Spain." New York: Eastern Economic Association, March 1992.

Sargen, N.P. "Commercial Bank Lending to Developing Countries." *Economic Review,* Federal Reserve Bank of San Francisco, (Spring 1976).

Saunders, A., and M. Subrahmanyan. "LDC Debt Rescheduling: Calculating Who Gains, Who Loses," in R. Kolb, *The International Finance Reader.* Atlanta: Kolb Publishing, 1991.

Shepherdson, I.C. "The Secondary Market in Less Developed Countries' Debt." National Westminster Bank *Quarterly Review,* November 1989.

Stigum, Marcia. *The Money Market.* New York: Dow-Jones Irwin, 1990.

Thompson, John K. *Securitization: An International Perspective.* Paris: Organization for Economic Cooperation and Development, 1995.

Truman, Edwin M. "U.S. Policy on the Problems of International Debt." *Federal Reserve Bulletin,* (November 1989).

Walmsley, Julian. *The New Financial Instruments.* New York: John Wiley, 1988.

PART FOUR

International Corporate Finance

*I*n this section we focus on the international financial activities of the multinational corporation and more specifically, the functions carried out in the corporate treasury area.
Corporate treasurers interact with bankers and portfolio managers in many different ways. It
is essential that students of global finance understand the activities, operating needs, and decision problems of the corporate treasury. In these five chapters we consider the field of foreign
direct investment, financing foreign subsidiaries, cash management in the global context,
management of foreign currency exposures, and capital budgeting.

ENVIRONMENT OF GLOBAL FINANCE

INTERNATIONAL FINANCIAL MARKETS

INTERNATIONAL BANKING

INTERNATIONAL CORPORATE FINANCE

INTERNATIONAL PORTFOLIO MANAGEMENT

CHAPTER 13

Direct Investment: Empirical Perspective, Motivations, and Country Risk Dimensions

INTRODUCTION

The multinational company (MNC) has played a crucial role in transforming the global economic system into an integrated and interdependent whole. This has occurred primarily through the overseas investment activities of MNCs, which are identified as direct foreign investment (DFI). Companies' investment activities abroad are considered direct foreign investment when: 1) there is control through substantial equity shareholdings, and 2) there is a shift of part of the company's assets-production-sales to a second country (host country).

In this chapter we define direct investment and examine the patterns for United States investment abroad and for British and Japanese investments in the United States. With this empirical overview we present a textured perspective on the causes of direct investment. Our objective here is not to give an academic treatise or to direct investment determinants. Rather, we intend to provide the reader with a basis for understanding direct investment and MNC investment behavior at a more intuitive level. We will approach the direct investment phenomenon first at a macro level and second, in terms of more specific business motivations. This presentation will draw upon several company analyses as illustrations. Risk dimensions for direct investment are set forth, including both global and country risks. Finally, we identify the steps that assist the MNC in controlling these risk dimensions.

LEARNING OBJECTIVES IN THIS CHAPTER

1. To define direct investment and understand its dimensions.
2. To outline the geographic distribution of direct foreign investment (DFI) throughout the world, focusing on the United States in particular.
3. To explain the motivation for DFI and its underlying determinants.
4. To contrast cases of British and Japanese DFI in the United States.

5. To present the concept of the investment locus to understand the DFI risk-return relationships.
6. To understand the three broad risk dimensions confronting the multinational corporation.
7. To describe measures that the MNC can use to control risk.

Direct Foreign Investment Defined

Direct investment is a complex activity consisting of four dimensions:

1. a transfer of capital
2. a control investment
3. a source of funds for foreign operations
4. a balance of payments flow

Direct foreign investment involves transferring capital from a source or home country to a host country. In comparison with other forms of international investment, the distinguishing feature for DFI is the element of control over management policy and decisions. Many companies are unwilling to carry out foreign investment unless they have full or 100% equity ownership and control. Others refuse to make such investments unless they have at least majority (51%) control. Interestingly, in recent years direct investors have engaged more and more in DFI cooperative arrangements where several investing companies participate and no single party holds majority control. While there is agreement that equity investment conveys control, we note in the following discussion that both equity and debt financed capital transfers to foreign affiliate companies are included in the U.S. government estimates of DFI. Currently the U.S. Department of Commerce regards a foreign business enterprise as a U.S. foreign affiliate if a single U.S. investor owns at least 10% of the voting securities or other equivalent.

Direct investment is a source of funds for foreign operations. In this regard we consider a simple analysis of the sources and uses of funds of a foreign affiliate company. An American manufacturer of hardware has 100% ownership of Zurich Hardware Company, located in Helvetia, Europe. At present the affiliate has an asset total of 100 million Helvetian francs. Helvetian francs are currently valued at US $0.50/HF. The budget projections for next year (Exhibit 13.1) call for a 30% growth in assets, based upon a HF 20 million expansion in fixed assets and a HF 10 million expansion in working capital (cash, receivables, and inventories).

EXHIBIT 13.1	**Projection for Next Year—Zurich Hardware Company**

Sources of Funds		Uses of Funds	
	(MILLION HF)		
1. Retained profit from previous year	10	5. Increase in working capital	10
2. DFI from parent	9	6. Increase in fixed assets	20
3. Local bank loans	8		
4. Automatic increase in payables	3		
Total	30	Total	30

The sources of funds anticipated next year include the current year profit reinvested (HF 10 million), automatic financing provided by increases in wage and tax payables (HF 3 million), and local bank loans (HF 8 million). These funds together add up to HF 21 million, leaving a shortfall in financing of HF 9 million. The parent company can provide this shortfall via an increase in its investment (equity investment and/or intercompany loans) in the Helvetian affiliate of $4.5 million (needed to purchase HF 9 million at the rate of exchange US $0.50/HF).

Direct investment is a balance of payments flow. Here we use the U.S. Department of Commerce balance of payments definition of direct investment as capital flows (equity plus intercompany loans) plus reinvestment of profits earned by foreign affiliates. In Exhibit 13.1, the U.S. Department of Commerce would include Lines 1 and 2 (HF 19 million or $9.5 million) in the balance of payments definition and measurement of direct investment.

GLOBAL FLOWS AND THE PATTERN OF U.S. DIRECT INVESTMENT

In this section we consider the size and growth of direct investment flows. First, we examine United Nations data. Then, we look in greater detail at U.S. Department of Commerce data concerning U.S. DFI flows. On an overall basis the United States is the largest participant nation in direct investment. Finally, we look at British direct investment in the United States. On a historical basis British-U.S. direct investment flows in both directions have been the largest single part of the global pattern of DFI.

GLOBAL DIRECT INVESTMENT FLOWS

The United Nations Center on Transnational Corporations (CTC) assembles and analyzes data concerning the global flow of direct investment. In Exhibit 13.2 we present a summary of the principal source countries for direct investment flows over the period 1985–1994. As we observe, the global total increased sharply in this period, from $58 billion in 1985 to $222 billion in 1994. This growth reflects the acceleration

EXHIBIT 13.2	Direct Investment Outflows—Global Total and Principal Source Countries		
	($US BILLION)		
Source Country/Region	**1985**	**1988**	**1994**
Global Total	58.4	168.0	222.3
Japan	6.4	34.2	17.9
United States	13.4	14.3	45.6
France	2.2	14.5	22.9
West Germany	4.9	12.7	20.6
United Kingdom	11.1	37.4	25.1
Sweden	1.2	7.2	6.1
Italy	1.8	5.6	5.1
Switzerland	4.5	8.7	6.8
Canada	3.7	5.8	4.8
Australia	1.7	4.9	6.0
Netherlands	3.2	6.8	11.4
Taiwan	0.1	4.1	2.0
Subtotal (12 Countries)	54.2	156.2	174.3
Subtotal as % Global Total	92.8%	93.0%	78.4%
Developing Countries	1.1	6.0	14.8

SOURCE: United Nations, Center on Transnational Corporations.

in DFI in the 1980s brought on by a surge in cross-border acquisitions, an increasing interest in investment in the United States partly due to a declining dollar in the foreign exchange markets, the opening of China to foreign investment, and the wave of corporate consolidations in Europe in anticipation of the unified market, "Europe 92".

Exhibit 13.2 presents the 12 largest investing countries ranked in order of their respective direct investment outflows in 1994. The United States led the list in 1994, but its aggregate DFI over the previous years represented in Exhibit 13.2 was below that of Japan and of the United Kingdom. The Group of Seven industrial nations is included among the 12 largest investors (United States, United Kingdom, Japan, West Germany, France, Italy, and Canada). In addition the list includes the Netherlands, a traditional foreign investor. Taiwan is included on the list and enjoys a massive international liquidity position that has financed its growing foreign investment. Finally, Switzerland and Sweden—both relatively small nations—have companies that traditionally carry on a disproportionately high amount of DFI.

The 12 countries account for approximately 78% of global direct investment in the period covered in Exhibit 13.2. Developing nations provided more than 14% of direct investment in 1994, and their importance as investors is growing rapidly.

In Exhibit 13.3, we present a summary of the direct investment inflows to host countries over the period 1985–1994. Here the focus is on the 12 largest recipient countries in 1994 along with the amounts of total DFI inflows each year. Traditionally the largest recipient countries are the United States, the major European nations, Canada, and Australia. Not surprisingly the top 12 recipients include Hong Kong, based on its traditional competitive position in manufacturing and its role as an entry point into mainland China and as a business/financial services center for the region. China has also enjoyed a significant growth in DFI inflows, given the opening of its economy to foreign investment in the 1980s and its membership in the World Bank.

As a group, the 12 leading recipients of direct investment took between 65% and 82% of the total global inflow. In 1994 developing countries received more than 35% of the global direct investment inflow.

EXHIBIT 13.3	Direct Investment Inflows—Global Total and Principal Recipient Countries		
	($US BILLION)		
Recipient Country/Region	**1985**	**1988**	**1994**
Global Total	48.9	162.0	225.7
United Kingdom	4.6	21.4	10.2
France	2.5	8.5	16.9
United Sates	19.1	59.4	49.5
Spain	1.9	7.0	8.2
Italy	1.0	6.8	3.6
Belgium-Luxembourg	1.0	5.2	6.0
Canada	−1.7	3.8	6.0
Australia	2.0	7.7	2.8
Netherlands	1.4	5.1	3.2
China	1.6	3.2	33.4
Mexico	0.5	2.6	4.4
Hong Kong	−0.1	2.7	2.0
Subtotal (12 Countries)	33.8	133.4	146.2
Subtotal as % Global Total	69.1%	82.3%	64.8%
Developing Countries	13.2	30.0	84.4

Source: United Nations, Center on Transnational Corporations.

DATA ON U.S. DIRECT INVESTMENT

Stocks and Flows   In this section we consider several dimensions of U.S. investment. The first is the U.S. investment *position* that we define as the past accumulation of direct investment. As the second dimension, we consider the *flow* of direct investment in a particular year. The investment position is a *stock* concept, in contrast to the annual flow.

We focus on the U.S. direct investment position for several reasons. First, the United States continues to be the largest participant nation, both as investor and recipient of investment. Second, the shift in the 1980s and 1990s toward acquisitions as compared with de novo or "greenfield" direct investment plays an important role in the U.S. direct investment experience. Finally, the United States appears destined to continue to play a key role in light of the acceleration of direct investment flows.

Exhibit 13.4 illustrates the relationship between the DFI position and the DFI flow. As measured by the U.S. Department of Commerce, the DFI flow incorporates three basic elements: outflows of capital in the form of equity investments to foreign affiliates; outflows of capital in the form of loans (intercompany debt) to foreign affiliates, and reinvestment of earnings by foreign affiliate companies. In 1994 U.S. companies as a group increased their equity investments in overseas affiliates by $11.7 billion, and increased their loans to these affiliates by $3.0 billion. Reinvested earnings aggregated $33.1 billion.

The change in direct investment position includes 1) direct investment capital flows (balance of payments concept) plus 2) valuation adjustments of existing investments. In 1994 the increase in the U.S. direct investment position was $52.4 billion including $47.7 billion of outflows and $4.7 billion of valuation adjustment.

Direct Investment Position of the United States   The direct investment position of the United States includes the accumulation or stock of U.S. direct investment abroad (Line 1, Exhibit 13.5), and the accumulation of foreign direct investment in the United States (Line 2). The difference between these two magnitudes yields the net position of the United States (Line 3). Direct investment estimates are presented on a historical-cost basis. Thus these numbers reflect prices at the time of investment rather than prices of the current period. It is likely that the use of book value significantly understates the direct investment estimates. For the United States the understatement of outward investment probably exceeds that of inward investment, since the former is more mature. The U.S. Department of Commerce

---

EXHIBIT 13.4	Stocks and Flows in U.S. Direct Investment Position Abroad, 1993–94 (Historical-Cost Basis)

1. U.S. Direct Investment Position Year End 1993		$ 559.7 billion
2. U.S. Direct Investment Outflows in 1994 (BOP Concept)		47.7 billion
Of Which:		
a. equity flows	11.7 bill	
b. intercompany debt	3.0 bill	
c. reinvested earnings	33.1 bill	
3. Valuation Adjustments		4.7 billion
4. Change in DI Position During 1994		52.4 billion
5. U.S. Direct Investment Position Year End 1994		$ 612.1 billion

SOURCE: U.S. Department of Commerce, *Survey of Current Business.*

has recently begun to report direct investment using alternative approaches.* In this text, we adhere to the traditional book value approach for several reasons:

1. Historical cost is the accepted basis for company accounting records.
2. International comparisons are facilitated, since most countries carry their direct investment position at book value.
3. Current cost and market value estimates are difficult to obtain in a consistent manner across both countries and industries.

The data in Exhibit 13.5 represents DFI positions at year end based on past accumulations from direct investment flows. The net position of the United States as a direct investor increased substantially over the period 1960–1980. However after 1980 the net investment position of the United States declined considerably. This decline occurred due to rapid growth in foreign direct investment in the United States during the 1980s. We elaborate on this trend in the discussion that follows.

In Exhibit 13.6 we have the geographic breakdown of the U.S. direct investment position in 1994. U.S. companies' direct investment activities show a high concentration in two regions, the European Union ($251.1 billion) and Canada ($72.8 billion). Direct investment in developing countries is concentrated in Latin America and other Western Hemisphere nations. Direct investment in Japan is surprisingly low at $37.0 billion.

Foreign direct investment in the United States comes from two regions, principally, the European Community and Japan. These two sources and the Middle East have a positive net direct investment position in favor of the United States (Column 3, Exhibit 13.6).

In Exhibit 13.7 we present the direct investment position of the United States by industrial sector. From the point of view of U.S. direct investment abroad, the largest sectors are manufacturing ($220.3 billion) and finance and insurance

---

EXHIBIT 13.5	U.S. International Position on Direct Investment, 1960–1994. (Millions of U.S. Dollars, Historical-Cost Basis)							
	1960	**1965**	**1970**	**1975**	**1980**	**1985**	**1990**	**1994**
1. U.S. Direct Investment Abroad	31,900	49,500	75,480	124,050	215,375	230,250	424,086	621,109
2. Foreign Direct Investment in United States	6,910	8,797	13,270	27,662	83,046	184,615	396,702	504,401
3. Net Position	24,990	40,703	62,210	96,388	132,329	45,635	27,384	107,708

SOURCE: **U.S. Department of Commerce,** *Survey of Current Business* and *Statistical Abstract of the United States.*

---

* Under current U.S Department of Commerce procedures, the direct investment positions are valued on three alternative bases: a) current cost (replacement cost) basis incorporating adjustments for reported depreciation, depletion, expensed exploration and development costs, and valuation changes; b) market value basis, reflecting equity price appreciation, capital inflows, and exchange rate changes and other adjustments; and c) historical cost basis.

   Under the historical cost approach, the position is the book value of U.S. direct investors' equity in, and net outstanding loans to, their foreign affiliates. A foreign affiliate is a foreign business enterprise in which a single U.S. investor owns at least 10% of the voting securities or the equivalent.

EXHIBIT 13.6	**Source and Host Country Distribution of the U.S. Direct Investment Position 1994**

(Billions of U.S. Dollars, Historical-Cost Basis)

Source and Host Country	U.S. Direct Investment	Foreign Direct Invest. in U.S.	Balance
Canada	72.8	43.2	29.6
Europe	300.2	312.9	−12.7
European Union	251.1	273.7	−22.6
Other Europe	49.1	39.2	9.9
Japan	37.0	103.1	−66.1
Australia, N.Z., S. Africa	25.1	8.1	17.0
Developing Countries	173.5	47.1	128.4
Latin America and Western Hemisphere	115.0	24.0	91.0
Other Africa	4.5	0.8	3.7
Middle East	6.7	5.6	1.1
Other Asia-Pacific	47.3	14.7	32.6

SOURCE: U.S. Department of Commerce, *Survey of Current Business.*

EXHIBIT 13.7	**Distribution of Direct Investment by Industrial Sectors, 1994**

(Billions of U.S. Dollars, Historical-Cost Basis)

Sector	U.S. Direct Investment Abroad	Direct Investment in U.S.
Manufacturing	220.3	184.5
Petroleum	65.7	34.1
Wholesale Trade	67.3	65.8
Banking	29.5	36.7
Finance and Insurance	175.1	76.1
Services	23.0	36.5
Other Industries	31.2	70.7
Total	612.1	504.4

SOURCE: U.S. Department of Commerce, *Survey of Current Business.*

($175.1 billion). The industrial sectors in the United States that have received the largest inflows of foreign direct investment are manufacturing ($184.5 billion), finance and insurance ($76.1 billion), and wholesale trade ($65.8 billion).

Motivation for Direct Investment

ROLE OF DIRECT INVESTMENT VERSUS ALTERNATIVES

Direct investment is one of several approaches that business enterprises can use in gaining foreign markets. The following is a common sequence that companies use to develop foreign markets for their products:

"This progression is heavily driven by company and industry strategic plan dynamics." Vice president for corporate strategy, at a Fortune 50 MNC.

1. *export* of merchandise produced in source country;
2. *licensing* a foreign company to use process or product technology;
3. foreign distribution of product through *affiliate entity*; and,
4. *foreign production*.

The third and fourth steps generally involve direct investment. Moving from step 1 to step 4 requires larger commitments of resources and in some respects greater risk exposure. While this sequence may be a chronological path for developing foreign sales, it is not necessary that all four steps be taken; in some cases companies jump immediately to step 3 or 4.

In some cases a company either can seek to export or to produce in a foreign location. The choice may be very close in terms of profitability and opportunities for market growth. Regional trade agreements tend to induce companies headquartered in countries outside the region to use local production affiliates within the regional trade area. For example, the European Union (EU) has attracted considerable U.S. and other direct foreign investment due to the common external tariff imposed by the EC on goods exported into its market area and the absence of trade barriers on intra-European trade.

Production cost levels and possibilities of scale economies also affect the choice between export and foreign production. For many years MNCs have undertaken direct investment in Singapore and Hong Kong due to low production costs available in these nations. Because of this cost advantage, these countries traditionally export goods to third country markets.

Scale economies limit the scope of direct investment in industries where costs are subject to these influences. This trend is particularly evident in the motor vehicle, construction equipment, and transportation equipment industries. One rarely will find examples of inward direct investment in small country markets within these industry sectors. This factor is due to the need for long production runs where scale economies of production must be realized.

BUSINESS-ORIENTED MOTIVATIONS

In one perspective we can view direct investment as an activity that satisfies basic business needs. In this section we consider firm-specific motivations, and in the following section we consider broader more economically oriented factors.

We can account for most foreign investment activity by considering company efforts to satisfy five basic needs. These include:

1. need for markets
2. need for production efficiency
3. need for raw materials
4. need for information and technology
5. need to minimize or diversify risks

Many multinational enterprises give primacy in their business strategies to seeking markets, and a large number of cross-border investments are prompted by the need to expand and diversify markets on a global basis. Market seeker-type companies generally fall into the consumer nondurables category, including food processing, beverages, tobacco, and soap and toiletries sectors. These companies tend to spend a relatively high percentage of sales revenues on advertising and rely on a strong and distinct marketing effort to maintain or increase market position.

Coca-Cola is a good illustration of a market seeker company. Information provided by the company indicates that it is the world's largest soft drink company, with 45% of the world's market share, and sales in more than 200 countries (Exhibit 13.8).

Despite its success at expanding internationally, Coke believes its most underserved market is southern California in the U.S.

EXHIBIT 13.8   **The Global Beverage Company—Coca-Cola**

The Coca-Cola Company is an international soft drink firm headquartered in the United States. The company labels itself as the only global soft drink producer, with an international market share over 45%. In many international markets, low per capita consumption rates offer opportunities that are reinforced by demographic trends and the expanding reach of the mass media. The company's share in many national markets exceeds 60% (see exhibit following for company details).

The Coca-Cola system is truly global, operating in more than 200 countries. In each of these countries the company has strong local bottling partners who work under the global trademark system. The system includes more than 1,000 local bottlers.

This unique worldwide network has made the Coca-Cola Company the world's largest soft drink enterprise. Its market share on a global basis is double that of the closest rival. Soft drinks are the fastest-growing beverage in the world. Market leadership in a growing worldwide business creates financial strength and shareholder wealth. Based on the company market value at 1995, Coca-Cola was the 4th largest publicly held U.S. company with a market value of stock outstanding of $93 billion (year end 1995).

The company distributes its products in more than 200 countries and uses approximately 48 functional currencies, in addition to the U.S. dollar. The company employs derivative financial instruments as a way to reduce its exposure to adverse fluctuations in interest and foreign exchange rates. Objective measurement systems, well-defined market and credit risk limits, and timely reports to senior management are employed according to specific guidelines. In 1995, approximately 82% of operating income was generated outside the United States.

Share of Soft Drink Sales: Selected Countries

	Market Leader	Leadership Margin*	Second Place
Australia	Coca-Cola	3.9:1	diet Coke
Belgium	Coca-Cola	7.7:1	Coca-Cola light
Brazil	Coca-Cola	3.3:1	Brazilian Brand
Chile	Coca-Cola	4.6:1	Fanta(another Coke brand)
France	Coca-Cola	4.3:1	French Brand
Germany	Coca-Cola	3.1:1	Fanta
Great Britain	Coca-Cola	1.9:1	diet Coke
Greece	Coca-Cola	3.8:1	Fanta
Italy	Coca-Cola	3.1:1	Fanta
Japan	Coca-Cola	2.3:1	Fanta
Korea	Coca-Cola	2.1:1	Korean Brand
Norway	Coca-Cola	3.3:1	Coca-Cola light
South Africa	Coca-Cola	4.1:1	Sparletta(another Coke brand)
Spain	Coca-Cola	3.0:1	Spanish Brand
Sweden	Coca-Cola	3.8:1	Fanta

* Over second-place brand.

SOURCE: The Coca-Cola Company, *Annual Report (1995)*.

The need for production efficiency motivates companies to produce in countries where resource inputs are relatively low priced. Considerations of production efficiency have led American companies to invest in manufacturing establishments in Mexico (especially in the so-called Maquiladora Zone), Taiwan, and Thailand for labor intensive production.

The need for raw materials underlies foreign investment in many industrial sectors including petroleum, metals mining, forest products, and plantation activities. Countries that have served as hosts for foreign investment of this type include

EXHIBIT 13.9	**Hoffman La Roche and Genentech Spliced Together**

Genentech Inc.—the crown jewel of the United States biotechnology industry—announced in early 1990 that it would sell a majority of its shares to Roche Holding, a large Swiss health products company. Under the agreement Roche, a company of vast drug and chemical expertise, spent $2.1 billion in cash for a 60% share of Genentech. Genentech's main products are a drug that helps to dissolve blood clots after heart attacks and a genetically engineered protein to combact cystic fibrosis.

The agreement that shocked the industry was viewed favorably on Wall Street. This acquisition is one of many deals in which pharmaceutical companies have combined to meet the growing costs of developing new drugs and the need to sell products abroad. The agreement came at a time of increasing concern about foreign firms' purchase of American technology companies. The biotechnology industry is a largely American business populated by dozens of small enterprises.

Genentech—whose stock price had been severely depressed because sales did not live up to Wall Street expectations—decided that linking with a foreign partner would be a better way to raise money than going to Wall Street. Officials of Genentech and Roche foresaw no problems with their agreement, because Genentech would be operated autonomously, and its stock would still be traded publicly. Roche gets only two seats on Genentech's board that has 13 members. These precautions have helped to preserve Genentech's entrepreneurial spirit and to prevent the company's scientists and managers from leaving, a tendency often occurring when larger companies acquire small, new high technology businesses.

Under the arrangement, Roche purchased half of the outstanding Genentech shares and in addition injected $492 million in new capital into Genentech to buy new shares, bringing its total ownership to 60% and providing Genentech with a total cash hoard of more than $700 million to invest in research.

Officials of both companies said the agreement could eventually give Roche access to Genentech's strong scientific expertise that is considered the best in biotechnology. Although the companies will operate independently for now, they may also arrange to sell one another's products, giving Genentech a stronger marketing ability in Europe. The companies said that such cooperative arrangements would be forged through "arm's length" negotiation.

Consolidation in the pharmaceutical industry has already produced the merger of the SmithKline Beckman Corporation of the United States, and the Beecham Group P.L.C. of Britain. Other pharmaceutical mergers include Bristol-Myers Company and the Squibb Corporation, both American, and the combination of Rhone-Poulenc S.A. of France and Rorer Group of the United States.

Canada (petroleum, forest products, metals mining), Australia (metals mining), Malaysia (plantation), and Chile (metals mining).

The need for information and technology has motivated foreign investment in U.S. companies manufacturing computer software and hardware and U.S. and non-U.S. pharmaceutical companies. Exhibit 13.9 demonstrates this pattern in the case of a Swiss investment made to acquire U.S.-based Genentech.

A second illustration of multinational collaboration in technology development is a European and American consortium set up to develop advanced high definition television (HDTV). Exhibit 13.10 describes this arrangement in detail. Leading European consumer electronics companies and the National Broadcasting Company (an affiliate of the General Electric Company) will pool their resources to develop the technology.

The need to minimize or diversify risks has led to foreign investment in countries considered more stable and offering lower political risk. This move explains some of the direct investment entering the United States in the 1980s. Some companies based in Hong Kong have sought to diversify their operations due to uncertainties regarding the return of Hong Kong to Chinese authority in 1997. One such

EXHIBIT 13.10	Consortium for Advanced Technology TV

Early in 1990 two rival consumer electronics manufacturers and the National Broadcasting Company (NBC) announced they would join forces to produce the next generation of television technology. The Philips Consumer Electronics Company, Thompson Consumer Electronics Inc., and NBC said they had formed a consortium to develop a system for high definition television (HDTV) that is expected to produce pictures as sharp in detail as movie images. Philips is the world's largest producer of television sets including brands like Magnavox, Sylvania, and Philco. Thompson is a division of the French electronics industry. Industry analysts reacted, noting that the combination would pose a formidable challenge to the Japanese companies that until recently had gained control of the development and production of consumer electronics in the United States and were far ahead of the rest of the world in developing HDTV technology.

HDTV is an expensive research area. More than 20 research groups including Philips, Sarnoff, and Zenith had been competing to develop a high definition system that the Federal Communications Commission will designate as the industry standard in the United States. A number of these companies withdrew in 1989 because of the costly research investment required. The FCC indicated that it started testing proposed HDTV systems in 1991 to select a standard. Current television pictures in the United States consist of 525 horizontal lines. HDTV pictures would have about 1100 lines and produce pictures that would be twice as clear. Broadcasters would have to make relatively minor changes in their production and transmission equipment to send high definition signals. Consumers would still receive these signals on their current sets, but they will have to buy new sets to receive the enhanced reception.

True high definition images would come later if demand warranted, after consumers had a chance to try the enhanced system. Development of true HDTV, the second phase of this process, was the subject of the agreement announced by the Philips-Thompson-NBC group.

Thompson purchased General Electric's consumer electronics business in 1987 and still places the RCA and General Electric brand names on television sets, videocassette recorders, and other electronic devices. General Electric acquired RCA—and thus NBC—in a multibillion dollar deal in 1986. Together Thompson and Philips account for about 40% of the television sets sold to American consumers.

---

illustration is the Jardine Group whose activities in Hong Kong extend back many decades. Basically, a Bermuda-based holding company was established that holds more than half of the ownership in Jardine Strategic Holdings (a Hong Kong company). In turn, Jardine Strategic maintains substantial shareholdings in other members of the group, as well as in the Bermuda holding company (see Exhibit 13.11). Similarly, during the 1980s the Hong Kong and Shanghai Banking Corporation acquired interests in companies outside of Hong Kong, as indicated in Exhibit 13.12. In December 1994 Hong Kong Shanghai Bank ranked 18th in Moody's listing of the 100 largest banks in the world.

ECONOMIC ANALYSIS

While firm-specific factors are important in understanding what motivates certain types of enterprises to engage in direct investment, it is also necessary to look beyond individual firms. Industry-wide influences, trends in broad product markets, and other factors can also play a role in encouraging (or discouraging) direct investment.

Modern finance theory holds that firms operate in a manner consistent with maximizing the market value of the enterprise of the shareholders. If this theory is true, direct investment activity must promote greater sales, market share, and/or

---

EXHIBIT 13.11   **Acquisition and Diversification Investments of Hong Kong Shanghai Banking Corp.**

1986	Acquired James Capel & Company, U.K. stockbrokers.
1986	Established Hong Kong Bank of Australia (80% owned).
1986	Acquired most of the assets and liabilities of Bank of British Columbia, Canada.
1987	Acquired remaining shares of Marine Midland Bank, New York, making this a wholly owned subsidiary.
1987	James Capel, a subsidiary of Hong Kong Shanghai Bank, acquired 82.4% of Amsterdam stockbroker, Effectenbank Van Meer, and a 35% interest in the Toronto stockbroker Brown, Baldwin, Nisker.
1987	Rivkin James Capel became a wholly owned subsidiary and was renamed James Capel Australia.
1988	Acquired 15% ownership of Midland Bank, U.K.
1989	Acquired Kidde Credit Corp. (U.S.) from Hanson P.L.C. (U.K.) for $60 million via a U.S. subsidiary Concord Commercial Corp.
1992–1994	Completed the takeover (more than 50% interest) of Midland Bank. Result: the second largest non-Japanese bank in the world, and the largest in the U.K

---

profit. We consider four approaches based on economic analysis to explain how DFI takes place. All four approaches can be reconciled with the modern theory of finance and the maximization of shareholder value.

The four approaches are:

1. Market imperfections
2. Role of government
3. Internalization and the Eclectic Theory
4. Portfolio Theory

Market Imperfections   Much of the literature on DFI focuses on imperfections in product and factor markets, stemming from the work of Hymer and Kindleberger and others who have contributed to this approach. While the main body of these writings focuses on manufacturing investment, related theories based on financial market imperfections have appeared.

Market imperfections may be naturally arising, for example, as a result of limited amounts and locations of certain mineral deposits. More often they are related to the activities of firms seeking to gain market advantage, or to the policies of governments. Oligopolistic firms create competitive advantage through product differentiation, obtaining patents and copyrights, franchising, or gaining government support and protection (tariffs on imports). Governments create market imperfections by imposing tariffs and nontariff barriers on imports, tax incentives, subsidies, and controls on financial transactions.

What is important to the MNC is its ability to exploit market imperfections, especially where the MNC operates differently across nations, as seen in Exhibit 13.13. The degree of monopolistic pricing can vary considerably across product and factor markets from country to country. This dimension alone provides profitable opportunities for MNCs. Given these imperfections, the MNC can operate in such a way as to allow all units to benefit from market imperfections.

EXHIBIT 13.12   Jardine Group Has One Foot in Bermuda

This example is a case of a corporate reorganization and direct investment aimed at minimizing political risk. The reorganization created a Bermuda-based holding company that effectively protects against political changes anticipated in Hong Kong with the reversion of the city to Chinese sovereignty in 1997. The Jardine Group also delisted itself from the Hong Kong Stock Exchange and switched share trading in its main subsidiaries to Singapore. At the same time the company has sought to maintain some elements of its business in Hong Kong, for example, in 1996 to gain a share in the Hong Kong overseas shipping container business.

Jardine Matheson Holdings Ltd. The company was incorporated in Bermuda 9 April 1984, and under reorganization became the holding company

of the Jardine Group. With the reorganization, all shares in Jardine Matheson & Company Ltd. (JM&Co) were cancelled, and shareholders received shares in the company on the basis of one share for each share held in the predecessor company (JM&Co).

Jardine Strategic Holdings Ltd. This company was incorporated 16 November 1986 as Hong Kong Investors Ltd. in anticipation of the major restructuring of Jardine Matheson. The company subsequently acquired stakes in Jardine Matheson Holdings Ltd., the Hong Kong Land Co. Ltd., and Dairy Farms International Holdings Ltd. It merged with Jardine Securities Ltd., and the present name was adopted in 1987. The company is effectively owned 55% by Jardine Matheson.

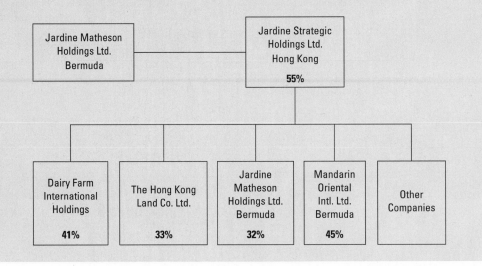

Role of Government   Governments create market imperfections. These can operate through regional trading groups such as the Common Market in Europe in 1958 and the European Single Market in 1992. Governments also create imperfections by providing subsidies to foreign investors. Each of the 50 states in the United States seeks to attract foreign investors by offering low cost land sites, tax deferral, and other subsidy benefits to foreign investors. In the case of the Volkswagen investment in western Pennsylvania, Gordon and Lees estimated that state and local governments provided substantial subsidies, as seen in Exhibit 13.14.

Internalization and the Eclectic Theory   To more fully explain DFI, it is necessary to draw on different elements of analysis. In 1977 John Dunning noted this

EXHIBIT 13.13	Multinational Companies Exploit Market Imperfections

Essential Characteristics of MNC	How MNC Exploits Imperfection
1. Able to exploit differences in national economic environment.	a. U.S. firms use low labor costs in offshore assembly. b. MNCs borrow in low cost Euromarkets.
2. Operates all units to achieve system objectives.	a. Divides production between affiliates to minimize costs. b. Allocates profit between affiliates to minimize global taxes. c. Shifts currency exposures among affiliates to minimize system exposure.
3. Able to internalize firm-specific advantages.	a. Uses proprietary information to develop better products. b. Manufacturer of transport equipment uses process technology in several affiliates around the world. c. Petrochemical firm employs prior technology base to develop improved method of manufacturing.

EXHIBIT 13.14	Volkswagen in America: DFI Under Subsidy

Multinational companies employ a variety of strategies in their efforts to enlarge market share and global profitability. The Volkswagen investment in a U.S. production facility in the late 1970s is a specific example of how a MNC adapted to shifts in its international competitive position.

Volkswagen was the largest foreign supplier of automobiles to the United States, with annual export sales to the United States exceeding 500,000 units in the early 1970s. The VW market share was based on a strong export position, an overvalued dollar, and the emphasis of American manufacturers on large cars. A sharp decline in U.S. market share in the period 1972–1975 led Volkswagen to reappraise corporate strategy. By 1975–1976, the German parent company was working on plans to establish a production facility in the United States. Volkswagen made the 1977 investment under the following conditions:

1. Volkswagen received considerable investment incentives from state and local government units in Pennsylvania. The net present value of these subsidies exceeded $111 million. The subsidy benefits raised the estimated internal rate of return of the Volkswagen investment in the United States from 18% to 23.5%.

2. As a MNC operating production and distribution units in a number of countries, VW is able to engage in various financial and other activities that provide substantial cash flow and profitability benefits. These activities include transfer pricing and profit-tax advantages. In the late 1970s there were specific currency relationships that afforded opportunities for favorable transfer pricing practices.

3. At the time of the investment in the United States, VW was manufacturing automobile components in West Germany, Latin America, and the United States. Under this configuration, the Pennsylvania project provided an opportunity to transfer profits between these units.

4. In the case of the Volkswagen investment in the United States, transfer pricing opportunities included sale and servicing of components between parent and overseas subsidiaries, loan interest and repayment of loan principal to the West German parent, sale of used capital equipment to Volkswagen America, and management fees charged the U.S. affiliate.

EXHIBIT 13.15	Risk-Return Properties of U.S. Domestic, Three Foreign Investment Projects, and Mixed Portfolios			
	Mean Return, %	Standard Deviation	Correlation of Return with U.S.	Covariance of Return with U.S.
Projects				
Canada Project	25	12	1.0	144
British Project	20	8	0	0
Australian Project	20	10	−1.0	−120
U.S. Domestic	18	12		
Portfolios:				
U.S.-Canada	21.5	12.0		
U.S.-British	19.0	7.2		
U.S.-Australia	19.0	1.0		

NOTE: Portfolios are weighted 50-50 U.S. and foreign.

Eclectic theory addresses directly the choice between export and licensing on the one hand and foreign production on the other.

diversity in his development of an "eclectic theory" of DFI. At that time, Dunning offered a theory that brought together several aspects of economic analysis, including industrial organization theory, international trade theory, the theory of the firm, and the theory of international competitive advantage (ownership, internalization, and locational advantages of the firm).*

To serve particular markets, according to Dunning, the firm must possess ownership advantages that are exclusive to that firm. These advantages consist of firm size, existing market position, access to resources, and possession of intangible assets (patents, copyrights, and organizational skills). The firm benefits more by using these advantages internally, rather than by selling or leasing them to others. The firm exploits its ownership advantages by extending its operations through DFI. Multinationals serve foreign markets and simultaneously allocate productive resources according to their own control procedures. Firms can bypass the market and internalize their ownership advantages.

Dunning's eclectic theory draws on a wide range of factors to explain how MNCs make DFI decisions. In this regard, his approach appears to be more realistic than the approaches of others.

Portfolio Theory Portfolio theory is another perspective by which to understand direct investment and the incentives of companies to engage in DFI. Consider an American manufacturing company that plans to invest in a new plant that can be located either in Britain, Canada, or Australia. Exhibit 13.15 presents the expected mean return, standard deviation (risk), and correlation of returns with those in the United States. When the investment is made, the weighted composition of assets, sales, and profits will be 50% United States, and 50% foreign.

Company boards of directors will frequently emphasize the diversified portfolio approach.

Portfolio theory tells us that a diversified portfolio may provide better overall outcomes than one that is not well diversified. Analogously, MNCs that diversify their operations internationally may achieve a better risk-return outcome than

---

* This theory is summarized in Dunning, John. "Trade Location of Economic Activity and the NME: A Search for an Eclectic Approach," in Bertil Ohlin, Par-Ove Hesselborn, and Per Magnus Wijkman (eds). *The International Allocation of Economic Activity.* New York: Holmes and Meier, 1977, pp. 395–418. The internalization theory was first expounded in Buckley, Peter, and Mark Casson. *The Future of the Multinational Enterprise.* London: Macmillan, 1976.

| **EXHIBIT 13.16** | **Risk-Return Properties of Investment Portfolios and Projects** |

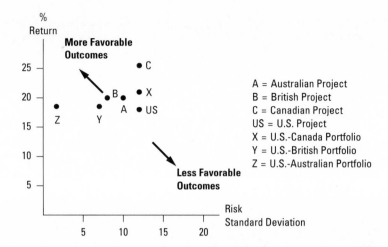

companies that operate purely as domestic entities. We can visualize this by referring to Exhibit 13.16 that portrays possible risk-return outcomes. As we note in the following discussion, a suitable portfolio of investment projects can generate a superior outcome.

Returning to the threefold choice available to the American company, in Exhibit 13.15 we see that the risk-return properties of the three foreign investment projects are fairly close. However, when we project the risk-return properties of the portfolios (MNC with 50% U.S. and 50% overseas), we have the risk-return characteristics outlined in the lower part of Exhibit 13.15.

Taking the case where the American company decides to invest in the Canadian plant, the enlarged firm's expected return will be:

$$R_e = W_{US} \times R_{US} + W_{Cdn} \times R_{Cdn}$$
$$= .50 \times 18\% + .50 \times 25\%$$
$$= 9.0\% + 12.5\%$$
$$= 21.5\%$$

Note that we have weighted the return of each component of the enlarged firm by its weight in the portfolio. Similar calculations are applied for the case where the American company decides to invest in the British or Australian plants. In these cases, the weighted return is 19%.

We can calculate portfolio risk (standard deviation) by use of the following relationship:

$$\text{Portfolio Standard Deviation} = \sqrt{W^2_{US}\,\sigma^2_{US} + W^2_{Cdn}\,\sigma^2_{Cdn} + 2W_{US}W_{Cdn}(COV_{US,Cdn})}$$

In this case W_{US} and W_{Cdn} represent the percent weight of portfolio in the United States and Canada, s_{US} and s_{Cdn} represent the standard deviation of return on the U.S. and Canadian investments respectively, and $COV_{US,Cdn}$ is the covariance of returns between the U.S. and Canadian investments. We apply this equation to the calculation of the portfolio standard deviation as follows:

$$\text{Portfolio Standard Deviation} = \sqrt{.5^2 12^2 + .5^2 12^2 + 2(.5)(.5)(144)}$$

$$= \sqrt{36 + 36 + 72 = 144}$$

$$= 12$$

Note that there is no risk reduction when the American company invests in a Canadian plant. This factor is due to the assumed perfect positive correlation of returns for the U.S. and Canadian investments. A decision to locate the plant where the correlation of returns is low or even negative can provide considerable risk reduction. When investing in Australia, the portfolio standard deviation (risk) is 1. Chapters 18–20 explain portfolio construction and *portfolio risk reduction* in greater detail.

The investment in Australia provides the least risky (most stable) overall return to the enlarged firm. We can obtain a clearer picture of the risk-return outcomes in the three alternative foreign investment cases in Exhibit 13.16. Here we plot risk-return for each of the three foreign investments projects (A, B, and C), the U.S. domestic operation, and three portfolios (X, Y, and Z). It is clear that the Z portfolio (50% U.S. plus 50% Australia) provides a superior risk-return outcome.

BRITISH INVESTMENT IN THE UNITED STATES: A REMARKABLE SEVEN YEARS

This historical episode provides considerable insight into factors affecting MNC direct investment choices.

Importance   British outward direct investment has increased rapidly since the late 1970s, in part coinciding with the liberalization of foreign investment under the Thatcher government. The seven-year time period from 1979 to 1986 deserves special attention in our study of DFI determinants. During this period the stock of British direct investment abroad increased more than fourfold, from £17.9 billion to £74.6 billion. After 1979 British DFI shifted toward the United States, which came to account for half of the total stock of British direct investment.

British investment in the United States has taken the form of acquisitions, more than de novo or greenfield operations, and has been highly diversified. According to J. Hamill in the period 1976–1986 there were at least 1572 direct investment transactions in the United States by British investors.* Taking the same period for the 784 transactions where the value of the investment is known, the total value of British direct investment in the United States was $36.6 billion. The industrial sector breakdown of these investment transactions in the United States includes the following: manufacturing, 48%; wholesale and retail trade, 20%; and financial and other services, 19%. Within the manufacturing sector, British companies have invested fairly evenly across a range of industries in the United States with a large number of investments made in chemicals, electrical and electronic equipment, machinery, printing and publishing, metal manufacturing, and the food-drink-tobacco

---

* Hamill, J. "British Acquisitions in the United States," *National Westminster Bank Quarterly Review* (August 1988): 2–17.

sector. British companies carried out significant investment in building products, oil, and transport equipment.

Pattern and Type of Investment   British companies have used the *acquisition of U.S. enterprises* as the dominant entry mode for investing in the United States. As presented in Exhibit 13.17, over the period 1976–1986, 719 of 1253 or 57% of total transactions were acquisitions. By contrast de novo plants have been a relatively less important mode of entry, involving 106 transactions or 8% of the total.

More than 300 British parent companies have engaged in direct investment in the United States, including many small- and medium-size companies. There is a high correlation between the size of U.S. acquisitions and the size of the British parent company. The largest acquisitions generally are made by the largest British parent companies. Exhibits 13.18 and 13.19 broadly depict this pattern. Exhibit 13.18 describes the major British investment acquisitions in the U.S. in the period 1978–1986. Several large British firms appear a number of times as investors (BAT, Grand Metropolitan, Hanson).

Analysis of the investment transactions by type of British parent company provides insight into the strategic motivations underlying these investments. Exhibit 13.19 presents five types of British companies, estimates of the value of their investment transactions, and their chief characteristics. Large conglomerate/holding companies represent the largest size group of British investors. Seven conglomerates have made more than 125 separate U.S. investments with a total value in excess of $8 billion. Most investments have involved acquisitions in printing and publishing, food and tobacco, restaurants, and hotels. Several examples of these are presented in Exhibit 13.18.

Oil companies have been the second largest group of British investors in the United States with 46 investments totaling $3.4–$4.0 billion. British Petroleum is the most important investor in this sector, with more than three-fourths of the total value.

British banks represent the third major type of investor. In this case there have been a limited number of high-value strategic acquisitions of United States banks, including Natwest-National Bank of North America, Barclay's-Aetna Business Group and the Beneficial Corporation, and Lloyd's-Talcott National.

The manufacturing sector represents the fourth type of investor and displays the greatest diversity of activity in the United States. A small number of the largest British manufacturing companies have made substantial investments in the number of transactions and overall value. The fifth company type, nonmanufacturing, includes British investors in insurance services, advertising, and retail outlets. The

EXHIBIT 13.17	**British Direct Investment Transactions in the United States, by Type, 1976–1986**

(Number of Transactions)

	Acquisition	Joint Venture	New Plant	Plant Expansion	Equity Increase	Other	Total
No.	719	58	106	52	73	245	1253
%	57	5	8	4	6	20	100

SOURCE: Hamill, J. "British Acquisitions in the United States," *National Westminster Bank Quarterly Review* (August 1988): 2–17.

| EXHIBIT 13.18 | Major British Acquisitions in the United States (Excluding Real Estate): 1978–1986 | |

Year	British Company	United States Company	Value ($m)
1978	BOC	Airco. Inc.	298.7
	BAT	Appleton Papers	280.0
1979	National Westminster Bank	National Bank of N.A.	429.0
	ICI	Corpus Christi	375.0
1980	Imperial Group	Howard Johnson	630.0
	Grand Metropolitan	Liggett Group	415.0
	Barclay's Bank	Aetna Business Corporation	165.0
	Lloyds Bank	Talcott National	118.0
1981	British Petroleum	Kennecott Corporation	938.1
	Midland Bank	Crocker National Bank	820.0
	Grand Metropolitan	Intl. Hotels	500.0
	Legal and General	GEICO Life Insurance	740.0
	Hanson Trust	McDonough Corporation	112.1
1982	Goldsmith, Sir J.	Diamond Intl.	455.0
	BAT	Marshall Field	365.0
	European Ferries	Andrau Airpark	300.0
	Rowntree	General Mills (Tom's Food Division)	215.0
1984	Pilkington Bros.	Libbey-Owens Ford	108.2
	BAT	Peoples Drug Stores	320.0
	Grand Metropolitan	Quality Core Inc.	125.0
	Saatchi and Saatchi	Hay Group	100.0
	Hanson Trust	U.S. Industries	469.2
1985	ICI	Beatrice Cos. Chemical Div.	750.0
	Rio Tinto-Zinc Corporation	Martin Marietta Corporation Plants	400.0
	Grand Metropolitan	Pearle Health	386.0
	United Kingdom, Government of	Gulf Oil Corporation's Assets	380.0
1986	Prudential Corporation	Jackson National Life Insurance	608.0
	Boots	Baxters Travenols Flint Division	555.0
	United Kingdom, Government of	Purina Mills Inc.	500.0
	Saatchi and Saatchi	Ted Bates Worldwide Inc.	450.0
	Cadbury Schweppes	RJR's Soft Drink subs.	230.0
	Rowntree Mackintosh	Sunmark Inc.	230.0
	Robert Maxwell	Providence Gravure Holdings	152.5
	Rio Tinto-Zinc Corporation	Celanese Special Resin Inc.	138.0

SOURCE: Ibid.

largest investor in this group has been Saatchi and Saatchi with 12 separate investments totaling approximately $700 million.

Motivations   To fully understand the growth of British direct investment in the United States during this period, we must consider that these investments occurred at a time of rapid increase in all DFI entering the United States. The United States became the largest single recipient of direct investment in 1980 among the world's major industrial countries. At that time the stock of direct investment in the United States reached $68 billion. The U.S. Department of Commerce has identified ownership and location factors as important determinants in the growth of DFI inflows.* Six major factors appear to have contributed to this growth:

1. wide recognition among non-U.S. MNCs of the size of the U.S. market, and a growing perception of the United States as a safe haven in a turbulent world;

---

* "International Direct Investment: Global Trends and the U.S. Role," U.S. Department of Commerce, International Trade Administration, 1984.

EXHIBIT 13.19	**Investment Transactions in the United States and Type of Parent Company: 1976–1986**

Company Type	Main Companies and (No. of Transactions)	Estimated Value of Transactions	Investment Characteristics
Conglomerate/ Holding Companies	BAT (42) Thom. Tilling (29) Hanson Trust (10)	$8b–$9b	Large-scale investment in the United States mainly through acquisitions. Acquired companies active in a range of industries including manufacturing, retail, hotels, etc.
Oil	BP (38) Burmah (4)	$3.5b–$4b	Large-scale investments in the United States since late 1970s, mainly through the acquisition of companies in oil, petroleum, and mining sectors.
Banks	Lloyds (10) Midland (5) Barclays (9) Nat West (3)	$2.25b–$2.5b	Limited number of investments, but large in value terms, mainly through strategic acquisition of U.S. banks. Investments largely confined to banking sector.
Manufacturing	Large Investors BOC (35) GEC (12) ICI (20)	$3b–$3.5b	Large-scale investments in terms of both the number and value of investments, mainly acquisitions of U.S. companies operating in same industry as parent company.
	Medium Investors Racal (12) Reed Int. (12) Thorn-EMI (12) RTZ (14)	$1.5b–$2.5b	Large number of investment but limited in terms of value, mainly acquisitions of U.S. companies in related sectors.
	Single Investors Acorn Computers Boots Granada Serck		Investment in the U.S. limited to single, small-scale investments, mainly through the acquisition of U.S. companies in related sectors.
Nonmanufacturing	Large Investors Saatchi and Saatchi (12)	Approx. $700m	Major acquisitions of U.S. advertising companies since 1982.
	Small Investors Debenhams Habitat/ Mothercare	<$50m	Limited investments in the U.S. in terms of both number and value, mainly acquisitions of U.S. companies in related sectors.

Source: Ibid.

2. emergence of non-U.S. MNCs with the ability to compete successfully in the United States market;

3. depreciation of the U.S. dollar against a number of leading foreign currencies, reducing the foreign currency cost of acquiring U.S. companies, building new factories, and expanding existing ones;

4. narrowing of the gap in production costs between the United States and foreign locations, making investment in the United States more attractive compared to exporting;

5. concern regarding possible U.S. protectionist measures; and

6. relatively nonrestrictive U.S. policy toward inward direct investment, together with the active promotion of such investment by individual state governments.

British and Japanese Direct Investment Compared   Japanese direct investment in the United States has been a latecomer compared with British DFI. However, in the late 1980s Japanese DFI entering the United States accelerated rapidly. Several reasons can be offered to explain this late surge, including the need to circumvent increasing U.S. restrictions on Japanese exports and the continued appreciation of the yen against the dollar in the foreign exchange market.

Hamill notes that while Japanese MNCs have invested in the United States to exploit some competitive advantages over U.S. enterprises, it is unlikely that this is the situation for most British MNCs. He notes that the rapid rise in British direct investment in the United States has occurred "against the background of a substantial deterioration in the international competitiveness (declining ownership advantages) of British industry."[†] British MNCs are technologically weak in many industry sectors. The growth of British DFI in the United States is not explained by an improvement in the ownership advantages of British over U.S. companies. For many British companies, U.S. investments represent part of a long-term strategy of geographical diversification away from stagnant or slow-growing markets.

The main objectives underlying British companies' recent U.S. expansions have been geographic diversification and pursuit of growth through acquisitions in well-proven industries. Companies following these strategies include conglomerates (BAT and Hanson Trust), oil (British Petroleum), finance (Barclay's), manufacturing (ICI), and business services (Saatchi and Saatchi). In contrast, Japanese investment that has been heavily based on ownership advantages is motivated in part by fear of increasing trade friction and the consequent need to shift from an export-based a to DFI-based competitive strategy. Japanese companies have developed a distinct internal managerial culture, well-suited to low cost production processes and total quality management principles. For these reasons Japanese companies have preferred de novo investments to acquisitions.

Risk Analysis

Generally the global investment opportunities offering the highest expected returns are those entailing the greatest risks and uncertainties. In this regard the simple axiom that "high risk takers can be the biggest gainers" may be globally applicable. In this section we have two purposes. First, we place risk and return into a framework of analysis where these dimensions can be viewed as important and necessary tradeoffs. Second, we consider the need for the MNC to control or minimize risk.

RISK AS A TRADEOFF

The idea that risk is a tradeoff for return is prevalent through the literature of international finance and investment. For example, if a company is contemplating several alternative investment projects, expected return would tend to be higher in cases where risk is also higher. Companies willing to assume higher degrees of risk in their foreign investment may also have expectations of higher return.

Portfolio Versus Direct Investment   The U.S. Department of Commerce uses the 10% equity ownership level as a line of separation between direct investment and portfolio investment. For purposes of making balance of payments estimates,

---

[†] J. Hamill, "British Acquisitions in the United States," 12.

foreign investments into or from the United States involving less than 10% owner-ship are considered to be portfolio investments. The agency defines direct invest-ments beginning at the 10% control level and above.

The Department of Commerce approach provides a simple and easily applied distinction between direct and portfolio investment, based on the concept of "control." Control investment implies that some degree of discretionary decision making by the investor is present in management policies and strategy. For exam-ple, this control may occur through the ability of the investor to elect or select one or more members on the board of directors of the foreign company or foreign affiliate.

While equity market purchases can be the conduit for portfolio transactions, such transactions are not necessarily part of the process where direct investment is involved. In fact it is possible to distinguish between the so-called control market for shares, and the noncontrol or portfolio share market. During the 1980s the for-mer market expanded rapidly, and in the United States control type transactions on the New York Stock Exchange and other equity for market sectors resulted in net retirements (or reductions) in outstanding shares exceeding at times $100 billion an-nually. These control transactions included acquisitions of interests in U.S. compa-nies by foreign direct investors, mergers between domestic firms, leveraged buy-outs, and share repurchases by companies. The growth in importance of control transactions in the United States equities market was transmitted to the Canadian, British, and other stock markets in the later years of the 1980s.

Investment Opportunity Locus We can analyze the risk-return relationship in the form of an investment opportunity locus (IOL). The IOL provides a two-dimen-sional picture of the investment outcomes available for investors depending upon the risk level they are willing to assume. For example, in Exhibit 13.20A the IOL in-dicates that investors in Helvetia have the opportunity to make investments gener-ating returns of OA accompanied by a risk level of OC, or to make investments gen-erating returns of OB accompanied by a risk level of OD.

Several observations are in order regarding this investment opportunity locus. First, it portrays optimal investments and therefore can be considered equivalent to an *efficiency frontier.* Second, it is not possible to enjoy more favorable outcomes, since by definition the efficiency frontier is the locus of optimal investments at dif-ferent risk levels. Third, there is no distinction between returns available at a given risk level for portfolio versus control investors.

In Exhibit 13.20A portfolio and control investors are assumed to have the same or identical investment opportunities available to them. Under certain conditions, however, portfolio and control investors may have different investment opportuni-ties such as investment opportunities generating different levels of return. This situ-ation occurs when there are market imperfections that block portfolio investors from certain types of investments, allowing the possibility of higher returns for con-trol investors. Investment opportunities also may differ when market imperfections are such that different investors (portfolio and control) face dissimilar investment opportunities (Exhibit 13.20B).

Several types of imperfections can operate to provide dissimilar investment op-portunities to portfolio and control investors. These include:

1. Product Differentiation Oriented.   The ability of large MNCs to spend substan-tial amounts on advertising and product differentiation gives the MNCs advantages over smaller rivals. With this control they can earn higher returns based on domi-nant market share. Coca-Cola is an example of a company that can earn a high

Control investments bring a much higher level of economic, financial, and management integration across countries; in a phrase, more complete globalization.

EXHIBIT 13.20   **Investment Opportunity Locus, Under Conditions of Perfect and Segmented Capital Markets**

A.   Perfect Market
(Domestic)

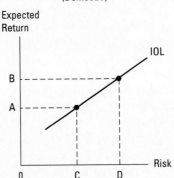

B.   Segmented Market
(Domestic)

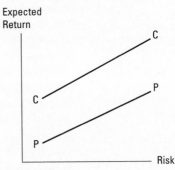

A. No distinction between returns available for portfolio and control investors.

B. CC reflects returns available to control investors, and PP reflects returns available to portfolio investors.

C.   Segmented Market
(International)

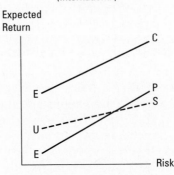

C. EC and EP reflect returns in Europe available to control and portfolio investors, respectively. US reflects returns available to U.S. investors. This reflects Ragazzi thesis, applicable to the situation in the 1970s.

return on its investment abroad via large expenditures aimed at product differentiation. The important point is that portfolio investors outside the United States willing to invest in local firms competing with Coca-Cola will find the local company unable to earn as high a return as the large direct investor.

2. Technology Oriented.   Improved technology can lower costs (process technology), or increase revenues (product technology). In either case, the MNC can undertake control (direct) investments in host countries that should earn the MNC a higher return than will be available to local portfolio investors who purchase the securities issued by domestic (lower technology) companies.

3. Capital Market Oriented.   Some MNCs have enjoyed access to lower cost capital, based on home country capital market conditions. This situation was the case for U.S. MNCs until the early 1970s, and since the early 1980s has been the case for Japanese MNCs. In such conditions these MNCs can earn a higher return on their global control investments than local competitor companies. In addition MNCs with lower cost of capital are able to undertake investments offering marginally lower returns than their rivals, based on the capital market axiom that investments must earn at least the firm's cost of capital. In either case the MNC can undertake control investments in host countries that should earn the company a higher return than will be available to local portfolio investors who purchase the securities issued by domestic companies with higher cost of capital.

All of these illustrations show MNCs as enjoying lower costs or access to higher revenue totals due to incomplete arbitrage across input, product, and/or financial markets. In turn MNCs may earn higher returns (in the same risk class) than domestic firms due to the existence of these imperfections. Under these conditions, domestic portfolio investors receive lower returns on the securities issued by local firms, but control investors earn higher returns on their ownership in domestic firms. This lower expected return to domestic portfolio investors may be due to lack of information about companies or to smaller size stock markets subject to wider fluctuation. The disadvantages of inefficient capital markets may be avoided through direct investment. The MNC control investors (direct investors) earn higher returns than domestic portfolio investors.

The Ragazzi perspective shows the special role and motivations for control investment.

Ragazzi Thesis Applied to the 1980s   In 1973 Ragazzi published an analysis of U.S. direct investment entering Europe, based upon the separation of the investment opportunity locus for control versus portfolio investment.* This analysis demonstrated that European equity markets suffer from imperfections, producing separate control and portfolio IOLs (Exhibit 13.20C). These capital market imperfections in Europe were based in part on the ability of American direct (control) investment companies to make large-scale investments in Europe that were closed to European companies for any of several reasons (lack of capital, technology, or marketing skills). Ragazzi noted that U.S. MNCs were able to undertake these large manufacturing investments and could therefore operate on the EC curve (Exhibit 13.20C). This curve was dominant to the U.S. portfolio IOL. Also note that the U.S. IOL (US in Exhibit 13.20C) is dominant to most segments of the European portfolio IOL (EP).

Since the publication of Ragazzi's study, a number of changes have taken place to reverse the flow of DFI. Beginning in the 1980s European and Japanese direct investment flows to the United States have grown to exceed the U.S. outward flow of direct investment to these regions. The reasons for this reversal in direction of net flows of direct investment are: 1) the separation of the U.S. IOL into two separate control and portfolio loci; and 2) the unification of the European IOL into a single investment locus (Exhibit 13.21). Exhibit 13.22 provides detailed reasons for this reversal of net flows of direct investment.

COUNTRY RISK AND DIRECT INVESTMENT

Decomposition of Risk   In the preceding section we considered risk as an unavoidable tradeoff within the framework of a risk-return analysis. In that discussion

---

* Ragazzi, Giorgio. "Theories of the Determinants of Direct Foreign Investment," *IMF Staff Papers,* (July 1973): 471–98.

EXHIBIT 13.21 **Segmented U.S. Investment Opportunity Locus**

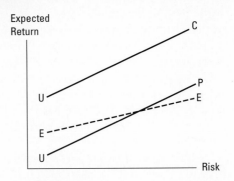

A. UC reflects returns available to control investors in the United States.
B. UP reflects returns available to portfolio investors in the United States.
C. EE reflects returns available to European investors.

EXHIBIT 13.22 **Reasons for Shift of Net Direct Investment Flows Between Early 1970s (Large Net Outflows from United States) and Late 1980s (Small Net Outflows from United States)**

REASONS FOR SEGMENTATION OF U.S. IOL:

1. Reagan administration relaxes antitrust enforcement and embarks on active program of deregulation in many sectors (airlines, banking). European investors perceive these changes as offering opportunities for more profitable operations in the United States. American investors do not share these perceptions, and the U.S. control IOL rises above the U.S. portfolio IOL, as in Figure 13.3.
2. The coming of the European Single Market in 1992 causes European companies to place a high premium on developing fully global operations, including the development of a substantial base of operations in the United States.
3. Increasing intensity of trade frictions between the United States and Japan and the growing fear among Japanese businessmen that U.S. trade restrictions will result in the Japanese placing a high premium on U.S. production versus exporting to the United States as a means of supplying the North American market.
4. Increasing volume of U.S. domestic takeover and merger activities results in a substantial expansion of control-oriented stock market activity in the United States, and a growing dichotomy in the valuation of shares for control as contrasted with portfolio investment activity.

REASONS FOR UNIFICATION OF EUROPEAN IOL:

1. The "growing up" of the large European MNCs gives them the ability to engage in control investments that are similar to those formerly reserved to U.S. MNCs Growing up includes growth in size, access to multiple sources of capital, and international orientation.
2. Expansion and integration of the European capital markets so that there are no longer substantial cost of capital advantages for corporate borrowers in New York as compared with London, Paris, and Frankfurt.

---

risk was treated as an invariant factor. That approach is valid when we view the MNC as seeking to achieve an optimum global portfolio of operating investments. We now look at risk differently from a managerial perspective. This perspective requires that we consider risk as subject to decomposition, where various elements of risk can be controlled or even eliminated.

EXHIBIT 13.23		**Decomposition of MNC Risk**
Related to Internal Structure of MNC	I.	**Corporate Financial Structure:** financial risk of becoming unable to service debt, and translation exposures of MNC system
Related to Global Environment	II.	**Global Systemic:** risk of change in global environment such as unfavorable commodity prices, and global business slowdown
Related to Specific Country Factors	III.	**Country** (Unsystemic)**:** transfer risks, business cycle risks, expropriation, translation exposures, transaction exposures, economic exposures

In Exhibit 13.23 we consider three broad elements of risk to which the MNC is exposed. The first is corporate financial structure. Two important risks included here are financial risk (inability to service company debt) and translation exposures. Translation exposures relate to the foreign currency denominated assets and liabilities of the MNC. When foreign exchange rates change, these translation exposures can generate gains or losses for the company. We deal with currency exposures and their control in Chapter 16.

A second broad element of risk refers to the global systemic dimension. This element includes the risk of change in the global environment (particularly economic change) in which the MNC operates. This risk includes unfavorable international commodity price trends, a global business slowdown, and adverse changes in the international institutional environment. An example of the latter is the shutting down of special IMF credit facilities to assist nations that encounter severe balance of payments difficulties.

A third broad element includes the specific country (unsystemic) risks to which the MNC may be exposed. Generally these risks will consist of a range of economic and political factors. More specifically they may take the form of transfer risks (possible blockage of outward payments by the host country), country business cycle movements, expropriation, foreign currency transaction exposures, and foreign currency operating exposures.

Country Risk   For the MNC engaging in foreign investment, country risk assumes pivotal importance. We discussed country risk analysis in Chapter 12, in connection with international lending and the need for lenders to evaluate country risk. There we pointed out that country risk analysis may require a special focus, depending on whether the users are bank lenders, exporters, or direct foreign investors. Direct investors generally tend to develop a long-term relationship with the host country, and for that reason the appropriate country analysis is one that evaluates the host country from this long-term perspective.

The major country analysis concerns of the direct investor will be as follows:

1. stability of local economy, and absence of high inflation;
2. fair and equal treatment from the host government;
3. freedom from arbitrary and changing government regulation;
4. free transfer of profit from the host country; and
5. ability to sell or liquidate investment and, subsequently, to withdraw funds from the country.

"It is imperative that both operations managers and central MNC management achieve a high information base regarding developments in countries abroad." Chief Executive Officer, of an international management consultancy.

There are a number of sources of information concerning country risk. These include the reports of Frost & Sullivan that provide a mix of quantitative and qualitative information. In addition International Reports publishes the monthly *International Country Risk Guide* covering approximately 80 countries. On a semiannual basis, Institutional Investor publishes the results of a survey of bankers concerning their subjective ratings of debtor countries.*

Two major problems with these country evaluation systems are 1) their reliance on past performance to estimate future prospects and 2) the possibility that isolated events (political or other) will have a strong impact on company operations and profit.

An example of a country risk situation arose for several U.S. automobile companies in 1996 in Indonesia. This case is driven by an Indonesian government decision to undertake a "national" automobile industry, and is described in greater detail in Exhibit 13.24.

Measures to Control Country Risk Efforts to control country risk must begin before the investment is made, continue while the investment is negotiated with the host government, extend through the investment and operational period, and may be concluded some time after the investment is liquidated or sold.

The measures used vary from case to case. The following provides a brief consideration of a few selected approaches.

1. Prenegotiation. Important areas of prenegotiation with the host government include size and form (equity-loan) of initial investment, amount required of local labor employed in the project, sourcing of inputs (local vs. imported), tax burden, ease and cost of local financing, remittance amount and composition (dividends, interest, and fees), and protection given to original investment and any accumulated profits.

2. Joint Venture. A joint venture is a case in which two or more investors undertake a cooperative investment in a project, sharing risk and return. We can view joint ventures as a form of risk reduction where the parties reduce their exposure in the project by providing only a fraction of the total funds required. Local joint venture partners may also have political clout that can reduce the likelihood of adverse government actions. MNCs have participated in many joint ventures in developing countries. In the late 1980s joint ventures in Eastern European countries became popular; in 1989 joint ventures registered in East Europe numbered 3300. Joint venture arrangements are also common in the East Asian countries. For example, the Kia Motors Corporation of South Korea joined to provide technical know-how for the pioneer auto project in Indonesia, as described in Exhibit 13.24.

3. Operating Strategies. A variety of strategies are available to cope with country risk. One is to plan on exporting a substantial part of production, where currency weakness threatens the long-term hard currency value of local profit and cash flows. Another strategy is to maximize local content to reduce the problem of foreign exchange costs, especially when there is the expectation of repeated local currency depreciation. High inflation environments can pose difficult operating problems. In such cases financial operating strategies will call for minimizing cash and other asset holdings subject to the risks of inflation and declining real values.

---

* These country risk evaluations are provided by: Frost & Sullivan, Inc.; Washington, Bowker Associates; International Reports, Inc., Guenter Reimann, editor and publisher, New York, Drake Publishers; and *Institutional Investor,* International Edition, Institutional Investor, Inc., New York.

EXHIBIT 13.24   **Country Risk: Foreign Automobiles in Indonesia**

In 1996, the Indonesian government announced its plan to give strong backing to its "pioneer auto project," which was intended to develop a locally owned auto company, clearly to be favored by government policies.

This announcement led several American companies to curtail investment activities in that nation. General Motors, which had invested $110 million in a small Indonesian assembly plant, was clearly hurt the most by this change in government policy. With the government announcement, GM suspended plans for further investments, instead shifting its SE Asia focus to a $750 million assembly plant in Thailand, even with only limited concessions from the Thai government. According to Donald T. Sullivan, the GM vice president for the Asian and Pacific region, "We have put our future investment in Indonesia on hold because we want to get a better understanding of where the Indonesian government is heading on their policy."

In a similar reaction, the Chrysler Corporation canceled its plans to assemble its small Neon cars from kits in Indonesia. The Ford Motor Company, which was on the verge of building a small assembly plant, also announced that it "was not moving forward with any plant at this date."

The new pioneer auto project is a joint venture controlled by a son of President Suharto. The Kia Motors Corporation of South Korea is a minority partner in the joint venture.

Japan, the European Commission, and the United States all criticized the Indonesian national car program. Under a principle of international trade law known as national treatment, members of the World Trade Organization must not enact tax laws and other legislation that favor domestic companies at the expense of foreign companies in such a way as to impede trade. Indonesia is a member of the WTO and a signer of the General Agreement on Tariffs and Trade.

---

4. Risk Insurance.   Most developed nations sponsor government agencies that can insure against country risks, including expropriation restrictions on the transfer of remittances and the inconvertibility of assets, and war and civil strife. This is done in Japan, for example, by the Ministry of International Trade and Industry (MITI); in Germany by Treuarbeit; in the United Kingdom by the Export Credits Guarantee Department (ECGD); and in Canada by the Export Development Corporation.

OPIC
Overseas Private Investment Corporation.

In the United States, the Overseas Private Investment Corporation (OPIC) provides investment guarantees for U.S. business investors in developing countries. To be eligible for OPIC coverage, the investment must be a new project in the country, and the host country must have concluded an investment agreement or treaty with the United States.

MIGA
Multilateral Investment Guarantee Agency.

In 1985, the World Bank established the Multilateral Investment Guarantee Agency (MIGA) as the first truly global agency to insure foreign investment against political risks. The use of MIGA has been growing. For example, the agency signed 54 guarantee contracts in 1995, compared to 39 in 1994.

5. Dispute Resolution Mechanisms.   Corporate risk control managers should include in their plans the use of dispute resolution mechanisms that are available through international treaty arrangements. One such procedure is incorporated in the North American Free Trade Agreement (NAFTA). The General Agreement on Tariffs and Trade (GATT) sets forth arrangements for dealing with disputes involving international trade and competitive practices.

ICSID
International Center for Settlement of Investment Disputes.

Disputes between foreign investors and their host nations may also be submitted to the International Center for Settlement of Investment Disputes (ICSID). This is an affiliate of the World Bank that was established by an international convention in 1966. To date, the convention has been signed by 98 nations, all of which are World Bank members.

SUMMARY

In direct foreign investment the investing company gains managerial control through equity shareholdings. Also the investor shifts part of the company's assets, production, and/or sales to a second (host) country. Direct investment is a complex activity including transfer of capital, control investment, a source of funds for foreign operations, and a balance of payments flow.

Firm-specific factors that encourage direct investment include need for markets, need for production efficiency, need for raw materials, need for information and technology, and need to minimize and diversify risks. Economic factors that explain why direct investment takes place include market imperfections, role of government, internalization and the eclectic theory, and portfolio theory.

The United States continues to be the largest participant in direct investment, both as investor and recipient of investment. During the 1980s the United States experienced a shift from de novo to acquisitions type investment. As measured by the U.S. Department of Commerce, the DFI flow incorporates three basic elements: outflow of capital in the form of equity investment, outflow in the form of loans to foreign affiliates, and reinvestment of earnings by foreign affiliate companies.

Direct investment involves control investment. We distinguish between the control and noncontrol (portfolio) market for shares. Also we can analyze the risk-return relationship for investors as an investment opportunity locus (IOL). The IOL, a two-dimensional picture of investment outcomes, portrays optimal investments and therefore is considered equivalent to an efficiency frontier. As control investors, MNCs may enjoy better IOL opportunities than noncontrol investors.

We can also identify various elements of risk for the MNC. Such risk dimensions include financial risk, translation exposures, country risk, and global systemic.

REVIEW QUESTIONS

1. How is direct investment defined?

2. When should a company prefer exporting to a country in contrast to undertaking direct investment in that country? Under what conditions would direct investment (local production) be preferred over exporting to a given country market?

3. Which are the more important factors in explaining the motivation for direct investment?
   a) business-oriented motivations
   b) economic motives

4. How would you define the MNC in terms of its essential characteristics? How does this definition fit with Dunning's explanation of direct investment?

5. A U.S. multinational company can invest in Europe or Latin America. Essential investment performance information is as follows:

	Return	Risk	Correlation with U.S. Returns
European Project	20%	20%	.50
Latin American Project	20%	10%	1.00
U.S. Domestic	10%	10%	—

Which investment, when mixed 50-50 with the U.S. domestic operation, will yield a lower risk portfolio?

6. How can you account for the sharp growth in global DFI flows in the 1980s?

7. How important are developing countries as recipients of direct investment? As providers of direct investment capital? Why is there such a difference in these two roles?

8. Distinguish between direct investment stocks and flows. What are the elements of the annual change in the direct investment position of the United States?

9. What role has British direct investment played in the United States? Does this reflect more firm-specific or location-specific factors?

10. The U.S. Department of Commerce has identified six factors as important determinants of direct investment inflows. What are these factors?

11. Does an analysis of a company's geographic segments reveal anything about its multinationality? Explain.

12. Explain how the investment opportunity locus can be used to demonstrate how direct investment takes place. Ragazzi uses this approach to explain U.S. DFI into Europe in the 1970s. Is his analysis still relevant?

13. Under what conditions might control investment offer higher returns to shareholders than portfolio investment?

14. Describe the types of risks to which MNCs are exposed. Which are related to the external environment of the MNC?

15. Give an example of an operating strategy used by an MNC to control country risk.

EXHIBIT 13.25   **The World's Biggest Industrial Corporations**

In 1993 the 100 largest industrial corporations of the world included 32 from the United States, 23 from Japan, 3 from Germany, 6 from France, and 5 from the United Kingdom. The table from *Fortune* (August 5, 1995) provides a list of the Top 50 along with other pertinent data concerning these companies.

Based on this information and your reading of this chapter, formulate a theory of each of the following:

1. Why do MNCs from certain countries hold a lead in the size rankings among industrial corporations.

2. Why is the industrial sector representation heavily biased toward certain sectors (see small table following). What sectors are not represented, and why?

Sectoral Representation of Top 50 Industrial Companies, 1995

Motor Vehicles	11	Scientific-Photographic Equipment	2
Petroleum Refining	10	Metals	2
Computers and Electronics	10	Tobacco	1
Chemicals	6	Soaps, Cosmetics	1
Food	4	Industrial and Farm Equipment	1
Aerospace	2	Total	50

(Continued)

Exhibit 13.25 (*Continued*)

			$million	Profits $million	Assets $million	Stock-holders' Equity $million	Employees Number 1
1	MITSUBISHI	JAPAN	184,365.2	346.2	91,920.6	10,950.0	36,000
2	MITSUI	JAPAN	181,518.7	314.8	68,770.9	5,553.9	80,000
3	ITOCHU	JAPAN	169,164.6	121.2	65,708.9	4,271.1	7,182
4	GENERAL MOTORS	U.S.	168,828.6	6,880.7	217,123.4	23,345.5	709,000
5	SUMITOMO	JAPAN	167,530.7	210.5	50,268.9	6,681.0	6,193
6	MARUBENI	JAPAN	161,057.4	156.6	71,439.3	5,239.1	6,702
7	FORD MOTOR	U.S.	137,137.0	4,139.0	243,283.0	24,547.0	346,990
8	TOYOTA MOTOR	JAPAN	111,052.0	2,662.4	106,004.2	49,691.6	146,855
9	EXXON	U.S.	110,009.0	6,470.0	91,296.0	40,436.0	82,000
10	ROYAL DUTCH/ SHELL GROUP	BRIT/ NETH.	109,833.7	6,904.6	118,011.6	58,986.4	104,000
11	NISSHO IWAI	JAPAN	97,886.4	(259.5)	46,753.8	1,998.2	17,005
12	WAL-MART STORES	U.S.	93,627.0	2,740.0	37,871.0	14,762.0	675.000
13	HITACHI	JAPAN	84,167.1	1,468.8	91,620.9	29,907.2	331,852
14	NIPPON LIFE INSURANCE	JAPAN	83,206.7	2,426.6	364,762.5	2,241.9	89,690
15	NIPPON TELEGRAPH & TELEPHONE	JAPAN	81,937.2	2,209.1	127,077.3	42,240.1	231,400
16	AT&T	U.S.	79,609.0	139.0	88,884.0	17,274.0	299,300
17	DAIMLER-BENZ	GERMANY	72,256.1.	(3,959.3)	63,813.2	9,038.0	310,993
18	INTL. BUSINESS MACHINE	U.S.	71,940.0	4,178.0	80,292.0	22,423.0	252,215
19	MATSUSHITA ELECTRIC INDUSTRIAL	JAPAN	70,398.4	(589.2)	74,876.9	31,753.2	265,538
20	GENERAL ELECTRIC	U.S.	70,028.0	6,573.0	228,035.0	29,609.0	222,000
21.	TOMEN	JAPAN	67,755.8	46.2	22,365.6	1,049.6	2,943
22.	MOBIL	U.S.	66,724.0	2,376.0	42,138.0	17,951.0	50,400
23	NISSAN MOTOR	JAPAN	62,568.5	(916.1)	66,276.6	12,679.2	139,856
24	VOLKSWAGEN	GERMANY	61,489.1	247.0	58,610.7	7,332.2	242,420
25	SIEMENS	GERMANY	60,673.6	1,268.0	57,346.6	14,666.0	373,000
26	DAI-ICHI MUTUAL LIFE INSURANCE	JAPAN	58,052.4	1,732.2	256,010.3	1,578.7	70,038
27	BRITISH PETROLEUM	BRITAIN	56,981.9	1,770.7	50,258.8	18,353.0	56,650
28	METRO HOLDING	SWITZERLAND	56,459.0	403.5	25,061.1	4,158.5	178,594
29	U.S. POSTAL SERVICE	U.S.	54,293.5	1,770.3	48,921.2	(4,191.0)	870,160
30	CHRYSLER	U.S.	53,195.0	2,025.0	53,756.0	10,959.0	126,000
31	PHILIP MORRIS	U.S.	53,139.0	5,450.0	53,811.0	13,985.0	151,000
32	TOSHIBA	JAPAN	53,046.9	936.5	51,967.1	11,236.1	186,000
33	TOKYO ELECTRIC POWER	JAPAN	52,361.5	536.9	131,485.4	13,842.2	43,448
34	DAEWOO	SOUTH KOREA	51,215.3	N.A.	63,597.8	9,460.3	196,000
35	NICHIMEN	JAPAN	50,841.9	44.3	19,765.9	1,393.7	2,443
36	SUMITOMO LIFE INSURANCE	JAPAN	50,710.5	1,871.6	218,593.3	1,735.6	70,000
37	KANEMATSU	JAPAN	49,838.5	3.5	16,232.1	744.6	11,759
38	UNILEVER	BRITAIN/ NETHERLANDS	49,738.0	2,324.7	30,077.3	8,732.2	308,000
39	NESTLE	SWITZERLAND	47,780.4	2,468.4	38,354.4	15,588.4	220,172
40	SONY	JAPAN	47,581.5	562.1	47,156.3	10,926.9	151,000
41	FIAT	ITALY	46,467.6	1,318.0	64,300.1	13,532.6	237,426
42	VEBA GROUP	GERMANY	46,279.9	1,336.3	47,229.7	12,193.1	125,158
43	DEUTSCHE TELEKOM	GERMANY	46,148.7	3,678.8	111,709.3	17,237.4	220,000
44	ALLIANZ HOLDING	GERMANY	46,044.9	592.4	164,654.8	8,250.9	67,785
45	NEC	JAPAN	45,557.3	799.5	43,767.5	8,213.6	152,719
46	HONDA MOTOR	JAPAN	44,055.6	733.5	32,860.9	10,696.6	96,800
47	ELF AQUITAINE	FRANCE	43,618.4	1,009.2	49,453.6	16,063.7	85,500
48	ELECTRICITE DE FRANCE	FRANCE	43,507.8	246.8	139,841.0	32,617.6	116,909
49	UNION DES ASSURANCES DE PARIS	FRANCE	42,004.2	(413.9)	183,861.8	7,273.9	51,284
50	IRI	ITALY	41,903.2	391.7	115,041.0	3,869.6	263,063

| **EXHIBIT 13.26** | **Dow Chemical Company—Geographic Segments** |

The Dow Chemical table presents the geographic segment reports of the company for a three-year period.

1. Is Dow well diversified geographically? What additional information would you require to answer this question more completely?

2. Transfers between areas totaled $2,697 million in 1995. These transfers represent slightly more than 13% of sales to unaffiliated customers. Explain the importance of these transfers between areas.

3. Using the following formula, calculate the operating margin for each geographic segment for each of the three years.

Operating Margin = Operating Income ÷ Sales

Are there trends for the company on a consolidated basis?

Are there similar or dissimilar trends for each segment?

How might you account for these differences?

The Dow Chemical Company and Subsidiaries, in Millions US$

	United States	Europe	Rest of World	Corporate Eliminations	Consolidated
1995					
Sales to unaffiliated customers	$9,035	$6,411	$4,754	—	$20,200
Intersegment transfers	1,728	515	454	$(2,697)	
Operating income	1,603	1,112	1,176	—	3,891
Identifiable assets	10,127	6,914	6,541	—	23,582
Gross plant properties	12,416	7,466	3,336	—	23,218
Capital expenditures	1,008	295	114	—	1,417
1994					
Sales to unaffiliated customers	$8,093	$4,809	$3,840	—	$16,742
Intersegment transfers	1,424	447	341	$(2,212)	—
Operating income	1,024	237	559	—	1,820
Identifiable assets	9,399	5,516	4,867	6,763	26,545
Gross plant properties	11,729	6,725	3,337	1,419	23,210
Capital expenditures	692	234	148	109	1,183
1993					
Sales to unaffiliated customers	$7,486	$4,299	$3,267	—	$15,052
Intersegment transfers	1,042	325	304	$(1,671)	—
Operating income (loss)	795	(23)	302	—	1,074
Identifiable assets	9,475	5,010	4,034	6,986	25,505
Gross plant properties	11,326	5,901	3,165	1,216	21,608
Capital expenditures	762	266	176	193	1,397

SOURCE: Dow Chemical Company, *Annual Report,* (1995).

SELECTED BIBLIOGRAPHY

Baker, James. "Global Foreign Investment Insurance: The Case of MIGA with Comparisons to OPIC and Private Insurance," *Managerial Finance,* vol. 21, no. 4, (1995): 23–39.

Buckley, Peter, and Mark Casson. *The Economic Theory of the Multinational Enterprise.* London: Macmillan, 1985.

Dewenter, K.L. "Do Exchange Rate Changes Drive Foreign Direct Investment?" *Journal of Business,* vol. 68, no. 3, (July 1995): 405–33.

Dunning, John H. "The Eclectic Paradigm of International Production: A Restatement and Some Possible Extensions," *Journal of International Business Studies,* (Spring 1988): 1–31.

_____."Foreign Direct Investment in the European Community: A Brief Overview," *Multinational Business,* no. 4, (Winter 1989): 1–9.

_____."Trade Location of Economic Activity and the MNE: A Search for an Eclectic Approach," in Bertil Ohlin, Per-Ove Hesselborn, and Per Magnus Wijkman (eds). *The International Allocation of Economic Activity*. New York: Holmes and Meier, 1977, 395–418.

Fahim-Nader, M., and W.J. Zeile. "Foreign Direct Investment in the United States," *Survey of Current Business,* vol. 75, no. 5, (May 1995): 57–81.

Fitzgerald, Jr, Thomas. "Protecting Against Credit and Political Risk," *Journal of Accountancy,* vol. 181, no. 1, (January 1996): 66.

Gordon, Sara L., and F. Lees. *Foreign Multinational Investment in the United States: Struggle for Industrial Supremacy*. Westport, CT: Quorum Books, 1986.

_____."Multinational Capital Budgeting, Foreign Investment under Subsidy," *California Management Review,* (Fall 1982): 22–32.

Hamill, Jim. "British Acquisitions in the United States," *National Westminster Bank Quarterly Review,* (August 1988): 2–17.

Hultman, C.W., and L.R. McGee. "Factors Affecting Foreign Direct Investment in the U.S.: A Review of Recent Developments," *Rivista Internationale di Scienze Economiche e Commerciali,* vol. 40, no. 10–11, (October–November 1993): 931–40.

Lowe, J.H. "Direct Investment Positions on a Historical-Cost Basis, 1994: Country and Industry Detail," *Survey of Current Business,* vol. 75, no. 6, (June 1995): 61–68.

Madura, Jeff. "A Valuation Model for International Acquisitions," *Management Decision,* vol. 29, no. 4, (1991): 31–38.

Parry, Thomas G. "Internalization as a General Theory of Foreign Direct Investment: A Critique," *Weltwirtschaftliches Archiv,* vol. 121, no. 3, (September 1985): 564–69.

Ragazzi, Giorgio. "Theories of the Determinants of Direct Foreign Investment," *IMF Staff Papers,* (July 1973): 471–98.

Scaperlanda, A.E., and L.J. Mauer. "Determinants of U.S. Direct Investment in the E.E.C," *American Economic Review,* (September 1969): 558–68.

Scholl, Russell. "The International Investment Position of the United States in 1994," *Survey of Current Business,* vol. 75, no. 6, (June 1995): 52–60.

Westerberg, John. "Hague Tribunal and ICSID Case Law: An Increasingly Important Source of Rules for Resolving International Investment Issues," *Middle East Executive Reports,* Vol. 17, no. 2, (February 1994): 8–15.

CHAPTER 14

Foreign Affiliates Financing, Taxation, and Cost of Capital

FINANCING ALTERNATIVES FOR THE MNC SUBSIDIARY—AN OVERVIEW

Financing the MNC can take a wide range of forms. Traditionally in discussions of strictly domestic corporate finance, the distinction is made between debt and equity. Equally important for Multinational Corporation (MNC) subsidiaries is the distinction between intracompany loans and financing sources external to the MNC. Internationally finance can traverse both foreign exchange and national boundaries.

This chapter presents foreign affiliate financing alternatives and the taxation dimensions in international financial management. These subjects are brought together at a more abstract level in the after-tax concept of the cost of capital for the MNC. We will explore the application of these concepts in international cash management, foreign exchange exposure, and international capital budgeting in depth in Chapters 15, 16, and 17.

Exhibit 14.1 presents the range of dimensions of financing for the MNC's subsidiary in Iceland. For example, it is possible to have equity finance that derives from intracompany sources or from external sources. In the latter case, we would view the MNC as a "joint undertaking" with another firm, or alternatively, such financing may derive directly from individual investors or stockholders. In the case of debt this financing also may derive from either intracompany or external sources. With regard to intracompany financing, whether the firm elects debt or equity, a transfer of financial resources occurs that is internal to the MNC from another part of the MNC worldwide financial network. Through such internal transfers, the MNC exercises considerable control over subsequent developments in that subsidiary. Thus the effect of the linkage from financial control to managerial control is quite strong, whether the intra-MNC financing is conveyed in the form of equity or debt. We usually assume that the control linkage is strongest in the equity case. However, intracompany debt financing provides a mechanism for the regular payment of interest and principal, and therefore for the regular "repatriation" of cash flows generated by that subsidiary.

EXHIBIT 14.1	**Financing Dimensions for Subsidiary in Iceland**		
Sources	**Jurisdictional Dimensions**	**Legal Forms**	**Characteristics**

• Intra-MNC
  - Parent
  - Sister affiliates,
    including retained
    earnings of affiliated
    companies
  - Retained earnings
    of Iceland subsidiary
 	
• External Financing
	• Parent country sources
	  - through corporate parent
	  - directly
	
	• Icelandic (local)
	  sources
	
	• Third Country sources
	  - directly
	  - sister affiliates
		• Debt, owed to
		  - corporate parent
		  - sister affiliates
		  - banks and financial
		    institutions
		  - Eurocurrency market
		  - International bond
		    market
		  - Icelandic (local)
		  - Third country
		    financial markets
		
		• Equity, owned by
		  - corporate parent
		  - sister affiliates
		  - unaffiliated joint
		    venture partners
		  - individual Icelandic
		    (local) investors
			with parent guarantee
			no guarantee
			
			Icelandic (local) currency
			parent country currency
			third country currency
			
			FX hedge
			not hedged
			
			short-term
			- trade finance
			long-term
			
			cash
			real goods

LEARNING OBJECTIVES IN THIS CHAPTER

1. To present the wide array of financing alternatives available to the MNC.
2. To show MNC remittance strategies and parent guarantees.
3. To describe the differences between various national tax regimes and the impact of taxation on the MNC.
4. To explain in detail how the United States taxes an MNC's foreign operations.
5. To illustrate how the MNC manages remittances.
6. To show the cost of capital for the MNC and how that compares to a strictly domestic firm.

FINANCING DIMENSIONS

External Funds

Financing source from outside the MNC company system.

For the MNC both internal and external sources of funds can vary over a range of dimensions including maturity, currency of denomination, geographical sourcing and institutional sourcing. We can view these dimensions according to the nature of the capital market sources. Thus funds can come from national capital markets where instruments for short- and medium-term funds may include overdrafts, bridge loans, and discountable medium-term loans. Alternatively, sources may be long-term in nature with sourcing from longer-term bank lending, lease financing, or in the form of bonds or equity. The alternatives to national capital markets are the international capital markets that have been described in depth in previous chapters. Among these are the Eurocurrency markets and the international bond markets, including both Eurobonds and foreign bonds. The choice among the sources for the MNC will rest on the following issues: 1) the need to maintain or strengthen the extent of MNC parent managerial control; 2) the need of the MNC parent to receive regular and contractual cash inflows from the subsidiary; 3) the purpose for the financing (fixed assets, net receivables financing, etc.); 4) other business strategy elements including minimizing global tax liabilities and developing business ties or relationships with national or international financial institutions; 5) expectations of MNC financial managers concerning the future course of interest rates and exchange rates and other financing costs across the markets that the MNC can regard as financing sources; and, 6) desire to minimize exposure to various types of risks, including financial risks, currency risks, and political risks.

In reference to intrafirm financial sourcing, the distinction between debt and equity becomes substantially blurred. With both debt and equity, the funds provided to the subsidiary must be raised elsewhere within the MNC's global financing network. There are decisions in both cases that must be made concerning the source country and the currency of issue. For a subsidiary located in a specific national jurisdiction, e.g., Iceland, special considerations may apply that cause the firm to prefer equity to debt. In a number of countries, notably Iceland and many developing nations, local governmental authorities insist on a commitment to a certain proportion of equity financing before approving the establishment of the subsidiary within that governmental jurisdiction. These nations typically require the MNC's demonstration of commitment to operate within their nation. For this assurance, the authorities may insist on the "posting" of an equity stake to ensure a degree of permanence.

Complexity of MNC decision making increases significantly in the case of external debt financing. Here the locus of decision making will vary depending upon MNC parent policy. The common practice is for longer-term debt financing to be the primary responsibility of the regional treasury or of the MNC parent finance organization. Local subsidiary managers are typically responsible for working capital finance.

Internal and External Funds

On a year-to-year basis, each subsidiary will have a need for external (to the subsidiary) funds. This need is related to 1) the generation of internal funds from profits and depreciation cash flows and 2) the growth rate of the subsidiary. It is conceivable that slow growth-high profit subsidiaries may be cash generators and have no external funds requirements. By contrast low profit-high growth subsidiaries may be substantial cash absorbers, requiring substantial external funds. Some subsidiaries may require little or no external finance, due to their profitability and ability to generate cash flows in excess of incremental financing needs. By contrast other subsidiaries may require considerable external finance, given the high growth rate of assets and limited cash flows.

In the case of subsidiaries that are cash generators, a basic question is "from which subsidiaries should remittances be extracted to cover MNC system fund requirements?" (We will examine this issue in the Taxation of International Operations section.) From a purely tax basis, the firm should arrange remittances in a manner that minimizes global tax liabilities of the system. But profit remittance in the form of dividend distributions involves both a legal and a financial transfer. Multinational enterprises are skilled at separating legal and financial transfers. Alternatives to the cash generator subsidiary paying large dividends to the parent company include the following:

1. Provide longer repayment terms to sister subsidiaries when selling to them on open account.

2. Repay sister subsidiaries over a shorter time span when buying from them on open account.

3. Use transfer prices to shift funds from cash generators to cash absorbers.

In the case of subsidiaries that are cash absorbers, the firm may have to seek funds from outside the MNC system. In such cases the source utilized may depend on whether funds are required in the short-term (Eurocurrency loan or local bank loan), or in the medium-or long-term (Eurobonds or medium-term bank loan). In cases where short-term needs are to be covered, local bank loans denominated in local currency may be desirable if currency risk avoidance ranks high in priority. Alternatively, where interest costs have become burdensome for the subsidiary as well as the MNC system, the firm may prefer low-interest rate Eurocurrencies. In cases where medium-term funds are needed, there will be an inevitable tradeoff between low cost (borrow hard currencies) versus minimum currency risk (borrow soft currencies).

MOBILIZING SYSTEM FUNDS

The MNC system is a complex organization with several types of organizational units. Each pair of units within the system can have numerous transaction type linkages within the pair. Exhibit 14.2 presents an overview of system financial linkages. With a system encompassing a parent, a regional financial headquarters, and two operating subsidiaries, there are six broad financial linkages. With a larger number of units in the system, the number of linkages expands geometrically. Within each financial linkage there are numerous transaction types. For example, in linkage

---

EXHIBIT 14.2   **MNC System Financial Linkages**

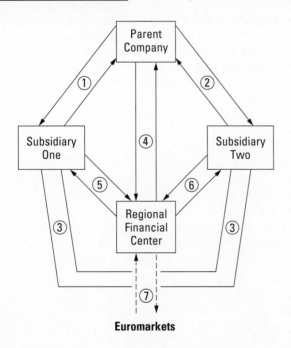

① Parent-Cash Generating Subsidiary
② Parent-Cash Using Subsidiary
③ Subidary-Subsidiary
④ Parent-Regional Financial Center
⑤ Cash Generating Subsidiary-Regional Center
⑥ Cash Using Subsidiary-Regional Center
⑦ System-Euromarkets

Linkages include dividend and interest remittances, borrowing-lending-repaying, equity investments, royalty and management fees, changes in account receivable finance terms, and transfer pricing.

number 1 there can be: a) parent equity investment, b) parent loans, c) purchases-sales on open account, d) lengthening or shortening of terms on open account, e) fixed asset sales to the other unit, f) transfer pricing, g) dividend remittances, h) loan repayments, i) interest payments, and j) fees payment.

Alternative Strategies and the Financial Environment

We have observed that numerous funding alternatives are available for the MNC (Exhibit 14.1). Also, each MNC system may differ in the pattern of financing that it requires. This decision may be a question of risk aversion, generation of internal funds, and the differences in the various financial environments in which the MNC system operates. In the following, we consider models or alternative strategy sets that could be adopted by the MNC. This discussion is intended to be demonstrative, as a way to show the role of strategies in financing alternatives. Funds management strategies are covered in greater depth in Chapter 15.

REMITTANCE MANAGEMENT

The MNC system generates a high percent of fund requirements in the form of internal cash flows. We refer to this approach of allocating these cash flows as remittance management.

Subsidiaries differ with respect to their profitability and ability to self-finance. Subsidiaries that are cash generators enjoy cash flows that exceed funds needs. Subsidiaries that are cash absorbers have funds needs that far exceed internal cash flows. The MNC system reallocates surplus cash flows to units in need of external finance, subject to constraints. These constraints include considerations of tax structure, the financial markets environment, and the need to control risks. Risks include currency, country (political and economic), and financial dimensions. The MNC can advance funds to operating subsidiaries from a system pool, provided that the system does not take on excessive currency exposure. Country risk considerations may mandate borrowing from local banks, even if more costly. The firm may seek to minimize global tax liabilities that impose constraints on profit remittances from units subject to low tax rates. Remittances can take the form of dividends, loan repayment, interest and fees, and even funds received as a result of transfer price strategies.

Global Tax Burden

The total (net) tax bill paid by the MNC on a worldwide basis.

WIDE INTEREST RATE AND CURRENCY DIFFERENTIALS

The many subsidiary units of the MNC system spread across countries where there are wide differences in interest costs and inflation rates, for example, as presently exist among many of the countries in Eastern Europe and in emerging market nations. It is possible to analyze parity conditions in the several countries or currencies in which subsidiaries operate. Through this analysis financial managers should identify disconformities to these conditions. We should remember that parity conditions (Chapter 4) tell us whether to consider currencies as overvalued or undervalued, and whether real interest rates are higher or lower in any countries where subsidiaries are located. The "real effective rate" is the exchange rate adjusted for price level changes in the respective countries. The general rule should be to borrow overvalued currencies and repay loans denominated in undervalued currencies, after considering

EXHIBIT 14.3	**Parity Conditions—Overvalued and Undervalued Currencies**

We can use the data in the following table to illustrate the so-called parity conditions for the respective currencies. the purpose in this case is to determine the most attractive currency of denomination of borrowing for the U.S.-based MNC system. The four countries are ranked by their inflation records over the past 12 months. We will assume that these inflation trends will continue indefinitely. Exchange rate movements against the U.S. dollar reflected these inflation differentials in part with the Spanish peseta index down and the rise in the deutsche mark index. In Spain and the United Kingdom where inflation has exceeded the inflation in the United States, the peseta and pound have declined against the dollar. By contrast, the deutsche mark has appreciated in Germany. Germany has had lower inflation than the United States.

Interest rates tell us what the market sees in the future. Interest rates are higher in the United Kingdom and Spain than in the United States, indicating past inflation in those countries relative to the United States and the expectation that this inflation will continue. Interest rates in Germany are lower, reflecting the expectation of lower inflation than in the United States.

In the lower section of the table, we observe that a comparison of inflation and exchange rate changes suggests that relative to the U.S. dollar the pound is slightly undervalued, and the deutsche mark and peseta are overvalued. A comparison of the exchange rates and interest rates suggests that all three currencies are overvalued in comparison with the U.S. dollar. The signs (+ and −) are indicative of how the market gauges expected future currency rate movements.

	United States	**United Kingdom**	**Germany**	**Spain**
Inflation Rate (past 12 months)	4%	7%	2%	10%
Exchange Rate Change	—	−4	+4	−1
Interest Rate	8	14	5	11
Inflation Rate Differential*		+1	−2	−5
Interest Rate Differential†	—	−2	−1	−2

* Inflation rate differential (U.S. - foreign) minus Exchange Rate Change

† Interest rate differential (U.S. - foreign) minus Exchange Rate Change

adjustments for interest rate levels. The example in Exhibit 14.3 demonstrates this concept.

MNC Parent Guarantees

In all cases irrespective of the locus of decision making, financial managers must consider the question of parent company guarantees of the subsidiary's debt financing. The practice of granting guarantees varies considerably among companies. As indicated in a survey by Robbins and Stobaugh, MNCs with "small" foreign sales (of less than $100 million) tend not to guarantee their affiliates' loans.* For these companies the extent of their foreign sales is generally not of sufficient size to require such guarantees. Also the nature of the business tends to be more oriented toward sales and representative offices rather than full and integrated manufacturing facilities. Consequently, there simply is less long-term debt to be "guaranteed." Middle-size firms are typically willing to provide guarantees. In doing so, these firms may achieve a small reduction in the cost of borrowing or other beneficial

---

* Sidney Robbins and Robert Stobaugh, *Money in the Multi-National Enterprise* (NY: Basic Books, 1973): 67–69.

elements in the loan agreement. A number of prominent large firms (sales greater than $500 million) generally prefer not to provide guarantees. Companies in this category are of sufficient size to be able to persuade their banks to accept this arrangement without significant additional costs associated with loan agreements. In addition should parent company guarantees not be provided, there would be an additional control of the "agency costs" associated with the MNC subsidiary. The extent of this gain, however, is probably of small magnitude in most MNCs. We draw this conclusion from the fact that, for the preponderance of medium and large MNCs, company guarantees are provided.

Agency Costs

These costs occur when the senior management in a subsidiary chooses to pursue objectives that differ from the shareholder value maximization goal of the parent corporation.

Taxation of International Operations

MNC FINANCIAL OBJECTIVES AND TAX CONSIDERATIONS

The problem of how to fund the activities of the multinational corporation is inherently more complex than that of the firm operating within a single country. As in the case of the domestic firm, the MNC faces a trade-off between the objective of minimizing the expected after-tax cost of financing and of keeping risks within acceptable levels. With regard to risk factors, the financial manager focuses on reducing those risks that are specific to the industry, to the country of operations, and to the firm itself. In accomplishing these objectives for the subsidiary, the firm must first reach a decision regarding the proportion of the subsidiary's financing needs to be satisfied from internal (i.e., intrafirm) as opposed to external sources. Internal funds sources can be either from the subsidiary itself in the form of retained or reinvested earnings or from elsewhere within the MNC's worldwide financing network.

Tax considerations, both in the United States and abroad will influence MNC decisions toward reinvesting cash flows that the subsidiaries generate. In all countries reinvestment can occur through cash flows generated from depreciation charges. Generally, such cash flows are not subject to corporate income taxes. In addition, foreign source net income can be subject to a tax shield depending on the tax regulations of the MNC parent's home country. The next section describes the wide range of tax approaches and types of taxes.

NATIONAL TAX SYSTEMS

National tax systems can be classified under two broad approaches. The first is that of the territorial exemption. Under this approach the home country excludes foreign income from its tax base entirely. Countries that follow this approach also will permit no deduction against home country taxable income for expenses incurred outside of the home country. Countries that have adopted this approach are Venezuela, Brazil, Australia, South Africa, Belgium, Netherlands, Canada, Italy, Sweden and Denmark.

A second approach is the *worldwide credit* system. Under this alternative, earnings that are repatriated to the home country are subject to full taxation with a credit given for foreign taxes paid in the country of the MNC's subsidiary. This approach—followed by France, Germany, Ireland, Japan and the United States—applies to repatriated investment income (usually including dividends, interest, rents, and royalties) of controlled foreign corporations. Some analysts have criticized this system, saying that it encourages the accumulation of earnings in tax

Territorial Exemption approach versus Worldwide Credit system.

Deferral of Tax Liability

For qualifying foreign source income, such income not subject to U.S. tax liability until dividend paid (or deemed paid) to U.S. parent.

Withholding Tax on Dividends

Approach that taxes remittance dividend payments to foreigners.

haven or low-tax countries. In their view these accumulations are seen as interest-free loans made by the home country (e.g., the United States) on the deferred taxes.

Wide variations exist in tax systems among countries. These variations apply to the types of taxes levied and the tax rates applicable within each tax category. MNCs can initiate cash flows between subsidiaries to move funds toward nations with low-income tax rates, and minimal profits are then accumulated in high-income tax jurisdictions. In addition to corporate income taxes, many national tax systems use the general sales tax or turnover taxes as well as taxes on property and capital. Some national tax systems focus their attention on the movement of funds internationally and apply high withholding tax rates on dividends, royalties, and interest payments to foreign entities, i.e., to the MNC parent company. Exhibit 14.4 shows the breadth of this variation for 15 countries. These tax differences, from a global efficiency viewpoint, contribute to distortions in international capital flows. Most economists expect that national governments' actions to harmonize tax systems among countries—such as in Europe 92, the effort to remove restrictions on capital flows among the major EU nations—will result in national income gains to the participating nations.

The incidence of taxation is a special issue for multinational companies. In many instances wide disparities in national taxation provide opportunities for companies to exploit the environment. As indicated in Exhibit 14.4, there are substantial differences in tax rates applicable to MNCs, foreign shareholders, and investors.

EXHIBIT 14.4   Comparative Corporate Tax Rates (%)

Country	Corporate Income Tax (Basic Tax)	General Sales or Turnover Tax	Tax on Capital	WITHHOLDING CORPORATE TAX RATES[1]		
				Dividends	Interest	Royalties
Australia	39	10–20 Sales	None	30	10	39
Brazil	30	10–15 VAT	None	25	15	25
Canada	28	7 GST	0.3–0.532	25	25	25
France	34	18.6 VAT	None	25	45	33.33
Germany	50 Undistributed Profits 36 Distributed Profits	14 VAT	0.6 Net Assets	25	25	25
Hong Kong	16.5	0.5 Gross Sales	None	None	None	1.65
Italy	50	19 VAT	None	32.4	30	21
Japan	37.5	3 VAT	None	20	20	20
Korea	34	10 VAT	None	25	25	25
Mexico	35	10 VAT	None	None	35	35
Poland	40	25 Turnover	None	30	30	30
Russian Fed.	32	28 VAT	None	15	15	15
Spain	35	13 VAT	None	25	25	25
Sweden	30	20 VAT	None	30	None	None
Switzerland	3.63–9.80	6.2 Endusers 9.3 Retailers	.0825 Federal .26–.12 Cantonal	35	35	None
Taiwan	25	5 VAT	None	20	20	20
U.K.	33	17.5 VAT	None	25	25	25
U.S.	34	1–12 Local Sales Tax	None	None	None	None

[1] Withholding taxes often reduced by tax treaties.

SOURCE: Various country reports.

Such differences provide an incentive to the MNC to locate cash and short-term investments where after-tax returns are most favorable. Also, these different tax rates cause MNCs to find alternative ways to move funds. One alternative avenue is for the MNC parent to explicitly identify the management services or intellectual property rights that it provides to the subsidiary. When these services and rights are defined, the MNC can enter management service contracts and establish licensing and royalty agreements with the subsidiary that can serve as alternative vehicles for such international funds movement.

A few countries operate economic systems in which it is difficult to separate decision making and policy planning in the private and public sector. In these systems "indicative" planning is often stressed, or government ownership of large enterprises is extensive. This arrangement is also the case in countries that have long maintained a policy of close partnership between business and government to achieve national goals. For example, Japan has followed a policy of coordinating the private and public sectors via the national economic plan. In Japan the public sector is much more prepared than the private sector to achieve plan objectives.

Consequently, some analysts view Japan as a national corporate system, in which private sector activities and public sector activities are carried out with careful thought to the implications of the effects of one sector on the other. A careful analysis of the Japanese fiscal system and the myriad of detail that goes into supporting and subsidizing specific economic sectors via central government expenditures adds validity to this interpretation. Included among these systems are special tax concessions such as accelerated depreciation for enterprises deriving income from overseas transactions, ability to "cost" overseas market development through a reserve created for that purpose, and tax sheltering income by setting up an overseas investment loss reserve.

The government of Japan derives approximately 24% of tax revenue from corporate income taxes, and this revenue source is equivalent to more than 7% of Japan's gross domestic product.* Given the close working relationships between industry and government at the planning level, it is clear that there must be strong pressures on Japanese corporations to locate profits where the national government will enjoy primacy over other governments in receiving tax revenues. This close relationship between government and industry has a significant influence on Japan's economy, especially given the fact that the Japanese tax system is based on a worldwide approach.

IMPACT OF TAXATION ON MNC

The multinational corporation operates across a number of different national tax environments. The tax environment in host countries will differ from that in the home country in several respects, including the types of taxes applicable to the MNC's profits and the level of tax rates. In the following discussion we address the issue of how differing tax environments affect decisions and policies in the MNC.

We consider four dimensions or policy areas in which the tax environment can impact the MNC (Exhibit 14.5). These areas include investment decisions, form of organization, financing decisions, and remittance policies.

---

* OECD, *Taxing Profits in a Global Economy* (Paris, 1991): 71–75, 82–83, 228.

EXHIBIT 14.5   **Impact of Taxation on Key Decision and Policy Areas**

Decision-Policy Area	Applicable or Relevant Tax Treatment	Expected Company Decision or Policy Response	Alternative Company Decision or Policy Response
Investment Decisions "Where to Locate"	Tax relief is provided by host country.	Decision is reached to locate operational facility in one of several potential host countries.	Decision is to locate facility in the country offering the greatest tax relief.
Form of Organization	Home country treatment of branch vs. affiliate income	Affiliate form is preferred where high profit expected.	Branch form is preferred where losses are expected.
Financing Decisions	Host allows interest to be deducted as expense.	Finance foreign affiliate with parent debt when tax rate higher in host than home country.	Debt repayment is generally treated as return of capital, not subject to tax.
Remittance Policies	Host vs. home country tax treatment	Extract remittances from country with smallest incremental tax liability.	On year-to-year basis, mix of countries from which remittances are extracted will vary, based on sources of profit and tax rates.

Value-added tax (VAT)

System that levies tax at each level of productive process, based on the value added at each level.

Once an MNC has decided to invest in a particular region of the world, it must choose in which country it will locate the new operating unit. One consideration in deciding where to locate will be level of tax burden. Most host countries offer some form of tax relief to new investors. The question of level of tax burden can be complex, as noted in Exhibit 14.4. If we compare France and Germany as possible alternative host countries for a U.S. MNC, we find that German taxes on undistributed profits are considerably higher than French taxes. However, this difference tends to be offset by higher French VAT or value-added tax, and higher French withholding tax on royalties and interest. To further complicate the comparison, German taxes on distributed profits are lower than French taxes that do not distinguish between distributed and undistributed corporate profits.

Exhibits 14.4 and 14.5 suggest several possible models for the use of tax havens by foreign investor companies to locate profits outside the United States. A fairly general application of the tax haven takes place when the foreign investor company's home country uses the territorial exemption system. Under this approach, a European parent company can shift income to a tax haven subsidiary outside the United States and defer tax liability indefinitely. This pattern is suggested by the relatively higher nominal tax rates in several investor countries and the low ratio of corporate income to gross domestic product reported in the cases of Germany, Belgium, and Australia.

A second possible pattern of tax haven use arises with France. In France's case, dividends from foreign sources are tax exempt (95% of dividend) if there is more than 10% share ownership. Under these circumstances, the French parent can set up a U.S. operating subsidiary and a tax haven affiliate. Shifting income to the tax haven affiliate and subsequent payment of dividend to the French parent leaves virtually no tax liability in France. Dutch parent companies may employ the tax haven in a similar pattern, where a comparable exemption applies.

Foreign multinationals can also carry on financial or interest rate arbitrage, especially where tax treatment facilitates this practice. One practice is to have the U.S. subsidiary take out borrowings that are deductible against U.S. tax, investing them at higher returns in the United Kingdom where the taxable interest can be offset against advance corporation tax payable on dividends.*

The tax filings of foreign corporations with income derived from U.S. sources indicate an inordinate amount of interest paid. Over the period 1983–1987, interest paid ranged between 50.5% and 64.7% of total receipts, averaging $24,826 million. Over the same period, in the aggregate these corporations filed deficit net income each year, averaging $883 million.† Therefore, over this five-year period, on average interest paid was 28.1 times as large as the aggregate yearly deficit.

Foreign Subsidiary

A foreign affiliate that is separately incorporated under the host country's law.

Selection of organizational form for the foreign company can also be influenced by tax considerations. Here, home country taxes play an important role. Often the MNC can select either the affiliate or branch organizational form. The foreign subsidiary form may confer the benefit of payment deferral of any home country taxes. The branch form generally cannot offer this advantage. Since it is not a separate corporate entity, branch earnings are considered part of the parent organization's taxable profits in the year earned. In such cases MNC managers may prefer the affiliate form when high profit levels are expected, and when the deferral of home country taxes is important. By contrast managers may prefer the branch form when operating losses are expected. Thus many U.S. MNCs have followed the approach of establishing their initial overseas operations using the foreign branch organizational form, since the startup phase is when losses are most likely to occur. Later, after the foreign operation establishes itself as profitable, the MNC can convert its organizational form to that of a subsidiary or other type of foreign affiliate.

Foreign Branch

A foreign-based affiliate which is a legal and operational part of the parent MNC.

Financing decisions also require consideration of tax consequences. In most instances the host country allows interest to be treated as a deductible expense. However, in the United States and many other countries, dividend payments are not tax deductible. Therefore in situations where the MNC parent company provides financing for a foreign subsidiary company, parent loans may be preferred to parent equity. The tax advantage from financing the foreign subsidiary with parent loans will be greater in cases where the corporate income tax rate is higher in the host country than in the home country. Finally, tax authorities generally treat the repayment of loan principal as a nontaxable return of capital to the parent company.

Remittance policies can also be very much affected by tax considerations. Tax consequences influence policies concerning the form of remittance (dividend versus interest), as well as the choice of subsidiaries from which remittances are best obtained. Where remittances take the form of tax deductible expenses—for example, royalties and interest on debt—managers may prefer these over dividend remittances.

In all cases of dividend remittances, MNCs endeavor to extract these funds so as to minimize the global tax burden. This practice can be seen in Exhibit 14.6. The top part of the table outlines the tax burden on $1 million of income of each of four foreign subsidiaries for a U.S. MNC. The second part illustrates the global tax burden on the $4 million of foreign source earnings of the U.S. MNC, given a dividend remittance of $1 million from only one of the four subsidiaries, and assuming earnings are retained in the other three subsidiaries. The calculations indicate that when the U.S. parent wishes to extract a $1 million dividend from one of the four subsidiaries, the global tax burden is minimized in the case where the dividend comes

---

* Andrew Jack, "Foreigners Keep Their Cool on U.S. Tax Threat," *Financial Times,* (6 November 1992): 6.

† U.S. Treasury, *Statistics of Income Studies of International Income and Taxes* (Internal Revenue Service, Compendium Studies on International Income and Taxes, 1988): 13.

EXHIBIT 14.6	Dividend Remittances to Minimize Global Tax Burden $1 Million from Each Country Available for Remittance

Applicable Tax Rates:	Tax on Undistributed Earnings	Tax on Distributed Earnings	Host Withholding Tax	Residual U.S. Tax[1]
German Subsidiary- 56% Undistributed 36% Distributed 25% Withholding	$560,000	$360,000	$160,000	$ 0[2]
Netherlands Subsidiary- 42% Rate; 25% Withholding	420,000	420,000	145,000	0[2]
LDC Subsidiary- Tax Holiday; No Withholding	0	0	0	340,000
Hong Kong- 18% Rate; No Withholding U.S. Parent Tax Rate: 34%	180,000	180,000	0	160,000

GLOBAL TAX WHEN DIVIDEND PAID TO U.S. PARENT FROM[3]
TAXES PAID ON EARNINGS PLUS WITHHOLDING TAXES

	Hong Kong	LDC	Netherlands	Germany		Residual U.S. Tax		
LDC Country:	$180,000	$0	$420,000	$560,000	+	$340,000	=	$1,500,000
Hong Kong:	180,000	0	420,000	560,000	+	160,000	=	$1,320,000
Netherlands:	180,000	0	565,000	560,000	+	0	=	$1,305,000
Germany:	180,000	0	420,000	520,000	+	0	=	$1,120,000

[1] United States uses foreign tax credit where foreign taxes paid give rise to tax credit against U.S. tax liability.

[2] Creates an excess tax credit U.S. company may be able to use against tax liability from other foreign source income.

[3] Global tax on $4 million foreign source income, when $1 million dividend paid to U.S. parent from one of the subsidiaries; earnings retained in the other three subsidiaries.

from the German subsidiary. This outcome is due to the interaction of a number of factors specific to how each subsidiary incurs tax liabilities, and also to how the MNC parent company is taxed. The LDC tax holiday makes the tax cost of dividend remittance from this subsidiary extremely high. The relatively low tax rate in Hong Kong also discourages extracting dividends from Hong Kong. The deciding factor tends to be the wide difference in tax rates applicable in Germany on distributed and undistributed earnings. Exhibit 14.6 illustrates the interaction of the factors that MNCs consider in making the decision with reference to dividend remittances and earnings retention.

U.S. TAXATION OF FOREIGN OPERATIONS

This section focuses on taxation of business income under the U.S. tax code. In the international context, the business income of a foreign subsidiary of a U.S. MNC may be subject to taxation in two ways. First, the host country may tax all income earned in that country, irrespective of whether the income is earned by a foreign-owned or controlled company or a domestic company. Thus if an American company earns income in France, it must pay French income tax. The second source of tax liability arises from the parent MNC's country of origin, under the philosophy that residents of a country should pay taxes on their income, wherever earned. Under this approach an American company earning income in France must pay

EXHIBIT 14.7	**Calculation of U.S. Tax on Foreign Subsidiary Income—Foreign Subsidiary Located in Latin American Country with 25% Tax Rate**

(100% OF INCOME REMITTED AS DIVIDEND COMPARED WITH 50% REMITTED)

	I **100% Dividend**	II **50% Dividend**
I. Foreign Subsidiary:		
1. Taxable Income	$1,000,000	$1,000,000
2. Foreign Income Tax (25%)	250,000	250,000
3. Net Income after Tax	750,000	750,000
4. Gross Dividend	750,000	375,000
5. Dividend Withholding Tax (5%)	37,500	18,750
6. Net Dividend Received by Parent	712,500	356,250
II. Taxable U.S. Income:		
7. Net Dividend to Parent	712,500	356,250
8. Foreign Income Tax	250,000	125,000
9. Dividend Withholding Tax Paid	37,500	18,750
10. Foreign Income Tax Payable in U.S. (Grossed Up)	1,000,000	500,000
III. U.S. Taxes Payable on Foreign Source Income		
11. Foreign Income Taxable	1,000,000	500,000
12. Tentative U.S. Tax (34%)	340,000	170,000
13. Foreign Tax Credit[1]	287,500	143,750
14. U.S. Taxes Payable	52,500	26,250

[1] In Column I where a 100% dividend is paid, all foreign income taxes and withholding taxes can be claimed as foreign tax credit. In cases where less than 100% of earnings are paid as dividend to the parent, the foreign tax credit is allocated in proportion to the percentage of earnings available that are paid as dividend relative to total earnings available for dividends. In Column II this is 50% of the total.

Double Taxation

When foreign source income is taxed abroad and taxed a second time when remitted as dividend to the MNC parent.

American income tax on these earnings. With these circumstances in the host and parent countries, the possibility of double taxation of foreign source income poses serious problems for MNCs and calls for careful tax strategy and tax planning.

U.S. taxation of foreign business income of U.S. MNCs is designed to achieve an effective tax rate no lower than that which would apply if the income was earned in the United States, but also to avoid or minimize the possibility of double taxation. This outcome is accomplished by use of the following:

1. worldwide basis of taxation
2. foreign tax credit

U.S.-based companies are subject to U.S. income taxes on their worldwide income. However, taxes paid to foreign governments can be used as credits applicable against U.S. tax liabilities.

Foreign Tax Credit—Calculations for Foreign Subsidiary   To demonstrate how the foreign tax credit works, we use as an illustration a foreign subsidiary of a U.S. MNC that is subject to a 25% income tax rate by the host government. In addition the host government levies a 5% withholding tax on dividends paid. As shown in Exhibit 14.7, the foreign subsidiary generates $1 million in taxable income (dollar translated amount).

Foreign taxes paid on the subsidiary's income include $250,000 income tax, and $37,500 withholding tax (Exhibit 14.7, Lines 2 and 5, Column I). The gross dividend paid to the U.S. parent is reduced to a net dividend of $712,500 as a result of the withholding tax.

Grossing Up

MNC income is increased by foreign income taxes paid on foreign subsidiary earnings.

Taxable U.S. income is calculated by a procedure referred to as grossing up. The reason for this procedure is to establish a uniform treatment for calculating U.S. taxable income and foreign taxes eligible for the foreign tax credit. We take the net dividend received by the U.S. parent company, and allocate the foreign taxes paid. This is done *pro rata,* meaning that if the dividend paid the U.S. parent is less than the full amount available from current earnings, there must be a proportionate allocation of foreign income taxes paid to calculate the foreign tax credit. This calculation is evident in Column II of Exhibit 14.7, where only 50% of available earnings is paid as a dividend to the U.S. parent.

Deemed Paid Foreign Tax Credit

Tax credit allowed against U.S. income tax for foreign taxes paid on foreign-source earnings.

Returning to the illustration in Column I, the grossing up yields a U.S. taxable income of $1,000,000. Applying the U.S. tax rate (34%) to this income, the tentative U.S. tax is $340,000. The applicable foreign tax credit is $287,500 that includes 100% of foreign taxes paid. This difference leaves an amount of $52,500 as the amount of U.S. taxes remaining payable. The effect of the foreign tax credit is to prevent total (global) tax liabilities from exceeding the U.S. tax payable. An exception to this practice would be the case where foreign tax rates exceed U.S. tax rates. Under such conditions the U.S. company has an excess tax credit that may be applicable against tax liabilities related to income from other foreign sources.

Deferral of U.S. Tax Liability   As noted at the beginning of our discussion of taxation, an important difference in the taxation of foreign branch vs. foreign subsidiary (or affiliate) income is that branch income is automatically included in the U.S. parent company's taxable income. This situation is true, irrespective of remittances or branch transfers of income flows. By contrast foreign subsidiary income generally does not ordinarily become subject to U.S. tax liability until the subsidiary has paid a dividend from income, or until a dividend can be deemed to have been paid.

Deferral of U.S. tax liability is an important advantage for the U.S. multinational and becomes one of the key controlling factors in MNC cash management, as well as in tax planning. It is a truism to state that U.S. MNCs may prefer to borrow at relatively high cost to meet cash needs in one part of the world, while in another part of the world subsidiaries are accumulating funds through profit generation. However, the funds accumulated may enjoy low (or zero) tax rates due to the deferral privilege. It is clear that it can be advantageous for a U.S. MNC to make use of the deferral privilege indefinitely, given application of low taxes in the host country and the existence of relatively high income tax rates in the home country.

Revenue Act of 1962

Added Subpart F to the U.S. Internal Revenue Code dealing with foreign source income.

The U.S. government has modified the deferral privilege in one important respect through provisions incorporated in the Revenue Act of 1962, reaffirmed in the Tax Reform Act of 1986. Prior to the 1962 law, U.S. MNCs were able to defer U.S. tax liabilities on significant parts of their overseas revenues through the combined use of tax haven subsidiaries and the concentration of remittance income and export sales revenues. Many congressional legislators were led to believe that the operation of tax haven subsidiaries provided opportunities for excessive and permanent deferral of U.S. tax liability.

Tax haven subsidiaries are established where the following needs are satisfied:

1. low tax rate on business and investment income
2. low withholding tax on remittances (dividends and interests)
3. stable currency and/or absence of exchange controls
4. good communications for efficient banking services
5. political and social stability

"Compared with companies in Europe and Japan, U.S. MNCs have limited tax alternatives." senior vice president-taxation, with a major MNC.

Subpart F of the Internal Revenue Code

The section of the U.S. IRC which sets the rules applicable to MNC foreign source income.

The Revenue Act of 1962 removed the tax advantages of tax haven subsidiaries. At the same time the deferral privilege was retained for subsidiaries operating as manufacturing and sales units. This act added Subpart F to the Internal Revenue Code that deals with taxation of foreign source income. Over the years the tax code has maintained this feature; the Tax Reform Act of 1986 again maintained this important tax dimension.

Subpart F Income   Subpart F focuses on certain types of undistributed income of controlled foreign corporations. A controlled foreign corporation is one in which U.S. shareholders own more than 50% of the voting stock. In addition, U.S. shareholders must each control 10% or more of the voting shares for the subsidiary to be considered a controlled foreign corporation. In such cases, the U.S. parent could be taxed on certain types of undistributed income.

Subpart F income refers to certain types of income of a controlled foreign corporation that are taxable for the U.S. shareholder. This tax applies whether or not the corporation distributes the income to the U.S. shareholder. The types of this income that are taxable under Subpart F are deemed to have been distributed as a dividend to U.S. shareholders. Specifically, Subpart F income includes: 1) passive income such as dividends, interest, rents, royalties, net foreign currency and commodities gains, and gains from the sale of certain investment property; 2) certain income from insurance, shipping, financial services, and oil-related activities; 3) income from the performance of managerial or other services, and 4) export (from the U.S.) sales income.

When foreign earnings from these sources are subject to Subpart F treatment, the following regulations apply:

1. Such income is deemed to have been distributed to the U.S. shareholder. When dividend remittance is made from the controlled foreign corporation out of earnings that have been previously taxed, the distribution is not again subject to U.S. tax.
2. Foreign base company income does not include certain income from less developed countries when reinvested in these countries.
3. If foreign income is blocked by a host country because of foreign currency restriction, it is excluded from the profits of the controlled foreign corporation for Subpart F purposes.

Subsidiary income from sources other than those qualifying under Subpart F may enjoy the privilege of deferral of U.S. tax liabilities until the subsidiary remits those earnings in the form of dividend income to the MNC parent.

REMITTANCES UNDER ALTERNATIVE TAX REGIMES

Differences in national tax environments provide opportunities for MNCs to develop remittance strategies that can yield considerable tax savings. These differences become apparent from an examination of the three columns at the extreme right of Exhibit 14.4. We should understand the following points with respect to the complexity involved in formulating an appropriate remittance strategy.

1. The range of withholding tax rates varies considerably on dividend remittances. In addition, there are equally large variations in withholding rates when comparing to interest and royalties. Therefore one must carefully analyze these differences to determine *from which country* a particular form of remittance should be extracted.

2. Within a given country the differences in withholding tax rates between alternative remittance forms are considerable. For example, in the case of Mexico, the differences in withholding tax rates between dividends and interest and royalties is 35% (35%–0.0%). In the case of Switzerland, there are wide differences between withholding tax rates on royalties and interest (35%).

3. Generally, choosing between a dividend versus a royalty or interest remittance form involves creating tax shelter expenses (in the case of royalties and interest) that can reduce taxes overall. The alternative is paying a remittance with after-tax money (in the case of a dividend remittance).

Exhibit 14.8 presents the tax consequences of using alternative remittance forms for six countries. In each case, a $1 million remittance is possible from the subsidiary operating in each country. Column 1 indicates the reduced tax that results from tax shelter effects of the remittance (royalty and interest only). Column 2 indicates the increased tax (withholding tax). Column 3 indicates the net effect on tax liability in the host country. In Italy, the lowest withholding tax applies to interest on bonds (issued by the subsidiary to the parent company). The highest withholding tax applies to dividend remittances (32.4%).

Column 4 indicates the residual U.S. tax, applicable when the parent receives the remittance. Generally, no additional tax liability exists with respect to dividend

---

EXHIBIT 14.8   **Net Tax Effect from Alternative Remittance Forms, Seven Selected Countries ($1 Million Remittance)**

	Reduced Tax 1	Increased Tax 2	Net Change 3 = 1 − 2	Residual U.S. Tax 4	Net Tax Effect 5 = 3 + 4
Italy					
Dividend	—	324,000	324,000	0	324,000
Interest	360,000	300,000	−60,000	340,000	280,000
Royalty	360,000	210,000	−150,000	340,000	190,000
Mexico					
Dividend	—	0	0	0	0
Interest	350,000	350,000	0	340,000	340,000
Royalty	350,000	350,000	0	340,000	340,000
Australia					
Dividend	—	300,000	300,000	0	300,000
Interest	390,000	100,000	−290,000	340,000	50,000
Royalty	390,000	390,000	0	340,000	340,000
Switzerland					
Dividend	—	350,000	350,000	0	350,000
Interest	96,000	350,000	254,000	340,000	594,000
Royalty	96,000	0	−96,000	340,000	244,000
Hong Kong					
Dividend	—	0	0	160,000	160,000
Interest	165,000	0	−165,000	340,000	175,000
Royalty	165,000	0	−165,000	340,000	175,000
United Kingdom					
Dividend	—	250,000	250,000	0	250,000
Interest	330,000	250,000	−80,000	340,000	260,000
Royalty	330,000	250,000	−80,000	340,000	260,000

NOTES: Column 1 derived from tax shelter effects for subsidiary related to expense of interest or royalty. Column 2 derived from withholding tax against remittance. Column 4 derived from U.S. foreign tax credit and U.S. residual tax on foreign source earnings.

SOURCE: Exhibit 14.4.

remittances, unless the local (host country) tax rate is lower than the U.S. tax rate. In the case of Hong Kong, there is additional U.S. tax liability due to the very low tax rate (16.5%).

Column 5 indicates the net effect on tax liability from each remittance form. In Italy the dividend remittance produces the highest additional tax liability. In Australia the highest additional tax effect comes from use of the royalty form. This result is due to the very high withholding tax rate on royalty payments, and the low withholding tax on interest. In Switzerland the highest additional tax effect comes from the use of the interest form of remittances. This effect is due to the absense of withholding tax on royalties and equally high rates of withholding on dividends and interest.

The tax consequences of remittances are complex and require careful analysis when the MNC seeks to develop a tax sparing strategy. The preceding analysis illustrates the important role played by taxes in MNC remittance strategies and cash management.

The Cost of Capital and the MNC

COST OF CAPITAL AND RETURN ON INVESTMENT

The cost of capital is an important concept in the understanding of MNC financial decisions. In a later chapter we will see that this concept plays a critical role in capital budgeting that in turn drives financing decisions. At this point in the presentation of international corporate finance, we employ the cost of capital concept as a way to gain an overview of the MNC financing process. Further discussion of these concepts will be reserved for Chapter 17.

Traditionally the cost of capital has played a pivotal role in understanding how firms allocate or should allocate financial capital. A rich literature exists on this subject in a "purely domestic," or noninternational, setting. The reader is encouraged to review a presentation of this literature before proceeding into the treatment of the subject from the standpoint of the MNC.*

The cost of capital is traditionally viewed as the sum of the cost of debt financing and the cost of equity. The theory underlying this concept focuses on factors influencing the firm's choice between debt and equity. For the purely domestic firm these factors are: 1) the avoidance of bankruptcy/ liquidation and its implied consequences for company shareholders and central management; 2) the fact that interest-related expenses on debt can be deducted in the calculation of corporate income, while taxing the shareholder on income received as dividends; 3) management perspectives toward agency-related costs. An example of the latter is the expectation that a higher proportion of debt financing will reduce the range of alternatives open to central management, forcing a closer adherence to profit-related objectives.

When we shift focus to the multinational corporation, the firm is confronted with a wider range of alternatives. Internationally, there are considerable variations

---

* For example, see: Stanley B. Block and Geoffrey A. Hirt, *Foundations of Financial Management,* 7th ed., (Homewood, IL: Irwin, 1994): p. 317-ff; Burton A. Rolb and Richard F. DeMong, *Principles of Financial Management,* 2nd ed. (Plano, TX: Business Publications, Inc., 1988): p. 314ff; James C. Van Horne and John M. Wachowicz, Jr., *Financial Management and Policy,* 9th ed. (Englewood Cliffs, NJ: Prentice Hall, 1995):238ff. A more advanced presentation is found in: James C. Baker, "The Cost of Capital of Multinational Companies, Facts and Fallacies," *Managerial Finance* (September 1987): pp. 12–17.

among corporate income tax rates (e.g., Germany, 50%; U.S., 34%), conveying greater tax advantages to debt in the high tax nations. Bankruptcy laws and their effective enforcement also vary greatly among nations. Stricter enforcement of creditor rights will ensure higher penalties on management, for example in Germany where management is typically replaced by a receiver during the "workout" period. Under bankruptcy laws in the U.S., in contrast, management retains substantial rights during the proceedings.*

In addition to tax and bankruptcy considerations, the MNC, which sources funds across foreign currency boundaries, must consider the potential influence of exchange rate changes on the cost of capital. A simplified analysis for a U.S.-based MNC will illustrate the role of exchange rates. Assume that the MNC issues equity solely in the U.S. and that debt to finance new projects is issued both in the U.S. and in the foreign country, Iceland. Debt issued in Iceland will be denominated in the local currency, the Icelandic pound. Further, assume that neither the U.S. nor Iceland impose withholding taxes on dividend and interest payments. And finally assume that the MNC parent services all debt from a U.S. dollar base. In this framework fluctuations in the exchange rate between the Icelandic pound and the U.S. dollar will affect the cost of debt.

The exchange rate/interest rate factor can be incorporated to form the total pre-tax cost of debt for the MNC

total pre-tax cost of debt	=	cost of debt sourced in Iceland, in $	+	cost of debt sourced, from U.S.

$$R_D = \frac{DL}{D} \times R_{DL} \times \left(1 - \frac{L\$}{100}\right) + R_{D\$} \times \frac{D\$}{D} \tag{1}$$

where

R_D = weighted average cost of total debt
R_e = annual % cost of equity
R_{DL} = annual interest rate for debt sourced in Iceland, in pounds
$R_{D\$}$ = annual interest rate for debt sourced in the U.S., in dollars
D = dollar value of total debt; $D = DL + D\$$
DL = dollar value of debt sourced in Iceland, issued in Icelandic pounds; expressed in dollar terms (historical basis)
$D\$$ = dollar value of debt sourced in the U.S. (historical basis)
$L\$$ = expected % annual appreciation in U.S. dollar exchange rate, in terms of Icelandic pounds (depreciation, "−")

When the debt cost component R_D is combined with the equity component R_e, the overall cost of capital for the MNC is as follows:

$$K_c = \frac{E}{V} \times R_e + \frac{D}{V} \times R_D \times (1 - t_{us}) \tag{2}$$

where

K_c = cost of capital (after-tax basis)
E = $ value of equity

---

* For an interesting summary in this area, see R.G. Rajan and L. Zingales, "What Do We Know about Capital Structure? Some Evidence from International Data," *Journal of Finance.* vol. 50, no. 5, December 1995, pp. 1421–1460.

$$V = E + D$$

t_{us} = relevant marginal U.S. tax rate

Because the cost of capital incorporates the cost of debt R_D, the cost of capital for the MNC is dependent on the financial decision maker's expectations about the future value of the pound/dollar exchange rate L$. When the dollar appreciates against the Icelandic pound, the cost of debt sourced in pounds will fall. Conversely, when the dollar depreciates in pound terms, the cost of Icelandic debt will rise.

For this analysis, the marginal cost of capital can be considered for different levels of new financing requirements for the firm. The cost of capital will remain constant for a time as new financings rise. However, as the firm places progressively greater demands on the capital markets, the suppliers of capital will require higher yield incentives to provide additional funds.

Closely related to the cost of capital is the marginal return on investment schedule. For this analysis the firm considers the relevant investment possibilities. The marginal return on investment is defined as the rate of return on new investment expenditures open to the firm. For each increment of investment spending, the contribution to earnings is related to the investment requirements to yield a rate of return. When the investment project rates of return are arrayed in descending order, these define the negatively sloped marginal return on investment schedule.

The reference footnote in this section presents further background sources on the derivation of the marginal cost of capital and marginal return on investment functions. These concepts are used in Exhibit 14.9 in the next section.

Marginal Cost of Capital (MCC)

At the margin, the sum of the proportionally weighted costs of different sources of financial capital for the MNC.

Marginal return on Investment (MRI)

The return on the marginal investment project for the MNC.

FINANCING DECISION: COSTS AND RISKS FOR THE MNC

This framework can be used to compare the MNC's behavior toward investment in Iceland with that of a comparable, but strictly domestic, firm in Iceland. For this comparison assume that both firms face identical marginal return on investment (MRI) functions. Further assume that the MNC investment opportunities in Iceland involve production and marketing projects that are confined strictly to the country. Finally assume that Iceland is a country of moderate size with a domestic financial market that is not highly integrated with other national and international financial markets.

Because of the limited size of the Icelandic capital market and its lack of integration with other national financial markets, the cost of funds is higher for companies that have access only to the Icelandic financial market. The MNC, however, has the additional option of financing from capital markets that are outside of this country. Because it has a worldwide funds-sourcing network, the MNC will be able to obtain financing at significantly lower cost than the purely domestic firm, resulting in a marginal cost of capital schedule that is uniformly lower than that of the domestic firm. Consequently the MNC's flexibility to proceed with the investment will be greater than that of the domestic firm. Exhibit 14.9 illustrates these relationships.

Exhibit 14.9 also portrays MNC behavior toward investment in the case where the MNC does not incur special costs—for example, costs associated with hedging and insurance—arising from the fact that the company is multinational. For this case the relevant cost of capital schedule becomes "MCC, MNC, no risk abatement." By comparison, the cost of capital for the purely domestic firm is presented as "MCC, DOM." As indicated, the MNC investment F* exceeds F' for the comparable

EXHIBIT 14.9   **Comparison of Marginal Cost of Capital (MCC), Domestic Case, with Risk Abatement, and Without Financial Costs Related to Risk Abatement**

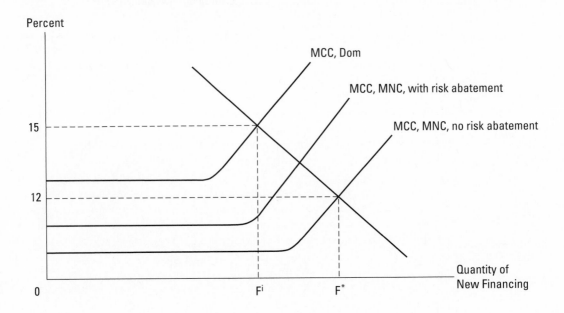

domestic firm. Correspondingly, the MNC is able to finance this investment at a lower cost of capital rate.

The MNC may incur hedging costs when sourcing funds from financial markets denominated in currencies other than that of the Icelandic pound. Also, special political and country risks that the MNC bears when operating in Iceland may cause additional insurance costs. The "MCC, MNC, no risk abatement" case shown in the diagram applies to the unhedged and uninsured MNC marginal cost of capital. This cost lies significantly below the "MCC, DOM" case for the strictly domestic firm. When the additional costs of hedging and insurance are taken into account, the MCC shifts upward somewhat to "MCC, MNC, with risk abatement," but will typically remain below that for local finance. Hedging approaches using futures, options, and swaps are presented in Chapter 5. Under the conditions applicable to Iceland, the MNC will obtain finance at lower cost and will have a larger new financing budget than will purely domestic firms.

As described in this section, MNC financial managers can significantly influence the firm's cost of capital. In the typical MNC, the management of sourced funds is an active process, which is described in greater detail in Chapter 15, International Cash Management.

ILLUSTRATIONS OF MNC FINANCIAL RISK ABATEMENT

The MNC decisions toward hedging and political risk insurance are matters of managerial discretion and policy. From the financial manager's perspective, decisions to hedge and insure depend on the extent to which such elements are "recognized in the market." Key to the use of these techniques is the MNC financial manager's

EXHIBIT 14.10	**Sensitivity Analysis of Currency Rate Changes on Cost of Financing: Zeta Chemical Company**

1 Amount To Be Repaid (Guilder) Million)	2 Exchange Rate (Guilder Per Dollar)	3 = (1 ÷ 2) Amount To Be Repaid ($ Million)	4 Principal Amount Borrowed	5 = (3 − 4) Effective Cost (Interest ± Exchange) ($ Million)	6 Effective Cost as Percent of Amount Borrowed	7 = (5 − $1.4 mil.) Exchange Rate Effect ($ Million)
64.2	2.60	24.7	20.0	4.7	23.5%	3.3
64.2	2.80	22.9	20.0	2.9	14.5%	1.5
64.2	3.00	21.4	20.0	1.4	7.0%	0
64.2	3.20	20.1	20.0	0.1	0.5%	−1.3
64.2	3.40	18.9	20.0	−1.1	−5.5%	−2.5

decision as to the "fairness" of the market prices for hedging and insurance on which such risk abatement would be based. If the cost of hedging or political risk insurance is accepted as "fair," the MNC would then have the option of reducing risk (gaining certainty of values) by entering into hedge or insurance agreements.

One way to control risk when borrowing is to select the "correct" currency in which to denominate the loan. Consider a situation where Zeta Chemical Company needs a loan of $20 million to fund operations for the next budget year. One alternative for Zeta is to borrow this sum from its U.S. bank for one year at 12% interest; all interest and principal would be repaid at the end of the year. An alternative loan proposal, made by a Dutch bank, is to provide 60 million in guilders at 7% interest. The exchange rate is DG 3.0/$, and Zeta can borrow the guilders, convert them to dollars, and have the required $20 million. At year end, Zeta would have to repay DG 60 million principal plus DG 4.2 million interest (for a total of DG 64.2 million).

At 7%, the guilder loan carries a lower nominal interest rate. If Zeta's financial officer could be guaranteed that the exchange rate would not move from its current level, the selection of currency decision would be simple—borrow in guilders from the Dutch bank. Unfortunately, the exchange rate relationship is not likely to remain stabilized at current levels.

To focus on this problem, we undertake a sensitivity analysis where we consider the dollar cost of financing at five alternative exchange rates.

As we observe in Exhibit 14.10, an appreciation of the guilder against the dollar from 3.00 to 2.80 (a change of 7.2%) more than doubles the effective cost of financing (Column 5).

If the MNC wishes to avoid the risks arising from possible changes in the guilder/dollar exchange rate, the financial manager should consider buying guilders forward against dollars. If the forward guilder can be obtained at a forward discount of less than 5%—that is, a value above DG 2.85/$—then the cost of the Dutch bank loan proposal would be more attractive than the U.S. bank loan, and foreign exchange market risk would be dispelled.*

In this example the U.S. MNC recognizes the cost of hedging as a required element in project finance. This hedge cost can be incorporated into its strategic decision plan toward investments.

---

* This example uses the one-year time period as illustrative only. In the case of long-lived capital projects, financing is typically longer term in nature.

In the actual execution of the investment, the corporate treasury would ordinarily undertake the task of deciding whether or not to hedge. That decision, a tactical one, will rest on the level of expertise and knowledge that treasury management has toward the guilder/U.S. dollar currency relationship.

A second way to deal with risks in a foreign investment is through political risk insurance. For example, the Overseas Private Investment Corporation (OPIC), an agency of the U.S. government, can issue policies to insure for political risk elements, including currency inconvertibility, expropriation, war, revolution, insurrection, and civil strife. Several private insurance companies also provide policies addressing political and country risk, for example, the AIG Corporation and the Chubb Group. Again at the strategic planning stage in evaulating potential foreign investments, it is appropriate to factor in the cost of such insurance when weighing the project's costs and benefits. Projects will appear less attractive in country locations where political risks are particularly high. This procedure at the strategic level need not be followed in the actual implementation of the investment. MNCs may wish to "self-insure" depending upon the financial manager's judgment concerning the risks relative to the insurance premiums.[†]

SUMMARY

There are fundamental differences between multinational companies and domestic companies with respect to financing operations. These include differences in financial environment related to domestic monetary expansion and exchange rate behavior, interest rate levels, and inflation rates. In addition, national tax rates differ, further influencing comparisons of after-tax cost of capital.

The essential characteristics of the MNC are that it is a system-oriented unit for planning and operation; it has the ability to internalize competitive advantages; and it can exploit environmental differences. Given the extensive variations in the international financial environment, MNCs can enjoy considerable opportunities to operate at competitive advantage over purely domestic companies.

MNC financing of international operations can take a wide range of forms. These forms call for choices between equity and debt, external source and intracompany financing, local and international financial markets, long-term versus short-term funds, and foreign currency versus local currency funds. The choice among these sources will rest on issues of 1) need to strengthen managerial control, 2) need to receive cash inflows from subsidiaries, 3) purpose of the financing, 4) business strategy elements, 5) expectations concerning financial environment, and 6) desire to minimize risk exposure.

The taxation of international operations can have an important impact on MNC operations and decisions in the following areas: investment decisions, selection of organizational form, and financing decisions. Double taxation is an ever-present hazard.

The U.S. government minimizes the possibility of double taxation of income for U.S. companies through foreign tax credit. Under some circumstances, foreign operating subsidiaries of U.S. MNCs may be able to defer U.S. tax liability by reinvesting profits overseas.

---

† Further discussion concerning country risk and risk insurance is presented in Chapter 10.

MNC control over cost of capital is subject to greater flexibility due to several factors. First, there are more diverse sources of capital for MNCs as compared with domestic companies. Second, financial risk managers can opt for risk abatement actions, and the cost can be factored into cost of capital calculations. By comparing the marginal cost of capital and the marginal return on investment, we are able to determine the optimal investment financing level for the MNC.

REVIEW QUESTIONS

1. Compare and contrast the world of two countries and two products (often used in presentations of comparative advantage) with the world of complex products, services, and markets. What implications are there for financing the MNC and its subsidiary units?

2. What alternative formats are available for MNCs to develop or exploit overseas market opportunities? How do the financing requirements differ among these cases?

3. Describe the evolution of the MNC headquarters organization as its foreign subsidiary operations grow in importance.

4. Distinguish between internal and external fund sources for the foreign subsidiary of the MNC.

5. Which has access to a broader range of funds to finance expansion, the foreign subsidiary or the total MNC system? Explain in detail.

6. How do legal factors affect the flexibility of the MNC system to finance its needs?

7. Which is the riskier method of financing the foreign subsidiary of the MNC:
   a. retained earnings from the subsidiary
   b. parent debt
   c. parent equity

8. Distinguish between cash generating and cash absorbing subsidiaries. Suppose an MNC had only cash generators, what problems would it face? Suppose an MNC had only cash absorbers, what problems would it face?

9. MNCs face very little flexibility in mobilizing system funds. Evaluate this statement.

10. For what reasons might MNCs be unwilling to make frequent use of guarantees for subsidiary borrowings?

11. For what reasons might we expect an MNC firm to have a declining (downward to right) MRI curve?

12. For what reasons might we expect an MNC firm to have a rising (upward to left) MCC curve? Compare MCC curves for MNC and purely domestic firms, under *otherwise unchanged* conditions.

13. Explain how taxation of international operations can influence investment and financing decisions.

14. Explain how taxation of foreign source earnings can influence the organizational format used to develop overseas operations.

15. A U.S. MNC has French, Italian, and U.K. subsidiaries. The corporate income tax rates in these three countries are 50%, 30% and 25%, respectively. Italy

levies a 10% withholding tax on dividend payments. The U.S. corporate income tax rate is 34%. From which subsidiary should a dividend remittance be extracted to minimize global tax liability? Assume that each subsidiary generates $10,000,000 in pre-tax profits, and a full dividend is to be paid (all of after-tax income).

16. What is the purpose of the foreign tax credit?

17. Gramco has a subsidiary in Latin America where the income tax rate is 30% and the dividend withholding tax rate is 10%. Calculate the foreign tax liability and U.S. tax liability in a year when the subsidiary earns a profit of $5,000,000, which is 100% remitted as a dividend.

18. The Matrix Corporation has annual intersubsidiary sales as indicated in the table. Profit margin on sales is 5% for each subsidiary. Tax rates on profits are: Belgium 30%, France 40%, Italy 50%, and U.K. 25%. Calculate the tax savings possible for Matrix by utilizing transfer prices to shift profits to the lowest tax countries. In this case, assume intersubsidiary sales prices can be shifted up or down no more than 20% by the respective subsidiary companies.

Intersubsidiary Sales Matrix, All Revenue in U.S. Dollars

	DESTINATION COUNTRIES			
Origin Countries	**Belgium**	**France**	**Italy**	**United Kingdom**
Belgium				
Revenue		500,000		300,000
Units	xx	5	xx	3
France				
Revenue	600,000		400,000	
Units	12	xx	8	xx
Italy				
Revenue	100,000	160,000		120,000
Units	50	80	xx	60
United Kingdom				
Revenue	5,000,000	7,000,000	1,000,000	
Units	50	70	10	xz

CASE 1

Zeta Europe's Choices

Zeta Chemical Company, a U.S. parent, has a subsidiary in Europe that needs $10 million in additional funds. The European subsidiary will use these funds for a five-year period, at which time the loan will be repaid. The financing alternatives are as follows:

1. Borrow U.S. dollars for five years at an interest rate of 10%.

2. Borrow deutsche mark for five years at an interest rate of 7%.

3. Borrow under a Eurocurrency revolving bank loan agreement, where the currency borrowed can be changed at the six-month interval when the floating rate is reset. Current rates are Eurodollars 9.5%, Eurosterling 12.5%, Euro Dmark 7.0%, Euro French franc 10.5%

What are the advantages and disadvantages of each alternative?

CASE 2

Where To Locate A Financial Headquarters in Southeast Asia: Hong Kong or Singapore?

As we go to press, Hong Kong is in the process of reverting to Chinese sovereignty. This case is provided based on the expectation that the city will retain its international financial center status in the years ahead.

Early in 1994 Mr. Victor Blanchard was given the assignment of preparing a background study concerning an overseas regional office. Mr. Blanchard was an officer in a medium-sized European manufacturing company in the packaged foods business. His company found that it could obtain needed inputs in the Far East. Approximately 10% of its production capacity was located in the Far East (Thailand and Malaysia). Another 30% was located in the U.S., with the remainder in Europe. It was projected that the Far East production would double in the next four years, with expansion in existing plants and the construction of new facilities in Indonesia and possibly the Philippines.

With these plans the following needs could be serviced from a regional administrative and finance headquarters: medium-term borrowing, currency hedging, trade finance, search for acquisition of companies in the region, development of regional banking relationships, and management and control of operating units in the region. Corporate management considered Hong Kong and Singapore both qualified, but a choice had to be made. The global system had aggregate resources of $1.7 billion. Prior to writing his report and recommendations, Mr. Blanchard made a brief summary of the major comparison points.

Advise Mr. Blanchard on this matter, defending your preferred choice.

Singapore	Hong Kong
(1) Paternalistic social and economic system	(1) Free competition and market orientation
(2) Large, well-developed Asian dollar market	(2) Large, well-developed Asian dollar market
(3) Lack of domestic finance activity and base	(3) Access to Mainland China business; project finance and trade finance business
(4) Low political risk	(4) High political risk. Unification with China in 1997
(5) In past capital market development hindered by government institutions. Central Provident Fund plays dominant role in market; capital financing supported by large dollar tax on payrolls.	(5) Financial institutions in Hong Kong aggressively working to build capital market, based on Asian dollar business.
(6) Interest rates kept low due to inflow of neighboring countries	(6) Interest rates volatile due to funds from alternating waves of fund inflows and outflows
(7) Money market growth supported by monetary authority with large T-Bill market.	(7) Lack of monetary authority, and lack of T-Bill market.
(8) Stock market overlaps with that of Malaysia market	(8) Stock market susceptible to property development cycles
(9) Growth of economy related to service of financial needs of region	(9) Growth of economy related to trade and investment links with Mainland China

SELECTED BIBLIOGRAPHY

Baker, James C. "The Cost of Capital of Multinational Companies, Facts and Fallacies." *Managerial Finance,* (September 1987) 12–17.

Booth, Lawrence David. "Taxes, Funds Positioning, and the Cost of Capital for Multinationals." *Advances in Financial Planning and Forecasting,* Vol. 4, Part B, (1990): 245–270.

Choi, Jongmoo Jay. "Diversification, Exchange Risk, and Corporate International Investment." *Journal of International Business Studies,* (Spring 1989): 145–155.

Corporate Taxes, A Worldwide Summary. New York: Price Waterhouse, 1996.

Fay, Jack, and Judson Stryker. "An Update on Foreign Taxes." *CPA Journal,* Vol. 65, No. 10, (October 1995): 28–29.

Feldstein, Martin, James R. Hines, Jr., and R. Glenn Hubbard, (ed). *The Effect of Taxation on Multinational Corporations.* A National Bureau of Economic Research Project. Chicago and London: University of Chicago Press, 1995.

Frisch, Daniel J. "The Economics of International Tax Policy: Some Old and New Approaches." *Tax Notes,* (April 30, 1990): 581–591.

Jack, Andrew. "Foreigners Keep Their Cool on U.S. Tax Threat." *Financial Times,* (November 6, 1992): 6.

Kidwell, David S., M.W. Marr, and C.R. Thompson. "Eurodollar Bonds: Alternative Financing for U.S. Companies." *Financial Management,* (Winter 1985).

Lee, Kwang Chul, and Chuck C.Y. Kwok. "Multinational Corporations vs. Domestic Corporation: International Environmental Factors and Determinants of Capital Structure." *Journal of International Business Studies,* (Summer 1988): 195–217.

Mataloni, R.J., Jr. "U.S. Multinational Companies: Operations in 1993." *Survey of Current Business,* (June 1995): 31–51.

McCauley, Robert N., and S.A. Zimmer. "Explaining International Differences in the Cost of Capital." *Federal Reserve Bank of New York Quarterly Review,* (Summer 1989): 7–28.

Park, Young S. "Currency Swaps as a Long-Term International Financing Technique." *Journal of International Business Studies,* (Winter 1984).

Rajan, R.G., and L. Zingales. "What Do We Know About Capital Structure? Some Evidence from International Data." *Journal of Finance,* Vol. 50, No. 5, (December 1995): 1421–1460.

Ranzal, Gerald. "The Foreign Provisions of the Tax Reform Act of 1986: an Overview." *The Tax Advisor,* (December 1986): 768–776.

Shao, Lawrence. "An Evaluation of the Financial Structure Policies of European Affiliates." *Review of Business,* Vol. 17, No. 1, (Fall 1995): 34–39.

Shao, Lawrence, Iftekhar Hasan, and Alan T. Shao. "Determinants of International Capital Structure for U.S. Foreign Subsidiaries." *Multinational Business Review,* Vol. 3, No. 2, (Fall 1995): 67–77.

Sherman, H. Arnold. "Managing Taxes in the Multinational Corporation." *The Tax Executive,* (Winter 1987): 171–181.

Stanley, Marjorie T. "Capital Structure and Cost of Capital for the Multinational Firm." *Managerial Finance,* Vol. 16, No. 2, (1990): 13–16.

U.S. Corporations Doing Business Abroad, New York: Price Waterhouse, 1996.

U.S. Treasury. *Statistics on Income Studies of International Income and Taxes,* Internal Revenue Service, Compendium Studies on International Income and Taxes. 1988.

CHAPTER 15

International Cash Management

INTRODUCTION

Multinational corporations must make cash management decisions toward financial flows both within the money payments systems of specific countries and between countries. In this chapter we review international cash management decisions in relation to the objectives of corporate management, the strategies and mechanisms available for effective cash management, and the problems that arise in this area. It is difficult to consider international cash management separately without taking into account the many other financial decisions that the MNC must make. We examine cash management in detail, first with emphasis on the "between country" dimension and then from the "within country" perspective.

Traditionally, multinational organizations focus on cash management in four ways—through cash collections, cash mobilization, disbursements, and management of liquid assets relating to working capital. This chapter focuses on all four of these elements.

LEARNING OBJECTIVES IN THIS CHAPTER

1. To understand the importance of cash management to the MNC.
2. To identify corporate objectives for MNC cash management.
3. To describe MNC strategies and mechanisms for system-wide and affiliate cash managers.
4. To review the special cash management problems MNCs encounter when dealing with blocked funds and extremely high inflation.
5. To illustrate how an MNC derives benefits from intrasystem transactions based on environmental, operational, and systemwide factors.

Cash Management and Financial Management

International cash managers must operate in relation to other areas of financial decision making. MNCs must make interrelated financial decisions for cash management, capital budgeting, and capital structure.* These decisions are the major links between operations, i.e., the parts of the company specializing in production and sales and the corporate treasury. Of these decisions, the area with the closest link to day-to-day operations is cash management.

Often the typical MNC treasury approaches the cash management, capital budgeting, and capital structure problem areas as if these are independent issues. One procedure for making these decisions is to proceed in a sequential fashion, resolving capital budgeting and capital structure issues first, and then deriving the implied cash management policy. This sequential ordering carries the implicit assumption that the firm's best investment opportunities lie in the area of capital budgeting. While this priority may at times be appropriate for strictly domestic companies, it is not normal ordering for an internationally-oriented company. This priority ordering is different for MNCs for the following reasons:

1) On a country-to-country basis, MNCs face different patterns in the rates of return that they can earn on fixed assets and working capital. Therefore MNCs must distinguish carefully between longer-term capital budgeting and the shorter-term cash management decisions. 2) MNCs operating in high inflation countries frequently encounter the highest rates of asset returns from effective cash management. Therefore they must give the highest priority to this decision area. 3) In the past 20 years, interest rate yield curve inversions have dominated world financial markets for protracted periods. Under these conditions, the firm's fortunes can be heavily dependent on effective cash management techniques, with a high opportunity cost of cash that may exceed that of longer-lived assets. Consequently, the cash management function cannot be subordinated to other financial decisions.

Corporate Objectives

MNC System

The subsidiaries, affiliates, or strategic business units over which MNC central management has operating control.

Multinational corporations must consider a constellation of cash management goals. First, MNCs aim at optimizing cash holdings—balancing system needs and opportunities against the more specialized requirements of operating affiliates. Second, they seek to minimize finance and transaction costs. In part this goal requires internalizing many of the MNC's money transfer and international settlement activities. Third, they must avoid foreign exchange losses, mobilizing foreign exchange for deposit in strong currencies and reducing FX holdings in weak currencies. Fourth, multinationals must consider the effects that their cash management activities have on tax liabilities. For example, a dividend remittance may remove funds from an inflation environment where foreign exchange rate risks are high, but in the process may generate additional tax liabilities. Finally, political and regulatory conditions can change in a country, warranting a reevaluation of cash management approaches and techniques.

The importance of cash management varies among industries and also depends on national and international economic conditions. Companies in some industries

---

* This way of viewing MNC financial decisions is suggested by J.C. Edmunds, "Working Capital Management in Multinational Companies: An Integrated Approach," *Management International Review,* Vol. 23, No. 3, 1983, pp. 73–80.

EXHIBIT 15.1	A System of Cash Management		
Corporate Goals	**Strategies and Mechanisms**	**Problems and Risks**
	System Approaches	
1. Optimal Cash Holdings	Regional financial head- quarters	Currency Rate Changes
	Centralized depositories	
2. Minimum Finance and Transaction Costs	Payments netting	Government Action
	Intrasystem loans	
	Transfer pricing	
	Dividends and remittances	Tax Incidence
3. Avoidance of Foreign Exchange Losses	International finance affiliate	
	Reinvoicing center	Inflation
	Individual Affiliate Approaches	
4. Minimum Tax Burden	Cash forecasting	Interest Rate Changes
5. Avoidance of Loss from Political and Economic Risks	Leads and lags	Blocked Funds
	Local money market operations	
	Local credit practices	Political Risk

typically have a higher percentage of their total assets in working capital. Because of the importance of working capital, companies in the retail and wholesale industries find that they must give a greater priority to cash management. In contrast companies in the heavy manufacturing sector have a smaller share of their total assets allocated to working capital; for these firms, cash management tends to play a secondary role relative to capital budgeting.

National and international economic conditions can also influence the importance of cash management for the MNC. From a strictly national perspective cash requirements are smaller for company operations in more static economic settings. For example, company operations in socialist nations typically require smaller cash balances than similar operations in the more dynamic Western market economies. From an international perspective, high interest rates in world money markets can also raise the priority that the firm's financial managers assign to the corporate treasurer's cash management activities. High interest rates were evidence in the major financial markets during the period 1980–1982. For example, short-term interest rates in several major international financial markets were above 12% during most of that period. In contrast rates were in the 6% range during the 1975–1978 and 1986–1996 periods.

In the discussion that follows we consider corporate objectives in cash management from two perspectives:

1. system view of cash management
2. needs of overseas affiliates

These two perspectives do not require mutually exclusive approaches toward cash management. However, by looking at cash management from these alternative corporate points of view we can provide a broader understanding of the need to reconcile differences in approach within the multinational corporation.

Finally, cash management approaches may include the use of derivative instruments for foreign exchange hedging purposes. However, straightforward FX hedging is sometimes difficult to employ when considerable change is possible in the underlying operations areas of the MNC. For example, considerable variability can occur in a foreign-based subsidiary's demand for parts and raw materials and in the cost and productivity of equipment inputs and labor. For this reason MNCs have evolved cash management techniques that go well beyond simple financial hedging approaches.

SYSTEM VIEW OF CASH MANAGEMENT

The system view considers the multinational corporation as an organizational totality, within which there can exist components that function differently. As an organizational totality, the MNC's objectives are straightforward. Profitability must be pursued on a systemwide basis. This totality implies that the parent MNC requires individual units (affiliates) to sacrifice their profit aspirations for the good of the whole.

Cash Cows

MNC subsidiaries that consistently generate net surplus funds for use elsewhere in the MNC system.

We can visualize three basic types of components within the MNC from the perspective of within-system fund flows: fund generators, fund users, and financial coordinators. Fund generators, known as "cash cows" in some circles, are affiliates that have limited investment requirements, but large sales and cash flow positions. These are typically older, established units. Fund users are affiliates that have substantial investment requirements and limited sales and cash flows (newer, rapidly expanding units). Finally, financial coordinators provide financial services for the system in the form of maintaining banking relationships, assisting in the management of foreign currency exposures, and providing other services.

Financial coordinators play an important role in working toward corporate goals (described in Exhibit 15.1). As central coordinators they are able to optimize cash holdings. Also, their centralized focus can facilitate the avoidance of foreign exchange losses and promote effective control over transaction costs.

NEEDS OF OVERSEAS AFFILIATES

Individual operating affiliates of the multinational corporation may have a different understanding and perspective of how cash management should work. Compared with the system view, the affiliate will focus more on its performance and the ability to budget and plan for more narrowly conceived objectives. Clearly system objectives and affiliate objectives will overlap and will include optimal cash holdings, lower financial costs, and lower incidence of tax liabilities and foreign exchange losses. The difference comes in the definition and implementation of these objectives.

A simplified illustration may make this clear. American Manufacturing Corporation (Amacorp) has several overseas affiliates. Among these are Amacorp France and Amacorp Germany. Exhibit 15.2 summarizes the relevant financial environment and operations data for these affiliates. The two affiliates sell to one another on a regular basis, invoicing in the seller's currency. The affiliates offer one another terms of open account, with 30 days to make payment.

We may refer to the operational aspects of the affiliates' activities as "arm's-length dealing," where there is no effort to enhance the profitability and performance by shifting profits or reconfiguring financing, currency exposures, or other operating variables. Now let us assume that these two affiliates abandon the arms-length approach, and seek to gain by adjusting their methods of operation to exploit the financial environmental differences in their respective host countries.

The possibility of improving the financial performance for each of these two affiliates depends upon their ability to generate benefits from environmental factors,

EXHIBIT 15.2	**Financial Environment and Operational Data, Amacorp France and Amacorp Germany**		
	Amacorp France	**Amacorp Germany**	**Amacorp System**
Financial Environment:			
Local cost of borrowed funds	9.2%	6.3%	
Cost of Eurobond financing	8.7%[1]	6.4%[2]	7.1%[3]
Cost of swap, dollars to	1.3%[4]	−0.9%[5]	
Corporate profit tax	40 %	46 %	
Operational Data:			
Sale of components monthly			
Amacorp France to Amacorp Germany	$6.4 mill.		
Amacorp Germany to Amacorp France		$7.2 mill.	

NOTES:

[1] Denominated in French francs

[2] Denominated in deutsche marks

[3] Denominated in U.S. dollars

[4] Dollars to French franc

[5] Dollars to deutsche marks

EXHIBIT 15.3	**Benefits of Non Arms-length Transactions, Based upon Environmental, Operational, and System-wide Factors**

1. **Environmental Factors**

   French subsidiary can request extended (60 day) terms of sale in its purchases from German subsidiary. Also, German subsidiary can accelerate payments made to French subsidiary.

   Financial savings equal the difference between current cost of financing receivables, less cost of financing under new strategy. Current cost is 6.4×9.2 plus $7.2 \times 6.3 = \$1{,}042.4$ thousand. Cost under new strategy is $14.4 \times 6.3 = \$907.2$ thousand. Financial savings equal $135.2 thousand ($1042.4 − $907.2) yearly.

2. **Operational Factors**

   Transfer pricing can shift profits to a lower tax unit of the multinational company. Tax savings equal the tax rate differential times the amount of income shifted.

   Financial savings equal tax rate differential (6%) times income shifted ($13.6 mill. $\times$ 0.2). The 2% price adjustments shift income of that amount from Germany to France. Tax savings equal $195,840 yearly, obtained as follows: $13.6 \times 12 \times .02 \times .06 = 195{,}840$.

3. **System-wide Factors**

   Eurobond financing where a dollar issue costs 7.1%, swapped into deutsche mark for a 0.9% profit lowers cost to 6.2%. This is a full 3.0% lower than the cost of French franc financing (9.2%). Where $13.6 \times 3.0\%$ equals a $408,000 interest saving.

SOURCE: Exhibit 15.2

operational factors, and systemwide factors. A benefit from environmental factors could take the form of shifting the financing base away from the affiliate with relatively high borrowing costs, to the affiliate with lower borrowing costs. Exhibit 15.3 outlines the implementation of this plan in detail. Basically, the German affiliate offers 60-day open account terms instead of 30 days and accelerates repayment of balances due in purchases from the French affiliate.

A benefit from operational factors could take the form of using transfer pricing to shift profit from a high income tax environment to a lower income tax environment.

Here the German affiliate is in the high income tax environment. Therefore it would be desirable to shift profits to the French affiliate. One way of achieving this shift is by use of transfer prices—altering the prices used in sales transactions carried out between the two affiliates. The German affiliate would lower prices in sales to the French affiliate. In turn, the French affiliate would raise prices on sales to the German affiliate.

A benefit from systemwide factors would take the form of using global system financing capabilities. The Amacorp system can finance by issuing dollar-denominated Eurobonds (at 7.1% interest). These funds can be swapped into deutsche marks for an effective cost of 6.2% (7.1% − 0.9%). This achieves greater financial cost savings than in the case of the German affiliate.

Strategies and Mechanisms for Effective Cash Management

As we have noted in the preceding discussion, among the complications that can arise in intercountry cash management are:

1. the interaction of two or more financial systems offering different interest rate returns and costs of funds;
2. different foreign exchange regimes, including the possibility of government controls on specific categories of transactions and blocked funds;
3. changing foreign exchange rates and foreign interest rates, and the expectations of such changes; and
4. wide variations in national tax regimes.

When two different national financial systems perform the collections or disbursements functions, lags in cash flows may develop. These lags are more likely when payments instruments, customs, and conventions differ widely between the two nations. Under these circumstances the MNC may accelerate collections by dealing with an international bank that has branches in both countries, and therefore is able to transmit payments instructions more easily and accurately between the two banking systems.

The foreign exchange rules that governments impose can differ widely. The United States, Japan, and the major European nations have adopted foreign exchange systems that are substantially free market oriented, with little continuous government presence in the markets. In contrast, detailed central bank rules and market intervention play an important role in most less developed countries (LDCs) that operate centrally administered foreign exchange rate regimes. In the LDCs, for example Mexico and Brazil, there is an effort to maintain foreign exchange rates close to market equilibrium levels. In contrast in the Dominican Republic, the authorities may choose to impose quite severe rationing procedures on foreign exchange flows. Under these conditions the MNC subsidiary may face conditions of blocked funds, especially for funds to be remitted as dividends from the subsidiary to the parent corporation. Where there is the threat of blocked funds, the MNC must find ways to avoid cash accumulations.

SYSTEMWIDE AND REGIONAL APPROACHES

We now examine approaches followed on systemwide and regional bases to improve cash management. These typically occur within the strategic framework of a centralized organization that might be a central MNC depository, or alternatively a regional treasury function. With this approach subsidiaries prepare cash flow forecasts and send all funds in excess of basic transaction needs to the central depository. In turn the central authority has the responsibility to place those funds into currencies and money market investments best suited to the system's need. Many large MNCs do this using sophisticated computer driven systems which allow integration of the company units and their systemwide and also country specific banking relationships.

A key element in centralizing the international treasury function is shifting of currency risk management to the center organization. Alternatively, currency risk may remain the responsibility of the operating affiliates. The decision as to whether to decentralize this function will rest on the organizational ability of the affiliates to afford and retain a high level of financial expertise sufficient to effectively conduct currency risk management. With the exception of the largest MNC affiliates, the centralized treasury function is preferred.

Benefits derived from the centralized approach to treasury management include:

1. More efficient levels of cash held in operating affiliates;
2. Better management of risk generated by cross border currency flows;
3. Ability to accelerate or slow collection disbursements to meet system needs and market expectations; and
4. Improved ability to coordinate internal funds availabilities and bank borrowing to minimize funding costs.

Centralized depository systems have long been used by large MNCs based in the United States, Europe, and Japan. In recent years, many medium and smaller companies based in Europe have found themselves operating in multiple locations within the European Union. During the past 20 years, periodic breakdowns in the European Rate Mechanism have occurred, leading many of these smaller European MNCs to pursue centralized treasury systems. These developments may give these Europe-based companies a foundation in the future to be more effective in pursuing business initiatives outside the EU.

Within the framework of the centralized treasury function, a number of cash management approaches are used. Those include 1) intracompany netting, 2) international finance affiliates and reinvoicing centers, 3) transfer pricing, and 4) intrasystem loans.

Intracompany netting

The cash management process that results in transferring only net settlement values between company units.

Intracompany netting   Intracompany netting is a technique used by MNCs to reduce foreign exchange transactions: affiliates in the system generate a large number of foreign exchange transactions between themselves. Basically this practice involves viewing the foreign exchange claims generated between sister affiliates as a matrix of payments. Clearing and settlement occurs through a central pool in much the same way that local banks in the United States clear checks through a local clearing house.

The effect of netting systems is a reduced number of intracompany funds transfers and the commissions and fee payments associated with such transfers, including the spread on foreign exchange purchased and sold. Netting also reduces the value dates and float that are otherwise lost to the international banking system. In addition, both treasury management and the MNC senior management gain timely access to otherwise unavailable information on company operations, both within and between business-line groups.

International Finance Affiliates and Reinvoicing Centers   The cash management approaches that require more substantial organizational changes are the use of reinvoicing centers and international finance or factoring companies. For the reinvoicing center, financial management establishes a centralized organization, as in Europe. The reinvoicing company agrees to purchase billings from the MNC's European subsidiaries in foreign currencies and then rebills those purchases to operating subsidiaries in local currencies. Under this structure the center manages the MNC's European foreign exchange positions and also has complete control over the timing of cash flows and cash accumulations. Because of this centralized control, sophisticated expertise in foreign exchange and cash management systems can be combined to achieve company objectives.

The international finance company (IFC) provides an alternative to the reinvoicing center without the administrative overburdens associated with the reinvoicing process. Under this approach the IFC buys or factors invoices from the MNC's operating subsidiaries, on either a recourse or nonrecourse basis. With this system the IFC can also assume the foreign exchange risks associated with billing. Thus a French subsidiary of the MNC with a deutsche mark denominated invoice could sell that billing to the IFC and receive payment in its French franc equivalent. The IFC would provide the finance and also take the currency risk. With the reinvoicing center the IFC would have control over the timing of cash flows and cash accumulations.

Transfer Pricing Transfer pricing is an important and widely used technique for transferring funds between MNC subsidiaries. This procedure involves fixing prices on intracompany transactions in ways that may differ from economic or arms-length market values. Transfer prices may differ from arm's-length prices since the transaction does not take place in a competitive market environment. The transfer is internal between units of the MNC. The underpricing of goods sold from country A to country B has the effect of transferring funds from A to B. Overpricing goods sold from A to B has the effect of transferring funds in the reverse direction.

Transfer pricing that has the effect of transferring funds and assisting in cash management also serves other functions. For example, management can employ transfer pricing to influence the location of profits and tax liabilities, to affect the cost of imports and tariff duties, and to facilitate funds positioning to achieve currency risk reduction. Exhibit 15.3 shows a situation where cash management and tax reduction are achieved simultaneously by transfer pricing.

In 1991, the U.S. Internal Revenue Service issued its most recent regulations regarding Section 192 of the Internal Revenue Code governing acceptable transfer pricing methodologies. Under this code there are several methods for determining an appropriate price for tangible property transferred between "related parties" such as MNC subsidiaries. A recent survey of 143 U.S. industrial companies showed that market-based transfer pricing techniques are used in intracompany transactions more often than either cost-based or negotiated price approaches.* In addition to the United States, most developed nations have rules governing MNC cross-border transfer pricing. However, some nations are notably lax in enforcement. Ireland, for example, is recognized as combining lax enforcement with a relatively low corporate income tax environment, as a way to attract MNC plant locations to that nation.

Remittance Strategies Remittances play a key role in cash management because they allow funds shifts from one location to another. Moreover, the form of the

Arm's-length pricing

In the U.S. the IRS allows methods based on: comparable uncontrolled prices, resale prices, cost plus, and comparable profits.

---

* Roger Y.W. Tang, "Transfer Pricing in the 1990s," Management Accounting, Vol. 73, No. 9, February 1992, pp. 22–25.

remittance can have important tax consequences. Remittances occur through the forms of dividends, interest, royalties, or fees. Where remittances take the form of dividends to the parent company, the paying affiliate is using fully taxed cash flows, and the parent company is receiving fully taxable income. Where remittances take the forms of interest, royalties, or fees on intracompany loans to the parent, the paying affiliate is using cash flows that become sheltered from taxes where interest expenses are tax deductible, and the receiving parent company or affiliate is receiving fully taxable income. In addition, where the parent company is receiving interest income, it may also receive repayments of principal originally loaned. Generally this latter cash flow is a nontaxable receipt of funds for the recipient.

Intrasystem Loans   Intrasystem loans can play an important role, both in cash management and as a means of pursuing other corporate strategies and objectives.

EXHIBIT 15.4	**Basic Types and Patterns of Flows within the Global MNC System**

Note: Financial flows can take any of the following forms:
1. Dividend payment
2. Interest payment
3. Royalty payment
4. Payment of management fee
5. Repayment of loan
6. Provision of loan
7. Payment for merchandise
8. Sale of financial claim (discount, factoring)
9. Purchase of shares

"For me, there is little difference between corporate treasury lending and equity positions in the subs." International Treasurer, large U.S.- based MNC.

An affiliate in a soft currency country working to transfer funds out may sell exports to a sister affiliate with longer credit terms granted on the export sale. In this way the MNC system has the opportunity to repay later in depreciated currency. An affiliate in a low interest rate country may borrow aggressively and release excess cash to the regional financial center.

The important point is to understand that there is a global MNC system that mobilizes cash and allocates it to the best purposes of the system (Figure 15.1). Each of the operating units is located in a country offering a different financial, foreign exchange, and taxation environment. Therefore management can plan for and carry out advances of cash from one unit to another that provide benefits to the system as a whole.

MNCs tend to plan their remittance flows carefully in order to benefit from the tax status of different forms of remittances. At the same time they structure remittances to provide greater flexibility in their future cash flows to solve cash management problems.

INDIVIDUAL AFFILIATE STRATEGIES

Considering cash management from the perspective of the "within country" dimension, there can be significant differences in the way specific country financial systems operate. For example, the major industrial nations have a relatively well-developed complement of financial institutions, markets, and instruments. In contrast most less developed countries do not have financial infrastructures that are as advanced. In addition national economic environments can differ widely—for example, between low inflation and high inflation countries—also contributing to substantial environmental and institutional differences between countries. These considerable differences in national financial systems require that the MNC adopt cash management approaches suited to specific country circumstances.

In the discussion that follows, we consider 1) cash forecasting, 2) cash collections and local credit practices, and 3) individual affiliate's use of leads and lags.

Cash Forecasting A basic information input for the MNC is the cash forecast of individual operating affiliates. These forecasts are important components of the MNC's control system. They point toward how changes in domestic activities of affiliates will influence that unit's cash position. The cash forecasts can then be assembled on a regional or global basis for implementation.

Centralized cash management requires data inputs from scattered (decentralized) sources. In Exhibit 15.5 we have an illustrative cash forecast provided by the European affiliates of IGT Corporation, covering a four-week period. During the

Cash Forecasting
Projection of subsidiary and systemwide changes in cash (and cash equivalents) resulting from operations, investing, or financing activities.

EXHIBIT 15.5	**IGT Corporation Cash Flow Forecasts— European Region—Four-week Period**				
($U.S. Million)					
	Week 1	Week 2	Week 3	Week 4	Total
West Germany	30	−80	−20	50	−20
Italy	−20	50	−10	15	35
France	−10	−5	−25	5	−35
Netherlands	15	−25	−10	−45	−15
European Region	15	−10	−65	25	−35

first week covered there will be an overall cash surplus of $15 million, but for the entire four-week period the forecast calls for a net cash outflow of $35 million.

As noted in the preceding section of this chapter, a centralized depository will make use of the information in Exhibit 15.5. The central depository will plan for drawings on bank credits as the cash deficits materialize. Conversely, the depository will pay down outstanding loans at times when net cash inflows take place.

Cash Collections and Local Practices   The second within country cash collection and management dimension that we examine relates to cash collections and local credit practices. From this perspective the collections process has four components: order-invoice, credit terms, accounts receivable, and collections instruments. The order-invoice component is set in motion when the customer initiates an order. The procedures typically trigger a sequence of actions: credit confirmation and invoicing, shipment, and inventory control. The primary issue for the MNC as regards the order-invoice component is the extent to which centralization of this function can occur. Greater centralization will result in increased treasury control over the collections process, though at greater costs in terms of information and communications requirements. As the collections process is computerized at most MNCs, there has been a shift toward greater centralization of this function in business practice.

The credit terms component requires the MNC to strike a balance between two conflicting objectives. On the one hand, marketing and sales managers ordinarily have a great interest in using credit terms to support their efforts to sell product. In contrast MNC management must justify trade credit offered to customers, since this credit is inherently a source of additional financing costs. Because of the divergent interests of these two groups of managers, MNC credit policies must strike a compromise between length of the credit time period, the per customer credit limits, the form of the credit, and the mechanisms for monitoring and enforcing credit terms.

Of these credit policy dimensions, the forms of credit are perhaps the most basic. There are four categories of trade credit used in international business: open account, "near" drafts, full drafts or bills of exchange, and documentary collections. Of these, the open account offers the least security to the MNC; accounts receivable are essentially unsupported. The near draft form offers somewhat greater surety to the MNC. The near draft, in use in a number of countries, can involve special signed invoices, as in Italy, or invoice copies that are filed with the seller's bank as security, as in Brazil.* Full drafts or bills of exchange represent unconditional obligations for the purchaser to pay by a fixed date. Finally, documentary-based collections are of two types: payment against defined documents and the letter of credit opened by a bank on the purchaser's behalf. Both are conditional on the seller meeting the specified requirements of the collection agreement. When using the letter of credit, the bank's credit is substituted for the purchaser's credit. Documentary collections are more thoroughly discussed in Chapter 10.

In the accounts receivable component, the MNC managers must balance the customer relations factor against costs arising from interest expense and administration expense. The administration cost arises from monitoring and following up on overdue customer accounts. The economic environment of specific countries can greatly affect the balance between these factors. For example, accounts receivable practice and control systems will differ greatly between noninflation countries like Germany and the higher inflation environments of Spain and Greece.

---

* John Giannotti and Richard Smith, *Treasury Management* (New York: John Wiley and Sons, 1981):22.

There are three types of collection instruments in wide use in today's commercial world: bank transfers, checks, and drafts or bills of exchange. Within the limits set by commercial practice in specific countries, the MNC treasury attempts to select the collections instruments and procedures that minimize collections costs, including those imposed by procedural delays (such as advice transmission and clearing processes), cash fees (including those arising from taxes, bank commissions, and advice costs), and internal administrative costs.

Bank transfers, in wide use in continental Europe, involve the remittance of funds from the buyer's bank account to that of the seller without the creation of a negotiable instrument. The payer initiates transfers through the banking system; most countries employ national clearing systems. Bank float refers to funds tied up in the clearing and value-dating process. Float varies depending on country-specific banking practices and the number of clearing centers used in the bank transfer. Transfers between national clearing centers can involve onerous time delays.

Float

Usually one or two days during which value is conveyed as a transaction clears the banking system. In emerging economies and in Eastern European countries, the time for clearance can be several days.

The "check" is an unconditional order by the payer instructing his or her bank to pay a stated amount to the payee. The delay elements associated with check collections are the mail delay and internal handling delays within the seller's organization. Checks are the dominant collection instrument in Canada, the United Kingdom, and the United States. They are also widely used in Continental Europe. In the United States "lock boxes" result in reduced mail delay. These are post office boxes, accessed by the seller's bank, to which customers are instructed to mail checks.

In countries where the discount of trade paper is a major source of working capital finance, business practice has emphasized drafts and near drafts. With drafts, delays can occur in the time required for the buyer to receive the draft, to accept, and to notify the seller. A second source of delay can occur in the collection of the draft on maturity in the time required to provide the seller with advice of the collections receipt.

Leads and Lags   Leads and lags involve timing funds transfers to achieve desired objectives. Firms can accelerate or slow down the timing of payments to shift funds from countries with weak currencies or that have blocked accounts. Such transfers may occur either between affiliated or independent companies. The effect of these practices is to change the assets and liabilities in one corporate affiliate with an opposite change taking place in the assets and liabilities of the other corporate affiliate. Typical types of lead-lag activities include: transfers from low interest to high interest rate countries, and transfers from soft currency to hard currency countries. Many countries seek to limit corporate use of leads and lags.

Special Problems

Cash management involves many detailed aspects of international financial operations. In the discussion that follows we consider two of these special aspects, namely, the incidence of blocked funds and high inflation.

Blocked funds

Host country government authorities prevent the transfer of funds to the parent MNC. One mechanism is through not permitting currency convertibility.

BLOCKED FUNDS

Many multinational companies operate in countries with exchange control systems. In such instances there is the perennial problem of blocked funds. The multinational may need to finance the affiliate, remit profits, or simply move funds for reasons of safety or more effective employment. Various approaches are:

Transfer pricing

The use of transfer pricing to move funds out of countries with exchange controls may depend on operational patterns. An affiliate that manufactures components locally for export can utilize this method. This procedure involves invoicing in the local currency (blocked currency). Here financial management can frequently purchase blocked currency at favorable rates outside the country.

Loans through banks

Financial management may wish to move funds into a blocked currency country in order to provide needed finance to a local affiliate. Reliance on an international bank may provide greater assurance that the loan will be repaid. Use of this technique can reduce country risk, since countries do not like to block debt service payments to international banks. Blocking payment to the multinational corporation would not have as negative an impact on the international credit standing of the country as blocking payments to an international bank.

Reinvestment

One alternative—not one always voluntarily selected by the multinational company—is reinvestment. Blocked funds that remain in the host country will take the form of an asset (physical or financial). Temporary blockage calls for short-term investment, perhaps in the local money market if reasonably attractive opportunities exist. In such circumstances government securities (perhaps indexed to the inflation rate) or bank deposits may prove suitable. Where such money market instruments are not available, alternatives could include physical assets (inventory, fixed assets) or deposits placed with international banks that can offer compensating advantages. These advantages might include low interest loans in other parts of the world or financial services. Management can also use back-to-back loans as a way to reinvest blocked funds. For example a U.S.-based MNC operating in the Dominican Republic may be able to lend its blocked funds in that country to another MNC that has a need for funds in the Dominican Republic to undertake an expansion of its business.

Country Risk Insurance

As discussed in Chapter 12, several agencies provide political and country risk insurance to MNCs. The risk of currency inconvertibility or blocked funds is typically included in the coverage. While limitations on MNC eligibility and the extent of coverage exist, if funds blockage can be anticipated, it is possible for the MNC to insure against this risk dimension.

Inflation

The importance of effective cash management techniques is probably greatest in high inflation countries. For example, in 1993 Brazil's inflation ran in excess of 1000% per annum, or approximately 30% per month assuming monthly compounding. Interest rates were running in double digits, well above 30% per month. Under these circumstances, a company's financial health will be greatly influenced by its ability to manage its cash and working capital.

In Brazil a highly sophisticated financial market system has been developed, in part as a response to the needs of companies, investors, and lenders that have to cope with this problem. The system offers diverse solutions to multinational companies. First, Brazil has adopted a system of indexation and monetary correction that permits companies to reconstitute their fixed asset and net worth accounts according to price level changes. This system avoids the decapitalization of companies that often accompanies inflation. Second, the system of monetary correction provides for the adjustment in value of specified financial assets such as bank deposit accounts and government securities. In this way, the central bank and government can assure the holder of that asset a positive real rate of interest. Exhibit 15.6 presents a sampling of such asset returns in Brazil at mid-year 1993.

Two other asset categories offer multinational companies the opportunity to hold inflation-hedge assets. In Brazil corporations are free to trade in gold bullion. Many companies engage in this practice. Second, inventories provide another type of inflation hedge. Also imported inventories provide an additional hedge against any exchange depreciation that would follow from domestic inflation. In Brazil the government's resort to price controls that can be in effect for relatively long periods of time usually complicates corporate treasurer efforts to minimize inflation and currency depreciation problems.

In a high inflation environment such as Brazil a foreign subsidiary must adopt procedures that safeguard financial interests. For example there is a strong incentive for banks to allow float to grow. One technique that the subsidiary may select is a regionally centralized system for handling collections and disbursements. Such a system may involve a different bank in each region of the country to maintain the MNC's contacts among banking alternatives. This approach, simple though it may appear, has greatly enhanced the leverage over float that the subsidiary has within the overall banking community.

EXHIBIT 15.6   **Return on Investments in Brazilian Money Market**

1. Domestic Federal Government and Central Bank Debt
"Titulos Publicos"—basis for overnight rate in money market.

	Month	**Day**
June 1, 1993	40.97%	1.365667%
Covering:	Treasury financing bills	
	Central bank bills	
	Central bank bonus certificates	

2. Operations between Financial Institutions
"Mercado Interfinanceiro"—cost of funds in the interbank and interfinancial institution markets.

Overnight rates on certificates of deposit (interbank)

	Median	**Daily rate, monthly basis** **Modal**
June 1, 1993	40.99%	40.99%

3. Savings Rate
"Poupanca"—basic cost of deposit funds for the banking system.

	Nominal	**Real**
April 1993	29.32%	0.14%
May 1993	28.86%	0.09%

SOURCE: *Gazeta Mercantil* (4 June 1993): 16–17.

Brazil's commercial banks have responded well to the problems of customer cash management. They operate highly efficient computerized cash clearing and settlement systems. These systems clear payments against accounts promptly, allowing the corporate treasury in Brazil to manage cash positions on a daily basis. Since the largest Brazilian banks operate on a nationwide basis, centralized clearings cover all payments irrespective of the location of payer and payee.

Parallel Internal System

An intracountry cash management approach most effective under conditions of high inflation.

A second approach toward maintaining pressure on banks for efficient clearing of collections is setting up a parallel internal system between regional offices within the country and the subsidiary's country headquarters. This parallel system requires that regional offices report daily on account status. Management reconciles these reports daily against reports from the subsidiary's regional concentrator banks.

On the disbursements side the subsidiary headquarters can maintain strict control over payments by issuing a daily list of payments authorizations to be made by specific banks. Under this system if a regional office of the subsidiary requests a release of funds in excess of the daily authorizations to pay, the bank for that regional office would refuse to accept that request. This "double checking" system assures that the MNC country headquarters maintains tight control over payments made by the regional subsidiary offices.

SUMMARY

Financial managers must consider international cash management in relation to other areas of financial decision making. On a country-to-country basis MNCs face different patterns in the rates of return they can earn on assets. MNCs operating in inflation countries frequently encounter the highest rates of asset returns from effective cash management.

MNCs seek to optimize cash holdings, minimize finance and transaction costs, avoid foreign exchange losses, and balance cash management needs against the impact on tax liabilities. In addition, they must continually monitor changing conditions. MNCs generally take a system view of cash management. Parent company management may require individual units to sacrifice their profit aspirations for the benefit of the MNC system. Interaffiliate transactions may be conducted on a non arm's-length basis.

Approaches followed in the pursuit of systemwide and regional cash management include 1) use of centralized depositories, 2) use of international finance affiliates and reinvoicing centers, c) transfer pricing, d) remittance strategies, and e) intrasystem loans. Individual affiliates must make effective use of specific cash forecasting, cash collections, and lead-lag techniques.

REVIEW QUESTIONS

1. What are the basic objectives of international cash management?
2. Explain how a systemwide approach to international cash management can provide improved results.
3. Give detailed illustrations of environmental differences that MNCs can utilize in their international cash management.
4. What are the benefits derived from the use of reinvoicing centers as compared with international finance affiliates?

5. You are the local corporate treasurer in the Brazilian affiliate of a U.S. company. Local projections are for the inflation rate to accelerate. What approaches will be available for local cash management?

6. Ultra Corporation has operating subsidiaries in Britain, Netherlands, and Italy. These subsidiaries finance local operations with local bank loans. They are also responsible for the temporary management of idle cash funds. The following financial environment operates. Discuss some of the cash management strategies that might be applied under these circumstances.

	Great Britain	Netherlands	Italy
Local interest rate	11%	5%	12%
Local inflation rate	7%	2%	10%

7. The Troy Corporation has a Dutch and French subsidiary. Each subsidiary has been selling components to the other subsidiary each month worth $20 million. Payment terms have been open account due 60 days. Short-term interest rates in Holland and France are 7% and 11%, respectively. The international treasurer has advised that the two subsidiaries alter their credit terms as follows:

Troy Holland sells to French subsidiary with 120 days payment due.

Troy France sells to Dutch subsidiary for cash payment.

What will the Troy Corporation financial savings be annually from this change in intersubsidiary payment terms?

8. Explain how a U.S. MNC can determine which remittance form to use when extracting income from a foreign subsidiary.

9. Abrak Corporation has a Latin American subsidiary generating local currency profit equivalent to US $30 million annually. The government has been blocking profit remittances. Abrak has the following alternative measures available to deal with this problem. Which measure appears most feasible?

   a. The country produces many agricultural products that may have an export market potential. The plan is to develop a special agricultural export marketing division that can be helpful in moving funds from the country.

   b. Develop a new product line exclusively for export. Management intends to use underinvoicing to shift financial resources from the country.

   c. Make an equity investment in a local company.

SELECTED BIBLIOGRAPHY

Avi-Yenah, Reuven S. "The Rise and Fall of Arm's Length: A Study in the Evolution of U.S. International Taxation." *Virginia Tax Review,* Vol. 15, No. 1, (Summer 1995): 99–159.

Edmunds, J. C. "Working Capital Management in Multinational Companies: An Integrated Approach." *Management International Review,* Vol. 23, No. 3, (1983): 73–80.

Garverick, Rob. "OPIC Supports U.S. Investors in LDCs and Emerging Democracies." *Business America,* Vol. 112, No. 20, (October 1991): 14–18.

Giannotti, John, and Richard Smith. *Treasury Management.* New York: John Wiley & Sons, 1981.

Grubert, Harry. "Taxes, Tariffs and Transfer Pricing in Multinational Corporate Decision Making." *Review of Economics and Statistics,* Vol. 73, No. 2, (May 1991): 285–293.

Horst, Thomas. "American Taxation of Multinational Firms." *American Economic Review,* Vol. 67, No. 3, (June 1977): 376–389.

Lees, Francis, Rubens Crysne, and James Botes. *Banking and Financial Deepening in Brazil.* New York: St. Martins Press, 1991.

Levy, Haim. "Optimal Portfolio of Foreign Currencies with Borrowing and Lending." *Journal of Money, Credit, and Banking,* Vol. 13, (August 1981): 326–341.

Long, Robert B. "Speed Collection of Foreign Currency Receivables." *Business Credit,* Vol. 94, No. 10, (November/December 1992): 4–5.

Madura, Jeff. "International Cash Management: An Argument for Diversification." *Journal of Cash Management,* Vol. 11, No. 5, (September/October 1991): 50–53.

Robinson, Jean Hardy. "International Cash Management: Problems and Opportunities." *Journal of Cash Management,* Vol. 10, No. 5, (September/October 1990): 34–36.

Sato, M., and R. Bird. "International Aspects of the Taxation of Corporations and Shareholders." *IMF Staff Papers,* Vol. 22, No. 2, (July 1975): 384–455.

Shapiro, Alan. "Payments Netting in International Cash Management." *Journal of International Business Studies,* (Fall 1978): 51–58.

Sherman, W. Richard. "International Transfer Pricing: Application and Analysis." *Ohio CPA Journal,* Vol. 61, No.1, (August 1995): 29–35.

Soenen, Luc A. "Cash and Foreign Exchange Management: Theory and Corporate Practice in Three Countries." *Journal of Business Finance and Accounting,* Vol. 16, No. 5, (Winter 1989): 599–619.

Srinivisan, Venkat, and Yong Kim. "Payments Netting in International Cash Management: A Network Optimization Approach." *Journal of International Business Studies,* (Summer 1986): 1–20.

Tang, Roger Y. W. "Transfer Pricing in the 1990s." *Management Accounting,* Vol. 73, No. 8, (February 1992): 22–25.

Thunell, L., J. S. Kydel, and P. Mees. "International Cash Management" in Abraham George and Ian Giddy, *International Finance Handbook.* New York: John Wiley & Sons, 1983: 8.11A.1–8.11B.25.

U.S. Corporations Doing Business Abroad. New York: Price Waterhouse, 1996.

Van der Klost, Nicholas. "Foreign Treasury Center Activities of U.S. Multinationals: U.S. Tax Implications." *Tax Management International Journal,* Vol. 21, No. 7, (July 1995): 311–323.

CHAPTER 16

Foreign Currency Exposure and Its Management

INTRODUCTION

The major difference between the multinational corporation and the strictly domestic corporation is the substantially greater vulnerability of the MNC to incur earnings fluctuations as a result of foreign exchange rate changes. As indicated in Chapter 2, with the rejection of the fixed exchange standard in 1971 and 1973 and the subsequent adoption of floating exchange rates, foreign exchange rate fluctuations have increased in frequency and magnitude. This volatility has become a serious risk problem for the multinational corporation.

Under the floating rate system, substantial exchange rate changes can take place within relatively short periods of time. For the typical manufacturing MNC, since 1980 several three-month periods have occurred when losses from foreign exchange rate changes more than offset profit growth over the previous three to four years. Over the past ten years we have observed circumstances of severe currency overshooting, where the foreign exchange value of major currencies has moved persistently in one direction for an extended period of time. This trend has also increased the degree of risk inherent in the system, has made exchange rate forecasting more difficult, and has posed serious challenges to MNC financial management.

This chapter addresses how management can deal with the changes and problems associated with foreign currency exposures. Most companies over a certain size find their business activity and commercial success affected in some way by foreign exchange rate changes. These effects may be direct or indirect. The strictly domestic corporation, in part because of its orientation, may be less aware of such effects. However, during times of extreme and prolonged local currency strength in the foreign exchange markets, a surge of import competition has typically occurred. This circumstance, seen in the United States from 1980 to early 1985 and in Mexico prior to the 1994 peso crisis, should leave no doubt as to the vulnerability of even strictly domestic companies to foreign exchange exposures.

Foreign exchange exposure is a fundamental business dimension in the same way as interest rate exposure. And, like interest rate exposure, foreign exchange exposure affects corporations in both operational and financial ways. Depending upon the foreign exchange exposure dimension considered, foreign exchange gains and losses will affect the operations of the corporation, will be recorded in accounting terms, and will be subject to tax regulations.

Historically there has existed a large gap between practitioners and academicians in the area of foreign exchange management. One factor contributing to this difference of views is conflicting lines of thinking that have developed within the academic community. One line of academic thinking suggests that financial managers do not need to manage foreign exchange exposures, because foreign exchange risks either do not exist or need not be hedged. This line of reasoning* is based on the assumptions of continuous purchasing power parity equilibrium, the CAPM theory, and the efficient markets hypothesis. Within this framework the presumption is that foreign exchange market equilibrium is maintained, and hedging efforts are not needed.

CAPM
Capital Asset Pricing Model.

Of course this framework is very abstract. Most foreign exchange market practitioners give great importance to information and analyses, transactions costs, explicit and implicit contract periods, and other obstacles to instantaneous price adjustments. Practitioners also recognize that deviations from purchasing power parity and the domestic and international Fisher effects can persist over rather lengthy time periods—witness the violent effects seen in the U.S. during the protracted period of U.S. dollar strength in the early 1980s.

Given these circumstances most multinational corporations have developed systems for addressing foreign exchange exposure management. However it is also widely acknowledged that substantial differences in practice exist among the MNCs. In part this variation occurs as a result of the natural differences among companies with international operations. Thus foreign exchange rate changes will affect the rate of return on investment in companies in different ways depending upon various factors. These factors include the relative importance of exports versus imports for those companies, whether foreign sales activities dominate foreign operations, whether there are foreign manufacturing operations, and whether such manufacturing operations rely in turn on international sourcing and sales.

The approach presented in this chapter will focus first on identifying foreign exchange rate risks in terms of "modalities." We will identify the types of foreign exchange exposure for which there is broad agreement both within the academic community and among business practitioners. Following this discussion we will examine the policies and objectives of exposure management and their implementation.

LEARNING OBJECTIVES IN THIS CHAPTER

1. To define three types of foreign exchange exposures: transaction, operating, and translation.
2. To compare and contrast dimensions of the three foreign exchange exposures.

---

* Gunther Dufey and S.L. Srinivasulu. "The Case for Corporate Management of Foreign Exchange Risk." *Financial Management,* (Winter 1983): 54–55.

3. To understand approaches for managing transaction exposures using forwards and futures contracts, money market instruments, currency swaps, and options.
4. To illustrate operating exposure management for production reconfiguration.

Types of Foreign Exchange Exposure

In this section we discuss several dimensions of foreign exchange exposure more specifically. We begin by recognizing the essential goal of corporate financial management: maximizing the value of shareholder investment in the firm. Within this framework there are two approaches. The first focuses on the role of the market in determining the value of the firm. According to this view, the net present value of future cash flows measures the value of the firm, based on the theory that the value of the company's equity will be adjusted in the stock market depending upon the market's perceptions of those future cash flows. Within this framework, foreign currency exposure management can increase the value of the firm through: 1) increasing the present values of future cash flows accruing to the corporate system on a global or consolidated basis, or 2) reducing the year-to-year variability in cash flows, thereby reducing the riskiness of the global enterprise.

It is important for foreign exchange management purposes to make a distinction between two types of future cash flows. The first category refers to flows that are "contractual;" such future receipts and disbursements will be called, for our purposes, "transactions exposures." A second cash flow category is longer term in time perspective, addressing cash flows in the time period beyond those that are presently known contractually. What we identify as "operating exposure" is fundamentally different from transaction exposures in that consideration is also given to the firm's long run ability to generate cash flows.*

The second broad approach to the value of the firm arises in an accounting context and focuses on the balance sheet value of the parent company's equity. Balance sheet values can be affected by changes in the value of foreign currency assets and liabilities, when restated in the parent's base currency. This change appears as an adjustment to equity required to reconcile each foreign entity's balance sheet when restated in the parent company's currency. For purposes of our discussion we will refer to this as the "translation" approach.

Some perspective on these two approaches—cash flow and accounting—for foreign exchange exposure management is in order. Cash flows that are reduced as a result of a foreign exchange rate change are gone forever. These losses are tangible and final and cannot be regained as a result of a subsequent change in the foreign exchange rate to its original value. In contrast in the case of translation exposure, the value of assets can fluctuate in value without cash flow implications. Thus the return of the foreign exchange rate to its prior value can reverse an earlier adverse translation effect.

Exhibit 16.1 presents a comparison of cash flow and translation concepts. These points of comparison will be clarified through the rest of this chapter.

---

* Michael Moffett and Jan Karlsen, "Managing Foreign Exchange Rate Economic Exposure," *Journal of International Financial Management and Accounting,* Vol. 5, No. 2, June 1994, p. 161.

EXHIBIT 16.1 **Foreign Currency Exposure Dimensions**[1]

CASH FLOW EXPOSURE		TRANSLATION EXPOSURE
Transaction	**Operating**	
1. Static concept that refers to a particular point in time, the contract date.	1. Dynamic concept that refers to all relevant futures.	1. Static concept that refers to a particular point in time, the date of financial statements.
2. The extent of transaction exposure is the volume of outstanding contracts denominated in specific currencies. These contracts will be affected by structure of operations.	2. The extent of operating exposure is determined by a firm's position in its product and input markets; effect is due to nature of operations (source of input, destination of output, debt policy).	2. The extent of translation exposure is determined by accounting conventions such as FAS No. 52.
3. Easy to compute the extent of exposure and the exact consequences of a given exchange rate change; if not reversed, an exchange rate change will result in transaction gains/losses at the time of contract maturity.	3. Effects of an exchange rate change will be reflected in successive future income statements; difficult to compute.	3. Easy to compute the extent of exposure and the exact consequences of a given exchange rate change; if not reversed, an exchange rate change will result in translation gains/losses at date of financial statements.
4. MNC policies: usually financial hedging is recommended; tactical decisions; the extent of transaction exposure can be quickly changed; short-term perspective.	4. MNC policies: strategic decisions; longer lock-in effects are involved; takes time to develop new technology, sources, products, or to rationalize production on a global basis; long-term perspective.	4. MNC policies: tactical; the extent of translation exposure can be quickly changed; short-term perspective.
5. Avoidance may forego opportunity gains in the form of increased cash flows.	5. Avoidance may increase translation exposure; opportunity loss is to be avoided by proper operational changes.	5. Avoidance may increase cash flow exposure; a purely paper loss may be avoided at the cost of reduced cash flows.
6. Considers all contracts, both on- and off-balance sheet, that will affect future cash flows; likely to be the center of management's attention in the short term.	6. Focus is on future cash flows and their variability; long-term, strategic.	6. Does not consider exposure of contracts not appearing on the balance sheet (e.g., leases, purchase/sale contracts for future delivery); likely to be the center of management's attention in the short term.
7. Management of transaction exposure is usually the responsibility of the treasury.	7. Management of operating exposure can involve virtually all functions including marketing, productions, logistics, sourcing, and the treasury.	7. Management of translation exposure is usually the responsibility of the treasury.

[1] Michael Adler and Bernard Dumas: "Exposure to Foreign Exchange Currency Risk: Definition and Measurement," *Financial Management,* Spring 1984, pp. 41–50.

TRANSACTION EXPOSURE

Transaction exposure rises from the need of the multinational corporation to make payments or to receive funds denominated in foreign currency in the future. More precisely, transaction exposure measures the degree to which the value of the firm's known future cash transactions can be affected by exchange rate fluctuations. As indicated transaction exposure is one of two cash flow exposure dimensions. The distinction between transaction exposure and operating exposure is that the latter focuses on how exchange rate changes work themselves out through effects on cash flows, not contractually specified, in terms of underlying supply and demand adjustments. Thus transaction exposure is specific to a transaction where the only uncertainty is the value of the future foreign exchange rate, usually in terms of the parent company's base currency.

Transaction exposure is sometimes interpreted to include anticipated contractual exposures.

As an illustration of transaction exposure, consider the case of the Kingsbran Corporation's U.S. subsidiary that has the following expected cash flows one year from today. This example is a simplified payments netting system, as described in Chapter 15, International Cash and Country Risk Management.

ACCOUNTS RECEIVABLE

Italian lira	20,000 million
Deutsche mark	100 million
Mexican peso	9,500 million

ACCOUNTS PAYABLE

Italian lira	10,000 million
Deutsche mark	200 million

LONG-TERM DEBT

Japanese yen	400 million

When these transactions are taken together, the subsidiary's treasury is faced with the following *net* transaction exposures:

Positive Exposures		Negative Exposures	
IL	10,000 million	DM	100 million
MP	9,500 million	JY	400 million

In this example, a positive exposure is a net asset exposure, whereas a negative exposure is a net liability exposure.

For these exposures, the current exchange rates against the U.S. dollar are: IL 1300, MP 1500, DM 1.8100, and JY 145.00.

Over the next year, Kingsbran's international treasurer forecasts the following exchange rate changes as applicable to these exposures:

1. U.S. dollar to rise in value by 100% against the Mexican peso; this rise will reduce the dollar value of Mexican peso receivables.
2. U.S. dollar to fall in value by 10% against the deutsche mark; this fall will raise the dollar value of Kingsbran's net negative deutsche mark exposure.
3. U.S. dollar to rise in value 10% against the Japanese yen; this increase will reduce the dollar value of Kingsbran's net negative yen exposure.
4. U.S. dollar to remain unchanged against the Italian lira.

Based on these projections for each currency exposure, the treasurer can compare the current value of the exposure in U.S. dollars with the value expected one year forward under his projections:

CURRENCY EXPOSURE	DOLLAR VALUE OF PROJECTED EXPOSURE		
	Today's FX Rates	FX Rates One Year Later	Transaction Gains or Loss
Positive Exposure			
Mexican Peso	$6.3 million	3.2 million	$3.1 Loss
Italian Lira	7.7 million	7.7 million	
Negative Exposure			
Deutsche Mark	$55.3 million	61.4 million	6.1 Loss
Japanese Yen	2.8 million	2.5 million	0.3 Gain
		Overall Transaction Loss	$8.9 million

Accordingly, the treasurer is faced with projected losses of $3.1 million and $6.1 million on the MP and DM transaction exposures, and transaction gains of $0.3 million on the JY transactions exposure. These shifts could produce overall transaction losses of $8.9 million on all currency exposures taken together, if the projected exchange rate changes materialize. Thus a failure to deal with these exposures in a timely manner will affect the profitability of Kingsbran's U.S. operations unfavorably. In this way transaction exposures can pose a serious direct problem for a multinational corporation.

OPERATING EXPOSURE

The concept of operating exposure has been introduced. The essence of this concept is that unexpected changes in foreign exchange rates can affect the long-term ability of the MNC to generate cash flows by altering the cost of a firm's inputs and the revenue derived from its outputs. The extent to which exchange rate changes will have these effects depends upon the underlying price elasticities for supply and demand in the input and product markets as well as competitor reactions in these markets. As these changes occur there will be shifts in the relative competitive position of the multinational corporation across its product and market segments. Operating exposure, in contrast to transaction exposure, applies to the entire investment. Therefore unlike transaction exposure, we are led to view operating exposure in a longer-term perspective. Management can alter the nature and extent of operating exposure by a change in the company's operating context, that is, through a change in the choice of products, markets, input sourcing, technology, and financial sourcing via long-range planning.

Operating exposure is presumed to encompass the reaction of competitors to currency changes.

Consider, for example, the case of an MNC subsidiary that manufactures product in Belgium using Belgian-sourced component inputs. Finished product is exported to the United Kingdom. Under these conditions Belgian franc appreciation will place this subsidiary at a disadvantage when selling into the U.K. markets relative to U.K. local competitors. This effect will be sharpest when the Belgian company adjusts its British prices (denominated in pounds) to reflect the full change in the exchange rate.

Assuming full adjustment in British prices, the extent to which U.K. sales revenues are affected will depend on the price elasticity of demand that the Belgian subsidiary faces in the U.K. market. Should the price elasticity be low, approaching zero, the franc appreciation (pound sterling depreciation) will have little negative effect on sales. If, however, the price elasticity is high, a significant decline in sales can occur.

Under conditions of low price elasticity of demand, a company may fully reverse the impact on itself of an adverse exchange rate change. As described in the example, this reversal is done through an increase in the prices that the MNC charges in the host country market. However even in this simple and uncommon case, typically there will be time lags in implementing such local market price increases. Until the time is reached when margins are restored for the company, the

MNC will experience a short fall in local currency cash flows. This short fall in cash flow is lost to the MNC forever.

This principle is shown for the French subsidiary of the U.S. based Queensbran Corporation in Exhibit 16.2. The presentation involves the simple case where an unexpected increase in local currency price fully offsets the adverse cash flow effects of local currency depreciation. In this hypothetical case the MNC is able to raise its French franc (FF) prices to an extent that it preserves its cash flow in U.S. dollar terms. In this illustration we assume it takes three time periods to raise FF prices. In addition there is a receivables turn of one period. The lag in raising FF prices can come from several sources. The company must first determine the effect of the exchange rate depreciation on its markets. This effect may be unclear, for example, where companies produce a wide range of products, as in the case of the manufactured components industries. In most markets companies must notify their customers when price changes are to take effect. Usually this notification sets a forward date as the time point when the price increase occurs. With time lags in FF price adjustment, and with lags inherent in receivables collection, a short fall in cash flow generation can occur, even though the company is fully able to offset the impact of the FF depreciation by raising FF prices. Thus as shown in the example, Queensbran experiences an operating exposure in periods three through six.

The presentation in Exhibit 16.2 focuses on a relatively simple case. In the real world the MNC may or may not be able to fully offset the adverse effects of unexpected foreign exchange rate changes. These effects can occur through changes both in prices/costs in parent company terms and through changes in sales volumes.

EXHIBIT 16.2   **Queensbran Corporation: Operating Exposure for the Subsidiary in France**

SIMPLE CASE WHERE INCREASE IN FF PRICES FULLY OFFSETS ADVERSE CASH FLOW EFFECTS OF FF DEPRECIATION[1]

ASSUMPTIONS

Sales per period:	100 units
Initial sales price:	FF 10
Cost per unit:	FF 5
Initial FX rate:	$1 = FF 1
After FX depreciation at end of 2nd period:	FF 1 = $0.5 or $1 = FF 2
Lag in FF price adjustment	3 periods
New sales price:	FF 15
Receivables turnover	1 period

CASH FLOWS IN $

Period	1	2	3	4	5	6	7
Price in FF	10.0	10.0	10.0	10.0	10.0	15.0	15.0
Price in $	10.0	10.0	5.0	5.0	5.0	7.5	7.5
Units	100	100	100	100	100	100	100
Sales ($)	1000	1000	500	500	500	750	750
Receipts ($)	1000	1000	500	500	500	500	750
Payments ($)	500	500	250	250	250	250	250
Cash Generated ($)	500	500	250	250	250	250	500
Cash Flow Effect of FF Depreciation ($)	0	0	−250	−250	−250	−250	0

[1] John Gianotti and Richard Smith, *Treasury Management,* New York: John Wiley & Sons, 1981, p. 209.

The full effects of local currency depreciation on subsidiary revenues measured in dollar terms can occur both through price and quantity changes. Again the overall revenue effects will be greatest under conditions of relatively high price elasticity of demand for the products of the MNC subsidiary in the host country. In cases where the price elasticity of demand is low, the subsidiary will have a greater latitude in raising prices in the face of adverse foreign exchange rate changes.

In the real world the MNC subsidiary has a wide range of ways to adjust to reduce operating exposure. These include not only the possibility of raising local currency prices, but also substituting domestic inputs for more expensive imported inputs, altering the mix of product lines, altering promotional and market selection strategies, and changing plant location. In these more complex cases, an adjustment period is required. During that time—even assuming eventual full offset—the MNC subsidiary may experience losses resulting from operating exposure.

More generally, operating exposures can arise from any cross border cash flows including product flows, input and component flows, company remittance requirements, and financing. Given this broad orientation, the management of operating exposures typically requires coordination among the MNC's senior management, strategic planners, and international treasury. To minimize operating exposure, multinationals frequently employ the following strategies:

1. Invest in countries where the dollar value of cash flows can be preserved; for example, countries with currencies that have shown a persistent trend toward appreciating against the parent company's base currency, the so-called "hard currency" nations.

2. Source components from countries where hard currency costs are projected to be low.

3. Develop markets in countries where the dollar value of sales revenues and dividend remittances can be easily protected.

4. Finance company needs in ways that limit currency exposures and the possibility of company losses.

TRANSLATION EXPOSURE

Translation exposure is related to the need of multinational companies to report their global operations on a consolidated basis. In this regard and in contrast to the other exposure concepts, translation exposure is accounting oriented and therefore will be subject to accounting definition and measurement.

Translation exposure is also called accounting exposure.

In the United States, multinational companies must present their consolidated financial statements of worldwide operations on the basis of rules prescribed by the Financial Accounting Standards Board. In this case the Financial Accounting Standard (FAS) 52 is the relevant statement concerning the consolidation of foreign currency accounts and the reporting of foreign source income. Under FAS 52 American multinationals are to use the current rate method of translating and reporting foreign activities, under which all balance sheet items (assets and liabilities) are considered to be exposed. This method leaves the net worth of the foreign subsidiary subject to an exchange adjustment based on the gains or losses incurred in translation. Under FAS 52 these translation gains and losses are also to be reported as an adjustment directly to the consolidated equity account of the American parent company, leaving the reporting of consolidated earnings for the American parent

> **• EXHIBIT 16.3**   **Analysis of Exposure: Princebran's German Subsidiary[1]**

Balance Sheet Account	COLUMN A DM Amount	COLUMN B Dollar Amount DM1 = $.500	COLUMN C Dollar Amount DM1 = $.375
Cash	50	25	18.8
Accounts Receivable	300	150	112.5
Inventory	200	100	75.0
Fixed Assets	250	125	93.8
Total Assets	DM800	$400	$300
Accounts Payable	210	105	78.8
Notes Payable	300	150	112.5
Long-Term Debt	150	75	56.3
Translation Gain or (Loss)			(17.6)
Net Worth	140	70	70
Total Liabilities and Capital	DM800	$400	$300

[1] Values in millions of currency units

FAS 52

Financial Accounting Standard No. 52.

unaffected by specific translation adjustments. There are no cash flow implications from this accounting method.*

These principles can be best illustrated through an example. Consider the German subsidiary of the Princebran Corporation. Assume for simplicity that the German company has no cross border flows, and that all earnings are retained at the subsidiary level. The specific balance sheet magnitudes in deutsche mark terms for this subsidiary are set forward in Exhibit 16.3, Column A. At current rates of exchange ($1 = DM2 or equivalently, DM1 = $.50), the German subsidiary has a balance sheet total of $400 million, as shown in Column B.

Now assume that the deutsche mark's value falls to $0.375. The corresponding dollar-valued balance sheet is presented in Column C. Under the new exchange rate, the dollar value of assets in the German subsidiary falls to $300. However, since net worth is carried at the book value of $70 (or DM140), the reduction in the value of the balance sheet must be "plugged" with a translation loss, here $17.6. On consolidation, this translation adjustment is registered in the equity account of the Princebran Corporation's consolidated balance sheet. Under FAS 52, this adjustment to net worth does not appear in Princebran's consolidated income statement. Translation adjustments are maintained on a cumulative basis in the consolidated balance sheet until the foreign subsidiary is liquidated or sold. At that time the corporation's consolidated income statement will record the difference from book value as a gain or loss. This treatment is tantamount to reserving translation gains and losses.

As an historical note, prior to 1975 when the first FASB accounting standard for foreign subsidiaries and affiliates was adopted, fully 75% of the U.S.-based MNCs maintained reserves against adverse changes in exchange rates.

When a reserves approach of the type described is used, businesses feel little pressure to hedge translation exposure. Surveys of MNC hedging patterns in recent years suggest that companies rarely hedge their balance sheet exposures. Accordingly, we

---

* This brief description of FAS 52 rules is, strictly speaking, applicable to nonhyperinflation countries. The temporal translation method applies for MNC operations in high inflation environments, and certain other cases where the U.S. dollar is used as the functional currency. See *Statement of Financial Accounting Standard No. 52,* (Stamford, CT: Financial Accounting Standards Board, 1981).

place little emphasis on translation exposure management practices. The following sections examine the management of transaction and operating exposures.

Managing Transaction and Translation Exposure

COMMON ELEMENTS

Previous sections in this chapter have presented the concepts of transaction, operating, and translation exposures. The focus of those discussions has been to identify each exposure concept and to show how the concept of exposure can be measured. As indicated in the previous section, it is unusual for companies to hedge translation exposure. Therefore our FX exposure management discussion will focus on transaction and operating exposures. However, it should be pointed out that balance sheet translation exposure is similar in basic ways to transaction exposure. In both, the MNC has a specific time point to which the exposure is referenced. In the case of the transaction exposure, that time point is the maturity date of the transaction. In the case of translation exposure, the time point is the date on which the financial statement is to be reported.

> Companies in financial distress may choose to hedge translation exposures if debt covenants are in danger of being breached.

For both the transaction and translation cases, the exposures are neutralized by entering into foreign currency transactions that exactly offset the amount of the exposure. The mechanics of such hedging actions, as well as illustrations of their use, are presented in detail in Chapter 4, Foreign Exchange Market and Chapter 5, Currency Futures, Options, and Swaps. The reader is encouraged to review these supporting complementary presentations.

FORWARD (FUTURES) CONTRACT APPROACH

Typically the MNC will have a sizeable stream of foreign currency transactions. As indicated in Chapter 15, the extent of exposure is the net volume of transactions in a specific currency. For simplicity let us assume that the U.S.-based Jacksbran Corporation has just one exposure in sterling. This situation arises from a pound sterling receivable due to a large export order from the United States to a British company for the amount of one million pounds to be settled by the British company in 360 days. One mechanism that can create an offsetting pound sterling payable from pounds to dollars is a forward contract selling pounds against dollars one-year forward, or an alternative mechanism through equivalent operations in money market instruments, futures, swaps, or foreign currency options.

The senior management at Jacksbran have operated for some years under a policy of selective hedging. Jacksbran has a rather sophisticated international treasury staff; in addition, the company has a strong regional treasury network in Europe. With this expertise the firm has a historical record of practicing selective hedging with successful results. To achieve these results, the international treasury managers form expectations or forecasts concerning the future course of exchange rates. In the case of the one million pound receivable, the treasury provides the following foreign exchange rate configuration.

Current Exchange Rate:	£ 1 = $1.80
Current Forward Rate, 1 Year:	£ 1 = $1.85
Jacksbran Treasury Forecasts 1 Year Forward:	£ 1 = $1.83

Under these rates the pound sterling is selling at a premium in the forward market. The extent of the premium exceeds the value of the international treasury's projection of the pound's value one-year forward. With forward sterling trading at a premium, it is possible for Jacksbran to lock in a small increases in value over the current spot rate by hedging.* The effect of the hedge will be to assure certainty in the dollar value of the receivable at the end of the year. This outcome is seen in the following table that presents four possible results: the fall of the value of the pound to $1.70; no change in the pound's value from the current spot; a rise in the pound's value to the current, one-year forward rate; and a rise in the pound's value to $1.90.

Ex Post Turnout after 360 Days	Receivable in Dollar Terms	Gain or (Loss) on Forward Contract	Dollar Value of Hedged Receivable
£ 1 = $1.70	$1,700,000	$1,50,000	$1,850,000
£ 1 = $1.80	$1,800,000	$50,000	$1,850,000
£ 1 = $1.85	$1,850,000	0	$1,850,000
£ 1 = $1.90	$1,900,000	($50,000)	$1,850,000

In all cases, the dollar value of the hedged pound receivable is $1,850,000.

"Opportunity Loss" as opposed to cash loss.

Because the Jacksbran treasury forecasts a spot rate one-year forward of $1.83, it is possible for the company to lock in a more favorable rate by hedging, that of $1.85. If in fact the actual or ex post spot rate after one year lies below $1.85, Jacksbran would benefit by the hedge. However, if the ex post rate turns out to be above $1.85, this hedging action would result in an "opportunity loss," determined by the difference between the spot rate turnout and the $1.85 forward rate value. For example, a spot rate turnout of $1.90 results in an opportunity loss of $50,000.

Money Market Instruments

Money market hedging, futures contracts, and currency swaps are less well suited for medium- and small-sized companies.

Another approach to hedging the pound receivable is through the use of money market instruments as a way to create foreign currency cash flows that exactly offset the transaction exposure. Continuing the example with Jacksbran, we may calculate the premium on the pound over the 360-day period using the formula for direct foreign exchange rate quotations, as given in Chapter 4. Using that calculation, the premium on the pound is 2.78% over the next 360 days. It is known that the relevant money market interest rate in the United States is 8%. Under the assumption of interest rate parity, the money market interest rate in the United Kingdom will be 5.22%.

With this information the Jacksbran treasury manager can create a pound payable which will offset the £1 million receivable. This transaction can be done by borrowing £950,390 (= £1,000,000 ÷ 1.0522) in the United Kingdom. This loan to Jacksbran will be made at the relevant money market interest rate of 5.22%. The borrowed sum is then exchanged for U.S. dollars at the current exchange rate of £1.80. The resulting sum of $1,710,665 can then be invested in the United States for one year at the relevant interest rate of 8.0% to yield $1,847,419 at maturity. This value is close to the $1,850,000 value of the forward contract hedge.

In addition to hedging through the forward exchange and the money market avenues, Jacksbran can consider a similar hedge by working through the futures market for pound sterling. As discussed in Chapter 5, it may be possible to approximate

---

* If the pound was selling at a discount relative to the spot rate, the opposite case would apply. That is, relative to the spot rate, the forward hedge would "cost you money."

the value of the one million pound receivable by a combination of pound futures contracts. As indicated in that chapter, however, forward contracts have a greater flexibility in that they can be customized to the exact amount and date of the pound receivable, and thus, from the standpoint of a large multinational corporation, they are generally the preferred hedging instrument.

CURRENCY SWAPS

Currency swap arrangements may also be used as a way to achieve this hedge. Under these circumstances the Jacksbran Corporation could reach an agreement to swap a net pound sterling payable of approximately the same amount in 360 days. In situations where interest differentials between the countries are substantial, additional fee compensation may be required.

FOREIGN CURRENCY OPTIONS

Another approach to hedging transaction exposure is the use of foreign currency options. These options differ in a fundamental way from other hedge instruments such as forwards, futures, swaps, and money market instruments. The latter instruments offer ways to hedge foreign currency receivables or payables of a known value; in contrast, options hedging is applicable in situations where the volume and need to hedge foreign currency is uncertain in magnitude. An example of such a case would be where Jacksbran offers a bid on a project in the United Kingdom. Should Jacksbran win the bid, the company will have a £1 million receivable. However, it will not be known for 12 months whether this bid has been accepted. If Jacksbran entered into a forward contract to sell £1 million against dollars in 360 days, the hedge would be in place in the case where its bid was accepted. However, should the Jacksbran bid not be accepted, and the company hedged using a forward contract, the company would then face the problem of locking itself in an uncovered forward contract and its attendant risks.

An options contract provides a way to guarantee a minimum price for the firm's contribution to the project should its bid be selected. Should the bid not be selected, Jacksbran will have its loss limited to the price that it has paid for the options contract. In this example, Jacksbran would buy put options to sell £1 million in 12 months. The price of this option might be $50,000 at the strike price of $1.80. By purchasing this option Jacksbran is assured that if the company wins the bid, it will receive a minimum value of $1,750,000. However should the bid not be selected, the loss to the company will be limited to $50,000.

Foreign currency options are an attractive vehicle in cases where the volume of foreign currency to be hedged is uncertain. However in practice many companies find that they are able to duplicate the benefit of options by using a combination of forwards and open positions. When these positions are actively managed, the result can be a lower cost as compared to the currency options case.

The company's choice among these several hedging avenues will depend on a number of considerations. Foremost of these factors is the extent of foreign exchange market development. Foreign exchange markets for the currencies of the major industrial nations are fully developed in the sense that these markets have achieved adequate market breadth, depth, and resiliency. For most of these currencies, futures, swaps, and options have developed as parallel markets and instruments.

Beyond the ten currencies of the major European industrial countries, the United States, Canada, and Japan, the extent of foreign exchange institutional development is quite limited. For the currencies of these other nations, the forward exchange and ancillary markets are limited or can be entered only by incurring very high costs. In these cases companies must rely on the money market approach and swap arrangements, where these are available.

THE LIMITATIONS OF HEDGING

The traditional view of hedging is that financial instruments—as described in the previous section—can be used to offset transaction exposure. However, this works only when the maturity of the hedging contract matches the company's decision horizon. Most MNCs have foreign currency cash flows that are regular, frequent, certain, and that arise from the normal pattern of business. Because these flows are ongoing for the foreseeable future, the MNC has essentially a long-term exposure that cannot be addressed using the traditional financial hedging approaches.

This is most clearly seen in situations of long-term foreign exchange rate trends. Consider, for example, the case of a subsidiary of a U.S.-based MNC that is located in Spain and that sources key inputs from Germany for production, with sales in Spain. There are no other suppliers of this key input due to the patent coverage held by the German firm. Assume that the peseta has maintained a secular trend of depreciation against the deutsche mark. Further assume that the sourcing relationship calls for the payment of input purchases on six-month credit terms in deutsche marks. Under these circumstances, successive hedges of the six-month payables will not offer protection against the long-term depreciation of the deutsche mark/peseta exchange rate since, at the end of each six-month contact period, the forward hedge will be reset at the new lower peseta exchange rate value. Thus the Spanish subsidiary will be under constant pressure from rising costs in peseta terms associated with its sourcing from the German supplier.*

The fact that the Spanish company engages in hedging does not remove its vulnerability to the long-term trend of peseta depreciation. This circumstance cannot be approached as a transaction exposure problem. Rather, it must be interpreted as an operating exposure problem, the resolution of which is addressed in the next section.

Operating Exposure Management

In most cases, the management of operating exposure requires expertise from the MNC's international treasury department and from other areas of the firm as well. In most large companies, this responsibility is usually shared through a cooperative effort between the corporate strategic planning department and the international treasury.

One approach to operating exposure management is passive and involves seeking a high level of diversification of company operations across a range of currencies. Thus in targeting markets internationally, in locating production facilities, input sourcing, and financial sourcing, the MNC should seek currency area locations that are not highly positively correlated.

As described, diversification across currencies is sometimes called "green" hedging.

Beyond this passive approach, when an unexpected change occurs in a key exchange rate relationship, the MNC can react in ways to offset the effect of the

---

* Luc Soenen, "When Foreign Exchange Hedging Doesn't Help," *Journal of Cash Management,* 1991, Vol. 11, no. 6, pp. 58–62.

adverse development. This action is illustrated in the following example involving a reconfiguration of the locus of production.

Baronsbran Corporation, a U.S.-based MNC, wishes to determine the extent to which it may be affected by foreign exchange rate changes. The focus for this analysis is on Baronsbran's subsidiary in Italy. Mr. George, the treasury manager at Baronsbran corporate with responsibility for foreign exchange exposure management, has been troubled by the exposure environment that his Italian subsidiary faces.

Baronsbran's Italian subsidiary produces super scepters for sale both in the domestic Italian market and also in Germany. The selection of this marketing pattern was made to provide the company with a range of options, should unexpected exchange rate relationships occur. At the time of Mr. George's analysis, the Italian subsidiary has an input configuration involving component inputs from Germany and from the domestic Italian economy. The super scepters manufacturing process requires a labor-intensive assembly operation that was incorporated in the Italian operation. Exhibit 16.4 summarizes these relationships.

The company's motivation for establishing the Italian subsidiary some years ago was to take advantage of relatively low labor and component costs in that nation. However in recent years weak monetary policy and related inflation trends have contributed to make this an undesirable situation, and these policies are projected to continue over the next five years. Projected inflation rates are:

INFLATION RATES P.A.

Italy	25%
U.S.	5%
Germany	3%

With much more virulent inflation in Italy than in the United States and Germany, Italian central bank authorities have been reluctant to allow the Italian lira to depreciate in line with the relative inflation rates. That is to say, the Italian monetary and government authorities have been acting in a manner that prevents purchasing power parity conditions from being established. The authorities are

EXHIBIT 16.4	**Baronsbran Corporation: Italian Subsidiary**		
All values in millions of US$	Col. 1	Col. 2	Col. 3
	Year 0	Year 5 Projections with no change in operations structure	Year 5 Projections with shift in assembly locus to Germany
Total revenues from super scepters sales	1000	800	1100
Sales in Italy	500	500	600
Sales in Germany	500	300	500
Component inputs from Italy	150	150	
Component inputs from Germany			200
Product assembly labor expense in Italy	400	400	
Product assembly labor expense in Germany			500
Cash flow	450	250	400
Projected operating exposure relative to year 0[1]		200	50

[1] In this example, it is assumed that Baronsbran cannot avoid these exposures through internal company adjustments other than the reconfiguration of production.

aided in this effort by a secular rise in net capital inflows to Italy, projected to continue. Exchange rate trends over the next five years are forecast as follows:

	Projected FX Rate Change (per annum)	FX Rate Change (per annum) Under PPP Conditions
U.S. Dollar/IL	−15%	−20%
DM/IL	−18%	−22%

Mr. George determines that should these trends continue, the structure of the Italian subsidiary operations will become increasingly untenable. As deviation from purchasing power parity continues, company sales in Germany will deteriorate. His projections are presented in Column 2 of Exhibit 16.4. Given this "best guess" projection to year five, Mr. George determines that his projected operating exposure relative to year 0 will be $200 million. After discussions with Baronsbran's international economists and the corporate-level strategic planners, Mr. George develops an alternative set of projections through year five that are based on a shift in the labor-intensive assembly operation from Italy to Germany.

In the German environment both component inputs and labor costs will be more expensive than in Italy. However these higher costs will be more than offset by higher revenues, since this change will allow Baronsbran to maintain its sales revenue in Germany and will also provide the company with a cost advantage in selling back to Italy. This change will permit a higher level of revenues from Italian sales as measured in U.S. dollar terms. Under this alternative configuration, the operating exposure relative to year 0 will be reduced to $50 million, as opposed to $200 million in the case of no change in the operating structure. Based on this analysis, Baronsbran reconfigures the Italian subsidiary by locating its assembly operations in Germany.

SUMMARY

The concepts of cash flow exposure and translation exposure are developed based on the concept of the "value of the firm." The focus on cash flow exposure has the "market value" of the firm as its emphasis, as measured by the value of equity recorded in the stock market. This, in turn, was seen to have two components: transaction exposure and operating exposure. In contrast translation exposure has as its focus the value of the firm as recorded through accounting statements. Both cash flow and translation dimensions have legitimate roles in the practice of financial management.

When financial managers are concerned about short-term financial objectives, the primary focus tends to be on transaction and translation exposures. However, companies must also necessarily be oriented to longer-term considerations. And for this reason operating exposure must be given significant weight. MNCs can ignore the operating exposure dimension only at their peril.

It is the responsibility of senior management in most firms to set company policies for managing foreign exchange exposure that strike a balance between the operating dimension, on the one hand, and the transaction and translation exposure dimensions on the other. When this is done, most large MNCs will find their important exposures to be of a longer-term operating nature. To deal with these the MNC should create flexible and diversified business configurations that will allow the company to offset unexpected adverse exchange rate changes. Financial management and strategic planners should work together to address these problems as they are identified.

REVIEW QUESTIONS

1. With reference to Exhibit 16.2, what is the operating exposure impact of a rise in the French franc exchange rate to FF1 = $1.30?

2. With reference to Exhibit 16.3, calculate the translation gain for Princebran's German subsidiary that develops from an appreciation of the deutsche mark to DM1 = $1.00.

3. Jacksbran expects a £1 million receivable in three months. The treasury manager elected to hedge this receivable by selling £1 million for dollars three months forward at the price of $1.85/£. The spot market turnout three months later was $1.90/£ . What was the opportunity loss associated with this hedge decision?

4. In problem 3, how does a hedging opportunity loss affect management decision making? If the receivable was not hedged and the turnout was $1.70/£, what was the financial loss incurred? How would that loss be likely to affect management decision making?

5. Explain the relationship between transaction and translation exposures from the foreign subsidiary standpoint. What differences arise when this relationship is considered from the standpoint of the consolidated parent?

6. Prattline Corporation, a U.S.-based MNC, has a subsidiary in the Netherlands that produces machine tools, the principal market for which is the United States. Each machine tool incorporates a key component accounting for 40% of the total value of the finished machine tool product that is purchased in the United States. All other inputs for the Dutch operation are purchased in the Netherlands. When the U.S. dollar strengthens against the guilder, we would ordinarily think this strength would improve the earnings of the Dutch subsidiary with its selling efforts in the U.S. market. This presumption is based on implied assumptions concerning the underlying elasticities of supply and demand in the U.S. market for machine tools and in the U.S. market for the key component. Construct a numerical example for the Dutch subsidiary that illustrates conditions under which this is true. Express your results in U.S. dollar terms, assuming low inflation conditions in the Netherlands.

7. Mitsubishi Motors (Japan) has just agreed to supply to Mitsubishi (U.S.) 2,000 automobiles for a total value of Y2,640 million. The sum is to be paid in three months. The following data pertain:

Spot rate	Y110.10/$
90-day forward rate	110.45/$
U.S. 90-day interest rate	3.25% per annum
Japanese 90-day interest rate	4.50%
Call Option, Y, 90 days	
Strike price	111.00/$
Premium	0.5%
Expected Spot rate in 90 days	110.11

What course of action do you suggest to the Mitsubishi (U.S.) financial manager to assure certainty of value for yen payable?

8. The Woolworth Corporation's French subsidiary is committed to the following transactions

in 90 days:

—make interest payment to U.S. bank of $100.

—receive DM 160 for goods sold to German retailer.

in 180 days:

—receive $100 in payment for sales to a U.S. manufacturer.

—make DM 160 payment to German supplier for product.

The spot exchange rate today is DM 1.60/$. Other foreign exchange and interest rate data are:

90-day forward	DM 1.630
180-day forward	DM 1.650
90-day interest rate, Germany	9.5% per annum
180-day interest rate, Germany	8.25% per annum
90-day interest rate, U.S.	2.0% per annum
180-day interest rate, U.S.	2.5% per annum

Demonstrate how the French subsidiary can achieve certainty of value for its future payables and receivables.

9. The GTE Corporation has entered a forward contract to sell French francs (FF) 1 million in one year against dollars at the rate of FF5.60/$. The contract was negotiated for the purpose of hedging French franc receivables. On the day the forward contract matured, the spot rate for the dollar against the French franc was FF5.40/$. What was the opportunity loss of the hedging strategy for GTE?

SELECTED BIBLIOGRAPHY

Adler, Michael, and Bernard Dumas. "Exposure to Foreign Exchange Currency Risk: Definition and Measurement." *Financial Management,* (Spring 1984): 41–50.

Benet, Bruce A. "Commodity Future Cross Hedging of Foreign Exchange Exposure." *Journal of Futures Markets,* Vol. 10, No. 3, (June 1990): 287–306.

Collier, P. "The Management of Currency Risk: Case Studies of U.S. and U.K. Multinationals." *Accounting and Business Research,* Vol. 20, No. 79, (Summer 1990): 206–210.

Griffiths, Susan H. "Foreign Currency Management: Part IV—Treasury Considerations." *Journal of Cash Management,* Vol. 10, No. 1, (Jan/Feb 1990): 41–44.

Jorion, Philippe. "The Exchange-Rate Exposure of U.S. Multinationals." *Journal of Business,* Vol. 63, No. 3, (July 1990): 331–345.

Kaepplinger, Peter. "Foreign Currency Hedging Transactions under Section 988 Temporary Regulations." *CPA Journal,* Vol. 60, No. 7, (July 1990): 72–74.

Khoury, Sarkis J., and K. Hung Chan: "Hedging Foreign Exchange Risk: Selecting the Optimal Tool." *Midland Corporate Finance Journal,* (Winter 1988): 40–52.

Luehrman, Timothy A. "The Exchange Rate Exposure of a Global Competitor." *Journal of International Business Studies,* Vol. 21, No. 2, (Second Quarter 1990): 225–242.

Madura, Jeff. "The Impact of Financing Sources on Multinational Projects." *Journal of Financial Research,* Vol. 13, No. 1, (Spring 1990): 61–69.

Moffett, Michael, and Jan Karl Karlsen. "Managing Foreign Exchange Rate Economic Exposure." *Journal of International Financial Management and Accounting,* Vol. 5, No. 2, (June 1994): 157–175.

Perold, André F., and Evan C. Sulman. "The Free Lunch in Currency Hedging: Implications for Investment Policy and Performance Standards." *Financial Analyst Journal,* (May-June 1988): 45–50.

Soenen, Luc A. "When Foreign Exchange Hedging Doesn't Help." *Journal of Cash Management,* Vol. 11, No. 6, (1991): 58–62.

Statement of Financial Accounting Standard No. 52. Financial Accounting Standards Board, Stamford, CT: 1981.

Stulz, René, and Clifford W. Smith. "Determinants of Firms' Hedging Policies." *Journal of Financial and Quantitative Analysis,* (December 1985): 391–405.

Sucher, Pat, and Joanna Carter. "Foreign Exchange Exposure Management Advice for the Medium-Sized Enterprise." *Management Accounting,* Vol. 74, No. 3, (March 1996): 59–61.

CHAPTER 17

International Capital Budgeting

INTRODUCTION

Financial managers in multinational corporations must make decisions regarding investments in fixed assets. This decision process is called capital budgeting. The dominant characteristic of such decisions is that assets will be acquired that have a long useful life and will influence company cash flows for many years in the future. Thus correct capital budgeting decisions will have a long-term positive influence on the MNC, and conversely, incorrect decisions will result in a long-term negative influence. In this chapter we analyze investment decisions made by companies that extend around the world. Further, we develop an understanding of how international capital budgeting contrasts with domestic budgeting practices.

LEARNING OBJECTIVES IN THIS CHAPTER

1. To explain MNC capital budgeting decisions and the complexities of the international ramifications.
2. To describe the differences and congruencies of the parent and subsidiary perspectives on international capital budgeting.
3. To review alternative approaches to capital budgeting.
4. To identify methods to account for risk and uncertainty in capital budgeting.
5. To understand the role of macroeconomics and industry-level assumptions in international capital budgeting.
6. To demonstrate the role of business assumptions and tax dimensions.
7. To show how, using sensitivity analysis, varying inflation conditions can have a significant effect on a project's financial requirements.

The MNC Organizational Context

Capital budgeting is a key financial decision for both purely domestic companies and MNCs. However the importance of the capital budget in the international business arena may be more crucial in certain ways. MNCs are typically large and capital intensive. For such firms, capital budgeting is a critical decision area.

International capital budgeting is applied to projects that are located geographically in countries (host countries) other than the home country of the investor company. These international projects differ from purely domestic ones in a number of ways. International projects have an inescapable foreign currency dimension and are subject to a number of factors, including differing inflation rates between countries and special risk dimensions unique to the countries in which the projects are to be located.

Because capital budgeting involves substantial expenditures, approvals of major projects are usually required at several levels within the MNC. Furthermore, the capital budgeting analysis will require information inputs from many sources located in different parts of the MNC organization. Typically the company's operating divisions initiate project proposals. The treasury managers are called upon to evaluate or rank these proposals from a finance perspective, and senior management must determine the strategic consistency of these proposals given overall corporate goals and objectives. The corporation's chief executive officer is responsible for final signoffs on specific projects. Given the involvement of these diverse groups within the MNC, many companies have established strategic planning systems to integrate these organizational perspectives. The strategic planning staff members work closely with financial managers in evaluating capital budgeting proposals. This evaluation takes place at an early stage in the company's annual strategic planning cycle.

Many studies have surveyed the practices that multinational firms use in international capital budgeting over the past two decades. Studies using survey techniques have been undertaken by: Baker and Beardsley (1973); Oblak and Helm (1980); Stonehill and Nathanson (1980); Bavishi (1981); Kelly and Philippatos (1982); Stanley and Block (1983); Kim, Farragher, and Crick (1984), and Cheng (1994). A common thread that emerges from these studies is that the typical multinational company employs several different techniques in assessing international capital budgeting projects.

One reason why practitioners rely on several techniques is that the decision process within the typical MNC, as indicated above, involves a number of management groups with different backgrounds, orientations, and objectives. And some techniques are simply better suited to the thinking of particular groups. For example, the operating subsidiary that will have to run the proposed project when it is established will typically focus greater attention on the marketing and production aspects, as well as on the risks and uncertainties of revenues, costs, and net cash flows associated with the project itself. Although the operating subsidiary will develop the detailed revenue and cost data, managers at the corporate level will provide other information inputs and perspectives.

The corporate treasury staff managers will be responsible for the financial factors that enter the decision—the financial methodologies applied to evaluate the project, including the choice of discount and cost of capital rates selected. At the corporate senior management and board of directors levels, the orientation is toward seeing a given project as one of several potential alternative applications of corporate resources, where the range of alternatives can include both nonfinancial and financial investments. And finally, the strategic planning group within the parent corporation, although strongly oriented toward the senior management perspective, will usually focus more on how a given project "fits" or complements the major strategic directions of the MNC. That is, the planners focus on the benefits and externalities that the proposed project might convey to other divisions and subsidiaries within the MNC. The divergent views of these participants in the international budget process appear to be met in practice by providing several evaluation techniques and measures for a given project.

Project Cash Flows

MNC projects can have a number of cash flow and product/input configurations; Exhibit 17.1 presents the range of possibilities for these flows. This figure illustrates that sales revenues to the subsidiary can originate in third countries and in the United States, as well as in local markets in the subsidiary's host country. In addition, inputs to the subsidiary can originate from the United States and from third countries as well as from local host country sources. Whenever the subsidiary's revenues and input cost flows originate from outside the host nation, foreign exchange dimensions are inescapably encountered. Capital budgeting involving such cross border flows must consider not only foreign exchange rate changes, but also differential inflation rates among countries in the configuration and differences in nominal and real interest rates.

EXHIBIT 17.1   **Product, Input, and Cash Flows for U.S.-based MNC**

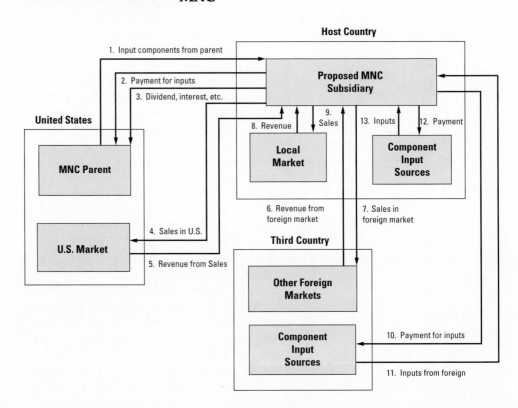

Different types of MNC operations will take different cash flow configurations. For example, a bauxite mining operation in Guyana may require a tight integration with the U.S. parent's alumina refining and marketing activities. As such, the cash flows for this operation will be described by items 1), 3), 4), and 10) in Exhibit 17.1. Similar flows would characterize a manufacturing operation in Haiti established to take advantage of the country's low labor costs. In contrast many MNC manufacturing projects are established on a more stand alone basis. This situation can result from political pressure within the host country to achieve a high percentage of domestic content in total value added in the subsidiary. Alternatively, this type of project can take place as an MNC seeks to become established within the European Community in order to avoid the EC's common external tariff. In this case, the operation will be characterized by cash flows 3), 9), and 12).

Parent Versus Foreign Subsidiary Viewpoints

When considering a proposed project, the MNC can evaluate cash flows associated with the project from two perspectives. The first is the net impact of the project on the MNC's consolidated cash flows. The second perspective is to view the proposed project on a stand alone or unconsolidated basis. Of the two, the first is conceptually correct. However, there is a tendency on the part of operating managers at the subsidiary level to not fully appreciate the ways in which their proposed project may benefit the overall MNC organization. This tendency is reinforced by executive incentive programs in some MNCs that base the bonus package for operation managers on the net income or operating income performance of their MNC subsidiary, as opposed to the subsidiary's net contribution to the consolidated performance of the overall MNC organization.

This divergence in viewpoints is seen most sharply when considering the extreme case in which cash flows generated at the subsidiary level are not transferable to the parent MNC. This circumstance may occur, for example, in the case of an investment in a developing nation that encounters severe balance of payments problems and is forced to ration its scarce foreign exchange. These situations have been known to continue for years, as occurred in many Latin American countries following the international debt crisis of the 1980s.

Divergencies between parent and subsidiary cash flows can also arise from the nature of the MNC's revenue/cost configuration. Thus where the MNC sells license rights or management services to the foreign subsidiary, these are net benefits to the parent MNC while the subsidiary counts these rights and services as costs. This method is also used where other MNC units sell raw materials or key components to the subsidiary. Again, sales from other units of the company may be counted as contributions toward the MNC's consolidated net income, while the subsidiary regards such sales as costs. The captial budgeting example presented later in the chapter will focus on the corporate allocation expense as illustrative of this form of externality that should be understood as generically similar to more complex linkages.

A second issue in international capital budgeting that arises from this divergence in viewpoints between the subsidiary and the MNC parent concerns the currency of denomination for the evaluation analysis. In the case of the U.S.-based MNC, the parent viewpoint toward the project will be in U.S. dollars. However, the subsidiary perspective will be in terms of the local currency of its host country. As will be illustrated later in this chapter, the selection of the currency of analysis can lead to divergencies in judging the merits of specific proposals, since in general foreign exchange translation rules are seldom neutral in their effects. Such divergencies, for example, can arise from differential inflation rates and from foreign exchange rate changes between the host country and that of the MNC parent.

Finally, different parent and subsidiary viewpoints can arise in the selection of the discount rate used for the capital budgeting analysis. From the foreign subsidiary perspective the appropriate discount rate should relate to the cost of funds borne by the subsidiary's local competitors, after adjusting for differences in the credit ratings for the companies. The perspective of the parent MNC is ordinarily toward the average cost of capital in its operations worldwide as the relevant discount rate. This rate is not related in any necessary way to local credit conditions that the foreign subsidiary's competitors face in the host country. In the capital budgeting example developed later in the chapter, we will present project evaluations based on both the parent and subsidiary discount rates as a way to illustrate these dimensions.

Capital Budgeting Approaches

Analysts and practitioners have developed a broad and rich literature in the area of international capital budgeting in recent years. It is not our intention to review this extensive technical work here.* However, we examine three traditional capital budgeting approaches that are widely used in international capital budgeting analyses: the net present value (NPV), the internal rate of return (IRR), and the payback period (PBP). These approaches are summarized briefly in the following section. We can apply the criteria for evaluating capital budgeting proposals to the project's cash flows, either in terms of U.S. dollars or in terms of the currency of the country in which the proposed project is to be located. In terms developed in this literature we will focus our presentation on "new" investment, as opposed to the "replacement" investment decision. However, it should be recognized that the principles developed are readily applicable to the replacement case.†

Surveys over the past 15 years indicate that larger firms work with the IRR measure more than smaller firms.

The net present value approach takes as its basic premise that the firm wishes to maximize its net worth. Under this assumption, the approach compares the cost of the proposed investment with the present value of cash flows associated with the investment. If the discounted cash flows exceed the cost of the investment, the NPV criterion calls for accepting the project. More technically, this calculation is presented as follows:

$$NPV = -I_0 + \sum_{i=1}^{n} \frac{C_i}{(1 + k)^i} + \frac{T_n}{(1 + k)^n}$$

---

* The interested reader is referred to the references at the end of this chapter.

† The focus for this analysis will be on investment projects where the project alternatives are mutually independent, not mutually exclusive.

EXHIBIT 17.2	**Illustration of NPV and PBP Approaches-Helvetia Manufacturing Projects**

We can illustrate the calculation of NPV and PBP using the following example. Axsensor, a U.S.-based MNC, is evaluating two alternative investments in manufacturing plants in Helvetia, a European country. Each project calls for a $30 million investment by the U.S. parent. Cash flows are indicated below. There is no terminal value.

We calculate the PBP as follows:

Payback Period Project A = 3 1/3 years (9 + 9 + 9 + 3 = 30)
Payback Period Project B = 3 2/3 years (4 + 6 + 10 + 10 = 30)

In this case Project A has a somewhat shorter PBP, and therefore shorter exposure of initial investment before cash flows enable recovery of investment.

We calculate NPV with the following information. Three possible discount factors (cost of capital) are used. At 10%, Project B is clearly preferred. At a discount rate of 14%, Project B continues to be preferred, and there is very low positive NPV for Project A. At a discount rate of 20% Project A has a negative NPV and is rejected; Project B has a very small positive NPV.

PAYBACK PERIOD METHOD

Year	Project A	Project B
1	$9	$4
2	9	6
3	9	10
4	9	15
5	9	25
	45	60

NET PRESENT VALUE METHOD

	AT 10 PERCENT			AT 14 PERCENT			AT 20 PERCENT		
Year	Discount Factor	A	B	Discount Factor	A	B	Discount Factor	A	B
1	.9091	8182	3636	.8772	7895	3509	.8333	7499	3333
2	.8264	7437	4958	.7695	6926	4617	.6944	6250	4166
3	.7513	6762	7513	.6750	6075	6750	.5787	5208	5787
4	.6830	6147	10247	.5921	5329	8882	.4823	4341	7235
5	.6209	5588	15523	.5194	4675	12985	.4019	3617	10047
		34116	41865		30900	36743		26915	30568
		−30000	−30000		−30000	−30000		−30000	−30000
		4116	11865		900	6743		−3085	568

where:

NPV = net present values of the project
I_0 = the cost of the initial investment
C_i = after-tax project cash flows in year i
T_n = terminal or salvage value of investment in year n
n   = anticipated life of the project or planning period
k   = cost of capital applicable to the project[†]

Examples of NPV calculations can be found in Exhibit 17.2.

The internal rate of return criterion focuses on the comparison of the project's internal rate of return with the IRRs associated with alternative projects and/or

---

[†] This approach conceptually will allow k to vary over time; the cost of capital is developed in Chapter 14, Foreign Affiliate Financing, Taxation, and Cost of Capital.

same minimum rate of return standard such as the cost of capital. Technically, the IRR calculation is as follows:

$$I_0 = \sum_{i=1}^{n} \frac{C_i}{(1 + r)^i} + \frac{T_n}{(1 + r)^n}$$

where r is defined as the IRR, and is calculated given the other known inputs to the equation.

The third investment criterion that we will examine is the payback period approach. In this analysis the question asked is: "How long will it be before the initial cash outlay of the project is recouped?" The presumption in this analysis is that investments will be undertaken that have "acceptably short" payback periods. To calculate the PBP, the following formula is used, assuming for ease of exposition that the annual cash flows C_i associated with the project are of equal magnitude:

$$PBP = \frac{I}{C_i}$$

For example, for an initial investment of $1 million and annual cash flows of $300,000, the payback period will be 3.3 years.* Exhibit 17.2 demonstrates the PBP calculation in comparison with the NPV approach.

The three decision frameworks described are widely used in evaluating proposed international investment projects. However, it is important that we gain perspective on these so that we understand the strengths and weaknesses of each approach. The first two—the NPV and IRR—are viewed as preferred from the standpoint of modern financial theory, because both incorporate adjustments to future cash flows that reflect the time value of money. This time value dimension is fundamental to modern financial analysis and is not satisfactorily incorporated in the PBP analysis as previously presented. More specifically, the difficulty with the PBP approach is that this analysis ignores cash flows from the investments that occur after the PBP timepoint.† In contrast the NPV and IRR approaches consider all of the cash flows associated with the project on a discounted basis.

Between the first and second approaches, the NPV is traditionally taken as the most theoretically satisfactory. The principal difference between the NPV and the IRR is the implied assumption each uses regarding the reinvestment rate for cash flows. In the NPV case the implied reinvestment rate is the cost of capital that can be interpreted as an approximation of the opportunity cost for reinvestment. In contrast under the IRR approach the implied reinvestment rate is the IRR for the project itself. And there is no necessary relationship between a project's IRR and the MNC's opportunity cost of investment. Still, use of the IRR as a capital budgeting

One PBP variation is to consider the payback period using discounted cash flows, rather than the approach presented in the text.

---

* In cases where cash flows vary from year to year, the analysis is somewhat more complicated. Assume the cash flows in the first three years of the $1 million investment were, respectively: $300,000, $400,000, and $500,000. Under these circumstances, the payback period would be 2 years plus

$$\frac{\$300,000}{\$500,000}$$ or 2.6 years.

† One variant of the PBP involves the use of discounted cash flows in determining the PBP, where the discount factor can be a cost-of-capital rate. This approach softens considerably this criticism of the PBP approach.

evaluation measure is widespread in MNCs, particularly at the senior management level. At that level the IRR as a measure that summarizes the project in terms of a percentage yield is readily comparable to yield measures on other investments including financial instruments.‡**

INTERNATIONAL CAPITAL BUDGETING: RISK ELEMENTS

When considering the international capital budgeting problem at a less theoretical level, risk and uncertainty elements pose serious problems, as compared to similar investments that might be made in the parent company's domestic economic environment. Both domestic and international investments have business (or credit) risks associated with these undertakings. Such risks are specific to industries and product lines and involve the likely evolution of markets and competitor behavior. The MNC may perceive the business risks for international projects as exceeding those of comparable domestic projects. However, this distinction is often one of degree, not order of magnitude, and usually arises because less is known about the international market and production environments.

In addition to business risk, international capital budgeting projects have an additional risk element, the country risk dimension. Country risk, as indicated in Chapter 12, is the risk of an adverse outcome to the investment project that arises from factors beyond the control of the foreign subsidiary or its industry. Country risk is usually viewed as arising from changes in government policies and typically focuses on the effects of those policies on the MNC subsidiary's operating environment at a microeconomic level. For example, policies that create inflation without offsetting foreign exchange depreciation may pose substantial risks to subsidiaries that source materials and components locally and produce to sell in export markets. Similarly, subsidiaries relying on critical imports from abroad may be at risk should a country adopt widespread import controls.

The country risk dimension should be viewed as added to, and may indeed multiply, perceived business risk elements associated with international, as opposed to domestic, investment proposals. The more complex risk environment on the international side should be understood in the context of the nature of capital budgeting. Capital investments are inherently long-term, and thus capital budgeting

---

‡ At a more technical level, it can be shown that projects with cash flow patterns that include positive flows and negative flows can yield multiple IRRs. The ambiguity that arises from such situations is another reason to prefer NPV analysis.

**A modification of the net present value approach has been suggested by Donald R. Lessard, called the adjusted present value (APV) method, applying the principle of value additivity. Here, the value of the proposed international investment project is viewed as consisting of several components, including: 1) the present value of project cash flows after taxes but before financing costs; 2) the present value of tax savings on debt financing; and 3) the present value of savings on interest costs associated with project-specific financing. Component 1 is discounted using the cost of equity rate, while 2 and 3 are discounted at the before-tax cost of dollar debt. See Donald R. Lessard, "Evaluating International Projects: An Adjusted Present Value Approach," in Crum and Derkindern, (eds.), *Capital Budgeting Under Conditions of Uncertainity*, Martinus Nijhoff Publishing, 1981, pp. 118–137.

As compared with NPV, the APV approach allows a sharper focus on project complexities such as financing subsidies and other forms of assistance provided by the host government. Provided all project dimensions are taken into account, the NPV and APV methods have been shown to be equivalent by Lawrence D. Booth, "Capital Budgeting Frameworks for the Multinational Corporation," *Journal of International Business Studies* (Fall 1982): 113–123. In addition, surveys of MNC practice cited in the chapter show only limited useage of the APV approach. For these reasons, we have proceeded with the primary focus on the NPV, IRR, and payback period approaches.

analyses must focus on long-range projections of revenues, costs, and financial factors that influence the future cash flows of the proposed project. But in today's fast changing international business environment, the uncertainties associated with such projections can be very high. This uncertainty is evident at the very "macro" economic and political levels. A partial list of sources of such shocks would include: changes in the systemic operation of the foreign exchange markets; the rapid evolution of attitudes in the industrialized nations toward LDC indebtedness; changes in the foreign policies of major nations such as the United States, Russia, and China; changes in tax laws both in the United States and abroad; and changing roles for the world's international economic institutions such as the IMF and the World Bank. Beyond these factors, during the 1980s and 1990s many countries have been undergoing great internal social, political, and economic changes. In the midst of these sweeping changes, it is difficult to have high confidence in projections going forward ten to fifteen years. This point of view is felt most keenly at the operating and subsidiary level, where managers face the foreign operating environment in its greatest detail, and where the estimates for cash flows, revenues, and costs are formed in local currency terms as basic inputs to the capital budgeting process.

Certainty equivalent cash flows

Cash flows over time adjusted by the associated degree of risk.

The theoretically preferred way of accounting for risk elements in capital budgeting is to incorporate all that is known about such risk outcomes through adjustments in cash flows (the C_is), that is, to achieve "certainty equivalent" cash flows. This approach may be demonstrated using the following equation for net present value. There, the p_t factors are the certainty equivalent factors in year t applicable to the cash flows in those respective years. The certainty equivalent factor q_n is applied to the terminal or salvage value of the investment in year n.

$$\text{NPV}_{\text{CE}} = -I_0 + \sum_{i=1}^{n} \frac{p_i \times C_i}{(1 + k)^i} + \frac{q_n \times T_n}{(1 + k)^n}$$

where $0 \le p_i \le 1$
and $0 \le q_n \le 1$
and NPV_{CE} is the certainty equivalent net present value.

Under this formulation the p_i can vary over time to reflect what is known about relevant business uncertainties. Ordinarily, uncertainties rise as years farther into the future are considered; thus $p_t > p_{t21}$. Recognizing that uncertainties can rise rapidly over time for most foreign investment projects, the reader should appreciate why many companies employ the payback period approach as a "shorthand" way of incorporating the risk dimension.

The certainty equivalent approach is most appropriate when applied to business (or credit) risks, since more is known about how specific projected events will impact the firm. However, one range of possible events, projected changes in foreign exchange rates and inflation differentials, is particularly complex and requires further discussion.

The international capital budgeting literature refers to changes in foreign exchange rates and inflation as "monetary" changes. The effects on the foreign subsidiary of these monetary factors is one important difference between international budgeting and its domestic counterpart. As indicated in Chapter 14, these monetary changes can exert impacts on company operations in two ways: through accounting exposures and through economic exposures. Thus proposed investment projects with such exposures may be affected by projected changes in exchange rates and inflation rates that in turn can have a significant impact on decisions to accept or reject proposed investments.

It is challenging for MNCs to account for the implications of monetary changes on financials of the project. The economic exposure dimension takes on special importance when significant monetary changes are projected. Adequately capturing the range of economic effects associated with foreign exchange and inflation changes is difficult. Estimating these effects presumes a reasonably high level of technical expertise in economics that frequently is not available in the thinly staffed foreign subsidiary within the typical MNC. It is usually at that level that subsidiary managers adjust the basic cash flow estimates to reflect the economic effects of monetary changes.

The adjustments for risk described to this point—adjustments to cash flows, the C_i—are best suited for dealing with business risk. In the case of country risk, however, analysts generally know far less about the timing of adverse events and how specific risk dimensions might impact the proposed project. Under these circumstances an alternative approach is to apply a risk premium to the firm's relevant discount rate, that is the cost of capital in the NPV analysis. The MNC should ideally apply this country risk factor in a systematic way across the countries for which investment projects are proposed. Thus many MNCs maintain at the corporate level a system for monitoring country risk and assigning country risk premiums for use in evaluating proposed international investment projects.

Another approach to incorporating risk and uncertainty elements in the capital budget process is the use of sensitivity analysis. Here analysts can systematically change key assumptions of the analysis to determine the effects on the evaluation measures: NPV, IRR, and PBP. This approach allows the MNC staff to see the effect on the proposed project of a continuum of change, for example, a 6% local currency (LC) depreciation, a 20% LC change, a 30% LC change, and so on. Projects whose evaluation measures stand up in the face of such changes, especially in foreign exchange rates and inflation rates, can be expected to have a greater probability of success in volatile foreign business environments.

A final approach to uncertainty has been proposed for managers who may not feel comfortable with the described methods of risk evaluation. Such executives may wish to place a greater emphasis on the payback method as an evaluative approach. This method, incomplete as it is from the standpoint of financial theory, does have the advantage of providing a concrete, cash-oriented measure of risk: how long the corporation's funds will be tied up in the project under consideration. Thus from a risk management standpoint we may prefer a project in Brazil with payback in 2.6 years to one with a PBP of 5 years in the same environment. With this "risk-bounding" interpretation, some MNCs use the PBP analysis as a constraint to be satisfied before accepting the project.*

INTERNATIONAL CAPITAL BUDGETING: AN EXAMPLE

Project Framework   The ABC Corporation, a U.S.-based MNC, is considering establishing a new subsidiary in the country of "Host." This nation is a member of the common market arrangement, the Archipelago Economic Community (the AEC) that is patterned after the European Economic Community. ABC produces a line of manufactured goods sold in nations throughout the world. The production

---

* James C. Van Horne, *Financial Management and Policy,* 10th ed. (New York: Prentice-Hall 1995): 150.

process for the company is proprietary and closely guarded. It has been determined that production costs do not increase significantly after a certain minimum scale of operations, and the proposed project for Host will have a scale well in excess of that minimum level.

ABC's industry follows a pattern of oligopoly behavior. This has resulted in considerable relative price stability within specific national markets over an extended period of time. A pattern of price stability also prevails in the input markets for ABC. The ABC Corporation is a relatively small participant in its industry in the United States, in the Host country, and worldwide. Thus ABC can change its sales levels in these markets without provoking reactive changes in price by rivals. These assumptions assure that ABC's relative price structure will not be affected by its decision to go forward with the proposed investment in the Host country.

The project in Host is expected to have an effective economic life between five years and ten years. The ABC management team that is charged with evaluating this project has chosen five years for its analysis. Thus the challenge to the management team is that of projecting cash flows relevant to this project and evaluating the resulting data to determine whether the proposed investment in Host meets the appropriate criteria for approval with ABC. It is assumed that all cash flows are estimated on a "certainty equivalent basis," incorporating the business risks of the proposed venture. The treatment of the country risk dimension is discussed further at a later point in the example. An estimate will be made of the project's salvage value in the fifth year. It is assumed in the analysis that the salvage value will be repatriated to the U.S. parent at that time. Finally the ABC team decided to focus first on developing a "base case." Following this, we undertake sensitivity analyses aimed at varying the project's macroeconomic assumptions to examine the resiliency of the proposed project to those changes. Throughout the analysis, the capital budgeting project evaluation is to proceed at two levels: U.S. dollars and local currency.

ABC has decided to consider locating in Host rather than serving the market via exports from its U.S. production facilities. This form of product flows configuration is applicable to a wide range of MNC manufacturing companies, for example, in pharmaceuticals and many nondurable consumer goods. Host government officials would like to increase the number of jobs in the local manufacturing industry and have encouraged the company to establish production facilities in Host. Host officials have extensive leverage over the ABC project, because the government requires that all products sold in this industry receive government approval. This requirement is justified within Host on the grounds that the approval process will preserve public safety. However, we cannot ignore the fact that the approval process is a powerful lever that the government can wield in influencing MNCs in this industry.

In addition to conforming to the Host government's requests, the ABC Corporation has its own rationale for wishing to locate in Host. By this action, the company can take advantage of the AEC common external tariff. This common external tariff system, unfortunately, has seriously discouraged exports to the AEC from the United States.

Macroeconomic Environment   The macroeconomic policies followed by the Host government have been quite different from those of the United States. These policies have resulted in rather rapid inflation in the Host, at a rate of 20% per annum, and this trend is expected to continue. In contrast inflation in the United States is projected over the planning period at the rate of 6% per annum.

The Host officials pursue a foreign exchange rate policy that maintains relative purchasing power parity between the Host currency, called Local Currency (or LC,

The Old Treasurer's dictum: "If you don't make it in local currency, you don't make it." Assistant Treasurer, International, for a major U.S.-based MNC.

for short), and the U.S. dollar. Thus the value of the LC has been falling at a rate equal to 14% per year (the Host inflation rate minus the U.S. inflation rate). It has been Host's experience that this crawling peg exchange rate policy has served to control destabilizing expectations that can arise under conditions of higher inflation.

The monetary and exchange rate policies in Host also are calibrated to hold real interest rates in the 2% range. Thus with a 20% rate of inflation in Host, LC money market interest rates are 22%, and this trend is projected to continue. Interest rates in the United States are estimated to be in the 10% range, implying a 4% real interest rate over the planning period.

For this example we assume that the foreign exchange rate ratio is initially: LC1 = $1. This exchange rate assumption, as we will see, greatly simplifies our analysis.

Focus on macroeconomic factors—relevant to most countries in Latin America, Africa, and Southeast Asia.

Business Assumptions   The managers in ABC's international division base their interest in investing in Host on their intuitive feeling of a favorable balance between revenues generated and costs incurred. To more concretely address the proposed Host investment, the ABC management team compiled information required for a formal capital budgeting analysis. Then, using a computer model developed for this purpose, the ABC team converted these data into income statements, investment summaries, and cash flow statements for the project in both LC and U.S. dollar terms. The underlying assumptions on which this analysis is based are now described.

INCOME STATEMENT: ABC-HOST

We find the income statement for ABC-Host in Exhibit 17.3.

- Sales Revenues (A1) and Marketing Expense (A5). The number of ABC units sold over the five-year planning period is multiplied by the LC price per unit expected in each year to derive sales revenues by year in LC terms. These are presented in the Income Statement for ABC-Host in Exhibit 17.3. With Host inflation running at 20% per year, the 30% annual gain in net sales reflects a projected 15% real gain per annum. Marketing expense is at a rate of 2% of sales throughout the period.
- Direct Materials and Labor (A2). These are variable cost items that are incurred by ABC's proposed Host subsidiary. These elements are assumed to rise in value over the period at a rate consistent with the rate of Host inflation.
- Manufacturing Period Costs (A3). These are fixed costs associated with manufacturing and are assumed at a rate of LC 1,800,000, during the period.

EXHIBIT 17.3	**Income Statement: ABC-Host (in LC 000s)**				
	Year 1	**Year 2**	**Year 3**	**Year 4**	**Year 5**
A1 Net Sales	10,954	14,788	19,964	26,951	36,384
A2 Direct Materials and Labor	7,000	8,400	10,080	12,096	14,515
A3 MFG Period Costs	1,800	1,800	1,800	1,800	1,800
A4 Depreciation	250	250	250	250	250
A5 Marketing Expense	219	296	399	539	728
A6 U.S. Royalty Expense	657	887	1,198	1,617	2,183
A7 Interest Expense	1,012	1,366	1,845	2,490	3,362
A8 Profit before Tax	16	1,788	4,392	8,159	13,546
A9 Income Tax to Host	2	268	659	1,224	2,032
A10 Net Income	13	1,520	3,733	6,935	11,514

- Capital Expenditures and Depreciation (A4). The proposed Host investment calls for an equity investment of $2.5 million that is used to finance fixed assets. These outlays are to be made at the beginning of the project. No other capital spending inputs are required during the five-year planning period. Depreciation of fixed investment is at a straight line rate of 10% per year.

- U.S. Royalty Expense (A6). The ABC Corporation has long followed the practice of charging its foreign subsidiaries for a significant share of the development cost of its proprietary technology. Experience has shown that these charges are 6% of net sales. Some nations levy taxes on royalty payments to the parent company; however, the Host government does not. The role of this cost item in the capital budgeting analysis is, from a financial statement standpoint, similar to the more complex case of a subsidiary importing a key input component from its U.S. parent.

- Financing Requirements and Interest Expense (A7). Total working capital is required for the planning period in a fixed ratio to underlying sales activity of .42. This conclusion is based on the company's historical analysis of patterns of days receivables, days raw materials, days finished goods, and days payables. Since the ABC parent company has provided equity financing for fixed assets, additional financing is required only for Total Working Capital. Some financing will be provided by Funds Generated/(Required) (B7). The remainder must be obtained as debt financing. Given that the proposed subsidiary will be purchasing primarily local inputs for production directed to the Host market, it was decided that the subsidiary's debt financing would be sourced from Host financial markets. Thus debt service payments will be in LC terms.

- Taxes (A9). Income earned in Host is subject to a 15% corporate income tax imposed by the Host government; the Host tax regulations do not permit tax-loss carry forwards. The U.S. authorities will grant a full tax credit for taxes paid to Host.

- Net Income (A10). The LC income statement incorporating the previous items shows that net income for this project is negative through year 1, thereafter registering positive numbers in a rising trend. The ABC senior management has chosen to remit as dividends 100% of the net income generated by the Host subsidiary.

CASH FLOW SUMMARY: ABC-HOST PERSPECTIVE

We find the cash flow summary for ABC-Host in Exhibit 17.4.

We can use the data described in Exhibit 17.4 to calculate cash flows, as opposed to income flows. For this analysis, depreciation is taken as augmenting ABC-Host's cash flows, since it produces a tax shield for income earned elsewhere in the ABC Corporation. The Host project's salvage value will also increase cash in the final year, assumed available on the last day of that fiscal year. Technical estimates suggest that the project's fixed assets will last somewhat longer than five years. Therefore it is likely that some salvage value can be realized by sale at the end of the five-year time period. It is assumed that no capital gains are realized on these assets.

The funds generated (required, when negative) by the project are presented in line B7 of Exhibit 17.4. The capital budgeting evaluation measures described earlier in this chapter can now be applied to these cash flows. This analysis will permit us to judge the desirability of the proposed project from the ABC-Host subsidiary's standpoint. The steps are presented in this table. On line B10 the net present value

EXHIBIT 17.4	**Cash Flow Summary: ABC-Host (in LC 000s)**					
	Year 0	Year 1	Year 2	Year 3	Year 4	Year 5
Requirements:						
B1 Capital Expenditure	2,500	0	0	0	0	0
B2 Working Capital: Additions	0	4,601	1,610	2,174	2,935	3,962
B3 Total Working Capital	0	4,601	6,211	8,385	11,319	15,281
FINANCE REQUIRED (B1 + B2)	2,500	4,601	1,610	2,174	2,935	3,962
Internal Sources:						
B4 Net Income		13	1,520	3,733	6,935	11,514
B5 Depreciation		250	250	250	250	250
B6 Salvage Value						2,500
Total Sources:	0	263	1,770	3,983	7,185	14,264
Funds Generated/(Required):						
B7 After Salvage Value	(2,500)	(4,337)	160	1,809	4,250	10,302
Net Present Value in LC Terms:						
B8 PV Factors at 22%	1.0000	0.8197	0.6719	0.5507	0.4514	0.3700
B9 PV Funds Gen./(Req.)	(2,500)	(3,555)	108	996	1,914	3,812
B10 Cumulative NPV	(2,500)	(6,055)	(5,947)	(4,951)	(3,032)	779
B11 IRR 26%						
B12 Payback Period 4+ years						
B13 PV Factors at 27%	1.0000	0.7874	0.6200	0.4882	0.3844	0.3027
B14 PV Funds Gen./(Req.)	(2,500)	(3,415)	66	883	1,634	3,115
B15 Cumulative NPV (27%)	(2,500)	(5,915)	(5,849)	(4,966)	(3,332)	(214)

of the project, evaluated at a discount rate of 22% is positive at LC 779,000. This discount rate is selected as applicable to ABC's local competitors operating in this industry in Host. However, when the NPV discount rate is raised by a 5% factor to reflect country risk elements at work within Host, the project's NPV falls to LC-214,000, which does not indicate support for this project. Based on the 22% discount factor, this project is marginally acceptable on a stand alone basis, that is, where the subsidiary in Host is not considered as part of ABC's business network worldwide.

This conclusion is also reached by using the internal rate of return evaluation approach. For this analysis the project's IRR is 26%, well above the 22% LC discount rate. However, when the hurdle discount rate is raised to account for country risk considerations, the IRR analysis does not support the proposed project in Host.

The payback period for the project is a little over four years in length. ABC-U.S. will have to be comfortable with a funds recovery period that is nearly as long as the life of the project.

Our discussion now shifts to evaluating the ABC-Host project from the more meaningful viewpoint of the decision makers who must ultimately approve the project—ABC's senior management. This perspective considers ABC-Host within the consolidated framework for ABC worldwide. One of the additional elements that enters our analysis at the consolidated level is the tax treatment accorded dividends reviewed by ABC-U.S. from the Host investment.

TAX TREATMENT OF INCOME RECEIVED BY ABC-U.S. FROM HOST

We find the analysis of tax liability in Exhibit 17.5. Corporate tax law in the United States has been developed to reduce problems of double taxation that U.S.-based multinationals encounter. One such problem involves income that U.S. parent companies receive from their foreign subsidiaries. This income is typically subject to

EXHIBIT 17.5	**U.S. Taxes Due on Income from ABC-Host (in US $000s)**					
	Year 0	Year 1	Year 2	Year 3	Year 4	Year 5
C1 Exchange Rate LC/$	1.00	1.14	1.30	1.48	1.69	1.93
Net Income ABC-Host in LC		13	1,520	3,733	6,935	11,514
C2 Equals Dividends: ABC-US		12	1,169	2,522	4,103	5,966
C3 Foreign Deemed Paid Tax		2	206	445	724	1,053
C4 Gross Dividends		14	1,376	2,968	4,828	7,019
C5 U.S. Income Tax before Foreign Tax Credit		5	468	1,009	1,641	2,386
C6 U.S. Income Tax after Foreign Tax Credit		3	261	564	917	1,334

income taxes and withholding taxes levied by foreign governments. It is to avoid double taxation of these income flows that the U.S. tax law has incorporated the "deemed-paid foreign tax credit." A U.S. corporation holding at least 10% of the voting power of a foreign corporation can claim this foreign tax credit.

The deemed-paid credit, introduced in Chapter 14, is best understood in terms of an illustrative computation using the ABC example. The Host country in this example is assumed to levy a 15% income tax on businesses such as the proposed ABC project. For simplicity Host is assumed not to apply a withholding tax to dividends paid to nonresidents. However, the reader should appreciate that withholding taxes are in wide use throughout the industrial and developing nations of the world.

The deemed-paid tax computation involves "grossing up" the dividend reported from the foreign subsidiary to include the amount of the tax paid to the Host government. This calculation is presented in Exhibit 17.5. In the ABC-Host example the reader will recall that the dividend payout ratio was 100%. Under this condition all of the income tax paid to the Host government can be applied toward the tax credit. Gross dividends are presented on line C4 as the sum of dividends to ABC-U.S. (Line C2) and Foreign Deemed-Paid Tax (Line C3) (the U.S. dollar value of income taxes paid in Host). The U.S. income tax rate is assumed at 34%, and the associated tax amount is listed on line C5. The "U.S. income tax after the Foreign Tax Credit" (Line C6) is calculated by subtracting the total creditable taxes (Line C3) from U.S. Income Tax before Foreign Tax Credit (Line C5).

CASH FLOW SUMMARY: ABC-U.S. CONSOLIDATED PERSPECTIVE

We find the cash flow analysis for ABC-U.S. in Exhibit 17.6. In reviewing the proposal for ABC's investment in Host, the most important question of the U.S. parent company's senior management is "what will be the effects of this project on ABC's consolidated financial position?" The effects of the project on ABC's consolidated cash flows from the subsidiary's perspective are presented in U.S. dollar terms in Line D2. To these must be added the payments by ABC-Host toward ABC's assigned U.S. royalty expense (Line D3). And from Exhibit 17.5 the U.S. income tax after foreign tax credit (Line C6) must be deducted. The resulting dollar cash flows (Line D5) will be the net effect of the proposed subsidiary on the ABC parent's consolidated position. These cash flows can now be subjected to evaluation using NPV, IRR, and payback period analyses.

Considering first the net present value analysis, we must recognize that since our cash flows are now denominated in U.S. dollars, the appropriate discount rate must be drawn from the parent company's financial environment. The discount rate selected for this analysis is the average cost of capital for ABC-U.S., currently at

EXHIBIT 17.6	**Cash Flow Summary: ABC-U.S. Consolidated (in US $ 000s)**					
		Year 0	**Year 1**	**Year 2**	**Year 3**	**Year 4**	**Year 5**

		Year 0	Year 1	Year 2	Year 3	Year 4	Year 5
D1	Exchange Rate LC/$	1.00	1.14	1.30	1.48	1.69	1.93
	Funds Gen./Req.)						
	after Salvage in LC	(2,500)	(4,337)	160	1,809	4,250	10,302
D2	Subsidiary: Funds						
	Gen./(Req.)	(2,500)	(3,805)	123	1,223	2,515	5,338
D3	U.S. Royalty	0	577	683	809	957	1,131
D4	U.S. Income Tax after						
	Foreign Tax Credit	0	3	261	564	917	1,334
D5	Funds Gen./(Req.)	(2,500)	(3,226)	1,067	2,596	4,389	7,803
	NET PRESENT VALUE IN U.S.$ TERMS-						
D6	PV Factors at 10%	1.0000	0.9091	0.8264	0.7513	0.6830	0.6209
D7	PV Funds Gen./(Req.)	(2,500)	(2,933)	882	1,950	2,998	4,845
D8	Cumulative NPV	(2,500)	(5,433)	(4,551)	(2,601)	397	5,242
D9	IRR 33%						
D10	Payback Period 4+ Years						

10%. Under this rate the NPV for the project is positive at $5,242,000. At the year 5 exchange rate LC/$, this NPV is several times higher than the comparable LC amount calculated from the "subsidiary's perspective" analysis. This higher NPV results primarily from the corporate allocations expense.

As in the "subsidiary's perspective" case, we can take country risk into account by incorporating the assigned 5% factor into the NPV discount rate. In this case the discount factor rises to 15%. Under this higher discount rate, the project's NPV falls to $3,597,000—still positive and relatively large. Thus from the consolidated perspective the company's managers can make a strong case for undertaking the proposed investment in ABC-Host, even though the project is marginal at best when the subsidiary is considered on a stand alone basis.

This same conclusion is arrived at from IRR analysis. Using that approach the project's IRR calculation yields a 33% rate. When comparing this IRR with the discount rate of 10%, we conclude that the project is attractive and should be undertaken.

Finally, as in the "subsidiary's perspective" analysis, the payback period is calculated at 4+ years. Again the corporation should expect to recover its initial investment only at a time point close to the end of the five-year time period.

SENSITIVITY ANALYSIS: VARYING INFLATION CONDITIONS

Throughout the capital budgeting analysis, the ABC-U.S. management team was quite concerned about the possibility of unstable macroeconomic conditions in Host. To resolve this issue, the group decided to apply the technique of sensitivity analysis. This analysis entails systematically varying the assumptions of the capital budgeting analysis and examining the associated effect of this variation on the capital budgeting evaluative measures.

Computer spreadsheet methodology allows "tests" of many assumptions using sensitivity analysis.

Since economic conditions in Host have varied greatly over the past several years, the team selected two extreme scenarios to compare with the base case presented in the previous section. The key assumptions for the analysis relate to inflation. Recall that the base case maintained an inflation rate in Host of 20%, compared to inflation in the U.S. of 6%. The LC discount rate in Host was 22%. Thus Host LC borrowers, such as ABC-Host, must pay a real (inflation adjusted) rate of interest of 2%. In contrast the 10% discount rate applicable for ABC in the United States implies a 4% real cost of funds.

The high inflation scenario called for Host inflation to occur during the planning period at a rate of 30% per annum. U.S. inflation and the real discount rates in both countries were assumed the same as in the base case. The (nominal) discount rate in Host was 32%. As in the base, case purchasing power parity was assumed. Accordingly the LC/$ exchange rate is required to rise in value by the differential between the Host and U.S. inflation rates, in this case 24% per annum.

Under the low inflation scenario the inflation rate in Host declines to become equal to that in the United States, or 6%. Real discount rates in both countries are assumed to be the same as in the base case. So, the relevant nominal interest rate in Host is 8%, while that in the United States is 10%. Purchasing power parity is maintained, and therefore there is no change in the LC/$ rate during the planning period.

Financial management can examine the results of the three scenarios—high inflation, base case, and low inflation—to gain insights into the impact of differential inflation rates on company operations. The theory suggests that inflation can have contradictory effects from inflation on company cash flows. If inflation had an identical effect on all income statement and balance sheet items for the proposed subsidiary, then the translation of these items from LC currency units to US$ currency units would be entirely neutral in effect under conditions of purchasing power parity. In fact, inflation does not generally affect income statement and balance sheet items in an equal way. There are two contradictory forces at work.

One force arises from a project's fixed costs that do not increase as inflation rises. In the ABC-Host example, such fixed components were depreciation and manufacturing period costs. When all income statement items including fixed cost lines are subsequently deflated by the exchange rates, the effect is to increase net income and net cash flows from the project in US$ terms.

A second and offsetting effect arises because rising inflation requires a more than proportional growth in the project's working capital needs. This growth results in raising cash requirements directly and indirectly in raising interest expense. This result occurs under the assumption that working capital is financed using short-term borrowing, for example, from commercial banks.

The importance of each of these effects will vary from project to project. The net of the effects will determine whether rising inflation will, on balance, improve or erode the viability of a given project.

In the case of the proposed ABC-Host investment, Exhibit 17.7 presents NPV, IRR, and PBP evaluation results in US$ terms and from the ABC-U.S. consolidated perspective. The NPV measure for Exhibit 17.7 is calculated using as the discount rate the ABC-U.S.'s average cost of capital not adjusted for country risk.

The outcome of this investigation for the ABC project indicates the dominance of cash-using forces as the inflation rate rises. Both the NPV and the IRR move

EXHIBIT 17.7	**Sensitivity Analysis: Inflation ABC-U.S. Viewpoint**		
Host Inflation	**NPV**	**IRR in $**	**PBP**
6%	$12,952,000	60%	3+ years
20%	$ 5,242,000	33%	4+ years
30%	$ 1,343,000	17%	4+ years

progressively lower as inflation rises. In contrast the PBP measure shows little sensitivity to rising inflation. From the NPV and IRR criteria, under the 6% and the 20% inflation rates, the project from the perspective of ABC-U.S. is resoundingly supported at the selected discount rate of 10%.

In all three inflation scenarios, the project is supported by the NPV and IRR criteria. However, there is a marked decline in the project's viability as inflation moves from lower to higher rates. Given this demonstrated sensitivity, if company decision makers were concerned about a significant acceleration of inflation, they may wish to not proceed with this project. This outcome would be reinforced, should the company use a higher discount rate to reflect country risk considerations.

SUMMARY

The capital budgeting example that we have dealt with in this chapter takes place in a mythical country called Host. This country has been relatively free of market imperfections and arbitrary government actions. However in the real world many countries—particularly among the developing nations—are not so free market oriented. Many countries offer inducements to attract foreign direct investment in order to secure the benefits of these projects, jobs and work skills, for their citizens. One way this investment can be secured is through offering the MNC tax incentives such as the reduction or elimination of tax obligations for an agreed period of years. Another approach is to offer project-specific financing at subsidized or below-market interest rates. One study that illustrates this approach and the benefits that a plant location can bring to the host country was undertaken by Gordon and Lees. This study focuses on a major investment in the state of Pennsylvania by Volkswagen of America. In terms of capital budgeting analysis, the preferred way to handle subsidies is to add the subsidy effects to annual cash flows for the years in which the relevant subsidies are applicable. Under this approach, the relevant discount rate for the U.S. dollar analysis would remain the parent's weighted average cost of capital.

At a less favorable level, governments—particularly in cases of severe balance of payments problems—also have been known to limit the ability of foreign direct investors to transfer funds out of the country. Thus dividends to the parent and other funds transfers may be prohibited. This circumstance known as blocked funds was prevalent among the nations of Latin America and Africa during the international debt crisis of the 1980s. From an historical perspective, blocked funds situations are almost never permanent. Such restrictions on funds movements are usually eased as the nation's balance of payments position improves. Nevertheless the senior management of multinational companies almost always views blocked funds constraints as serious impediments to investment. If there is a probability of blocked funds for a specific MNC investment, the implications of that circumstance for the project's viability can be examined by employing the assumptions appropriate to this scenario. In most cases the blocked funds impose opportunity losses on the MNC. The cash flows from the proposed project can be reduced by these opportunity losses to determine the impact that such blocking might have on the project's viability.

The final real-world complication relates to the difficulty in estimating a project's salvage value. For example in the ABC-Host illustration presented earlier in the chapter, the salvage value of the project played a critical role in the project's viability. If that salvage value had not been taken into account (that is, held at zero), the project's NPV in both LC and U.S. dollars would have been negative.

The estimation of salvage values is, at best, an imperfect art. There are no well-developed markets for used, specialized manufacturing and office equipment. Estimating real property values is somewhat easier, but is still subject to wide variation in expert opinion. One approach to soften this problem is to undertake the capital budgeting analysis under high best guess, and low values for salvage. This form of sensitivity analysis will reveal how vulnerable the project is to this critical project dimension.

REVIEW QUESTIONS

1. How does international capital budgeting differ from that focused on domestic projects?
2. Why are approvals of major capital expenditures required at several levels within the MNC?
3. How might foreign project cash flows differ from parent company cash flows?
4. A U.S. company is evaluating an investment project in the United Kingdom. The expected useful life of the investment is ten years, $20 million will be invested, and annual cash flows are projected at $5 million after tax (dividends with which the U.S. foreign tax credit will not be subject to any additional taxation in the United States). The parent company discount rate on such projects is 18%. What is the net present value? There is no liquidation value of the project at the end of ten years.
5. In the same situation as in the previous question, what is the payback period? What is the IRR?
6. It has been suggested that an MNC can diversify its international investments, so that local (country) risks play an unimportant role. Under what conditions may this viewpoint be valid or invalid?
7. How might each of the following affect country risk evaluation:
    a. Persistently high rate of inflation
    b. Export instability
    c. Diversified industrial base
    d. Government dominated by military
8. Why might the discount rate applied to local currency (project) cash flows be different from the discount rate applied to parent cash flows?

CASE 1

Calculating NPV for Investment in a Philippines Hotel

Pacrim, a Hong Kong-based property development and hotel management company is considering investing in a new hotel in the Philippines. The initial investment required is $HK 80 million, or Phil peso 240 million (current exchange rate of Phil peso 3/$HK). Profits for the initial five-year period will be reinvested. At the end of this five-year period, Pacrim expects to sell the hotel property for Phil peso 700 million. It is projected that the exchange rate at that time will be Phil peso 3.5/$HK.

1. Calculate the NPV in Hong Kong dollars, assuming the present exchange rate is correct, and that Pacrim uses a discount rate of 14%.
2. Apply a sensitivity analysis using alternative exchange rates of 3.2, 3.7 and 4.0 pesos per $HK.

CASE 2

Multicon International

The Multicon International Corporation, a U.S-based multinational, has been invited by the government of Thailand to open a toy manufacturing operation. Multicon has successfully exported its toy sets to the Thai market for a number of years. If Multicon makes the investment, the company will be allowed to operate the plant for five years and then must sell the building and equipment to Thai investors at *net book value* at the time of sale *plus the current amount of any working capital*. Multicon will be allowed to *repatriate all net income and depreciation funds to the United States each year.*

Multicon's anticipated outlay in 1998 would be as follows:

Building and equipment	$1,000,000
Working capital	$1,000,000
Total	$2,000,000

Thai depreciation and investment recovery will allow the building and equipment to be depreciated over five years on a straight-line basis. At the end of the fifth year, the $1,000,000 of working capital may also be repatriated to the United States, as may be the remaining net book value of the plant.

Sales price. Locally assembled toy sets will be sold for the Thai baht equivalent of $60 each.

Operating expenses per toy set.	
Materials purchased in Thailand (dollar amount of baht cost)	$20 per set
Raw materials imported from U.S. parent	$10 per set
Variable costs per toy set	$30 per set

The $10 transfer price per set for raw materials sold by Multicon to its Thai subsidiary consists of $5 of direct costs incurred in the United States and $5 of pretax profit to Multicon. There are no other operating costs in either Thailand or the United States. Taxes. Both Thailand and the United States have a corporate income tax rate of 40%.

Cost of capital. Multicon uses a 15% discount rate to evaluate all domestic and foreign projects.

Assume the investment is made at the end of 1998 and all operating cash flows occur at the end of 1999 through 2003. Inflation in Thailand has been proceeding at the rate of 25 percent per year; inflation in the U.S., 5 percent per year. These inflation trends are expected to continue for the foreseeable future. The Thai baht is adjusted monthly to maintain purchasing power parity with the U.S. dollar.

As a management consultant to Multicon, what issues do you identify as relevant to this proposal? As with any case, you may have to introduce additional assumptions to your analysis. What do you recommend to Multicon's management?

SELECTED BIBLIOGRAPHY

Baker, James C. "Capital Budgeting in American and European Companies." *Mid-Atlantic Journal of Business,* Vol. 22, No. 2, (Summer 1984): 15–28.

Baker, James C., and Laurence J. Beardsley. "Multinational Companies' Use of Risk Evaluation and Profit Measurement for Capital Budgeting Decisions." *Journal of Business Finance,* Vol. 5, No. 1, (Spring 1973): 38–43.

Bavishi, Vinod B. "Capital Budgeting Practices at Multinationals." *Management Accounting,* (August 1981): 32–35.

Booth, Lawrence D. "Capital Budgeting Frameworks for the Multinational Corporation." *Journal of International Business Studies,* (Fall 1982): 113–123.

Caves, Richard E. *Multinational Enterprises and Economic Analysis,* Cambridge (England): Cambridge University Press, 1996.

Cheng, C.S. Agnes. "The Applicability and Usage of NPV and IRR Capital Budgeting Techniques." *Managerial Finance,* Vol. 20, No. 7, (1994): 10–36.

Dotan, Amihud, and Arie Ovadia. "A Capital Budgeting Decision—The Case of a Multinational Corporation Operating in High-Inflation Countries." *Journal of Business Research,* (October 1986): 403–410.

Freeman, Mark. "Capital Budgeting: Theory Versus Practice." *Australian Accountant,* Vol. 61, No. 8, (September 1991): 36–41.

Goddard, Scott. "Political Risk in International Capital Budgeting." *Managerial Finance,* Vol. 16, No. 2, (1990): 7–12.

Gordon, Sara L., and Francis A. Lees. "Multinational Capital Budgeting: Foreign Investment under Subsidy." *California Management Review,* (Fall 1982): 22–32.

Holland, John. "Capital Budgeting for International Business: A Framework for Analysis." *Managerial Finance,* Vol. 16, No. 2, (1990): 1–6.

Kelly, Marie E. Wicks, and George C. Philippatos. "Comparative Analysis of the Foreign Investment Evaluation Practices by U.S.-Based Manufacturing Multinational Corporations." *Journal of International Business Studies,* (Winter 1982): 19–42.

Kim, Suk, Edward Farragher and Trevor Crick. "Foreign Capital Budgeting Practice Used in the U.S. and Non-U.S. Multinational Companies." *The Engineering Economist,* (Spring 1984): 207–215.

Lessard, Donald R. "Evaluating International Projects: An Adjusted Present Value Approach." in Crum and Derkindern (eds). *Capital Budgeting under Conditions of Uncertainty.* Martinus Nijhoff Publishing, 1981: 118–137.

Oblak, David J., and Roy J. Helm, Jr. "Survey and Analysis of Capital Budgeting Methods Used by Multinationals." *Financial Management,* (Winter 1980): 37–41.

Rugman, Alan M. "Strategic Capital Budgeting, Decisions and the Theory of Internalization." *Managerial Finance,* Vol. 16, No. 2, (1990): 17–24.

Rusth, Douglas. "The Budgeting Process of a Multinational Firm." *Multinational Business Review,* Vol. 2, No. 2, (Fall 1994): 59–63.

Stanley, Marjorie, and Stanley Block. "An Empirical Study of Management and Financial Variables Influencing Capital Budgeting Decision for Multinational Corporations in the 1980s." *Management International Review,* Vol. 23, No. 3, (1983): 61–71.

Stonehill, Arthur, and Leonard Nathanson. "Capital Budgeting and the Multinational Corporation." *California Management Review,* (Summer 1968): 38–54.

Thomadakis, Stavros. "Foreign Project Financing in Segmented Capital Markets: Equity Versus Debt." *Financial Management,* Vol. 20, No. 4, (Winter 1991): 42–53.

Van Horne, James C. *Financial Management and Policy.* 10th ed., Englewood Cliffs, N.J: Prentice Hall, 1995.

Wilson, Mark. "Empirical Evidence of the Use of a Framework of Risk and Return in Capital Budgeting for Foreign Direct Investment." *Managerial Finance,* Vol. 16, No. 2, (1990): 25–34.

PART FIVE

International
Portfolio Management

*I*n Part V we analyze the opportunities for cross-border portfolio investment in the leading stock and bond markets around the world, as well as in the stock and bond markets of the emerging countries. We consider incentives and obstacles to portfolio investment in detail. International capital asset pricing is analyzed with respect to how cross-border investment influences asset prices. Leading theoretical contributions supporting international diversification are analyzed. Individual and institutional investor management is described from the point of view of the instruments utilized and various strategy approaches.

ENVIRONMENT OF GLOBAL FINANCE

INTERNATIONAL FINANCIAL MARKETS

INTERNATIONAL BANKING

INTERNATIONAL CORPORATE FINANCE

INTERNATIONAL PORTFOLIO MANAGEMENT

CHAPTER 18

International Investment and Capital Markets

INTRODUCTION

In this chapter we consider the major capital market sectors that international investors can use. Our focus for this discussion will be on the leading stock and bond markets, as well as the emerging stock and bond markets. We begin by examining the strong growth in international portfolio investment since the mid-1970s and the reasons for this growth.

LEARNING OBJECTIVES IN THIS CHAPTER

1. To develop an overview of the historical, regulatory, economic, political, and other factors that promote and constrain international portfolio investment activity of institutional and individual investors.
2. To comprehend the differences and similarities between the leading stock markets because they affect the opportunities and costs of participating in these markets.
3. To appreciate the dynamic changes taking place in the world's stock and bond markets in recent years and how these changes impact investor opportunities and activities.
4. To understand the role and importance of the leading bond markets, the important differences between currency segments of these markets, and the rationale for bond investing.
5. To develop an understanding of the role and status of the emerging bond and stock markets and the chief characteristics that affect their use by international investors.

KEY TERMS AND CONCEPTS

- accounting standards
- bearer shares
- Big Bang
- bolsa
- capitalization
- emerging markets

- foreign listing
- International Stock Exchange
- Kursmakler
- liquidity
- portfolio suppression

- registered shares
- segmented markets
- transparency
- universal banks

ACRONYMS

ADR	American Depository Receipt	**IFC**	International Finance Corporation
CATS	Computer Assisted Trading System	**SEAQ**	Stock Exchange Automated Quotation System
CONSOB	Commissione Nazionale per la Societa e la Borsa	**SIB**	Securities and Investments Board
FIRB	Foreign Investment Review Board	**SICAV**	Sociétés d'Investissement à Capital Variable
GAAP	Generally Accepted Accounting Principles	**SRO**	Self Regulatory Organization
IASC	International Accounting Standards Committee	**TSE**	Tokyo Stock Exchange

Segmented or Integrated Markets

One of the questions that arises at the outset of a discussion concerning international portfolio investment is the extent to which the global capital markets are segmented or integrated. Various writers have attempted to focus on this question. It is our view that the most practical approach to this question is to consider these capital markets as follows:

1. Strong linkages have developed between the three largest equity markets (United States, Japan, and United Kingdom), but these links do not necessarily mean that these markets are fully integrated. Currency rate changes between the dollar, sterling, and yen can be substantial. At best the stock markets of these three countries are partially integrated.

2. The leading bond markets display strong independent performance and variability due to the tendency for interest rates in national capital markets to move according to domestic trends and external forces. Large and persistent balance of payments disequilibria have required that countries experiencing these disequilibrium positions apply opposite pressures to their money and interest rate mechanisms to accommodate these disequilibria (e.g., over the period 1986–1991 it was necessary that U.S. interest rates be substantially higher than interest rates in West Germany and Japan, due in part to U.S. payments deficits and German and Japanese payments surpluses).

3. Over the period 1981–1990, leading bond markets experienced a tendency for convergence. As a result, yields on bonds in leading countries (United States, United Kingdom, Germany, France, Japan, and Canada) began to exhibit more

parallel movements. Forces leading to this integration of bond markets include 1) expanded role of Eurobond new issue and secondary trading, 2) governments encouraging foreign borrowers, 3) cross-border investing by financial institutions, and 4) development of new financial instruments such as the global bond (first issued by the World Bank, and subsequently by companies such as Matsushita).

4. Intermittent shocks have slowed or even reversed these integrative forces. These shocks include the unification of Germany, the breakup of the former Soviet Union, the September 1992 crisis in the European Exchange Rate Mechanism leading to the exit of several currencies (pound sterling) from the fixed rate arrangement, the August 1993 widening to 15% of allowed currency rate variations in the European Monetary System, and the December 1994 devaluation and float of the Mexican peso.

5. Some industrial country stock markets are only at the early stages of becoming integrated into any type of world equity market.

6. As long as major nations of the world rely on floating currencies to provide adjustment to their respective balance of payments positions, currency rate movements will be large and difficult to forecast, and capital markets will demonstrate independent behavior.

Emerging markets

Stock and bond markets of developing and transitional economies.

7. There has been a tendency for the emerging stock and bond markets to become more closely integrated into a world stock market system. Nevertheless, some of the countries in which these markets are located still limit foreign investor participation.

8. The growing importance of multinational companies suggests that they can provide an integrating force in the world's capital markets. However, MNCs do not in any way directly reduce or level down currency instability, trade barriers, or obstacles to foreign investment. If they merely "exploit environmental differences," these differences will persist and may prove to be obstacles to increased capital market integration.

Historical Overview of Portfolio Investment

PAST RECORD

International portfolio investment is not a new invention of the past 25 years. It has been going on for many centuries. If we were to compare the nineteenth and twentieth centuries (the latter up to 1975) on the basis of the relative importance of international portfolio investment, we would give a slight edge to the nineteenth century during which time this type of activity was more important. At that time, British and other European portfolio investment around the world represented a dominant aspect of global capital flows. Portfolio investment dominated foreign direct investment, in large part because the multinational corporation is more a creature of the twentieth century. In the 1800s London served as a world center for international bond issues, and British bankers and investment trusts dominated world finance as much as U.S.-based financial markets and institutions have since World War II.

International portfolio investment reached its zenith in the final days of British world financial hegemony immediately prior to World War I, when outward capital flows from Britain were equal to 7% of national income. The United States made a bid to establish itself as a major force in the 1920s, and a total of $12.8 billion in foreign loans was underwritten in New York over the period 1919–1929.[*] Unfortunately, the American experience was imperfect; poor loans were made, foreign lending fell precipitously after 1929, and many of these loans went into default.

After World War II the recovery of foreign lending and foreign bond issues was slow, in part due to the memory of past losses. Nevertheless, by 1959 annual foreign bond issues in New York exceeded $4.3 billion.[†] A renewed interest in foreign bond issues in 1960–1963 in New York coincided with a moderate deterioration in the U.S. balance of payments. Enactment of the Interest Equalization Tax (IET) in 1964 effectively closed New York from any significant amount of international portfolio investment until 1974, when the petrodollar crisis caused the American government to reopen the U.S. capital market to foreign issues. In the period since 1974, U.S. participation in international portfolio investment has intensified.

EVIDENCE OF RECENT GROWTH

On a global basis we might consider the decade of the 1980s as the "reawakening" in international portfolio investment. This decade stands out in terms of the increased activity in this area from a global perspective as well as from a United States perspective.

Evidence abounds on this point. On the American side institutional investors have moved strongly in the direction of internationally diversifying their common stock portfolios. In 1979 U.S. pension funds held less than 1% of their equity portfolios in foreign issues. By 1990 pension funds held 5–6% of their equity portfolios in foreign issues and this activity continues to expand in the 1990s. Similarly, individual investors have aggressively shifted into international and global mutual funds. Non-U.S. companies have cross-listed their share issues on the New York Stock Exchange and American Stock Exchange. In addition American Depository Receipts (ADRs) have been issued in New York for well over 1200 foreign equity issues. In 1996 non-U.S. companies raised $19.4 billion through 154 ADR offerings, representing a 50% increase from the number of offerings in 1995, and a 62% increase in dollars raised. Since 1983 more than four dozen closed end funds (mostly single country funds) have been listed on the stock exchanges in the United States.

Outside the United States the increased focus on international portfolio investment has been equally impressive. The stock exchanges in Europe, Japan, Canada, and elsewhere have been aggressive in modernizing their trading facilities. This modernization has included moving to flexible commissions, introducing derivative trading instruments (swaps, futures, and options), providing computerized information and trading, and extending trading hours and international linkages.

Similarly, multinational corporations have sought to list their securities on a number of national stock markets. Some multinational companies have also distributed blocs of shares in their overseas subsidiaries to local investors (in Brazil, Singapore, and other host countries).

American Depository Receipts

Issued in American stock market to represent foreign underlying shares traded on foreign stock exchange.

---

[*] Mikesell, Raymond F. *U.S. Private and Government Investment Abroad.* Eugene, OR: University of Oregon, (1962): 40.

[†] Mikesell, Raymond F. op.cit., p. 56.

Reasons for Growth

The rapid growth in international portfolio investment of the 1980s comes as a result of a number of factors:

Deregulation of Financial Markets In 1979 Britain abandoned the exchange controls that had been operative for several decades. Previously British portfolio investors had been restricted in their foreign investment activities to using the so-called "investment dollar" market. This market was a special window in the foreign exchange market where British investors liquidating foreign investments were required to sell investment dollars, and where British investors seeking to expand foreign investment were required to purchase investment dollars. Since 1979 London has prospered as a center for European portfolio investment activity, and British investors have been free to undertake outward portfolio investment through the mechanism of the unrestricted foreign exchange market in London. Similarly, Japan has liberalized outward capital flows of institutional investors to recycle dollars earned from a large trade surplus.

Desire of Institutional Investors to Improve Performance Institutional investors (pension funds and insurance companies) have been on the leading edge in the resurgence of international portfolio investment. This position has been prompted by concerns over improving portfolio return, as well as enhancing the diversification of risks.

Shift to Floating Currency Basis for Major Currencies Since 1975 the wide swings in currency rates have attracted the attention of portfolio investors and fund managers, who see additional opportunities from the point of view of enhanced returns and diversification of risk.

Growing Academic Literature on the Subject The academic literature concerning international diversification and portfolio theory has been incorporated into the strategies of portfolio management. This literature is reviewed in Chapters 19 and 20, beginning with the work of Harry Markowitz concerning efficient portfolios.

Modernization and Increased Competitiveness of Stock Exchanges In 1975 the NYSE switched from fixed commissions on securities transactions to flexible commissions. This switch brought on a steadily intensifying competition among and between U.S. stock exchanges, and between U.S. and foreign stock exchanges, to attract listing and trading activity. These forces led to the "Big Bang" in London, where the old London Stock Exchange was transformed into the more modern International Stock Exchange. Following the Big Bang the European continental exchanges have been modernizing to recapture security trading business that has traditionally flowed to London. The Madrid Stock Exchange experienced its "Big Bang" in July 1989 (see Exhibit 18.1).

Big Bang
Deregulation of stock exchange, allowing increased competition and market efficiency.

Expanded Pool of Liquidity Growth of the Eurocurrency market and national money markets has expanded the international pool of liquidity available to international investors. This expansion permits ready financing of portfolio investment and also provides a money market alternative to international stock and bond investments.

EXHIBIT 18.1	**Spain Braces Itself for Big Bang**

After nearly 160 years of virtually unchanged trading practices, 28 July 1989 was the last day that Spain's *Agentes de Cambio y Bolsa,* the licensed notaries who have a trading monopoly, traded on the floors of the bolsas of Madrid, Barcelona, Valencia, and Bilbao, as well as conduct as individual trades. This was Spain's Big Bang, the most sweeping financial market reform since the death of General Franco in 1975. After July 28th the *agentes* became limited companies. Most of the 51 new brokers and agents operating on the bolsas found powerful new domestic and foreign partners to back their operations.

In the short period of six weeks the stock exchanges underwent a complete transformation with new switchboards, desks on the floor, kiosks, telephones, and codes.

Reforms agreed upon by the Spanish Parliament have two aims to make the markets more transparent and to develop them as a source of long-term capital for industry. Individual investors conduct over half the stock market trading. A larger share of institutional investment is needed to compete against bank lenders and to provide an alternative to loan finance. Foreign investors account for nearly one-fourth of the trading volume in Spain. Many foreign investors have not participated in the Spanish market due to the lack of transparency.

Officials at the Madrid stock exchange assert that specific changes are necessary in the manner by which stock trading takes place. First, continuous trading on computers must replace ten-minute floor sessions to facilitate efficient movement of transactions. Second, turnover must increase to assure that investors will have liquidity. Finally, a streamlined settlements system must be made operative. The four Spanish stock exchanges have three months to connect up with each other electronically.

EXHIBIT 18.2	**Gazprom Share Offer**

Gazprom announced in October 1996 international offering of up to 9% of its shares. The Russian energy company holds hydrocarbon reserves equivalent to one-fifth the world's total, greater than Shell and Exxon combined. The over-the-counter market in Moscow, which is highly illiquid, values Gazprom, Russia's largest company, at about $4 billion. Western bankers value the gas group in the range of $26–200 billion.

The offering is the largest since the country cast off communism in 1991. Until 1996 the $230 million share issue by Lukoil held the record as the largest in Russia. The Gazprom issue consists of depositary shares through the Bank of New York. In 1995 there was speculation that a West European energy company such as Gaz de France might take a lead or managing investment position in Gazprom, but the risks of investing in the Russian conglomerate in the months leading to President Yeltsin's reelection probably appeared to be more than Western industrial companies wished to assume.

Appearance of Large Payments Deficits and Surpluses   Industrial countries have experienced large and intractable payments surpluses and deficits. These large shifts in financial position have induced governments to develop policies that "recycle" foreign exchange in a manner that would help finance or accommodate the large deficits and surpluses. As a result countries with large surpluses (or deficits) on trade have incurred large deficits (or surpluses) on capital account.

Privatization   During the decade of the 1990s privatization has spread from industrial to emerging market countries. Privatization widens the range of securities available for foreign investors in the country that carries out this process, and contributes to the growing depth and efficiency of the local capital market (See Exhibit 18.2).

Economic Opening and Increased Marketization   A number of countries have opened their economies and financial systems to foreign participation and competition. Over the past decade many Latin American and East European countries especially have initiated opening and marketization polices to increase productive efficiency and ultimately to attract foreign investors.

OBSTACLES TO FOREIGN INVESTMENT

International portfolio investment has expanded despite the many resistances that exist. At least four basic factors have operated to serve as obstacles to foreign investment. These include differences in risk and risk perception, differences in market mechanisms, differences in availability and quality of information concerning foreign investment opportunities, and differences in accounting standards.

Differences in Risk and Risk Perceptions   Is it really more risky to invest in foreign stock and bond markets than in domestic markets? To answer this question we must consider whether additional risks in international investment relate to degree of risk, qualitative factors, and/or investor perceptions. Investor perceptions often can be based on a fuzzy understanding of the nature of investor risk, and to lack of information concerning the conditions under which foreign investing takes place. In part concern over being exposed to higher risk in international investing may be due to perceptions that in turn can be attributed to lack of knowledge and understanding.

Notwithstanding, international portfolio investors can be exposed to political risks not present in domestic investment. A clear illustration of this political risk would be the sharp decline in the Hong Kong stock market in May-June 1989 that resulted from the Beijing student demonstrations, the government massacre of students at Tiananmen Square, and subsequent reprisals of the Chinese government against demonstrators.

Investors can also be subjected to currency risk. The decline of the pound sterling early in 1989 is illustrative of currency risk. The decline in sterling accompanied an upswing in the London stock market of almost equal magnitude. International investors are always at risk with respect to the possibility of adverse currency movements.

Concern over business and economic risks also can operate as an inhibiting factor against international investment. Property development cycles in Hong Kong and Singapore have added to the complex issue of risk analysis for investors focusing on these two markets. Business recession and slow economic growth in LDC debtor countries (Argentina, Brazil, Mexico, and Philippines) subsequent to the debt crisis of 1982, made investments in these capital market sectors subject to increased risks.

Finally, liquidity risk can be a problem in certain stock and bond markets. Some markets have smaller turnover, and investors can be exposed to a "drying up" of the market that can make it more difficult and more costly to liquidate their holdings under adverse market conditions.

Differences in Market Mechanisms   National stock market mechanisms differ from one another in a number of ways. These differences can operate as obstacles to cross-border investment.

In the previous section we noted that some capital markets lack liquidity. Added to this problem is the fact that daily trading activity in many stock markets is concentrated in the shares of a few large firms. For example, in Italy approximately 220 firms' shares are listed on the Milan Stock Exchange, but only two dozen of these are traded actively on a daily basis. One of these, Fiat, may account for as much as a fifth of total transaction volume on a given day. Similar concentrations of trading in one or several share issues take place in Brussels, Amsterdam, and Oslo. This concentration of trading volume causes foreign investors to remain less interested in these markets. In part this lack of interest is due to concern over limited liquidity, but also due to the belief that the pricing mechanism may be imperfect in cases of thinly traded shares.

A related problem exists where the stock exchange does not have a trading monopoly. In such cases off-exchange trading takes place, thus narrowing the base of exchange trading. This situation exists in Italy and Germany, where banks play an important role in securities dealing, and where off-exchange trading is permitted.

Provisions for settlement of transactions also differ from one market to another. In some cases settlement can take place many days after the trading date, causing day-to-day patterns of stock returns. This occurrence is referred to as one of the anomalies of stock price behavior yielding "seasonal" price patterns (on the London and Helsinki stock exchanges).*

Transaction costs also can serve as obstacles to international investment. This obstacle is especially the case where fixed commissions prevail, and where transfer taxes and other taxes are levied on securities trading. Finally, government regulation can serve as an obstacle to international investment. Some countries limit the extent of foreign investment in the shares of domestic companies (Thailand and Malaysia), or have restrictive rules or limitations (Taiwan and Korea).

Differences in Availability and Quality of Data   An investor must have access to appropriate information on a timely basis to deal with the complexity and dynamics of international investment. To monitor overseas stock markets, an investor needs a broad-based database containing information on economic factors, markets, and individual securities. Probably the most important requirement is that information should be updated frequently—preferably on a daily basis.

National financial markets differ in the extent to which information is generated and distributed. The three largest markets (New York, London, and Tokyo) lead all others in the volume and variety of information concerning portfolio investment opportunities. After these three markets, there exist wide differences in the volume, reliability, and speed at which information concerning portfolio investment opportunities is provided.

Differences in Foreign Versus U.S. Accounting Standards   Accounting standards and principles vary from country to country. Some countries such as Italy require companies to conform closely to local income tax laws in the preparation of their financial statements. Other countries, such as Brazil and the Netherlands, require companies to make greater use of general price level adjustments and current costs than is permitted under America's generally accepted accounting principles (GAAP).

There are many reasons for the lack of uniformity in accounting standards. These include:

1. lack of agreement on the objectives of financial statements;
2. different requirements under the company laws enacted by individual nations;
3. the influence of tax laws and differential tax systems; and

---

* Hawawini, G. *European Equity Markets: Price Behavior and Efficiency.* New York: New York University, Salomon Center, (1984): 137–143.

4. differences in the strengths and development of local professional accounting bodies in each country.

When U.S. companies consolidate financial statements that include the results of their foreign operating units, these statements are prepared in conformity with American GAAP. This regulation makes it necessary for U.S. companies to make adjustments to the original accounts of foreign units in order to bring these statements into conformity with American accounting standards.

Lack of uniform international accounting standards poses a major problem for international investors. Often the financial statements of companies located in different countries are not directly comparable. Exhibit 18.3 outlines some of the

EXHIBIT 18.3		Leading Accounting Problems Facing Cross-Border Investors
Category		**Description of Problem**
I. International Accounting Standards	1.	The lack of uniform international accounting standards greatly diminishes the usefulness of financial statements statements to users in countries other than the country on whose the accounting standards are based.
IA. Consolidation Practices	1.	The consolidation practices of groups of companies having international operations vary from one group to another, and groups headquartred in some countries do not consolidate at all.
IB. Disclosures	1.	Financial reporting and disclosure standards in many information areas are not uniform and in many countries they are inadequate. The information areas of concern include: revenue recognition, segment reporting, business combinations, research and development activities, and effects of changing prices.
II. Exchange Rate and Transaction Accounting	1.	Too many translation approaches now in existence around the world.
	2.	In a world of shifting exchange rates it is difficult to measure the economic effect of exchange rate changes on a particular company having dealings with foreign affiliates or other foreign operations, or the net effect of these rate changes on a system of interrelated companies in different countries.
	3.	In some cases the swings in the parities of currencies are unrelated to the operations of affiliated companies in those countries experiencing exchange rate changes.
III. International Auditing	1.	An auditor's report may not be easily or properly interpreted by readers in another country because it is prepared on the basis of the auditing standards and accounting terminology of another country.
	2.	It is difficult to determine the extent and competency of auditing performed by an auditor in another country, in part because of differing experience and admissions requirements for auditors.
IV. Accounting for Inflation	1.	Different rates and structural characteristics of inflation in different countries make it difficult to achieve comparability of financial status and results among companies in different countries for external financial reporting.
	2.	Lack of uniformity in approaches for inflation accounting hampers comparability among unrelated companies.

SOURCE: Smith, C.H., and H. Shalchi. "Multinational Accounting: Some Methodological Consideration," in F. Choi (ed). *Multinational Accounting: Research Framework*. Ann Arbor: UMI Research Press, 1981.

leading accounting problems facing cross-border investors. In the long run accountants hope that the International Accounting Standards Committee (IASC) will bring about a solution to this problem. This committee seeks to develop international accounting standards, and its members include the professional accounting associations of more than 40 countries. The IASC's ultimate goal—wide use of an international set of accounting standards—would contribute significantly to the efficient allocation of scarce resources throughout the world.

The United Nations Center on Transnational Corporations (UNCTC) has studied the financial reporting of multinational companies (the term transnational is equivalent to multinational). Price Waterhouse conducted a survey for the UNCTC, the results of which were published in 1991. Some 194 transnational corporations and other enterprises from 23 countries were selected. Financial statements from 1987 and 1988 were examined. Some of the results from this survey are included, along with findings from a similar study in Tonkin's *World Survey of Published Accounts*.

The results of these two studies are similar. Most corporations publish consolidated financial statements but often do not identify their main affiliates. These enterprises often do not include all their subsidiaries when consolidating. Tonkin notes that enterprises from the Federal Republic of Germany consolidate only domestic companies. Enterprises are also reluctant to give segment or line of business information. Half of the enterprises studied from Belgium and Japan do not disclose segmented information, and enterprises from developing countries rarely report segmentation.

Both studies confirm a lack of interest in inflation accounting. Tonkin's overall assessment is that over the period 1980–1988 there has been only little improvement in reporting practices.

Leading Stock Markets

AN OVERVIEW

Over the past decade there has been increased focus on the leading stock markets of the world. More attention and energy is devoted to measurement, analysis, and interpretation of these markets. In Exhibit 18.4 we present data from the International Finance Corporation developed to keep track of global stock markets. Several alternative measurement systems have been used. Morgan Stanley Capital International provides a similar information base, but covers fewer national stock markets. Morgan Stanley distributes the Capital International information in the United States. In addition, Strategies Research International and World-Vest-Base provide data on 21 national stock markets on a regular basis.

The data in Exhibit 18.5 presents market capitalization in U.S. dollars for 25 leading national stock markets. The data represents changes in this distribution over the period 1985–1994.

In Exhibit 18.4 we obtain a visual picture of the distribution of market capitalization in the leading stock markets. The United States market held the largest capitalization, with more than 38% of the developed markets' total. In 1994 the Japanese market held the second largest capitalization, and the three largest markets (Japan, United States, and United Kingdom) together accounted for 76% of the world total. Five other markets (Germany, France, Canada, Switzerland, and the

EXHIBIT 18.4

**Distribution of Global Stock Market Capitalization
Based on IFC Data on Leading Markets,
Year End 1994**

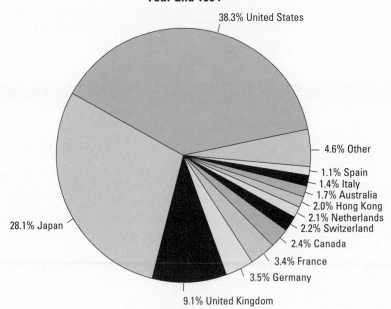

38.3% United States

4.6% Other

1.1% Spain

1.4% Italy

1.7% Australia

2.0% Hong Kong

2.1% Netherlands

2.2% Switzerland

2.4% Canada

3.4% France

3.5% Germany

9.1% United Kingdom

28.1% Japan

**Global Stock Market Capitalization
Not Including United States,
Year End 1994**

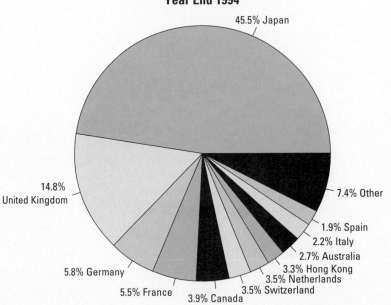

45.5% Japan

7.4% Other

1.9% Spain

2.2% Italy

2.7% Australia

3.3% Hong Kong

3.5% Netherlands

3.5% Switzerland

3.9% Canada

5.5% France

5.8% Germany

14.8% United Kingdom

EXHIBIT 18.5

World Market Capitalization: Leading Stock Markets 1985–1994

(US$ millions: End of Period Levels)

Developed Markets	1985	1986	1987	1988	1989	1990	1991	1992	1993	1994
Australia	60,163	94,713	105,709	138,283	140,956	107,611	144,867	135,451	203,964	219,188
Austria	4,602	6,656	7,411	8,862	22,261	11,476	7,689	21,750	28,437	30,272
Belgium	20,871	37,337	41,377	58,920	74,596	65,449	71,319	64,172	78,067	84,103
Canada	147,000	166,300	218,817	241,880	291,328	241,920	266,874	243,018	326,524	315,009
Denmark	15,096	16,284	20,181	30,178	40,152	39,063	44,841	32,635	41,785	54,399
Finland	5,855	11,692	19,698	30,179	30,652	22,721	14,271	12,202	23,562	38,278
France	79,000	149,500	172,048	244,833	364,841	314,384	348,083	350,858	456,111	451,263
Germany	183,765	257,677	213,166	251,777	365,176	355,073	393,454	348,138	463,476	470,519
Hong Kong	34,504	53,789	54,088	74,377	77,496	83,397	121,986	172,106	385,247	269,508
Iceland	—	—	—	—	—	—	—	—	—	484
Ireland	—	—	—	—	—	—	—	—	—	8,408
Israel	7,626	9,884	12,001	5,458	8,227	3,324	6,176	29,634	50,773	32,730
Italy	58,502	140,249	119,559	135,428	169,417	148,766	158,865	129,191	136,153	180,135
Japan	978,663	1,841,785	2,802,952	3,906,680	4,392,597	2,917,679	3,130,863	2,399,004	2,999,756	3,719,914
Kuwait	—	10,108	14,196	11,836	9,932	—	—	—	10,049	10,517
Luxembourg	12,658	26,163	38,277	44,808	10,348	10,456	11,308	11,936	19,337	28,511
Netherlands	59,363	83,714	86,240	113,565	157,789	119,825	136,158	134,594	181,876	283,251
New Zealand	8,761	22,215	15,713	13,163	13,487	8,835	14,336	15,348	25,597	27,217
Norway	10,063	10,122	11,818	14,332	25,285	26,130	22,043	17,821	27,380	36,469
Singapore	11,069	16,620	17,931	24,049	35,925	34,308	47,637	48,818	132,742	134,516
Spain	19,000	48,922	71,188	91,118	122,652	111,404	147,928	98,969	119,264	154,858
Sweden	37,296	63,354	70,564	100,083	119,285	92,102	97,495	76,622	107,376	130,939
Switzerland	90,000	132,400	128,527	140,527	170,936	160,044	173,881	195,285	271,713	284,092
U.K.	328,000	439,500	680,721	771,206	826,598	848,866	987,952	927,129	1,151,646	1,210,245
U.S.	2,324,646	2,636,598	2,588,890	2,793,816	3,505,686	3,089,651	4,099,479	4,497,833	5,223,768	5,081,810
All Developed Markets	4,496,503	6,275,582	7,511,072	9,245,358	10,975,622	8,812,484	10,447,505	9,962,514	12,464,603	13,256,635
World Total	4,667,766	6,513,885	7,830,394	9,728,493	11,713,685	9,424,144	11,299,573	10,846,418	14,055,683	15,185,607

NOTE: Table contains year end total market values of listed domestic companies.

Netherlands) accounted for another 13.6% of capitalization. The remaining 11% of market capitalization was distributed among another 17 national markets.

Market Capitalization   The distribution of market capitalization among national stock markets has been evolving in a dynamic way. This change can be seen in Exhibit 18.5 where we present the capitalizations of the 25 leading markets in dollars over the period 1985–1994. Changes in share of market capitalization have resulted from 1) changes in foreign exchange rate relationships, 2) expansion of individual markets via new listings of companies, 3) privatization and listings of privatized shares, and 4) appreciation in value (local currency) as a result of favorable national economic trends.

In examining Exhibit 18.5 we find that the most substantial changes in share of market capitalization involved the United States and Japan. The following table reflects this change, with Japan's share increasing from 21.8% in 1985 to 28.1% in 1994, and the U.S. share declining from 51.7% in 1985 to 38.3% in 1994. A considerable part of the redistribution can be explained by the depreciation of the dollar vis-a-vis the yen. In 1988 the Japanese market attained a share of 42.2% of the total capitalization of the 25 leading stock markets (U.S. share was 30.2%). Since 1988 the Japanese market has suffered a decline and the U.S. market has regained the top ranking. Over the period 1985–1994, the U.S. market experienced a 114% gain in total capitalization value.

	1985	1988	1991	1994
Japan	21.8	42.2	30.0	28.1
United Kingdom	7.3	8.3	9.5	9.1
United States	51.7	30.2	39.3	38.3
Total	80.8	80.7	78.8	75.5

Two other countries that gained in share of world capitalization were Spain and France. In the case of France, a series of privatizations and a favorable economic trend played a role in increasing market capitalization. Spain's stock market benefited from entry into the Common Market as well as from a strong economic growth rate. Over the period 1985–1994 the Netherlands and Swiss stock markets experienced a growth in capitalization and a modest increase in the share of their market in total capitalization.

Organization and Membership   G. Hawawini distinguishes between three forms of stock exchange organizations.* First, we have the exchanges that are privately owned and self-regulated. These exchanges include the NYSE, London, and Amsterdam exchanges. London and Amsterdam are free of government regulation, although since Big Bang London has developed a comprehensive system of self-regulation. Second, we have the state-controlled public institutions. Many European stock exchanges (France, Italy, and Belgium) follow this pattern. A government appointed body similar to the Securities Exchange Commission in the United States supervises these institutions. Finally, there are the semi-independent exchanges such as in West Germany. Here the exchanges are relatively free to establish their own rules and regulations, but are subject to government review and approval.

---

* Hawawini, G. op. cit., p. 25.

National stock exchanges differ from one another with regard to the role of brokers and dealers. Brokers function as agents and match buy and sell orders for customers. In return they are paid commissions. Brokers do not buy or sell securities for their account. Dealers act as principals, and make a market by holding an inventory of stocks from which they buy and sell to meet public demand. The dealer adjusts buying and selling prices (and the spread between these prices), and in this way controls the size of his or her inventory. Dealers derive profits from the spread and from changes in the value of the securities they hold in inventory.

On some stock exchanges member firms are allowed to act only as brokers. Typical of this practice are the Paris, Brussels, and Milan Stock Exchanges. On other exchanges members are permitted to perform both dealer and broker functions. Members acting in this dual capacity are found in the German and Netherlands markets and on the NYSE (specialists). Until Big Bang, members on the London Stock Exchange could function only in a single capacity. Since Big Bang this rule was changed to allow brokers to maintain continuous markets through their buying and selling activity.

Banks are not permitted membership on most exchanges. Important exceptions include Germany and Austria where the large banks play a central role in securities trading. Italian banks are active in stock trading, but not on the exchange. They trade off the exchange floor. This practice is possible since the Italian stock exchanges do not have a monopoly position in stock trading.

Price Determination   There are basically three systems of price determination on the stock exchanges. First, there are a number of markets where prices are determined through an auction system and where dealer participation is excluded (Paris, Brussels, and Milan). Brokers match up their overall buy and sell orders in each security, and the price is that which permits exchange of the greatest number of shares. The matchup process can be carried out by an exchange employee who aggregates the orders for a given security from all brokers, or by a periodic call (outcry) auction.

The opposite extreme involves use of jobbers (dealers) to provide a continuous market in shares assigned to them, as is commonly done in London. Finally, there are exchanges such as in Germany and the Netherlands where some members perform the roles of broker and dealer. Prices are first determined by a call auction similar to that operating on the Paris Stock Exchange. After this initial price fixing, active stocks are traded continuously through a combination of auctions and dealer activities.

SELECTED MARKETS

The discussion that follows offers a brief review and analysis of ten of the largest stock markets in the industrial nations. In a later section several of the emerging stock markets are examined.

To begin our review we provide a statistical analysis and comparison of these markets in Exhibit 18.6. In terms of market capitalization the three largest markets appear to dwarf the others. The U.S. market capitalization is ten times as large as that of Germany, and the Japanese market capitalization is more than 20 times as large as that of Italy. If we compare market capitalization with GDP we find that Hong Kong, United Kingdom, and Switzerland have the largest market capitalizations, in each case more than 100% of GDP. The U.S. market capitalization is only

EXHIBIT 18.6   **Comparative Analysis of 12 Leading Stock Markets**

	Market Capitalization (1)	Capitalization as % GDP (2)	Market Turnover (3)	Turnover as % Capitaliz (4)	Number Stock Listings (5)	Average Company Market Capitaliz (6)	Foreign Investm as % Total by Priv Pension Funds (7)	Concentration or Share Market Cap of 10 Largest Companies (8)	No. Foreign Compan- ies Listed (9)	Foreign Turnover as % Avg. Daily Turnover (10)
United States	5,081	79	3,592	77.2%	7,770	654	4	12	381	5
Japan	3,719	94	1,121	30.1	2,205	1,687	10	20	117	1/2
United Kingdom	1,210	120	928	76.7	2,070	583	20	23	522	43
Germany	470	26	460	97.3	417	1,128	4	39	594	2
France	451	32	615	136.4	459	983	2	27	222	2
Canada	315	64	161	51.1	1,185	266	9	25	—	—
Switz.	284	108	226	79.8	237	1,199	5	67	240	9
Netherl.	283	71	170	60.3	317	894	10	74	—	—
Hong Kong	269	298	147	54.7	529	509	—	44	27	1/10
Australia	219	73	94	43.2	1,144	192	15	41	—	—
Italy	180	14	117	65.5	223	808	—	52	—	—
Spain	154	28	61	39.2	379	409	—	56	—	—

NOTES: Market capitalization in billions of U.S. dollars. Market turnover in billions of U.S. dollars. Average company market capitalization in millions of U.S. dollars.

SOURCES: Securities Exchange Commission, *Internationalization of the Securities Markets*. International Finance Corporation, *Emerging Markets Factbook*, 1995. New York Stock Exchange, Research and Planning.

79% of GDP, close to the percentages demonstrated by Canada, Australia, and the Netherlands. Four countries exhibit low market capitalizations relative to GDP: Italy, Germany, France, and Spain.

Most stock markets have a turnover each year that is less than the capitalization of that stock market (Exhibit 18.6 Columns 3 and 4). Only the French stock market exhibits a larger turnover. Since 1982 most stock markets have experienced an increase in turnover as a percent of capitalization. In the case of the Netherlands, turnover tripled in the mid-1980s, whereas in the United Kingdom it more than doubled. In the United Kingdom foreign share turnover accounts for more than 40% of the daily average.

Foreign stock listings are very important in some markets (Switzerland, Netherlands). The United Kingdom has the largest number (522) of foreign listings. During the 1980s almost all stock markets were competing for foreign-share listings and market turnover on their respective exchanges.

Institutional investors play an important role on many of these stock exchanges. Column 7 of Exhibit 18.6 reflects the extent to which pension funds have undertaken foreign portfolio investment. In most cases foreign investment activity is moderate or large and growing at a rapid pace. U.K. pension funds have led the race with Australian, Dutch, and Japanese pension funds not too far behind. Foreign investment activity is an important reflection on the extent to which the stock market of the pension fund group can be integrated into the global equity market system.

Finally, stock markets differ in the concentration of market value. In Exhibit 18.6 (Column 8), the Netherlands and Switzerland display the highest concentration, with more than two-thirds of capitalization held by the ten largest stocks. The U.S. displays the lowest concentration.

United States   Until 1986 the stock market of the United States ranked first in market capitalization. Since then it was overtaken by the Japanese, but has subsequently regained top rank (1990). The U.S. market has served as a model for other countries to follow. In many cases stock market officials from Europe, the Pacific Basin, and Latin American countries have visited the United States to study how the U.S. market system is structured and how it operates.

Transparency
Wide availability of information concerning share prices and factors that influence specific ownership.

The U.S. market is probably unsurpassed in regard to transparency and liquidity. Market transactions and the underlying information base that gives rise to these transactions are widely available. These transactions are communicated to potential investors via a complex network of market-related (stock market tapes) and market-independent (news media) communications channels. A high degree of liquidity facilitates large block trades as well as retail transactions.

During the 1980s the dollar value of annual retirements of shares outstanding on average exceeded $100 billion. Despite this retirement figure, market capitalization increased from $2,324 billion in 1985 to $4,180 billion in 1991, and to $5,081 billion in 1994. These retirements resulted from company stock repurchases, mergers and acquisitions, and other corporate restructurings.

United Kingdom   The U.K. stock market traditionally has had a considerable international flavor. This international orientation was strengthened after the removal of exchange controls in 1979. As of Fall 1986, securities of companies and government agencies from at least 37 countries were listed on the exchange. By 1993 522 foreign equities issues were listed for trading. The International Stock Exchange (London) ranks third in the world in market capitalization ($1,210 billion at

December 1994). Disclosure requirements are fairly detailed and are generally comparable to the requirements in the United States. The ISE requires accounts of companies incorporated outside the United Kingdom to be prepared in conformity with international accounting standards as promulgated by the International Accounting Standards Committee.

The London market underwent a transformation with the Big Bang of November 1986. At this time Britain's Financial Services Act brought about a complete change in the method of operation of the stock exchange. The Act set new rules for investor protection, renamed the exchange (International Stock Exchange) to reflect the increased priority given to making the London market a truly international equities trading mechanism, and introduced a number of organizational changes.

One of the significant organizational changes was the removal of the distinction between brokers and jobbers. This change carried with it the responsibility that financial services firms be authorized to sell and trade investment products and to disclose information that investors need in order to evaluate these products.

The Financial Services Act set up the Securities and Investments Board (SIB). The SIB is subject to the authority of the Department of Trade and Industry. The SIB coordinates the activities of the five Self-Regulatory Organizations (SROs) that authorize firms—securities dealing, investment management, futures and options, and financial intermediaries—to carry out investment business in London. The SIB also must approve the operations of investment markets in London (International Stock Exchange and London International Financial Futures Exchange). SRO approvals of an investment firm's activities are based on individual activities. Therefore a firm may have to be a member of more than one SRO. For example after Big Bang, Kleinwort Benson was required to be a member of all five SROs with an annual membership cost of £200,000.

The Big Bang brought with it a screen-based automated quotation system (SEAQ) to facilitate retail trading. This system requires large market makers to advertise share prices on the automated screen system.

Growth of the London market has benefited from the large scale privatization program under Prime Ministers Margaret Thatcher and John Major. As a result the number of individual shareholders has been extended to several million new investors, and the base of listed shares in London has been broadened by a wide margin. Reforms proposed in 1996 will result in greater reliance on electronic matching of buy and sell orders on quote screens. Beginning in 1997 all intermediaries will be exempt from stamp duty on share trading, and there will be increased transparency of pricing. Trades bigger than six times the normal size should be disclosed immediately, rather than after a one hour lapse.

Japan The Tokyo Securities Exchange (TSE) is one of eight markets in Japan. It handles more than 80% of Japan's trading volume. The TSE is comprised of three sections, with the first being the oldest and the major market accounting for 96% of market capitalization. The second section handles new issues and those not traded over the counter. The third section encompasses trading in the over-the-counter market. The TSE has the second highest trading volume in the world, after New York, and in 1994 trading represented 30% of market capitalization. The number of domestic companies listed on the TSE is 2205.

The Tokyo stock exchange is a volatile market for several reasons. A great deal of cross-ownership exists between companies. In part this cross-ownership is based on business groups (keiretsu). This arrangement limits the possibility of corporate takeovers that are common in the United States.

The big four stock trading houses in Japan account for more than half of the activity in the stock market. These four houses wield considerable influence in the Tokyo market. In Japan there is not as much monitoring of market transaction activities as in the United States. Capital gains are generally exempt from taxation.

There are numerous differences between the Japanese and U.S. equities markets. First, price earnings ratios are much higher in Japan. This is partially due to accounting differences (nonconsolidated statements) and hidden assets. Second, interest rate movement and other economic indicators do not appear to have the same impact on the market as in the United States. Finally, investors who trade for speculative gain dominate the stock market in Japan.

Germany   The German stock market ranks fourth in capitalization among the leading stock markets. The West German securities market is relatively unregulated compared to those of most other developed countries. With a federal legal system, the governments of the respective states (Länder) are given jurisdiction over the establishment and supervision of stock exchanges in their states. There is a minimum of federal supervision, and the stock exchanges are self-regulatory. The Stock Exchange Act gives the exchanges jurisdiction over fixing of prices, listing of securities, membership, and prevention of fraudulent manipulation.

Until recently there were no restrictions on bank activities in the securities field. Banks participate freely in securities transactions with no distinctions made between investment and commercial banks. For this reason the large German banks have been given the name universal banks. German banks function as securities underwriters, market intermediaries who accept brokerage orders from the public. Public brokers such as those common in the United States do not exist in Germany.

Universal banks

Banks that function as securities underwriters and brokers, as well as deposit-taking institutions.

Prospectus disclosure requirements come from the Stock Exchange Act and the Notification of Admission of Securities (Zulassungbekanntmachung or "ZulBek"). The ZulBek is a federal implementing order that sets out the duties of the stock exchange listing committees and the standards that they must apply. These standards cover official trading on a stock exchange. Trades made off the exchanges are subject to minimal regulation. As a result there is considerably less regulation of transactions made on the market than on an individual exchange.

There are eight regional stock exchanges in Germany, but the largest and most dominant is located in Frankfurt. Three types of dealing take place on the exchanges: 1) official trading, 2) regulated market, and 3) free market (see Exhibit 18.7). Prospectuses are required for officially listed securities (larger companies). Kursmaklers who arrange transactions between members set official prices. Regulated dealing takes place on the exchanges between banks and/or friemaklers. Friemaklers (unofficial brokers) engage primarily in unofficial trading between members. Banks, also members of the exchanges, provide the link between the public and the stock exchange trading floor.

Trading may be over the counter (banks exchange bearer securities for cash). Prices are published by friemaklers and in private newsletters. There is no requirement that trading of listed shares be confined to the listing exchange, and these securities may be purchased in the unregulated unofficial market. The *geregelte* or regulated market was established in 1987. The government hopes to encourage medium-size companies to go public on this market.

EXHIBIT 18.7   **Stock Market Segments in Germany**

1. *Official Trading.* The Stock Exchange Act and Stock Exchange Admission Regulation set out the legal basis for the admission of securities to official trading. Principal conditions for admission are:

   A. Total volume of securities to be admitted must not be less than DM 2.5 million expected market value for share issues.

   B. Issuer of shares must have existed as a company for at least three years.

   C. Shares to be admitted must be widely owned. At least 25% of the total annual amount must be held publicly.

   D. Application for admission must relate to all shares of the same class.

   E. The prospectus must contain appropriate details.

   F. Issuer must publish an interim report.

2. *Regulated Market.* The legal basis for admission of securities to the regulated market is set down in the Stock Exchange Act and Rules of the Stock Exchange. Principal conditions are as follows:

   A. Minimum capital of nominal amount of DM 0.5 million must be available to the market.

   B. A company report must be published prior to introduction of shares. While this may be less extensive than the prospectus, it must be available at no cost.

3. *Free Market.* The free market merely serves the needs of securities dealing. The free market is governed by specific rules adopted by the Association of Frankfurt Securities Dealers. There are only a few formal admission requirements for the free market. Admission may not be granted if the issuer objects.

SOURCE: *Frankfurter Wertpapierbörse, History, Organization, Operation.* Frankfurt: Frankfurt Stock Exchange, 1990.

To some extent the German stock market has not attained its full developmental potential. Less than six percent of German private financial assets is invested in shares, compared with 35% in Sweden, 21% in the U.S., and 18% in the United Kingdom. Several factors explain this situation. First, not all potential domestic corporate customers use the German stock market since they find that fixed interest bank loans provide capital at favorable rates. Second, saving habits in West Germany tend to favor low risk assets including bank deposits and bank bonds. These types of assets minimize the role of individual investor participation. Third, much German capital for retirement purposes has been channeled through the comprehensive social security system.

The government seeks to encourage risk capital and opening of the financial markets through increased equity investment. A range of draft laws under discussion in 1995–1996 deal with capital market reforms (permit mutual funds to issue closed end funds and allow Anglo-Saxon type pension funds) and promotion of shareholder value (allow publicly quoted companies to buy back shares and reward executives with stock options). Also, moves are under way to develop a new market for small, capital-hungry companies. This Neuer Market parallels efforts in France and Brussels to develop a Nasdaq-type market for new technology sectors.

France   The French stock market enjoyed a period of favorable development during the 1980s. This growth can be attributed to the 1986 election of a conservative government and introduction of a privatization program, a series of takeover battles, and a positive economic climate. In 1978 the government provided a positive tax environment, permitting the deduction from taxable income of amounts invested in newly issued shares and SICAVs (Sociétés d'Investissement à Capital

Variable). The latter are open-end investment companies engaged in securities investment.

Ranking fifth in the world capitalization league, the French market also boasts second ranking after the United States in number of individual shareholders (9.5 million individual investors in the stock and bond markets).

France has seven stock exchanges, but the Paris Stock Exchange dominates with 98% of all trading. The regional stock exchanges trade securities of local interest. Each exchange comprises three different markets: the official list (cote officiale), the second market (second marché), and the over-the-counter market (marché hors-cote). By law a given security may be traded only on one market.

Trading is limited to stockbrokers (agents de change), who may buy and sell only for clients and not for their own account. Agents de change are licensed by the Finance Minister after passing professional examinations. There is no direct government regulation of stockbrokers, although the government supervises auditors, investment advisors, and intermediary brokers.

During the 1980s growth in trading volume strained the capacity of the French stock market, resulting in a shunting of some transactions to London and other centers. In 1989 the Paris market experienced its own Big Bang. Until then the large banks had been lobbying for access to the Bourse, because they originate a large proportion of stock trading orders. Reform of the Paris Stock Exchange opened the ownership of brokers to outside investors and provided for flexible stockbrokers' commissions. With large privatizations the value of the Paris Bourse tripled between 1984 and 1995. A large number of foreign companies list their shares in Paris. Parisian markets have struggled to attain a broader European base with Franco-German banks. This has not progressed well, in part due to disagreements over technology to be used in derivatives trading.

Canada   In terms of capitalization, the Canadian stock market ranks sixth (Exhibit 18.6), with a capitalization of $315 billion at year end 1994. In considering this ranking we should remember that the absolute size of the Canadian stock market is artificially constrained due to the enormous holdings of control shares by foreign investing companies. It can be roughly estimated that American companies have investments in Canadian industry equivalent to 40–50% of the total. If these shares were listed and publicly traded on the various Canadian stock exchanges, the capitalization market value of Canadian shares could be much higher. Also, the smaller domestic market in Canada constrains company growth, in part reflected in the average capitalization value ($266 million) of listed companions (Exhibit 18.6).

The focal point of Canadian stock market activity has shifted to Toronto. Twenty years ago, Montreal was the financial capital of Canada, but during the 1970s the provincial government declared that all business be conducted in French, the official language of the province of Quebec. Given the strong ties of the Canadian financial markets to New York and London, there was resistance to conducting business in a language other than English. This decree created a mass exodus from Montreal to the English-speaking city of Toronto.

Trading on the Canadian exchanges takes place in either of two fashions, the "open outcry" method where an auction takes place between buyers and sellers of stocks; or by CATS. CATS is the Computer Assisted Trading System developed in the late 1970s to allow for electronic execution by member firms. This has become a dominant aspect of trading, and is expected to lead to closing down of the Toronto exchange trading floor.

Shortly before the market crash of October 1987, the laws in Canada governing the structure of the securities industry were relaxed. Changes in the law allowed foreign ownership of broker-dealers, as well as ownership by banks. Canadian banks purchased the majority of broker-dealer firms, with a few of the broker-dealers having some foreign ownership.

Two factors stand out in the performance of the Canadian stock market. First, the Canadian economy and many of the companies whose shares are traded have a heavy dependence on natural resources activities (oil, mining, and agriculture). Second, there tends to be a high correlation in returns between the Canadian stock market and the U.S. market. It is rare to find as high a correlation. As a result, American investors seeking risk reduction in their portfolios might find the Canadian market less suitable than other markets with lower correlations of return with the U.S. market.

Netherlands At year end 1994, the Amsterdam Stock Exchange had a market capitalization of more than $283 billion, ranking eighth among the leading stock markets of the world. The Amsterdam market has one of the highest percentages of foreign companies listed (242 companies, or 47.7% of the total). The Amsterdam Stock Exchange is one of the most international of all the exchanges, and there is no restriction on foreign ownership of shares. Whereas the market turnovers compare favorably with countries such as Switzerland and Canada, this ratio can be deceptive. A large percentage of market turnover and capitalization is concentrated in a small number of companies. Close to three-fourths of turnover is concentrated in only ten stocks. Over a third of market capitalization resides in one company— Royal Dutch Petroleum.

The ASE is an efficiently operated exchange. This fact became evident in the weeks following the October 1987 crash. In a period of unprecedented trading volume, the ASE operated smoothly. There were no interruptions in trading, nor any back-office breakdowns or delays in clearing and settlements. Investors seeking liquidity by selling foreign stocks find the Amsterdam market able to absorb the supply.

On the ASE hostile takeovers are nonexistent. Most Dutch companies are protected against such events due to the existence of antitakeover devices that are built into corporate law. At present there is much discussion in the Netherlands concerning a revision of the corporate law that would make takeovers easier. Some members of the stock exchange community support this liberalization, arguing that it would protect shareholders from overly conservative management and lead to an increase in the attractiveness and value of shares.

Australia Australia has nine stock exchanges. The Sydney and Melbourne exchanges are the largest, accounting for 95% of turnover. In terms of market capitalization the Sydney Stock Exchange is the tenth largest in the world. In 1994 the capitalization of the Sydney exchange was more than $219 billion (Exhibit 18.2). Turnover as a percent of capitalization (43%) was the third lowest of the 12 leading markets.

Foreign investment plays a leading role in the Australian stock market, accounting for about 10% of all investment. The Foreign Investment Review Board (FIRB), an advisory body of the Commonwealth, screens foreign investments. Transactions subject to review by the FIRB include foreign acquisitions of the assets of, or substantial interests in, Australian corporations; proposals to invest more than five million dollars; and direct investments by foreign governments or other agencies.

There are no exchange control limitations on transactions by nonresidents on the stock exchanges.

Economic factors are a prominent backdrop to the Australian capital market. Foreign investors will typically consider prospects for the Australian dollar. In turn, the Australian dollar can be driven by changes in the current balance of payments, as well as by interest rate changes. Since Australia depends on foreign capital to close the perennial current account deficit, interest rates tend to be high relative to financial markets in other countries. The current account balance is subject to pressures that come from Australia's export position. As a natural resources exporter (coal, wheat, wool, iron ore, and meat), Australia is subject to changing world market conditions in these commodities areas. Weak commodities markets lead to a larger current payments deficit, necessitating higher interest rates and causing uncertainties in the stock market as well as foreign exchange market.

Switzerland   While the Swiss stock market ranks at a low seventh in market capitalization, its importance in global finance is considerably higher. This importance is reflected in 1) the high turnover of the market and 2) the large representation of foreign company listings, half of the total.

The Swiss market resembles the German market in one respect—the leading commercial banks play an important role in initiating trading in the market. Swiss banks hold and manage large blocs of shares listed on the Zurich and other markets for customer portfolios, whereas German banks hold large blocs of shares in German companies based upon their financial support and interests in these companies.

There are no federal laws restricting or prohibiting foreign firms or entities from engaging in securities transactions on a commercial basis in Switzerland. In Zurich and Basle, a cantonal license is required to engage in commercial transactions in securities.

Several types of shares are traded on the Swiss stock exchanges. Registered shares generally are held by (and restricted to) Swiss investors. Bearer shares generally are available for foreign investors to purchase. In part these distinctions have worked to protect Swiss companies from unwanted takeover attempts.

At year end 1994 the market capitalization of Swiss shares was $284 billion. At that time the average market value of Swiss companies (237 companies listed) was $1,199 million, second only to the Japanese average company market capitalization of $1,687 million. As many foreign companies list their shares as Swiss companies.

The main stock exchanges in Switzerland are located in Geneva, Basle, and Zurich. A substantial amount of share trading takes place off the exchanges, mostly by banks and financial institutions. There is no official over-the-counter market or quotation system. The Vorborse is an unofficial market for trading prior to official listing in the Zurich Stock Exchange, and the Ausserborse is an unofficial market dominated by the Swiss Bank Corporation and the Volksbank Willisan, Lucerne branch.

Registered shares

Ownership registered in official books maintained by company or trust bank. Specific ownership easy to trace.

Bearer shares

Issued in bearer form or street name. Difficult to trace specific ownership.

Like other Swiss firms, Nestle has distinguished between registered shares (available only to domestic investors) and bearer shares (available to foreign investors). Until 1989 Nestle divided its shares so that two-thirds were registered and held only by Swiss investors, and one-third were in bearer or street name and eligible to be held by foreign investors. Both types carried equal voting power. Over time, bearer shares advanced in value more rapidly than registered shares. Shortly before the October 1987 crash, bearer shares cost foreign investors 11,450 Swiss francs ($7230), or 21 times earnings per share. This amount is compared with SF 5,500 ($3450) or 10 times earnings per share for registered shares.

In November 1988 Nestle decided to "liberalize" the market for its shares, letting foreigners buy the registered shares. As a result the bearer shares fell in value, while the registered shares increased in value (Exhibit 18.8). Many foreign investors were burned on the bearer shares. The changes in share values between October 1987 and March 1989 are outlined in Exhibit 18.8. Domestic investors holding registered shares enjoyed a 23% increase in value, whereas foreign investors with bearer shares faced declines in value of 36%.

Italy The Milan Stock Exchange dominates the Italian stock market, accounting for 90% of trading. In 1994 market capitalization was $180 billion, ranking eleventh among the leading world stock markets. The stock market has grown impressively during the 1980s, in part fueled by the introduction of mutual funds.

Stock exchange membership is restricted to stockbrokers who are appointed by the Treasury after passing an examination. The controlling body is the Commissione Nazionale per la Societa e la Borsa (CONSOB), the Italian equivalent to the Securities and Exchange Commission in the United States. CONSOB was organized in 1974.

Numerous problems exist in the operation of the Italian stock market. First, government regulation is ineffective. This failure is due to the fact that much stock trading takes place outside of the official exchange. There is no obligation to use the stock exchange. Second, banks and securities dealers trade from their own inventories of stocks, and generally involve the brokers from the official exchange only when orders exceed their handling capacity. The existence of this dual market poses a problem as Italy struggles to upgrade and modernize its trading system. Third, some of the Italian exchanges are losing trading to London, especially with the advancement in 1989 of London's computer-assisted trading. Finally, there is a lag in information concerning Italian companies. Generally, annual reports are produced nine to ten months after close of the fiscal year.

In the past the Italian stock market was thinly traded. This has improved as reflected in Exhibit 18.6. Only a third of listed companies trade on a regular basis on the stock exchange. And while the domestic savings level is a high 24% of disposable income, Italian households put most of this into the purchase of government securities yielding high nominal interest rates. High levels of government deficits and borrowing has the effect of crowding out the investor demand for equity securities.

In the past government-owned and privately-owned financial holding companies controlled vast amounts of equity securities. For example, IRI (Institute for the Reconstruction of Industry), the state industrial holding company, acquired large equity holdings in the course of financing and bailing out enterprises in the industrial sector. Similarly, IFI (Istituto Finanziario Industriale), a holding company for the Agnelli family fortune, held investments close to 20% of the total capitalization of the Milan exchange. These investments include a large stake in Fiat, the dominant auto company in Italy.

EXHIBIT 18.8	**Change in Market Price of Nestle Bearer and Registered Shares**		
	Registered Shares	Bearer Shares	Premium of Bearer Shares
October 1987	SF 5,500	SF 11,450	108%
March 1989	SF 6,740	SF 7,325	9%
Percent Change	23%	−36%	

During the 1990s the Italian government initiated a comprehensive privatization program. By 1996 the government was planning final sales of shares in INA, the insurance enterprise, and IMI, the state banking group. Together these sales could raise more than $1.1 billion. The government was also finalizing plans to sell a second tranche of shares in ENI, the oil-gas-chemical group. Further into the future there were developing plans to sell a 64% stake in STET the telecommunication holding company, and the first stage of privatization of ENEL, the state electricity producer. Sale of the INA stake will be achieved through an innovative issue of government bonds which can then be exchanged for INA shares. This method avoids having to place INA shares at a price lower than that of the initial offering in 1994.

Leading Bond Markets

As bond markets around the world have been growing, fixed income investors have taken a more global outlook. As is outlined in Chapter 19, bonds can play an equally important role with equities in constructing internationally diversified portfolios. In this section we provide basic data concerning the size of the world bond market and the possible scope of international diversification via bonds. Also we outline the basic rationale for including bonds in the process of international diversification.

How Big is the Bond Market?

Based on readily available data, the world bond market is larger than the world stock market (Exhibit 18.9). At year end 1994 the combined capitalization of the leading stock markets represented approximately 82% of the combined value of the leading bond markets.

The bond market research departments of leading investment bankers regularly publish information on the world bond market. Here we make use of information provided by Salomon Brothers titled, "How Big is the World Bond Market?"

At year end 1994 the nominal value of bonds issued and outstanding in the 22 leading markets plus the international bond market was $18,482 billion. More than 41% of this amount was in central government issues, 14.8% in government agency and government-guaranteed bonds, and 12.4% in corporate (Exhibit 18.10).

Exhibit 18.10 indicates the currency composition of the major components of the world bond market. Not surprisingly, in 1994 the U.S. dollar component represented more than 43% of the total, with the Japanese yen (19.9%) and deutsche mark (10.6%) components ranked second and third, respectively. The Italian lira

EXHIBIT 18.9	Comparison of World Bond and Stock Markets		
	World Bond Market	World Stock Market	World Stock Market as Percent of World Bond Market
1985	$ 5,933	$ 4,551	76.7%
1988	$ 9,763	$ 9,404	96.3%
1991	$14,028	$10,760	76.7%
1994	$18,482	$15,185	82.2%

Amounts in billions of U.S. dollars.

Sources: Salomon Brothers and International Finance Corporation. Total includes leading equity markets and leading bond markets plus international bonds.

EXHIBIT 18.10

Size of Major Bond Markets at Year End 1994 (Nominal Value Outstanding; Billions of U.S. Dollars or Equivalent)[a]

Bond Market	Total Publicly Issued	As a Pct. of Public Issues in All Markets	Central Govt.	Central Govt. Agency and Govt. Guaranty	State and Local Govt.	Corp. (Incl. Cvts.)	Other Domestic Publicly Issued	INTL. BONDS[b] Foreign Bonds	INTL. BONDS[b] Euro-Bonds	Private Place. Unclass.
U.S. Dollar	$8,023.1	43.4%	$2,422.1	$2,195.1	$904.2	$1,509.0	$235.6	$137.5	$619.6	$689.4
Japanese Yen	3,669.3	19.9	1,906.6	197.5	90.3	382.8	784.5	81.0	226.6	—
Deutschemark	1,963.5	10.6	656.4	65.8	72.8	2.0	925.0	$241.5[c]	—	433.9[e]
Italian Lira	955.7	5.2	752.4	21.1	—	3.7	131.9	1.4	45.1	—
French Franc	891.4	4.8	402.6	215.5	3.8	144.3	—	6.2	119.1	—
U.K. Sterling	501.8	2.7	331.0	—	0.1	28.6	—	6.2	135.9	—
Canadian Dollar	404.4	2.2	162.9	—	111.0	51.5	0.8	0.6	77.6	—
Belgian Franc	347.1	1.9	179.2	7.7	—	13.2	119.9	26.6	0.5	—
Dutch Guilder	280.5	1.5	162.0	—	2.7	68.4	—	5.6	41.7	90.0
Danish Krone	251.0	1.4	90.9	—	—	—	156.7	—	3.4	—
Swiss Franc	231.0	1.3	23.0	—	17.6	32.3	63.6	94.6	—	0.0[e]
Swedish Krona	210.3	1.1	77.3	—	1.0	8.2	120.2	—	3.7	—
Spanish Peseta	171.0	0.9	119.4	—	8.7	19.8	12.5	10.5	—	—
European Currency Unit	154.6	0.8	61.8	—	—	—	—	—	92.8	—
Australian Dollar	123.6	0.7	59.9	24.9	—	15.5	—	—	23.3	—
Austrian Schilling	108.3	0.6	42.7	2.5	0.4	3.8	56.6	2.4	—	6.7
Norwegian Krone	45.8	0.2	16.5	2.6	6.5	3.2	16.2	0.8	0.0	—
Finnish Markka	43.9	0.2	20.0	—	1.5	6.3	14.5	—	1.5	—
Portuguese Escudo	34.1	0.2	22.7	—	0.6	3.6	4.5	2.8	—	—
Greek Drachma	30.0	0.2	29.7	—	—	—	—	0.2	0.1	—
Irish Pound	23.8	0.1	22.3	0.4	—	0.5	—	0.2	0.5	—
New Zealand Dollar	17.7	0.1	12.9	1.3	—	2.4	—	0.2	0.9	—
Total	**$18,482.0**	**100.0%**	**$7,574.1**	**$2,734.5**	**$1,221.2**	**$2,299.2**	**$2,642.4**	**$2,010.6[d]**		**$1,220.1[e]**
Sector as a Pct. of Public Issues in All Markets	100.0%		41.0%	14.8%	6.6%	12.4%	14.3%	10.9%		

a Exchange rates prevailing as of December 31, 1994: ¥99.74/US$; DM1.5488/US$; Lit1,629.7/US$; Ffr5.346/US$; £0.64/US$; C$1.3884/US$; Bfr31.838/US$; Dfl1.7351/US$; Dkr6.083/US$; Sfr1.3115/US$; Skr7.4615/US$; Pta131.74/US$; Ecu0.8129/US$; A$1.2873/US$; ATS11.095/US$; Nkr6.762/US$; Fmk4.7432/US$; Esc159.09/US$; Dr240.1/US$; Irf0.6464/US$; and NZ$1.5564/US$.

b Includes straight, convertible, and floating rate debt.

c The German bond market does not distinguish between Euro and foreign international issues.

d Includes both foreign and Eurobond totals.

e In addition, an unspecified amount of privately placed issues of the private sectors exists.

and French franc components ranked fourth and fifth, respectively. The lira component was one-half as large as the deutsche mark component, and the French franc component was one-fourth the size of the yen component. The sterling component represents 2.7% of the market, or $501 billion in outstanding bonds. Much of this is in the U.K. gilt (government securities) market centered in London, a fairly active and liquid market. During the 1980s budget surpluses in the United Kingdom (and in Sweden, Switzerland, and Australia) led to declines in the overall growth of central government and government agency debt in the world bond market. That situation was reversed in the 1990s.

The international bond sectors continue to be the fastest growing. Primary issues of Eurobonds and foreign bonds have been at a high level since 1985. As a result, international bonds outstanding increased from $499 billion in 1985 to $2,010 billion in 1994, in the latter year representing 10.9% of total bonds outstanding.

The composition of the 22 currency sectors differ somewhat. In Italy, the United Kingdom, France, and Spain, central government issues dominate, representing 81%, 66%, 69%, and 70% respectively (Exhibit 18.11). In the U.S. dollar sector, corporate issues are more important, representing more than 18% of outstanding bonds. By contrast, in Germany there are virtually no corporate bonds outstanding due to the practice of banks providing direct credits. Foreign bonds account for close to half of the Swiss market, reflecting the high utilization of this market by well-placed international borrowers. In the Canadian dollar sector, provincial and local

---

EXHIBIT 18.11   **Share of Outstandings in Central Government and Government Agency and International Markets in Each of the World's Major Bond Markets,[a] 1983–1994**

Bond Market	CENTRAL GOVERNMENT AND GOVERNMENT AGENCY BONDS						INTERNATIONAL BONDS					
	1983	1988	1991	1992	1993	1994	1983	1988	1991	1992	1993	1994
U.S. Dollar	54.7%	55.6%	55.0%	55.7%	56.0%	57.5%	6.8%	10.6%	10.0%	9.5%	9.1%	9.4%
Japanese Yen	68.3	63.6	57.8	57.1	56.9	57.3	2.2	5.0	6.9	6.8	7.3	8.4
Deutschemark	20.1	30.0	30.7	33.1	35.4	36.8	10.1	14.8	13.3	12.9	12.8	12.3
Italian Lira	70.3	79.9	80.8	81.0	80.7	80.9	0.1	0.9	2.8	3.3	4.0	4.9
French Franc	77.1	79.3	76.1	75.1	72.5	69.3	1.9	3.2	7.2	9.7	12.9	14.1
U.K. Sterling	90.1	72.1	59.3	62.0	64.6	66.0	3.9	21.4	34.0	31.5	29.6	28.3
Canadian Dollar	34.1	38.3	37.4	38.2	38.1	40.3	3.6	13.5	16.7	16.3	19.4	19.3
Belgian Franc	49.2	57.6	54.6	55.6	55.4	53.9	2.6	4.3	5.9	6.7	7.2	7.8
Dutch Guilder	52.8	60.2	66.4	65.4	62.5	57.8	10.4	12.3	10.2	12.1	14.5	16.9
Danish Krone	37.6	30.7	31.9	33.2	32.1	36.2	0.0	2.4	2.1	1.6	1.3	1.3
Swiss Franc	8.7	4.4	4.6	7.0	8.6	10.0	37.6	49.2	45.4	42.6	41.5	40.9
Swedish Krona	50.7	35.4	27.0	29.1	33.1	36.7	NA	0.1	1.6	1.6	1.5	1.8
Spanish Peseta	16.6	49.8	60.0	61.4	70.0	69.8	NA	1.4	7.3	7.6	6.6	6.2
European Currency Unit	39.4	30.6	31.6	29.8	34.6	40.0	60.6	69.4	68.4	70.2	65.4	60.0
Australian Dollar	98.9	60.4	57.2	60.7	63.6	68.6	1.1	35.7	26.7	23.0	17.1	18.8
Austrian Schilling	26.0	27.5	34.5	37.4	39.3	41.7	1.2	1.0	2.4	2.9	2.8	2.2
Norwegian Krone	52.2	46.2	33.4	38.8	39.6	41.7	0.4	1.5	1.4	1.2	0.7	1.8
Finnish Markka	41.9	30.8	23.4	26.3	37.8	45.6	NA	3.2	6.4	5.3	3.5	3.5
Portuguese Escudo	76.2	63.0	71.3	68.3	69.4	66.5	NA	0.5	4.4	4.9	6.2	8.1
Greek Drachma	NA	100.0	100.0	100.0	100.0	99.0	—	—	—	—	—	1.0
Irish Pound	100.0	99.6	97.5	96.6	96.0	95.5	NA	0.4	1.8	2.0	2.0	2.6
New Zealand Dollar	100.0	67.5	74.8	74.3	79.0	80.1	0.5	32.5	25.2	15.5	8.8	6.1

[a] Percentage of publicly issued debt. NA Not available.

SOURCE: Salomon Brothers Inc.

government borrowers represent close to 30% of issues and the corporate sector represents 13% of issues.

RATIONALE FOR BOND INVESTING

In this short section we present the basic arguments that support inclusion of bonds in the perspective of global investors.

Liquid market

Capital market sector in which turnover is large enough to accommodate large institutional investors.

1. The world bond market is larger than the world stock market, offering opportunities for "big players" (large institutional investors) to deal in a fairly liquid market.
2. Bond market sectors are driven by a somewhat different mix of factors than stock markets. Therefore profit opportunities on bond markets are likely to experience different timing patterns than stock markets. The return to a bond investor can include appreciation in value as interest rates decline, coupon interest, and currency gains (Exhibit 18.12). These returns can provide investors with favorable alternatives at times when major equity markets appear to offer less favorable opportunities.
3. Bond markets offer opportunities for selective risk reduction (currency risk, sectoral risk), as well as broader portfolio risk reduction.

EXHIBIT 18.12   **London Investor Rides New York Bond Cycle**

Mr. Albert Hardwick had completed a telephone discussion with a client whose investment account he managed. Mr. Hardwick has been with his employer, a London banking institution, for 15 years. The client wanted to invest in the U.S. Treasury bond market, noting that yields had reached a six-year high. The investor noted that the dollar had been strong in recent weeks and thought that this could add to the overall return on investment. The following market quotations were noted:

April 14, 1989:	Coupon Maturity	Price	Yield
U.S. Treasury bonds	8 7/8......2019 Feb 1	97.00–97.10	9.14%
NY FX Market.....................Spot pound		$1.6985	
	3 Mo. pound	$1.6862	

Transactions:

Purchase $973,125.00 on FX at $1.6985 per pound	£572,930.00
Purchase 1,000 bonds at 97.10 ($973,125 per bond)	$973,125.00

The following market quotations were noted on July 14, 1989:

U.S. Treasury bonds	109.06–109.10 (Yield 8.04%).
Spot pound	$1.6200

Transactions:

Sell 1,000 bonds at 109.06 ($1,091.875 per bond)	$1,091,875.00
Plus accrued interest of 8 7/8% for 3 months.	
$88.75 × 1,000 = $88,750	
$88.750 ÷ 4 = 22,187.50	22,187.50
Total Dollar Receipts	$1,114,062.50
Sale of dollar receipts at $1.6200	£687,690.00
Less original sterling investment	£572,930.00
Profit in sterling	£114,760.00
Rate of profit	20.03%
Rate of profit annualized	80.12%

4. Like stock investments, investment in bonds can be combined with programs aimed at currency risk neutralization via hedging in currency futures, forwards, and options.

5. Bond markets can offer investors favorable liquidity due to the high volume of market transactions. For non-U.S. investors, the U.S. Treasury bond market provides this liquidity on a 24-hour basis (see Exhibit 18.13).

EXHIBIT 18.13   **Day Traders Take Over the Field**

TWENTY YEARS AGO, ONLY "GENTLEMEN" PREFERRED BONDS. NOW THE MARKET HAS BECOME SPECULATIVE, SHORT-TERM, GLOBALIZED, AND HUGE

A joke familiar to Treasury bond traders in the United States sums up how dramatically the market for Treasury bonds has changed since the beginning of the decade. It says, very simply, that a long-term investor is someone who holds his position overnight.

The day of the buy-and-hold customer is gone from the once staid and slow-moving market reserved for pension funds and insurance companies. Now, it is a market for day traders, speculators, and foreign investors. Consequently, up to US $100 billion in bonds may be traded daily, making the market for 30-year T-bonds the most actively traded in the world.

It is no longer the sleepy repository for inherited wealth that it was 20 years ago when "gentlemen preferred bonds." "It is now a huge, globalized, speculative, short-term, and responsive market."

Investors flock to this market for a number of reasons. T-bonds are backed by the United States government and as such, are default-free. Because an investor assumes increased risk over time, T-bonds offer higher returns than their short-term counterparts. For traders, the main attraction is the market's liquidity. "You can get in and out of the U.S. Treasury market any time you want, 24 hours a day."

The United States is the world's largest debt market for government securities and offers the additional attraction of selling the only default-free, 30-year maturity instrument. Traders also like the homogeneity of the market and the regularity of the issues.

T-bond traders and investors are not the only ones interested in how the market fares. "the bell-weather long bond is a barometer of the nation's financial health," said one New York-based trader. "If rates are rising, the long bond may go up more than the shorter bond; that is a vote from the market saying that the authorities are not doing a good job of running the economy."

Almost all other fixed-income issues, such as mortgage-backed securities and corporate bonds are priced off, or react to, the 30-year T-bond price.

The volatility that attracted large numbers of traders and investors to the bond market began in the 1970s, when the U.S. Federal Reserve decided to focus on controlling money supply instead of interest rates. At the same time, the United States ran its first peace-time trade deficit, and traders and speculators saw the chance for big profits in the pending interest rate and bond price fluctuations.

Countries worldwide noticed the potential for profit. As recently as 1984, there was no Japanese retail market and no overnight market in London. Now, each major U.S. investment house has an overseas bond trading desk manned by traders fluent in foreign languages. All major non-U.S. players have trading desks in the United States, and some are primary dealers as well.

Even though the market's principal action occurs during U.S. trading hours, the maintenance of 24-hour portfolios is now mandatory. "My main job is to fill the gap between Tokyo and New York to protect our exposure," says a London-based trader. "I service the Japanese retail and European retail buyers pre-New York."

Japan, in particular, has become one of the biggest players. "The talk around auction time is always how much are the Japanese going to buy," notes Anthony Karydakis, money market economist at Mitsubishi Bank. "Life insurance companies and trust banks in Japan have a large appetite for longer-maturity, default-free securities."

Continued

EXHIBIT 18.13 (*Continued*)

Clearly, traders thrive on the market's volatility, liquidity, and variety of players. These features, however, carry an inherent potential for risk as well as for reward. Thus in 1977, the Chicago Board of Trade (CBOT) launched its T-bond futures contract. Based on an 8% bond, a dozen players initially traded the contract in a 10 sq. ft. corner of CBOT's Ginnie Mae pit.

In contrast, 66.8 million T-bond futures contracts were traded last year by some 600 traders each day.

The power of the futures contract as a hedging tool was driven home in 1979. This was the year that Salomon Brothers caught Wall Street's attention by using futures to effectively hedge a US $500 million underwriting of IBM bonds. T-bond futures gained almost immediate acceptance. "It has made a huge difference in what we can trade," notes one trader. "If I get in trouble, I know I can turn to the futures market and work the spread. Every bond trader these days is a basis trader to a degree."

While no one denies the importance of the CBOT contract, there are strong opinions as to what role it serves in price discovery. According to a March 1989 article in the *New York Times Magazine* "The prices 'discovered' here are arguably the most important in the world. . . . People who have to know where prices are going will increasingly look to Chicago for information as the years pass."

To this account, one cash market trader responds: "That's complete nonsense. Chicago is driven by technicians and chartists, and price discovery comes off the charts. I'm a fundamentalist and I don't believe in charts. It is the dollar flows and the economic fundamentals that truly determine where the market goes."

Regardless of whether cash or futures leads in pricing, there are a number of pending changes that will certainly affect the T-bond market. One of the most important is CBOT's move into nighttime trading. In response to this increasingly evident need for round-the-clock trading, Telerate has joined forces with Intex Holdings Ltd. to design fully automated, 24-hour global trading systems. The systems will be marketed to any exchanges interested in extending their trading hours.

Emerging Stock Markets

The emerging stock markets include those of the developing countries. The International Finance Corporation (IFC), an affiliate of the World Bank, has collected and analyzed data concerning these stock markets since the early 1980s. The purpose of this activity is to monitor and promote the development of these stock markets as a means of furthering the financing of economic development among LDCs. The IFC publishes an annual *Factbook* that contains statistical information concerning the emerging stock markets.

Periodically the IFC has extended its country coverage, and in 1995 included 60 countries. The indexes are expressed in U.S. dollars and computed from the component stocks of the IFC Emerging Markets Data Base. Exhibit 18.14 provides market capitalization for 60 emerging markets covering the period 1985–1994.

From 1981–1987 the IFC calculated its emerging markets indexes using a methodology of equally weighting indexes on the average of value changes of the stocks from each market.* This method was used instead of a market capitalization weighting because it gives equal weight to returns from both small and large capitalization stocks. These indexes were designed to take account of the great size disparities among actively traded stocks in some emerging markets. Beginning in 1987 the IFC implemented a system of market capitalization weighting of indexes. This system is comparable to the method applied to other major stock market indexes.

---

* International Finance Corporation. *Emerging Markets Factbook* (1992): 6.

Also it has the advantage of representing the performance of a fully invested, passively managed portfolio.

SIZE AND GROWTH

The term "emerging markets" comprises three categories of stock markets. These include 1) older established markets (Greece, Spain, Argentina, Brazil, India, and Zimbabwe); 2) markets that have developed in part due to special situations and circumstances (Hong Kong and Singapore due to their roles as regional financial centers in the Far East, and Jordan due to the influx of OPEC money); and 3) newer markets based on rapid economic development and the need to foster growth through financial development and modernization (South Korea, Taiwan, Philippines, Thailand, and Indonesia).*

The aggregate market capitalization of the emerging stock markets at year end 1994 was $1,928 billion (Exhibit 18.14), approximately 12.7% of the world total. In 1994 the largest capitalization emerging market was Taiwan, with more than $247 billion. Second and third ranking were South Africa ($225 billion) and Malaysia ($199 billion).

Comparative data on 14 of the largest emerging stock markets is provided in Exhibit 18.15. Eight markets show market capitalization in 1994 exceeding $100 billion. Several markets exhibit favorable overall liquidity based on turnover (Taiwan, Malaysia, Korea, and Brazil) or as a ratio of market capitalization (Taiwan, Korea, and China). Two markets (South Africa and Chile) exhibit low turnover as a percent of market capitalization. Several markets indicate low concentration of market capitalization (share of ten largest stocks), including Taiwan (25%), Malaysia (33%), Korea (30%), Thailand (29%), and India (20%).

SEGMENTED AND SUPPRESSED MARKETS

From the perspective of international investors, the emerging stock markets tend to operate as partially segmented capital markets. There are many obstacles to foreign portfolio investment. These problems include lack of relevant information, differences in accounting practices, and capital controls.

According to Vihung Errunza, "A set of unique conditions that characterize a developing economy has contributed to the existing state of capital markets in LDCs."† These conditions he labels "portfolio suppression," and includes: religious and social practices that have negative effects on the development of financial inter-

Portfolio suppression

Factors that hinder the evolution and development of capital markets.

mediaries; political and economic instability; inappropriate monetary and fiscal policies (often leading to inflation); interest ceilings on loans and bank deposits; preferential treatment given to government issues on the securities markets; and lack of capital market institutions and high costs of flotation and transactions.‡ This portfolio suppression has resulted in

1. lack of supply and demand for new stock issues on primary markets;
2. inefficient markets, where security prices do not reflect all available information;

---

* This three-fold distinction is based in part on V. Errunza, "Emerging Markets: A New Opportunity for Improving Global Portfolio Performance," *Financial Analysts Journal* (September-October, 1985): 51–52.

† Errunza, V.F. "Gains from Portfolio Diversification into Less Developed Countries Securities," *Journal of International Business Studies* (Fall/Winter 1977): 94

‡ Errunza, V.F. op. cit., pp. 94–95.

EXHIBIT 18.14 World Market Capitalization: Emerging Stock Markets 1985–1994

(US$ millions; End of Period Levels)

Market	1985	1986	1987	1988	1989	1990	1991	1992	1993	1994
Emerging Markets										
Argentina*	2,037	1,591	1,519	2,025	4,225	3,268	18,509	18,633	43,967	36,864
Armenia	—	—	—	—	—	—	—	—	—	—
Bangladesh	113	186	405	430	476	321	269	314	453	1,049
Barbados	—	—	—	—	—	280	307	259	328	518
Botswana	—	—	—	—	—	—	261	295	261	377
Brazil*	42,768	42,096	16,900	32,149	44,368	16,354	42,759	45,261	99,430	189,281
Bulgaria	—	—	—	—	—	—	—	—	—	52
Chile*	2,012	4,062	5,341	6,849	9,587	13,645	27,984	29,644	44,622	68,195
China*	—	—	—	—	—	—	2,028	18,255	40,567	43,521
Colombia*	416	822	1,255	1,145	1,136	1,416	4,036	5,681	9,237	14,028
Costa Rica	195	246	—	—	—	—	311	475	434	428
Côte d'Ivoire	302	332	458	437	531	549	567	336	415	514
Croatia	—	—	—	—	—	—	—	—	—	—
Cyprus	—	—	—	—	—	—	1,296	1,184	1,071	1,335
Czech Republic	—	—	—	—	—	—	—	69	—	12,589
Ecuador	—	—	—	—	—	—	—	—	1,620	3,499
Egypt, Arab Republic	1,382	1,716	2,150	1,760	1,713	1,835	2,527	3,259	3,814	4,263
Ghana	—	—	—	—	—	—	76	84	118	1,873
Greece*	765	1,129	4,464	4,285	6,376	15,228	13,118	9,489	12,319	14,921
Honduras	—	—	—	—	—	—	40	—	—	49
Hungary*	—	—	—	—	—	—	505	562	812	1,604
India*	14,364	13,588	17,057	23,623	27,316	38,567	47,730	65,119	97,976	127,515
Indonesia*	117	81	68	253	2,254	8,081	6,823	12,038	32,953	47,241
Iran, Islamic Republic	—	—	—	—	—	—	30,509	—	1,304	2,770
Jamaica	266	536	631	796	957	911	1,034	1,370	1,469	1,753
Jordan*	2,454	2,839	2,643	2,233	2,162	2,001	2,512	3,227	4,891	4,594
Kenya	—	—	—	474	499	453	638	3,365	1,418	3,081
Korea*	7,381	13,924	32,905	94,238	140,946	110,594	96,373	607	139,420	191,778

Lithuania	—	—	—	—	—	—	—	—	—	41
Malaysia*	16,229	15,065	18,531	23,318	39,842	48,611	58,627	94,004	220,328	199,276
Malta	—	—	—	—	—	—	—	—	—	52
Mauritius	—	—	—	—	—	268	312	416	791	1,514
Mexico*	3,815	5,952	8,371	13,784	22,550	32,725	98,178	139,061	200,671	130,246
Morocco	255	279	357	446	621	966	1,528	1,909	2,651	4,376
Namibia	—	—	—	—	—	—	—	326	3,450	9,574
Nepal	—	—	—	—	—	—	—	—	—	264
Nigeria*	2,743	1,112	974	960	1,005	1,372	1,882	1,221	1,029	2,711
Oman	—	—	—	—	983	1,257	1,506	1,544	1,599	2,135
Pakistan*	1,370	1,710	1,960	2,460	2,457	2,850	7,326	8,028	11,602	12,263
Panama	—	—	—	—	—	—	—	241	421	763
Peru*	760	2,322	831	—	931	812	1,118	2,630	5,113	8,178
Philippines*	669	2,008	2,948	4,280	11,965	5,927	10,197	13,794	40,327	55,519
Poland*	—	—	—	—	—	—	144	222	2,706	3,057
Portugal*	192	1,530	8,857	7,172	10,618	9,201	9,613	9,213	12,417	16,249
Russian Federation	—	—	—	—	—	—	—	—	—	30,000
Saudi Arabia	—	—	—	—	—	—	—	—	—	38,693
Slovak Republic	—	—	—	—	—	—	115	—	—	1,093
Slovenia	—	—	—	—	—	—	434	—	—	594
South Africa*	55,439	102,652	128,663	126,094	131,060	137,540	168,497	103,537	171,942	225,718
Sri Lanka*	365	421	608	471	427	917	1,936	1,439	2,498	2,884
Swaziland	—	—	—	—	—	17	27	111	297	338
Taiwan, China*	10,432	15,367	48,634	120,017	237,012	100,710	124,864	101,124	195,198	247,325
Thailand*	1,856	2,878	5,485	8,811	25,648	23,896	35,815	58,259	130,510	131,479
Trinidad and Tobago	463	374	388	268	411	696	671	510	485	663
Tunisia	600	595	662	608	638	533	711	814	956	2,561
Turkey*	—	935	3,221	1,135	6,783	19,065	15,703	9,931	37,496	21,605
Uruguay	15	35	40	24	27	38	44	368	251	170
Venezuela*	1,128	1,510	2,278	1,816	1,472	8,361	11,214	7,600	8,010	4,111
Zimbabwe*	360	410	718	774	1,067	2,395	1,394	628	1,433	1,828
IFC Index Markets	167,672	234,004	314,231	477,892	731,207	603,536	808,885	866,186	1,567,474	1,801,991
All Emerging Markets	171,263	238,303	319,322	483,135	738,063	611,660	852,068	883,904	1,591,080	1,928,972
World Total	4,667,766	6,513,885	7,830,394	9,728,493	11,713,685	9,424,144	11,299,573	10,846,418	14,055,683	15,185,607

NOTES: Table contains year end total market values of listed domestic companies. Asterisks indicate IFC Index markets in 1994.

EXHIBIT 18.15   Basic Characteristics of Selected Emerging Stock Markets

	Market Capitalization (1)	Market Capitalization as % GDP (2)	Market Turnover (3)	Turnover as % Capitalization (4)	No. Domestic Companies Listed (5)	Average Company Size (6)	Price-Earnings Ratio (7)	Concentration of Market Capitalization (8)	Total Return (9)	Volatility (10)	PRICE CORRELATION WITH U.S. Market (11)	UK Market (12)	Japanese Market (13)
Taiwan	247	117	711.3	288%	313	790	36	25%	28%	37%	.14	.24	.22
South Africa	225	202	15.9	7	640	353	21	—	38	42	.21	.41	.01
Malaysia	199	280	126.4	63	478	417	28	33	36	26	.39	.38	.24
Korea	191	51	286.0	149	699	274	34	30	14	30	.20	.33	.34
Brazil	189	34	109.4	58	544	348	13	38	56	81	.28	.15	.13
Thailand	131	92	80.2	69	389	338	21	29	44	25	.38	.27	.12
Mexico	130	35	82.9	64	206	632	17	44	10	49	.35	.24	.12
India	127	43	27.2	21	7000	29	26	20	16	18	-0.08	-0.01	-0.18
Chile	68	131	5.2	8	279	244	21	47	32	11	.29	.14	-0.12
Philippines	55	86	13.9	25	189	294	30	45	50	25	.36	.30	.08
Indonesia	47	27	11.8	25	216	219	20	42	35	32	.27	.23	-0.04
China	43	8	97.5	226	291	150	—	—	neg	60	.05	.00	-0.02
Argentina	36	13	11.3	31	156	236	17	61	8	43	.36	.12	-0.07
Russian Fed.	30	8	—	—	200	150	—	—	—	—	—	—	—

Note: Columns 1 and 3 in billions of U.S. dollars. Column 6 in millions of U.S. dollars. Column 8 reflects share of ten largest stocks in market capitalization. Column 9 covers period 1992–1994. Column 10 calculated by dividing mean value into hi-lo range.

Sources: IFC, *Emerging Markets Stock Fact Book,* and World Bank, *World Development Report.*

3. lack of stock market liquidity, except for the securities of the largest corporations; and

4. inadequate market regulation, security registration, and disclosure practices.

Given these market conditions in LDCs, investor time horizons are short. Shareholders tend to place a higher premium on current dividend income, rather than future capital gains.** In some cases LDC stocks tend to have high current yields, especially when compared with developed country stocks that retain and reinvest a substantial proportion of earnings. Both Errunza and Errunza and Bar Rosenberg found that dividend yields on samples of LDC stock markets were much higher than dividend yields in many developed country stock markets. This difference in dividend yields narrowed during the 1980s.

Errunza and Rosenberg have analyzed business and financial risk in LDCs, and conclude that business risk can be lower than in industrial countries, and that financial risk perceived by investors also may be lower.* They explain that the lower business risk is due to less intense competition, the role of the government (subsidies) in facilitating industrial finance, the group structure, and a lower rate of cultural change. Often business groups operate across many different industry sectors. These groups may be informal, based on closely knit circles of family, relations, friends, and associates. They may be more formal, where a holding company structure links the different component companies. These arrangements result in vertical and horizontal integration, diversified activities, and a lower risk. Concentration of activities leads to partitioning of markets among groups, resulting in monopolies and captive markets. Given these conditions, investors may perceive the financial risk arising from leverage to be low.

BASIC CHARACTERISTICS

The emerging stock markets present the international investor with opportunities as well as challenges. Exhibit 18.15 contains information reflecting the basic characteristics of selected markets. Here we can observe the opportunities for above average returns (Column 9), with a median of 32%. High returns are associated with Brazil, Philippines, Thailand, South Africa, Malaysia, and Indonesia. At the same time low correlations with the United States stock market (Column 11) suggest that considerable risk reduction can be possible. Correlations are low compared with the United Kingdom and Japanese markets, and in several cases negative correlations are indicated.

These markets continue to present a challenge to large institutional investors. Market liquidity is low. Less than half of the countries have satisfactory turnover from the viewpoint of large institutional investors. In one case (India, Exhibit 18.16), the small turnover is spread among 7000 listed companies. These markets also pose a challenge in that in many cases there are substantial withholding taxes on interest and dividend payments. In most of these countries, withholding taxes on interest and dividends are between 10% and 35%.

EFFORTS TO DEVELOP EMERGING MARKETS

Over the past decade efforts have been made to develop the emerging stock markets. The IFC has been central to this development. The onset of the international debt crisis

---

** Errunza, V.F., and Barr Rosenberg. "Investment in Developed and Less Developed Countries," *Journal of Financial and Quantitative Analysis* (December 1982): 753–755.

* Ibid., p. 753.

EXHIBIT 18.16   Capital Markets in India

In the 1950's India's capital markets helped to mobilize financial resources for the corporate sector. The importance of these markets then diminished because subsidized credits were available from commercial and development banks. In addition, equities had to be issued at a discount substantially below market value, the capital market lacked liquidity, and investor safeguards were inadequate.

A reform of the Foreign Exchange Regulations Act in the early 1970s limited the expansion of foreign-owned and foreign-controlled companies. In response, many companies decided to become Indian companies. This trend led to the issue of substantial quantities of company shares at low prices. The market's revival continued in the 1980s, as various measures were introduced to stimulate both demand and supply. Incentives for equity and debenture issues included reducing the corporate tax rate for listed companies and fixing the permitted interest rate for debentures above that for fixed deposits, but below that for bank loans. The government also authorized the use of cumulative, convertible preference shares and equity-linked debentures and gave generous fiscal incentives to investors.

The growth of the Indian capital markets has been impressive. Equity market capitalization is reflected in the following table. The number of listed companies on the Bombay Stock Exchange increased from 1259 in 1985 to 4413 in 1994. New issues of debentures also multiplied. However there were also abuses, such as the use of misleading prospectuses and insider trading. In addition, the processing of new issues that were heavily oversubscribed because of their low prices was plagued by delays in share allocation.

In April 1988 the Securities and Exchange Board of India was established to oversee and regulate the markets. In August 1988 a credit rating agency was established to grade capital issues. In January 1989 proposals were published regarding the appointment of market makers offering bid-and-asked quotations; the responsibility of stock brokers for vesting companies before listing; the opening of stockbroking to banks and other financial institutions; and the creation of a second tier market for smaller enterprises with less onerous listing requirements. The measures were intended to improve market liquidity and transparency and to provide adequate protection to investors.

Market Capitalization—Indian Stock Exchanges (Billions of U.S. Dollars)

Year	Value
1985	14.3
1987	17.1
1989	27.3
1990	38.5
1991	47.7
1992	65.1
1993	97.9
1994	127.5

In 1994 Indian companies carried out 41 Global Depository Receipt (GDR) equity issues, raising more than $3 billion. During that year the government announced guidelines for companies offering international issues, limiting the number of new issues and the timing of repatriation of issue proceeds into India. In 1996 the government initiated budget revisions, including a minimum alternative tax to bring more than a thousand companies into tax-paying states, allowing companies to issue nonvoting shares up to 25% of paid-up capital, and budget tightening to bring the fiscal deficit to 5% of GDP. Budget tightening is required to reduce government borrowing that tends to push interest rates higher and dampen stock market prices. During 1996 there was an increase in the volume of GDRs in the Euro-equity markets.

SOURCE: World Bank, IFC, Financial Times..

provided a strong stimulus when it became clear that LDC nations needed a larger amount of foreign risk capital instead of medium-term loans from international banks.

IFC efforts have focused on 1) providing more information on the status and trends in the emerging markets, and 2) promoting investment funds that channel foreign capital for investment in the emerging markets. As a result, the Emerging Markets Fund and other country funds were established. These activities aim at integrating the emerging markets with the world equity markets.

Efforts to develop emerging markets include creation of sophisticated derivatives products that give investors better access to these markets. In 1996 a new derivatives product was introduced to allow investors access to the Czech, Hungarian, and Polish stock markets without buying shares directly. These warrants on indices of selected stocks from these markets were introduced by Bankers Trust. The index return certificates are based on the three country markets indices compiled by the IFC.*

Bankers Trust said it had issued 42 million for the Czech, 12 million for Hungary, and 50,000 for Poland. The certificates are denominated in deutsche marks based on current exchange rates. They are to be listed on the Freiverkehr markets in Frankfurt, Berlin, Dusseldorf, Hamburg, and Stuttgart. Bankers Trust indicated readiness to make a market for the certificates.

Also in 1996, Salomon Brothers launched new call warrants allowing international investors easier access to the Russian equity market. This allows investors to circumvent local stock custody, which can make buying physical stock complicated and time consuming.

The 12.5 million European-style warrants have been issued on a basket of five shares (Chernogorneft-oil, Irkutskenergo-utilities and electric, Lukoil-oil, Mosenergo-utilities, and Rostelecom-telecoms).

The warrants have a multicurrency structure and can be traded and exercised in dollars, deutsche marks, escudos, and Swiss francs, the likely origins of demand for the product.

Salomon has applied for listing the warrants in Frankfurt and other German exchanges. Minimum trading size of the calls is 500. These can only be exercised on the day they mature.

Individual nations have acted to develop their own stock markets. In general they have enacted laws that provide for more effective regulation of the stock markets and stock market trading. In addition they have promoted the development of institutional investors (pension funds and stock mutual funds) that provide an institutional base for the market. Some nations have encouraged foreign portfolio investment through specialized vehicles (foreign investment funds). Finally, some countries have provided incentives for the conversion of external debt (held by international banks) denominated in U.S. dollars into local equity shares. This incentive tends to increase the demand for shares, facilitating additional corporate finance via new equity issues.

Chile is an example of a country that has encouraged growth of its stock market in part through the swapping of external debt for equity investment. Similarly, the Mexican stock market has enjoyed a strong expansion since 1989 as a result of more positive economic reforms, debt exchanges, a more open policy toward the rest of the world, and preparation for a North American free trade agreement (NAFTA) with the United States and Canada.

Poland embarked on a mass privatization program in 1993, implemented in 1995 and after. In 1995 Poland offered each adult (27.4 million) opportunity to purchase a freely marketable investment security for 20 zloty (2% of average monthly salary). These "universal share certificates" are exchangeable for one share in each of the National Investment Funds (NIFs). Fifteen NIFs were created as potential holding companies for privatized company shares. Each NIF is led or managed by Western financial services firms.[†]

---

* Boland, Vincent. "Novel E. European Derivatives Product," *Financial Times,* (May 30, 1996): 22.

† Puntillo, Richard. "Mass Privatization in Poland and Russia: The Case of the Tortoise and the Hare?," *Journal of Emerging Markets,* (Spring 1996).

By year end 1995 Poland had chosen 512 state owned enterprises (SOEs) to be portfolioed to the 15 NIFs, using a selection or draft procedure similar to that used by American professional sports teams for drafting college graduates. In this procedure each SOE will have one NIF as its core or main investor, initially owning one-third of the stock. As early as 1996, all 15 NIFs and some of the privatized companies are to be listed on the Warsaw Stock Exchange. Trading in share certificates is scheduled to begin on the Warsaw and over-the-counter markets later in 1996.

Promoting Emerging Markets with Stock Indices   The Barings Group head-quartered in London is owned by ING Bank. This group operates worldwide, and nearly half its directors and staff are located outside the United Kingdom.

ING Barings is one of the leading stockbroker and analysis companies in the emerging markets. Regional teams cover all significant emerging countries with local analysts familiar with the fine details of these markets. Additionally Barings provides services in derivatives, funds coverage (including closed end funds), primary equity markets, and trading.

The Baring Securities Emerging Markets Index was launched in October 1992 and in 1996 included 395 equities from 18 countries weighted by market capitalization. It acts as a performance measure for international investors in emerging markets.

The Baring Emerging Markets Index (BEMI) allows investors to compare market performance. This performance can be seen in Exhibit 18.17 where the BEMI is

---

EXHIBIT 18.17   **Comparison of BEMI, EAFE and S&P 500 January 1987–March 1994**

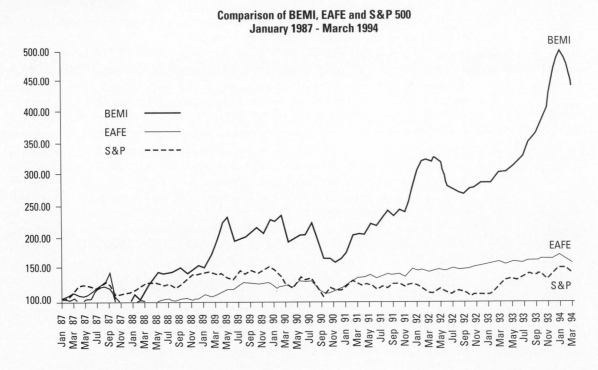

Comparison of BEMI, EAFE and S&P 500
January 1987 - March 1994

Source: Baring Securities, Inc.

compared with the EAFE (non-U.S. markets) and S&P 500 over the period 1987–1994.

Exhibit 18.18 indicates the country coverage and weights of BEMI as of April 1994. We should note that the coverage is restricted to countries where nonlocal investors have access. This weighting is reflected in the column indicating percent of market capitalization available and in the column indicating available capacity in U.S. dollars. Other indexes of emerging markets have wider coverage but include countries where foreign investor participation is narrowly constrained.

In addition, the BEMI has strict liquidity criteria at both the country and stock levels. At a country level, a minimum $2 billion market value traded in one year. At a stock level the criteria include minimum free float of 10% and a minimum average daily traded value of $100,000.

Emerging Debt Markets

A vast new bond market has emerged from the debt crisis of the 1980s. Sovereign borrowers with less than top quality credit ratings are floating sizeable amounts of debt in the global market. The catalyst for this was the Brady Plan, discussed earlier. In return for undertaking structural reforms supported by the International Monetary Fund and World Bank, emerging market countries in Latin America, East Europe, Africa, and Asia received assistance in obtaining debt relief.

By year end 1995 13 countries had issued Brady Bonds with a cumulative face value of more than $150 billion. With improving credit strength, these countries began to borrow in the Eurbond market. Also, private sector issuers in the emerging countries floated public bonds on international markets. In 1995, for example, close to 150 sovereign or private bonds were issued, denominated in currency such as the U.S. dollar, yen, deutsche mark, Swiss franc, and others.

| EXHIBIT 18.18 | Baring Securities Emerging Markets Index Country Weightings as of April 30, 1994 |

	Number of Securities	Index Weight (%)	Available Index Cap (US$)	Total Index Cap (US$m)	Percent Available
Argentina	19	7.80	11,878	33,270	35.7
Brazil	21	14.68	22,073	44,575	49.5
Chile	12	6.34	9,539	25,280	37.7
Greece	14	1.85	2,783	5,788	48.1
Indonesia	20	2.15	3,240	19,787	16.4
Korea	23	3.99	8,004	65,740	12.2
Malaysia	22	15.79	23,736	81,588	29.1
Mexico	24	25.45	38,273	83,000	46.1
Pakistan	10	0.74	1,106	3,276	33.8
Philippines	11	3.32	4,998	13,627	36.7
Portugal	14	3.08	4,625	9,724	47.6
Taiwan	30	6.70	10,075	101,806	9.9
Thailand	22	7.43	11,177	56,370	19.8
Turkey	22	0.57	858	3,529	24.3
Asia	138	40.23	60,338	342,193	17.7
Europe	50	5.50	8,265	19,008	43.5
Latin America	76	54.27	81,762	186,125	43.9
Total Market Cap.	264	100.0	150,647	547,326	27.5
China	26		2,593	3,106	83.5
India	24		8,327	35,315	23.6

PROBLEM AREAS FOR INVESTORS

Global money managers have a vested interest in considering how to use the growing emerging debt markets in the asset allocation process. However, they face several practical problems in this respect. These include:

1. Problems of limited data. In the absence of several decades of return volatility data, it is difficult to determine proper portfolio weighting. We do not have data covering several complete business cycles, and therefore cannot calculate correlation of returns between emerging debt and other investments such as select categories of U.S. Treasury bonds and various international equity indices.

2. Possible lack of stationary stability. The limited evidence available suggests that the correlations between emerging debt and U.S. Treasuries may vary widely over time. After the 1994 Federal Reserve monetary tightening, emerging debt traders found the debt sector moving more closely with Treasuries than before. Since early 1994 this degree of interdependence between U.S. Treasuries and emerging debt has shifted up and down.

3. Differing Sectoral Maturity. Each country component of emerging debt is experiencing its own somewhat unique life cycle. Early in 1996 it may be possible to categorize Russian debt as preemerging, while other country debt might deserve labels of mature emerging (Mexico), and middle stage (Brazil).

4. Changing Liquidity. The trading volume in the emerging debt markets is an approximate measure of the liquidity of the market. The market consists of many sectors, based on country of issues or type of market instrument. Each sector experiences substantial shifts in market turnover and liquidity. Therefore investors may experience at times a downward trend in trading volume in a given sector of the market, and greater difficulty in trading in that sector.[**]

What solutions might portfolio managers utilize, given these problems? Given data constraints, investment managers seeking optimal positions on efficient frontiers must consider special approaches. One possible alternative is to focus on maximum concentration limits. This emphasis on controlling risk is featured in mutual fund prospectuses. Users of the concentration limit method specify a maximum permitted exposure.

The concentration limit is a low technology approach, and typically not conditioned on expected returns. A bond fund may prescribe a flat 15% ceiling on less liquid securities. The purpose of such limits is to put a ceiling on risk.

Capping risk requires that an investor 1) define its risk tolerance, and 2) determine the worst case outcome in that asset class. To quantify worst case returns we must define the asset class precisely. Does it (emerging debt) include Eurobonds, noninvestment grade corporate issues originating in investment grade countries such as China? The answers to such questions become somewhat subjective.

As noted, the short performance record of the emerging debt sector makes reliance on average returns and standard deviations problematic. Martin Fridson quantifies worst case performances during the fixed income debacle of 1994, when Latin American Eurobonds in full year 1994 returned −12.9%, and Brady issues (for all countries) returned −19.9%. Fridson notes that emerging debt compares well against several other major asset categories such as intermediate government bonds

---

[**]Ishandar, Samer. "Salomon Issues Russian Equity Call Warrants," *Financial Times,* (July 16, 1996): 14.

and mortgage backed securities. For example, in July 1996 Brazilian Brady Bonds were yielding 12% compared with less than 7% on U.S. Treasury bonds.

SUMMARY

Strong linkages have developed between the largest equity markets, but these links do not necessarily mean the markets are fully integrated. At best the stock markets are partially integrated. In addition, the leading bond markets can display strong independent performance.

The decade of the 1980s witnessed a reawakening in international portfolio investment. Growth in international portfolio investment came as a result of financial market deregulation, desire of institutional investors to improve performance, shift to floating rates, growing awareness and literature concerning cross-border investment opportunities, modernization of national stock exchanges, expanded global liquidity, and large payments surpluses and deficits.

Distribution of market capitalization among national stock markets has been changing due to foreign exchange rate shifts, new listings of companies, privatization, and differences in national economic trends. National stock markets differ from one another based on the role of brokers and dealers, ownership and regulation of exchanges, membership, and method of price determination.

On a global basis the aggregate market value of the bond markets is somewhat larger than the combined value of the stock markets. The international bond market sector is the fastest growing. The rationale for bond market investing is related to its larger size relative to stock markets, unique profit opportunities, liquidity, and opportunities for risk reduction.

The emerging stock and bond markets include those of the developing countries. The IFC collects and publishes data on these stock markets, and the Emerging Markets Traders Association does the same for the emerging debt markets. Some of these markets suffer from portfolio suppression, resulting in lower supply and demand for new stock issues, lack of liquidity, and inadequate regulation and disclosure. Nevertheless, these markets can provide above average returns and opportunities for risk reduction through diversification.

REVIEW QUESTIONS

1. Compare and contrast international investment patterns and experience between the nineteenth and twentieth centuries.
2. What is the best evidence indicating that international portfolio investment has experienced strong growth since the late 1970s?
3. What factors or developments explain the surge in cross-border portfolio investment?
4. Why is the volume of international portfolio investment not as large as domestic investment?
5. Explain how investors use leading stock market indexes.
6. Why might individual and institutional investors carry out cross-border investment in different ways (use different channels or instruments)?

7. An American investor purchases an ADR of a European company in New York for $35 a share. The European company stock is traded in Frankfurt. The rate of exchange is $0.50 per DM. What should be the deutsche mark price of the underlying shares? If the $/DM rate becomes $0.70 and the ADR is priced at $42 in New York, the deutsche mark price must be what?

8. Why might regulations of the stock market be important? Is this a factor for cross-border investors?

9. Why do you think the capitalization of the Swiss stock market is smaller than that of the U.S. market (in dollar value), but larger as a percent of GDP?

10. Why might foreign companies list their stocks in New York? Why might U.S. companies list their stocks in Frankfurt?

11. Select one of the ten leading stock markets and draw as many parallels as you can find between the stock market development and structure and the socioeconomic conditions of that country.

12. A French investor can purchase U.S. Treasury bonds. Given present conditions in the U.S. and French bond markets and conditions in the currency markets, is this purchase recommended?

13. Why do you think the world stock market remains smaller than the world bond market?

14. Do the global bond markets offer international investors any important advantages? Explain.

15. What is meant by emerging market? Are these markets more or less risky than the leading markets?

16. What is portfolio suppression? How does it affect the international investor?

17. The following data reflect yields available on long-term government bonds in selected country bond markets.

	Yield to Maturity
United States	8.1%
Germany	9.2%
United Kingdom	10.5%
France	8.9%
Netherlands	7.7%

   a. Should an American investor select primarily the highest yielding bonds (e.g., United Kingdom and Germany)? Why or why not?

   b. Are there any reasons, practical or theoretical, that can explain these differences in yields on government bonds from country to country?

   c. Does your answer in b suggest any investment strategies to be followed? Explain.

18. Mr. Smith purchased German government bonds with face value of DM 10 million at a price of 96. At the time the $/DM rate of exchange was $0.60. Now, one year later, Mr. Smith contacts his New York broker to sell the deutsche mark bonds. They are selling at 98, and the deutsche mark is valued at $0.56. Interest was paid on the bonds just a few weeks ago (7.0% coupon). At that time the deutsche mark interest funds were converted to dollars at $0.57.

   a. What is the total dollar gain/loss on the transaction?

   b. What part is related to interest income, foreign exchange gain/loss, or capital gain/loss?

"Perfect Portfolios Designed by Money Managers"

The following few pages provides you with a 13-country summary of the investment outlook as seen by economic forecasters and money managers in September 1993. They are not in full agreement concerning what constitutes the perfect portfolio. However, they do agree that the best performing stock markets tend to be located in countries with high growth rates.

You also have information concerning the movement of stock markets, bond and money markets, commodity prices, trade balances, and currency rates in the months leading up to September 1993. The forecasts are real GDP growth, consumer prices, and current account in the balance of payments.

1. Which of the countries covered by the forecasts appear to offer opportunity for equity investing? Give an explanation for your answer.
2. Which of the countries covered by the forecasts appear to offer opportunities for bond investors? Give an explanation for your answer.
3. Select one of the 13 countries that appears to offer the least favorable opportunities for any type of investment (equity or bond) and write an explanation concerning the problems in this country for portfolio managers.

Economic Performance—13 Countries, September 1993

Country	GDP Growth	Industrial Production	Consumer Prices	INTEREST RATES 3 Month	INTEREST RATES Government Bond Yield	Trade Balance	CURRENCY UNITS/$ Now	CURRENCY UNITS/$ Year Ago	Stock Market % Change
Australia	4.7	3.3	1.5	4.8	6.6	+0.2	1.48	1.45	+24
Canada	3.6	4.3	2.0	3.9	7.5	+8.4	1.31	1.27	+22
France	2.7	2.8	1.7	6.5	6.2	+10.2	5.70	5.45	+23
Germany	1.4	1.5	3.0	6.1	5.6	+25.8	1.65	1.58	+36
Hong Kong	5.3	5.9	5.8	—	—	—	7.72	7.70	+71
Italy	0.9	4.9	3.8	8.7	7.8	−9.5	1620	1440	+35
Japan	−0.2	−1.1	0.7	2.0	3.3	+136.2	111	123	−2
Singapore	4.6	4.9	1.9	—	—	−8.5	1.51	1.52	+46
South Africa	3.8	4.4	9.1	—	—	+3.1	4.50	4.32	+12
Spain	0.7	6.5	4.8	8.9	8.2	−16.8	137	114	+36
Switzerland	1.2	6.2	0.4	4.1	4.1	+1.9	1.46	1.41	+31
U.K.	2.2	2.7	2.6	5.3	6.6	−18.3	0.66	0.64	+13
United States	3.1	4.3	2.5	3.3	6.3	−112.1	—	—	+9
World									+14

NOTE: All data pertain to latest 12 month period. Interest rates are current (Sept. 1993). Stock market data is percent change in latest year period. South African exchange rate refers to financial Rand.

SOURCES: International Monetary Fund and World Bank.

Consensus Forecasts—13 Countries (Sept. 1993–Sept. 1994)

	GDP Growth (Percent)	Consumer Prices (Percent)	Trade Balance (Year)	Change in Official Reserves (12 months)
Australia	4.1	3	−1	—
Canada	4.4	1	7	—
France	3.5	2	12	+2
Germany	1.7	5	22	—
Hong Kong	5.5	7	—	—
Italy	1.3	9	−10	−1
Japan	1.5	1	130	+10
Singapore	4.9	2	−6	+1
South Africa	3.9	8	3	—
Spain	2.5	9	−18	−3
Switzerland	1.6	0	2	+3
U.K.	2.4	3	−15	+3
United States	3.2	6	−120	−15

SELECTED BIBLIOGRAPHY

Black, F. "Universal Hedging: Optimizing Currency Risk and Reward in International Equity Portfolios," *Financial Analysts Journal,* (July-August 1989).

Bruce, Brian R., Heydon D. Traub, and Larry L. Martin. "Global Passive Management," in R. Aliber and B. Bruce (eds). *Global Portfolios.* Homewood, IL: Irwin, 1991.

Economist. "Bourses for Courses," (July 17, 1996): 81–82.

Errunza, V.F. "Emerging Markets: A New Opportunity for Improving Global Portfolio Performance," *Financial Analysts Journal,* (September-October 1985).

Errunza, V., and Barr Rosenberg. "Investment in Developed and Less Developed Countries," *Journal of Financial and Qualitative Analysis,* (December 1982).

Ferson, W.E., and C.R. Harvey. "The Rich and Predictability of International Equity Returns," *Review of Financial Economics,* (1993).

Fisher, Andrew. "Germans Urged to Take a Risk for Jobs," *Financial Times,* (February 12, 1996): 2.

Fridson, Martin S. "International Emerging Markets Debt in the Asset Allocation Process," *Journal of Emerging Markets,* (Spring 1996).

Gapper, John. "Stock Exchange Set for Overhaul," *Financial Times,* (July 25, 1996): 6.

Grossman, Sanford J., and Joseph E. Stiglitz. "On the Impossibility of Informationally Efficient Markets," *American Economic Review,* (June 1980).

Hawawini, G. *European Equity Markets: Price Behavior and Efficiency.* New York: New York University, Salomon Center, 1984.

Hill, Andrew. "Rome Prepares More State Sales," *Financial Times,* (June 10, 1996): 19.

Ibbotson, Roger G., and Gary P. Brinson. *Global Investing.* New York: McGraw-Hill, 1993.

Ibbotson, Roger G., and Laurence B. Siegel. "The World Bond Market: Market Values, Yields, and Returns," *Journal of Fixed Income,* (June 1991).

International Finance Corporation. *Emerging Markets Factbook,* Annual, (1992–1995).

Journal of Emerging Markets. "Debt Trading Volume Stabilizes in Emerging Markets," (Summer 1996).

Mikesell, Raymond F. *U.S. Private and Government Investment Abroad.* Eugene, OR: University of Oregon, 1962.

Peat, Marwick. *Worldwide Financial Reporting and Audit Requirements,* (January 1986).

Puntillo, Richard. "Mass Privatization in Poland and Russia: The Case of the Tortoise and the Hare?," *Journal of Emerging Markets,* (Spring 1996).

Roll, Richard. "The International Crash of 1987," *Financial Analysts Journal,* (September-October 1988).

Salomon Brothers. *How Big is the World Bond Market?* New York, August 1995.

Sinquefeld, Rex A. "The Gains From International Small Company Diversification," in R. Aliber, B. Bruce (eds)., *Global Portfolios.* Chicago: Richard D. Irwin, 1991.

Solnik, Bruno. *International Investments.* Reading, MA: Addison-Wesley, 1996.

Stanley, Marjorie T. *The Irwin Guide to Investing in Emerging Markets.* Chicago: Richard D. Irwin, 1995.

Stulz, R. "The Pricing of Capital Assets in an International Setting: An Introduction," *Journal of International Business Studies,* (Summer 1984).

Thompson, P., J. Thompson, B. Allworthy, and D. Roden. *BZW Equity-Gilt Study.* London: Barclays de Zoete Wedd, 1989.

United National Center on Transnational Corporations. *International Accounting and Reporting Issues: 1990 Review,* New York, 1991.

CHAPTER 19

International Portfolio Diversification

INTRODUCTION

In this chapter we address the theory and application of portfolio diversification in a global context. We first present a simplified model that applies the portfolio diversification concept in a two-country example. Subsequently this model is generalized to the multicountry case. Market efficiency is then considered. Finally, we review the results of several major studies of these concepts applied in an international setting. This review of the conceptual work provides the reader with a sense of the importance of international portfolio diversification in general, and of its several dimensions.

LEARNING OBJECTIVES IN THIS CHAPTER

1. To define the role and importance played by concepts and theory in developing an approach toward international portfolio investment.
2. To create an understanding of how construction of international portfolios is based upon key information pertaining to return, risk, and correlations of returns of securities that become components of these portfolios.
3. To appreciate the impact of cross-border investing on capital asset prices.
4. To understand how we can explain differences in stock valuation and bond yields on a country-to-country basis utilizing theoretical concepts such as rational expectations, risk aversion, and capital market theory.
5. To review and understand the empirically based studies that support international diversification in equities and other securities.
6. To realize the role of bonds in enhancing international diversification, both for equity and bond portfolios.
7. To develop the ability to analyze multi-asset portfolio investment strategies in an international context.

KEY TERMS AND CONCEPTS

- arbitrage pricing theory
- beta
- Capital Asset Pricing Model (CAPM)
- Capital Market Line (CML)
- continuous trading
- correlation of return
- covariance
- dominant portfolio
- efficiency frontier
- investment opportunity locus

- market portfolio
- Multiasset strategy
- Multicountry Model
- optimum portfolio
- overshooting
- PE ratio
- random walk
- rational expectations
- risk-free rate
- systematic risk

International Diversification and Capital Asset Prices

Correlations

Degree to which returns on two or more securities move together or not, or degree to which returns on security moves together or not with return on market portfolio.

Risk

Variability of return from one holding period to another.

Return

Gain from holding security over given holding period. Can consist of change in value (price) of security, dividend or interest, and change in currency value if traded in offshore market.

Correlation-covariance matrix

A matrix table, one part denoting correlations of returns on securities, and another part denoting covariances of returns on these securities.

PE ratios

Price earnings ratio is obtained by dividing price of an equity security by earnings per share.

In this section we focus on the effects of international diversification on capital asset prices. We use simplifying assumptions: namely, the currency factor plays a minimal role (fixed exchange rate system with equilibrium conditions in the foreign exchange market), cross-border securities transactions are unregulated, and national capital markets are informationally efficient.

A Two-Country Model

We take a four-security, two-country model with the required information relative to portfolio construction summarized in Exhibit 19.1. Investors in the United States have securities 1 and 2 available to them, with the return, risk and correlations indicated. Investors in the United Kingdom have securities 3 and 4 available to them. The price basis of these securities also is indicated, with the PE ratios, earnings per share, and prices of the securities. A correlation-covariance matrix is also included in Exhibit 19.1.

The properties of two security portfolios are presented in Exhibit 19.2. These include domestic portfolios (A and B), and international portfolios (C, D, E, and F). All portfolios are weighted 50-50. Two portfolios appear to dominate, C and B. This can be observed in Exhibit 19.3.

Capital Asset Prices

Before any cross-border investing takes place, capital asset prices are as indicated in Exhibit 19.1. PE ratios are uniformly 10 in the United States and 5 in the United Kingdom. When we introduce the possibility of international portfolios, cross-border investment flows take place. Of the six possible two-security portfolios in Exhibit 19.2, the dominant portfolios are C and B.

The dominance of portfolios C and B affect the relative strength of demand for securities included in and excluded from these two portfolios. Securities 1 and 3 are included in portfolio C, and securities 3 and 4 are included in portfolio B. Security 2 is not included in either of these portfolios.

EXHIBIT 19.1   **Return, Risk, and Correlations in a Two-Country, Four-Security Model**

	Portfolio Data Return	Risk	CAPITAL ASSET Pricing Data P-E Ratio	Price	EPS
United States:					
Security 1	20	6	10	$200	$20
Security 2	10	4	10	$100	$10
United Kingdom:					
Security 3	20	6	5	£200	£40
Security 4	10	5	5	£50	£10

Correlation-Covariance Matrix:

		1	2	3	4
	1	—	.70	.60	.20
	2	16.8	—	.30	.80
	3	21.6	7.2	—	0
	4	6.0	16.0	0	—

EXHIBIT 19.2   **Return and Risk for Two Security Portfolios**

Portfolio	Composition	Return	Risk	P-E
A	1 and 2	15	4.62	10
B	3 and 4	15	3.9	5
C	1 and 3	20	5.37	7.5
D	1 and 4	15	4.27	7.5
E	2 and 3	15	4.1	7.5
F	2 and 4	10	4.27	7.5

NOTE: The method for estimating portfolio risk (standard deviation) is described in the appendix to this chapter. Refer to this material in reading through this section and subsequent sections of the chapter where portfolio risk is mentioned.

EXHIBIT 19.3   **Two-Country, Four-Security Model, Dominant and Dominated Portfolios**

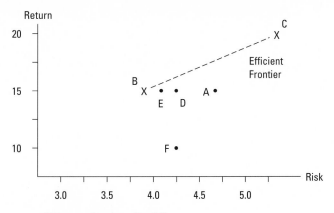

X Denotes Dominant Portfolio
• Denotes Dominated Portfolio
SOURCE: Exhibit 19.2

It is possible to generalize from the preceding information. Security 3 will experience a substantial increased demand because it is included in portfolios C and B. This demand should bring about an increase in the price of security 3 and its PE ratio.

Securities 1 and 4 will experience moderate increase in demand because they are each included in one of the so-called dominant portfolios. This demand may bring about a moderate increase in the prices of securities 1 and 4 and their respective PE ratios.

Security 2 will experience a decline in demand because investors will be shifting their funds to portfolios that do not include security 2. This decline should bring about a reduction in the price of security 2 and its PE ratio.

All of the described changes in price of the four securities will bring about further adjustments in expected return on these securities. Securities that rise in price should experience a reduction in expected return. Securities that fall in price should experience an increase in expected return. These changes in securities prices and expected returns will continue until a new capital market pricing equilibrium is attained.

A Multicountry Model

In this section we outline the assumptions of the Capital Asset Pricing Model (CAPM), and introduce the Multicountry Model as an improvement over CAPM. Finally the Arbitrage Pricing Model is described.

CAPITAL ASSET PRICING MODEL

The Capital Asset Pricing Model (CAPM) is a model of market equilibrium. It allows us to take a simplified view of the world of securities markets while retaining focus on the major components. In this way we can obtain a better understanding of the operation of these markets.

Important assumptions of CAPM are as follows:

1. Investors are concerned about risk and return. Each investor is more or less risk averse, and willing to trade off risk against return.
2. Investors in the market have a point of view concerning expected return and risk for all assets traded.
3. Investors operate on the basis of nominal returns, denominated in their own home currency.
4. Investors have available to them a risk-free rate at which they may lend or borrow.
5. Investors are not subject to transaction costs or taxes.

The CAPM draws us to the conclusion that there is a market portfolio of risky assets. This portfolio consists of all assets traded. In equilibrium investors hold a mix of more risky and less risky assets. This mix may include some risk-free assets. The equilibrium-expected return of an individual asset should be equivalent to the risk-free rate plus a premium. This risk premium is proportional to the covariance of the asset return with the return available on the market portfolio (beta). This calculation is represented in Eq. (19.1), where E_i reflects the expected return on a

Sidebar (margin definitions)

Dominant portfolio

Portfolio with highest return given the level of risk, or with lowest risk given the level of return.

Capital Asset Pricing Model (CAPM)

A model of market equilibrium in which the return on a given security is related to the risk premium on that security. In turn the risk premium is related to the covariance of the asset return with the return available on the market portfolio.

Risk-free rate

Rate of return earned on risk-free asset, generally a central government debt obligation.

Market portfolio

Portfolio of all risky securities in the market. In international context includes all national equity markets.

Beta

A measure of risk attached to individual securities.

security, *RFR* is the risk-free rate, *B* is the beta (measure of risk) attached to the individual security, and *M* is the expected return on a market portfolio of securities.

$$E_i = RFR + (BM) \qquad (19.1)$$

Assume an investor can earn a risk-free rate of 5%, the expected rate on the market portfolio is 10%, and the beta of a risky security is 1.2. Applying the formula yields an expected return on the risky asset of 5% + 1.2 (10) = 17%.

A basic problem with the CAPM is that it requires us to identify the market portfolio (assets and their weights). Also, it does not consider that investors in different countries may have different currency and investor (asset holding) preferences.

To apply the CAPM to the real world of cross-border investing requires two difficult assumptions. First, that investors all over the world have identical preferences, and second, that purchasing power parity is the standard in every country (exchange rates perfectly reflect inflation differentials).

Applying the CAPM model to international diversification requires that we use a beta that measures risk relative to the world market portfolio, showing the volatility of the asset relative to a world market index. The difficulty we face is that the return on most risky assets is influenced primarily by domestic market factors. Bruno Solnik introduced a solution to this problem—the multicountry model.*

THE MULTICOUNTRY MODEL

According to Solnik, each security is influenced by its domestic market factor, which in turn is influenced by the single world market factor. Therefore national market risk may be broken down into 1) risk caused by the world factor, and 2) risk specific to the country. The sensitivity of a country to this world factor results from many influences including importance of foreign trade, monetary policy, government regulation of the economy, and cross-border capital flows.

The world beta of a security (B_{iw}) is the result of its domestic beta (B_i) and the sensitivity of the domestic security factor to the world market factor (B_{cw}). Therefore each security's expected return is proportional to its world beta (B_{iw}) and its domestic beta (B_i). All of these relationships can be considered consistent with the basic model of CAPM.

Multicountry model

Seeks to describe complex international stock price behavior by use of a world stock market factor and national stock market factor. Each country stock market is sensitive to the world market factor based on several considerations—foreign trade, monetary policy, and cross-border capital flows.

The multicountry model leads to a top-down approach in international investment where the portfolio manager seeks to exploit inefficiencies within a global framework. The implementation steps are summarized as follows:

1. Forecast national market return and currency movements.
2. Make international asset allocations, with underweighting or overweighting of countries or sectors based on results of step 1.
3. Value individual securities within their national markets.
4. Estimate beta coefficients.
5. Select stocks based on betas and forecasts of national market returns. Where optimistic or bullish on a stock market, select stocks with high betas for that market. Where bullish on the currency (and uncertain about the market), select low beta stocks in that market.

---

* B. Solnik, *International Investments* (Reading, MA: Addison-Wesley, 1991):134–137.

To illustrate application of the multicountry model the following table can be constructed. Here we have forecasts of the risk-free interest rate, return on domestic stock market, and currency rate changes (against dollar). In the case of overweighting or underweighting stock markets, the choice is clear. The most bullish market return forecast is for the Netherlands; therefore this market should be overweighted in the portfolio, and high beta stocks should be included. The least bullish market return forecast applies to France. However, the currency projection is moderately bullish. In this case the fund manager should underweigh France in the portfolio and select low beta stocks. In the case of Italy where a bullish market forecast is available but currency uncertainties exist, the fund manager should be ready to apply currency hedges where possible.

Illustration of the Multicountry Model: Top-Down Approach

	Risk-Free Rate	Domestic Stock Market Return	Currency Value Against Dollar
United States	5	10	—
Netherlands	6	14	+5
France	9	2	+4
Italy	12	12	−2

The multicountry model has its own limitations. First, a world CAPM is not easily defended on theoretical grounds. Second, the definition of a world market portfolio meets numerous practical problems. Finally, a single world factor model does not describe international stock price behavior. The multicountry model is an improvement, since the national market factor in each case reflects the real and monetary influences on assets traded in the national market. The multicountry model is a step in the direction of describing the complexity of international stock price behavior. However, it needs refinement. A logical extension is the arbitrage pricing theory (APT).

ARBITRAGE PRICING THEORY

Arbitrage Pricing Theory (APT)

Focuses on relative pricing of securities based on common factors. Risk premiums are associated with each factor, and affect pricing of individual countries accordingly.

Arbitrage pricing starts with a simple descriptive model where the return on a risky asset is determined by a number of common factors. APT focuses on relative pricing of securities, not a world market portfolio. The common factors that influence returns are exogenous.

In APT there are a number of factors common to all securities that influence the relative returns (and prices) of these securities. Each factor has its own sensitivity to be estimated against the required return of the security. For a given factor this sensitivity (beta) may be higher or lower for each security, depending on the sensitivity relationship.

The expected return on a security is a linear function of these betas:

$$E(R) = R_o + B_1 RP_1 + B_2 RP_2 + \ldots B_K RP_K \qquad (19.2)$$

where RP_i is the risk premium associated with factor i and R_o is the risk-free rate.

Factors that determine return on a security must be estimated. There is no simple theoretical model from which factors can be selected. Several sets of factors are generally used by analysts.

1. *Real economic factors.* These measure economic growth, industrial production, and energy use.
2. *Monetary factors.* These could include interest rate changes or rates of inflation.
3. *Domestic factors.* These could include variables reflecting the domestic economy's deviation from trends that persist on a world basis.
4. *Industry factors.* These could include a set of factors common to companies in the same industry (industry-wide factors).

Market Efficiency in the International Context

MARKET EFFICIENCY AND IMPERFECTIONS

An important question influencing the potential benefits from international diversification is that of market efficiency. If international asset prices are determined in efficient financial markets, then all available information has been used in pricing these assets. As a result, prices are based on rational expectations of investors, and investors may experience difficulty when seeking undervalued securities. Consequently, they will not be able to outperform the market index.

If we consider that many internationally oriented institutional investors have implemented an index approach to portfolio management (see Chapter 20 for discussion of the index approach), we might conclude that these investors place a relatively high degree of credence in the efficient markets hypothesis. An alternative interpretation might be that these investment managers are minimizing opportunities for criticism of their portfolio performance by locking all or a substantial part of portfolio funds managed in a market-index driven portfolio.

Formal studies have generated results indicating that individually the large financial markets (New York, London, Tokyo, and others) satisfy the statistical tests of market efficiency. That is, price movements of their shares appear to conform to a random walk. Hawawini goes further, noting that few studies have been undertaken that are aimed at verifying international securities market efficiency.

While individual national stock markets exhibit efficiency by a statistically defined and measured random price behavior, these same markets can exhibit certain types of imperfections and differences in operation and structure.

Informationally efficient

Available data concerning a given security is incorporated into the pricing of that security.

A stock market is informationally efficient if available data is incorporated into the pricing of the securities (assets) traded in that market. There can be substantial differences between available information and complete information. Regulatory agencies, such as the Securities and Exchange Commission in the United States and similar bodies in other countries, try to reduce the gap between available information and complete information. Also, they seek to prevent the improper use of undisclosed information (insider information). The fact that Italian and Norwegian regulations do not mandate as much disclosure as is required in the United States does not necessarily make the Italian and Norwegian stock markets less efficient than the U.S. market. As long as Italian and Norwegian investors fully use the information available in pricing stocks, we can argue that these markets are also efficient.

Imperfections in stock markets are generally not considered to cause less efficiency, as we have defined it. Nevertheless, these imperfections are important to the investor. These imperfections include the following:

1. Extent to which continuous trading takes place. As noted in Chapter 18 in some stock markets there may be one or two market price settings at which trading

takes place at a uniform price established through participant outcry. Subsequently there may be only limited trading through designated market makers.

2. Concentration of trading may be high. In some stock markets trading in the five or ten most active stocks may account for over half of total market volume. As a result the majority of listed and traded share issues are only very thinly traded and are subject to relatively high price volatility.

3. Size of market and capitalization value of leading stocks may be fairly small. In some stock markets there may be very few share issues that have a market large enough to allow institutional trading without causing destabilization of the market.

THE CURRENCY FACTOR

The currency factor holds an important position in the question of international market efficiency. The foreign exchange market links the national capital markets and provides the mechanism through which investment funds move from one nation's capital market to another.

There are two disparate viewpoints that are not easily reconciled in discussions concerning how the currency factor bears on securities market efficiency. These viewpoints can be summarized as follows:

1. Country differences in return on stocks and bonds reflect anticipated currency rate movements. Therefore they can be considered as satisfying the conditions of the International Fisher Effect with investors operating within an environment of efficient markets. In this case international capital markets can be regarded as satisfying the conditions of equilibrium and efficiency.

2. Currency markets are inherently unstable and prone to overshooting. Under these conditions international investors must be viewed as operating in situations that do not satisfy conditions of efficient markets. Equally important, investors are subject to disequilibrium conditions, meaning that forecasting takes on a high priority.

According to the first viewpoint, changes in foreign exchange market values can be considered as only temporary departures from efficiency. In this view global capital market efficiency is regarded more as a question of equilibrium, where temporary (ex ante) departures from equilibrium occur. However, equilibrium is viewed as being restored quickly as new perceptions and information concerning currency valuations are brought into the process of pricing capital market assets.

The second viewpoint emphasizes the disequilibrium orientation of the foreign exchange market, and the tendency of floating currencies to fluctuate around, and even beyond, their equilibrium levels. This tendency can be seen in Exhibit 19.4, where the foreign exchange valuation rises, moving through the equilibrium zone (defined as P_aP_b), and moving well above the equilibrium zone. Subsequently, the foreign exchange valuation declines, again moving through the equilibrium zone, and falling well below this zone. This currency overshooting baffles foreign exchange rate forecasters.

RATIONAL EXPECTATIONS AND INTERNATIONAL ASSET PRICING

One of the apparent anomalies of international portfolio management is the differential pricing of capital market assets. This differential can be seen if we compare price earning ratios in different national stock markets, and if we compare yields on

EXHIBIT 19.4   **Currency Overshooting Above and Below an Equilibrium Zone**

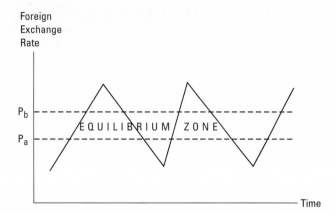

long-term bonds in different national bond markets. There are several reasons for this differential pricing.

One possible reason for differential pricing of international capital market assets would be expectations concerning changes in foreign exchange rates. Investors are assumed to behave rationally. Therefore these investors formulate reasonable estimates of future movements in financial asset prices related to changes in foreign exchange rates, bond prices, and interest rates. These rational expectations should result in market transactions and market arbitrage that price securities in a manner whereby there can be no profit from further arbitrage. In this case we expect the International Fisher Effect to operate. Any international differential in asset pricing can be attributed to perceived currency risk. Therefore this basis of determining prices is rational.

A second reason for differential pricing of international capital market assets would be differences in risk aversion in partially segmented capital markets. Investor clientele in one country (Sweden) place a greater premium on low risk assets such as government bonds than investor clientele in another country (United Kingdom). As a result, risk averse investors in Sweden bid up bond prices thereby driving down bond yields. The opposite takes place in the United Kingdom, where risk-oriented investors shy away from government bonds. As a result, government bond prices remain low, offering U.K. investors higher yields. This relationship can be depicted in Exhibit 19.5 where separate Capital Market Lines (CML) are used to depict the equilibrium positions in Sweden and the United Kingdom, respectively. The following section explains the significance and use of the CML.

We should note that the CML for the United Kingdom intersects the vertical axis at a relatively higher risk-free rate as compared with Sweden, denoting the higher premium for risk preferred by United Kingdom investors. Also, the CML for the United Kingdom has a different slope than the CML for Sweden, suggesting that Swedish investors are willing to trade off additional return for increased risk, where the increment to risk is relatively modest. Finally, we depict the market equilibrium where Swedish investors accept much lower risk levels than U.K. investors.

Capital Market Line (CML)

Depicts equilibrium position in a given capital market where investors can hold varying proportions of their assets in the risk-free asset and market portfolio. Borrowing and lending is assumed to take place at the risk-free rate.

EXHIBIT 19.5	**Comparison of Market Equilibrium Positions where Investors Display Different Degrees of Risk Aversion**

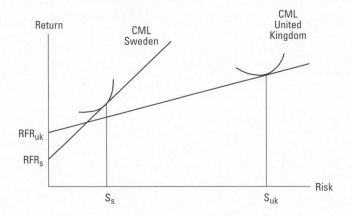

THE CAPITAL MARKET LINE (CML)

Capital market theory builds on the Markowitz portfolio model. According to this model 1) all investors are Markowitz-efficient and want to be somewhere on the efficient frontier, 2) investors can borrow or lend any amount of money at the risk-free rate, 3) investors have homogeneous expectations (regarding future rates of return) and apply the same one-period time analysis, 4) investments and investment securities are infinitely divisible (continuous curves), 5) there are no taxes or transactions costs in buying or selling assets, 6) there is no inflation or shifting in interest rates, and 7) capital markets are in equilibrium.

Efficient frontier

Investment portfolios producing optimal combinations of risk and return.

RISK-FREE ASSET

Investors can acquire a risky asset or a risk-free asset. A risk-free asset is one for which there is no question regarding expected rate of return; the standard deviation of returns equal zero. This return might be analogous to the long-term real growth rate of the national economy. The portfolio of risk-free assets is depicted in Exhibit 19.6 at the point RFR, where expected return equals the *RFR* and the standard deviation of return is zero.

Since the covariance between two assets is equal to the correlation of their returns multiplied by the standard deviation of return of the two securities, the covariance of the risk-free asset with that of any risky asset or portfolio of assets must be zero, as indicated in the following equation.

Covariance

Equal to the correlations of returns between two securities multiplied by the standard deviation of their returns. Covariance reflects correlation, but in numbers based on measuring percent returns.

$$\text{Cov}_{i,rfr} = \text{Correl}_{i,rfr} \yen SD_i \yen SD_{rfr} \qquad (19.3)$$

When we combine the risk-free asset with a risky portfolio, the expected return is the weighted average of the two asset returns.

When we combine the risk-free asset with a portfolio of risky assets, the variance of return of the risk-free asset is zero. Also the correlation between the risk-free asset and risky asset is zero. Therefore the standard deviation of a portfolio that combines the risk-free asset and a portfolio of risky assets is linear, having a

EXHIBIT 19.6   **Illustration of CML and Leveraged Portfolios**

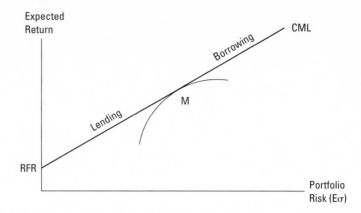

value related to the standard deviation of the risky asset, and in proportion to the relative size of the risky asset in the total portfolio. Hence the CML in the diagram is a straight line from the point RFR.

THE MARKET PORTFOLIO

The market portfolio includes all risky assets (bonds, stocks, real estate, gold, etc.) in proportion to their market value. In this portfolio all unsystematic risk is diversified away. Unique risk of each asset is offset by the unique variability in returns of other assets in the portfolio. The only risk that remains is systematic risk. This systematic risk is measured by the standard deviation of return of the market portfolio.

Investors can invest all their resources in the market portfolio (point M in Exhibit 19.6). Alternately they may lend (invest) some of their resources at the risk-free rate and invest the remainder in the market portfolio. In this case investors may expect an investment outcome somewhere between points RFR and M. Alternately they may invest all their resources in the market portfolio and borrow money at the risk-free rate, investing the proceeds in the risky market portfolio. Return and risk will increase in a linear way along the CML. In effect the CML becomes a new (dominant) efficient frontier. All portfolios on the CML are perfectly positively correlated.

Studies Supporting International Diversification in Equities

The models of portfolio selection of Harry Markowitz and James Tobin provide us with a theoretical basis for diversification of risky assets. As noted earlier in this chapter the extent of risk reduction through diversification depends in part upon the correlations of returns of the securities in the portfolio. Low correlations of return permit considerable risk reduction. High correlations of return result in minimal risk reduction, even when diversification involves including a large number of securities in the portfolio.

EARLY STUDIES ON DIVERSIFICATION

Within a single nation economic phenomena and economic variables generally move in unison. Therefore intranational equity returns can be highly correlated. Empirical studies tend to find correlations of return of .50 to .60 for domestic equity securities of a single national stock market. The relatively high degree of positive correlation among domestic equity securities in a single national stock market suggests that there are practical limits to risk reduction. However, the extent of risk reduction can be significantly increased when diversification is carried out on an international basis. In an early study published in 1968 Herbert Grubel constructed an efficiency curve (frontier) based on the return, risk, and correlations of return of national stock market indexes for 13 countries.* Two years later Haim Levy and Marshal Sarnat extended this approach to 28 countries for the period 1951–1967. Levy and Sarnat calculated mean rates of return and risk (standard deviation) in dollars. A correlation matrix was estimated. The range of returns was a high of 17.8% (Japan) to a low of −1.5% (Spain). Four countries had standard deviations greater than 30% while seven countries had standard deviations below 13%.

Utilizing the Sharpe-Lintner model, optimum portfolios were chosen assuming risk-free rates of return of 2, 3, 4, and 6%, respectively (Exhibit 19.7). It should be noted that stock market indices for only nine countries were included in the four optimum portfolios depicted in Exhibit 19.7. In part this result was due to the low or negative correlations of returns between and among these nine countries (14 of the 36 country-paired correlations were found to be negative). Investments in the United States and Japan account for a majority (50 to 70%) of the optimal portfolios. With the exception of Austria, the portfolios virtually exclude the developed countries of Western Europe. Perhaps the most striking feature of the composition of the diversified international portfolios is the high proportion of investments in developing or borderline income countries such as Venezuela, South Africa, New Zealand, and Mexico.

EXHIBIT 19.7	**Composition of Optimal Portfolios for Selected Interest Rates**			
	INTEREST RATES (in percent)			
Country	**2**	**3**	**4**	**6**
Austria	3.43	6.99	9.03	12.06
Denmark	—	2.06	0.01	—
Japan	14.68	16.71	17.65	20.86
Mexico	4.03	4.32	4.53	—
New Zealand	13.16	6.27	2.59	—
South Africa	10.37	12.51	13.83	12.86
United Kingdom	0.18	—	—	—
United States	36.57	40.99	42.79	51.06
Venezuela	15.51	11.72	9.57	3.16
Total	100.00	100.00	100.00	100.00
Mean Portfolio Rate of Return	9.5	10.5	11.0	12.5
Portfolio Standard Deviation	5.72	6.41	6.82	8.39

The remaining 19 countries are not included in any of the optimal portfolios.

SOURCE: Levy, H., and M. Sarnat. "International Diversification of Investment Portfolio," *American Economic Review,* (September 1970).

---

*Grubel, H.G. "Internationally Diversified Portfolios: Welfare Gains and Capital Flows," *American Economic Review,* (December 1968): 1299–1314.

The four portfolios depicted in Exhibit 19.7 are based on alternative interest rate assumptions. In Exhibit 19.8 we can observe optimum portfolios at points a and b, depicting interest rates of 3% and 6%, respectively.

Investment opportunity locus

Indicates combinations of risk-free asset and market portfolios, and their respective return and risk properties.

The investment opportunity locus r_1 starting from the 3% intercept on the Y axis reflects the assumption that lending or borrowing can take place at this rate. Similarly, the investment opportunity locus r_2 reflects the assumption that borrowing or lending can take place at 6%. The optimum unleveraged portfolio for a given interest rate is the point at which the respective investment opportunity locus is tangent to the efficient frontier (points a and b in Exhibit 19.8). We should note that the slope of the investment opportunity locus measures the tradeoff between expected return and risk for all investors, and it therefore uniquely determines the optimal unleveraged share portfolio for all investors operating where the risk-free interest rate applies.

Levy and Sarnat found substantial gains from international diversification. Exhibit 19.9 summarizes their findings, with mean rates of return and standard deviation of the optimal portfolios for each subset of equity markets.*

| **EXHIBIT 19.8** | **Optimum Portfolios at 3% and 6% Interest Rate Levels** |

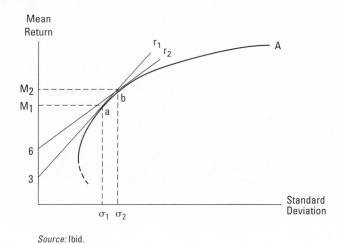

Source: Ibid.

| **EXHIBIT 19.9** | **Mean Rates of Return and Standard Deviations of Optimal Portfolios for a 5% Interest Rate** |

In Percent

	Mean Rate	Standard Deviation
Developing Countries	5.0	26.5
Common Market	15.5	25.0
Western Europe	15.5	23.5
High Income Countries	13.0	12.5
All Countries	12.0	8.0

* Levy, H., and M. Sarnat. "International Diversification of Investment Portfolios," *American Economic Review* (September 1970): 674.

EXHIBIT 19.10   **Relative Position of Six Optimal Portfolios for a 5% Interest Rate**

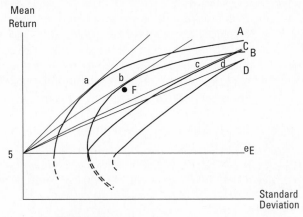

A – 28 Countries
B – 16 High Income Countries
C – 11 Western European Countries
D – 5 Common Market Countries
E – 9 Developing Countries
F –   United States

In the case of a portfolio created of equities in the developing countries only, investors would have received a 5% return with a 26.5% standard deviation (point e on Exhibit 19.10) as compared with a 12% return and standard deviation of 8% for the all countries portfolio (point a on Exhibit 19.10). While an American investor might not wish to restrict his portfolio to developing countries alone, inclusion of these countries in the opportunity set improves his risk-return position.

According to Levy and Sarnat, exclusion of the common market countries and Canada from optimal portfolios for American investors is based on their relatively strong correlations of return with the U.S. stock market. See Exhibit 19.11 for a discussion of reasons to expect high correlations among equity markets.

Levy and Sarnat conclude their article by commenting on the probable degree of imperfection in the international capital markets. They note that in the absence of artificial barriers we can expect an optimal portfolio to contain securities from all countries. That is if a country is not included, its share prices should fall (and rates of return rise) to levels where it would be included in the optimal portfolio. The results (ex post) of their study show other combinations of equities to be dominant, suggesting that restrictions on international trade and/or capital flows have a significant effect on the pattern of security returns and permit inefficient markets to persist.[†]

Duncan Ripley takes a different view on the possibilities of risk reduction and correlations of returns among national equity markets (Exhibit 19.11). Countries may tend to have higher correlations of return for several reasons. These include extensive trading linkages, within-area capital flows, and dominant financial centers. Based on a statistical study, Ripley identified three factors that account for a

---

[†] Ibid., p. 675.

EXHIBIT 19.11	**Reasons to Expect High Correlations Among Equity Markets**

We have indicated that international diversification can reduce portfolio risk where low positive or negative correlations exist between national stock markets. Now let us turn the question around and consider why we might observe some degree of correlation, perhaps even moderately high correlations between national stock markets.

Correlations between stock markets may arise in many ways. They may reflect a similarity in economic structure between national economies. Or, correlations may indicate a relationship in structure between two stock markets.

Countries that trade extensively with one another may be expected to have strong economic ties. Currency areas may reinforce stock market linkages by strengthening the relationship between domestic economic variables and by encouraging similar exchange rate expectations for the countries within the area.

According to Duncan Ripley, "A dominant financial center within a multinational area may stimulate correlation . . . by facilitating within-area capital flows, relative to capital flows to and from the area."* This tendency can operate through parallel interest rate movements and/or through stock price arbitrage.

Another possible source of covariation is where two countries have stock markets in which shares of the same group or similar groups of multinational companies are traded. If capital flows were not hindered, expectations and pricing of securities might be effectively equalized by these capital flows.

In 1973 Ripley published the results of a study of the linkages between national stock markets. Using factor analysis, he analyzed monthly data for 19 developed country stock markets covering the period 1960–1970. Ripley sought to identify "sources of common movement" affecting national stock market indexes. These "factors" are constructed as a weighted sum of the original variables. In his paper Ripley identified three factors that account for a substantial part of the common movement (covariation) between stock markets.

The first factor accounted for over half of the common movement. Countries with large weights in the calculation of this factor are "those whose stock markets are well-developed and appear to be reasonably open to capital flows." These are markets on which the shares of multinational companies are traded, including the Netherlands, Canada, Switzerland, and the United States. According to Ripley this grouping results from international capital flows and the composition of shares traded.

The second factor has large weights in the United Kingdom, Ireland, and New Zealand, and to a lesser extent on South Africa and Australia. According to Ripley these countries," are linked financially through the London financial market."

The third factor is dominated by covariation between the American and Canadian stock price indexes, and accounts for 26% of the movement of the American index and 21% of the movement of the Canadian index. Stock market indexes of most other countries are not significantly influenced by this factor, representing a covariation unique to the North American stock market. To a small extent the movement of the German and Italian stock markets was negatively correlated with that in the United States and Canada.

Ripley found that the first three factors described "account for almost 80% of the common movement." The four countries in the sample with high levels of common movement were the United States, Canada, Switzerland, and the Netherlands. Countries with exceptionally low levels of common movement included Finland, South Africa, and Denmark. The British and German stock markets were positioned midway between the former two groups of countries.

*Ripley, Duncan M. "Systemic Elements in the Linkage of National Stock Market Indices," *The Review of Economics and Statistics,* (1973): 357.

substantial part of the common movement between stock markets. These are 1) well-developed stock markets open to capital flows where shares of multinational companies are traded, 2) linkages of the London financial market, and 3) North American common variation (United States and Canada). These three factors account for almost 80% of the common movement of equity markets.

INTERNATIONAL DIVERSIFICATION REDUCES RISK

In 1974 Bruno Solnik demonstrated that systematic risk can be reduced by international diversification. Solnik generated a number of domestic and international portfolios. He demonstrated how increasing the number of securities in a portfolio removes diversifiable risk, leaving a residual (systematic) risk for the domestic investor. He pointed out that each domestic stock market has its own level of systematic risk. In some cases this risk is higher (Switzerland, Germany), and in some cases this risk is lower (Netherlands, Belgium, and United Kingdom).

One diagram in particular in Solnik's presentation has been widely used as a way of demonstrating the benefits from international diversification (Exhibit 19.12).

The curve for the U.S. market reflects the ability of domestic investors to reduce risk by utilizing a large number of securities in the portfolio. According to Solnik, nondiversifiable risk for the U.S. market is only 27%, whereas in Germany it is 44%. An internationally well-diversified portfolio would be only half as risky as a well-diversified portfolio of U.S. stocks.

Writing in 1974 shortly after the dollar devaluations of 1971 and 1973, Solnik noted that American holders of foreign equities greatly benefited from the dollar devaluations. An uncovered international portfolio is certainly a good hedge against devaluation of the dollar. Nevertheless Solnik correctly notes that the risk of a portfolio unprotected against exchange risk is larger than for a covered portfolio. However, its *total risk* can be much smaller than for a comparable domestic portfolio. This result follows from the low or negative correlation of return between domestic and foreign stock markets.

WORLD, COUNTRY, AND INDUSTRY RELATIONSHIPS

In an article published in 1976, Donald Lessard distinguishes between world, country, and industry factors in achieving international diversification and reduction of portfolio risk.*

Lessard views international equity investment as differing from its domestic counterpart in three important respects:

1. The covariances among securities within national markets are much higher than among securities in different national markets. National factors exert a strong impact on security returns relative to any world factor.
2. Barriers to international investment (taxation, currency blockage) may segment national financial markets to an extent so that they are priced in a domestic rather than international context.
3. Exchange rates between currencies fluctuate, raising the problem of exchange risk in international investment.

Lessard seeks to answer three basic questions: 1) what are the salient elements in the covariance structure of equity returns internationally? 2) Do world, country, or industry factors dominate? 3) What does the covariance structure suggest about gains from international diversification, under the alternative assumptions of integrated and segmented securities markets?

Lessard subjects world, national, and industry elements to statistical tests. He notes that previous studies found that national market indexes, representing

---

* Lessard, D. "World, Country and Industry Relationships in Equity Returns: Implications for Risk Reduction Through International Diversification," *Financial Analysts Journal* (January-February 1976): 2–8.

EXHIBIT 19.12   **Risk Reduction Compared—U.S. Stock Portfolio and International Stock Portfolio**

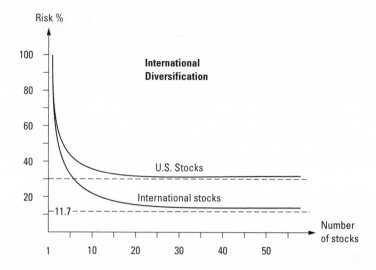

systematic (domestically undiversifiable) risk explain a substantial part of the variance of returns on individual stocks. In general a low proportion of variance is explained by world market factors for the country stock markets included in his study.

To test for industry elements, returns for 205 individual stocks were regressed against a world index and the residuals of the country or industry indexes were obtained by regressing these on the world index. The results show that there is a world element in returns. However stock returns represent stronger country effects together with important, but relatively weaker, industry effects. Lessard found industry factors large relative to country factors for only Australia, Japan, and the United Kingdom, and attributed this in part to the importance of multinational company stocks in total industry capitalization.

Lessard distinguishes between segmented market and integrated market conditions. The magnitude of gains from international diversification will depend on which of these conditions prevails. In the case of segmented markets, assuming the validity of the capital asset pricing model, securities prices and expected returns will be determined by undiversifiable (systematic) risk of each security in the respective national portfolio. In the case of integrated markets, prices and expected returns will be determined by the undiversifiable risk of each security in the world market portfolio.

In the case of integrated capital markets, low correlations between national stock market returns may overstate the benefits to be derived from international diversification. Since a few large countries make up the bulk of the world market value (e.g. Japan, United States, and United Kingdom), risk elements characteristic of these countries will dominate the risk of the world portfolio. Because asset prices in an integrated world market will adjust to induce investors to hold the world market portfolio, alternative portfolios with more complete diversification of these country elements will be inefficient in terms of any tradeoff between risk and expected return.

A more complete diversification of country effects will be feasible for segmented markets, while U.S. investors will evaluate foreign security portfolios in the context of the U.S. market for segmented capital markets. The return that the U.S. investor will require depends on the systematic risk of the foreign portfolio in the context of the U.S. market.

Lessard concludes by noting that actual market outcomes are "more consistent with the assumption of segmented markets than the assumption of integrated markets."[*] Most national stock markets have provided higher returns than the U.S. market. However, markets cannot in fact be regarded as totally segmented, since there is a measurable flow of international investment. This fact suggests that the actual outcome lies somewhere between the two assumptions.

Bond and Stock Portfolios

In Chapter 18 we noted that international investment in bonds offers opportunities for efficient diversification. The market capitalization of major bond markets exceeds that of the major equity markets. Bonds are an effective means of diversifying exposures to domestic monetary and other financial uncertainties. Reporting in 1986, K. Cholerton, P. Pieraerts, and B. Solnik (CPS) noted that foreign bond holdings of U.S. pension funds were less than $2 billion as compared with close to $15 billion in foreign equities. Nondollar bond markets are growing rapidly, and new issue activity in Eurobonds is comparable to the domestic U.S. market.

This CPS study is one of the earliest that provides detailed information concerning correlations with stock market returns. In the discussion that follows we present the main arguments of the CPS study regarding investment in foreign currency bonds. The CPS study considers investment in foreign currency bonds from 1983–1985, and a longer period (1971–1984).

In the period 1983–1985 the six major bond markets exhibited positive but weak correlations (Exhibit 19.13). The correlations between these bond markets range from a high of 0.72 (deutsche mark—guilder) to a low of 0.17 (Swiss franc—sterling).

EXHIBIT 19.13 **Correlation and Volatility of Monthly Rates of Return—1 January 1983–30 April 1985**

(Domestic Government Bond Indexes in Local Currency)

	US Dollar	Swiss Franc	Deutsche Mark	Pound	Dutch Guilder	Yen	Mean Return % Per Month	Volatility % Per Month
US Dollar	1	0.28	0.44	0.39	0.38	0.47	0.63	2.18
Swiss Franc		1	0.54	0.17	0.27	0.54	0.13	0.61
Deutsche Mark			1	0.38	0.72	0.59	0.63	0.94
Pound Sterling				1	0.23	0.49	0.92	2.32
Dutch Guilder					1	0.55	0.57	1.10
Japanese Yen						1	0.73	0.81

SOURCE: Cholerton K., P. Pieraerts, and B. Solnik. "Why Invest in Foreign Currency Bonds?", *Journal of Portfolio Management* (Summer 1986): 5.

---

[*] Lessard, D. op. cit. p. 37.

Based on monthly data, the local currency returns and risk are highest in the case of U.K. government bonds (return 0.92% and risk 2.32%).

Without exception the domestic and Eurobond markets in the same currency exhibit high correlation (CPS find a correlation of .84 for the U.S. government and Eurodollar bond markets).

However, the correlations across currencies is usually low, less than 0.5 in most cases. For example the R^2 between domestic pound sterling and Dutch guilder bonds is .23, implying that the two markets have less than 25% common price variation. Also CPS found that the volatility of non-U.S. government bond markets was much smaller than that of the U.S. market, with the exception of the United Kingdom (Exhibit 19.13).

Taking all rates of return in a common currency (U.S. dollars), the CPS study calculated correlation coefficients for short-term (1983–1985) and longer-term (1971–1984) periods. These coefficients are displayed in Exhibit 19.14. The correlation figures are even more striking than those found in the estimates restricted to local currency. Clearly the correlations between the various bond markets are low, and long-term interest rates are not well synchronized, giving considerable opportunity for risk reduction.

These results are not confined to the period under study. The CPS study has extended to a longer-term period (1971–1984), and the results are included in Exhibit 19.14. In all cases the comovement of each foreign bond market with the U.S. market is low (R^2 of less than 0.33).

The authors also find strikingly weak positive or even negative correlations between foreign bonds and the U.S. stock market (Exhibit 19.14, Columns 3 and 4). This lack of correlation is not surprising given the independence between national economic and monetary policies. Foreign monetary policies have little impact on U.S. economic growth and U.S. share prices. Therefore foreign bonds offer considerable diversification potential to a stock portfolio manager.

The long-term performance of the leading government bond markets appears in Exhibit 19.15. The following summarizes the main findings of the CPS study.

EXHIBIT 19.14   **Correlation of Non-U.S. Government Bond Indices with U.S. Bond Index and with S&P 500 Index**

	CORRELATION OF U.S. AND NON-DOLLAR GOVERNMENT BOND INDICES (US DOLLARS)		CORRELATION OF GOVERNMENT BOND INDICES AND S&P 500 INDEX (US DOLLARS)	
	1	2	3	4
	1983–1985	1971–1984	1983–1985	1971–1984
U.S. Bonds	1.00	1.00	0.45	0.30
Swiss Franc Bonds	0.03	0.21	0.06	0.09
DM Bonds	0.08	0.29	−0.02	0.19
Sterling Bonds	0.09	0.23	0.09	0.10
D. Guilder Bonds	0.09	0.31	−0.03	0.19
Yen Bonds	0.19	0.21	0.19	0.10

Columns 1 and 2: With U.S. bond markets

Columns 3 and 4: With U.S. stock market

SOURCE: Ibid.

EXHIBIT 19.15	Long-term Performance of Government Bond Markets, January 1971–December 1984. Dollar-Oriented Investor

	Mean Total Return % per year 1	Capital Gain % per year 2	Yield % per year 3	Currency Contribution % per year 4	Volatility in $ % per year 5	Volatility in Local Currency % per year 6
BONDS						
U.S. Dollar	6.80	−2.70	9.50	0	8.92	8.92
Swiss Franc	9.41	0.41	5.10	3.89	14.90	4.48
Deutsche Mark	9.77	0.09	8.56	1.12	14.46	7.02
Pound Sterling	6.33	−0.45	12.54	−5.76	11.78	9.38
Dutch Guilder	9.29	0.01	9.18	0.10	13.57	7.11
Japanese Yen	12.60	0.86	8.91	2.82	14.48	6.15
U.S. Stocks	7.96	3.18	4.478	0	15.43	15.43
HEDGED BONDS						
Swiss Franc	11.42	0.41	11.01	0	4.48	4.48
Deutsche Mark	12.56	0.09	12.47	0	7.02	7.02
Pound Sterling	9.86	−0.45	10.31	0	9.38	9.38
Dutch Guilder	12.09	0.01	12.08	0	7.11	7.11
Japanese Yen	12.54	0.86	11.68	0	6.15	6.15

SOURCE: Cholerton, K., P. Pieraerts, and B. Solnik. "Why Invest in Foreign Currency Bonds?", *Journal of Portfolio Management*, (Summer 1986): 6.

1. Over the period 1971–1984 dollar performance of foreign bond markets has been better than that of the U.S. bond market.
2. While foreign bond markets have tended to be less volatile in local currency terms, currency volatility strongly increases the potential risk of the U.S. investor (Columns 5 and 6, Exhibit 19.15).
3. When we add currency-induced volatility, each foreign bond market is individually more volatile than the U.S. bond market (Columns 5 and 6).
4. Nevertheless the addition of foreign bonds to a U.S. bond portfolio would have reduced the total risk while improving performance. This benefit is derived from low correlation between markets.

An illustration of the results from constructing internationally diversified bond portfolios can be found in Exhibit 19.16. CPS add nondollar bonds by increments of 10%, the foreign bonds equally distributed among the five major nondollar markets. The graph illustrates the changes in return and standard deviation of each portfolio. Starting from a purely domestic portfolio with 100% allocated to U.S. bonds, we are at the lowest point on the curve (Exhibit 19.16). A substitution of 10% in nondollar bonds increases the return from 6.80% to 7.18% and reduces the risk from 8.92% to 8.47%. The minimum risk portfolio is between 30% and 40% foreign bonds.

Multiasset Strategies

International investing provides opportunities to employ strategies whose success depends on complex economic and financial processes. These relationships are well illustrated in an article published by Solnik and Noetzlin in 1982.* Solnik and

---

* Solnik, B. and B. Noetzlin. "Optimal International Asset Allocation," *Journal of Portfolio Management* (Fall 1982).

EXHIBIT 19.16   **Risk-return Tradeoff for International Bond Portfolios**

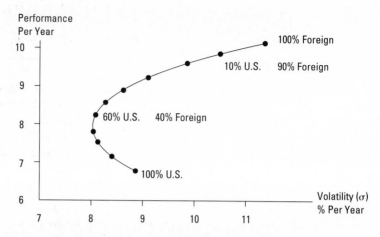

The indexes used here come from local publications in the various countries. They are either government bond indexes calculated locally or are reconstructed from published yield-to-maturity data on government securities.

SOURCE: Same as Exhibit 19.13

Bernard Noetzlin compiled a database reflecting investment outcomes for the period 1970–1980, encompassing 36 major investment vehicles and cutting across 17 currencies. The investment vehicles include 17 national stock markets, eight bond markets, eight money markets (Eurocurrencies or fixed rate deposits), and three gold-based assets. The authors employ mean-variance optimization (risk-reward) methodology and calculate returns and risks from the perspective of an American investor working from dollars.

RETURN AND RISK MEASURES

Solnik and Noetzlin computed performance and volatility of all 36 vehicles over the full ten-year period and in various subperiods. Annual stock returns ranged from a high of over 25% (Hong Kong) and 21% (Japan), to a small negative return (Spain) (Exhibit 19.17). The return consisted of capital gain, dividend income, and exchange gains. Risk on stocks consisted of two elements, domestic (systematic) risk and exchange risk. The differential in volatility (risk) in dollars (Column vii) and local currencies (Column viii) is due to the low or negative correlation between security price and exchange rate movements. Except for the United States, the major stock markets on which institutional investors trade generated annual gains ranging between 10% and 25%, broadly outperforming bond markets.

Solnik and Noetzlin found that exchange volatility makes short-term commitments very risky. The average risk for an American investor was 24% annually on stock markets, about 13% on bonds, and about 9% on short-term investments.

In Exhibit 19.18 we summarize their estimates of performance on broad-based portfolios. Exhibit 19.18 indicates that the U.S. stock market (S&P 500) provided lower returns with relatively high risk. The U.S. stock and bond market had returns of only 60% of the world stock and bond indexes, but reflected comparable risk

EXHIBIT 19.17   Risk and Return for U.S. Dollar Investors, December 1970–1980

Vehicle	Total Performance I %	Annual Return II % per annum	Capital Gain III % per annum	Div./Int. Income IV % per annum	Exchange Gain V % per annum	Total Risk VI % per annum	Domestic Risk VII % per annum	Exchange Risk VIII % per annum
STOCKS								
Germany	183.27	11.07	−0.06	4.48	6.65	18.39	13.87	11.87
Belgium	219.89	12.44	−2.11	9.58	4.97	18.76	13.25	11.02
Denmark	272.49	14.18	5.71	5.98	2.49	17.65	15.41	10.25
France	160.10	10.12	2.17	5.79	2.16	25.81	22.00	10.24
Italy	23.31	2.14	3.24	3.11	−4.22	26.15	14.21	8.58
Norway	205.45	11.92	4.59	3.74	3.58	29.92	28.61	8.89
Netherlands	242.70	13.22	0.86	6.58	5.79	18.91	16.37	10.97
United Kingdom	229.92	12.79	7.00	5.91	−0.12	31.61	28.94	8.84
Sweden	169.57	10.52	3.62	5.06	1.84	18.06	15.05	8.89
Switzerland	223.34	12.56	0.11	2.82	9.63	21.40	16.80	14.67
Spain	−5.19	−0.54	−5.42	6.17	−1.29	20.26	16.71	9.10
Australia	192.88	11.45	6.02	4.89	0.53	27.15	24.62	9.15
Japan	583.91	21.40	11.89	2.82	6.65	19.55	16.39	10.42
Hong Kong	853.28	25.53	21.20	4.74	−0.41	45.80	47.95	5.63
Singapore	372.08	16.94	18.35	3.29	−4.69	36.03	35.82	6.52
Canada	227.03	12.69	10.07	4.50	−1.88	20.29	18.92	4.16
United States	91.71	6.78	2.34	4.45	0.00	16.00	16.00	0.00
BONDS								
Germany	261.98	13.85	−1.19	8.23	6.81	14.35	6.91	11.87
France	178.41	10.88	−1.90	10.61	2.17	11.80	4.39	10.24
Netherlands	227.29	12.70	−1.72	8.66	5.76	13.61	7.16	10.97
United Kingdom	159.66	10.10	−2.18	12.39	−0.12	16.29	12.30	8.84
Switzerland	326.70	15.76	0.70	5.15	9.91	15.33	4.33	14.67
Japan	285.65	14.67	−0.62	8.98	6.31	14.36	6.53	10.42
Canada	40.50	3.49	−3.78	9.00	−1.73	7.93	6.16	4.16
United States	72.56	5.66	−2.48	8.13	0.00	8.96	8.96	0.00
CASH								
Germany	219.81	12.44	0.00	5.71	6.73	11.83	0.74	11.87
France	230.76	12.82	0.00	10.61	2.21	10.33	1.10	10.24
Netherlands	233.18	12.90	0.00	7.13	5.77	11.11	0.92	10.97
United Kingdom	222.59	12.54	0.00	12.66	−0.12	8.96	1.11	8.84
Switzerland	250.90	13.49	0.00	3.78	9.71	14.72	0.80	14.67
Japan	268.91	14.07	0.00	7.79	6.28	10.44	0.84	10.42
Canada	95.10	6.97	0.00	8.76	−1.78	4.26	0.79	4.16
United States	136.74	9.08	0.00	9.08	0.00	0.95	0.95	0.00
GOLD AND GOLD-RELATED VEHICLES								
Gold Mines in US$	1517.59	32.40	21.21	11.19	0.00	44.91	44.91	0.00
Indexed Loans in FFr	1853.23	34.95	29.59	2.72	2.64	18.61	13.93	10.24
Bullion in US$	1449.28	31.83	31.83	0.00	0.00	29.45	29.48	0.00

Source: Solnik B., and B. Noetzlin. "Optimal International Asset Allocation," *Journal of Portfolio Management* (Fall 1982): 1.

EXHIBIT 19.18	**Index Performance Comparisons in U.S. Dollars, 1970 to 1980**	
	Total Return (Percent)	**Annual Volatility (Percent)**
World Stocks	9.4	14.2
World Stocks and Bonds	9.4	9.6
EAFE Stocks[1]	13.4	17.3
EAFE Stocks and Bonds	13.7	11.8
U.S. Stocks	6.8	16.0
U.S. Stocks and Bonds	6.1	9.0

[1] Refers to Non-American stocks

SOURCE: Same as Exhibit 19.17.

level. The world stock and bond index matched the performance of the world stock index, yet showed significantly less volatility.

Solnik and Noetzlin found that the currency impact on investment return can be either positive or negative, but more importantly, can represent a substantial proportion of total return (Exhibit 19.17, Column v). They note that the impact of exchange gains and losses must be judged at the level of an international portfolio.

They found that exchange risk is always significantly smaller than the systematic risk of the respective stock markets. However, it is often higher than the local currency volatility of the corresponding bond market (Exhibit 19.17, Columns vii and viii). Market risk and exchange risk do not compound together. There is usually a weak or negative correlation between currency and market volatility.

OPTIMAL ASSET ALLOCATION

Solnik and Noetzlin computed the most effective investment approaches over the full ten-year period and for subperiods. This analysis was based on two assumptions:

1. A world universe of investments (including U.S. securities).
2. A non-U.S. universe (including the foreign part of the portfolio).

The efficient frontiers they calculated (bonds and stocks only) are presented in Exhibit 19.19 and Exhibit 19.20. Passive diversification along the lines of the Capital International World Stock Index (world stocks) involves less risk than a purely U.S. portfolio (risk of 14% instead of 16%), and provides a 50% higher return. International diversification in stocks and bonds provides lower risks despite the volatility of bonds. The world stocks and bonds index they compiled enjoyed the same performance as the world stocks-only index with less volatility (10% volatility).

OPTIMAL STRATEGIES

Optimal asset allocation depends on the universe of securities, whether it includes or excludes U.S. securities, bonds, or gold-related assets. Exhibit 19.21 depicts optimal asset allocations for the full ten-year period. Four universes are shown, starting with stocks only and finally encompassing four categories of securities. Exhibit 19.21 shows minimum risk and target return (16% in this case) portfolios for each universe.

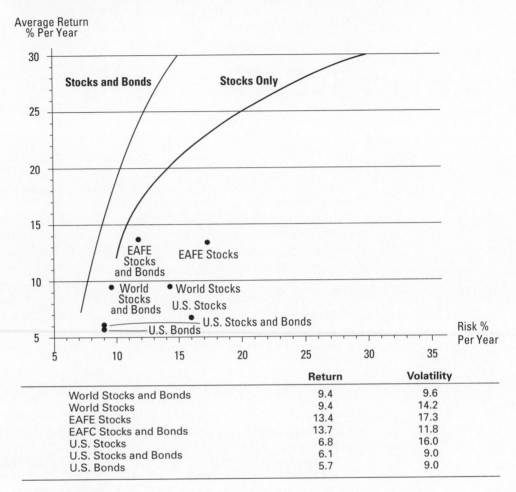

EXHIBIT 19.19   **Efficient Frontiers with U.S. Securities, December 1970–December 1980**

	Return	Volatility
World Stocks and Bonds	9.4	9.6
World Stocks	9.4	14.2
EAFE Stocks	13.4	17.3
EAFC Stocks and Bonds	13.7	11.8
U.S. Stocks	6.8	16.0
U.S. Stocks and Bonds	6.1	9.0
U.S. Bonds	5.7	9.0

SOURCE: Ibid., p. 16.

The information in Exhibit 19.21 permits us to estimate the contribution of each type of financial instrument (stocks, bonds, gold assets, cash) to the return, risk, and composition of the portfolio.

In analyzing Exhibit 19.21 the following central points emerge, relative to the development of appropriate portfolio strategies.

1. When the investment universe consists solely of equities, the minimum risk allocation is close to the index fund approach.

2. More aggressive strategies call for wider exposure to more volatile markets (Far East and gold mining stocks).

3. Once a broader universe of securities is allowed (bonds, money market assets), allocations to equities become more selective.

4. A mixed strategy covering equities, bonds, and other categories of assets makes greater market selectivity feasible while providing a means of controlling risk.

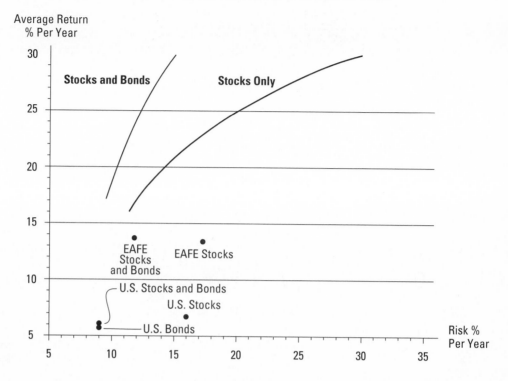

EXHIBIT 19.20   **Efficient Frontiers Without U.S. Securities, December 1970–December 1980**

5. Gold assets offer the twin appeals of a hedge (risk diversification) and a means of speculation (small gold holdings of 2–3% of the portfolio represent a hedge position).

6. U.S. bonds can represent core holdings for low risk portfolios.

7. Bonds serve as a low risk means of achieving currency diversification.

8. Short-term deposits position investors to benefit from exchange gains.

EVALUATION

The findings of the Solnik and Noetzlin study, or of any study of portfolio outcomes must be considered in light of the period covered. The ten-year period of their study was unique in several respects. First, it includes the international financial crises of 1971 and 1973 that led to two-dollar devaluations and to an abandonment of the fixed exchange rate system. In turn this led to massive speculation on gold-based assets, and a 15-fold increase in the price of gold. Second, the period was marked by strong inflation with price increases approaching double digit rates in countries such as the United States and the United Kingdom. Oil price increases in 1974 and 1978–1979 injected speculative shifts in the foreign exchange markets and contributed to inflation. Finally, interest rates moved upward strongly in the latter half of this period, bringing about higher returns on cash assets and sizeable capital losses on bonds (if and when liquidated from portfolios). Rising interest rates contributed to a relatively weak performance of many of the leading stock exchanges.

By contrast the decade of the 1980s provided a very different environment for international diversification. Inflationary pressures in industrial countries subsided.

EXHIBIT 19.21		**Optimal Asset Allocations for Various Investment Universes**						
	A. STOCKS ONLY PORTFOLIO		B. STOCKS AND BONDS (GOLD ASSETS EXCL.) PORTFOLIO		C. STOCKS, BONDS, AND GOLD		D. STOCKS, BONDS, CASH AND GOLD	
	Min. Risk %	16% Return h%	Min. Risk %	16% Return %	Min. Risk %	16% Return %	Min. Risk %	16% Return %
Return (% p.a.)	12.0	16.0	6.3	16.0	6.7	16.0	9.2	16.0
Risk (% p.a.)	13.2	13.9	7.0	11.3	7.0	9.2	0.9	4.9
Stocks								
America	49.6	36.8	5.1	10.1	5.3	4.7	0.0	0.0
Far East	21.7	39.8	0.0	28.7	0.0	18.6	1.0	19.8
Europe	25.8	15.8	0.0	0.0	0.0	0.0	0.2	0.0
	97.1	92.4	5.1	38.8	5.3	23.3	1.2	19.8
Bonds								
America	0.0	0.0	70.3	4.3	70.8	28.1	1.7	0.0
Far East	0.0	0.0	6.2	17.2	6.3	13.5	0.6	0.0
Europe	0.0	0.0	18.3	39.7	15.3	19.1	0.7	5.3
			94.9	61.2	92.4	60.7	3.0	5.3
Gold Assets	2.9	7.6	0.0	0.0	2.3	16.1	0.0	17.6
Cash								
America	0.0	0.0	0.0	0.0	0.0	0.0	95.8	54.2
Far East	0.0	0.0	0.0	0.0	0.0	0.0	0.0	3.1
Europe	0.0	0.0	0.0	0.0	0.0	0.0	0.0	0.0
							95.8	57.3
Total	100.0	100.0	100.0	100.0	100.0	100.0	100.0	100.0

SOURCE: Ibid., p. 17.

This stability contributed to a much better stock market performance in most of the leading stock markets. Also, the 1980s did not witness any significant changes in the structure and operation of the international monetary relationships. Currency overshooting became a more apparent phenomenon in the foreign exchange markets, leading to greater interest in taking investment positions to benefit from such movements. Interest rates subsided during the period 1982–1987, providing a global bull market for bond investors. The crash of October 1987 ended a prolonged stock market upswing and raised many questions concerning the efficiency and safety of international diversification. Nevertheless, stock market advances resumed in the period from 1988 onward.

Investing in Emerging Markets   As major industrial countries experience slow growth in the 1990s, investors are turning their attention to the stock markets in developing nations. Despite potential gains through international diversification, Errunza points out in 1994 that less than 5% of the assets of U.S. pension funds were invested internationally. This suggests high potential for investing in emerging markets. Studies report on the low correlation of returns among emerging markets and major stock markets. For example, in an article in 1993 Mullin points to low correlations and potential for risk reduction.

Stanley describes the high returns historically evident in these markets, based on data included in the International Finance Corporate (IFC) stock indexes. The IFC emerging markets indexes outperformed industrial country stock market indexes in virtually all time periods. According to Marjorie Stanley, over the period 1984–1993 there were 22 instances in which an emerging market (based on 17 country markets) showed an annual return of 100% or more.

Stanley further notes that higher returns in emerging markets generally are accompanied by high risk as measured by standard deviation of returns. But the IFC composite, Latin America, and Asia indexes all had a better return/risk relationship than developed country market indexes in terms of unit of return per unit of risk. The IFC composite provided seven times as much return for the same level of risk as the Morgan Stanley Capital International Europe/Australia/Far East (EAFE) developed markets index.

While emerging stock markets exhibit higher risk as measured by standard deviation of return, they also exhibit much lower correlations of return with leading markets. M. Ratner and R. Leal conducted causality tests for the Latin American emerging markets. Examining the correlation structure between the U.S. and emerging market indexes, they find the generally low value of the correlation coefficients consistent with benefits from international diversification. Closer inspection reveals that frequency of data yields distinct results. From the U.S. perspective, emerging equities based on daily or weekly data indicate excellent risk reducing properties with low correlation coefficients. On a monthly basis the portfolio benefits of the emerging markets appear to diminish.

SUMMARY

International portfolio diversification can affect capital asset prices. International diversification enables investors to construct portfolios offering risk-return characteristics that may be dominant over purely domestic portfolios.

In the multicountry model developed by Solnik, risk is broken down into risks specific to the world factor and risks specific to the country. Sensitivity of a country to this world factor results from foreign trade, monetary policy, and cross-border capital flows. The multicountry model leads to a top-down approach in international investment. In this approach initial steps are to forecast national market returns and currency movements. International asset allocations are made with underweighting and overweighting of countries or industry sectors. Problems in using the multicountry model include theoretical difficulties with a world CAPM and difficulties in defining a world market portfolio.

In the international context it is important to understand the significance of market efficiency. If international asset prices are determined in efficient financial markets, all available information has been used in pricing assets. Wide use of the index approach to international investing suggests that many investors place high credence in the efficient markets hypothesis. While individual stock markets exhibit efficiency, these same markets also exhibit imperfections. Imperfections include a lack of continuous trading, concentration of trading in a few share issues, and small capitalization relative to the needs of institutional investors.

The currency factor is interpreted in two ways. One view is that country differences in returns on securities indicate anticipated currency rate movements (International Fisher Effect). A second view is that currency markets are inherently unstable and prone to overshooting.

Studies supporting international diversification in equities trace back to Grubel, who constructed an efficiency curve based on data covering 13 countries' stock markets. Levy and Sarnat extended this work to consider the role of interest rates in selecting optimal portfolios.

Lessard distinguished between world, country, and industry factors in achieving international diversification.

Studies of correlations of returns between stock and bond markets indicate low correlations and significant potential benefits from mixed bond and stock portfolios.

Analysis of multiasset strategies suggest significant benefits from specific mixes of these assets. Capital market conditions differed widely between the 1970s and 1980s, suggesting that different portfolio mixes would achieve better portfolio performance in each period.

APPENDIX

ESTIMATION OF PORTFOLIO RETURN AND RISK
TWO-SECURITY PORTFOLIO

Given two securities and their respective return, risk, and correlations of return, we can estimate the characteristics of two-security portfolios. The portfolio return is estimated by taking the individual security return and multiplying by the weights in the portfolios. For example, when securities 1 and 2 are to be weighted 70-30, we use

$$20 \,(.70) + 10 \,(.30) = 14 + 3$$

$$\text{Portfolio Return} = 17$$

Exhibit 19.22 provides calculations of mean return for portfolios with various weights of securities 1 and 2.

Also, we can estimate portfolio standard deviation as follows:

Referring to the Exhibit 19.23, we see that with a 50-50 weight, the portfolio return is 15 $(.50 \times 20 + .50 \times 10 = 15)$, and the standard deviation is 5. Using the formula for the standard deviation of portfolio:

$$\sqrt{w_1\sigma_1^2 + w_2\,\sigma_2^2 + 2(w_1w_2)\text{Cov}_{12}}$$

EXHIBIT 19.22	Mean Return, Standard Deviation, and Variance for Security 1 and Security 2	
	Security 1	**Security 2**
Mean Return	20	10
Variance	36	16
Standard Deviation	6	4

| EXHIBIT 19.23 | Mean Return and Standard Deviation of Portfolios of Securities 1 and 2. Given Alternative Correlations of Return |

PORTFOLIO COMPOSITION		Mean Return of Portfolio	ALTERNATIVE CORRELATIONS		
			+1	0	−1
1	**2**		Standard Deviation of Portfolio		
100−	0	20	6	6	6
70−	30	17	5.4	4.37	2.97
50−	50	15	5	3.6	1
30−	70	13	4.6	3.33	1
0−	100	10	4	4	4

The covariance is the correlation multiplied by the standard deviation of the two securities:

$$Cov_{12} = +1.0 \times 6 \times 4 = 24$$

Substituting in the equation for portfolio standard deviation:

$$\sqrt{.5^2 36 + .5^2 16 + 2(.5 \times .5)24} = 5$$

EXHIBIT 19.24A	Investment Opportunity Locus where Correlation of Returns is +1.0

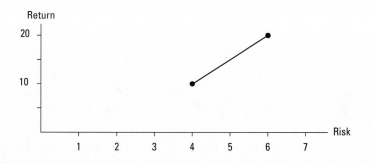

EXHIBIT 19.24B	Investment Opportunity Locus where Correlation of Returns is 0

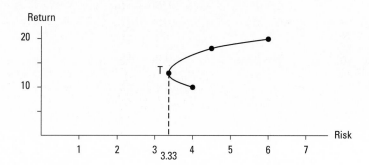

EXHIBIT 19.24C	Investment Opportunity Locus where Correlation of Returns is −1.0

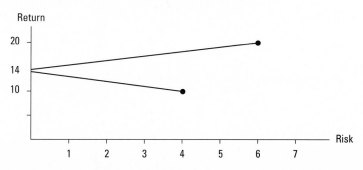

REVIEW QUESTIONS

1. Explain how international diversification affects international capital asset prices.
2. Explain what is meant by dominant and dominated portfolios.
3. It is said that the multicountry model developed by Solnik required specific implementation steps. What are they, and what is their importance?
4. Distinguish between market efficiency and market imperfections.
5. What approaches can be used to explain differential pricing of international capital market assets?
6. What were the major contributions of the Grubel and Levy and Sarnat studies? What did they demonstrate that had not been demonstrated previously?
7. What are the sources of high correlation of returns among national equity markets?
8. According to Lessard, international investment differs from domestic investment due to three factors. What are they? What is Lessard's major contribution to the analysis of international investment?
9. List the major arguments favoring inclusion of international and foreign bonds in diversified portfolios?
10. Solnik and Noetzlin find certain appropriate or optimal investment strategies. What are they? Is an index approach recommended? What role do they see for gold assets? Short-term deposits?
11. Solnik and Noetzlin compared return and risk for four different asset categories. Summarize their findings.
12. How does the time period of the Solnik and Noetzlin study (1970–1980) compare with the period 1980–1990? Could this affect the optimal investment strategy? How?
13. Given the data that follows:
    a. Complete the tables, estimating PE ratios and covariance.
    b. Estimate return and risk, PE ratios for two-security portfolios weighted 50-50 (six portfolios).
    c. Plot the risk-return positions of the six portfolios in (b) in a two-dimensional plane.
    d. Comment on the portfolios that are dominated and dominant.

	Return	Risk	Price	EPS			Correlation Matrix			
							1	2	3	4
U.S.	1	25	7	$100	10	1	—	.60	.80	.30
	2	15	5	50	5	2		—	.20	.70
France						3			—	0
	3	25	7	FF600	30	4				—
	4	15	6	300	15					

14. Using the data in the previous question, estimate the portfolio return and risk for the following two-security portfolios, with weights of 100-0, 70-30, 50-50, 30-70, 0-100. Plot the return and risk of each portfolio in the usual manner.
    a. 1 and 3   b. 1 and 4   c. 2 and 3   d. 2 and 4
15. If you follow the multicountry model, how would you structure your portfolio given the following information? In this case the American portfolio manager is

focused on dollar return. The forecasts for the next year are presented in the following table.

Forecast Information—Four National Stock Markets

Country and Equity Security	Expected Return	Beta
United States:		
Risk-Free Rate	8	
Domestic Stock Market	12	1.0
Common Stock 1	14	1.2
Common Stock 2	12	1.3
Common Stock 3	10	0.8
Germany:		
Risk-Free Rate	0	
Domestic Stock Market	14	1.0
Common Stock 4	17	1.8
Common Stock 5	15	1.1
Common Stock 6	11	0.9
Exchange Rate ($/DM)	+4	
Hong Kong:		
Risk-Free Rate	12	
Domestic Stock Market	18	1.0
Common Stock 7	20	2.0
Common Stock 8	17	1.2
Common Stock 9	13	0.7
Exchange Rate ($/HK$)	−3	
Australia:		
Risk-Free Rate	10	
Domestic Stock Market	16	1.0
Common Stock 10	19	1.1
Common Stock 11	17	1.4
Common Stock 12	11	0.8
Exchange Rate ($/A$)	+6	

CASE 1

Organizing an Equity Research Department

PART I: MR. BOWEN'S OFFER*

Mr. David Halvestrom enjoyed his meeting with John Bowen, the chief executive of a medium-sized Wall Street brokerage firm. Mr. Bowen had given Mr. Halvestrom an invitation to head up a new-to-be-formed London-based equity research department. This department was to focus on researching European equities, particularly in the expanding European Community (EC). Mr. Halvestrom was to begin his new job immediately. He had given notice to his former employer three weeks ago. This employer was a small British fund manager of unit trusts that was managing approximately £ 900 million invested in equities and bonds. Over one-third of this amount was allocated to non-U.K. equities.

Mr. Bowen had outlined the strategy of his firm, Delta Investment Managers, which was based in New York with retail branches in Chicago and on the West Coast. It had become increasingly difficult for his firm to hold clientele, since many had expressed interest in foreign stock markets, a subject that was beyond the research capabilities of his New York staff. The New York staff included 12 analysts, covering more than 1500 U.S. companies and most of the bond market sectors. Mr. Bowen's firm served as investment advisors for a closely-affiliated mutual fund group, with five different funds in operation and almost $1 billion under management. While it was considered desirable to offer new funds to the public (especially an international or global

*Part II: Mr. Halvestrom's plan follows Chapter 20.

(Continued)

(Continued)

fund), this step had not been taken, due to concern over having adequate research capacity.

Further, Mr. Bowen pointed out that one of his associates had read a report suggesting that by 1998 there would be no more than 40 internationally-oriented stock and bond fund managers around the globe. Between 1990 and 1998 over a hundred small- and medium-size stock brokerage and fund management firms would be absorbed through mergers or forced to find other lines of activity.

PART I: MR. BOWEN'S OFFER

Mr. Bowen requested that Mr. Halvestrom develop a plan of action for development of a London-based equity research department. He also suggested that he come to New York the following week to present the report to Mr. Bowen and his associates.

Mr. Halvestrom found the following article in a leading London financial newspaper. It gave him much food for thought.

"A WEAPON IN THE BATTLE"

The business of researching European equities is enjoying something of a renaissance. Demand from U.K. and overseas institutions for European equities is such that international banks and securities houses are fast expanding their European research departments, both in the numbers of markets and stocks covered, and the numbers of analysts employed.

Behind the growing investor interest in European equities are a variety of factors. The consistently strong performance of the continental European markets has attracted the attention of fund managers searching for new profit opportunities, while the U.K. market languishes. The approaching unification of European markets in 1992 highlights the potential for joint ventures and mergers that require greater information on European industries and companies.

The widespread deregulation of financial markets throughout the Continent has improved access to European equities, while the growth in trading on the London Stock Exchange's SEAQ international system has stimulated interest in a far wider range of European stocks among international investors.

All the big firms accept that equity research departments are an important weapon in the battle to win a slice of this fast-expanding market that in London alone sees roughly £ 40 billion-worth of shares turned over in one year.

Considerable amounts of money and time have been spent in the past two years on building up research facilities to meet the demand from investors for information on European equities.

Most houses now cover the leading stocks in seven countries: West Germany, France, Switzerland, Italy, Netherlands, Sweden, and Norway. A growing number offer research on Spain, Finland, and Denmark, while several provide coverage of more outlying markets such as Austria, Portugal, and Greece. Analysts, previously counted on the fingers of one hand, now number in the teens, while most firms worth their salt claim to research several hundred European stocks.

However there is a problem over what firms mean by "coverage." As some European fund managers find to their cost, a broker that claims to cover several hundred European stocks can often supply full analysis of only blue chip issues, while research on others—particularly second-line stocks—is sketchy at best, and nonexistent at worst.

A quick straw poll among European fund managers found that most were satisfied with the quality of research on leading stocks in the big continental markets. However, they were unhappy about the lack of coverage of second-line stocks, where research can be, at best, sketchy.

One such fund manager is Mr. Lester Woodfield of Edinburgh-based Global Management, who commented, "The amount of time and resources devoted to researching smaller companies in Europe is still pitiful."

Mr. Woodfield's thoughts are echoed by another European fund manager, who said, "Coverage of Europe is still relatively modest with too many firms covering the same stocks. London houses will usually only look at one or two second-liners, yet this is precisely the area where there's outperformance, and where we want to invest."

This lack of coverage of second-line stocks forces fund managers like Lester Woodfield into the arms of the

CASE 1

(*Continued*)

smaller continental brokage houses such as Germany's Bankhaus Reuschel or France's Rondebanque.

These often independent brokers may lack the ability to provide a comprehensive analysis of national and pan-European markets, but can provide information on local, lesser-known companies that their larger competitors cannot possibly offer.

Yet the research from continental brokers, both small and large, is often criticized for being too narrowly focused, too parochial. "London is streets ahead in putting the research into a European context," said one fund manager, "unlike say in France or Germany where firms fail to put together a truly pan-European product."

The lack of a tradition of comprehensive stock analysis is perhaps one reason why continental research is regarded as inferior to the U.K. variety. Pay and the lack of training are two others. Mr. Marc Peloit, chairman of Peloit-Bry, the London research operation of French broker Rondebanque, agrees that the quality of research in France is not as good as in the U.K. He explained that in France good analysts rarely remain in their jobs for long; they will very quickly be promoted to fund management if successful at analyzing stocks.

Analysts are neither paid enough on the Continent, nor do they enjoy the same status as their U.K.-based counterparts. "The French do not realize that a good analyst should remain a good analyst, and should be paid properly for it," commented Mr. Peloit.

Although some European houses have attempted to improve the quality of their research by acquiring U.K. brokerage firms (BNP's purchase of Quilter Goodison and ARK Securities, for example), most of the traffic of acquisitions goes the other way.

In Paris alone there have been at least four acquisitions by large U.K. houses in recent years: BZW of Puget Mahré; Warburg Securities of Bacot Allain; County NatWest of Sellier; and James Capel of DKL. James Capel has also bought Amsterdam firm Van Meer, while Warburg recently purchased a controlling stake in Munich stockbroker Berwein Wertpapierhandels und Börsenmakler.

In the rush to provide the best service to their clients, some firms are offering a new approach to equities research—cross-border analysis. In contrast to the traditional practice of dividing analysts into country specialists, the new approach organizes analysts on sector or industry lines.

The result is that fund managers are offered analysis of sectors where international forces are particularly at play. The industries that are most commonly researched on a cross-border basis are insurance/banking, chemicals/pharmaceuticals, motor, electronics and oils.

The growing technical complexity of industries makes specialization necessary, say supporters of cross-border analysis. Critics claim that the new approach is unnecessarily expensive and poorly tailored for the needs of fund managers.

One head of a U.K. research department that sticks to the old approach claims to have found no real demand for cross-border analysis among his clients. "Ninety-five percent of funds managers classify their

Top 10 London-based Firms Research Continental European Equities*

	Stocks	Markets	Analysts
Barclay's de Zoete Wedd	228	7	26
BNP Securities	175	12	13
James Capel	240	10	27
County NatWest	350	9	20
Hoare Govett	300	13	12
Kleinwort Benson	353	12	15
Smith New Court	350	6	8
Swiss Bank Corporation	200	7	12
UBS Phillips & Drew	200	12	17
Warburg Securities	521	11	14

* In alphabetical order, in terms of numbers of stocks and markets researched and analysts employed.

(*Continued*)

CASE 1

(Continued)

portfolios by country, so if you want to run a profitable and effective business, you have to organize it on a national basis. Anyway, sectoral analysis imposes a whole new layer of costs, because sector analysts tend to be additional to those who research national markets."

However no firm yet relies solely on cross-border analysis; most try to manufacture a happy mix of the two styles, with the emphasis still favouring the traditional country-by-country approach. "At the moment stock prices are moved more by local market conditions than cross-border conditions," explained one senior analyst.

A team of well-respected analysts can help a U.K. firm win new business from U.K. clients, or a U.S. firm win more from American clients; but can good research attract business from French, German or Swiss institutions? It is, as yet, a largely untapped and potentially huge market.

The answer so far seems to be no. Most investing institutions remain loyal to their local securities houses when looking for research on domestic stocks. And when they need information on lesser-known overseas companies, they tend to go to a firm from the country in which that company is based.

As one head of a London research operation put it: "I think that we are still some way from the day when a fund manager in Germany calls up a broker in Spain about a stock in Italy."

SELECTED BIBLIOGRAPHY

Chan K.C., G.A. Karolye, and R. Stulz. "Global Financial Markets and the Risk Premium on U.S. Equity," *Journal of Financial Economies,* (October 1992).

Cholerten, K., P. Pieraerts, and B. Solnik. "Why Invest in Foreign Currency Bonds?" *Journal of Portfolio Management,* (Summer 1986).

Divecha, A., J. Drach, and D. Stefek. "Emerging Markets: A Quantitative Perspective," *Journal of Portfolio Management,* (Fall 1992).

Errunza, V.F. "Emerging Markets: Some New Concepts," *Journal of Portfolio Management,* (1994).

Grubel, H.G. "Internationally Diversified Portfolios: Welfare Gains and Capital Flows," *American Economic Review,* (December 1968).

Ibbotson, R., L. Siegel, and K. Love. "World Wealth: Market Values and Returns," *Journal of Portfolio Management,* (Fall 1985).

Jorion, P., and L. Rossenberg. "Synthetic International Diversification," *Journal of Portfolio Management,* (Winter 1993).

Lessard, D. "World, Country and Industry Relationships in Equity Returns: Implications for Risk Reduction Through International Diversification," *Financial Analysts Journal,* (January-February 1976).

Levy, H., and Z. Lerman. "The Benefits of International Diversification of Bonds," *Financial Analysts Journal,* (September-October 1988).

Levy, H., and M. Sarnat. "International Diversification of Investment Portfolios," *American Economic Review,* (September 1970).

Mullen, J. "Emerging Equity Markets in the Global Economy," Federal Reserve Bank of New York *Quarterly Review,* (Summer 1993).

Odier, P., and B. Solnik. "Lessons for International Asset Allocation," *Financial Analysts Journal,* (April 1993).

Park, Keith K.H., and Antoine W. Van Agtmael. *The World's Emerging Markets.* Chicago: Probus, 1993.

Ratner, M., and R. Leal. "Causality Tests for the Emerging Markets of Latin America," *Journal of Emerging Markets,* (Spring 1996).

Ripley, Duncan M. "Systematic Elements in the Linkage of National Stock Market Indices," *The Review of Economics and Statistics,* (1973).

Roll R. "The International Crash of October 1987," *Financial Analysts Journal,* (September-October 1988).

Solnik, B., and B. Noetzlin. "Optimal International Asset Allocation," *Journal of Portfolio Management,* (Fall 1982).

Solnik, B. *International Investments.* 3rd ed. Reading, MA: Addison-Wesley, 1996.

Solnik, B. "Why Not Diversify Internationally Rather Than Domestically?" *Financial Analysts Journal,* (July 1974).

Speidell, L., and R. Sappenfield. "Global Diversification in a Shrinking World," *Journal of Portfolio Management,* (Fall 1992).

Stanley, Marjorie T. *The Irwin Guide to Investing in Emerging Markets.* Chicago: Richard D. Irwin, 1995.

Wainscott, C.B. "The Stock-Bond Correlation and Its Implications for Asset Allocation," *Financial Analysts Journal,* (July-August 1990).

CHAPTER 20

Investment Management and Evaluation

INTRODUCTION

The focus of this chapter is the operational aspect of international portfolio investment. Here we make distinctions between the investments of individuals and those of financial institutions, and explore the techniques and approaches that each uses to carry out their respective investment activities. We analyze portfolio construction from the perspective of active and passive management approaches. Finally, we consider approaches to the problem of evaluating investment performance.

LEARNING OBJECTIVES IN THIS CHAPTER

1. To develop a sense of the special problems faced by individual and institutional investors in implementing international investment.
2. To acquire a knowledge of the basic mechanisms available to investors to carry out overseas equity investment.
3. To understand the alternative strategies utilized by global investors and their implications with respect to expected return, risk, and costs.
4. To perceive the various dimensions involved in evaluating international investment performance, including theoretical as well as institutional aspects.

KEY TERMS AND CONCEPTS

- active management
- closed end
- efficient frontier
- excess return
- global fund
- index fund
- international fund
- modified active management
- open end
- passive management
- portfolio insurance
- Sharpe measure
- single country fund
- systematic risk

- ◆ top-down approach
- ◆ Treynor measure
- ◆ unit trust

- ◆ unsystematic risk
- ◆ world market portfolio

ACRONYMS

TAM	Tactical Asset Management	**CFTC**	Commodities Futures Trading Commission
GIC	Guaranteed Investment Contract	**SML**	Security Market Line
		UTA	Unit Trust Association

Investment Vehicles and Individual Investors

Individual investors face a number of problems in implementing international investment. The major problem facing the individual investor arises from the typically small scale of investment operations. Second, individuals wishing to benefit from the advantages of international investment must develop reliable sources of information flows as the basis for managing their internationally diversified portfolios. Third, judgments must be made on specific securities in selected industries, especially in foreign exchange environments. Fourth, experience must be obtained from associations and contacts. Finally, individual investors must develop administrative procedures for carrying out investment transactions and for meeting the requirements of securities custody. These can prove to be onerous requirements for individual investors. For these reasons individuals have sought investment vehicles that are adapted to resolving many of these difficult international investment dimensions.

In Exhibit 20.1 we describe five alternative investment vehicles for overseas equity investment that are available to individual investors. These are: direct purchase of securities in overseas markets, the use of American Depository Receipts (ADRs), and three managed fund approaches—the single country fund, the international fund, and the global fund. The first two vehicles do not provide the investor with significant reductions in transaction costs, professional portfolio management, or asset diversification. Managed fund approaches do provide some of these benefits.

DIRECT PURCHASE OF SECURITIES

The first mechanism described in Exhibit 20.1, direct purchase of securities in overseas markets, requires that the bank or securities firm carrying out the purchase or sale has a branch or correspondent securities firm authorized to transact in the overseas stock market. Two sets of commission or transaction costs will be involved, one for the foreign exchange transaction and one for the stock exchange commission or dealer spread.

Investors purchasing individual securities issues are exposed to four types of risks: country, currency, systematic, and unsystematic. In the international portfolio context, these types can be summarized as follows:

1. *Country*. Relates to economic and political developments in the country that have adverse effects on securities prices, or interfere with the ability of the investor to liquidate investment on a favorable basis.

EXHIBIT 20.1   Five Mechanisms for International Securities Investment

Type Mechanism	Characteristic of Mechanism	Advantages	Risks to Investor	Cost Factor	Specific Problems
1. Direct Purchase in Overseas Market	Use broker or bank to purchase shares in foreign stock market.	Purchase in market where lowest price available. May offer only alternative.	Unsystematic, Systematic, Country, Currency	Local market price plus transaction costs (FX spread plus stock exchange commission)	Can incur relatively high transaction costs.
2. American Depository Receipt (ADR)	Depository receipts issued for underlying shares. Bank holds underlaying shares.	Low transaction costs. Avoid flowback problem. Facilitates portfolio diversification.	Unsystematic, Systematic, Country, Currency	Dollar ADR price determined by price in local primary market in local currency, multiplied by dollar value of local currency.	Local liquidity problem, especially in period of day when primary market is closed. Generally excludes smaller companies.
3. Single Country Fund	Investments restricted to shares of single country. Closed-end fund.	Can gain access to market otherwise closed to foreign investors.	Systematic, Country, Currency	Net asset value plus or minus premium or discount.	Concentration of country and currency risks.
4. International Fund	In United States, internationally diversified excluding American shares. Open-end fund.	Low management costs. Diversified portfolio.	Modified systematic risk.* Risk of dollar appreciation.	Net asset value. Annual management fee.	
5. Global Fund	In United States, internationally diversified including American shares. Open-end fund.	Low management costs. Diversified portfolio.	Global Market Risk*	Net Asset Value. Annual management fee.	

* The difference between the international and global fund is the inclusion of U.S. equities in the global fund and exclusion of U.S. equities in the international fund. An international fund is viewed as having lower systematic risk than any country fund. A global fund offers still greater risk diversification benefits, due to the inclusion of U.S. equities. Global Market Risk is based on the concept of a unified world equity market, offering the greatest diversification opportunities and lowest systemic risk.

2. *Currency.* Relates to an adverse trend in value of investment currency in foreign exchange markets. Can apply to currencies on a fixed rate as well as floating rate system.

3. *Systematic.* This type is also referred to as market risk. National stock and bond markets have a propensity to offer variable returns from one holding period to another based on market fluctuations. Each national market carries its own level of market risk. For example, the Hong Kong market experiences greater variability of returns over time than either the New York or London stock markets. Systematic risk is not diversifiable in a portfolio of securities.

4. *Unsystematic.* Refers to the variability of returns of a single security. Individual securities exhibit their own pattern of variability. Companies that sell construction goods or capital goods tend to exhibit greater unsystematic risk in their securities returns than companies that sell nondurable goods. Unsystematic risk is diversifiable in a portfolio of securities.

Investors can earn returns on individual securities consisting of several components. We can define these returns from individual securities as follows. On a foreign currency basis they include capital gains/losses plus dividends. On a home currency basis they include currency appreciation/depreciation, plus capital gains/losses, plus dividends. An illustration will make this breakdown clear.

A German investor purchases 1000 General Motors shares at $50. The DM/$ exchange rate is DM/$ = 1.60. During the holding period the investor receives dividends of $2.00 per share, and at the time dividends are received the exchange rate is DM/$ = 1.70. At year end the investor sells the GM shares at $53 with the exchange rate DM/$ = 1.75. Aside from commissions and taxes, the breakdown of returns is outlined in Exhibit 20.2.

AMERICAN DEPOSITORY RECEIPT

American Depository Receipt

Issued by an American bank certifying it holds underlying shares issued by a foreign company.

The second vehicle, the American Depository Receipt (ADR), is a receipt issued by an American bank certifying that the bank holds an equivalent number of shares issued by a foreign company. The primary providers of ADRs are large commercial banks such as the Morgan Guaranty Trust Company, Citicorp, and the Bank of New York. These banks provide a custodian function and receive a small fee for their services.

U.S. securities brokers provide the market-making function in ADRs. The market price of an ADR is the price of the underlying security in the primary market (in foreign exchange terms), multiplied by the dollar value of local currency, and adjusted for the number of underlying shares included in one ADR. The following illustrates this calculation. The pound sterling price of the security is multiplied by the dollar value of the pound, and this is adjusted for the number of shares equal to one ADR.

Market Price of ADR	=	Price of Underlying Security	×	$ per Foreign Currency Unit	×	Multiple of Shares per ADR
$18.00	=	£1.20	×	$1.50	×	10

EXHIBIT 20.2	**Investor Return in Dollars versus Deutsche Marks**

Dollar-Measured Return

Purchase Cost	$50,000
Dividend	2,000
Sales Proceeds	53,000
Gross Amount Received	55,000
Profit	5,000 ...... (10.0%)
Percent from Dividend	40%
Percent from Capital Gain	60%

Deutsche Mark Measured Return

	Total Amount	Gain from Currency	Original Dividend	Pure Capital Gain[5]
Purchase Cost	80,000			
Dividend	3,400	200[1]	3,200[1]	
Sales Proceeds	92,750[2]			
Value Increase	12,750	7,950[3]	—	4,800
Total Profit	16,150[4]	8,150	3,200	4,800
Percent of Total	100.0	50.5	19.8	29.7

[1] On basis of original exchange rate of 1.60.

[2] $53,000 \times 1.75 = 92,750$.

[3] $53,000 \times 1.60 = 84,800$. Also $92,750 - 84,800 = 7,950$.

[4] $3,400 + 12,750 = 16,150$. Total profit is 20.19% of investment.

[5] Based on assumption no change in exchange rate.

The ADR mechanism can be regarded as a variation of the direct purchase approach with some marginal advantages. The advantages include 1) avoidance of any direct or explicit foreign exchange transaction costs, 2) ability to trade the foreign securities during regular stock market trading hours of the investor's stock market, as contrasted with the trading hours of the market where the underlying security is listed and traded.

Between 1985 and 1995 the number of ADRs traded in New York more than doubled to over 1200 issues. Countries whose companies are well represented by ADR issues in New York include Australia, Japan, South Africa, and the United Kingdom. The largest number of ADR issues is traded over the counter. NASDAQ is an important market for ADR listing and trading, but not as heavily represented with ADRs as OTC. The New York Stock Exchange also provides a market for ADRs. Small capitalization companies are for the most part excluded from this market.

In 1995 the 115 foreign securities listed on the NASDAQ trading system as ADRs realized a share volume of 2,065 million, and a dollar volume of $47.4 billion (Exhibit 20.3). Trading volume leaders included well-known companies such as LM Ericsson and Reuters.

Data provided by Bank of New York, one of the leading banks issuing ADRs, indicates that trading of ADR instruments increased 25% in 1996 as compared with 1995. Trading of Depository receipts in the U.S. totaled 10.9 billion, valued at $345 billion. Non-U.S. companies raised a total of $19.4 billion through 154 offerings, representing a 50% increase from the number of offerings in 1995 and a 62% increase in dollars raised.

EXHIBIT 20.3	**ADR Trading and New Issues, 1996 All U.S. Markets**
Share Trading Volume	10.9 billion
Dollar Value of Trading	$345 billion
New Funds Raised	$19.4 billion
New Offerings	154 issues

SOURCE: *Wall Street Journal*, "ADR Offerings Trading volume Increased in 1996," (January 3, 1997): A5B.

EXHIBIT 20.4° **Single Country Funds, Comparison of Market Price and Net Asset Value 2 April 1993**

Fund	Stock Exchange	Net Asset Value	Stock Price	Percent Premium (−Discount)
Austria Fund	NYSE	7.79	8.25	5.91
Brazil Fund	NYSE	16.13	15.125	−6.23
Chile Fund	NYSE	31.96	34.50	7.95
Emerging Germany	NYSE	8.14	7.25	−10.93
1st Austral. Fd.	AMEX	9.75	9.375	−3.85
1st Phillipine	NYSE	14.59	10.75	−26.32
France Growth	NYSE	11.84	11.25	−4.98
Germany Fund	NYSE	10.67	11.25	5.44
Indonesia	NYSE	8.76	10.25	17.01
Italy Fund	NYSE	7.86	8.75	11.32
Japan Fund	NYSE	12.78	12.00	−6.10
Korea Fund	NYSE	10.78	12.75	18.27
Malaysia Fund	NYSE	15.84	15.25	−3.72
New Germany	NYSE	12.15	10.50	−13.58
Portugal Fund	NYSE	9.47	8.50	−10.24
Singapore	NYSE	11.96	11.875	−0.71
Spain Fund	NYSE	9.05	8.75	−3.31
Swiss Helvetia	NYSE	15.62	15.25	−2.37
Taiwan Fund	NYSE	20.42	23.875	16.92
Thai Fund	NYSE	20.27	18.50	−8.73
Turkish Invest.	NYSE	6.20	6.625	6.85
United Kingdom	NYSE	10.89	9.50	−12.76
REGIONAL FUNDS				
Asia Pacific	NYSE	13.21	14.625	10.71
Europe Fund	NYSE	11.18	11.125	−0.49
1st Iberian	AMEX	7.68	6.75	−12.11
Latin Amer. Eq.	NYSE	14.98	14.375	−4.04
Latin Amer. Inv.	NYSE	19.46	19.125	−1.72
Morgan Stanley Emerging Mkt.	NYSE	16.83	18.875	12.15
Scudder New Asia	NYSE	16.43	18.00	9.56
Templeton Emerging Mkt.	NYSE	14.12	18.125	28.36

SOURCE: *New York Times,* (5 April, 1993).

CLOSED-END FUNDS

The third investment vehicle indicated in Exhibit 20.1 is the single country fund. This fund is typically closed end with investments restricted to the shares of companies of a single country. Examples of single country funds are provided in Exhibit 20.4. The closed end fund is an excellent way to enter a specific country market, especially where that market may lack sufficient breadth, depth, and resiliency.

EXHIBIT 20.5	**Open-End Funds—Global and International**		
Fund	**Expense Ratio**	**Largest Holding**	**Assets $ Mil.**	**% Change 1990–1991**
Fidelity Intl. Growth and Income	1.89	Repsol	58	74%
G.T. International Growth	1.80	Hutchison Whampoa	465	35
G.T. Global Growth and Income	1.85	Electrabil	86	210
Kleinwort Intl. Equity	1.78	Telefonos de Mexico	66	−8
Laxington Global	1.60	May Dept. Store	54	6
Putnam Global Growth	1.47	Pfizer	660	18
Scudder International	1.29	Telekom Malaysia	965	20
Scudder Global	1.81	Union Bank of Switz.	299	26

SOURCE: *Business Week, Guide to Mutual Funds.* 2 ed. New York: 1992.

Because the number of shares is fixed, there is a limit to the amount of money the fund can bring to a specific country market. The prices of single country fund shares in the closed-end case will rise or fall depending on supply-demand factors for the fund's shares. As can be noted, closed-end funds can be priced at premium or discount relative to their net asset value.

Several closed-end funds are not restricted to a single country, but are regional in nature. That is, they invest in the shares of companies traded on stock exchanges in several countries within a geographic region. Examples include the Europe Fund, Latin America Equity, and Scudder New Asia (Exhibit 20.4).

OPEN-END FUNDS

Open-end funds are available as international or global funds. International funds and global funds differ in one respect. Global funds include U.S. equity securities while international funds do not.* In the United States both types of funds are issued by large organizations that offer and manage a variety of open-end funds. These funds tend to be cost effective in that they sell shares and redeem shares at net asset value. Many do not levy a sales charge. The annual management fee (expense ratio) varies from one fund to another (Exhibit 20.5).

We characterize the risk related to the international fund as modified systematic risk, and the risk related to the global fund as global systematic. We have defined systematic risk in a preceding section, where it is equated to market risk or the variability in return of a national stock market. We can also depict systematic risk as the lowest level of risk attainable by diversifying (adding securities) to a portfolio within a given national stock market. Exhibit 20.6 depicts systematic risk for Mexico (27), Norway (18), and the United States (13) as a larger number of securities is included in the diversified portfolio. The different levels of

Closed- end fund

Limited number of shares can be issued to investors. Can be priced at premium or discount relative to net asset value.

Open- end fund

No limit on number of shares issued to investors, are priced at net asset value.

Global fund

Includes U.S. securities as well as foreign securities.

Global systematic

Risk related to volatility of securities included in global capital market.

Systematic risk

Market risk related to volatility of securities traded in that market.

---

* To be correct, international funds are defined to include no more than 24% U.S. securities, while global funds are limited to no more than 50% holdings in U.S. assets.

EXHIBIT 20.6	**Portfolio Risk Comparisons**

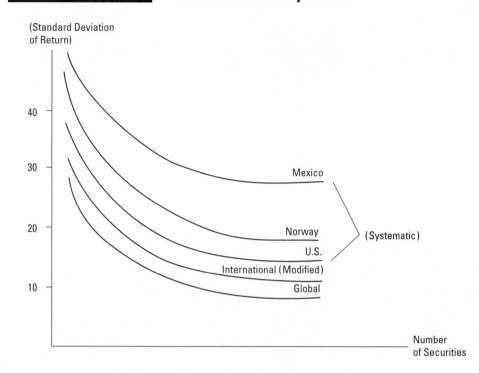

Modified systematic

Risk related to international fund that largely excludes U.S. securities and therefore enjoys only limited diversification.

World market portfolio

Portfolio that includes securities from all market components around the world.

systematic risk reflect structural and operational differences between national stock markets.

An international fund leaves the investor with modified systematic risk. That is, international diversification reduces risk below the level of risk experienced in most or all national markets. We refer to this as "modified systematic." A global fund can reduce risk even further, since addition of a U.S. stock component provides still greater diversification. The global fund approximates a world market portfolio. Therefore it should exhibit a risk level related to a world market portfolio.

Alternative Approaches for Institutional Investors

INSTITUTIONAL REQUIREMENTS

Institutional investors also may wish to gain the benefits of international diversification. The requirement of such institutions will be similar to those of individuals: low costs for transactions and custody procedures, efficient administrative systems, reliable information, and professional expertise. In addition, unlike the case of individuals, institutional investors face the problems of finding market sectors that are large and liquid enough to allow them to participate in that market sector without causing substantial price level changes, or even price disruption in that sector. This limitation can restrict many institutional investors to the largest national stock and bond markets. Generally individual investors are not restricted in this way. The leading global stock and bond markets available for institutional investors are described in Chapter 18.

At the same time, institutional investors have options available to them that typically are not open to individuals. For example, institutional investors often are large enough to separately develop adequate information flows to be able to manage their internationally diversified portfolios. They are also able to "buy" information through the "soft dollars" expended on commissions paid to securities brokers. Any direct expenses incurred to compensate analytical staff and to acquire international information services may represent a very small percentage of assets managed. For example, an institution managing $1 billion in assets could expend $4 million for staff and international information services, and that would represent only 0.4 of 1% of assets.

Despite the availability of greater resources, midsize institutional investors in the United States typically employ the services of other companies that specialize in international portfolio investment. These portfolio management needs are best met through tailoring the services. Following this mode domestically-oriented institutional investors will rely less on ADRs and single country funds. Most common in achieving international diversification is to follow the international and global funds management approaches.

In addition to the arrangements for settling transactions, investors need administrative systems to service their international investments. These services include: securities handling and basic custodial functions, receiving income, filing for tax refunds, and processing corporate actions. Services can cover portfolio valuations, capital and income transactions summaries, custody statements, dividend advice, and consolidated tax certificates.

INSTITUTIONAL PORTFOLIO STRATEGIES

The world securities markets are becoming globalized as institutional investors continue to seek better results through cross-border investing. According to estimates made by Salomon Brothers, world investment in foreign stocks increased from $300 billion in 1985 to $1,600 billion in 1989. This reflects gross flows into and from countries. Net flows are considerably lower. This growth in cross-border equity investment is driven by the desire of institutional investors to 1) enhance returns, and 2) reduce market risk. In Chapter 19 we review the theoretical basis of this approach—modern portfolio theory.

World Bank data indicates that net private investment flows to developing countries increased from $40 billion in 1990 to $150 billion in 1993, and to $160 billion in 1995.* These investment flows include a mix of portfolio and direct investment. In many developing countries the portfolio component is considerably larger than the direct investment component.

In the following discussion we note that the current pattern of global investing is likely to produce a shift in the efficient frontier available to cross-border investors. In turn this shift will require an adjustment in the strategies employed to achieve optimally diversified international portfolios.

Two Strategies   The current pattern of financial institutions toward global investing can be described by referring to Exhibit 20.7. Two strategies dominate. The first, passive indexation, has been increasingly utilized since the mid-1980s. International fund managers concentrate their investments on approximately 1000

---

* World Bank. *Global Capital Supply and Demand.* Washington, D.C.: (1996): 4.

EXHIBIT 20.7	**Current Pattern of Global Investing by Institutions**[1]		
Type Strategy		**Basis for Portfolio Allocations**	**Number of Share Issues**
Strategy I	Index the Portfolio to Large Markets	Percent capitalization shares of major world stock markets. Employ benchmark indices of Morgan Stanley Capital International or FT Actuaries.	1,000[1]
Strategy II	Aggressively Switch In and Out of Market Sectors	Broad economic forecasts and currency forecasts. Based on forecasts, selective allocation of portfolio to national stock markets.	1,425[2]

[1] A third strategy can be described. This strategy can be named Global Approach. In this case investors must estimate risk, return, and correlation with global market portfolio measured in investor currency. Over 13,000 share issues are available following the Global Approach (including almost 7,000 share issues in the Emerging Markets). Some of these share issues suffer from illiquid markets.

[2] The sum of share issues in leading stock market indices of 14 countries (United States, Japan, United Kingdom, Canada, Switzerland, Germany, France, Netherlands, Sweden, Italy, Belgium, South Africa, Australia, and Hong Kong.

large capitalization share issues. These share issues are components of the leading market indices (S&P 500, FT-SE 100, Nikkei 225, FAZ, All Ordinaries). At present more than one-fourth of U.S. pension assets are indexed to major international stock indices. Given that portfolio performance is compared against benchmark indices, fund managers can minimize criticism by following an index (passive) approach.

A second strategy emerged in the 1980s. We refer to this strategy as Tactical Asset Management (TAM). Applied on a global basis, TAM is based on a broad economic analysis of conditions in countries with leading stock markets. This analysis is extended to currency markets as well. Investment decisions are based on this economic analysis, as well as the resulting forecasts of growth in production, sales, and corporate profits by country. These decisions are modified by related forecasts of currency strength and weakness. Using these inputs, fund managers switch in and out of national markets and market sectors. This trading is facilitated by market liquidity and index derivatives (options/futures trading of market indices).

The year 1995 was a difficult period for active investment managers. The 37.6% return from the S&P 500 index in the U.S. proved a tough target to beat. Markets outside the United States presented difficult problems. Investors in Tokyo lost most of their gains if they left their Yen exposure unhedged. With the exception of Switzerland, dollar-based investors lost if they went outside the United States.

Practical difficulties arise in implementing simple investment strategies. The highly concentrated nature of some indexes is a case in point. The top 10 names in the S&P 500 make up 17% of the index. The biggest four of the 24 countries in the emerging markets index represent more than 48%. Therefore the active manager starts off with a more genuinely diversified portfolio but the resulting tracking error can work against the portfolio manager. In this case the lower return is a product of lower risks.

An index portfolio involves a buy and hold strategy. The initial weights are momentum driven. The index will be overweighted in situations that have shown strong relative performance and underweighted in situations of weak performance.

Internationally, index weights will be driven by supply considerations unrelated to investment value. A rise in the level of initial public offering activity or privatization of state enterprises will boost aggregate market capitalization without adding to the investment attractiveness of a stock market sector.

This view leads to the conclusion that a capitalization weighted index rides the country up and down. By contrast, a contrarian/rebalancing approach will trim back the strong performers and add to the weak performers, thus boosting return while reducing risk.

Impact of Strategies   Employing the strategies described in Exhibit 20.7 usually results in a concentration of institutional investment. This concentration is likely to distort the relative valuation of shares. When the distortion becomes pronounced there must inevitably be a correction in relative values. Such corrections take place in the case of individual share issues when these issues are added to or deleted from a major market index. These corrections also take place with respect to broad market components—witness the October 1987 crash in the U.S. and foreign markets, and more recently the 60% decline in the Tokyo share market from 1989–1993.

The following criticisms can be made of the two strategies currently in use:

1. While international investment by fund managers has tended to make equity markets more efficient, the concentration of investment in large capitalization issues can result in distortions in relative market values. This distortion may require market corrections of a significant magnitude.

2. International fund managers espouse a "global" approach, but the number and range of stock issues they focus on is relatively narrow. At present, managers focus on approximately 1000 share issues listed and traded on major national stock markets. Nevertheless, they are following strategies that include a major part of present world equity market capitalization.

3. As institutional investors acquire a larger percentage of outstanding shares among the 1000 large capitalization issues, they will make it more difficult to achieve liquidity. In some cases U.S. pension funds collectively own 60–70% of specific share issues.

Portfolio Construction

In the discussion that follows we focus on three basic approaches to portfolio construction. Each approach has different requirements regarding forecasting inputs. Each approach also carries certain implications for the portfolio manager relative to the rapidity of portfolio turnover and to transaction costs associated with managing the portfolio.

BASIC APPROACHES

International portfolio management can be carried out on an active or passive basis. Various in-between mixes of active and passive management can be implemented. For our purposes we describe three approaches: 1) active management, 2) passive management, and 3) modified active management.

Passive management

Portfolio approximates index of the stock market.

Passive management has its theoretical support in the efficient markets hypothesis. If the market has priced securities according to all available information, and the markets respond to this information in a rational manner, it may be difficult if not impossible to perform any better than the market or the market index. Passive management follows an index fund approach.

In the international context, modified active management requires a basic amount of forecasting in the direction of providing risk, return, and correlation data for each of the securities and/or national market indexes. Based on this information set, an efficient frontier can be estimated and used as a basis for portfolio selection and construction. This method is demonstrated in Chapter 19.

Active management

Portfolio selection based on forecasts of superior performance for securities included.

Active management requires considerable analysis and forecasting. The forecaster must provide detailed forecasts of the following:

1. national economic trends and their influences on each national market (15–20 national markets) in terms of expected return and risk; and
2. industrial trends on a worldwide basis and their implications for return and risk of specific company share issues in each of these respective industries (25–30 industry sectors).

Clearly the active management approach demands considerable research capacity, staff, and budget.

Passive Management

Passive management can be implemented through the index approach to investing. That is, the portfolio manager invests the portfolio, or a major part of it, in the market index or in a mixture of securities that can be expected to perform in a manner very similar to the market index. In the case of domestic investment a broad-based national stock market index is used. In the United States this might be the S&P 500 or the Wilshire 5000. In the United Kingdom this might be the Financial Times All Share Index.

Selecting the appropriate index raises several questions for the international investor. 1) Which world market index should be used? Several are available, including the Morgan Stanley Capital International Perspective and the FT-Actuaries World Indices. 2) How do we deal with the questions of stock market efficiency in the international context? Whereas many studies have demonstrated the market efficiency of the larger national stock markets, there is some question concerning efficiency among some of the smaller emerging markets. Also, the wide foreign exchange rate swings among the principal currencies raise questions concerning efficiency for investors seeking international diversification.

Despite these problems, world and regional market indexes are typically employed as reference points that international investors use in the following ways:

1. direct comparison of market and portfolio performance;
2. estimates of comparative national stock market liquidity, based on aggregate capitalization and turnover data;
3. comparisons of market volatility and riskiness; and
4. the latter, as a basis for calculating degree of stock market comovements that in turn furnish estimates of portfolio risk.

In its purest form passive management involves allocating portfolio funds to the leading 20–25 national stock markets in proportion to their respective weights in the world market index. In this respect there is little forecasting input required except the shares of world market capitalization for each component of the index. The data in Exhibit 18.5 provide us with the changing weights of market capitalization in leading world stock markets. As can be observed over the relatively short period

1985–1994, there were substantial changes in the weights (percentages of total world market capitalization) of many national markets. The most noteworthy changes were as follows:

1. The U.S. share declined from 51% to 38%.
2. The Japanese share increased from 22% to 28%.
3. The United Kingdom share increased from 7% to almost 9%.

MODIFIED ACTIVE MANAGEMENT

Modified active management involves constructing an efficient frontier of portfolios from the 20 or more national stock market indexes of the leading equities markets. Modified active management requires a basic amount of forecasting and analysis. The analyst must provide portfolio managers with estimated returns, risks, and correlations for each national market component. Considering that as many as 20 or more national stock markets are potentially eligible for inclusion in the portfolio, as a minimum the financial analyst must provide risk-return and correlation inputs for all of these components.

A basic problem in carrying out this required forecasting is the lack of stationarity in the variables themselves. Return on a given national stock market can vary considerably from one holding period to another. Similarly, risk and correlation with other markets can vary from period to period.

ACTIVE MANAGEMENT

Active management requires considerable analysis and forecasting. If we consider that the manager of a global stock fund may cover 20 countries and 30 industry sectors, there is a global matrix with 600 individual cells. The analyst must consider 600 company stocks if there is only one company represented in each cell of the matrix, 1200 if there are two, and 1800 if there are three in each cell.

In the case of a 20 country × 30 industry matrix, the analyst may be expected to provide 600 separate estimates of return, and 600 estimates of risk, as well as correlations of return with a market index.

If a top down approach is taken by the manager of the global fund, the manager considers national stock market selection and diversification as the primary objective. Industry selection and diversification plays a subordinate role. Forecasts of national stock market performance are used to select the better performing national markets, and these are given heavy weighing in the portfolio. Selection of stocks in specific industry sectors comes in the second round of portfolio selection. To some extent this selection can reduce the number of items to be forecasted. Nevertheless, considerable detailed forecasting is required.

By contrast the bottom-up approach considers industry selection and diversification as playing a primary role. National stock market selection is considered to play a subordinate role. Forecasts of industry performance are used to select the better performing industry sectors, and these are heavily weighted in the portfolio. Selection of stocks in specific national stock markets comes in the second round of portfolio selection. Exhibit 20.8 provides an illustrative matrix of the country and industry classifications of more than 200 company share issues.

The provider of international investment management services is typically a globally diversified financial institution, large in size, and with a market presence in

EXHIBIT 20.8   Country-Industry Matrix of Share Issues

Industry Sector	United Kingdom	Japan	Germany	France	Netherlands	Canada	Switzerland	Belgium	Sweden	Spain	Hong Kong	Italy
Food Processing	United Biscuits Schweppes Unigate Cadbury	Nissin Food Maruka		BSN DANOM	Unilever		Nestle J. Suchard					FERRUZZI
Beverages and Tobacco	Guinness Allied Lyons Grand Met, BAT	Kirin Brewery		Perrier LVMH	Heineken	Labatt Seagram	Eichhof					
Banking	Natwest Barclay's Lloyd's-TSB	Bank Tokyo Sumitomo Daiwa Fuji Sanwa	Deutsche Dresdner Commerz	Paribas Suez BNP	ABN-AMRO Bank ING Group	Royal Bank Bk Montreal Royal Trustco	Union Bank Swiss Banking Corp Credit Suisse	Kredietbank Banque Bruxelles Lambert	Skandinav. Handels BK. Skandinav. Enskilds	Banco Bilbao Banco Central	Hong Kong Shanghai Bank Hang Seng Bank	BCI Banca Naz del Lavoro Mediobanco
Insurance	Legal and General Royal and Sun Alliance Prudential	Fuji Fire and Marine Chiyoda Fire and M	Allianz	AXA VAP	Nationale Nederlanden AEEON		Winterthur Zurich Versich	Fortiz	Skandia			Assicurazioni Generale
Airlines	British Airways	JAL All Nippon	Lufthansa		KLM	Air Canada	Swissair				Cathay Pac.	
Retailing	Marks and Spencer Inchcape Sainsbury Tesco	Aozama Shimachu	Karstadt Kaufhof	Euromarche	Konin-Klÿke	Sears Canada		Colruzt			Wing On	

(Continued)

EXHIBIT 20.8 (*Continued*)

Industry Sector	United Kingdom	Japan	Germany	France	Nether-lands	Canada	Switzer-land	Belgium	Sweden	Spain	Hong Kong	Italy
Property Development, Construction	Barlows British Land	Daikyo Mitsui Fudosan Kajima		Euro-tunnel Bouy-gues	Rodamco				Skanska	Dragados	H.K. Land Sun Hung Kai Cheung Kong Henderson New World Dev	
Conglomerate Holding Co	Hanson Trust			Bic			Holder-Bank Sulzer	Société Générale de Belg.	Esselte Investor		Swire Pacific Hutchison Whampoa Jardine Math Wharf Holding	
Motor Vehicles, Parts, Tires	Abbey Panels	Toyota Mazda Nissan Denso	Volks-wagen Daimler Benz BMW Conti-nental	Peugeot Michelin Renault	DAF				Saab Scania Volvo	Motor Iberica		Fiat Pirelli
Publishing and Printing	Pearson Reed Intl. Reuters		Axel Springer	Lagardere	Elsevier Wolters	Moore Thomson						Ferruzzi
Chemicals	Imperial Chemical	Sumitomo Chemical Asahi	Schering Hoechst Henkel BASF	Air-Liquide Rhone Poulenc	Akzo DSM		Ciba-Geigy	Solvay Gevaert				Montedison
Pharmaceutical	Zeneca Glaxo-Wallcome Smithkline	Green Cross Taisho Sankyo	Bayer	Sanofi			Roche Sandoz		Astra			

	UK	Japan	Germany	France	Netherlands	Canada	Switzerland	Belgium	Sweden	Spain	Italy	Hong Kong
Metals, Metal Products, Mining	British Steel	Nippon Steel Kobe Steel	Thyssen F. Krupp Degussa Kloeckner VIAG	Pechiney Imetal Usinor-Sacilor	Hoogovens	Noranda Falconbridge Inco Alcan Alum	Alusuisse	Bekaert	SKF Sandvik	INI		
Petroleum Refining	British Petrol.	Nippon Oil	Veba	Total Elf Aquitaine	Royal Dutch	Imperial Oil		Petrofina		CEPSA Repsol	ENI	
Electronics and Telecom	GEC British Telecom Cable and Wireless Racal	NTT Sanyo Toshiba Matsushita Sharp	Siemens	Thomson CGE Moulinex Alcatel France Telecom	Philips Royal PTT Ned KPN	Northern Telecom Bell Canada (BCE)	ABB ASEA Brown Boveri Elektrowatt		L.M. Ericsson Electrolux	Telefonica	IRI Telecom Italia TIM	Hong Kong Telecom
Computers		NEC Hitachi	Nixdorf	Bull							Olivetti	
Industrial Eq. and Materials	BTR	Kawasaki Komatsu	Mannesmann Deutsche Babcock AEG MAN	Schneider Saint-Gobain Lafarge Coppee			Sulzer Schindler		Alfa Laval ASEA Copco Aga Aktiebolog			
Aerospace	British Aerospace			Aero-spatiale Snecma Matra	Fokker	Bombardier						
Cosmetics	Boots			L'oreal								
Broadcast and Media, Entertainment	Bret-Sky EMI Grenada	Nintendo										

a large number of major national financial markets. Consistent with the previous description of strategies toward portfolio construction, this provider has identified services products that may include: corporate cash management, master trust and custodial responsibilities for defined-benefit-plan assets, products oriented to defined contribution plans (for example, in the United States, for the 401(k) pension programs), portfolio management in the form of the "guaranteed investment contracts" (GICs), and performance measurement consulting. These services are provided on a fee basis, and hence are viewed as attractive by the global financial institution. Services are frequently adapted to the specific needs of the client investor, for example by the selection of specific procedures balancing active and passive management techniques. Obviously from the service provider's viewpoint, the wider the range of products offered and clients served, the greater the critical mass and competitive position that the provider achieves.

INDEX FUNDS AND PORTFOLIO INSURANCE

In an earlier section of this chapter we described the general merits and demerits of indexation as a portfolio management strategy. Beyond the question of investment strategy, indexes of leading markets (or market components) can be used as a reference base for achieving portfolio insurance.

Portfolio insurance

Methods used to hedge against losses in portfolio value.

Portfolio managers have developed the use of futures and options contracts to provide a hedge or insurance against broad portfolio risks. Often "portfolio insurance" is a simple hedge taken against a change in the value of some type of market index. This index could be related to interest rate changes, or to movements in broad stock indexes. During the 1980s markets for such futures and options contracts spread rapidly from the United States to London, Continental Europe, and Far Eastern centers. As a result fund managers around the world now can utilize these portfolio insurance approaches on a widespread basis.

Stock index funds are investment funds set up to match the performance of a broad stock market index such as the S&P 100, S&P 500, or Dow Jones averages. Financial research has found that some portfolio managers do not consistently generate returns superior to those of the aggregate stock market. For this reason it is preferable to engage in passive management and to invest in a portfolio that closely matches and performs like the market average.

Stock index options have developed as a hedge or insurance mechanism, often used in connection with the management of a wholly or partially indexed portfolio. Stock index options have been introduced in a number of countries. Stock index options give the holder a call or put on the level of that particular broad market index. Some options are tied directly to an index value (CBOE, NYSE), and others are options on futures contracts of stock indexes (NYFE, CME).

Options provide fund managers with a unique opportunity to insure portfolios against a decline in value, but also to benefit from positive performance potential. The following illustrates the use of put options in the case of a British fund manager wanting to insure a dollar equity fund, where the S&P 100 is considered to be a suitable stock index option.

S&P Put Options 19 November 1991

Strike Price	December 1991 Expiry	NY Close
355	7 1/2	354.9
350	5 3/8	354.9
345	4	354.9

In this case the British fund manager has a diversified portfolio of $1 million of stocks listed on the NYSE. It is believed that the S&P 100 will serve as an adequate hedge mechanism. On 19 November 1991 cash market for the S&P 100 is at a level of 354.9, and the premium on the December 1991 put option with strike price 355 is 71/2. The British manager fears a decline in share prices and decides to buy 28 put options with a December maturity, strike price 355. With a premium of 71/2, the total cost is:

$$\$7.50 \times 100 \times 28 = \$21,000.$$

Each S&P 100 contract covers 100 units, with dollar level equivalent. Each of the 28 contracts will cover $355 \times 100 = \$35,500$ stock value. The 28 contracts will cover the $1 million of American stock market exposure as indicated below:

$$\$1 \text{ million} \div \$35,500 = 28.1$$

If the S & P 100 rises in value by December, the options will be worthless. However, if the S&P 100 declines in value, the portfolio will generate a profit on the cash settlement of the options contracts.

Options on the index have been more popular than options on index futures. The Commodity Futures Trading Commission (CFTC) regulates options on stock index futures in the United States. Brokers must register with the CFTC to trade options on stock index futures. Alternatively, the Securities and Exchange Commission (SEC) considers options on stock indexes to be securities. Brokers registered to trade common stock options may also trade options on stock indexes. There are more sales representatives registered to trade stock index options than stock index futures.

Equity Fund managers may utilize equity index futures as well as stock index options to hedge portfolio positions. In Exhibit 20.9 we find price and other market data published in the *Financial Times* (August 16, 1996) referring to the Footsie 100 stock index. The FT-SE 100 futures contract specifications are summarized in Exhibit 20.10.

Equity index futures contracts are contracts on the basket of shares making up the index. The FT-SE 100 U.K. equity index has only 100 shares that enable traders to replicate the futures contract with a portfolio of underlying shares. Fund managers make frequent use of this contract to hedge portfolios of the FT-All share (750 share issues) as well as FT-SE 100. The contract is cash settled (Exhibit 20.10). It is priced at £25 per index point, so that if Mr. Silver purchased one equity index futures contact for September 1996 delivery (Exhibit 20.9) at the closing price of 3878, he would be buying into a portfolio of shares currently worth $3878 \times £25 = £96,950$. Tick size for the FT-SE 100 share index futures contract is 0.5 of an index point, or £12.50. If the futures price rose 20 index points or 40 ticks, Mr. Silver would profit by $40 \times £12.50 = £500$. The LIFFE exchange insures that the futures price converges to underlying cash price at expiration of the contract by defining the futures price on expiration to be the underlying or cash price.

Exhibit 20.9 provides two tables of FT-SE 100 option prices. The top FT-SE 100 index option gives American options prices, and the lower EuroStyle FT-SE 100 gives European options prices. U.K. fund managers who like to sell (write) options and to avoid early exercise against them use the European style option.

Options on the FT-SE 100 differ from options on individual shares in that the index options are cash settled. Second, options on the index are based on a notional sterling amount of the contract that varies directly with the level of the index. By

EXHIBIT 20.9 FT-SE 100 Futures and Options

FT-SE 100 INDEX FUTURES (LIFFE) £25 per full index point

	Open	Sett Price	Change	High	Low	Est. vol	Open Int. (APT)
Sep	3841.0	3845.0	+9.0	3855.0	3840.0	9113	62253
Dec	3861.0	3865.0	+8.0	3872.0	3861.0	472	4813
Mar	3878.0	3877.0	+9.0	3878.0	3878.0	40	310

FT-SE MID 250 INDEX FUTURES (LIFFE) £10 per full index point

	Open	Sett Price	Change	High	Low	Est. vol	Open Int.
Sep	4373.0	4373.0	+23.0	4378.0	4373.0	391	3490

FT-SE 100 INDEX OPTION (LIFFE) (*3836) £10 per full index point

	3650 C	3650 P	3700 C	3700 P	3750 C	3750 P	3800 C	3800 P	3850 C	3850 P	3900 C	3900 P	3950 C	3950 P	4000 C	4000 P
Aug	189½	1	139½	1	89½	1	40	1	2½	15	1	65	1	115	1	165
Sep	203½	8	159	13½	116½	22½	80	36	51	56	28	84½	13½	121½	4½	165½
Oct	220	20	177	28	138	39½	104½	56	74	75½	50½	102	32	134½	18	172
Nov	233½	20	195	42	157	53½	124½	71	94	91	70½	117	48½	146½	32½	181
Dec†			216	56½			153	89			95½	133½			53½	194½

Calls 10,738 Puts 4,446

EURO STYLE FT-SE 100 INDEX OPTION (LIFFE) £10 per full index point

	3675 C	3675 P	3725 C	3725 P	3775 C	3775 P	3825 C	3825 P	3875 C	3875 P	3925 C	3925 P	3975 C	3975 P	4025 C	4025 P
Aug	164½	1	114½	1	64½	1	17	3	1	35½	1	85½	1	135½	1	185½
Sep	178½	10	135½	16	96½	27	63	43	36½	66½	18	97½	7½	137	3	182
Oct	195	21½	155	31½	119	44½	87½	62½	60½	85	40	114	24	148	13	186½
Dec			201½	64½			135	95½			83	142			46½	203
Mar†			244½	98			185½	135½			136	182			95	237½

Calls 7,034 Puts 9,618 *Underlying index value. Premiums shown are based on settlement prices.

† Long dated expiry months.

Source: *Financial Times*, (August 16, 1996).

EXHIBIT 20.10	**Contract Specifications for FT-SE 100 Futures Contract**
Unit of Trading	£25 per full index point.
Delivery Months	March, June, September, December.
Quotation	Index points.
Minimum Price Movement	
Tick size	0.5
Tick value	£12.50
Contract Standard	Cash settled against average FT-SE 100 Index on last trading day.
Initial Margin*	£2,000

* Subject to change.

contrast, individual stock options are acquired on a fixed number of units of shares. For example, if 200 call options were bought on the FT-SE Index at the level of 3850 quoted in Exhibit 20.9, the underlying share value would be

$$200 \times 3850 \times £10 = £7,700,00$$

To buy the 200 3850 September calls quoted at 51, an investor would pay

$$200 \times 51 \times £10 = £102,000$$

we must remember the £102,000 cost covers a portfolio exposure worth £7.7 million.

Evaluating International Performance

This section describes how to evaluate investment performance, given the investment vehicle and related portfolio objectives. Managers aim at deriving superior returns, assuming that the level of acceptable portfolio risk is already established. They further strive to achieve sufficient diversification so that all (or the desired level) of the unsystematic risk is eliminated.

In this regard the portfolio manager may find it necessary to:

1. establish a strategy that maximizes the likelihood of attaining investment objectives.
2. predict market turns.
3. shift assets from one sector to another (e.g. equities, bonds, cash, real estate, metals).
4. select undervalued securities.
5. evaluate the effects on portfolio risk given changes in the composition of the portfolio.
6. establish a strategy that balances forecasting inputs (costs) with the value to be derived from these forecasts.

PROBLEMS IN EVALUATING PERFORMANCE

A basic question that must be considered in evaluating portfolio performance is, are we evaluating portfolio performance or the ability of the portfolio manager? Portfolio performance may be judged "very good" for the following reasons:

1. superior manager
2. favorable economic environment
3. minimal constraints imposed on manager and portfolio strategy used.

As we can understand, portfolio performance may be given high marks because a favorable economic environment operated, and/or there was a minimum of constraints imposed on portfolio strategy. Comparison of portfolio performance with that of the market portfolio is likely to neutralize the effects of changing economic environment. In a later section we discuss some of the constraints that managers of institutional portfolios face.

Portfolio managers confront several problems in their efforts to achieve superior performance. First, an appropriate benchmark is required with which to compare performance. Domestically the appropriate benchmark may be considered to be the market portfolio. In the case of domestic equity portfolios, the S&P 500 might be suitable for American-based investors, or the Financial Times 100 Index for U.K.-based investors. When the analysis is made in terms of excess returns over the risk-free rate, the U.S. or U.K. Treasury bill rates might apply (in the United States and United Kingdom, respectively).

Internationally, an appropriate benchmark becomes more elusive. We should note that the efforts of Ibbotsen-Siegel-Love to provide a world market wealth portfolio have met with only limited success.* There were several gaps in their wealth portfolio, particularly from the point of view of the non-U.S. investor. Where equity-only portfolios are concerned, the problem of an appropriate benchmark becomes less acute. World equity portfolios can be approximated by the Morgan Stanley Capital International and FT Actuaries Indices.

A second problem concerns itself with the definition of risk and the various levels of risk encountered in alternative portfolios. Is the appropriate risk level total risk or systematic risk? High risk portfolios may earn a higher return, but does this mean that the portfolio manager has been more successful than in the case of a low risk-low return portfolio? What is needed is a risk-adjusted evaluation.

As will be noted in the following evaluation approaches, the Sharpe and Treynor measures of performance use total risk and systematic risk, respectively. However, the difference may prove to be unimportant since well-managed portfolios can remove virtually all unsystematic risk.

A third problem is that different types of investors may face unique constraints and operating problems. This situation is clear if we examine and compare institutional investor groups. If we contrast pension fund with stock mutual fund management, the former must consider benefit payment goals, whereas the latter has no such concern. In this sense we might argue that pension fund asset allocation should be viewed as liability driven, on the basis of an analysis of the benefits that a

---

* Ibbotson, Roger, Laurence Sieglel, and Kathryn Love, "World Wealth: U.S. and Foreign Market Values and Returns," *Journal of Portfolio Management,* (Fall 1985).

fund is likely to be called upon to finance over the years ahead. Mutual funds do not face this type of constraint.

Furthermore there can be fundamental differences among pension funds. Pension schemes may pay benefits linked to final salary, or they may be constructed on a money purchase basis where benefit payments depend strictly on portfolio return. Among final salary pension schemes there can be important differences in the liability structure. Trustees of pension schemes of fast-growing, young companies can be relatively unconcerned about portfolio liquidity knowing that significant out-payments will not develop for many years. By contrast, trustees of mature company pension funds face high out-payments and must be concerned with maturity structure and liquidity.

BASIC EVALUATION APPROACHES

In this section we examine two basic performance evaluation approaches, the (William F.) Sharpe and (Jack L.) Treynor measures. Treynor developed the first in a *Harvard Business Review* article.[†] In this article he distinguishes between systematic risk that is risk produced by general market fluctuations, and unsystematic risk that is risk resulting from fluctuations unique to the securities in the portfolio. Treynor proposes using a measure based upon the ratio of return to risk. The numerator of this ratio is based on the excess return of the portfolio over the risk-free rate. The denominator is based on the risk of the portfolio, measured by its beta (systematic risk):

$$TRN_i = \frac{R_i - RFR}{B_i}$$

where

TRN_i = the Treynor measure of portfolio risk.
R_i = the average rate of return for portfolio i over a given period of time.
RFR = the risk-free rate of return over a given time period.
B_i = the systematic risk of the portfolio i.

The larger the *TRN* value, the higher the evaluation of portfolio management. This ratio holds irrespective of risk level and risk preference. In this sense *TRN* provides a risk-adjusted measure of performance. Since the numerator indicates the risk premium return (excess return) and the denominator indicates the level of risk, *TRN* reflects the portfolio return per unit of risk.

The *TRN* measure can be applied to the performance of the market portfolio. Accordingly we can determine whether a given portfolio would lie above the Security Market Line (SML)*. The following expression indicates application of the Treynor measure to the market portfolio.

$$TRN_m = \frac{R_m - B_m}{RFR}$$

Treynor measure

Evaluates portfolio performance related to systematic risk.

[†] Treynor, Jack L. "How To Rate Management of Investment Funds," *Harvard Business Review*, (January-February 1965).

[*] The Security Market Line differs from the Capital Market Line as follows: The SML utilizes beta as a normalized measure of systematic risk, while the CML utilizes portfolio standard deviation as a measure of risk.

In this case B_m should equal 1.0 (the market beta) that is the slope of the SML. If a portfolio has a higher *TRN* value than the market portfolio, it will plot above the SML. Exhibit 20.11 demonstrates the use of *TRN* in evaluating funds management on a comparative basis. Exhibit 20.12 indicates that fund manager A performance is inferior (below the SML), whereas fund managers B, C, and D performance is satisfactory (above the SML).

Sharpe measure

Evaluates portfolio performance related to total risk.

Sharpe also developed a measure of performance related to earlier work on the Capital Asset Pricing Model (CAPM). The Sharpe measure (SHP) is:

$$SHP_i = \frac{R_i - RFR}{SD_i}$$

where

SHP_i = the Sharpe measure of portfolio *i* performance.
R_i = the average rate of return for portfolio *i* over a given time period.

EXHIBIT 20.11   **Comparative Evaluation of Four British Fund Managers**

Over the recent five-year period the average annual return on the market portfolio (FT Actuaries) was 12% (R_m = 12), and the average rate of return on government T bills was 7% (RFR = .07). Assume you are the administrator of a British pension fund that has been divided between four money managers. You must decide how well the four money managers have performed. Assume the following:

Fund Manager	Average Annual Return	Fund Beta
A	11	0.90
B	12	0.90
C	15	1.10
D	16	1.50

Calculation of TRN values for each of the portfolio managers and the market portfolio is as follows:

$$TRN_m = \frac{.12 - .07}{1.005} = .0500 \text{ TRN value}$$

$$TRN_a = \frac{.11 - .07}{0.90} = .0440 \text{ TRN value}$$

$$TRN_b = \frac{.12 - .07}{0.90} = .0555 \text{ TRN value}$$

$$TRN_c = \frac{.15 - .07}{1.10} = .0727 \text{ TRN value}$$

$$TRN_d = \frac{.16 - .07}{1.50} = .0600 \text{ TRN value}$$

These results indicate that fund manager A ranked lowest of the four managers and did not perform as well as the market portfolio. The performance of B, C, and D was satisfactory, outperforming the market portfolio. Exhibit 20.12 provides a clear indication that fund manager A lies below the SML, and fund managers B, C, and D lie above the SML.

EXHIBIT 20.12	**Comparative Evaluation of Portfolio Performance of Market Portfolio and Four Fund Managers**

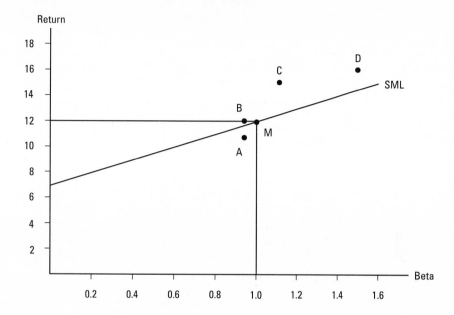

RFR = the risk free rate of return over a given time period.

SD_i = the standard deviation of the rate of return for portfolio i over a given time period.

The Sharpe measure resembles the Treynor measure, except that in the Sharpe measure risk is represented by the standard deviation rather than beta. Sharpe uses total risk rather than systematic risk, and therefore portfolios are compared with the CML (not the SML as in the Treynor measure).

The Sharpe measure evaluates the portfolio manager on the basis of return per unit of risk, but there is an added element. That is, Sharpe also discriminates concerning portfolio diversification. In the Treynor measure it is possible to have a satisfactory evaluation even if the portfolio is poorly diversified. Poor diversification could yield higher unsystematic risk that tends to be excluded in the Treynor measure. On the basis of the Sharpe measure, total risk figures into the denominator of the equation so that poor diversification will be reflected by higher total risk. The two measures (Sharpe and Treynor) provide somewhat different information. For that reason both should be used.

LEAGUE TABLES

At the outset of our discussion concerning evaluating performance we distinguished between evaluating portfolio performance and evaluating the ability of the manager. In the case of pension fund investment, the perceived ability of the fund manager will affect the share of total managed funds under his or her jurisdiction. If we can assume an "efficient market" for the services of fund managers, league tables provide a market driven evaluation.

League tables indicate on a yearly basis which fund managers have increased the amount of funds under management, as well as the number of clients served. Yearly changes in amounts and relative rankings are watched carefully. Three distinct types of fund managers compete in the U.K. pension fund market. These include merchant banks that are leaders in the field, clearing bank affiliated managers such as Barclays de Zoete Wedd, and independent boutiques (Gartmore, Murray Johnstone). Among the merchant banks, Schroder Investment Management remains an independent, while Baring Investment Management was acquired by ING Bank in 1995.

EVALUATING PERFORMANCE OF FINANCIAL INSTITUTIONS

In previous sections we described several approaches toward evaluating portfolio performance. One of the problems in this area is that within a given institutional investor group there can be substantial differences in the form of constraints on operational flexibility that seriously affect the ability of the fund manager to achieve above average investment results.

In this section we focus on three types of British institutional investors: investment trusts, unit trusts, and pension funds. In each case we note the need to consider special constraints or differences in operational flexibility.

PENSION FUNDS

U.K. pension fund management has become a mature industry. Over the period 1986–1988 new money inflows as a percent of market value averaged 5–6% (Exhibit 20.13). Nevertheless the year-to-year allocations of cash inflows by pension fund managers are subject to dramatic changes. As a group, U.K. pension fund managers shifted from overseas equities to U.K. equities in 1986–1987 and reversed this shift in 1987–1988. In the same period they reduced new bond investments and increased and then reduced new cash holdings.

The following outlines the different investment practices followed by U.K. pension funds. These practices are based on needs related to special operating constraints.

1. There is a fundamental difference between pension schemes that pay benefits linked to final salary and those that are constructed on a money purchase basis.

EXHIBIT 20.13	U.K. Pension Funds, Annual Cash Flow Allocation (Percent)									
	79	80	81	82	83	84	85	86	87	88
U.K. Equities	29	33	29	24	21	37	37	48	91	55
Overseas Equities	11	23	24	25	17	−6	28	25	−16	26
U.K. Bonds	41	30	26	22	31	24	22	6	−9	−15
Overseas Bonds	—	—	—	—	—	—	—	−2	−1	7
Index Linked	—	—	—	9	10	10	9	7	−9	−2
U.K. Property	13	15	16	15	9	10	7	2	−5	7
Overseas Property	—	—	—	—	—	—	—	−1	0	1
Cash/Other	6	−3	3	4	13	24	−4	18	49	21
New Money (%) of Initial Market Value	20	19	15	13	12	9	8	7	5	5

SOURCE: The WM Company.

Where the pension liability is linked to final salary, a specific premium must be paid into the fund, based upon carefully determined actuarial estimates of return. In this case, asset commitments must be prudently driven by liability considerations. In the case of a money purchase scheme, somewhat greater risks (and flexibility) are possible.

2. Mature and immature pension schemes require different investment management. Similarly, permitted risk levels will vary. In the case of fast-growing, young companies, it is understood that significant pension liabilities will not crystallize for many years. Such immature schemes will be highly invested in equities or property that offer the best long-term returns. Volatility and liquidity scarcely matter. By contrast, in the case of mature schemes with a higher element of scheduled maturity, fixed income (bonds) securities will be required.

Unit Trusts

As of 1991 more than 1300 British unit trusts in the United Kingdom held approximately six percent of U.K. equities. Unit trusts differ markedly from one another in form, size, and investment objectives. Given the growing emphasis on performance, the job of ranking unit trusts in order of performance is a daunting task.

Unit trusts need to be placed into homogeneous categories that identify the nature and purpose of the fund. The Unit Trust Association has set up a standard set of categories for funds, on which performance evaluation can be based. The first set of categories was issued in 1982 and has been revised. The categories issued in 1989 are described in Exhibit 20.14. A reasonable approach in evaluating performance is to compare funds that are in the same unit trust category.

EXHIBIT 20.14   New System of Categories for Unit Trusts

On 1 August 1989 the Unit Trust Association (UTA) introduced a new system of categorizing unit trusts, intended to simplify performance comparisons. The objective is to place unit trusts into roughly homogeneous groups, making it easier and more valid to compare investment performance. Trusts are divided by geographical region, asset type, and investment objectives. The UTA categories are:

- UK Funds—all trusts with at least 80% of investments in the United Kingdom and subdivided into General, Equity Income, Growth, Gilt and Fixed Interest, and Balanced.
- International—trusts in which less than 80% is invested in any one geographical area, and subdivided into Equity Income, Growth, Fixed Interest, and Balanced.
- Japan

- Far East (a) including Japan, and (b) excluding Japan.
- Australia
- North America
- Europe—includes funds with a U.K. content not exceeding 80% of the fund.
- Specialist—Commodity and Energy, Financial and Property, Investment Trust Units, Fund of Funds, and Money Market.
- Exempt Unit Trusts—Funds exempt of tax, available only to approved pension funds and charities.
- Personal Pension and FSAVC Unit trusts.

With the single European market in UCITS, developing the UTA will have to integrate with its counterparts in continental Europe to produce a mutually agreed upon European classification.

INVESTMENT TRUSTS

The first British investment trust, Foreign & Colonial Investment Trust, was organized in 1868. Since then this form of investment has grown in importance. The investment trust provides management and diversification to investors who otherwise might not be able to provide these needs themselves. The investment trust business is claimed to have originated in Scotland, and the city of Edinburgh is home to a number of leading fund managers that specialize in this activity.

The investment trust resembles the American closed-end fund, with one difference. British rules allow these companies to be leveraged, which can affect their investment performance.

Originally investment trusts were designed to be active in cross- border investing to take advantage of higher bond yields overseas (6–8%) as compared with yields in the U.K. (2–3%). Recently this sector increased its emphasis on achieving a global perspective. We can use the Foreign & Colonial case as an illustration. The management company (Foreign & Colonial Management) was restructured in 1985 to widen its range of activities. FCM has joint ventures in international investment management with the Long Term Credit Bank of Japan and Banco de Investimentos Garantia in Brazil.

In 1989 a strategic partnership was formed with Bayerische Hypotheken-und-Wechsel-Bank of Munich (Hypo Bank). Hypo is the fifth largest commercial bank in Germany. The strategic objective of this partnership is to combine the Foreign & Colonial skills and experience with Hypo's strong retail base and distribution capacities in Germany. (Exhibit 20.15).

EXHIBIT 20.15 **Hypo Foreign and Colonial Structure**

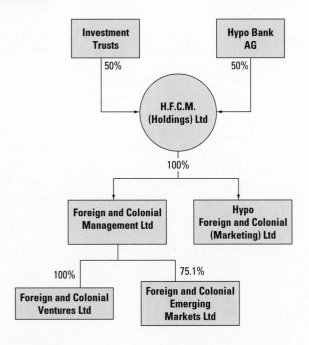

SOURCE: Hypo Foreign and Colonial

EXHIBIT 20.16

Growth of Assets under Management – Hypo Foreign and Colonial £billion

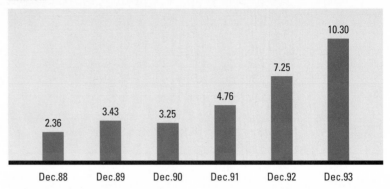

SOURCE: Hypo Foreign and Colonial

Hypo Bankers and the five investment trust shareholders control FCM and its sister company Hypo Foreign & Colonial (Marketing) through Hypo Foreign & Colonial Management (Holdings). In 1993 FCM merged Latin American Securities with its South East Asian business to form Foreign & Colonial Emerging Markets, in which it owns a 75.1% stake, making it one of the top five emerging markets money managers in the world. The group ownership structure is reflected in the previous exhibit. Given the new global strategy, funds under management have grown rapidly as indicated in Exhibit 20.16.

SUMMARY

This chapter focuses on the operations dimension of international portfolio investment. Individual and institutional investors face different problems and have different needs. Individual investors must operate at small scale and develop their own sources of investment information. They must also develop procedures for carrying out investment transactions.

Individual investors make use of the following investment channels: direct purchase in overseas markets, American Depository Receipts, single country funds, and international and global funds. In such cases they may be exposed to various risks, including country, currency, systematic, and unsystematic.

Institutional investors have options that are typically not open to individual investors. Information is more readily and inexpensively available. Moreover, institutional investors have larger overall resources to obtain information and investment services.

International portfolio management can be carried out in an active or passive basis. Passive management has its theoretical support in the efficient markets hypothesis and generally conforms to the index approach. Active management requires considerable analysis and forecasting of national and industry trends. Modified active management involves constructing an efficient frontier from available investment information.

Several approaches are used for evaluating portfolio performance. Problems are encountered in evaluating performance including: finding an appropriate benchmark, defining risk and its role in performance, and dealing with different constraints imposed on various types of investors. The Treynor and Sharpe measures of portfolio evaluation are useful. League tables provide a market driven evaluation.

REVIEW QUESTIONS

1. Describe the functional needs of individual investors undertaking internationally diversified investments.

2. What types of investment vehicles are available to individual investors? How do they compare in permitting investors to carry out investment in a satisfactory and efficient manner?

3. Compare and contrast the risks that individual investors are exposed to when using the following vehicles: a) single country fund, b) international fund, and c) global fund.

4. Describe the major problems that large institutional investors encounter in carrying out international investment.

5. Distinguish between passive, active, and moderately active portfolio management in connection with each of the following:
   a. amount of forecasting required and b) risks assumed.

6. It has been said that evaluation of international portfolio investment performance is at best an exercise in futility. Why might one make this statement?
   a. Describe the logic of Treynor's approach to evaluation of portfolio performance.
   b. How does the Treynor measure differ from the Sharpe measure of performance?

8. A mutual fund has a return of 16%, compared with the market return of 10%. The risk-free rate is 6%. The fund's beta is 1.6. Using the Treynor approach, evaluate the fund's performance.

9. In the previous case you also know that the standard deviation of return of the mutual fund is 0.20 and for the market index 0.08. Evaluate performance based on the Sharpe approach.

10. What special problems are encountered in evaluating the performance of a) fund managers and b) financial institutions such as pension funds?

11. A British investor buys 2000 shares of Philip Morris at $70. The exchange rate is pounds/$ = 0.56. During the next year the investor receives dividends of $2.20 per share, at which time the exchange rate is pounds/$ = 0.59. At year-end the investor sells the shares at $84. The exchange rate now is pounds/$ = 0.61. Aside from commissions and taxes, what is the overall return? What part of dollar profit is dividends? Capital gains? What part of the pound sterling profit is currency gain, capital gain, and dividends?

12. A German fund manager holds $10 million worth of U.S. stocks, all traded on the NYSE. The original cost of this portfolio is $6 million, and the manager does not want to sell at the present time. The German fund manager is concerned about a decline in the U.S. stock market, and is interested in hedging by buying a put on the S&P 100. Given the information in the table, he is interested in the S&P put at 350. The S&P currently is at a level of 360.

S&P Put Options	S&P Market Close	Premium on August Option
Aug 320	360	2¼
Aug 330	360	3⅛
Aug 340	360	5¼
Aug 350	360	6
Aug 360	360	9½

a. What will the hedge position cost?

b. What would be the difference if the German fund manager used the August 320 put option? Explain.

13. A European-based money manger holds $40 million worth of dollar- denominated Eurobonds. They have a face value of $35 million, are relatively illiquid, and have eight to ten years to maturity. The fund manager fears that U.S. interest rates will rise over the next year and decides to hedge using the U.S. Treasury bond futures. Can a perfect hedge be made? Explain what difficulties may be encountered.

14. United States-based investors have increased the extent of cross-border investing year by year. It is believed that there are certain key benefits from international diversification.

a. Using the return and risk information in the following table, explain the rationale for diversifying a U.S. dollar bond portfolio into foreign currency bonds.

b. Using the same table, explain the rationale for diversifying a U.S. institutional investor portfolio into foreign currency stocks and bonds.

Annual returns, recent 12-year period

Market	Return	Standard Deviation
Equities:		
United States	9.2%	13.2
United Kingdom	6.2	14.3
Germany	8.1	16.8
France	7.3	11.7
Netherlands	5.6	8.4
Hong Kong	13.1	28.2
Mexico	18.2	27.1
Bonds:		
U.S. Government	5.4	7.6
U.S. Corporate	5.8	8.5
U.K. Government	11.3	12.5
Germany Bank Bonds	6.4	9.8
France Government	9.5	10.4
Netherlands Corporate	6.5	9.6

15. An American fund manager believes the U.K. stock market will rise sharply over the next half year. Compare the advantages of buying FT-SE 100 options, FT-SE 100 futures, and actual U.K. shares.

16. Mr. Silver has a portfolio of U.K. shares whose returns correlate well with the returns of the FT-SE 100. The current level of the FT-SE 100 share index is 3800, the short-term interest rate is 10%, and the expected dividend yield is 3%. The FT-SE 100 futures contract due to expire in three months is 3900. Should Mr. Silver hold shares or switch to the futures market to have exposure to U.K. equities? Assume that round trip transaction costs are 1.60%. How would this influence any decision to sell shares and buy them back?

CASE 1

Organizing an Equity Research Department
(Continued from Chapter 19)

PART II: MR. HALVESTROM'S PLAN

Mr. Halvestrom had to make a critical decision in formulating his plan for the development of a London-based equity research office. Should an office be launched de novo, hiring financial analysts and other staff one by one? Or should the parent New York firm buy a large controlling interest in an existing firm?

Mr. Halvestrom had learned that a 50% interest in a small British merchant bank could be acquired for approximately $32 million. It has a total work force of 46 individuals, as follows:

Chief executive and two senior VPs	3
Bond traders and money market traders	15
Stock market traders (London Exchange)	5
Equity analysts	4
Economic research staff	3
Corporate liaison officers	2
Secretarial and clerical	14
Total	46

This firm has been operating at low profitability, and losses in recent years. The past five-year record (after tax) is as follows:

Year	£ Million
1986	+2.4
1987	−0.3
1988	+0.1
1989	−2.7
1990	−4.6

The British merchant bank already has an outside investor (a large Dutch bank holding a 15% equity stake).

The British merchant bank has a small office in Frankfurt with staff of two (one officer and one secretary). This office provided occasional investment analyses of German companies obtained from German financial institutions.

The alternative of opening a de novo office in London was expected to require an initial staff of 14, including eight equity analysts and one economist. The expected annual costs would be as follows:

Office rental and equipment	£ 820,000
Personnel	390,000
	£1,210,000

($1.64 = £1).

SELECTED BIBLIOGRAPHY

Arnott, R., and R. Henricksson. "A Disciplined Approach to Global Asset Allocation," *Financial Analysts Journal,* (March-April 1989).

Coggan, Philip. "Bull Run for Emerging Markets?", *Financial Times,* (August 19, 1996): 20.

Cumby, R.E., and J.D. Glen. "Evaluating the Performance of International Mutual Funds," *Journal of Finance,* (June 1990).

Halpern, Philip. "Investing Abroad: A Review of Capital Market Integration and Manager Performance," *Journal of Portfolio Management,* (Winter 1993).

Harges, Kent. "The Globalization of Trading and Issuance of Equities from Emerging Markets," *Journal of Emerging Markets,* (Spring 1997).

Howell, M., and A. Cozzini. *International Equity Flows: 1990 Edition.* New York: Salomon Brothers.

Ibbotson, Roger, and Gary Brinson. *Global Investing.* New York: McGraw-Hill, 1993.

Ibbotson, Roger, Laurence Siegel, and Kathryn Love. "World Wealth: U.S. and Foreign Market Values and Returns," *Journal of Portfolio Management,* (Fall 1985).

McNelis, Paul D. "A Neural Network Analysis of Brazilian Stock Prices: Tequila Effects vs. Pisco Sour Effects," *Journal of Emerging Markets,* (Summer 1996).

CASE 2

Sell, Hold, or Switch?

Mr. Ramirez, a New York stockbroker, had advised his customer to buy Pearson and Glaxo shares (London International Stock Exchange) early in 1989. At this time the exchange rate was \$1.80/£, with the price of Glaxo £10.60 (purchased 4000 shares) and price of Pearson £6.70 (purchased 5000 shares).

Ramirez came up with the following alternative suggestions.

1. Sell the stock and buy three-month U.K. Treasury Bills yielding 13.5%.

2. Sell the stock and buy 15-year U.K. Treasury bonds yielding 9.7%.

Cost:				
Glaxo	4000 shares @	10.60 —	£42,400 @ \$1.80	\$76,320
Pearson	5000 shares @	6.70 —	£33,500 @ 1.80	60,300
			£75,900	\$136,620
Value:				
Glaxo	4000 shares @	5.70 —	£62,800 @ 1.55	\$97,340
Pearson	5000 shares @	8.40 —	£42,000 @ 1.55	65,100
			£104,800	\$162,440

Seven months later (August 1989) Glaxo had climbed to 15.70 and Pearson to 8.40. However the pound had declined to \$1.55. While the local currency (sterling) profit was almost £29,000 or 38%, the dollar profit was only \$26,000 or 18%.

At this point the customer wanted to take the sterling profit. Mr. Ramirez pointed out that the dollar return was 18%, not 38%. After some discussion Mr.

3. Sell the stock and convert it to dollars.

4. Hold the stock for another three to six month period.

Which alternative might be preferable? What specific information would be required (as a forecast) to select the best alternative?

Moreira, Jose Carlos. "Why Invest in Brazil?" *Journal of Emerging Markets,* (Summer 1996).

Porter, Michael T. "Closed End Emerging Country Funds Review," in Keith K. H. Park and Antoihe W. Van Agtmael, *The World's Emerging Stock Markets.* Chicago: Probus, 1993.

Sharpe, W.F. "Mutual Fund Performance," *Journal of Business,* (January 1966).

Singer, B.D., and D.S. Karnisky. "The General Framework for Global Investment Management and Performance Attribution," *Journal of Portfolio Management,* (Winter 1995).

Singuefield, Rex A. "Where Are the Gains from International Diversification?", *Financial Analysts Journal,* (January-February 1996).

Stanley, Marjorie T. *The Irwin Guide to Investing in Emerging Markets.* Chicago: Richard D. Irwin, 1995.

Taylor, J.R., and A.M. Pietruska. "The Case for Active Currency Management," *Investment Management Review,* (January-February 1989).

Treynor, Jack L. "How to Rate Management of Investment Funds," *Harvard Business Review,* (January-February 1965).

Van Agtmael, A.W. "Investing in Emerging Markets," in Park and Agtmael, *The World's Emerging Stock Markets.* Chicago: Probus, 1993.

Wahab, M., and A. Khandwala. "Why Not Diversify Internationally With ADRs?", *Journal of Portfolio Management,* (Winter 1993).

Walmsley, Julian. *The New Financial Instruments.* New York: Wiley, 1988.

Glossary

Active management Portfolio selection based on forecasts of superior performance for securities included.

Adjustment mechanisms Processes in the economy that work to assure a nation's external economic equilibrium.

Agency Banking office similar to a branch, except not permitted to accept deposits.

Agency costs These costs occur when the senior management in a subsidiary chooses to pursue objectives that differ from the shareholder value maximization goal of the parent corporation.

AIM The Alternative Investment Market is a new market established by the London Stock Exchange in June 1995 for smaller, young, and fast-growing companies, domestic and foreign.

American depository receipts Issued by an American bank certifying it holds underlying shares issued by a foreign company. These represent shares of foreign stocks or bonds taken care of by American banks for U.S. residents who buy foreign securities without possession of the foreign securities.

Arbitrage Purchase of securities, including foreign exchange, on one market for immediate resale on another at a more advantageous price.

Arbitrage Pricing Theory (APT) Focuses on relative pricing of securities based on common factors. Risk premiums are associated with each factor, and affect pricing of individual countries accordingly.

Arm's-length pricing In the U.S. the IRS allows methods based on: comparable uncontrolled prices, resale prices, cost plus, and comparable profits.

Asian dollar market A market for buying and selling U.S. dollars among banks in Singapore (and sometimes in Hong Kong) for profit.

Asia Pacific Economic Cooperation (APEC) Countries around the Pacific Ocean in Asia, America, and Australia would meet from time to time for economic consultation and cooperation.

At the money An option where strike price is the same as spot price.

Balance of payments (BOP) Statistical estimate of the transactions between residents of one country and residents of the rest of the world.

Bankers acceptances A negotiable instrument (time draft) drawn to finance export, import, and domestic shipments. The phrase comes from when a bank writes the word "accepted" on the draft certifying its agreement to pay it at maturity.

Bankers sight draft Means by which foreign exchange bank issues draft drawn against its foreign currency balances on deposit in a foreign financial center.

Basic balance Sum of the current account and long-term capital account balances.

Basle Accord International agreement to impose minimum capital requirements for banks—related to riskiness of assets.

Bearer shares Issued in bearer form or street name. Difficult to trace specific ownership.

Beta A measure of risk attached to individual securities.

Big Bang Revolutionary structural changes in the U.K. securities markets under the Financial Services Act of 1986. Deregulation allowing increased competition and market efficiency.

Blocked funds Host country government authorities prevent the transfer of funds to the parent MNC. One mechanism is through not permitting currency convertibility.

Brady bonds Issued by developing countries and backed by U.S. Treasury bonds to replace commercial bank debt. Initiated in 1989.

Brady Plan Initiative to reduce debt by exchange of debt for a smaller amount of better quality and collateralized debt.

Branch Office that can carry out full range of banking activities.

Bretton Woods, NH Conference in 1944 establishing foundation for postwar international monetary system.

Call option Gives holder right to buy underlying asset at strike price.

Capital Accord International agreement that introduced minimum capital for banks relative to the riskiness of their assets.

Capital Asset Pricing Model (CAPM) A model of market equilibrium in which the return on a given security is related to the risk premium on that security. In turn, the risk premium is related to the covariance of the asset return with the return available on the market portfolio.

Capital controls Government regulations and legislation to influence foreign exchange market supply and demand.

Capital inflows Transfers of funds to the (home) country whose balance of payments is being estimated.

Capital Market Line (CML) Depicts equilibrium position in a given capital market where investors can hold varying proportions of their assets in the risk-free asset and market portfolio. Borrowing and lending is assumed to take place at the risk-free rate.

Capital outflows Transfers of capital funds (asset holdings) to other (host) countries.

CAPM Capital Asset Pricing Model.

Cash cows MNC subsidiaries that consistently generate net surplus funds for use elsewhere in the MNC system.

Cash forecasting Projection of subsidiary and systemwide changes in cash (and cash equivalents) resulting from operations, investing, or financing activities.

Cedel   An international clearing system, located in Luxembourg, created by a group of European banks in 1970.

Central exchange rates   The fixed par values, with respect to ECU, among exchange rates of participating countries.

Certainty equivalent cash flows   Cash flows over time adjusted by the associated degree of risk.

Closed-end fund   Limited number of shares can be issued to investors. Can be priced at premium or discount relative to net asset value.

Commodity Exchange Act   U.S. federal law that regulates commodities trading.

Common external tariff   For each commodity class, the EC countries maintain the same tariff rate for imports from outside the EC. There are no tariffs on trade among EC countries.

Common Market   In addition to economic benefits, CM brought countries of Europe closer politically.

Correlation-covariance matrix   A matrix table, one part denoting correlations of returns on securities, and another part denoting covariances of returns on these securities.

Correlations   Degree to which returns on two or more securities move together or not, or degree to which returns on security moves together or not with return on market portfolio.

Cost of capital   Return required on capital or bank funds, as determined by the capital market.

Countertrade   Generally refers to barter trade, counterpurchases, buyback agreements, and switch trade that can be flexibly used by traders in different countries for avoiding tariffs and quotas, and possibly can conserve foreign exchange.

Country exposure   Amount of hard currency lending of bank concentrated in a particular country.

Country risk   Possibility that country will be unable to service external loan due to political and economic conditions.

Covariance   Equal to the correlations of returns between two securities multiplied by the standard deviation of their returns. Covariance reflects correlation, but in numbers based on measuring percent returns.

Covered interest arbitrage   Swapping one currency into another on a hedged basis to benefit from interest differential.

Credit risk   Inability of borrower to service loan due to financial situation or status.

Cross rate   Rate obtained by multiplying two foreign exchange rates.

Currency substitution   A model that deals with the substitutability of currencies on the demand side.

Currency swap   Agreement between two counterparties to swap or exchange future cash flows denominated in two different currencies.

Dealer bank   Bank that makes a market in a financial asset, buying and selling at price differential (spread) that provides a profit margin.

Dealing room   Bank or securities firm service facility for trading a number of financial claims, equipped with advanced communication and computer facilities for rapid execution of transactions.

Debt crisis   Refers to 1982 and following period when many developing country debtors were unable to make service payments on external loans.

Debt service   Total debt at the year-end in percent of exports of goods and services in year indicated.

Debt service ratio   Ratio of annual service payments on loan paid by country debtor, to its annual export receipts.

Deemed Paid Foreign Tax Credit   Tax credit allowed against U.S. income tax for foreign taxes paid on foreign-source earnings.

Deferral of tax liability   For qualifying foreign source income, such income not subject to U.S. tax liability until dividend paid (or deemed paid) to U.S. parent.

Derivative instrument   Financial claims with value based on that of the underlying securities.

Devaluations and trade restrictions   Sometimes called "beggar thy neighbor" policies.

Dirty float   Central bank of a nation intervenes in the foreign exchange market under the floating exchange rate system without legitimate reason, purely for the benefit of its own currency.

Distant control membership   Securities firms in London and other European financial centers use electronic connections to trade securities listed on London Stock Exchange but outside Exchange.

Divergence indicator   The DI system is used to determine which nations are to alter economic policies to maintain the fixed parity values.

Dollar shortage   Protracted period after World War II when world demand for U.S. dollars exceeded supply.

Dominant portfolio   Portfolio with highest return given the level of risk, or with lowest risk given the level of return.

Double entry accounting   Every BOP transaction has two sides, a debit and a credit.

Double swap   Involves two separate swaps, back to back.

Double taxation   When foreign source income is taxed abroad and taxed a second time when remitted as dividend to the MNC parent.

Dual currency market   Market in which two currencies play important roles as borrowing and lending vehicles.

Economies in transition   Former communist countries in Eastern Europe and Russia which have gradually transformed their centrally-planned economies to free market economies in the 1990s.

ECU   European Currency Unit.

Edge Act corporations   These corporations are allowed under the Edge Act of 1919 to do international (not domestic) banking business such as trade financing, foreign exchange, and equity investment in foreign countries.

Effective cost   Includes nominal interest adjusted for factors (reserve requirements, deposit insurance) that also may influence basic cost of funds.

Efficient frontier   Investment portfolios producing optimal combinations of risk and return.

Emerging capital markets   Emergence of capital markets in developing countries resulting from their rapid economic growth have attracted international lenders and borrowers to these markets.

Emerging debt market   Market where debt of developing and transitional countries is issued and traded.

Emerging market debt   Refers to debt issued by all developing countries in Asia, Latin America, and Europe in 1980s and 1990s being traded in international financial markets.

Emerging markets   Stock and bond markets of developing and transitional economies.

Eurobank   Banks engaging in Eurocurrency, Eurobonds, and other Euro-transactions.

Eurobonds   Issued in one or more foreign countries but currency denominations are other than that of the country or countries where the bonds are issued.

Euroclear   An international clearing system located in Brussels created by Morgan Guaranty Trust Company in 1968.

Eurocurrency   A collective term applicable to any major currency deposited outside the currency issuing countries.

Eurocurrency Interbank market   Eurobanks trade Eurocurrency from each other for profit.

Eurocurrency market   Offshore money market in which term deposits denominated in several currencies are traded.

Eurodollar arbitrage   Buying and selling Eurodollars in different Euromarkets for profit based on price differentials of the dollars.

Eurograms   A variety of financial instruments by which both lenders and borrowers have freedom of choice in the Euromarket.

European Monetary Cooperation Fund   Provides EMS settlement resources, based on specified revolving swap arrangements.

European Monetary System   A monetary alliance among European Community members to maintain exchange rates within specified margins about fixed central rates.

Exchange control   Government has exclusive power to determine the allocation and use of foreign exchange.

External funds   Financing source from outside the MNC company system.

Factoring   An exporter sells his or her invoices to a factoring company at a discount on a with or without recourse basis. The factoring company will collect the face amount of the invoices from the importer.

FAS 52   Financial Accounting Standard No. 52.

Financial innovations   Process and product changes in the use and type of financial instruments.

Fisher effect   Nominal interest rate equals the investors required return plus the expected rate of inflation.

Fixed rates   Government establishes par value for currency, and actively intervenes in market to maintain this valuation.

Float   Usually one or two days during which value is conveyed as a transaction clears the banking system. In emerging economies and in Eastern European countries, the time for clearance can be several days.

Floating rates   Exchange rate is free to find its level based on demand and supply forces.

Foreign bonds   Issued in a domestic bond market by a nonresident borrower and are denominated in the local currency of that bond market.

Foreign branch   A foreign-based affiliate which is a legal and operational part of the parent MNC.

Foreign exchange   A financial claim denominated in a foreign currency.

Foreign subsidiary   A foreign affiliate that is separately incorporated under the host country's law.

Foreign trade as "an engine of economic growth"   Economic growth of a nation is primarily stimulated by exports that generate trade surplus that in turn stimulates domestic production, investment, employment, and economic growth.

Forfaiting   A short- and medium-term trade financing technique used by financial institutions for facilitating exports from industrial countries to transitional and developing countries. Exporters can sell the promissory notes guaranteed by the importer's bank to forfaiters at a discount and without recourse.

Forward curve   Trading curve on which one can buy/sell currency at various forward maturities.

Forward exchange   Contract to buy or sell a currency for future delivery.

Forward yield curve   Based on differential between cost of funds denominated in one currency at given maturity, and cost of funds denominated in a second currency at the same maturity.

Funding   Securing funds for short- and medium-term lending, managing foreign currency balances, dealing in money market, and obtaining international deposits.

Fund positioning   Taking long or short position in the money market or currency market to realize a profit. Based on expected change in interest rate and/or exchange rate.

Future options   Option contracts where the underlying asset is a financial futures contract.

FX futures   Contract trading foreign currency on an organized exchange where a standardized contract is utilized.

Gensaki   A market for repurchase agreements with government securities as collateral; it liberalized the Japanese money market in 1974 and in the years after.

Gilt-edged stocks   Bonds issued and guaranteed by the British government.

Global bonds   Large issues with one or more currency denominations sold simultaneously in the world's major capital markets. They combine the characteristics of Eurobonds and foreign bonds.

Global fund   Includes U.S. securities as well as foreign securities.

Global systematic   Risk related to volatility of securities included in global capital market.

Global tax burden   The total (net) tax bill paid by the MNC on a worldwide basis.

Grossing up   MNC income is increased by foreign income taxes paid on foreign subsidiary earnings.

Hedging   Covering an open or uncovered currency position.

Herstatt risk   Related to inability of a bank to make cash settlements at end of day's clearings.

ICSID International Center for Settlement of Investment Disputes.

IMF quota For each country, assigned under a complex formula based on national income, international monetary reserves, imports, and exports.

Immature creditor BOP phase with trade surplus and deficit on capital account.

Immature debtor BOP phase with trade deficit and surplus on capital account.

Imperial preferences Imports from British colonies favored; tariffs and quotas on noncolony imports.

Informationally efficient Available data concerning given security is incorporated into the pricing of that security.

Initial margin Cash payment required when futures position is taken, imposed by exchange on which such contracts are traded.

Interbank market Refers to the over-the-counter foreign exchange market, where dealer banks play a major role.

Interest arbitrage Borrowing one currency at a given interest rate, exchanging into a second currency for investment at a different interest rate.

Interest rate parity equilibrium Where there is no advantage to engage in interest arbitrage on covered basis.

International Banking Act Federal legislation in 1978 that first placed foreign banks under central government regulation.

International banking facility Conducts offshore banking activities in the United States.

International bonds Include both foreign bonds and Eurobonds.

International Fisher effect Equilibrium between present and future spot exchange rates based on interest rate difference between two countries.

International Gold Standard The golden years of the international monetary system.

International liquidity Foreign exchange reserves and gold held by the national government.

International repurchase agreements (repos) International repos are conducted by international financial institutions mostly with government securities similar to the domestic repos in the U.S. but sometimes involving central banks between nations.

International treasury report Report that provides banks with data helpful in carrying out a range of global money market transactions.

Intervention Central bank buying or selling its currency in the foreign exchange markets.

In the money An option that generates profit for the holder when exercised.

Intracompany netting The cash management process that results in transferring only net settlement values between company units.

Intrinsic value Financial benefit to be derived if an option is exercised immediately. Generally the difference between spot price and exercise price.

Investment banking Banking activities that focus on securities issuance and trading.

Investment opportunity locus Indicates combinations of risk-free asset and market portfolios, and their respective return and risk properties.

Inward arbitrage U.S. bank bids for Eurocurrency funds and moves them onshore for domestic use.

Jamaica Agreement, 1976 Formal adoption of floating rates.

Japan premium The retrenchment in Japanese banks' foreign lending due to their domestic financial problems led to strong expansion in international lending of other banking groups, notably German banks.

Keiretsu Group of companies where cross stock holdings reinforce cooperative behavior.

LIBOR Short-term interest rates charged to banks in London when they borrow funds from each other.

Liquid market Capital market sector in which turnover is large enough to accommodate large institutional investors.

Loan pricing Total interest charged to borrower, based on credit status, maturity, and other factors.

Loan syndication Method by which banks diversify risks by allocating parts of a large loan to a number of participating banks.

London club Negotiation for loan rescheduling with respect to commercial bank private credits.

Maastricht Treaty, 1992 Agreement among European Union nations to work toward full economic and monetary union.

Maintenance margin Cash payment required when price of futures contract moves up or down. Needed to maintain "equity" position of trader.

Managed float Governments and central banks intervene in the foreign exchange market to influence exchange rate value.

Marginal Cost of Capital (MCC) At the margin, the sum of the proportionally weighted costs of different sources of financial capital for the MNC.

Marginal Return on Investment (MRI) The return on the marginal investment project for the MNC.

Market portfolio Portfolio of all risky securities in the market. In international context includes all national equity markets.

Mature creditor BOP phase with trade deficit and surplus on foreign investment income account.

Mature debtor BOP phase with trade surplus and deficit on foreign investment income account.

Maturity gap Borrowing and lending funds at different maturities, leaving bank exposed to risks from shift in level of interest rates.

Maturity mismatch Arises when bank borrows and lends funds at different maturities.

Meiji Restoration A new era started by the Emperor of Japan in 1868 to make Japan a modern nation.

Merchant bank Carries out wide range of investment banking activities.

Mexican peso crisis Drastic decline in value of the Mexican peso in December 1994-early 1995 affected many emerging capital markets in Latin America including Mexico, Brazil, and Argentina.

MIGA Multilateral Investment Guarantee Agency.

MNC System The subsidiaries, affiliates, or strategic

business units over which MNC central management has operating control.

Modified systematic Risk related to international fund that largely excludes U.S. securities and therefore enjoys only limited diversification.

Monetary approach A model of exchange rate determination focusing on the impact of money creation and money demand.

Money market Financial market in which short term funds are bought (borrowed) and sold (loaned).

Multicountry model Seeks to describe complex international stock price behavior by use of a world stock market factor and national stock market factor. Each country stock market is sensitive to the world market factor based on several considerations: foreign trade, monetary policy, and cross-border capital flows.

Mundell-Fleming Model A model of exchange rate determination with floating rates and capital mobility.

NASDAQ National Association of Security Dealers Automated Quotations is a nationwide electronic quotation system that displays dealer quotations on terminals to securities firms across the United States for most actively traded OTC stocks.

National treatment Home country extends foreign firms rights of national or local investors.

Net advantage Difference between interest rate differential and cost of swap, resulting from interest arbitrage.

Nominal interest Cost of funds expressed as annual percent rate. Ignores cost of funds components that may influence real or effective cost such as reserve requirements.

North American Free Trade Agreement (NAFTA) The United States, Canada, and Mexico signed an agreement allowing free flows of trade and capital among these three countries in 1993.

Official settlements balance Net transactions by government of a monetary nature.

Offshore banking centers Special centers for international banking transactions with minimal government regulations.

OPEC Members are: Algeria, Iraq, Kuwait, Libya, Qatar, Saudi Arabia, United Arab Emirates, Gabon, Indonesia, Iran, Nigeria, Venezuela, and Ecuador.

Open-end fund No limit on number of shares issued to investors, are priced at net asset value.

OPIC Overseas Private Investment Corporation.

Option Gives holder right to buy or sell the asset traded at a fixed or strike price.

Option on futures Right to buy or sell futures contract.

Out of the money An option that generates loss for the holder when exercised.

Outward arbitrage U.S. bank borrows domestic funds and redeposits them in overseas branches.

Parallel internal system An intracountry cash management approach most effective under conditions of high inflation.

Paris Club Negotiation for loan rescheduling with respect to official creditors.

Passive management Portfolio approximates index of the stock market.

Payments transaction Transaction that results in payment of funds by a resident.

PE ratios Price earning ratio is obtained by dividing price of an equity security by earnings per share.

Petrodollar recycling U.S. dollars received by Organization of Petroleum Exporting Countries (OPEC) and deposited in international banks which, in turn, lend to oil importing countries for payments of their oil.

Petrodollars Dollar exchange earned by oil export nations. Increased rapidly in 1970s with petroleum price increases.

Placement power This refers to the strength and capacity of an underwriting group to place the bond issues with individual and institutional investors.

Plain vanilla swap A five- to seven-year swap of floating rate funds against fixed rate funds to avoid interest rate risk.

Plaza Accord, 1985 Joint intervention and efforts to lower U.S. dollar value.

Portfolio balance model A model of exchange rate determination that treats bonds denominated in different currencies as imperfect substitutes.

Portfolio insurance Methods used to hedge against losses in portfolio value.

Portfolio suppression Factors that hinder the evolution and development of capital markets.

Premium Price paid to writer of option contract.

Price-Earnings Multiple Ratio of price of bank common stock to earnings per share of common stock.

Primary capital Under Basle Accord, Tier 1 capital, or the initial four percent capital, satisfied only with certain types of capital.

Profit center Operating unit of a bank (money market dealing room) that seeks to generate profit based on overall operations.

Purchasing power parity Model that explains how exchange rate adjusts to differences in inflation, keeping prices of traded goods equal in all countries.

Put option Gives holder right to sell underlying asset at strike price.

Real profit pricing An exporter must price his or her product according to the domestic price index plus a margin for profit. This is intended to maintain a real profit margin, especially under inflation conditions.

Receipt transaction Transaction that results in receipt of funds by a resident.

Reciprocal rates A pair of currencies exhibit two rates of exchange in comparison with one another, which are reciprocals of one another.

Reciprocity Home country extends equivalent investment rights to foreign firms as are extended its own firms.

Registered shares Ownership registered in official books maintained by company or trust bank. Specific ownership easy to trace.

Representative office Office allowing contact with local customers, but with no operating privileges.

Return Gain from holding security over given holding period. Can consist of change in value (price) of security, dividend or interest, and change in currency value if traded in offshore market.

Revaluation Upward change in value of a currency. Opposite of devaluation.

Revenue Act of 1962 Added Subpart F to the U.S. Internal Revenue Code dealing with foreign source income.

Revocable letter of credit The importer's bank may amend or cancel the letter of credit at any time without approval by the exporter (beneficiary).

Revolving letter of credit One letter of credit to handle multiple shipments on a continuing basis instead of establishing an individual letter of credit for each shipment.

Risk Variability of return from one holding period to another.

Risk-based capital Capital requirement imposed by bank, weighted according to risk of assets.

Risk-free rate Rate of return earned on risk-free asset, generally a central government debt obligation.

Samurai bonds Yen-denominated bonds issued by foreign governments and corporations in Japan.

Securitization Transforming illiquid asset into a tradeable market security.

Sharpe measure Evaluates portfolio performance related to total risk.

Shogun Foreign-currency-denominated bonds issued by foreign governments and companies in Japan.

Sight deposits The "commodity" traded in the foreign exchange market.

Sight draft Order to pay, drawn on a party, bank or nonbank, payable at sight.

Smithsonian Agreement December 1971: "Gold as a reserve asset has an uncertain value. Central banks do not wish to have gold back again center stage." (Japanese financial adviser)

Special Drawing Rights (SDRs) A form of international reserve asset. Its value is based on a portfolio composite of widely used currencies, created by the IMF in 1967.

Speculation Taking an uncovered currency position for profit.

Spread Dealer banks quote bid and ask prices for a currency, the difference or spread providing a trading profit.

Stabilization program IMF loan to member country based on it adopting austerity measures.

Standby letter of credit A seller or exporter pays a fee to the bank in turn for the bank's promise to pay if the buyer or importer defaults on the obligation covered by the standby L/C.

Strike price Price fixed in the option contract, at which holder can buy or sell asset.

Subpart F of the Internal Revenue Code The section of the U.S. IRC which sets the rules applicable to MNC foreign source income.

Supplementary capital Under Basle Accord, Tier 2 capital, or the second four percent of capital, satisfied with a wide range of types of capital.

Swap Simultaneous spot purchase and forward sale of foreign currency. Simultaneous purchase and sale of financial claim at different maturities.

SWIFT Society for Worldwide Interbank Financial Telecommunications. Computerized message and pay-

ments instruction system operated by and for foreign exchange banks.

Syndicated bank loans A group of international banks join together and provide large amounts to international borrowers in the Eurocurrency market.

Syndicated lease Two or more international banks jointly purchase the equipment (such as an aircraft) from an exporter and lease to a user in another country.

Systematic risk Market risk related to volatility of securities traded in that market.

Term structure Shape and configuration of interest rate at different maturities within a given currency sector.

Time draft Order to pay, drawn on a party, bank or nonbank, with a stated future maturing date.

Time value Related to the possibility that the price of the underlying asset will change over remaining lifetime of the option contract.

Trade balance Goods exports minus goods imports.

Trade bloc Trade blocs such as European ommunity (EC) and North American Free Trade Agreement (NAFTA) are generally designed to protect (through a common external tariff) their internal trade from countries outside the blocs.

Transfer risk Inability of country to service external loan due to scarcity of foreign exchange.

Transparency Wide availability of information concerning share prices and factors that influence specific ownership.

Treasury management Sourcing and allocation of use of short-term funds, to achieve optimal cost-risk position.

Treynor measure Evaluates portfolio performance related to systematic risk.

Twin deficits The U.S. federal government deficits and the U.S. international balance of payments deficits.

Underwriting spread The profit resulting from buying and selling Eurobonds by the underwriting group of the Eurobond issues.

Universal banking Banks carry out deposit and securities trading activities.

Universal banks Banks that function as securities underwriters and brokers, as well as deposit-taking institutions.

Value-added tax (VAT) Levies tax at each level of productive process, based on the value added at each level.

Volatility Variability in price of the underlying asset. One factor that affects time value of option.

Withholding tax on dividends Approach that taxes remittance dividend payments to foreigners.

World market portfolio Portfolio that includes securities from all market components around the world.

Writer Party that writes or issues the option to another party.

Yankee bonds U.S. dollar-dominated bonds issued by foreigners in New York.

Zaibatsu A great industrial or financial combination in Japan between the First and Second World Wars.

Index